CW00345615

LANNER

A CORNISH MINING PARISH

SHARRON SCHWARTZ

ROGER PARKER

Whenever I find myself growing away, beyond my beginnings, there comes a need to bow my head, come down, and stabilise my rambling identity in the tangled fragrance of Cornwall, in case the slender vine which feeds me breaks and leaves me withering in the English air.
(*The Saffron Eaters*, N.R. Phillips, Devon Books, 1987, p.18)

HALSGROVE

First published in Great Britain in 1998

Note: Individual photographs are acknowledged to those who provided them for use, with © denoting the image is supplied Courtesy of the named individual or organisation. It does not necessarily always confirm ownership of copyright.

British Library Cataloguing-in-Publication Data
A CIP record for this title is available from the British Library

ISBN 1 84114 019 8

HALSGROVE
PUBLISHING, MEDIA AND DISTRIBUTION

Halsgrove House
Lower Moor Way
Tiverton, Devon EX16 6SS
Tel: 01884 243242
Fax: 01884 243325

DEDICATION

Sharron Schwartz (née Kessell) wishes to dedicate this book to the memory of Harry and Ida Polkinghorne of 'Hillside' Carn Marth, her maternal grandparents, who initiated a powerful desire to know about the past.
Roger Parker dedicates it to all those Lanner people, past and present, who have helped make a wonderful home for him and his family for a quarter of a century.

Printed and bound in Great Britain by Bookcraft Ltd, Midsomer Norton

Contents

Acknowledgements

This book could not have been written without the help and contribution of the following people, at home and abroad, to whom we wish to express our deep thanks: Mrs Sandy Albrant, Michigan, Mr and Mrs J. Allen, Mr Paul Annear, Mrs M. Barbarry, Mr P. Benbow, Mr and Mrs S. Bishop, Mrs Rhona Blatchford, Mr Chris Bosworth, Mr John Bray, Mr and Mrs Lance Bray, Mr Ivor Bryant, Mrs O. Burrell, Mr and Mrs Mike Buzza, Mr C. Caddy, Dr. F. Chappel, Mr Mike Cooper, Mr and Mrs Joseph Craze, Mrs Prudence Danby, Mr Bernard Deacon, Mr and Mrs T. Dudley, Newport, Gwent, Mr J.D.D. Eastman, Mr Roger Eslick, Mr Jack Evans, Mrs D. Fiol, Mr Rob Gibson, Mrs E. Gilbert, Miss Susan Gribble, Mrs Grigg, Mr J. Ham, M.B.E., Mrs J. Handley, the late Mrs Minnie Haughton, Mrs Hill, Mrs J. Hopkins, the late Mrs Mary Job, Mr Michael Job, Mr and Mrs B. T. Kessell, Mr Arthur Langford, Mr Paul Langford, Mrs Helen Lawn, New Zealand, Mr David Lean, Mr P. E. Lloyd, the late Mr Tommy Martin, Mrs J. Martin, Mr D. Menhenott, Mr and Mrs Ken Minson, Mr P. Mitchell, Mrs Sheila Mooney, Mr Roy Morton, Mrs Janeen Nelson-Watkins, Utah, Mr Geoffrey Olds, Mr J. Opie, Mrs A.M. Opie, Dr. Philip Payton, Mr Nigel Pender, Mr Joe Pengelly, Plymouth, Mrs S. Pooley, Mr M. Quintrell, Mr Paul Richards, Mr L. Rouse, Mr Chris Russell, The Reverend and Mrs Thomas Shaw, Mr C. Thurlow, Mrs I. M. Staat, Michigan, Mr C. Stephens, Mr Michael Tangye, Mr David Thomas, Mrs A. Todd, Mr and Mrs Michael Veall, Mr and the late Mrs Cyril Williams, Mrs Irene Williams and Mrs M. Williams. If we have inadvertently omitted anyone, we ask forgiveness.

Our sincere thanks to Christine North, County Archivist, for permission to publish material from the archive and to the staff at the Cornwall Record Office (CRO), Truro for their help and assistance. Thanks also to Roger Penhallurick for permission to use illustrations and photographs from the collection of the Royal Institution of Cornwall (RIC) and Angela Broome, H. L. Douch and Anne Knight of the Courtney Library, R.I.C., for their assistance. Sharron Schwartz would like to thank Moira Tangye and Dennis Martin at Murdoch House, Redruth, for access to the computer database of the Cornish-American Connection, and also the staff at the Morrab Library, Penzance. She wishes to express her special thanks to Terry Knight, Librarian, and his staff at the Cornish Studies Library (CSL), Clinton Road, Redruth, for their constant and cheerful assistance and help and for patiently bearing many difficult questions and requests. A big thank you must be extended to Joanne Hillman, for knowing exactly where everything 'lives' in the library and for her ability to track down the vaguest request, and to Kim Cooper, for faithfully booking her a place on a microfilm reader every Friday, and for ensuring that her library books were up to date!.

We would also like to thank the Lanner Parish Council for their financial support of this project and to the 'Q' Fund for a research grant. And we gratefully acknowledge the help given in the preparation of this book by Sheila Barnard who was instrumental in launching the idea to record the material presented at the exhibition, and who carried out some of the interviews on which the book is based. Our sincerest thanks to the late Dr. F. L. Harris O.B.E., who took so much interest in the writing of this book, and from whom we had the benefit of a lifetime's devotion to Cornish history and access to a vast personal archive. To Paddy Bradley and Derek Reynolds, for permission to publish photographs from their extensive postcard collections, and also to the Lanner Historical Society for the use of their photograph archive. Our thanks to the numerous people who have trusted us with treasured photographs and other items, and invited us into their homes to discuss old times. Last but not least, we wish to extend our gratitude and sincerest thanks to the following draft readers: John C. C. Probert, who offered valuable advice on the Religion chapter; John Tonkin for commenting on the China Clay and Brick chapter; Michael Veall for reading the Agriculture chapter; Allen Buckley for his assistance and input on the Mining chapters and particularly to Dr. Ronald Perry who read the whole text, offering valuable suggestions, assistance, advice and encouragement. He also honoured us by writing the Foreword to our book. But most importantly, we wish to thank our families for their help, advice and support. In particular, Sharron Schwartz would like to thank her daughter Keren, for patiently waiting for Mum to finish up on the computer, for enduring many quiet hours in local libraries and archives and for having to listen to her Mum talking for endless hours about Lanner, a Cornish Mining Parish.

Sharron P. Schwartz
Roger Parker
Lanner, 1998

FOREWORD

BY DR RONALD PERRY

This book is a parochial history with a difference, one that sees the wood as well as the trees. It results from years of painstaking documentary research, dozens of interviews with Lanner people and advice from experts in every facet of relevant knowledge. It tells a dramatic tale of a once insignificant moorland area that came into being as a parish when it found itself at the centre of the world's copper mining industry, attracting people from all parts of Cornwall and beyond. Later, quite suddenly, it became marginalised again, drained of its dynamism by mass emigration. Later still, it was re-populated by an influx of outsiders who were seeking, if not a life of leisure, at least a more leisured lifestyle.

Yet, in describing these traumas of industrialisation, de-industrialisation and post-industrialisation, the authors have not lost sight of underlying continuities of everyday Lanner existence. They bring vividly to life the detailed patterning of work in mines, quarries, clay-pits and brick works, on farms, smallholdings and in workshops. They portray the vigour of religious life in church, chapels, through Sunday School tea-treats and Methodist outings. They highlight the vitality of leisure activities, from hunting, hare-coursing and entertainment in the village inns in times past, to the rugby and cricket club, brass band and parades of carnival queens today.

At the same time - and this is where the book stands out from many parochial histories - it sets the Lanner story in a wider historical framework, one that is enlightened by the most recent advances in historical research made by such writers as Bernard Deacon and Philip Payton of Exeter University and the Institute of Cornish Studies. The chapter on emigration is a good example of this. Orthodox histories trace a simple trajectory of mining growth followed by collapse, mass emigration and economic stagnation. Yet, as Payton and Deacon have shown, people began leaving Cornwall in large numbers from the 1840s, when mining was booming, not only from the 1860s, when it was failing. This book explores the complex political, religious and cultural factors that help to explain this apparently puzzling phenomenon.

This chapter also plots the hair-raising adventures of Lanner folk in the lawless mining territories of North America, Australia and South Africa, to remote Andean and desert outposts in South America. Nor does it neglect the impact upon the local economy and the built environment of Lanner, of the fortunes that some of these pioneers brought back. In this context it provides new insights into a neglected facet of local history - the flowering of Redruth and district in late Victorian days, as an oasis of comparative prosperity in a desert of deprivation, an occurrence that resulted partly from the influx of mining incomes from abroad, which also stimulated Lanner's quarries and brick works.

Finally, through remembering Lanner's past, this book may help to regenerate its future. Shining through the history of dire poverty, the often drab existence of getting by and making do, is the resilience, initiative and courage that enabled the people of Lanner to survive troubled times. These qualities will stand them in good stead to face the twenty-first century with confidence.

Dr Ronald Perry
Cornish Economic and
Social Research Group
Truro, July 1998

I live at Trevarth
To the South of Carn Marth,
Near the village of Lanner
Where tin miners gather.

You can if you will
Visit Carn Marth Hill,
And see the place
Which Wesley graced.

In those old times
Were many mines,
But now 'The Pit',
Is where they sit.

(K.E. Gribble, *Trevarth Farm*)

INTRODUCTION

The inspiration behind the writing of this book was an event in the village organised by the Lanner Methodist Chapel in May, 1994. The '100 Years of Lanner' exhibition was a tremendous success which encompassed the help of all the village organisations and a number of individuals in putting together an exhibition to celebrate a century of life in this Cornish mining parish. Arranged by Michael Veall and a group of dedicated helpers, the exhibition was held in the Methodist Schoolroom and the Lower Vestry over three days, and almost two thousand people from near and far attended. The success of the exhibition and the interest it aroused focused attention on the history of Lanner. As this had never before been attempted, it was decided to prepare a written account of the material included in the exhibition and to build upon this with additional research in local archives and libraries thus creating a comprehensive book. Unsurprisingly, this turned out to a far bigger task than the original authors had expected. The problem with writing this book has not been what to include, but rather what to omit, and the following document represents contributions from many people and various written sources. Our aim has been to compile a book which combines an analysis of documented history, reminiscence and anecdote, which hopefully will appeal to the historically minded as well as the more sentimentally-motivated reader. On the brink of the twenty-first century, it seems doubly important to 'gather up the fragments before they are lost'. This has resulted in the telling of the dramatic story of a little known parish on the outskirts of Redruth – *Lanner - A Cornish Mining Parish.*

Michael Veall holding Foster Hooper's butcher's delivery bicycle, at the '100 years of Lanner' Exhibition, May 1994. (Courtesy © Packet Newspapers , Falmouth)

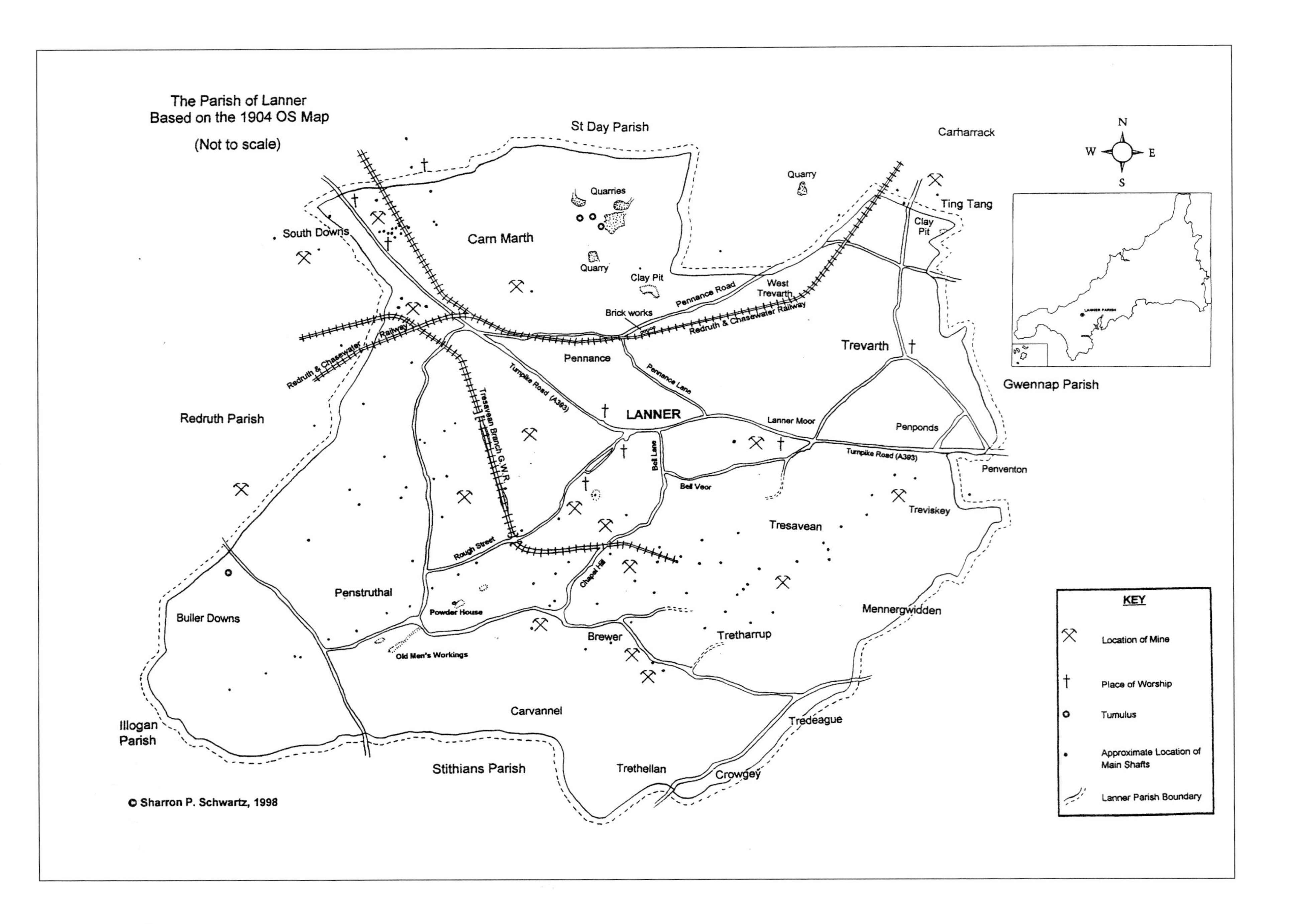

The Parish of Lanner
Based on the 1904 OS Map
(Not to scale)
St Day Parish
Carharrack
N
W
E
S
Quarry
Quarries
Ting Tang
Clay Pit
South Downs
Carn Marth
Quarry
Clay Pit
West Trevarth
Pennance Road
Brick works
Redruth & Chasewater Railway
Trevarth
Redruth & Chasewater Railway
Pennance
Pennance Lane
Gwennap Parish
Turnpike Road (A393)
LANNER
Lanner Moor
Penponds
Redruth Parish
Tresavean Branch G.W.R.
Turnpike Road (A393)
Penventon
Bell Lane
Bell Veor
Treviskey
Tresavean
Rough Street
Chapel Hill
Penstruthal
Mennergwidden
Buller Downs
Powder House
Brewer
Tretharrup
Old Men's Workings
Carvannel
Tredeague
Illogan Parish
Stithians Parish
Trethellan
Crowgey
© Sharron P. Schwartz, 1998
KEY
Location of Mine
Place of Worship
Tumulus
Approximate Location of Main Shafts
Lanner Parish Boundary

Chapter 1
A Brief History of the Area from Earliest Times

Before the nineteenth century, Lanner as a community did not really exist. 'Lannarth' lay in the ancient Parish of Gwennap and was merely the name of a tenement which eventually gave its name to the parish containing one of Cornwall's largest villages. Nevertheless, the area which later became Lanner Parish has probably been inhabited from prehistoric times, and one of the main reasons for settlement was most likely to have been to seek the tin which lay hidden in the earth, or concealed in the beds of nearby rivers. But for the archaeologist and historian searching for evidence of early man's past within Lanner and its vicinity, the task is a difficult one as many probable sites of habitation and possible remains have been obliterated by mining and quarrying. The earliest relics to have been unearthed to date appear to belong to the Mesolithic period (the Middle Stone Age, 8000–4000 BC), and the Neolithic period (New Stone Age, 4000–2500 BC).

Stone Age Finds

A microlith (a small flint that is a remnant of a Stone Age tool or weapon), was discovered in a garden at Penponds near Lanner Moor by W.A.D. Watson earlier this century, and was catalogued as belonging to the Tardenois Culture of Brittany, immigrants from Europe, particularly Western Brittany.[1] No further finds have been recorded in this location to date. There is also evidence to suggest that nearby Carn Brea was inhabited during the late Mesolithic period, as several microflints and microburins have been discovered there. It is thought that the flint to manufacture the small arrowheads and spears necessary for hunting was obtained from pebbles on the beaches of the nearby seashores. Hundreds have been found at Gwithian where traces of Mesolithic occupation have been detected. By all accounts, the Tardenois Period was an impoverished one, and there is little physical evidence for this early period of Cornwall's prehistory. A number of flint waste flakes have been found on the north-west slope of Carn Marth at Grambler, by Brian Tuck.[2] The name 'Grambler' translates from the Cornish as cromlech or dolmen, and might once have been the site of a Neolithic burial site similar to those found at Penwith, although no trace of it remains.

But a rather splendid example of a prehistoric weapon was discovered in the old workings of Tresavean Mine by Captain Edmund Michell in the last century. James gives the following description, supplied by the curator of the Victoria and Albert Museum, Exeter, where the axe was exhibited: 'The axe hammer is of a Neolithic type. It is of a fine grained quartz porphyry or similar rock pierced for a haft through the centre and partly smoothed and polished for an inch or so from the cutting edge. It measures six inches in length by two and a half inches in width, and is two inches thick through the hole.'[3] The find was presented to the museum in 1873, the date of its discovery unknown, and was thought to date from the transitional period between the late Neolithic and the early Bronze Age (2500–1700 BC).

During the Neolithic Period there seems to be evidence in Cornwall of an extensive trade in polished axe production. There have been six axe factories identified in areas where igneous rock, particularly greenstone, could be easily exploited. One of these sites is just south-west of Camborne and many axe heads have been unearthed at nearby Carn Brea, in Illogan Parish. Here a series of ramparts enclosed a hill top area covering 46 acres, making it one of the most important sites of its period now known in Western Europe. Perhaps the person who once yielded the Tresavean axe came from this settlement.[4]

The Bronze Age

No metal artefacts have been found in our area which can be positively included in the Bronze Age (2500–600 BC), but one possible Bronze Age sherd (fragment of pottery) was discovered by Brian Tuck in a field near Grambler to the south of the Manor of Trefula, which could suggest that the megalithic burial site already mentioned might have been utilised also for the burial of Bronze Age peoples.[5] The paucity of finds for this period in our area is hardly surprising, as much the same picture is presented for the remainder of the county. In the early Bronze Age, a trade grew up with Ireland where native copper was in abundance. As copper is a soft metal it was necessary to mix it with another metal such as tin, to create a more durable and tough alloy – bronze. Gold lunulae have been discovered at Padstow, St Juliot and at Gwithian, and were exchanged in barter for tin with the Irish. An extensive trade route was thus established which ran from Ireland across the Irish Sea to the Atlantic Cornish coastline, to sheltered estuaries such as Hayle and Padstow. The route crossed the Cornish peninsula, to St Michael's Mount, an important trading post, and continued across the Channel to Brittany, and on to the ports of the Southern Mediterranean. During this early Bronze Age period, Cornwall was at the heart of European trade.

However, by the middle Bronze Age, this Atlantic seaboard trade with Ireland came to an end, as new routes overland in Northern and Central England, less perilous than the lengthy sea passage to the Cornish coast, came into being. Cornwall became gradually peripheralised and entered a period of relative isolation and lack of prosperity. Little is found in the burial places from this era, as it appears that it had become unfashionable to inter the dead with grave goods, which explains the lack of finds in the county. Cremation became the general form of interment, the ashes of the deceased being placed inside biconical cinerary urns and buried under round barrows of earth and stone.

The summit of Carn Marth is the alleged site of three tumuli or barrows, which James claims belonged to the Iron Age.[6] In fact, it seems more likely that the tumuli in this location, and a further two, one of which lies inside the Lanner Parish boundary on the high windswept moorland opposite on the north slope of Lanner Beacon (now known as Buller Downs), are Bronze Age burial places. It was the practice in the Iron Age for bodies to be interred without any attempt at cremation, so the bones rotted away in the wet climate and sour soils of Cornwall leaving little behind for the archaeologist to examine. The nineteenth century poet and historian, William Francis, adds to our understanding of the site at Carn Marth by relating how in 1789 it was excavated, and in one of the barrows, two British urns were discovered containing burnt human remains.[7] The 1873 edition of the Harrod's *Royal County Directory* mentions that discovery of the previous century with the remark: 'There is also a hill called Carn Marth from which many vessels containing burnt bones have been dug'. This strengthens the case for supposing the site to be of the Bronze Age period, rather than the later Iron Age.

The sites of these pre-Celtic burial places on Carn Marth's summit, and at Lanner Beacon today, are impossible to substantiate, even from aerial photographs. The 1880 Ordnance Survey Map indicates that at the Carn Marth site, two tumuli stood on either side of the modern trig. point. The area is now covered by an early enclosure wall of field clearance, and the whole site is strewn with debris and quarry spoil.[8] The original position of the third tumulus is gone, obliterated by the expansion of the now filled quarry. And at Lanner Beacon, on the opposite side of the valley, early tin bounding, later deep lode mining and the gradual pillaging of the stone, have wiped away all traces of the two tumuli which once stood there.

Carn Marth, an Iron Age Hill Fort?

Iron gradually replaced bronze for the weapons of warfare and for farming implements from the seventh century BC. Waves of immigrants from Europe crossed the Channel in search of new land to colonise and develop. These immigrants may have been the Celts, who brought the new metal – iron – with them. They also ushered in a more unsettled era which woke Cornwall from its Bronze Age slumber. The La Tène Celts are said to have been an organised warrior people who overcame the more peaceful Neolithic communities established in Cornwall. The Iron Age is characterised in Cornwall by the construction of defensive sites such as cliff castles, defended farmsteads and hill forts. In the Lanner area, defended sites include those at Gear (which is derived form the Cornish 'ker' and means fort or round),[9] Trebowland, Busveal and Scorrier. A further defended site might formerly have existed at Carvannel, as the name in Cornish means 'fort of the wild broom', from the Cornish 'ker' and 'banathel' – broom[10] and so could relate to an earthwork covered by a specific vegetational growth.

James believed that Carn Marth was fortified during the Iron Age and twinned with nearby Carn Brea (which means hill fort), both places being of strategic geographical importance in a particularly violent era. A clue to the fact that Carn Marth might once have been fortified lies in the meaning of Carharrack as 'fort-height', from the Cornish 'arð'[11] – height, and 'ker' – fort. But any physical evidence to support this theory has been obliterated by quarrying at the summit and on the slopes of the hill. The removal of many thousands of tons of moorstone over the centuries and field clearance for agriculture have further disrupted the environment.

Yet according to the Reverend R. Polwhele, Carn Marth was thought to mark the boundary between two feuding Celtic tribes, the Damnonii, whose dominion, Dumnonia, stretched from the region of Exeter westwards to the dominion of the Carnabians of Redruth, who controlled the remaining areas of the peninsula. The Damnonii were eventually to prevail in this war.[12]

William Francis maintains that an echo from this bellicose era was continued into modern times with the vicious feuds and blood letting between neighbouring parishes, epitomised by the St Day Fight, which occurred until the eighteenth century, the antagonists being men from the parishes of Gwennap and Redruth.[13] But of course local rivalries of this kind were common in Cornwall and indeed in many other regions.

Roman 'Roads' and Milestones

Considerable excitement followed the discovery of a large granite block in 1942 at Menheer Farm, 550 feet above sea level on the north-facing slope of Carn Marth. It was 18 cm below the surface and approximately vertical. When examined, it was found to be quadrangular, 1 metre 10 centimetres high, 35x20 centimetres in section and was inscribed IMP. CAES GORDIANO PIO FEL. The translation of this being, 'to the Emperor, Caesar, Antonius Gordianus, Pious, Fortunate'. The find was believed to have been a Roman milestone, which tied in with the suggestion of a Roman road which was alleged to have run down the spine of the county from the region of Launceston, to an area close to Redruth. As Gordian III ruled from AD238–244, this makes the Menheer milestone the earliest of its type in

Cornwall.[14] Interestingly, the word Menheer is derived from the Cornish 'Men' – stone and 'hyr' – long.[15]

Little light has been thrown on the geography of Roman Cornwall, but the assumption that they came here in search of the rich alluvial deposits of tin is probably a correct one. Yet there are no Roman roads in Cornwall of the type found beyond Exeter. The Romans did however, make use of trackways which were already established, and the milestones which have been discovered in Cornwall were erected to commemorate the upgrading of these routes. Tradition claims that Rough Street, which runs up the western side of Lanner valley towards Penstruthal, was once one such Roman 'road'. It is of interest to note that Rough Street might well indeed be a part of a road which runs from Menheer in a fairly straight line to St Michael's Mount via Four Lanes, Praze an Beeble, Leedstown, Goldsithney, St Hilary and Marazion.[16] St Michael's Mount, alleged to have been known in ancient times as Ictis, was an important market and trading post for the exchange of tin, which was conveyed along the old trailways like Rough Street, to be traded by the indigenous population for various imported commodities.[17]

The Romans would certainly have been aware of Cornwall's mineral wealth, although there was little contact with the native population of Dumnonia until the mines in Spain, which had been extremely rich, ceased production in about AD250; the period following this date saw Cornish mines boom.[18] Several fine examples of pewter-ware have been discovered at Bath, where a temple dedicated to Sulis-Minerva was situated. These were created from lead mined in Somerset and amalgamated with tin, probably from Cornwall. It is claimed that another Roman road ran inland from the Fal to the rich mining area around Carn Brea. And it has been proven that there was early alluvial mining or tin streaming in the Carnon Valley which lay but a few miles from Lanner. In 1817, numerous brass coins were discovered there, which when examined were found to bear inscriptions to Domitian who ruled from AD81–96.[19] More Roman coins were found in the Carnon River in the last century bearing the inscription of Tetricus I, who was Caesar from AD270–3.[20] In addition, an urn and a Roman coin were found at Calvadnack near Carn Brea in about 1700 during the removal of an artificial heap of stone from a steep slope. Sadly, all the finds have been lost, but provide firm evidence of native contact with the Roman world in our vicinity.

The Carn of the Horse

Dumnonia enjoyed a relatively independent status under the Romans, largely determining its own affairs. One of the Kings of Dumnonia, alleged to have ruled in the sixth century AD, was King Mark. There is a strong possibility that this ancient Cornish king had a connection to Carn Marth, the most prominent hill in the Redruth area. Once a part of the ancient Variscides mountain range, this hill dominates the skyline standing 771 feet above sea level, and offers spectacular views.[21] This rocky granite hill has probably been continually inhabited as we have already noted, and the name Carn Marth is doubtless ancient. There is no debate about the translation to English of the noun 'carn', which in Cornish means rocky hill or tor; it is the meaning of the adjective 'Marth', which poses considerable controversy. 'Marth' has been translated as wonder or astonishment,[22] but there is no historical evidence to suggest that anything miraculous or wonderful occurred there.

One of the more likely explanations offered is that Marth is a personal name, in this case, that of the semi-legendary King Mark. Trevarth would then have the meaning of 'Mark's town place'. Romantics like to believe the legend that the Cornish king is buried there, the name Carn Marth forever commemorating this Cornish monarch. However, some scholars argue that 'Marth' has the meaning of horse, claiming Cornish surnames and place names often attempted to describe the local landscape and things peculiar to it, making the translation from the Cornish, 'horse's tor'. And one of the earliest references to the hill was by the sixteenth century map maker Norden, who wrote the following in 1584: 'Kern-Margh Beacon or Carn-Mairgh, signifyinge rocke wher horses shelter them: it is a heade beacon in Gwynop Parish'.[23] This description of Carn Marth, written just after the Middle Ages, seems to confirm the argument in favour of the adjective meaning horse, and this is what today's consensus prefers.

Yet of particular interest is the fact that King Mark appears in a Dark Age list of the Kings of Dumnonia, who ruled in the West Country. He is listed under the title of 'Cynwawr', which when translated into Latin becomes 'Cunomorus', the meaning of which is horse, a creature which was revered as sacred in Celtic mythology, which would have given him the title 'Mark the Horse'.[24] (Note the names of later English monarchs, such as Richard the Lionheart).

Although King Mark is unlikely to have been buried on Carn Marth, the more probable location for this being Kilmarth near Fowey, it is conceivable that this important Cornish king had some connection to such a strategic and prominent hill. The name might therefore be translated as 'The horse's tor', namely, 'Mark's tor'.

The 'Heade Beacon in Gwynop Parish'

As Norden's comment confirms, Carn Marth was used as a beacon from the earliest times. Long before the telephone and television, fires were lit on the summits of hills enjoying elevated positions to announce important occasions, the fiery message being rapidly disseminated throughout the land. This ancient use of the carn as a beacon probably dates from pre-Christian times.

The Bronze Age people who formerly inhabited the locality had a primitive religious system which venerated the forces of nature, particularly the dead, cremating their corpses in a ritualistic fashion. During the Celtic period, the most important celebration was that of Beltane, the great spring–summer fertility gathering held on 1 May which celebrated the resurgence of primeval life.[25] The occasion was marked by the burning of a large fire which maintained a link with ancestors of the distant past.

In the Middle Ages, the Church, mindful of the attraction of these ancient festivals, but keen to dispose of their pagan implications, decided to Christianise them into the 'Fires of the Feast of St John'. Huge fires were lit on the summit of hills such as Carn Marth, the Midsummer festival being highly popular amongst the mining population in the last century, continuing a custom stretching back to the dawn of history in our area. In 1929, the Redruth Old Cornwall Society rekindled the bonfire ritual which had become moribund in our area, with a ceremony in the ancient Cornish Language, although the future venue for the Midsummer events was changed in favour of Carn Brea.[26]

Ancient Trailways and Pilgrim's Routes

The Lanner we know today was once very different, as the topography of the landscape has changed enormously over the last few hundred years. An ancient deciduous forest, which had established itself after a change in climate sometime around 8000BC, lasted until Tudor times in the area which was later to become Lanner. The most popular species in this ancient forest was the sessile oak or durmast, a stumpy tree with tough, elastic wood. The valleys were densely wooded, and the only places exposed were the summits of the hills, such as Carn Brea and Carn Marth and the high land of Lanner Beacon, which were covered with grasses. The forest stretched from the lower slopes of these hills to the coast at Portreath, where today low tides occasionally expose the fossilised trunks and petrified roots of the ancient trees and the peat beds in which they grew. The woods at Tehidy are a vestige of this once great forest.[27]

Yet the memory of this ancient forest has been preserved in many local place names. The Cornish word for wood is 'cos'[28] which evolved into 'coit', 'coyse', and 'coose' amongst other regional variations. A look at a few local names immediately confirms this point. Burncoose comes from the Cornish, 'bron' and 'cos' meaning wooded hill, Pencoose, from 'pen' and 'cos' meaning head of the wood, Chycoose from 'chy' and 'cos' with the translation of house in the wood, Cusgarne from 'cos' and 'garan' meaning wood of cranes or herons, and Lanner, from the Cornish 'Lanherch' which when translated into English means glade or clearing, presumably in the midst of a wood.[29] The woods in our area disappeared during Tudor times (1485–1603) when they were systematically felled for use as a fuel in the tin smelting process in local blowing houses, or cleared to facilitate farming, particularly in the valleys in which the best farming land was found. Francis in his 1845 poem mentions that the roots of these ancient trees had been discovered on Carn Marth when croftland was being broken in during the eighteenth century. He also remarks that several oak corbels existed in the oldest dwellings at Skyburrier, a thing which struck him as very strange when moorstone (granite) was plentiful in the locality.[30]

Since the woods were so dense in places, trail ways tended to traverse the tops of hills and downs. The Roman 'road' already mentioned probably crossed Carn Marth and was used by pilgrims during the Dark Ages (c.AD476–1000) and the period prior to the Reformation en route from the famous shrine at Gorland, St Day, to St Michael's Mount, which besides being a trading post, was an important religious centre.

St Day, situated just a few miles away from Lanner valley on the north side of Carn Marth, was an epicentre of religious activity on this important route, for during the fifth and sixth centuries, Cornwall was visited by many Celtic Christian missionaries who came from Ireland, Wales and Brittany. These included Day, or They, a Breton saint who founded the Chapel of the Holy Trinity at St Day, and Wennep, who built a church and monastery on the site of Gwennap Parish Church about 1400 years ago. Little however, is known of Saint Wennap's life.

Many such early Christian missionaries founded churches and chapels where miraculous events were alleged to have occurred. Paul Annear states that Saint Day was held in veneration for healing powers over rheumatism, and the Chapel of the Holy Trinity housed a shrine (usually a cask or reliquary which served as a receptacle for the bones, hair, or garments of the original saint, and sometimes even pieces of wood which purported to be that of the true cross or other equally holy relics). By the late medieval period St Day had become the second most popular shrine in Cornwall, around which a thriving and prosperous commercial, cultural and spiritual centre grew up.[31] And all along the pilgrim's route between St Day and St Michael's Mount, and trailways joining it, lay various holy sites marked by wells, chapels and crosses.

For people travelling long distances by foot, the provision of water was of prime importance. A natural spring existed on Carn Marth which was at some point made into a well, the water within being of excellent quality. But if the well was ever considered holy, or its waters attributed with any curative or miraculous powers, this fact has been lost. Until recent times, girls would bring their dolls to the well to be baptised on Good Friday, although what pagan derivation this might have had is not known. The Carn Marth well is known by two names, that of Figgy Dowdy, or Margery Daw. Henderson's notes mention a curious local rhyme concerning it:

St. Margery Daw had a well
On the top of Carn Marth Hill,
She kept it locked by night and by day
Lest people should take her water away.[32]

James referred to the same rhyme, but he misquoted the original, and attributes the well to Figgy Dowdy. It has been argued that St Margery Daw might have been an early Christian missionary, which is more likely than the suggestion that Figgy Dowdy was a fertility goddess, but there is no conclusive evidence for either. Nevertheless, the well is obviously ancient, and roofed in the beehive fashion. Four

Fig. 1.1. *Figgy Dowdy's Well, Carn Marth, c.1900.* (© Lanner Historical Society)

granite steps lead down to the crystal waters, and the dimensions of the well are given by Henderson as '3 feet wide, 5 feet 3 inches deep, and at the further end about 9 feet high. It is entered by a doorway 4 feet high'.[33] (Fig 1.1.) Sadly the well's granite front has been considerably mutilated, but the clear water still flows within. It is situated in a bank beneath the lane leading to the amphitheatre quarry, and can be seen several metres before the entrance on the opposite side of the lane if approached from uphill. There are plans afoot to restore this ancient site.

The majority of trailways in our locality leading to the shrine at St Day were probably 'signposted' by crosses, wells and chapels. An exemplar might have been the cross of Penhalvyngan, erected for the soul of the Lord of Tolgollow, which was situated on the modern road which leads from Carharrack to Comford, and now stands in the grounds of Scorrier House. And there was an alleged chapel which gave its name to 'Chapel Hill', marked on a map of 1767, on the western side of Lanner valley. Two granite crosses thought to have belonged to this chapel were re-erected outside the entrance to Lanner Christ Church by the Reverend F. Buckler. One is the damaged head of a round-headed cross found in a hedge at Tredeague Farm. It is eighteen inches in diameter, and has been fixed on to a new rough-hewn pillar of granite. The cross head has a crucifix in high relief on both sides, and is encircled with a three-inch raised beading, a design which is very rare in Cornwall (Fig 1.2).

Fig. 1.2. *Cornish Cross with Christ figure, re-erected in Lannarth churchyard entrance.* (© The Paddy Bradley Collection).

The second is also a round-headed cross, but with a Latin cross on each side. It was found by Mr Shepherd on the Tresavean side of Bell Farm. On the front the cross is raised about half an inch, and on the back the cross is outlined by a groove about three-quarters of an inch deep. The height of the second cross is four foot six inches, and perhaps two feet of shaft are in the ground. The diameter of the head is fifteen inches.[34]

There does not appear to be any evidence to support the hypothesis that the name 'Lanner' signifies an early Celtic Christian settlement with a 'lann' or an enclosed cemetery. The chapel which formerly existed on the western side of the valley might have been erected as a wayside chapel for pilgrims, or alternatively for the private worship of the Brewer family of the Manor of Pensignance (see below), the place name 'Brewer' being not far from Chapel Hill.

The Reformation

The chapel which gave its name to Chapel Hill, like its famous counterpart at Gorland, St Day, was probably destroyed during the Reformation. With more than a whiff of revolution in the air and intensifying protest at the doctrinal elements of Catholic practice by the likes of Luther and Calvin, the unsettled atmosphere of the early sixteenth century enabled Henry VIII to break with the Papacy between 1530 and 1534 and thus begin the process of Tudor centralisation, the effects of which were felt in every corner of the kingdom.

In 1534 Henry assumed the position of the Supreme Head of the *Anglicana Ecclesia*, and secured for himself full power 'to visit, redress, reform, correct, and amend all errors, heresies, abuses and enormities which by any manner of spiritual authority may lawfully be reformed and redressed'. He was aided in this new spiritual jurisdiction by a vicar-general, Thomas Cromwell.[35] In the following six years, Henry made the breach with Rome final by crushing active opposition and by seizing the lands of the monasteries which he redistributed amongst the gentry of the day who had supported him. In Cornwall, the Arundell, Carew, Rashleigh, Prideaux and Treffry families all made gains through the dissolution of monastic holdings. Thereafter land came to be regarded as property to be bought and sold, as well as being derived by hereditary succession.

But the unsettled era for the Church did not end with Henry's death in 1547, for the very next year an angry mob in West Cornwall murdered a Protestant Commissioner, and in 1549 the Cornish people were provoked into rebellion. The arbitrary measures of the Council of Edward VI were greatly disliked and provoked a storm of protest in many local parishes, because they directly affected 'the penumbra of superstition and custom which was the religion of the people'.[36] Numerous age-old rites were abolished, such as the bearing of candles on Candlemas Day, ashes on Ash Wednesday, and palms on Palm Sunday. Creeping to the cross was no longer allowed, nor was the making of holy bread and holy water. Even more startling was the removal of all images, stained glass and frescoes from church interiors, which had provided the visual aids to faith. All future services were to be held not in Latin, but in English, and the first *Book of Common Prayer* in English was introduced. English, it must be remembered, was at this time a very foreign language in a land where Cornish was the mother tongue.

In addition, Edward ordered that parish records should be kept, which made the Cornish intensely suspicious as they suspected this to be merely another device to demand increased taxation from them. (The failed Cornish Rebellion of 1497 was an event which remained within living memory for some people.). And on top of this, a full inventory of all church plate, jewels, ornaments, bells and vestments made the impact of change all the more revolutionary and shocking.

James states that little of value was found at Gwennap Church, and mentions that just one chalice and paten were restored to the Church by Queen Mary; the rest had presumably been hidden to avoid seizure. Edward's measures had encountered stiff resistance in West Cornwall and the 'obnoxious tool' used by the Council of Edward VI to enforce their will, John Body, was murdered at Helston on 5 April 1548 as he attempted to remove 'Popish' images from the parish church. In the mob which killed Body were at least four Gwennap men: John Chykose, husbandman, Alan Rawe, husbandman, Laurence Breton or Franke, a Breton groom, and Michael Vian Bretton, a Breton husbandman.[37]

Opposition to the continuing march of the Reformation came to a head in 1549 with the Prayer Book Rebellion, which had almost the nature of a crusade, as hundreds of Cornishmen led by parish priests marched to demand the restoration of the old Catholic practices. The rebellion was crushed at a battle near Exeter, largely by foreign mercenaries recruited by Lord Somerset, regent for Edward VI. Tudor Queen Elizabeth I added another blow to the Church, in 1568, when she confiscated many of the ancient chapels with which our Cornish parishes abounded in the Middle Ages. These included the Chapel of the Holy Trinity at St Day, 'Gwenep Ground', very possibly the chapel and enclosure thought to have been situated to the south of the current Gwennap Parish Church, and perhaps that at Chapel Hill.[38]

The ultimate result of the Reformation in Cornwall was the alienation of the people from the Church. The clergy was seriously depleted in number and links with our Celtic, Catholic cousins in Brittany were severed. Moreover, the popular shrines and wayside chapels which had so characterised Celto-Catholic Cornwall were destroyed and the ornate interiors of our parish churches with their colourful stained glass and frescoes, and beautiful carved screens and images were obliterated, leaving places of worship gaunt and bare.

A gulf between Church and people opened in Cornwall, one that was ultimately filled by Methodism, which became the dominant religious force in Gwennap, as we shall see in Chapter 9.

The Ancient Manor of Pensignance

The first census and survey of English landowners and their property was made by order of William the Conqueror in 1085–86. Only two manors which appeared in the Domesday Survey have been positively identified in the Lanner area, that of Tolgolle (near St Day) and Tregoose (near Stithians). 'Gwennap' is first mentioned at the end of the twelfth century in a charter dated at Brionne in Normandy on 18 October 1199, in which King John confirmed to the celebrated Judge William Briwer, the Manor of Pentigenand and the right of presentation to the Church of Lamwenap which he had by gift of Godfrey, Bishop of Winchester.[39] It is not known how the latter acquired it. The judge in turn gave the advowson of the church in 1225 to the Dean and Chapter of Exeter Cathedral.

In this Charter, the church at Gwennap is referred to as the 'Church of Pensigenens' (Pensignance), which provides evidence that when the manorial system was first introduced into Cornwall, the ancient Church of South Wennap must have been attached to the Manor of Pensignance.[40] This manor was not mentioned in Domesday, and so must have formed a part of a much larger manor, but which is not known.

Considerable controversy has surrounded the location of the Domesday Manor of Chienmerc, which John Carne, in a paper of 1867, suggested referred to Carn Marth in Gwennap, held at the time of Domesday by Alward. He claims that this manor thereafter passed from Alward to Richard de Lucie and then to his co-heiress, Rohesia de Lucie, who then granted all her lands in Cornwall to William de Briwer.[41] However, recent research seems to prove his theory wrong. It now appears that Chienmerc in fact refers to Carmar or Kilmerigh in St Kew.[42] Yet sometime in the twelfth century, the original large manor which included our area, was split up and the Manor of Pensignance was created, with William de Briwer the landowner. Sometime afterwards, the manor passed to the Durant Family who held Pensignance until about 1513. In 1639, Richard Carew, in his *Survey of Cornwall*, noted that six Cornish acres as Knights' fees from each of the manors of Tallgollen and Pensignans were assigned to King Edward III, but more importantly, in 1402, Thomas Durant paid one fee Morton on the Manor of Penzenguans as Knights' fees to King Henry IV.[43]

On 6 February 1585, James Erysye of Erysye mortgaged his 'Manor of Pensugnans in the parishes of Guynop and Key' for £220 to 'Sir ffrances Drake of Buckland in the Countie of Devon, Knight'.[44] James Erisey later married the sister of the author Richard Carew, and after his death the manor reverted to his wife's family. James states that the Manor House formerly stood at the turning of the lane from the main road to the schoolroom, west of the belfry of Gwennap Church. It was dismantled in about 1765 and the site was later occupied by a public house until around 1800. In 1768 Jonathan Rashleigh came into possession of a much smaller Manor of Pensignance through his marriage to Jane Carew. James states that the manor then included lands which later became a part of the Parish of Lanner - Brewer and Trethellan.[45]

Other manors were created out of the original large Manor of Pensignance before the turn of the thirteenth century. These included Trevarth, Cusgarne, Tolcarne, Trevethan and Treskerby. Strangely, Trevince, one of the largest holdings, did not receive manorial status. The earliest reference to Trevarth seems to be that of 1281 where the names of John and Oliver de Trevart appear in a document relating to a Visitation by a Commissary of the Chapter, formed to arrange the income of the incumbent of Gwennap church.[46]

A further reference to the Trevarth Family is made in the Stannary Roll of 1305–6, when Johannes Margh was noted as having sent thirty shipments of tin to Truro, which clearly shows the antiquity of tin mining in our vicinity. The Bodrugan Family formerly held a part of the Manor of Trevarth, which was lost through forfeiture in 1485, the estate then passing to Sir Richard Edgcumbe whose descendant was created the Earl of Mount Edgcumbe in 1789.[47]

The Bodrugan land was sold to the Beauchamp Family of Trevince by the Earl of Mount Edgcumbe at the beginning of the twentieth century, and included Trevarth House with about 60 acres of arable land, and several acres of waste and mining dumps.

The Landed Gentry

During the sixteenth and seventeenth centuries, a complicated series of marriage dowries caused the division of local manors and estates and the families of Beauchamp, Rogers, Edgcumbe, Buller and Trefusis, who later became Lord Clinton, emerged as the principal landowners in our area. In Lanner, the Beauchamp Family held Penventon and Penstruthal, and jointly with the Rogers Family of Penrose, Bell Veor and Lannarth. Tresavean was held by the Buller and Rogers families. Trevarth was held jointly by Lord Clinton, and the Edgcumbe and Beauchamp families. Lord Clinton of Trefusis held the land at Carvannel solely, but Pennance was held jointly with the Buller family, as a part of their Manor of Tolgus. Tretharrup also formed a portion of the Manor of Tolgus. These wealthy and powerful landowners dominated life for centuries through their ownership of land. People wanting to acquire a smallholding would have to have purchased the leasehold, usually for a period of 99 years, under a system of three lives, and on top of this, agree to pay an annual rent and a heriot (fine) should one of the names die and another needed to be added. Ultimately the land and appurtenances thereupon reverted back to the landowner. In addition, many landowners had also apportioned the rights of tithe from the local church, which provided a further source of annual income.

But of far greater importance to the landed families, and the source of their immense wealth, lay with their claim to the mineral rights on their land. Gwennap, of which Lanner was once a part, became the 'copper kingdom' of the world in the late eighteenth century, and in addition, useful

Fig. 1.3. *Manorial markers at the summit of carn Marth. 'PT' signifies Pennance in the Manor of Tolgus, part of the Buller Estate.* (photo S.P. Schwartz).

amounts of tin were also discovered (see Chapter 3). Families such as the Rogers, Beauchamps, Clintons and Bullers made a fortune from the mineral dues paid to them by some of Cornwall's most famous mines which lay in our area - Wheal Beauchamp, Penstruthal, Tresavean and Wheal Buller. And that these great families once dominated the area is recorded in granite – the mineral markers and manorial boundary stones delineating their separate holdings, which may still be seen all around the Parish of Gwennap.

Several are sited at the summit of Carn Marth. One bears the crude initials CT on the side which faces St Day, indicating that it was a boundary stone delineating the lands of Lord Clinton of Trefusis, whilst the opposite face has the roughly carved inscription PT, indicating that the stone also marked the boundary between Pennance in the Manor of Tolgus, a part of the Buller estate (Fig. 1.3). It is Grade II listed, and probably dates from the early nineteenth century. Many more may be seen at Tresavean, bearing the marks of the Buller family.

These great families owned lands in the Lanner area until relatively recent times, but the introduction of Estate Duties in 1889 and Death Duties in 1894 signalled the start of the diminution of the great landowner's authority, as many landed families were forced to sell off their land to pay the crushing duties. And this process was quickened by the loss of life in the Boer and First World Wars, in which many sons of the gentry had served as officers. In the following decades, parcels of land in many of the large estates in our area were sold, an example being the lands comprising the Buller's Manor of Tolgus in 1917.[48]

After the First World War, the Rogers of Penrose sold off much of their land on the western side of Lanner valley. For the first time, many ordinary working people could own their own home and land. But the landowners did not forfeit the rights to the minerals which might yet lie deep underground, the basis of their former wealth.

Place Names

Many of the place names with which we are familiar have gradually emerged over the centuries, and it is interesting to attempt to discover when they first came into usage, and what they might mean when translated from the ancient Cornish language. Many local place names begin with the first element 'tre' which means farmstead or estate. So widespread is this prefix in Cornish place names, that Padel considers that in origin it must have had something to do with agriculture. 'The use of "tre" as a standard settlement term must go back to the Common Brittonic period: that is shown by its use in all Brittonic areas, including Southern Scotland and North West England... compare also the Welsh "tref" and Breton "trev".'[49] In other words, 'tre' dates from at least Celtic times. Local examples include Tresavean, Trethellan, Trevarth, Treviskey and Tretharrup.

The earliest recorded local place name appears to be that of the ancient manor, Pensignance, which translated from the Cornish means 'pen', head, 'segh', dry, 'nans', valley – head of the dry valley. A century later 'Trevargh', from the Cornish 'tre' and 'margh', appears in 1277, and thereafter as Trevare (1281), Trevarth (1613), Trevark (1767) and Trewrath (1768), with a possible translation of horse farmstead, from the Cornish 'margh' – horse. Other early place names include Bell Veor/Vean and Tresavean, first mentioned in 1336. The former, which appeared as Bel-Woles, could mean great mine, from 'meur' – great, and bal, mine; but Padel notes that 'Bell' could come from the Cornish 'pell' which in English means far, or distant. Could Bell Veor just mean great distance? Bell Vean might therefore be translated as 'little distance' from the Cornish 'vyghan' which means little.

The first written reference to Tresavean was also in the fourteenth century, as 'Treyusu'. It afterwards appeared as Tresowe (1588), Treyusow vyan and Tresovean (1608), Trusavean (1655), 'Tregevaen' (1755) and 'Trejeuvyan' in 1758. The meaning of Tresavean could be 'tre' plus a personal name, perhaps from Breton, and 'vyghan'. The great mine which was responsible for the growth and creation of Lanner Parish took its name from this early farmstead. Trethellan appears in 1350 as Tredyen, and thereafter as Tredelyn (1409), Trethelyn (1412, 1434, 1493, 1542 and 1601), and Trethellin in 1613. The meaning of the name is uncertain, but could incorporate a personal name, in this case, 'Dinan', giving Trethellan the meaning of Dinan's homestead.

Pennance is first mentioned in 1380, and means head or top of the valley, from the Cornish 'pen' head, and 'nans', valley, an apt description for a settlement high above the valley of Lanner. The earliest reference to Carvannel is 1390, and, as we have already established, means fort of the broom.

Lanner appears rather later as 'Lannarth' in the year 1542, and comes from 'lanherch', the Cornish for clearing or glade, and probably refers to the Lanner Green area. Tretharrup was also mentioned in 1542, and is derived from the Cornish 'tre' and 'gortharup', which means very pleasant, or unpleasant, farmstead or settlement. Penventon meaning spring-head, from the Cornish 'pen', head, and 'fenten', spring is also recorded in 1542. Bell from the Cornish 'pell', meaning far or distant, is noted in 1613 and Brewer in 1666, the latter named for William Briwer the medieval owner of Pensignance, mentioned above.

Penstruthal, or Bedstruthal is more recent, noted in 1819, with the possible meaning of top or end of the narrow moor, from the Cornish 'pen', top, 'stroth' narrow or constricted, and 'hal', moor.

Looking around Lanner Parish today, the signs of its modern mining past are evident everywhere, so that much of its early history has been obscured or obliterated in the march of industrial progress. Yet the antiquity of many of the above local place names points to the inhabitation of our area from early times. But the numbers living in these scattered communities was very small for many centuries, for it was not until the late eighteenth century that the population figures began to increase, and then rise dramatically, as deep lode mining took off at Tresavean and some of its satellite mines, causing a wave of in-migration to Gwennap which swelled the numbers of people living in small hamlets such as Lanner, as we shall see in the next chapter.

REFERENCES

1 James, C.C., *History of Gwennap* privately published, undated, p. 117.
2 Cornwall Archaeological Unit (CAU) Database, County Hall, Truro.
3 James, C.C., p. 117-118.
4 Weatherhill, C., *Cornovia, Ancient Sites of Cornwall and Scilly*, Cornwall Books, 1997, p. 55; see also Tangye, M., *Carn Brea*, Dyllansow Truran, Redruth, 1981, pp. 18-25 .
5 CAU Database.
6 James, C.C., P.118
7 Francis, W., *Gwennap, A Descriptive Poem*, J. May, Redruth, 1845, p. 116.
8 CAU Database.
9 Padel, O.J., *Cornish Place-Name Elements*, English Place Name Society, Vol LVI/LVII, 1985.
10 Ibid. p. 16.
11 Ibid. p. 9.
12 Francis, W., p. 123.
13 Ibid.
14 CAU Database.
15 Padel, O.J., p. 164.
16 James, C.C., p. 121.
17 Penhallurick, R.D., *Tin in Antiquity*, The Institute of Metals, London, 1986, p. 143-146.
18 Branigan K, and Fowler, P.J., *The Roman West Country, Classical Culture and Celtic Society*, David &Charles, Newton Abbot, 1976, p. 196.
19 Penhallurick, R.D., p. 194.
20 Ibid. p. 194.
21 Bristow, C., *Cornwall's Geology and Scenery*, Hillside Publications, St Austell, 1996, p. 91.
22 George, K., *Gerlyver Kernewek Kemmyn*, The Cornish Language Board, 1993, p. 213.
23 Francis, W., p. 116.
24 Wilson, J., *Cornwall Land of Legend*, Bossiney Books, St Teath, Bodmin, 1989, p. 37.
25 Sharkey, J., *Celtic Mysteries*, Thames and Hudson, 1984, p. 18.
26 Jenkin, A.K. Hamilton, *Cornwall and Its People*, David & Charles, Newton Abbot, 1970, pp. 439-440.
27 Tangye, M., *Carn Brea*, Dyllansow Truran, Redruth, 1981, pp 33-34
28 Padel, O.J., p. 66.
29 Ibid, pp. 32, 177, 77, 101, 142.
30 Francis, W., p. 177.

31 Annear, P., *The Church and Chapel of the Holy Trinity of St Day*, 1994, p. 8
32 The Henderson MSS, RIC, Truro.
33 Ibid.
34 Doble, G.H., *A History of the Parish of Gwennap*, Cornish Parish Histories, No.8, 1943, p. 8.
35 Mackie, J.D., *The Early Tudors, The Oxford History of England*, Clarendon Press, Oxford, 1988, p. 335.
36 Rowse, A.L., *Tudor Cornwall*, Dyllansow Truran, Redruth, 1941, p. 335.
37 James, C.C., p.18. Cornwall's links with Brittany grew out of trade and religious contact, as well as a similar Celtic tongue, and many Breton migrants settled in Cornwall. Names such as Tangye, Harvey and Britton reflect our common heritage. See Payton, Philip, *The Making of Modern Cornwall*, Dyllansow Truran, Redruth, 1992, p. 55.
38 Doble, G.H., *A History of the Parish of Gwennap*, Cornish Parish Histories, No.8, 1943, p. 6.
39 James, C.C., p.12.
40 Ibid.
41 *Journal of the Royal Institution of Cornwall*, Vol 2, 1867, p. 222.
42 Maxwell, I.S., *The Domesday Settlements of Cornwall*, Cornish Branch of the Historical Association, 1986, p. 24, also Padel, O.J., p. 46.
43 James, C.C., p.60.
44 Ibid., p. 64.
45 Ibid., p.66.
46 Ibid., p. 60.
47 Ibid. pp. 61-62.
48 The Sale Book of the Manor of Tolgus, in Private Possession.
49 Padel. O.J., p. 223.

Chapter 2
The Community in the Nineteenth Century

The development of steam-driven pumping machinery at the end of the eighteenth century which allowed mines such as Tresavean to be dewatered and worked to greater depths, gave a marked impetus to the local mining industry. F.L. Harris describes this exciting time in Cornish history as 'a renaissance of enterprise' in which all classes appeared to have been affected: 'The Cornish people were never more creative. The native industries, above all, mining, had developed their characteristics through the centuries, in all ranks, from the adventurer of means to the working miner who bargained for his pitch and worked it. Now the challenges of a new age brought them out vividly – the ready eye for a sign of opportunity, the vision of great achievement and reward, the willingness to labour with furious energy and devoted skill'.[1]

The Parish of Gwennap, of which Lanner was then a part, became a region specialising in copper mining. This industrialisation, centred on copper mining, created a region much different from that which existed before or since. In other parts of England, the same process was experienced, but on a much larger scale. The Midlands became synonymous with metalware production, Lancashire with cotton manufacture, Clydeside for shipbuilding, and so on. Hudson argues that in the eighteenth century, smaller proto-industrial (pre-industrial) regions had existed but in relative isolation from one another because of poor transportation and communication 'and lack of the economic complementarity which might stimulate major transport improvements'.[2]

Such regions disappeared from the mid eighteenth century to be replaced by distinct, internally integrated and economically more specialised regions whose extra-regional export base became an important foundation of their success. The success or failure of Gwennap, then, rested on its ability to export copper ore which was dispatched to the Swansea smelters, close to the coalfields of South Wales.

However, by the mid 1850s the warning signs of impending economic collapse in the county's copper industry were apparent enough for those who wanted to see them. Production was slowly declining at a time when the output from foreign countries such as Cuba, Chile and South Australia was increasing. Cornwall did not have an inexhaustible supply of copper, and many mines which hoped to produce tin, usually encountered below the shallower copper deposits, did not find economically viable quantities. A crisis ensued, one which Philip Payton has argued was born 'of the imperfect, incomplete and overspecialised industrialisation that Cornwall had experienced and which culminated in social and economic marginalisation'.[3]

Industrial progress slowly halted and Cornwall, in its far away corner of Britain, was gradually left behind the rest of the nation. Lanner, one in a constellation of mining villages around the old industrial towns of Camborne and Redruth, was subjected to a process of de-industrialisation to which its inhabitants seemed to have little or no answer beyond emigration.

Industrialisation and Growth

William Francis in his descriptive poem of Gwennap, composed in 1845, mentions the time when, just within living memory of some of the elderly members of the community, there were but six cottages along the route of the Redruth & Chasewater Railway, and the Turnpike Road from Redruth to Penryn was so little frequented, that it was 'regarded with fear by women and youth'.[4] How different the picture of Lanner Parish was by the middle of the nineteenth century:

Trevarth and Treviskey, Pennance, Tresavean,
I see with farms around them, and hamlets between:
A dense population now greets the glad eye,
Where stood lonely houses in ages gone by.[5]

Lanner had seen a remarkable growth from the beginning of that century due to the success of the mining industry within its vicinity, foremost among these mines being the highly productive Tresavean. Hundreds of people seeking work gravitated towards the villages and hamlets of the semi-rural Parish of Gwennap which lay at the heartland of the world's richest copper mining region.

Francis, describing Lanner's valley, provides a colourful description of the importance of the mining industry to Lanner's development:

'...employment is rife;
your ears are well greeted with clank and with clang
of machinery sounds, and also the bang
of the massive stamp heads, th' halvans all crushing...
...Some are building a boiler the sound is rap rap
Hills send back the echo through every gap'.[6]

Richard Thomas's map, dated 1819, depicts several buildings clustered around the village green with a further group of dwellings shown around the square, prominent among these being the Commercial Inn. Scattered farms and smallholdings dotted the hills surrounding the valley, and a few individual cottages were shown along the route of Rough Street. No terraced housing was indicated. The earliest terrace of cottages built were six at the bottom end of the row on the way up Lanner Hill on the right side, and were probably constructed in the early 1830s. Other early terraces indicated appear to have been the row of cottages almost opposite the village square, which included the Miners' Arms Public House, and the row with the old Post Office, now the Londis Shop. These were probably built at a similar date to those above. Lanner was separated from Lanner Moor by a stretch of low lying, boggy moorland. Close to the Turnpike Road, an array of devices had been erected to crush and dress the tin ore from local mines, the noise of which certainly made an impression on William Francis, as evidenced above. The course of the stream, later known as the 'leat', which ran through the valley had been diverted to power the waterwheels for several sets of Cornish stamps.

Pennance, a separate hamlet situated above Lanner on the south-facing slope of Carn Marth, contained even fewer houses than Lanner. Terraced housing here only appeared after the mid century. Trevarth, an old farming village also witnessing rapid growth because of mining, contained buildings mainly connected to farms which were considered to be of great age, and was separated from Pennance and Lanner by fields and a rough cart track which probably had its origins in antiquity. A map dated 1827 shows two rows of cottages, one of which appeared to contain about three houses along the course of Trevarth Lane (the road which leads to Penponds), and a smith's shop. These old terraces at Trevarth were constructed of cob and moorstone and have disappeared.

The Creation of Lanner Parish

The population of Gwennap increased sharply between the years 1821–1841, as people flooded into the villages, including Lanner, from elsewhere, most in search of work in the mines. Many of those who made Lanner their home in the first half of the nineteenth century had arrived from neighbouring parishes, as depicted by analysis of the 1851 census. Of those listed as moving to Lanner Parish to live, 21 per cent came from Wendron, over 15 per cent from Stithians, 11 per cent from Redruth, 9 per cent from Illogan and 4 per cent from Perranarworthal.[7]

This increase in population was the reason for the creation of Lanner Parish, as separate from Gwennap, on 3 December 1844 (see Chapter 9). In the middle of the nineteenth century the area was very much a neighbourhood of miners, as evidenced by the registers of baptisms and marriages for Lanner Christ Church. The first baptism, by the Revd John Tucker on 12 January 1845, was of Emily Holman, daughter of a miner of Lannarth, Josiah Holman, and his wife Elizabeth. Of the next seven names (Whitburn of Pennance; Harris of Carnmarth; Lawn of Carnmarth; Pascoe of Carnmarth; Canon of Ting Tang; Jorey of Pennance; Bessanco of The Stamps), all but one were the children of miners. The first wedding was also between the children of miners, Edward Moyle and Ann Dower, on 4 August 1845.[8] They signed the register with their marks, a cross.

To accommodate this increase in population, more rows of miners' cottages were built along the route of the Turnpike Road which ran through the village, thus ensuring Lanner would develop into a linear settlement. These terraces probably date from the mid 1830s–40s and include Bears Terrace (the cottages which are situated at Lanner Moor near the junction of the road to Trevarth), parts of Pennance Terrace which date from the late 1830s to early 1840s and further additions made to the row up Lanner Hill, built above those which already existed. Francis notes the appearance of these new rows of miners' cottages with the remark:

Improvements or mining may furnish the tale.
Long ranges of buildings substantial and neat,
With their fair verdant gardens all blooming complete.[9]

Built during the boom years of Tresavean Mine, and constructed of granite and killas, with slate roofs, these new dwellings were in many cases an improvement on the thatch and cob cottages in which many people had lived in the eighteenth century.

Further terraces were developed bit-by-bit during the nineteenth century; a terrace of three cob and moorstone cottages, named Pilcher's Row, was built on the eastern flank of Carn Marth close to the summit, probably during the late 1830s. Pentreath Terrace at Lanner Moor probably dates from the 1840s. Church Row was built in the late 1840s, and Grays Terrace was constructed in stages during the late 1840s to mid 1850s by Mr Gray, who designed number 7, the cottage with the crescent-shaped gateway in the garden wall, for himself. It was his intention to continue to build Grays Terrace which has 11 cottages, as evidenced by the large stones left sticking out of the wall of the one facing Falmouth. But the money he earned abroad to finance his endeavour ran out and his building plans were stopped.

Brays Terrace probably dates from the same period, and was constructed by Captain Bray who worked at Tresavean Mine (Fig. 2.1). Tresavean Terrace, opposite the Coppice, did not appear on the Tithe Map of 1845 and was probably built during the 1850s. The rows of cottages at Trevarth seem to have been constructed during the late 1860s, as they appear on a manorial map dated 1876. Later terraces include Woodlands Terrace, constructed in the 1880s on a parcel of waste land which was formerly the site of a set of stamps, and Prisks Terrace, which bears the construction date of 1889.

Building cottages in terraces was cheaper, because it meant that only three walls had to be constructed instead of four. There is evidence that the system of land tenure, whereby a landlord leased a plot of land upon which the

Fig 2.1. *Lanner village, turnpike road looking South. Bray's and Woodland Terraces on left.* (original photo by Caddy, © Lanner Historical Society).

lessee was permitted to build a cottage under the three lives system, was on the decline in neighbouring Redruth Parish before the mid nineteenth century.[10] Presumably the same could be said for Gwennap. As the population increased in the mining districts, so the availability of land began to decrease, thus placing pressure on the finite resource of suitable land. This meant that people were beginning to be increasingly housed in terraced cottages, which became as much a symbol of Cornwall's industrial era as the brick and grit stone rows of colliers' cottages were to the mining towns of South Wales and the Midlands.

Lanner and its satellite villages contained an interesting blend of housing by the end of the Victorian era and several residences of note, including West Trevarth Farm, Lambriggan House, Pennance House, Melrose House, Tregiffian, Lanner House, Clinton Villa and Glyngarth, each bearing witness to the affluence of a new but relatively small middle class which had emerged because of the success of the local mining industry.

Economic Collapse, Depression and the Advent of Peripheralism

The local economy grew steadily in the first decades of the nineteenth century. At this time Gwennap was the world's chief producer of copper ore and its mines were its life blood. However, by the 1840s there were economic storm clouds gathering on the horizon, in the shape of upheaval abroad. The revolutions which swept through the Continent in 1848, foremost of these being the second French Revolution, led to a collapse in the price of tin and copper on the world market, which in turn translated into lower wages and unemployment in Gwennap's great mines. This compounded the problems of a succession of poor harvests, and the failure of the potato crop, which led to soaring prices. The 1840s witnessed great suffering among the poor of Gwennap. In 1839 several gentlemen in the Parish of Gwennap had subscribed to a fund set up to alleviate suffering in the severe winter weather. Four hundred bushels of coal were given to the poor and needy families to alleviate the suffering caused by high prices and low wages paid in the mines.[11]

Poor families had become used to eking out a meagre living just above subsistence level on a spartan diet of watery broth made with minute quantities of meat, into which all manner of greens would be boiled, including sometimes stinging nettles, and 'milsey bread' (a moist, sticky bread made from partially fermented grain), or barley bread and skimmed milk, a meal which earned the sobriquet 'sky blue and sinker'. An old woman living in the late nineteenth century, wrote that she prayed the men would have a 'good catch of pilchards', as she, like most labouring folk, regularly ate 'pilchards and tatties (potatoes)' washed down with weak tea.

On rare occasions, such as when the family pig (or that of a neighbour) was slaughtered, a slice of fatty home-cured ham with a few home-grown vegetables would grace the miner's table. However, in the depressed economic times of the late 1840s, many poor families found themselves unable to cope.

A general subscription had commenced throughout Gwennap in 1847, and an application was made to the mining and landed proprietors for their charitable co-operation 'which it is hoped that by a rigorous and combined effort of all classes, we may be able, with God's Blessing to mitigate that severe suffering which now threatens to be universal'.[12]

In June 1848, Gwennap's Guardians of the Poor pleaded with the Board of Redruth to revert to the former practice of relieving the able-bodied poor with bread to prevent people from becoming ill and malnourished, and had put unemployed men from Gwennap to work on breaking up crofts to earn enough money to feed their families. Their wages were to have been paid out of the Highways' Rate as a matter of urgency.[13] But many of the poor in possession of smallholdings were compelled to sell their property because they could not pay their rates or rent. Unemployment, and dependence upon the failed potato crop to pay off the rent, spelt disaster for numerous people who decided to emigrate, heralding the beginning of the migratory trend from Lanner, which was actively encouraged by the parish overseers (see Chapters 7 and 8).

The 1850s were a period of transition within Lanner and district. The copper mining industry in Lanner was in trouble well before the calamitous crash of the mid 1860s. Tresavean was showing signs of decline in production and grade of ore mined throughout the 1840s, the last dividend coming in 1847. This precipitated an economic slowing down, the shedding of large numbers of its workforce and the streamlining of operations as a cost cutting exercise, with the management increasingly going over to contract work as opposed to tribute.

As long as tribute work continued the miner maintained some control over the pace of his labour and was free to spend his out-of-core (shift) time in the way he chose. But the decline in the amount of tribute work produced several subtle changes in the miner's lifestyle both socially and culturally. Less control over their free time to work smallholdings or allotments meant that the mining family became more dependent on a formal wage economy and increasingly lived in terraced housing, like their counterparts in many of the northern industrial regions of England. Those without

Fig.2.2. *Athanasius Pryor and Family, of Bell Veor House, Lanner, 1866. After being a mine agent, Pryor was appointed copper ore sampler and assayer in 1848, for Messrs Williams, Foote & Co, Swansea. He was a rigid Conservative, and dissenter, and this formal group illustrates the new social position of the managerial class at this time. The photograph is a copy of a copy made in 1890, of the original by Matthew Row, in 1866.*(© Royal Institution of Cornwall, Truro).

employment and who were divorced from access to land for the supply of food and fuel, found themselves at the mercy of the Guardians of the Poor for charity in the form of the dole. Culturally there was a decline in the observance of traditional rural leisure pursuits, such as the Midsummer celebrations, which used to merit a day off, but which by the mid century was on the wane.

The growth of an articulate, affluent and increasingly confident middle class which had made its money through the local mining industry was beginning to make its presence felt in the parish, playing a prominent role in the life of village institutions - the chapels, schools and philanthropic societies, a pattern which was mirrored in many of the other industrial towns and villages of the nation (Fig. 2.2).

At this time, Bernard Deacon has argued, Cornwall was nudged on to a more convergent path with such other industrial regions of Britain. However, he argues that this convergence was to be short-lived. The over-specialisation of the Gwennap area, reliant on the success of its export commodity, copper, proved to be its undoing.[14] The collapse of the copper industry was paralleled by a major outflow of people, and the limited diversification of the Cornish economy made the loss of the copper industry an even larger void which seemed incapable of being bridged. Similar scenes to those witnessed during the 1840s returned to the parish as great era of the 'Copper Kingdom' came to an end in the mid 1860s following the collapse of the price of copper on the world market, precipitated by the failure of bankers Overend and Gurney.

One by one the local 'bals' were 'knacked'. 'The distress which prevails would scarcely be believed but for the corroboration of the Scripture readers', wrote William Jenkin of Trewirgie House, Redruth in 1867, continuing: 'the Union House had never been so full'.[15]

The winter weather of 1866–67 was particularly severe. In Gwennap a general subscription of the landed and wealthy was organised and a committee of 4–5 people elected to provide aid to those who had been in receipt of parochial relief in the previous half year. A sum of £61 16s 4½d was distributed to 250 families, and bread, soup, coal and clothing, over double the amount usually distributed to the poor, was dispatched. In the Central Mining District (the area surrounding Camborne and Redruth), a list containing the names of 41 Gwennap families who had applied for relief, many headed by widows or women whose husbands were abroad, as well as sick, poorly paid or unemployed men, was received by the Guardians of the Poor. The 41 families had a total of 178 children between them.[16]

A huge emigration of people to South America, Canada, Australia, New Zealand and America is recorded, also to the coalfields of Wales and the Midlands, the lead mines of Derbyshire and iron mines of Scotland, Cheshire, Yorkshire and Lancashire. In 1871, it was noted that, since 1868, 2750 people had moved from Chasewater, Gwennap and Redruth to the North of England, hoping to find work in the cotton mills of Burnley, Bacup, Skipton and Oldham.[17]

In the 1870s the tin industry was hit hard by the vagaries of the international market which dictated prices. In 1875 the price for tin hit an all time low and prompted the closure of numerous marginal mines in the Central Mining District, further prompting migration. A surplus supply of labour was therefore removed, but this ultimately reduced the opportunity the Central Mining District had of meeting conditions necessary for a consumer market to flourish and a more diversified economic structure to appear. This, as Bernard Deacon has perceptively argued, was one reason, along with Cornwall's distance from major market centres, why it never attained the 'critical mass' needed to support consumer-oriented industries on a significant scale.[18]

It has been argued that marriage statistics provide a sensitive indicator of the state of the nineteenth century economy. If we follow the argument that in times of economic upswings, more people were likely to marry than in times of economic downturns and uncertainty, we should see a pattern emerge which will throw more light on how the local economy affected Lanner sociologically.

Using the Lanner Christ Church marriage register, we can see that the period up to the early 1870s was subject to wild fluctuations, with peak years for marriage in the mid 40s, mid 50s, early 60s and early 70s (Fig. 2.3). The lowest points came in the late 40s, early 50s, late 50s, mid 60s and mid 70s. These peaks and troughs, particularly those of the late 1840s – the time of the potato blight and recession on the mines, and the depressions of the mid 60s and 70s, following the collapse of the copper and tin mining industries – correspond directly to the ups and downs of trade cycles in the mining industry. After the mid 70s, the trend continues downward, punctuated by a few smaller peaks in the mid 80s and 90s as the economy improved.

Migration and the effects of mine closures and de-industrialisation conspired to keep the numbers of those marrying low in comparison to the 1840s and 50s. It is interesting to

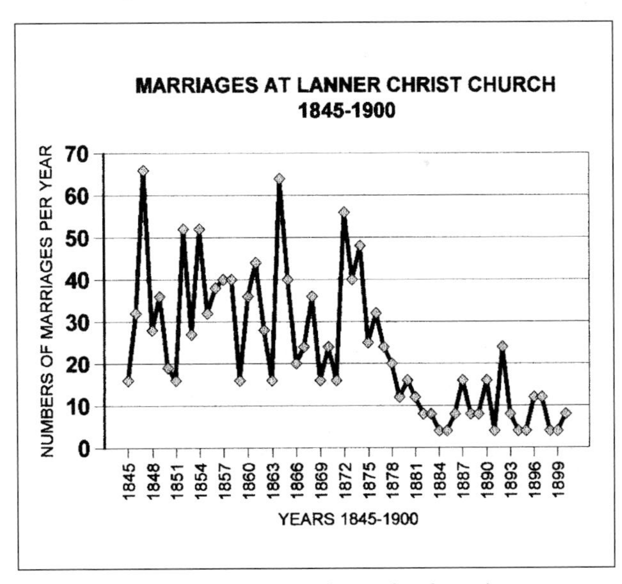

Fig.2.3. *Marriages at Lanner Christ Church, 1845–1900.*

note that Methodist revivals and chapel building, extensions and renovations, also appear to correspond to the swings in the local economy.

Lanner's False Dawn

After the hardship and trauma of the late 1840s and the disastrous collapse of the mining industry in the 1860s and 70s, the 1880s were a period of limited growth in the Parish of Lanner and district, which witnessed a mini building boom. Many village men found much needed employment in the Carn Marth quarries and the local brick works.

One of the main reasons for the development of Lanner at this time was a feel-good factor which had sprung from the reopening of the Tresavean Mines. 'There are many signs that this parish will again in some measure become as important and busy as it was some 20-30 years ago. In mining, the starting and working of Tresavean Mines have been the means of circulating a deal of money and giving employment to many in the parish,' ran a report in a local newspaper in 1883. 'Houses are, we hear, being let in the neighbourhood, which have been tenantless for years'.[19] Many plans for new buildings were promulgated, such as those published in the local press for a new tower and north aisle for Lanner Church.

This economic upswing in Lanner was further aided and enhanced by developments in nearby Redruth which underwent two decades of expansion, particularly in the southern part of the town, the area centred around Clinton Road. This gave a marked impetus to the Carn Marth granite industry.

During this time, Redruth made a transition from a dull and dingy mining town to a service and residential area, embellished with elegant villas and attractive public buildings. One reason for this building boom in Redruth during a period of industrial decline might have been the fact that many families which had made large fortunes in the local mines earlier in the century, or who had made money abroad, now had both the financial resources and opportunity of purchasing building plots or the leaseholds of ready built elegant homes for themselves in an area of the town which was considered highly desirable and respectable.

Sadly for Lanner, the collapse of mining at Tresavean in the late 1880s put paid to plans for proposed building programmes, but neighbouring Carharrack did receive a Church during this period. It was during this short boom that new rows of housing such as Prisk's Terrace, Woodlands Terrace and the terrace immediately to the south of it were built. This mini boom however, only sought to underline the fragile nature of the local economy which had been severely undermined by emigration and economic overspecialisation. Even new industries, such as the brick works at Trevarth and Pennance, closed because they were ultimately dependent on mines and foundries for the greater part of their income. Yet again we are reminded of the danger posed to a community completely dominated by one industry.

There is something almost pathetic in the tendency of the local populace to continue to cling to a belief that the area's mines would once again return to their former glory and provide prosperity for all. The lack of economic diversification, coupled with a large migration and financial dependence on South Africa in particular, was to cost the area greatly in the following decades, particularly post First World War.

But the building boom was only one aspect of a period of expansion in the Redruth area. In addition, many municipal improvements were made to towns and villages across the nation following the Public Health Acts of 1872 and 1875. This resulted in the introduction of sewers, pavements, piped water supplies and improved street lighting. In January 1894 a group of villagers gathered at the Commercial Inn, Lanner, to celebrate the turning on of the first public lights in the village. This was followed by a dinner and a performance by the St Day Amateur Operatic Society at Lanner School.[20] About 60–70 village middle class notables were at the dinner which was chaired by George 'Lawyer' Bray, with James Davey, farmer and butcher, occupying the Vice-Chair. Over 85 subscribers had helped to put the scheme into operation, which included C.A.V. Conybeare (a Radical politician and MP for the Mining Division), who was present, and Lord Clinton, who had offered 10 shillings and 6d per year. A house to house collection in 1895 had proved the widespread support the Lamp Committee enjoyed, as they were only refused a subscription in four houses. The story might have been somewhat different if the scheme had been a year later, as rising unemployment made life difficult for many villagers.

The idea to provide public lighting for the village came about because of the success of a similar scheme at nearby St Day. The lamps, which numbered over seven, were Vulcan central-draft, 45 candlepower and were supplied by Mr T. E. Courtis, ironmonger, of Fore Street, Redruth and the standards, by Messrs. Bartle of the Basset Foundry. By 1895, there were 14, and they had not been vandalised in the least. The custodian of the lamps was Edward Jennings.

It was felt by all those present at the dinner which followed the lighting of the lamps for the first time, that the village should be able to boast of a public institution, a scheme which had been mooted in the village for many years (see Chapter 12), a public reading room and a better sewerage system. The deficiency of these were noted by the President, who had made plans for a private subscription to raise £60 for the laying of sewerage pipes through the village without asking the parish 'for a single farthing'.[21]

The successful public lighting scheme was however, probably the first and last big project to unite the whole community, irrespective of religion, employment or class. Despite the commencement of a fund, plans to erect the institution were foiled by the political instability which prevailed in South Africa where much of the village's wealth was gained in the 1890s, and the much-needed sewerage system failed for the same reason. The latter was not to come about until the 1960s (see Chapter 11), due to a lack of finance continually blamed on the over dependence on the mining industry which ended for good in Lanner in 1928. A warning of the impending hardship and further economic decline and de-industrialisation which was to come in the next century was felt as hard times, yet again, returned to the village in the closing years of the nineteenth century.

In 1894, twenty people from Gwennap had been summoned to appear before the court at Penryn for neglecting to provide for the proper education of their children. 'Most of the defendants were miners', reported the *Cornubian*, continuing 'pitiful cases unfolded; large families in a starving condition. Small fines of 1–5 shillings were inflicted in the majority of the cases'.[22]

A Miner's Relief Fund had voted to grant £40 to the Parish of Gwennap in 1895 for the relief of the out-of-work miners who numbered about 173. This action occasioned much comment, as Illogan Parish with 100 unemployed miners, was given £55. The money was used to put them to work on road building, and some 20 men and boys were contracted to create a road from Rough Street to the south part of the parish. Their wages were 2 shillings a day for the able-bodied men, and 1 shilling and sixpence for lads, the wages being paid twice a week.[23]

In 1897 a meeting was held in neighbouring Carharrack to discuss the problems of continuing unemployment in Gwennap. It was noted that about 75 miners were out of work and the greatest number by far were from Lanner.[24]

The climate of political instability in South Africa and the closure of many of the mines there only increased the problem of local unemployment. The return of miners from the Rand was probably partially responsible for the frequent disturbances in the Village Square during the 1890s.

The nineteenth century closed on a bleak note for Lanner, with the year 1899 seeing the beginning of the Boer War, an event which had a profound effect on the parish, as will be discussed in Chapter 8. This war marked the onset of a very unsettled era, which saw two World Wars in the space of four decades, and long periods of economic depression.

Crime and Punishment

A large increase in population during the first half of the nineteenth century has been generally acknowledged to have been mainly responsible for a rise in crime. But this is an oversimplification. During the late eighteenth century and early nineteenth century there was a change in the definition of crime, which tended to be conflated in the eyes of the authorities with political conflict and social unrest, and it was therefore increasingly feared.[25] The result was a number of get-tough policies, which witnessed a marked criminalisation of the poor. Formerly in places such as Lanner and Redruth, old traditional shaming policies, such as use of the stocks, which in the Lanner area once stood immediately inside the western entrance to Gwennap Churchyard, near the Six Bells Inn, were used to deter offenders who were usually known to the rest of the community.

But such policies had a limited impact in a rapidly urbanising society subject to large population shifts, and therefore gradually disappeared (the stocks were last used at St Day in 1850 and at Redruth in about 1862). Such traditional retributive policies were superseded by reform policies of transportation and imprisonment as a key to reform of the individual. This mirrored the changes brought about by industrialisation which stressed the need for disciplined and industrious workers.

Reports of chapel events in the local papers give a warped impression of what Lanner was really like in the nineteenth century. Society was not as calm, respectable and law abiding as is often thought. In common with many other mining communities, Lanner was a rough place with a strong working class character, and markedly less religious than we tend to think (see Chapter 9). Scenes of violent confrontation, assault, cruelty and disorder appear at variance with a society perceived to be considerably more religious and law abiding than our own, and lead one to conclude that our nineteenth century forbears were in no way less culpable than members of today's society.

Miners' riots over the price of food, grain or copper periodically caused disturbances in Redruth Market. Reports of such violent assemblies were recorded from the late eighteenth century, and continued well into the nineteenth. Rioting was noted in Redruth Market in 1785, 1793, 1795, 1801, 1812, and 1847. The following report by Mr Jenkin of Trewirgie House describes the disturbances of 1801: '...I have had the disgusting sight of a riotous assemblage of Tinners from Gwennap who broke into the Market and are now compelling the people to sell Potatoes, Fish, Butter and Salt Pork etc. at the prices they chose to fix. Finding nobody to stop them (for we have neither Magistrate or Military here), they are likely to grow intoxicated with both liquor and success – and I dread the consequence.'[26]

Thompson argues that such food riots in the eighteenth and early nineteenth centuries marked the struggle for the defence of customary rights which were being eroded by increasing industrialisation and the rise of a wage economy (see Chapter 7).[27] Gwennap Parish was responsible for the annual selection and payment of its own constables, who numbered 17 in 1842, their wages being met out of the rates levied on all property owners.

Those paid constables in the Parish of Lanner were Edward Chegwidden, Edward Hales, James Morcom, Michael Chegwidden, William Tregonning and Almond Chipman. A salary of £26 per year was to be spilt between all 17 of Gwennap's constables; by 1845 their annual salary was £7 each, a paltry amount when compared to the average miner's monthly wage of £2, which perhaps suggests that their work might have been on a part-time basis only. Lanner had by far the most constables; St Day had 4 and Carharrack 3.[28] These constables were responsible for keeping law and order within the parish, and to prevent persons from assembling in the different villages and on public highways so as not to cause a nuisance to passengers and pedestrians. In 1836 for example, five men guilty of breaking the Sabbath were arrested and called before the Magistrate.

However, the constables' top priority was patrolling the parish's numerous pubs and beer houses, to ensure that the proprietors did not keep a rowdy house, pull beer at improper hours, or allow gambling or prostitution on their premises. Numerous examples of arrests in pubs, and of publicans being hauled before the magistrate for infringements of the law, furnish the Gwennap Vestry book: 'Capt. Richard Nicholls to call William Bray, Lanner Hill, before the Magistrates for disorder in his house and drawing beer at a late hour – also to enquire of the friends of the boys who were found gambling on Sunday last if they will account for them to be placed in the stocks'.[29]

Cases of thuggery and drunkenness were very prevalent in the area during much of the nineteenth century, and remained high, unlike the figures for serious crime. In the Gwennap area, drunkenness was a serious problem, with the infamous miners' Maze Monday being but one example of a society given to overindulgence in drink.[30]

Tresavean miners often repaired to 'Uncle Joe's (the Rogers' Arms Pub) or the Miners' Arms at the end of a 'core' (shift), where in the smoky atmosphere, pares (partners) divided their earnings, drinking was encouraged and fighting often broke out. The old mining towns and villages of Lanner, Redruth and St Day were rough places, and remained so well into the twentieth century.

In 1882 Joel Hosking and William Hocking, Lanner miners who had recently returned from South Africa, were involved in a drunken brawl which threatened to turn into a mini riot outside the Red Lion Inn at Redruth. During the fray a policemen was punched, a gold watch smashed and a valuable ring lost. The two men were later charged with being drunk and disorderly, and their actions were described as having 'sprung from an unwise indulgence in too much liquor over the reunion of old friends'. They were each fined £1. 3s 6d.[31]

The late Mrs Minnie Haughton remembered her father, Jim Harvey of Carn Marth, telling her that in his youth, when he and his brothers went to Redruth to the Saturday evening market, it was quite usual for him or one of his brothers to get involved in a fight in one of the pubs. Furthermore, it was not just men who were given to excessive drinking. The quiet of one Sunday afternoon in the winter of 1896 was shattered when Sergeant Noy was required to forcibly remove an inebriated woman, Janie Simmons, from the Miners' Arms opposite the village Square. A large crowd assembled to watch the scene as she was taken away by cab, appalled at her language which was said to have been of the most disgusting character.[32]

In 1890, an incident occurred at the Miners' Arms pub which was run at the time by Jane Pryor, and led to a man losing the sight of an eye. Bill Collins, a stonemason, was sitting in the kitchen of the pub by the side of the stove drinking a pint of small beer, when John Hocking, a retired publican and his friends, who were no doubt the worse for drink, began to aggravate and 'ransack' Collins, Hocking picking up a poker with which he set about making a hole in Collins' trousers. Being a small man Collins' only defence was to pick up a kettle of hot water, which he tried to throw over his attacker. Someone present at the affray suggested that lime was far better a thing to scald or burn, so Hocking ran out into the yard and took up a handful of newly slaked lime which he threw into Collins' face. The stonemason 'began to roar with pain, and it was then seen that the horseplay of Hocking had resulted in some serious way'. Collins lost the sight of his left eye, and Hocking had to pay the partially blinded stonemason the huge sum of £40 plus costs.[33]

The job of acting as a police constable in a rough, working class mining village was made all too clear in 1883, when Sergeant Trennery was savagely attacked and beaten about the head, face and body in Lanner Village Square outside the public house (the Commercial Arms) by a gang of men, after attempting to quell a drunken row. A miner called Cocking, who was supposed to be the ring-leader, was later apprehended at Wheal Uny near Redruth.[34]

Most of the incidents of crime reported in the nineteenth century in and around Lanner involved people who were caught stealing livestock, food, fuel or clothes, and in some cases the punishment was most severe. In 1839, we read of two local cases of theft, the first involving a youth of 15 employed as a railroad worker, named Thomas Davey. He was charged with having stolen a pair of gaiters and a jacket from miner William Wilkins. The suspect was caught wearing the items and sentenced to 14 days hard labour, which included one week's solitary confinement, and a recommendation that he should be privately whipped.

But a worse punishment awaited William Trewartha of Gwennap, who stole a quantity of candles from John Northey. Having been convicted of a similar offence before, he was sentenced to 11 year's transportation.[35]

In 1890, John Blight of Lanner was apprehended by Sergeant King and PC Bray on a charge of stealing a pair of boots from Josiah Bray of Gwennap at North Wheal Basset Mine. Blight took the boots underground at East Pool Mine the following day, where he was caught wearing them on coming to grass. He pleaded guilty and was fined £1, but in default of payment, he was sent to prison for a fortnight.[36]

During the early nineteenth century sheep stealing was quite common in Gwennap and Sir William Williams of Scorrier House, himself the victim of such theft, once found the following audacious notice placed on the gate of a field in which one of his flocks of sheep were grazing:

Pray Sir Billy, do not weep,
We've stolen one of your fat sheep.
For you are rich, and we are poor,
And when that's had, we'll come for more.[37]

Punishments in response to many of the above crimes of theft of other people's property were harsh. It has been argued that this signified a radically changing class-specific attitude to private property.[38] But with poverty a reality for many of the labouring poor of nineteenth century Gwennap, cases of opportune thieving were common, necessity far outweighing the risk of getting caught and subsequently punished. In 1861, three local women were caught red handed stealing coal from the United Mines which was the property of John Eddy. Elizabeth Moyle, who subsequently reported them, had spied the three from the door of the 'burning house' hurriedly gathering the coal under cover of darkness. Mary Ann Halse was filling a basket, while her two accomplices, Anna Maria Magor and Ann Blamey, were carefully filling their aprons. They were later apprehended and it was decided to make an example of them as so much coal had been stolen from the same place. Twenty-one days' hard labour was the result of their late night indiscretion, but the circumstances which had led the three to steal the coal was not mentioned. One can speculate that these were women who were probably struggling to rear large families, with little recourse to common land for gleaning, food and fuel.[39] By contrast, the perpetrators of a similar offence which took place in Lanner half a century later (discussed in Chapter 11), were not punished.

The radical *West Briton* took up the theme of poverty and its connection with stealing, poaching and plunder in an 1889 edition, and raised the question of responsibility. 'Who benefited from the privations of the poor? The people who were the main cause of this state of existence... and who mainly benefited thereby were the landlords'. The report concluded that, 'during the first half of the present century, landlordism was probably responsible for more crimes than all the other 'isms' put together in Cornwall'.[40]

This report is a valuable one, for it signals a clear departure from the predominant eighteenth-century view of landlords as defendants of traditional customary ways of life, which by the nineteenth century were giving way to an innovative market regime. The landed class had previously seldom come in for much criticism, which was instead vented on artisans, merchants and tradesmen; meddling innovators who were disrupting the social order in the interests of profits, epitomised at the time of food riots at Redruth Market. But as Hudson has argued, industrialisation eroded reciprocity and *noblesse oblige* fundamental to the stability of gentry–plebian relations.[41]

Violence against others was also common; for example in 1870 Pennance miner, Richard Halse, was attacked with a fire shovel when he attempted to collect overdue house rent from Elizabeth Andrew of Lanner Moor. The case went to court, where the ostentatious Mrs Andrew, adorned in all her finery, which included 'showy earrings' and a brooch, pleaded not guilty. The defendant, whose husband was in Chile, apparently had a reputation for 'doing a moonlight flit'; the collector commented that he 'could never find her twice in the same house!'[42]

In 1894 an old woman named Collins was viciously assaulted at Wheal Buller by a Lanner man who drove a cart for the Redruth Local Board. In 1896, Thomas Collins of Carvannel was charged £3 for a confrontation which turned ugly over some escaped fowls, resulting in Collins throwing stones at his neighbour, Mrs Martha Opie, one of which struck her in the face causing a deep cut and extensive bruising.[43] He was later apprehended and heavily fined.

Sadly, violent behaviour often extended to children. In 1879 farmer, John Tiddy, found a dead baby boy wrapped in a black apron. It was later proven to be the child of Elizabeth Harvey, aged 28, who was charged with concealment of birth. And in 1836 it was agreed to call Mary Manuel before the Magistrates, 'for abusing her daughter'.[44]

Large gangs of youths were often to be seen in the village square creating a din and intimidating passers-by, and in 1891 this all too regular disturbance led to much questioning as to where the policeman kept himself. It was reported that gangs of young men numbering from 60–100 had been frequently assembling in the square, 'for the purpose of beating tin pans, kicking up unearthly rows and otherwise making night hideous, much to the annoyance of the dwellers in the immediate vicinity.'[45]

Such congregations of young men were probably a result of unemployment, and their collective actions could thus be interpreted as acts of open defiance and protest at the seeming inability of the local authorities to remedy the lack of work. Perhaps the police constable, as a figure of authority, was too afraid to confront such a large group of restless youths, as we have already noted the attack on Sergeant Trennery above.

Acts of group violence were common in pre-industrial times, when society often took the law into its own hands, and was quick to mete out judgement on those thought to have erred. This judgement often took the form of effigy burning, a custom which had declined after the mid nineteenth century, so it was quite interesting to see an example of this in 1882. It came to be known that a farmer of Gwennap had deserted his wife and was found to have been living with a single woman. This blatant show of immorality was rewarded by the intimidating act of the effigies of the two involved being burnt on Carn Marth by some youths from Carharrack.[46]

However, not all crimes involved petty theft, drunkenness, or a breach of the peace. In 1836 Caroline Manuel, the daughter of Philip Manuel of Carn Marth, was shot in the neck by her father. Neighbours, summoned to give evidence before a jury, claimed the shooting occurred after Caroline and her sister Christian had been 'teasing' their father, calling him by his nickname 'Figgy' and throwing stones at him. Manuel was apparently given to violent outbursts bordering on insanity, and according to eye witnesses, it was during one such moment that he picked up his shotgun, gave chase to the two girls, and shot Caroline who was running some 40 feet ahead of him. She was attended by Dr Samuel Pellew from nearby St Day, who informed the jury that the poor girl had lived some 15 hours after the event. The jury were urged to return a verdict of 'wilful murder', and Manuel was committed to the assizes, and convicted for murder.[47]

In 1839 the area was thrown into considerable excitement by the news of the savage murder of the wife of Jesse Lean of Trevarth. Jesse and Loveday Lean were well known in the area as being thrifty and having set by 'a good round sum in the house'. This, it was supposed, had excited the cupidity of some person who decided to rob the couple. It was surmised that upon being disturbed, the perpetrator attacked Mrs Lean leaving her bleeding and moaning in agony. Passers-by who heard her crying out thought that she was in the process of finding peace with The Almighty and did not think that anything amiss had occurred (this was the era of revivals within the Methodist Churches). She later died from her horrific injuries, an event which so shocked and appalled the neighbourhood, that the Gwennap Vestry agreed to impose a rate of 1d in every pound 'to be collected for the purpose of offering a reward of £50 for the detection of the murderer of Loveday Lean'. Sadly, the chief suspect turned out to be her husband.[48]

Serious crime figures reached a peak countywide during the early 1840s and fell away later in the century, and Gwennap conforms to this pattern. The early years of the nineteenth century witnessed increased local crime as the population rapidly expanded as the mining industry grew. However, increased crime figures were also the authorities' response to a deep-seated fear about the working classes' threat to social order following the mayhem on the Continent due to the French Revolution. More people were being summonsed than previously. By the latter third of the nineteenth century, living conditions for many people had improved considerably, raising families above the subsistence level which had been common at the beginning of the nineteenth century. Despite industrial collapse, real wages gradually rose due to a flood of cheap imported food: beef from Argentina, barley from Russia, grain from the prairies of North America and refrigerated meat from Australia and New Zealand.

Emigration further helped reduce serious crime figures within Gwennap, by the turn of the twentieth century, as the group most likely to commit violent crime, young adult males, were migrating in numbers. Doubtless improvements in education and the influence of Methodism were also important contributory factors in crime reduction.

Poverty and the Poor Law

As we have seen, many of the petty crimes discussed above arose because of poverty. The 1601 Poor Law attempted to make provisions for the most needy; this legislation was administered for over 200 years, until the Poor Law Amendment Act of 1834. The provision of the poor was always considered the responsibility of the Church which held frequent Vestry Meetings for the purpose of discussing parochial matters. Each year the parish churchwardens and two to four property owners had to be appointed as overseers of the poor, to maintain them and set them to work. In Gwennap, these positions were usually occupied by the likes of the Williams' of Scorrier, and the Beauchamps of Trevince, as well as mine agents and men of successful commercial backgrounds – the new middle class. Funds were provided through the collection of rates, payable by the inhabitants of the parish who were owners of property and land. An act of 1722–23 authorised the parish officers to obtain workhouses (Gwennap's earliest was at Crousmeniggus, near Stithians) and to contract with enterprising businessmen to lodge, keep, maintain and employ the poor of a parish.

The 1601 Poor Law stipulated that parents must maintain their children, but those who were unable to do so after 1722 found their children 'bound out', taken on as apprentices by people deemed suitable by the parish overseers. The children had no choice with whom or in what trade. Failure by prospective employers to take 'prentices' could result in a heavy fine; by the early nineteenth century a sum in the region of £10 in Gwennap.

To make the choosing of apprentices appear as fair as possible, Gwennap used a lottery system. If for example 10 apprentices were to be bound out, twelve masters would draw lots, and inevitably two would draw a blank lot. A provision was made for each apprentice to have an outfit of clothes upon his or her being bound out to their master; a man was apprenticed until the age of 24, and a woman to the age of 21, or until such time as she married.

Many of the poor children of Gwennap were apprenticed to the copper mines. One such. James Michell. is bound out to Tresavean Mine in 1805, and typical entries read 'John Wasley aged 8 to Capt. Edmund Michell, 1799'; 'Mary Francis aged 15 to Capt. John Tregonning, 1802'. Individuals who took apprentices in the Lanner area in the early decades of the nineteenth century were James Holman of Bell, John Williams Junior of Trevarth and John Trevenna of Carvannel.[49] The lot of the parish apprentice was usually grim; they received no money for their labours and often had to subsist on the meanest of fare.

The Gwennap Parish Workhouse, which superseded that at Crousmeniggus, provided indoor relief and was formerly at Burnwithian, near St Day. A new Union Workhouse was built at Barncoose, Redruth, in 1838 to serve a combined parish population of 48 047 following the Poor Law Amendment Act. The very mention of the workhouse was enough to instil great fear in the poor, who dreaded the idea of ending up in this institution, where Victorian ideas on poverty and self-improvement made the regime for inmates extremely austere.

Outdoor relief of the needy, whereby the able-bodied poor received a monetary payment to make up the deficiency in their wages, which was paid out of the parish rates, was tied to the price of bread and when the cost of a loaf rose, the dole rose accordingly. Sometimes the poor were paid in kind – given goods when judged necessary. Most received both monetary relief and payment in kind and the majority of the poor were relieved in their own homes in early-to-mid nineteenth century Gwennap. Yet this policy, The Speenhamland System of Outdoor Relief, did little to improve the lot of the poor, for supplementing individuals' earnings did nothing to address the real problem of low wages. With plenty of labour available, the net result was that employers were less inclined to pay higher wages. And outdoor relief aided the destruction of the self-respect of the labouring poor, by making pauperism the shameless rule instead of the shameful exception.[50]

The 1851 Census for Lanner indicates several paupers living in the parish, which included the following: Jane Odgers of Lanner Moor, a 50 year old widow with six children, 70 year old Eliza Tippett who lived alone at Lanner Moor, Jane Oppy of Lanner, aged 88, who lived with her 16 year old grandson, Mary Nichols of Trevarth, a 68 year old widow, who lived with her daughter and grandchildren, Christian Oppy, also from Trevarth, a 77 year old widow. and Elizabeth Nicholls, aged 61, resident at Trevarth with her daughter, granddaughter and a lodger. No men are listed as paupers, and the women are all widows, the majority of them elderly.

Great concern was expressed at the implementation of the New Poor Law in Gwennap for the widows of the parish, and there were many. In Lanner in 1851, there were 128 households out of a total number of 522, or one in every four headed by women, and of the adult female population, 19.5 per cent were widows. By 1891, 105 out of 500 households in Lanner, or almost 32 per cent, were headed by widows. We see in the above examples that many of these women had children or grandchildren to care for.

The aim of the Old Poor Law was to follow the practice of allowing, in cases of necessity, weekly disbursements, both monetary and in kind, to widows for their youngest children, while the earnings of the children from ages 9–18 or 20 were generally sufficient to make up any deficiency. The younger children, as they grew up, were instructed in whatever labour became immediately available and thus, in course of time, the whole family ceased to be chargeable. The Gwennap Guardians of the Poor feared that if the New Poor Law abolished outdoor relief, and the families placed in the Workhouse, the children would lose the preference they had of obtaining work as the offspring of deceased or crippled miners. These children would therefore be unable to assist in the welfare of the family which would then become the problem of the parish which could not afford to keep large numbers of paupers without raising the rates.[51] In other words, the Guardians tacitly supported child labour.

With the implementation of the New Poor Law Act, widows were relieved by the parish through monetary payments, but parents found that the loss of outdoor relief in the form of bread bore heavily on them and therefore sent their children to the local mines in search of work, hoping to pass them off as older than they were. Child labour thus continued, and was in some cases magnified, resulting in children being put to work earlier than ever, as we will see later, in Chapter 4.

Gwennap parishioners in receipt of outdoor relief after 1805 and before the New Poor Law of 1834, had to walk to the Wheal Damsel Counting House on the outskirts of Carharrack for their handouts, with a different overseer making the disbursements every week. We read of Eliza Bray of Carn Marth being granted a gown and a 'body lineiry' in 1799; in 1802 she received two shillings and a pair of shoes, and in 1805 was given a further two shillings. Thomas Perry's wife was granted swaddling clothes, a 'shift' and an undercoat in 1801, and soldier Thomas Michell, home on a visit to his wife from the Napoleonic Wars, in 1802, was given a full set of clothes consisting of two shirts, a pair of shoes, a waistcoat and trousers.

John Morcom, of Lanner, in his 'necessity' received one shilling in 1805. John Bray, of Lanner, had his half year rent due at Christmas paid in 1807, and Mary Gregor was to receive 2 shillings per week in 1805; in 1807 she was granted one shift and a blanket. Ann Urin, of Lanner, a woman who appears to have been a widow with a large family, was in receipt of a 'swanskin waistcoat and trousers and 42 yards of dowlas for her 8-year-old son' in 1808; later that same year, she received 5 yards of dowlas and trousers for an 11-year-old son. Richard Jeffrey, a Pennance man, received a sheet, blanket and two shirts in 1808 and a further handout of two pairs of boys' shoes the same year. William Jose, of Carn Marth, was given a blanket and a sheet in 1808 in addition to some cloth for his 9 year old.[52]

To encourage a degree of self help, entries in the Poor Law Book for Gwennap dated 1799–1808, contain numerous references similar to the following entry of 1801: 'To Ann Eslick, a turn and cards'. Cards were instruments with iron teeth used to comb wool, and a turn was a spinning wheel, so we can deduce that the old cottage industry of manufacturing homespun cloth was still in evidence in the early 1800s in Gwennap, a good example of a traditional or proto-industrial handicraft which helped to give women a degree of independence. Yet it appears that this trade had died out in the area by the mid nineteenth century, as no spinners are mentioned on the 1851 Census. Spinning had perhaps become a victim of the rise of a formal wage economy, eclipsed by sweated labour in the tailors' shops at nearby Redruth, or home-dressmaking by groups of women, aided by mechanisation with the appearance of the first sewing machines in mid century.

To help to counter the effects of poverty, a munificent legacy, known as the Davey Charity, was founded by a will proved at Bodmin on 3 November 1882 after the death of John Davey, a native of Gwennap Parish and a successful middle class industrialist and mine agent. The capital was invested in Consols and Metropolitan Stock realising considerable annual interest, which was intended to benefit 'poor persons of good character whether in receipt of Poor-law relief or not', who were resident in the ancient Parish of Gwennap. Beneficiaries were subject to certain criteria: those men not less than 70 years old who had worked underground in a mine for a period of not less than five consecutive years; men of whatever age who from accident, sickness or infirmity were disabled from earning their living temporarily or permanently, and who at or shortly prior to the time of disablement were working underground in a mine, and miners' widows who were not less than 70 years of age, or who from accident, sickness or infirmity were disabled from earning their living temporarily or permanently.

Payment, in 1920, amounted to not less than 2s 6d and not more than 10s a week, which the Trustees were at liberty to fix from time to time, with regard to the needs and circumstances of the respective applicants. The Davey Fund, still operating today, is administered by a committee of management composed of local parsons and ministers from the Methodist Chapels and Church of England in the old Gwennap Parish. This charity doubtless helped many local families in times of economic hardship.[53]

Incredible as it might seem to the reader of today, many of the poor in the nineteenth century had but one set of clothes to wear. Often, children were sent to bed during the day in order that their mother might wash their linen which would then be clean to wear the following day. Richard Jeffery, a nine year old who worked at the Consolidated Mines, had never attended school of any kind because his mother could not afford to give him clothes to go in. The only thing the little boy had to wear, were the rags he wore to work at the mine.[54]

The Gwennap School Board Minutes contain numerous references to parents being unable to send their children to Lanner School for want of clothes or shoes (see Chapter 10). In this respect, things had not changed all that much by the early years of the twentieth century, as we shall discuss in Chapter 11.

For many years, after Christmas in the late nineteenth century, Lanner Church customarily gave away a large quantity of counterpanes, blankets, sheets, flannel and calico to the poor of the neighbourhood, irrespective of denomination, and as we shall see in Chapters 9 and 12, numerous self-help groups and organisations grew up in Lanner as a rational response to combat continuing poverty.[55]

Disease and the Great Cholera Epidemic

In the climate of poverty, malnutrition and periodic economic depression which characterised Gwennap Parish for much of the nineteenth century, diseases which thrived in unsanitary conditions were prevalent. In 1836 there was a severe outbreak of smallpox in Gwennap, in which Carn Marth man Nicholas Rogers died, followed by whooping cough in the summer of 1837. The years 1840–41 saw the return of a smallpox epidemic, and in 1842–43, scarlet fever was wreaking havoc among Gwennap parishioners. The summer of 1844 saw the diseases whooping cough and measles strike with disastrous results.[56]

However, in 1848–49, the parish was thrown into a panic by the recurrence of one of the diseases of the nineteenth century which was most feared - cholera. Cholera had been a pestilential disease which for generations had formed a daily hazard for the people of the Indian sub-Continent. The upsurge of cholera in India in 1817 was exceptional because it quickly spread to the Western world, and by the 1830s had struck terror into the people and governments of Europe. In 1831, it made its appearance on British soil, and by 1832 had appeared in Gwennap for the first time. The disease was characterised by copious watery diarrhoea, severe vomiting, with consequent rapid dehydration, muscular cramps from loss of salt, suppression of urine, and shock, proceeding in severe cases to rapid coma and death.[57]

The *cholera vibrio* thrived in communities similar to those we see in third-world countries on television today. Stinking middens (communal rubbish dumps) containing human and animal excrement, earth closets, choked drains and primitive soak-aways, cess pits, ash heaps, pigsties, unsanitary slaughter houses and foul leats (such as the one which formerly ran uncovered in Lanner), were responsible for regularly contaminating wells and sources of drinking water. These were often to be found in close proximity to people's living quarters, and animals, particularly pigs, often virtually cohabited with their owners.

Overcrowded houses with primitive sanitary arrangements, many neighbours sharing outside privies for example, allowed the *vibrio* to spread rapidly; it was for example, able to survive for several days on moist clothing and mattresses soiled with the contaminated body fluids of those afflicted.

In October 1848, the Gwennap Vestry appointed a committee for the purpose 'of removing all nuisances throughout the parish and making such sanitary arrangements agreeably to the provision of an Act passed in the last session of Parliament as may be found necessary for the prevention of cholera'.[58] Rubbish near the highways was removed, scavengers were prevented from moving middens and dung heaps, and the roads were cleansed in some areas.

However, these attempts were in vain, for by September 1849 cholera had made a second and more virulent visit to Gwennap, and steps were taken to try to halt the spread of the epidemic. Mr Govett of Mevagissey (a town which had been severely afflicted with the disease, killing 125 people that July), was appointed as a doctor and adviser to help Gwennap's medical officers cope with the epidemic. Posters were printed and displayed throughout the parish giving precise information of the names and places where aid and medicine could be obtained. Suitable rooms in the East Wheal Damsel Account House were fitted out to create a makeshift hospital for the cholera victims, and Messrs Bawden and Morcom were instructed to supply suitable nurses, with as little delay as possible, and to provide food, changes, beds and bedding to the hospital.

So great was the fear of contamination from those hapless victims who had succumbed to the disease, that it was decided by the Guardians of the Poor that no such victim was to be admitted into any of the parish churches for a burial service. Instead the service was to take place at the graveside, the hour of internment being decided upon by the medical officers.

Henry Strick, carpenter and undertaker of Trevarth, was instructed to make coffins for the cholera victims, for which he received the generous sum of 15 shillings for each adult corpse. He was required in every case to provide a tarred cloth in which to wrap the body and to place the corpse securely in the coffin. Emergency meetings were convened in the Gwennap Vestry Room, due to the 'exigencies of the disease', and extreme measures were resorted to in order to halt the spread of the epidemic, which included removing all children and others who were infected to the makeshift hospital at Wheal Damsel. Gwennap's attempts to limit the scourge of cholera seem to have been relatively successful. By October the parish was free from infection and the hospital closed.[59] But before the disease subsided, it had claimed 28 lives in Gwennap.

Some of the parish registers note cholera as the cause of death. Victims Mary Vincent, of Gordon, aged 60 and John Uren, of Lanner Downs, aged 18, were buried at Gwennap that September. There had been 140 cases of choleric diarrhoea and 592 cases of common diarrhoea, making 760 cases in all.[60] In the Redruth District (of which Gwennap was a part), the Registrar General's returns show that from a population of 48 047, there were 133 deaths. Locality played a large part in the figures for cholera fatalities which were commonly highest in unsanitary large towns and mining districts.[61]

After the epidemic a great effort was made to clean up Gwennap Parish, and Messrs Hicks and Morcom were empowered to remove all nuisances that had been complained of within the parish, including cleansing the premises of parties (to whom the property belonged) who had not been willing to do so themselves. A sum of £2.12s. 6d was set aside for the purpose in 1850. Further mention is made to a committee for nuisance removal in 1853, and butchers were required to ensure 'that all offal and everything offensive that comes from their slaughterhouses were moved to such safe distance from every dwelling house as shall meet the approval of the inspectors'. Cess pits and pools were filled in and the beginnings of a rudimentary sewerage system was begun at the worst places in St Day and neighbouring Carharrack.[62]

Sadly, not enough seems to have been done at Lanner to tackle a problem which continued to mar the salubrity of the village environment for over another century. Therefore diseases such as typhoid fever, smallpox, measles, influenza and diphtheria made all too regular appearances in the parish. Indeed cholera made a repeat visit to the area in 1853, and resulted in 3 fatalities. In 1893 Lanner School was closed for three weeks owing to an outbreak of scarlet fever, and this was not an isolated incident of disease forcing the school to close.

Smallpox occurred in Lanner once more, in 1896, causing the death of a 9-week-old baby and a young domestic servant, and in 1898, whooping cough was said to have reached epidemic proportions. Dr Permewan's Medical Report for the Redruth District commented on the primitive sewerage system in Lanner in 1894: 'The difficulty at Back Row has been dealt with and the new drain is working satisfactorily. Some work has been carried out at Church Row. The Long Row at Lanner Moor ought to be put into a more satisfactory state in this respect, but there are considerable difficulties in the way'.[63]

A step in the right direction had clearly been made as regards making the environment in Gwennap's villages a more salubrious one, but the process of de-industrialisation and subsequent unemployment in the closing decades of the nineteenth century prevented the large-scale scheme for the disposal of sewage in Lanner as envisaged by many of the village notables in 1896. Moreover, dirt and disease were by no means purely nineteenth-century phenomena, and even at the turn of the twentieth century, occasional reports of squalor in Gwennap reached the press, as we shall examine in Chapter 11.

It was only with increased public awareness of the connection of dirt with disease, municipal improvements, such as the new sewerage and water systems with which Lanner and villages like it benefited in the 1960s (see Chapter 11), plus universal inoculation, which finally confined some of the above diseases to the pages of history.

Few from Lanner could afford to summon the doctor or apothecary 150 years ago, and most people made use of traditional herbal remedies and recipes for cures passed down through the ages. People placed their faith in healers or 'pellars', quack doctors who claimed to be able to affect cures using potions, charms and healing. In Lanner, such a person was Uncle Will Martin, who lived at Lanner Green. He acquired a fine reputation for curing all manner of ills, and was once visited by ailing 'Lord B' (presumably Lord Beauchamp) whose doctors had been unable to effect a cure. Uncle Will uttered a few words over him and gave him a small bottle of medicine to take away. His Lordship's health was soon fully restored.

Some time later, Lord B sent his servant to Lanner Green to fetch the bill. Upon reading what Uncle Will had requested - £50, Lord B immediately took his carriage to pay him a visit and demanded to know why the bill for a small bottle of medicine was so large. Uncle Will, drawing deeply on his old clay pipe, answered him thus: 'Well, I've cured hundreds of people in my time and some pay me and some caant, and when the people that caant pay me anything are going away they do say "thanky Uncle Will, I'm feard I caant pay ee, but ef I don't pay ee, I hope the Loard will," and so I thot that as you wor the first loard that ever come to me to be cured I'd turn in awl the bill to you'. Lord B was reputed to have burst into laughter and immediately drew a cheque for Uncle Will for £50![64]

Of course the less amusing side of this is that many people died needlessly from curable ills, whilst many more succumbed to primitive methods such as 'bleeding', the lancing of wounds, and even kitchen-table abortions.

Housing Conditions of the Poor

We have seen that the diet and sanitary conditions of Lanner's labouring poor in the nineteenth century were not conducive to good health. Neither were the majority of their dwellings. Built in the midst of a barren district covered with 'poisonous rubbish thrown up in rugged heaps, a waste-land of stunted heath, in which the whitewashed miners' cottages which give the appearance of being dropt down *a-propos* to nothing',[65] many of the old miners' cottages which predated the new terraced homes were hastily built with any material which came to hand, and 'homers', materials purloined from the mines.

Cob or turf, with a lower foundation of roughly-hewn moorstone, formed the walls of the humblest abodes which were thatched with reeds. The thatched roofs of these primitive cottages often blew away in the storms and gales which characterise a Cornish winter. And slate roofs were sometimes so badly fixed that the stars could be seen through the gaps, and inevitably let in water.

There was unlikely to be much glass fitted into inordinately small windows and, as both windows and glass were subject to duty, there were people who resorted to dispensing with as many windows as possible, making bedrooms in particular airless and unhealthy. Yet blocking up windows was seldom done with bricks, as even these were taxed![66] What little glass there was, was probably that recycled from the bottoms of old bottles – 'dimples', which cast an eerie green half-light into the rooms. Lanner Methodist Chapel has some examples of such dimples. In a few homes rough hessian sacking and wooden shutters served to keep out the worst of the elements.

A percentage of the labouring poor lived in tenements in the early nineteenth century, and many more in lodgings, for which a few pence were paid each week for a crude bed and board. Conditions in accommodations of this type were usually cramped, unsanitary and sometimes flea and vermin ridden. Even the new rows of miners' cottages, several containing only two rooms, one up and one down, provided less than ideal living conditions and were expected to house large families.

The 1851 Census for Lanner shows a family of miners and bal maidens, numbering 12, by the name of Dunstan, living in a small cottage at Lanner Moor. Besides his own family of eight children, Joseph Dunstan had also taken in two nephews. And many Lanner families took in miners from other mining areas as lodgers, whose rent helped to increase the collective family income. Therefore the average household size in Lanner in 1851 was over 5 persons per dwelling. Today the figure is half this.

Overcrowding was a feature of life for many mining families, and it was not uncommon to find households of ten or more in a two-roomed cottage. Some of these cottages had but the most basic amenities, and many held numerous hidden dangers for children. Reports of youngsters scalded by boiling water in cramped cottage kitchens, or, like nine-year-old Lanner girl, Nanny Ingram, burnt to death in 1844, form depressing entries in the local newspapers. In the 1864 Commission on the Mines of Great Britain, a Tresavean miner was described as living in a very bad cottage, with two rooms, the upper one slanting to the roof which had two small windows incapable of being opened, in which nine persons, from adults to a baby slept together. The interior walls of such miners' cottages were customarily given an occasional coating of limewash. The late Mrs Minnie Haughton remembered how her aunt Kate Bray usually added a little 'bluing' to the limewash to give it some colour for interior decorating.

Floors were generally of flagstone or compacted earth, the latter surface sprinkled with clean sand, which was sold for about one penny a bucket. Earlier this century an old man named Billy Sand Man, who had been blinded in a mining accident, did this job in the Gwennap area. Mrs Haughton remembered seeing him come around with his donkey and cart at Pennance.

A small cob and moorstone cottage with a slate roof once existed behind the house named 'Carn Wartha' on Carn Marth, which typified the average miner's cottage in the last century. A large deal table covered with a heavy green table-cloth, a long form, a high backed wooden settle, a couple of chairs and a Cornish range with its wrought iron, black-leaded 'slab' or cooking surface, were the main items in the downstairs room. (These old ovens are becoming quite rare; Geoffrey Olds of Grays Terrace has one of the only surviving working Cornish ranges in the village in 1998.). The floor was of compacted earth.

This room doubled as the kitchen and living room, through which a small pantry was reached. The toilet was in a yard some 20 feet from the house. Upstairs were two small bedrooms, one of which had the luxury of a fireplace. An oaken 'press' contained the meagre family linen and Sunday best, and a large chest of drawers made a ready bed for a baby or infant if one of the bottom drawers was pulled out. A family of four children and three adults lived in this small cottage.[67] (Fig 2.4)

Few pictures adorned the walls of most miners' cottages, and those that did were usually of a religious nature. In Methodist households, a portrait of Wesley was a popular choice. Joseph Harvey, a Carn Marth quarry owner, thought little of pictures, but one was allowed pride of place over the mantel – a portrait of Queen Victoria. He enjoyed reading the Bible, and had read it cover to cover three times in his life. He would allow no carpets (or later linoleum) into the house, arguing that this encouraged fleas, preferring bare floorboards, scrubbed regularly.[68] Although he was a granite merchant and the employer of many men, Joseph Harvey still worked in the quarry with his workers, and there was nothing in his home to suggest that he aspired to be anything other than working class.

Few books made their way into the homes of the working class in the early nineteenth century, but the family Bible was usually prominent. There were no electric lights in those days, and in the poorest households the only illumination provided was that of a weak and somewhat ineffectual light of a tallow-dip rushlight candle in a glass jar, made from 'homers', candle ends from the mine. Those who could afford them owned oil lamps with ornate glass shades.

Fig.2.4 *The Polkinghorne Family, Carn Marth, c.1905. Left to right: Frank, David, Edie, Harry, Caroline (Carrie), Jack and Ann (née Trythall).* (© Sylvia Kessell, Redruth).

Many of these old miners' homes have disappeared, melted back into the landscape whence they came, the spot they once occupied betrayed only by a few ivy and bramble covered blocks of moorstone, or maybe a lilac tree marking the location of the long-vanished outside toilet, a clump of yellow primroses in spring, or a rambling dog rose in summer.

There are many such examples on Carn Marth, but the most noticeable is Pilcher's Row. This old row of three cottages, built in the early nineteenth century on the south-eastern flank near the summit of the carn, was bought by the Winn Family and renamed Winn's Terrace earlier this century, although due to their exposed position were jokingly nicknamed Three Winds! At Rough Street there were also once many miners' homes of cob and thatch, now vanished. But a fine example of a miner's cottage still intact can be seen on the south-eastern side of the carn not far from Martin's Quarry. (Fig. 2.5)

In Lanner, along the course of the A393, there are still several examples of a two-roomed terraced miner's cottage, 'one up and one down', albeit radically altered to provide the amenities of modern living. Renovation to some of these cottages has revealed the large open fireplaces, with massive granite lintels, at which the housewife of yesteryear would have cooked using a brandis, kettle and crock.[69]

Middle Class Housing

However, not everyone in the Lanner area lived in such basic circumstances in the last century. The new middle class were defined by their higher wages, which provided larger homes with well furnished contents and servants to care for their

Fig.2.5. *Miner's cottage, east of Carn Marth.* (photo. R.H.Parker).

families. But they were also defined by their dress, and working class people were often held up for ridicule or contempt by the classes above them for pretentious displays of clothing at Chapel or Church. This perhaps explains the controversy which surrounded the very dressy bal maidens, in particular, who were seen to be becoming indistinguishable from the class above them (see Chapter 4).

Middle class people were more likely to send their sons to schools such as Trevarth, an establishment tailor-made to suit their requirements (see Chapter 10). The rise of a middle class in the Gwennap area came about because of a rapid growth in the local mining population servicing the large mining towns and villages. Many merchants and dealers, as well as larger farmers, became quite wealthy, as did a number of the agents and mine captains who managed the local mines. Some made a fortune; most well known of these *nouveau riche* families were the Harveys of St Day, who made their money selling goods to miners on the truck system (payment of wages other than in money), and were elevated almost to the status of local gentry, marrying into the Williams Family of Scorrier, lower gentry, who had themselves become newly rich through their involvement in mining operations in parishes such as Gwennap in the eighteenth century.

In the first half of the nineteenth century, there were probably more *nouveaux riches* families in Cornwall than in any other county.[70] These new wealthy families came to play an increasingly important role in the life of communities such as St Day, Lanner and Carharrack, patronising village institutions, providing money and influence for charitable causes, sitting on various committees, and in effect pushing the older absent landed gentry, such as the Clintons, Rogers' and Bullers, aside in terms of local influence.

Added to these came the lower middle class: butchers, small farmers, grocers and shopkeepers and a variety of self-employed artisans. The list of people from Lanner nominated for the first Parish Council of Gwennap, in 1894, shows the involvement of the new middle class in the life of the parish: T. Born, Farmer; James Bray, Agent; Richard Johns, Commissions' Agent; James Osborne, Retired Miner; Richard Rendle, Mine Agent and Joshua Williams, Grocer.[71]

Middle class families were keen to show and enjoy the trappings of their success and, in 1877, an example of the household contents of a Lanner butcher, J. C. Mayne, was auctioned prior to his emigration to Chile. The furniture was said to be nearly new. The parlour consisted of a handsome walnut drawing room suite upholstered in green and gold silk rep, an oval table, a whatnot, 4 pictures, a pair of lustres, 3 vases, a gilt cornice, one pair of long curtains, a bronze fender, a fire set and tapestry carpet. In the sitting room there were six cane-seat chairs, a polished deal table, a pair of lustres, an American easy chair, more china ornaments, pictures, and a brand new lock-stitch sewing machine by Grover and Baker.

The dwelling had four bedrooms, the contents of which consisted of a very beautiful mahogany Tudor bedstead trimmed in crimson damask, iron bedsteads, feather beds, palliasses, mahogany and other chests of drawers, marble topped and other washstands, a mahogany night-commode, looking glasses, toilet tables, six cane-seat chairs, and kidder and other carpets. This aspiring gentleman also possessed an excellent milch cow seasoned in calf, a valuable grey colt, a pony and trap, and all the equipment necessary to carry on the butcher's trade.[72]

In 1892, T. R. Mills was instructed to auction the household effects of another Lanner butcher, John Nicholls, which included a mahogany half canopy bedstead with brocaded silk trimmings, a mahogany duchess table, several marble topped, tile-backed washstands, a walnut suite in plush, an elegant walnut-burr-top table and a Brussels carpet.[73]

The drawing room of John Hawken, headmaster of Trevarth Grammar School, was crammed full of furniture including a piano, a walnut suite upholstered in green damask, comprising a table, couch, chiffonier and six chairs, as well as side tables and an easy chair. The room was fitted with heavy damask curtains and a Brussels carpet. The walls were cluttered with mirrors, pictures and valuable engravings. Numerous china ornaments, flower arrangements, a unique Indian fire-screen and a magnificent case of extremely rare stuffed birds also graced the room. The light was provided by ornate lustres. The dining room contained a table, six chairs and a couple of side tables, and there were also ottomans, mirrors, numerous ornaments and heavy carpets and curtains. His sitting room boasted yet more mahogany in the form of a table and secretary, which also contained a flower stand and several valuable maps. In the hallway were two chairs, a hat-stand, a barometer and an eight-day clock. Three of his four upstairs bedrooms were furnished with high quality French and iron bedsteads trimmed in crimson or scarlet damask, with mahogany chests of drawers, night-commodes and washstands. Even the servants' quarters were well furnished. The garden contained a first-class greenhouse with vines.[74]

Hawken's home was typical of the decor of the mid nineteenth century middle class, with its dark rooms dusty from coal fires, cluttered with heavy mahogany furniture, exquisite 'bric a brac' and exotic glass-cased curios, furnished in dreary shades of green or red.

West Trevarth Farm was, in the late nineteenth century, the residence of the Blamey Family who succeeded the Tregonings. William Blamey, farmer and butcher, the son of retired Mine Agent John Blamey, continued to live in the property after his father's death. This house contained marble fireplaces and a stunning walnut staircase. The house had 14 rooms, a good office, wash kitchen and coal house, coach house and stable and a large conservatory containing five grape vines, plus a large orchard well stocked with choice fruit trees and extensive flower and vegetable gardens.[75] It also had a large, slate-lined underground water tank, providing water for bathing and an indoor WC.

G. Blamey, who spent his childhood holidays there in the early years of the twentieth century, remembers this

Victorian toilet as 'a handsome blue and white affair with splendid mahogany, and the 'pull' was upwards instead of downward. Water was not unlimited, so we boys had to go to the 'thunder-box' down by the coach houses'.[76]

Lanner House was another residence with a big water tank. Large homes containing furniture made from walnut and mahogany in particular, would have been far above the resources available to most of Lanner's inhabitants in the last century. In 1890, a 9-roomed dwelling house at Pennance with 7 acres of land and outbuildings attached, cost £23 and 10 shillings per year to rent. By contrast, the annual rental on a 2 roomed cottage with a garden, in the same area, cost a mere £2.

Changing Occupational Patterns in Lanner, 1851–1891

A comparison of the Census of Population statistics for 1851 and 1891 illustrates important changes that took place in the way people made their living. As the table below shows, the total working population fell by 29 per cent, but the drop was twice as great for men as for women.

LANNER WORKFORCE, 1851-1891

	MEN	WOMEN	TOTAL
1851	807	434	1241
1891	525	354	879
CHANGE	-282	-80	-362
CHANGE (%)	35%	18%	29%

Not surprisingly as (Fig. 2.6) shows, we see a society completely dominated by the mining and engineering industry for men in 1851. A staggering 80 per cent of the parish's male work force at this time was dependent on the mine for their livelihood. When compared with Cornwall, with an average of around 50 per cent, this provides a clear indication of the overwhelming importance of the copper mining industry to nineteenth century Lanner. All other employment categories are dwarfed by comparison. Within this category are included all those men who worked as tributers, tutworkers, tin streamers, at the surface of the mine, in the count house, as stationary engine drivers, assayers, engineers, mine captains and agents. There was a clear hierarchy characterised by skill, age and sex at the local mines, and the Mine Captain was always a man of importance and position in society, even after he had retired.

By 1891, as (Fig 2.7) shows, mining and engineering still remained the most important employment category for men at about 58 per cent, but showed a decrease of 23 per cent from the 1851 figure. (For women the drop of 21 per cent was equally pronounced. See below). However, it is probably more accurate to describe nineteenth century Lanner as a community dominated by mining, than as a mining community, for even when the miners were numerically dominant, they were viewed as members of a wider and interactive semi-rural community.

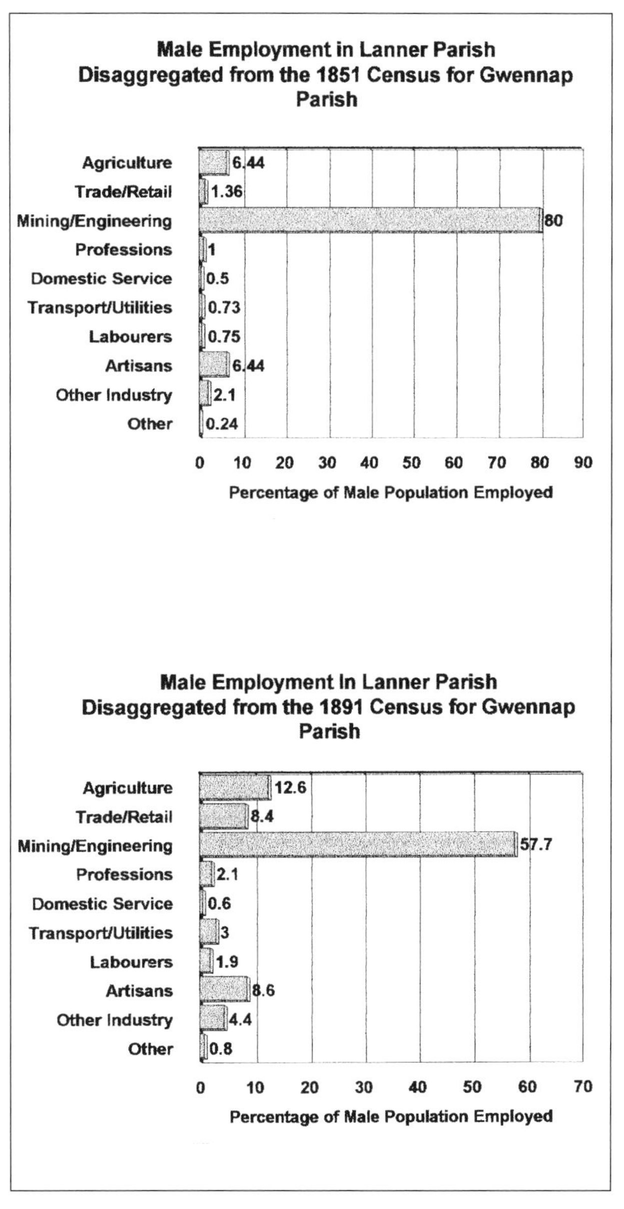

Figs.2.6 and 2.7. Male employment figures, 1851 (top) and 1891 (lower graph)

By 1891 changes in the mining industry were very apparent, with most men describing themselves as tin miners, as opposed to copper miners as in 1851, which provides further evidence of the calamitous collapse of the local copper mining industry.

The description of the men as tin miners also reveals an easily overlooked point, that of changing travel-to-work patterns. Lanner's mines were predominantly copper producers, as were those of Gwennap. Although miners had sometimes worked at mines quite distant from their homes, by the 1890s this had become the norm for Lanner men, who now found work in the tin mines of the Great Flat Lode near Camborne for example. This was, in effect, the beginning of a trend of working outside Lanner which was to become more evident in the twentieth century, with the long term result of a commuter-based economy and a dormitory village status. Other industries, such as quarrying and foundry work, the latter taking place outside the parish, showed a percentage of 23 per cent in 1851. The quarry industry was to become quite important in Lanner during the 1880s and early 1890s when the district saw a building boom of relatively short duration, and this is reflected by the increase of this category in 1891 which had doubled to 4 per cent, the majority of this percentage made up of stone masons and quarrymen, with the brick works at Pennance making a more limited contribution.

Men engaged in agriculture and those who were artisans – blacksmiths, wheelwrights, carpenters, masons, cordwainers and tailors, could only muster 7 per cent apiece in 1851. In 1891, agriculture almost doubled to 13 per cent, but was still below the county average of about 26 per cent. This increase is probably due to many men who were formerly miners switching their attention to farming their smallholdings as the local mining industry contracted. Nine per cent of the male work force in 1891 were described as artisans, an increase from the 7 per cent of 1851, but in real terms the numbers in this employment category did not change much at all, and if anything showed a slight decrease, probably explained by migration and the fact that many of the men described as artisans were, by their trade, connected to the copper mining industry in some capacity, which had shed large numbers of its workforce in the 40 years between 1851 and 1891.

Middle class occupations such as those employed as traders, merchants and shopkeepers amounted to just over 1 per cent, proving that in 1851 this branch of the middle class was still in its nascence in the parish. Not surprisingly, in 1891, this figure had risen to 8 per cent, as Lanner had evolved into a community with a variety of small shops and businesses operated by a growing middle class, serving the needs of a village just a little too distant from Redruth or St Day for many of its inhabitants to make use of the shops in either of them. Few male professionals had their homes in the parish in 1851, just over 1 per cent is recorded, which consisted of the parish priest, schoolmasters, clerks and accountants. By 1891 this had doubled to 2 per cent, representative of a small but influential group of men as we shall see when discussing the trade directories.

In 1851 transport and utilities employed just less than 1 per cent of the male population, but had witnessed a modest rise by 1891 to 3 per cent, as new roads and railways had been built in the district, making transportation easier and the population more mobile, which translated into more work for carriers. Labourers made up less than 1 per cent in 1851, but this figure had risen to 2 per cent in 1891, again due to contracting opportunities in the local mines and the need for men to labour on road building and croft reclamation.

Domestic service as an employment category for men failed to make an impact, amounting to a mere 0.5 per cent in 1851, with the situation not really changing by 1891, when it was 0.6 per cent. This should come as no surprise as there were not many large estates in the village or wealthy middle class families able to support numbers of male domestic servants as footmen, butlers, coachmen, valets, gamekeepers, gardeners or estate managers.

Female Employment

Before the advent of industrialisation, work for women took place mainly in the home. 'Her dignity depends on remaining unknown; her glory lies in her husband's esteem, her greatest pleasure in the happiness of her family', argued Rousseau in *Emile*, his classic work of 1762, articulating the thoughts and opinions of a patriarchal, male dominated world. This mind-set coloured men's attitudes to the opposite sex for well over a century. But although proto-industrial (the period which preceded and paved the way for large scale industrialisation) pursuits such as spinning or basket making represented low status, low waged employment in which women often worked within a family group, and probably did not see their earnings as individuals, Valenze has argued that women's labour played an indispensable economic role. For by working from home, women made a valid contribution to the family economy and helped to keep working class families above the subsistence threshold.

But in the late eighteenth century the advent of industrialisation was accompanied by acts of enclosure which drove women out of field labour and led to craft deskilling – the disappearance of traditional rural handicrafts, such as spinning, resulted in a degradation of women's traditional labour. Valenze argues that women's work was thus 'relegated in principle to the invisibility of domestic housework or, even worse, to a unique sub-proletarian purgatory of domestic service'.[77]

Analysis of the nineteenth-century census returns for Lanner give indications that many women were not a part of the formal wage economy and the figures we see for those Lanner women in the paid labour force were probably on the whole, young and elderly unmarried women or widows. Twenty-two per cent of the parish women are listed as being 'at home' or engaged in 'domestic duties' in 1851. (Fig. 2.8) By 1891 this had fallen to 6 per cent. We can speculate that a high proportion of the 1851 figure was made up of teenage girls who by 1891 were required to be in full time education until the age of 12 or 13. But it is highly likely that there was a degree of hidden earnings among Lanner's married women. Such women might have occasionally helped out in their husband's shop, took in extra washing or sewing, lent a hand in the fields on the family farm, or helped with childminding.

However, the advent of industrialisation had challenged the opinions of men such as Rousseau, and women increasingly sought work outside the home and therefore became more dependent on a formal wage economy. Even after industrialisation, the choice of occupations for women in Victorian Cornwall was restricted, but the clearest and preferred occupation for Lanner women was that of a bal

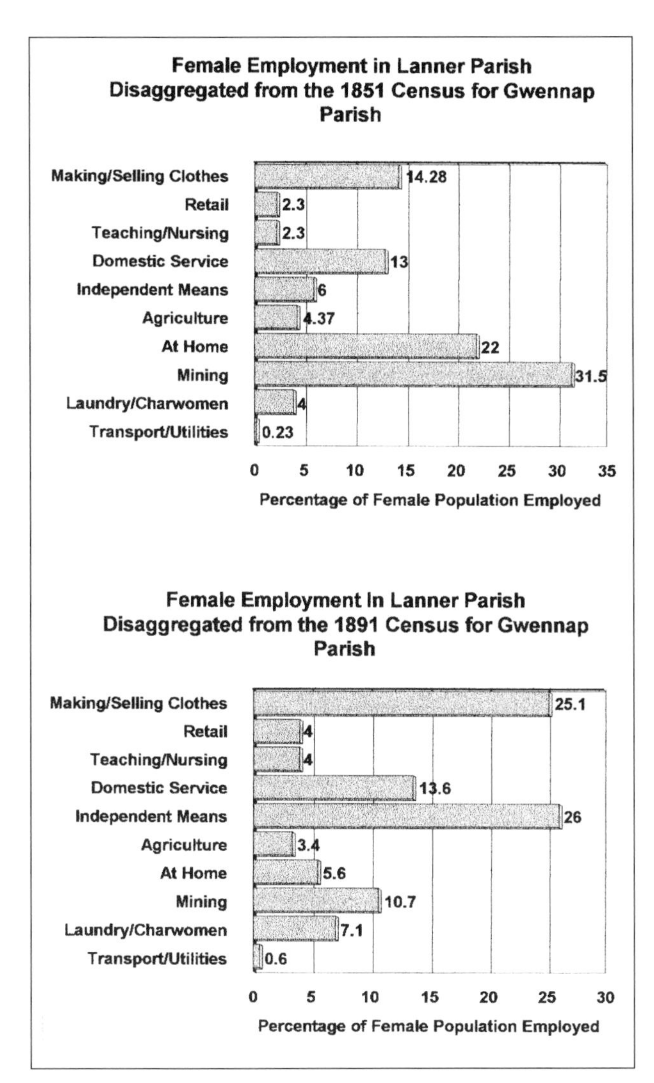

Figs.2.8 and 2.9. *Female employment figures, 1851 (top) and 1891 (lower graph).*

maiden. In common with the men, the mining industry was the chief and most important employment category for women in 1851, amounting to almost 32 per cent. (Fig. 2.9).

Wages were generally above those paid in agriculture, and we learn of some young women formerly employed as servants expressing a preference for their work at the mine, claiming it was easier than domestic service. This marks an important difference between the occupational opportunities for Lanner women and those in Cornwall as a whole. In 1851, in the heyday of mining, 52 per cent of females were in domestic employment compared with 32 per cent in Lanner. Many Victorian men, most notably George Henwood, a well known mining journalist of the time, became uncomfortable and concerned about the degree of independence women's work at the mines engendered, and the social implications of this are discussed in Chapter 4. Women found jobs at the mine's surface as bal maidens, but also as account-house cooks, servants and cleaners.

The collapse of the local copper mining industry affected Lanner's women perhaps more than the men, as the gradual switch to tin mining dispensed with the need for a large number of surface workers. Methods used to dress tin were not as labour intensive as that of copper, and this is reflected in the decline in importance of the mining industry for women by 1891, which had dropped from first to fourth position of importance, employing nearly 11 per cent of the parish's women. Once again, this was a higher figure than in Cornwall as a whole, where the proportion of female employment in mining dropped from 20 per cent in 1861 to a mere 1.5 per cent by 1901. The disappearance of the independent bal maiden was the major shift in employment opportunities for women in the period.

Making and selling clothes constituted 14 per cent of the female labour force in 1851. Many women describe themselves as dressmakers and seamstresses on the 1851 census, but from this it is not clear whether they were self-employed, or working for someone else outside the home. We know that some were working at small factories during and after this time at Redruth, such as Catherine Jose and her cousin Elizabeth Hitchens, who were seamstresses at Cummins Outfitting Establishment at Redruth.[78] But some women were working from other people's homes and supplementing their income by taking in extra work. An elderly resident of the village remembers being told how, in the last century, her granny used to walk from the village to Mount Ambrose just outside Redruth every day carrying a small Singer sewing machine to her place of work in someone's home there. In the evenings she needed the sewing machine at home so she could continue to work.

The Singer sewing machine was invented in 1851, and as the century progressed, such machines became cheaper and more readily available. We note John Evans Junior of Lanner advertising in the *Cornubian* of 1883 as a tailor, hatter and agent for sewing machines in the village (Fig. 2.10). Such small 'cottage factories' were evidently quite popular in the last century, and became more common after the collapse of the mining industry. Perhaps this is local evidence of the exploitation of women following the intensification of sweated labour in cottage manufactories which were prevalent and better known in the big towns and cities of England. Clearly, technological advances had not radically affected the type of work women did, nor the status of their work. Manufacturing clothes at home was poorly paid and of low status. Hudson argues this was more to do with ideology than biology and concerned with cheap labour, the association of women with the domestic sphere and responsibility of large families to rear, than with women's choices as to what they really wanted.[79] By 1891, 25 per cent of women were employed in this category which became the chief category for women in paid employment, work as a seamstress seeming to replace that of a bal maiden.

Domestic service is the third most important employment category for Lanner's women in 1851, at 13 per cent. In 1891 the figure stood at nearly 14 per cent, making it the second most popular employment category for women. The above figures show that this category remained almost

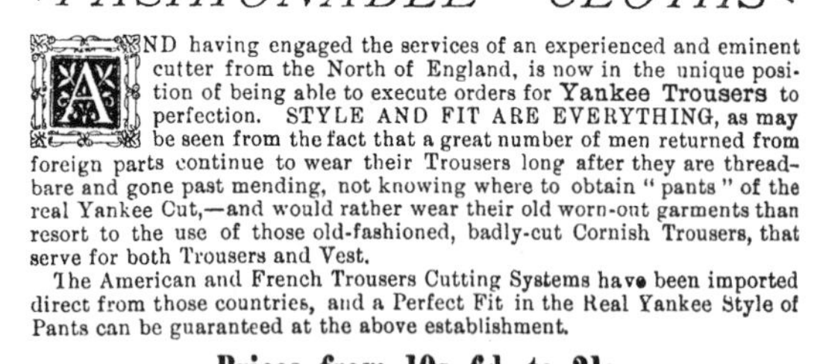

Fig.2.10. *John Evans, of Lanner, advertises his tailor's establishment, c.1878. He later moved to Tower House, Redruth.*

unchanged, but has an inherent weakness, in that it does not give a true representation of the importance of domestic service to nineteenth century Lanner women. In Cornwall as a whole it provided a half of all female employment and many young Lanner ladies were forced, by the absence of local wealthy families requiring servants, to move away from the area, some to local towns such as Falmouth, Redruth and Truro, but many more to Plymouth and beyond, to the large industrial towns and cities.

Leaving the village to seek work as a domestic servant undoubtedly accounted for a great deal of female migration in late nineteenth-century Lanner. Five of John Polkinghorne's six daughters left their Carn Marth home in the 1880s and 90s to enter service in Devon, at Exeter and Plymouth, and other South Western counties.[80] Moreover, a degree of caution must be exercised when analysing these figures for Lanner's female domestic servants, as such women were not always bona fide servants of the type found in a Catherine Cookson novel. Often we find that the young woman described as a servant is in fact a family member, who by necessity has had to move in with a relative, and was earning her keep by helping with the household chores. Such an example is that of the Brown Family, resident at Lannarth in 1851. The head of the household, Richard Brown, had his mother-in-law, Grace Lean, living with him, and Eliza Lean, an 18-year-old is shown, listed as a servant, who was in all likelihood a relative. John Oppy, a miner of Lanner, had his 13-year-old niece, Ann Thomas, living with his family as a 'servant'.

A small percentage of women were employed as old fashioned 'live in servants' to farmers, but were in fact better described as agricultural labourers, and were expected to perform a wide range of farm duties – milking, planting, cropping, hoeing, harvesting and threshing, as well as helping with cooking and keeping house. Only a percentage of more 'well to do' families, the new middle class, employed a lone female servant who was expected to perform a variety of chores, which probably included cooking, cleaning, carrying water, washing and running errands. In most instances the young woman would have been known to her prospective employer.

Examples include John Hodge, a mine agent, who employed 20-year-old Blanch Penhallurick, and Edward Pearse of Trevarth, also an agent, who employed Mary Ann Reed as a servant to care for his family, his wife and three children, in 1851. In 1891 Edwin Hosking, a 58 year old Mine Agent, employed 20 year old Nanny Uren, a Lanner girl, as a servant to keep house for himself, his wife and two teenage sons. A house help would have gone a long way towards liberating the lives of the wives of aspiring middle class gentlemen, who were freed from the tasks of domestic drudgery in the days before Hoovers, washing machines, central heating, and a variety of other time-saving devices. Middle class families were keen to show the trappings of their success, and being able to boast of a servant, or in some cases, more than one domestic, was a sign to the community that the family involved 'had arrived'.

In 1891, 40-year-old solicitor, George Skewes Bray (Lawyer Bray), employed a cook, Emily Light, and a house maid, Elizabeth Herring, to look after himself and his 33-year-old spinster sister Christiana. Very few local girls were fortunate to find work on Gwennap's estates of Trevince, Burncoose, Pengreep or Scorrier.

Just over 4 per cent of the parish's women were engaged in agriculture, and in 1891, just over 3 per cent. The figure might in reality have been much higher, as the wives and daughters of farmers would have worked on the farm with their husbands, sons and brothers. When later the Census for Cornwall, of 1911, included farmers' daughters, it more than doubled the statistical size of Cornwall's female agricultural work force. Agricultural wages were poor in comparison to those paid at the area's mines in 1851, and fewer women were attracted to farming, as new employment possibilities opened to them in dressmaking, trade and commerce, and domestic service, as the century progressed following the collapse of the local copper industry.

Four per cent of women in 1851 and 7 per cent in 1891, described themselves as working as washerwomen or charwomen. Within this category it was usual to find a high percentage of widows and some single women with illegitimate children, who had been forced by sheer necessity to take in washing, or grub for their neighbours, to earn a few shillings each week to avoid becoming inmates of the Union House. This work was also characterised by low wages and was very low status, but meant that unmarried or widowed women with small children could work from home, or take their children to work with them. The 1851 Census shows several such cases, including that of Abigail Barrett, a 48-year-old widow, working as a washer who had a family of five, the youngest just 8. Sixty-three-year-old widow, Anna Dower, is recorded as a laundress on the 1891 Census.

The 1891 Census returns shows a large increase in the number of charwomen, as the opportunity for employment on the mines had diminished, including 30-year-old Elizabeth Jane Blewett, working to support her three illegitimate children.

Numbers of women employed in trade and retail in 1851 shows a figure just under 2.5 per cent, slightly higher than the male percentage, indicating that perhaps some of these women ran a business while their husbands were employed in the mines or elsewhere. By 1891 the figure had almost doubled to 4 per cent, as the number of small shops and businesses in the parish increased. Interestingly, this form of employment featured more strongly for women than men by 1891, in Lanner as in Cornwall, and consisted in the main of grocery businesses run by widows such as Nannie Knuckey, but also married women whose husbands were absent, such as Jane Tregellas, age 43, who operated a grocery business at Pennance in 1891. But despite this growth in retail activity in the village of Lanner, however, female employment in retailing was much lower than in Cornwall as a whole, where it accounted for over a quarter of the total; evidence that Lanner was still quite dependent upon Redruth for shopping.

Teaching and nursing accounted for 2.30 per cent in 1851 and 4 per cent in 1891, with jobs such as village schoolmistress or midwife accounting for this total. The rise in this category is attributable to the need for more young ladies to work as schoolmistresses, pupil teachers and monitors, following the 1870 Education Act, and the construction of Gwennap's Board Schools. The wages of female teachers, however, were never on a par with those of their male counterparts, even though their jobs involved much the same level of skill and responsibility (see Chapter 10).

Women shown as living on their own means came to just 6 per cent in 1851, and included annuitants and those receiving remittances from absent husbands, some of whom had moved overseas to work in foreign mining fields, beginning a trend of emigration which was to have such an impact on the parish in the half century which was to follow. This category more than any other reveals the extent of the changes which were being wrought in the latter half of the nineteenth century in Lanner.

The collapse of the local copper mining industry prompted a large exodus of men, many of whom were employed in foreign mining fields for a period of a few years before returning home. Such men remitted money to their families back home in Lanner. The extent of Lanner's dependency culture is revealed in the startling jump in the figure for women of independent means, most recorded as 'living on own means' or 'living on husband's means' in the 1891 Census. A total of 26 per cent of Lanner women were described thus, making it the top category for female 'income' by the close of the nineteenth century.

Although the first half of the nineteenth century saw more women than ever before working outside their own homes, their work did not confer income or status comparable to their male counterparts, even for the 'independent' bal maiden. And at the same time, the nature of industrialisation saw the decline of many traditional female proto-industrial pursuits, which included gleaning on common lands, a variety of cottage-based industries (such as spinning), casual seasonal labour and petty market trading, which increased women's vulnerability and made them more dependent on their husbands, fathers or sons. Moreover, this trend was further compounded by early marriage which reduced the prevalence of women as independent economic agents.[81] Yet however much Victorian Lanner appeared to have been a man's world on the surface, many women had been forced by necessity into managing their finances independently of their absent husbands who were working overseas, successfully running small shops and businesses, keeping family farms and rearing their families single-handedly; evidence that Lanner was fast becoming a matriarchal community.

The Development of Trade and Commerce

The development of the Turnpike Road from Redruth to Penryn (now the A393), doubtless helped to aid Lanner's development in the nineteenth century. This road was originally built in the mid eighteenth century and had a turnpike gate at Comford, and a further one on the Redruth side of Lanner Hill, on the opposite side of the road just above the entrance to Sandy Lane. The date, 1742, above the door of the Fox and Hounds Pub at Comford, indicates the year of construction for this public house, which was probably built not long after the Turnpike Road. Francis wrote the following concerning the road in 1845: 'Oft tourists with glee travel onward this road from Redruth... the highway is teeming with animal life.'[82] Omnibuses – long four-wheeled spring carts, which were covered with canvas stretched over a framework, with curtains hung at the front and back, plied the route regularly. These cumbersome vehicles went along the road at snail's pace and were not at all comfortable, but provided a welcome respite from walking, especially for the elderly.

In the mid nineteenth century Matthews's Van departed Lanner for Truro at 10.00am on Mondays, Wednesdays and Saturdays, and to Falmouth daily at 10.30am and 6.30p.m. A service to Redruth for the weekly market was offered on Fridays only via St Day and Carharrack.[83] Along this important arterial road came all manner of goods on their way to

Fig.2.11. *The Redruth & Falmouth bus at South Downs, early twentieth century. The driver is Bert Tallack. Note the mine dumps of Wheal Buller on the left, Wheal Trefusis on the right.* (© The Paddy Bradley Collection).

Redruth Market from the Ports of Falmouth and Penryn, and the state of its surface was often described as deplorable in the nineteenth century. In 1888 it was reported that large stones, many of which were loose and too big, were causing severe discomfort to passengers and pedestrians alike (Fig. 2.11).

In the winter the roads in Lanner and district were often so awash with mud and mire that old women were sometimes seen clanking around on round 'pattens', iron frames attached to their boots to raise them above the filthy puddles which would have soiled the bottoms of their dresses. For those of us who know the present heavily used A393, it will be no surprise to discover that the old Turnpike Road was also very busy in Victorian times, carrying a tremendous amount of traffic, and accidents were frequent. In 1862, an inquest on the body of 7-year-old Joseph Gregor was held in the village. This Lanner lad had died from injuries he received after becoming caught in the wheels of a heavy cart belonging to Mr Wearn of Ponsanooth, being driven by Dick Richards to Redruth Market laden with sacks of flour. In 1869, an old woman, Martha Gray, was crossing the road in the dark when she was knocked over by a horse and trap, the driver of which drove on regardless. And in 1870 a boy named John Henry Jory fell under the wheels of a cart at Lanner Hill.[84]

Trade directories, such as those of Harrods and Kelly, provide further evidence of the development of business and commerce in Lanner in the nineteenth century, although it must be noted that not everybody who was engaged in business had their name in these directories (Fig. 2.12). However limited they might be, analysis of these trade directories help to provide proof of a thriving, virtually self-contained society, able to provide most of the necessities required by a community predominantly of miners. There is however, a lack of specialist shops such as would have been found in nearby towns; those wanting to purchase a piano, a velocipede (bicycle), a decent bottle of wine, jewellery or watches, a good clock, quality furniture or a fine chinaware, a journey to St Day, or more probably Redruth, would have been necessary. This applied equally to the services of a doctor, apothecary, surgeon or solicitor for much of the nineteenth

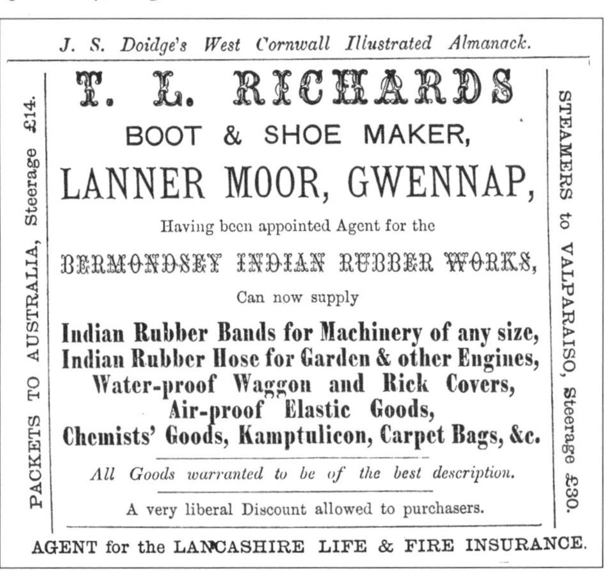

J. S. Doidge's West Cornwall Illustrated Almanack.

PACKETS TO AUSTRALIA, Steerage £14.

T. L. RICHARDS

BOOT & SHOE MAKER,

LANNER MOOR, GWENNAP,

Having been appointed Agent for the

BERMONDSEY INDIAN RUBBER WORKS,

Can now supply

Indian Rubber Bands for Machinery of any size,
Indian Rubber Hose for Garden & other Engines,
Water-proof Waggon and Rick Covers,
Air-proof Elastic Goods,
Chemists' Goods, Kamptulicon, Carpet Bags, &c.

All Goods warranted to be of the best description.

A very liberal Discount allowed to purchasers.

STEAMERS to VALPARAISO, Steerage £30.

AGENT for the LANCASHIRE LIFE & FIRE INSURANCE.

Fig.2.12. *T.L. Richards advertises his boot and shoemaking business in Doidge's Almanack of 1873. Note the advertisements for packets to Australia, and Steamers to Chile.*

century. And of course Lanner had no market, so people had to frequent that of Redruth to sell their produce. In 1898 Lanner followed Redruth's example of half-day closing; all Lanner businesses shut at 1.00pm on a Thursday afternoon.

Therefore a close link was maintained with the town of Redruth, and Lanner people benefited socially from interaction with members of the wider community, on a market day for example. In spite of the rise of a middle class, the numbers of people who could have been described as affluent in nineteenth century Lanner remained quite small. Lanner was still a poor neighbourhood, and we therefore find evidence of many small shops which sold a wide range of affordable basic goods, often making it difficult to differentiate between grocers, bakers, drapers and other shopkeepers in Victorian Lanner.

Kelly's Directory for 1856, the first edition of a trade directory in which Lanner is mentioned as a separate parish, confirms the overwhelming importance of mining to the area. Eleven people are mentioned in connection with the industry, including six mine agents and four assayers, among them Athanasius Pryor, a copper sampling agent. As we have already established, the importance of mining was to diminish as the nineteenth century wore on and the process of de-industrialisation began, but even in 1881, the village could boast two sampling agents for copper companies, John Evans of Lambriggan House, and Captain William Odgers of Treweek Cottage, Rough Street. By 1897 the decline in mining was very evident; only one person is listed as being employed in the industry and the Pennance brick works, managed firstly by John Thomas and later Thomas Fisher, was to close soon after.

As we have already deduced, there was a steady rise in the numbers of people involved in commerce in the village during the Victorian period; nine grocers and shopkeepers are noted in 1866, and the number rose to 13 in 1873, and to 16 in 1878. The rise in the numbers of people engaged in commerce from the late Victorian period can in part be attributed to the growth of Lanner as a settlement, but also because people had to find new occupations to replace those of bal maiden, tutworker and tributer.

One might suppose that the demise of the mining industry would mean fewer shops, but increased demand for consumer durables and meat and milk, created a general rise in the standard of living because of the rise in real wages. Such village 'grocery' shops usually sold anything from fruit and vegetables, dried and salted fish, jar and tinned goods, candy, loose grain and pulses, tea, spices, treacle, sugar, animal feed, flour, tobacco, bottled drinks, blocks of salt, dried fruit and cured meats. A huge range of household items including nails, fire shovels, buckets, tin baths and pans, enamelware, cloths, brushes, candles, furniture polish, black lead, oil, paraffin, starch, ointments, soap and matches could be purchased, as well as bolts of cloth, children's toys, books and stationery. Some even sold safety fuse and caps.

When William Combellack ceased trading from his grocery shop in the village in 1890, the whole of his shop stock and equipment was offered for sale by public auction. The latter consisted of brushes, tea canisters, brass scales and weights, a treacle cistern, a large weighing machine and weights, and flour scales. In addition, potential purchasers were alerted to large quantities of drapery, groceries, stationery and ironmongery.[85]

A well known grocery shop was that of Elizabeth Tregoning, who founded the family grocery business which

Fig.2.13. *Tregoning's Grocery Store (early 1900s). Now the Lanner Post Office.* (© Mr and Mrs M. Veall, Gwennap)

was to survive in the village well into the next century, and was situated where the village Post Office stands in 1998 (Fig 2.13). Chris and Sara Russell's lounge was once the store for the shop's barley and oats.

Similar village grocery businesses of the mid to late Victorian period included those of George Bennett, Colan Dunstan of Lanner Moor, George Reed, James Lawn and Mrs Elizabeth Hosking, who later became a mistress at the new board school built in 1878.

Not surprisingly three beer retailers are named in *Kelly's Directory* of 1856: Thomas Lean of the Commercial Inn, Samuel Gray, who kept a shop in addition to the Miners' Arms, and Stephen Williams, innkeeper at Lanner Moor. His wife was later to take over the pub, noted as Mrs Sarah Williams in *Kellys Directory* of 1873. The public house was an important social focus of village life, as we shall see in Chapter 12.

The Commercial Inn is shown on a map dated 1819, and probably started its life as a tavern after the Turnpike Road came through the village in the mid 1700s. A number of landlords in the nineteenth century are noted in the directories for this pub, among them John Prisk in the 1880s, and William Taylor in the 1890s. The public house at Lanner Moor, formerly the Tresavean Ale House of Stephen Williams, later became The Prisks Hotel named after its landlord, Uncle Joe Prisk. It afterwards became the Rogers Arms, the new name commemorating the Rogers of Penrose, the landed family on whose land the pub stood. The Gray Family and then the Pryors were, for a long time, landlords of the Miners' Arms pub in the square.

Three butchers are noted in Lanner in 1866, Thomas Rowe and John Faull of Lanner and James Davey of Lanner Moor. Davey, who also farmed on a small scale, began his butcher's business in 1861 at Lanner Moor. In 1875 he migrated to Chile where he continued his trade before returning to the village, around 1886, when he once again opened a butcher's shop adjoining the old Lanner Post Office.[86] (Fig. 2.14.).

The butchery business was obviously quite lucrative, as we have seen by the examples of some of their household contents above. The number of butcher's shops in nineteenth-century Lanner was never very high because poor people seldom bought butchers' meat, the purchase price for beef and pork being beyond the means of most working class families on a regular basis. Instead their table was supplemented with rabbit, hare and other game, and many mining families kept their own livestock of a few fowls and a pig, which were slaughtered if and when necessary. And cheaper cuts of meat were always available at the Saturday night market held at Redruth. The late Mrs Mary Job remembered that it was possible to get most things needed in Lanner, but that on Saturday nights she would go with her mother to Redruth because the 'stannins' (stalls) in the street would be selling off cheap beef.[87]

It is interesting to note the absence of a bakery business in Lanner, which only appeared in the early twentieth century.

JAMES DAVEY,

BUTCHER, LANNER,

Desires to return his sincere thanks to his numerous friends in

LANNER AND ITS NEIGHBOURHOOD,

for the very liberal support accorded him during the last 26 years, and begs to inform them that he intends

OPENING HIS

NEW SHOP

ADJOINING THE POST OFFICE,

On Friday, Dec. 10th, 1886,

and hopes by strict attention to business, and supplying the

BEST QUALITY MEAT

AT THE LOWEST POSSIBLE MARKET PRICES, still to retain those favours.

Prime Beef at from 5d. to 8d. per pound.

Fig.2.14. *James Davey advertises the opening of his new shop in Lanner.* (Redruth Independent, *3 Dec 1886).*

We must therefore conclude that the majority of nineteenth century housewives baked their own bread, cakes and buns.

One cobbler is named in 1866, Thomas Richards of Lanner Moor, who employed one man and two apprentices in 1851. He was also noted as an emigration agent by 1873, as the miners began to leave the village in increasing numbers to places world wide. Richards regularly made out tickets direct to faraway mining towns, and booked passages on the ocean liners which plied the routes between Liverpool and Southampton to the USA, Australia, New Zealand and South Africa. His interest in mining was also evidenced by his collecting and dealing in mineral specimens. We might speculate that some miners' passages could well have been paid for with stunning specimens smuggled out of the local mines (Fig. 2.15). He also acted as an agent for the Bermondsey Indian Rubber Works, and supplied Indian

GENTLEMEN FORMING CABINETS OF

British and Foreign

MINERAL SPECIMENS

Can be supplied on applying to

T. L. RICHARDS,

LANNER MOOR, GWENNAP.

Agent for the Lancashire Fire and Life, and for the Accidental Insurance.

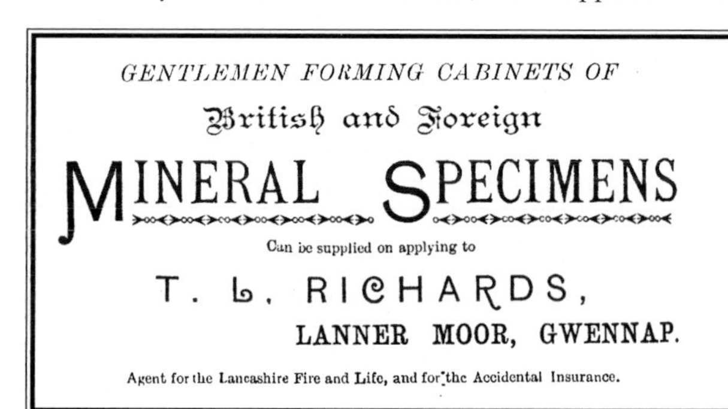

Fig. 2.15 *T.L.Richards advertises as a mineral collector in Doidge's Almanack, c.1870.*

rubber bands for machinery of any size, Indian rubber hose for garden and other engines, waterproof wagon and rick covers, waterproof elastic goods, chemists' goods, Kamptulicon and carpet bags, which were all offered at a liberal discount to customers.[88] (By 1878 another emigration agent and cordwainer, John Secombe Tonkin, is noted as also, in the 1880s, is John Evans, draper and tailor, as migration began to be a lucrative business in the village.).

In 1878, five cobblers are listed in Harrod's *Royal County Directory*, including Frank Trethowan and Edwin Walsh who had been village cobblers long before their names appeared in a trade directory. In the Victorian era, those who could afford it had boots made for them. People seldom threw out their footwear but had them regularly repaired, with hobnails fitted into the soles to increase their longevity, particularly in the case of children's boots which were handed down. Cobblers usually had plenty of work, and far more men practised this trade in nineteenth-century Lanner than the directories imply.

As early as 1856 James Hosking is listed as a tailor, resident in Lanner, and by the early 1880s, John Evans Junior, son of the middle class copper company agent, John Evans Senior, acquired a fine reputation as a tailor, hatter and draper, employing an experienced cutter from the North of England. He always had a splendid assortment of cloths in stock. Hats in all the newest shapes were advertised from 1s.6d to 6s.9d, as well as cashmeres from 1s.5d to 4s.6d. 'Collars, ties, braces, shirts, sheets, quilts, blankets, flannels, calicoes, shirtings and serges were advertised all at good low prices and very common cloths were left for other people to keep'.[89]

But the limitations imposed on shopkeepers who wanted to achieve a higher degree of commercial success than could have been realised in a predominantly poor, working class mining village like Lanner, became apparent to Evans. On Thursday 22 April 1886, after five years in Lanner, he relocated his business to Tower House, Redruth, where he continued to work as a tailor and emigration agent and quickly prospered in the climate of the more lucrative town market.[90]

The increasing popularity of coal as a domestic fuel is shown by the growing numbers of people engaged in coal dealing. From just one noted in 1866, William Richards, three entered the pages of the 1873 *Kelly's Directory*: William Carvolth, Henry Kneebone and Mrs Ann Richards, wife of William, above. Coal was formerly hawked around the village by Martha Williams, shown as a 55-year-old spinster on the 1851 Census, but her name never appeared in the directories.

The position of Post Officer was taken over by Nanny Lean from Richard Skewes in the 1870s. She also ran a shop, the premises of which is now the Londis Shop. Letters came through the Redruth Office, arriving in Lanner at 8.30am and 3.30pm, and were dispatched from the village at 6.30am and 4.15pm, and 8.30pm on Sundays, but Redruth was the nearest office for the purchase of money orders and for telegraph services. Postal orders could be purchased in Lanner, but not cashed.

In the late nineteenth century when the South African mail arrived, many local women would rush into Redruth to cash bankers' drafts remitted by their husbands and sons working in the mining camps there. On 26 February 1875,

Fig. 2.16. *Lanner Square, c1905.* (Photo by Bragg. © The Paddy Bradley Collection)

Fig.2.17. *Lanner village from the first tramway bridge, c.1914. This gives a good idea of the layout of the village about the turn of the century. Note the school in the centre-right.* (© The Paddy Bradley Collection)

the *Cornubian* noted that a condiment manufactory was situated at Lanner. Frank Savage's 'Anglo-Chilean Chutney Sauce' was reported to have been highly popular and successful, sold by S.T. Rowe, chemist, and Messrs Trounsons, at Redruth, and H.J. Harvey, grocer, of Falmouth. Yet the company never appeared in *Kelly's Directory* which might suggest that it foundered in the years following its inception.

John Willoughby was the village smith in the latter nineteenth century and ran his business from a shop which opened out on to the busy Turnpike Road almost opposite the square and just below the present day Londis Shop. (Fig. 2.16.). Blacksmiths comprised a large percentage of the total number of artisans in the 1851 Census for Lanner, but most of these were connected to the mines as 'bal smithies'.

By analysing the nineteenth century trades directories, Willoughby appeared to have held an unrivalled position as proprietor of the village's only blacksmith's business during most of the nineteenth century. His premises was remembered by elderly residents of the village in the early twentieth century as a veritable gossip shop, where men would drop in to enjoy a pipe of baccy and a chat close to the warmth of the forge, and where the idle whiled away their time. There were in reality many more smithies working in the community in the nineteenth century, including Ridgerald Willoughby, John's father, and John Paul who lived on the parish boundary with Carharrack, who employed one man in 1851. Henry Strick and Nicholas Jorey are listed as carpenters, the former employed as a builder and undertaker as well. The 1873 edition of the same directory also lists Joseph F. Letcher as a carpenter, and we find a mention of Philip Harvey and Sons, masons.

The Tiddy Family were also to become important village builders in the late nineteenth century, and were responsible for building some of the rows of cottages in the village, such at that at Lanner Green, named Tiddy's Terrace. The 1889 *Kelly's Directory* also lists Thomas Job as a mason. By 1897, three wheelwrights and carpenters are listed: William Williams, Joseph Pryor and William P. Martin.

Added to the artisans and traders of Lanner was a small but influential professional class, which included Richard Skewes, who provided the residents with certain medicines, being noted as a druggist and the village postmaster in 1866. In 1830, Pigot's Directory had noted John Paul of Trevarth as a surgeon. This highly esteemed gentlemen died in 1837 of apoplexy. He had earned an excellent reputation, gaining the goodwill and esteem of the mining people among whom he lived, and his death was a severe blow to the area's residents who then had to rely on a doctor from Redruth or St Day.[91]

George Skewes 'Lawyer' Bray (1850-1930) of Lanner House, a large shareholder in Pedn-an-Drea Mine, middle class solicitor of the firm Peter and Bray, Redruth, local magistrate, Guardian of the Poor, member of Cornwall County Council, leading light in Lanner Church and Chairman of numerous committees both within the parish and further afield, was to play a very important role in the area for many years. One former resident claimed he walked about the village wearing his high silk hat 'like he owned the place'.[92]

John Hawken and his successor, Richard Green, were the headmasters of the Trevarth Grammar School, both of whom were active members of various local groups and societies. The board school at Lanner in 1889 was noted as having John Richards as master and Miss Elizabeth Hocking as Mistress. In 1873, Miss Ellen Richards is recorded as running a day school in Lanner. We might add to these professional people, Charles Williams, the Registrar of Births, Marriages and Deaths for Gwennap and Stithians in 1856. The professional and middle class were never to be large in Lanner, which was overwhelmingly working class, but nevertheless they played many key roles in various village organisations and events.

Conclusion

The story of Lanner through the nineteenth century is one of rise and fall, boom and decline. By the mid nineteenth century, it had developed into a thriving village community with Tresavean Mine at its nucleus (Fig. 2.17).

However, the twentieth century brought the final closure of Tresavean which became just a memory in the minds of those who had grown accustomed to the rhythmic pounding of the stamps, toiled hard underground in its stygian depths, or listened intently for the two-tone hooter which heralded the tramp of the miners' feet through the village in their heavy boots.

With its sons and daughters scattered to the four corners of the world, with many of those who remained dependent on a banker's draft from the USA, or South Africa, Lanner at the close of the nineteenth century was a far cry from the confident, animated community of just over half a century before. Lanner was forced to confront the many problems arising from an unstoppable process of de-industrialisation and economic paralysis, leading to what Philip Payton has termed a 'fossilisation of the economy' and which was to endure until after the Second World War.[93]

REFERENCES

1 Rowse A.L., (ed.), Harris F.L., 'The Industrial Revolution in Cornwall', from, *The West In English History*, London, 1949.
2 Hudson, Pat, *The Industrial Revolution*, Edward Arnold, London, 1992, p.102. Proto-industrialism is taken to generally refer to a period which preceded industrialisation proper. The precursors of many modern industries have been traced to the countryside, where 'they existed in dynamic and flexible symbiosis with prevailing agrarian systems of production and manufacture'. Callum, D.H., Society and Economy in West Cornwall, c.1588-1750, Ph.D, University of Exeter, 1993, p. 19.
3 Payton, Philip, *The Making of Modern Cornwall*, Dyllansow Truran, Redruth, 1992, p. 99.
4 Francis, William, *Gwennap, A Descriptive Poem in Seven Cantos*, J. May, Redruth, 1845, p. 66.
5 Ibid.
6 Ibid, p. 87.
7 HO 107/1914; 1851 Census Returns for the Parish of Gwennap, C.S.L.
8 P112/1/4, CRO (Lanner Marriage Register, 1845-1933).
9 Francis, William, *Gwennap, A Descriptive Poem in Seven Cantos*, J. May, Redruth, 1845, p. 86.
10 Deacon, Bernard, 'Proto-Industrialisation and Potatoes', *Cornish Studies* 5, Philip Payton, (ed.,) University of Exeter Press, 1997, p. 69.
11 *West Briton*, 15/2/1839.
12 P 79/81/1; Vestry Meeting, 9/2/1847.
13 Ibid, Vestry Meeting, 7/2/1848.
14 Deacon, Bernard, 'Proto-Industrialisation and Potatoes', *Cornish Studies* 5, Philip Payton, (ed.,) University of Exeter Press, 1997, p. pp. 75-79.
15 Michell, Frank, *Annals of an Ancient Cornish Town - Redruth*, Dyllansow Truran, Redruth, 1978, p. 166.
16 *West Briton*, 12/4/1867; 11/10/1867.
17 Michell, Frank, *Annals of an Ancient Cornish Town - Redruth*, Dyllansow Truran, Redruth, 1978, p. 172.
18 Deacon, Bernard, 'Proto-Industrialisation and Potatoes', *Cornish Studies 5*, Philip Payton, (ed.,)University of Exeter Press, 1997, pp. 79-80.
19 *Cornubian*, 29/6/1883.
20 *Cornubian*, 2/2/1894.
21 *Cornubian*, 8/10/1896.
22 *Cornubian*, 27/7/1894.
23 *West Briton*, 21/2/1895.

24 *Royal Cornwall Gazette*, 27/2/1896.
25 Hudson, Pat, *The Industrial Revolution*, Edward Arnold, London, 1992, p. 207.
26 Michell, Frank, *Annals of an Ancient Cornish Town - Redruth*, Dyllansow Truran, Redruth, 1978, p. 66.
27 Thompson, E.P., 'Patrician Society, Plebeian Culture'. *Journal of Social History, VII*, (1974); Hudson, Pat, *The Industrial Revolution,* Edward Arnold, London, 1992, p. 205.
28 P 79/81/1, CRO.
29 P 79/81/1, Vestry Meeting, 2/12/1842.
30 Maze Monday was the first working day following pay day, when it was commonplace for many miners to be still too 'mazed', or madly drunk, from the effects of the weekend's carousing to return to work.
31 *Cornubian*, 13/1/1882.
32 *Royal Cornwall Gazette*, 27/2/1896.
33 *Cornubian*, 1/1/1890.
34 *Cornubian*, 9/2/1883.
35 *West Briton*, 29/3/1839.
36 *Cornubian*, 28/2/1890.
37 James, C.C., *History of Gwennap*, Undated, Privately Published, p. 93.
38 Hudson, Pat, *The Industrial Revolution*, Edward Arnold, London, 1992, p. 206.
39 *West Briton*, 31/5/1861.
40 *West Briton*, 21/11/1889.
41 Hudson, Pat, *The Industrial Revolution*, Edward Arnold, London, 1992, pp 203-4.
42 *Cornubian*, 7/10/1870.
43 *Royal Cornwall Gazette*, 22/7/1896.
44 P 79/81/1, CRO; *West Briton*, 30/1/1879.
45 *Cornubian*, 30/1/1891.
46 *Cornubian*, 27/1/1882.
47 *West Briton*, 4/3/1836.
48 *West Briton*, 8/2/1839; P 79/81/1, CRO.
49 P 79/81/1, CRO.
50 Trevelyan, G.M., *British History in the nineteenth century and After, 1782-1919*, Penguin Books, London, 1979, p. 156.
51 P 79/81/1, CRO
52 Bawden W.L., 'Transcriptions of the Poor Law Book of Gwennap' (P 79/81/2, CRO); swanskin - a thick cotton cloth with a nap on one side; dowlas - a coarse type of calico; shift - chemise or night shirt.
53 F.L. Harris Archive.
54 1841 'Commission on the Employment of Children'; Dr. Barham, p. 846.
55 *Cornish Telegraph*, 30/12/1886.
56 Gwennap Parish Registers, pre 1845, Transcribed by W.L. Bawden, C.S.L..
57 Rowe, J., and Andrews, C.T., 'Cholera in Cornwall', *Journal of the Royal Institution of Cornwall, New Series,* Vol. 1, part 2, 1974, p. 153.
58 P 79/81/1, Vestry Meeting, 18/10/1848.
59 P 79/81/1, CRO.
60 Ibid.
61 Rowe, J., and Andrews, C.T., 'Cholera in Cornwall', *Journal of the Royal Institution of Cornwall, New Series,* Vol. 1, part 2, 1974, pp 160-61.
62 P 79/81/1, Vestry, 31/10/1853.
63 *Cornubian*, 16/2/1894.
64 *Doidge's Almanack*, 1900.
65 Burt, Roger, *Cornwall's Mines and Miners*, (after George Henwood), Bradford Barton, Truro, 1972, pp. 91-2.
66 The window tax was introduced in 1696 and repealed in 1851. Excise duty on glass persisted from 1695-1845, and the excise duty on brick was in force between 1750-1850.
67 Information courtesy of Mrs J. Craze, Redruth, interviewed in 1996.
68 Information from the late Mrs Minnie Haughton, interviewed in 1996, aged 80.
69 Brandis - a heavy iron trivet; kettle - small iron bowl with 3 legs; crock - large three-legged iron bowl, used for boiling.
70 Chester, Veronica, 'Some Cornish Landowners. 1690-1760. A Social and Economic Study', unpublished MA, University of Oxford, 1957, p. 11, as quoted by Deacon, in *Cornish Studies* 5, p. 67, 1997.
71 *Cornubian*, 7/12/1894.
72 *Cornubian*, 16/3/1877.

73 *Cornubian*, 30/5/1892.
74 *Redruth Times*, 7/1/1870.
75 *Redruth Independent*, 14/5/1887.
76 Information courtesy of Mrs P. Danby, West Trevarth Farm.
77 Valenze, Deborah, *The First Industrial Woman,* Oxford University Press, New York, 1995, pp 3-12.
78 *Cornubian*, 24/2/1871.
79 Hudson, Pat, *The Industrial Revolution*, Edward Arnold, London, 1992, p. 230.
80 Research on Polkinghorne Family, S. P. Schwartz.
81 Hudson, Pat, *The Industrial Revolution*, Edward Arnold, London, 1992, p. 230 .
82 Francis, William, *Gwennap, A Descriptive Poem in Seven Cantos*, J. May, Redruth, 1845, p.86.
83 *Doidge's Almanack*, 1866.
84 *West Briton,* 15/11/1862; Cornubian, 15/1/1869.
85 *Cornubian,* 28/2/1890.
86 *Redruth Independent,* 5/12/1886.
87 Interview with the late Mrs Mary Job, in 1991, when aged 101.
88 *Doidge's Almanack,* 1873.
89 *Doidge's Almanack,* 1883, and 1884.
90 *Redruth Independent*, 16/4/1886.
91 *Royal Cornwall Gazette,* 24/3/1837.
92 Information courtesy of Mrs Rhona Blatchford.
93 Payton, Philip, *The Making of Modern Cornwall*, Dyllansow Truran, Redruth, 1992, p. 114.

Fig.3.1 *Pennance Consols Engine House, 1998. This building, on the west flank of Carn Marth, is the only engine house in the parish remaining in anything like its original state.* (Photo R.H.Parker).

Chapter 3
The Rise and Fall of Lanner Mining

Cornish tin mining has a long history – stretching back to the realms of myth and legend. Significant copper mining has a much shorter record, being more or less unknown in Cornwall before 1700 (the Mines Royal Company made an unsuccessful attempt to mine copper in the 1560s and 1580s, using German engineers), and virtually collapsing in the 1860s. Lanner, tucked away in its valley, has not had much impact in mining literature, remaining virtually unnoticed between the big mining activities of Redruth and Gwennap. Indeed, as Lanner was part of the Parish of Gwennap until the middle of the nineteenth century, many references to mining activity in Lanner were documented under the name of the older parish, where it is said that, around 1825, as much as one-third of the world's copper was produced. Nevertheless, Tresavean, one of Cornwall's great mines, is within the Lanner parish boundary and undoubtedly was the main reason for the development of Lanner village.

Although Lanner has produced some tin, copper was its main metal product, and most of that was mined in the first half of the nineteenth century, during which period Lanner grew from a few cottages to a village with a population of much the same size as it has today. According to Henwood, within a radius of two miles from the top of Carn Marth, about £30 million worth of minerals had been raised from the earth, and, without her mines, 'Cornwall, instead of her present active, teeming population, and highly prosperous state, would have been a howling wilderness and a desert, her sons barbarians, and her gentry paupers'.[1]

Tresavean Mine in the early nineteenth century lay at the heartland of the then richest known mineralised area in the world, 'Gwennap, the Copper Kingdom', and was at the forefront of the Industrial Revolution. This rapid industrialisation associated with Lanner's mines led to a sudden demographic growth which resulted in the development of the village, its subsidiary industries, its chapels, its school, its shops and businesses. When the mines closed one by one, Lanner was subjected to the painful process of de-industrialisation, made all the more acute by its over dependence on and overspecialisation in the copper mining industry.

A Brief Geological History

Cornwall is lying on a large mass of granite rock, known as a 'batholith'. This is considered to be at least 20 kilometres deep, and was once molten. Where the molten granite came into contact with sedimentary rocks, such as sandstones, mudstones and clays, near the earth's surface, these rocks were metamorphosed by heat and pressure to form altered rocks, often called 'killas' in Cornwall. Lanner village lies in a valley on killas rocks sandwiched between two granite outcrops; that of Carnmenellis in the south, and Carn Marth to the north. The granite of Carnmenellis is considered to have formed some 290 million years ago, but that of Carn Marth, a separate intrusion, is thought to be several million years younger.[2]

High temperature fluids, carrying metals in solution, penetrated the killas close to the granite, and crystallised out as metalliferous minerals in cracks in the killas, and in the granite bordering the killas. This is the origin of many mineral veins or 'lodes', the source of Cornwall's mining wealth. In our area, the lodes run mainly east-west, but are in places interrupted by faults, the result of one section of rock shifting in respect to another, causing a shearing effect, and thus displacing the lode. The metalliferous minerals of Lanner are largely to be found in the granite, close to its contact with the killas. This is why shafts, sometimes as deep as 2000 feet, had to be sunk into the granite outcrop, or through the killas, to intersect the mineral lodes.

Early Mining in Lanner - Tin Bounds

The earliest mining would have consisted of shallow excavations at the surface, known as 'coffans'. These 'old men's workings' resembled pits which had been excavated to follow a lode outcrop that had become exposed over many thousands of years due to weathering. Early mining records for Gwennap are scarce, but we have some evidence of the antiquity of tin mining in our area; a reference is made in the Stannary Roll of 1305–6, noting that Johannes Margh of Trevarth had sent 30 shipments of tin, probably to Truro; and in a Charter of 1400 relating to Trevarth, two 'stagnariæ', or tin works, are named – Monhek-Cam and Monhek de Nanscoryles.[3] Moreover, a thirteenth century list of the ornaments of Gwennap Church contains numerous items made of tin, no doubt manufactured locally.

From time immemorial the Cornish have had the right to mark out a claim on any unenclosed piece of waste land in order to seek tin by 'pitching bounds' there, paying the landowner a fixed proportion of the tin that might be won within these bounds as his 'toll tin', or 'dish'. Bounding involved the cutting of turves and placing them at the corners or angles of the ground to be worked, usually three to six turves in each corner (or sometimes stones). In many instances a couple of pits about two feet wide and deep would be dug in each corner of the bound. These bound marks had to be renewed annually on a specific day by the Lord's Toller, or the bounder, who would take a shovelful of soil from the pit near the markers and heap it on top of the turves.[4]

Some areas of bounded ground extended over several acres, whilst others were only a few perches in extent, but many were far from four-sided equilateral plots and often had side bounds added to them by claiming a triangular plot enclosed by one of the original sides. Some tin bounds crossed each other which made it necessary to record their exact location by recording the names of adjacent bounds, prominent landmarks or houses. Many of the tin bounds were not at all productive, but large areas of unenclosed land were bounded just in case tin lay beneath. In our area, Lanner Common or Beacon, Pennance Common, Trevarth Common, Penstruthal Common, Carn Marth, Tresavean, Brewer, Carvannel, Tretharrup and South Downs were all bounded. (Land which had been bounded and subsequently enclosed could continue to be bounded.).

Bounds were recorded in a tin bounds book by the Mineral Lord's agent, and their description is usually quite vague, with the majority of them having four corners, north east, south-east, south-west and north-west, so they were often described in that way:

Little Wheal Sawsen Vean or Wheal Sawsen.

S.W corner to the North of Croft North Bounds in Lanner Common West of the Redruth Road. N.W. corner joining Redruth Road a little to the South of Wheal Sawsen works East of the said road in Pennance Common. N.E. corner is up the hill a little under Pennance Road to Redruth and South of the train. S.E. corner is further south under the same road and joining near to the North East corner of Wheal Reeth Bounds in Pennance Common.[5]

This particular bound was at the top of Lanner Hill and straddled the present A393. Many of the tin bounds in the Lanner area mentioned in a tin bounds book of the eighteenth century appear to have been of great antiquity, as evidenced by their Cornish names: Wheal Callice at Penstruthal Common, from the Cornish 'cales' for hard; Wheal Dew at Lanner Common, 'du' in Cornish meaning black; Wheal Growan at Penstruthal, 'growan' translating to gravel; Wheal Nooth at Pennance meaning New Mine from the Cornish 'noweth'; Post Mean Bounds at Pennance, which translates from the Cornish 'mean' as stone post; Wheal Vark at Pennance meaning Horse Mine from the Cornish 'vargh' and Wheal Sawsen or Zawson, meaning the Englishman's Mine.

Other tin bounds had English names, such as Wheal Fatt at the top of Lanner Hill, Double Rose Bounds near Tresavean, and Wheal Just and Wheal Crab at Pennance, whilst some were named after the area in which they were located, such as Wheal Gordon, Tretharrup Lane and Croft and Brewer Mine and Stream.

Bounds were occasionally named after people, Wheal Hockin, at Lanner Common for example, whilst others were named after a geological feature, such as Wheal Clay Bounds, Great and Little Elvan Bounds at Penstruthal, or Wheal Caunter at Carn Marth. A few were named after Saints and maybe indicated the day on which the bounds were to be annually renewed, examples of which include Wheal St George at the top of Carn Marth and St Martin at the top of Lanner Hill.

Early maps of the Lanner area show numerous old men's workings along the course of lodes. These appear in the area below Lanner Hill Garage at South Downs, western Carn Marth, Trevarth Common, Tresavean and Penstruthal. In fact, evidence of some of these early workings are still visible, in spite of the later disturbance of the land when deep lode mining took off. At Penstruthal, to the east of the old Penstruthal Mine powder house, a series of shallow depressions mark the remains of 'coffans' made by tin bounders exploiting the rich tin lode which ran almost parallel to Rough Street (evidence of this may be found on the 1880 O.S. map).

At Carn Marth, to the west of Martin's Quarry, is a tunnel cut into the granite which in winter is partially flooded. Upon investigating the tunnel it was found to terminate some 120 feet into the hillside and was presumably an experimental drive made by 'the old men' who wished to see if they would encounter any metallic material. Their pick marks can still be seen on the tunnel wall in places. Because these pick marks are clear, it indicates that the tunnel probably dates from the seventeenth century before gunpowder became widely used. The same may be said for the adit at Bell Vean which offers well-defined pick marks, which clearly shows the antiquity of mining in the Lanner area.

Often bounds came to be held in shares, and local newspapers sometimes contained advertisements for the sale of shares in tin bounds. In 1821 shares in Wheal Gordon, Wheal an Nooth, and Great and West Wheal Fatt, which were situated at South Downs and the top of Lanner Hill, were offered for sale. Potential buyers were alerted to the possibility of purchasing shares in East and West Wheal Zawson tin bounds in 1826. 'Those with claims are requested to meet at the Count House of Wheal Buller and Wheal Beauchamp'. In the mid nineteenth century a list of 17 tin bounds near Wheal Beauchamp and Penstruthal were advertised for sale at the London Inn at Redruth by public auction. These included some which have already been mentioned, but others with strange names were listed: '2 pair long Luchanter; 2 pair Hoods; 2 pair Bounds Fosters, Michael Pen-Pons and Bounds Agar' (bounds were often described as a 'pair').

In 1767 it was recorded that the Earl of Godolphin had 11/24ths of a tin bound named 'Wheal Mareah in Carne Marth', but the majority of the bounds worked in the Lanner area belonged to John Williams Esq. The Williams', originally a family from Stithians, became one of Gwennap's greatest ever families, and made a fortune through their sagacious dealings in mines both within Gwennap and further afield, even acting as agents for mining concerns in Brazil, Haiti, Cuba and Mexico.

Gradually the practice of bounding ceased, mainly because of the pressure of land enclosure which restricted access to common land. Those bounders who challenged the legality of the right of landlords to enclose common land found it difficult to afford the costly lawsuits which resulted. However, the names of many ancient tin bounds were in some cases perpetuated by the naming of lodes within the mines of the nineteenth century. In Penstruthal there is a Wheal Gallish Lode, and Wheal Trefusis has a Gordon Lode. Wheal Fatt gave its name to the adit which formerly ran down through South Downs.

The earliest methods of extracting metals from the earth in Cornwall were for surface tin deposits, and a well established method was 'tin streaming', in which the natural tendency of the heavier tin minerals to separate out in a water stream was used. Eventually, it was discovered that breaking the ore to form fine mineral particles was necessary to release the tin, and 'stamps' were developed to break up the rock by pounding it with heavy weights. There is evidence that the stream which runs down through the village, today buried beneath the road, was deliberately diverted down the valley to power the waterwheels for such stamps. The earliest reference in the seventh year in the reign of Queen Anne, 1708, suggests that a set of stamps named 'Pennans' were probably operational in Lanner from at least the late seventeenth century, which were leased from James Buller of Shillingham to John Pearse (Parish of Stithians), at an annual rent of two shillings and sixpence in 1735.[6] On 16 September 1743, James Buller leased the stamps to James Hitchens of the Parish of Gwennap, and a lease was signed again in 1749. The Pennance stamps are also mentioned in 1859, in a lease between J. W. Buller and John Michael Williams, of Pengreep.

On 5 August 1855, Baron Clinton leased to Messrs Michael Williams of Trevince and William Williams of Tregullow, for a yearly rental of £10, the Pennance stamps, the Roskrow stamps and the Majors (or Blackers) stamps, situated on the north side of the Turnpike Road from Redruth to Penryn.[7] The Williams' then sublet these stamps to men who worked them.

The sites for the stamps are believed to have been at the bottom of what is now Pennance Lane, two sets, those of Major's or Blackers' stamps, and the Pennance Stamps, being sited near the present Lanner Bakery, another, believed to be Trewartha's Stamps, were formerly situated behind the northern half of Woodlands Terrace. Roskrow's Stamps were likely to have formerly stood to the west of what is now a dwelling named 'Glyngarth'. Local builders digging the foundations for extensions to some of the cottages at Grays, Brays and Woodlands Terraces, behind 'Glyngarth' and on the site of the Lanner Moor Garage, have discovered large quantities of crushed gravel-like material showing signs of secondary copper staining – the detritus from various stamps and dressing floors.

The deeds of the house 'Lambriggan' by Lanner Square indicate that a portion of the back garden was once the site of the Old Bell Stamps (leased in 1816 from John Rogers to Thomas Teague, an adventurer in Tresavean Mine),[8] and according to Richard Thomas's map of 1819, there was another stamping mill on or near the present site of the camper van centre, at Penponds, or Lower Trevarth.

But of far greater interest are two stones outside the Penventon garden centre (the Tresavean Adit discharges here) which have several hemispherical depressions on their surfaces. One rock is of granite and served as a long mortar stone, forming the base of a dry stamps in an ancient crazing mill. The other mortar stone is of metamorphosed killas, and has been turned over two or three times, as both of its surfaces are marked with circular pits. The stones were discovered during renovation of the mill house at Penventon and had been buried under the floor. Further finds – a circular granite mill stone, about three feet wide with a five inch hole in its centre – has a series of concentric grooves along its surface caused by constant grinding which indicates that before conversion to a grist mill, the site at Penventon appears to have been a medieval crazing mill. We know that from the 1500s such grinding stones were gradually superseded by wet stamps. This helps to prove the antiquity of the site at Penventon, and of tin mining in our area.

In the *Royal Cornwall Gazette* of 4 September 1825, the lease of Trevarth Stamping Mill was advertised, along with the houses, water course, floors, dressing places and appurtenances, then occupied by the Adventurers in Wheal Squire Mine, at a clear rent of £15 per year. Also advertised, was the residue of the lease of the Pennance Stamps, then unoccupied. James states in 1944 that the stamps at Penponds were powered by a water wheel fed by the adit stream flowing through Lanner, which eventually joins the River Fal below Bissoe. Irene Williams of Tresavean Estate remembers seeing the water wheels and dressing floors of this stamping mill in the late 1930s, operated by a company named Rodda and Sons who worked over the material which had escaped the mill at Tresavean Mine. The leat past Penponds formerly ran red because of the tin stream works.

These records of stamps indicate that there was considerable tin mining in the area, although stamps were never so important in copper mining, and were only used on value mineral which was locked and disseminated through extremely hard rock. Ore from local mines found its way to Lanner's numerous stamps; Wheal Buller, a great mine situated on the high downs between Lanner and Four Lanes, sent ore to be stamped at Lanner, a practice which only ended in 1866.[9]

When underground mining gained pace, it was assisted by blasting powder and water-driven pumps and whims (hoisting gear). A contract to build a water wheel at Wheal Buller, on the Redruth side of Lanner Hill, was advertised in the *West Briton* in 1819, and Tresavean Mine advertised for a water wheel in February 1828, but these water wheels were usually employed for crushing and stamping purposes at Tresavean.

Berg has argued that one of the distinctive features of the British economy was its reliance on coal resources from the late eighteenth century, arguing that the exploitation of the nation's coalfields allowed Britain to break free of the limitations imposed by organic, land-based materials.[10] Thus it was the expansion of the South Wales coalfields (where Cornwall procured the coal necessary to steam the pumping engines), plus the introduction of steam-driven pumps to keep the mines dewatered, which allowed the great development of copper mining in Gwennap Parish.

The area around Camborne and Redruth was a hot bed of industrial activity and experimentation. Many famous engineers were busy developing steam technology at this time, which ultimately was to benefit mines like Tresavean. At nearby Redruth, engineer William Murdoch had designed and tested a model steam-powered locomotive, and experimented with gas lighting. His home in Cross Street, Redruth, was the first in the world to be lit by gas. And at nearby copper mines, Boulton and Watt, Messrs Hornblower and Edwin Bull were competing to perfect the steam engine technology begun by Newcomen and Smeaton. By the early nineteenth century, Cornish engineer Richard Trevithick, born but a few miles from Redruth, successfully tested the world's first high pressure steam carriage, ushering in the dawn of steam traction.

Because the early engines of Newcomen and Smeaton were very expensive and inefficient, using a lot of coal, it was the advent of the more powerful and fuel-efficient engines of Boulton and Watt in the late 1770s which really gave Gwennap's mining its main driving force, allowing deeper mines to be developed.

Although there was natural drainage at Tresavean to a depth of 240 to 330 feet (40 to 55 fathoms, one fathom being equal to 6 feet, the measure of depth used in mines to this day), the mining had penetrated below this, and pumping was essential. Natural drainage was effected by driving a tunnel, known as an 'adit', into the earth, allowing water in the mine to flow away naturally. The lowest level to which such natural drainage could be effective was known as 'adit level'. Although the competition to Cornish mines offered by the Parys Mountain, a large, easily worked copper deposit discovered in Anglesey in 1768, had diminished rapidly by the turn of the century, Tresavean mine was only in small production between 1811 and 1819. Then came the massive growth of Tresavean, and also that of some of the smaller mines in its vicinity, and the community of Lanner grew with it.

The Gwennap area gradually became an rural industrial region specialising in metal mining, particularly of copper, and, as the ore was sent to Swansea for smelting, reliant on an export commodity for its economic well-being. For example, in 1819, about 7000 people were employed in 23 mines in Gwennap Parish. The Consols Mine has been said to have been an enterprise which compared in scale and turnover with the largest in any sector of industry and commerce, and enterprises such as Consols and Tresavean involved capital investment of tens of thousands of pounds (staggering amounts in today's money). In fact, pre-1840 Cornwall has been summed up as being 'a complex industrial society exhibiting early developments of banking and risk-sharing to deal with the particular needs of local industry as well as a remarkable attempt to cartelize copper in the 1790s'.[11]

Anyone owning land in the area of the Parish of Gwennap from 1700 to about 1850, or who was an in-adventurer in some of its successful mines, was in a position to amass a fortune from the mining of copper, which was found quite close to the surface, even though a mine may have originally been sunk for the purpose of obtaining tin.

A DETAILED SURVEY OF LANNER'S MINES

Bell, Lannarth and Bell Vean (OS grid ref: SW 715 397)

Thomas remarked in 1819 that Bell was an ancient mine, and was situated in the bottom of the valley, to the west of the Turnpike Road, now the A393. We have noted the position of the stamps of this former mine, as being behind Lambriggan House. Some work was done on the mine in 1837, and it was reported by William J. Henwood to have been employing six men in the year ending June 1838.[12] It reopened in 1842, and the company formed to work it had very rapidly spent £4000. However, by 1845, the 30-inch cylinder engine and other machinery were offered for sale. Work was quickly resumed the following year, but it is unclear whether this was in tandem with Lannarth Mine.

A lease dated 1784, granted by Joseph Beauchamp to William Paul of Gwennap, gave the lessee and his heirs the right to dig, work, mine and search for tin ore, copper ore and other minerals 'in upon and through the Tenement of Lannarth'. The boundary of the sett was described as 'so far south as to join the Tenement of Penstruthal, so far to the north as to join Wheal Beauchamp sett, so far east as the landmark near Bell Stamps and so far west as the land extends in and upon all and every courses, loads, and veins of tin and copper ore etc. which shall be cut and discovered'.

Good quality tin ore had already been found in tin bounds in a part of the Tenement of Lannarth, and in 1767, was reported to have been raised for two or three years.[13] The area in which the sett lay seems to have witnessed considerable mining activity prior to the granting of the sett to Paul, as mention is made to a deep adit which was being driven West. The lease was for a term of 21 years.[14] The sett was situated on west of the turnpike road as one leaves the village, and the *West Briton* reports that Lannarth Mine was worked briefly in 1836 by a company in 128 shares, and that some further work was done in 1849.[15] After this, it was worked in conjunction with Bell.

In June 1853, the first records of a concern named Bell and Lannarth United appear in the *Mining Journal*. Soon after its inception, the company commenced work on clearing and deepening the Bell Engine Shaft below the 38 fathom level, and had succeeded by the end of the year in sinking it 48 fathoms below adit. In January 1854, it was reported in the *Mining Journal*, that gold had been found by a Mr Perkes, and upon being assayed by Mr Mitchell, was reputed to have been equal to 2 ozs.2 dwts.1gr. of fine gold per ton of gossan.[16] This discovery came at the same time as the Welsh gold rush, and since no further mention is made of the discovery, it might have been a scam to attract up-country investment.

By the end of 1855, operations were small scale and mainly concentrated upon driving a deep adit north and south of the valley between the two mines, with the intention of draining the ground to a depth of 70 fathoms. In 1857 flat rods were built to the Western Shaft, and by 1858, £8450 had been expended. Ore had been discovered in the bottom of the flat rod shaft, and on the 24 level, but the low grade of the copper ore produced, 13 tons in 1854 and 10 tons in 1857, conspired to close the mine. The machinery was put up for sale in October 1859, including the 30-inch engine.[17]

Interest in Bell was resumed under the management of Captain J. Harris in 1873, and some of the old workings were cleared out.[18] In 1876, a new 21 year lease was granted at 1/18 dues effective on 24 July 1876. This lease was reported to have been made between a cost book company (a company of unlimited liability into which shareholders either paid 'calls' or shared profits) in 12 000 shares with 12 subscribers. It appears that this company was likely to have been West Tresavean.[19] The new company commenced work on rehabilitating Gobben's Engine Shaft and making necessary repairs to the engine house. In 1878, the name reverted to Bell Vean, the agent being Captain J. Brokenshire. A steam stamp battery was brought on to the mine and partially erected.

At the end of 1879 the Bell Vean Tin and Copper Mining Company Ltd. was formed with a capital of £24 000 in 12 000 shares of £2 each. The directors were William Hudspith Esq. of Northumberland, Henry Pritchard of Newcastle-on-Tyne, Jonathan Walton of Cumberland, Robert Crawford of Glasgow and William Burns of Ayrshire. The secretary was Mr David Burns and the offices were located at Haltwhistle by Carlisle.[20] The company was formed for the purpose of purchasing, working and more extensively developing the Bell Vean Tin and Copper Mine, Gwennap.

The original cost book shareholders, Thomas Parkyn, David Burns, Jacob Walton, Robert L. Barr and John M. Clark, wanted to increase the available capital and so formed the limited company. Here we have evidence of the changing nature of investment, which was now in the hands of men from outside the county, replacing the old style adventurer who was often a local man. The purchase price was '£1000 in cash to be paid out of the net profits and not otherwise, except at the option of the company or the Directors, and £5000 fully paid up shares, leaving £12 000 to equip and fully develop the mine'.[21]

At the beginning of 1881 the horse whim was moved from Bell Shaft to Mitchell's. That spring an engine was erected on the refurbished Gobben's Shaft. The adit between Bell and Mitchell's Shafts was cleared out and used as a haulage-way. In autumn of 1881, the stamps engine was erected and Gobben's Shaft was deepened. The following year the mine produced 4 tons of black tin (the concentrated tin minerals, ready for the smelter). However, in March 1883, the entire plant was put up for sale, including a 24-inch double-acting rotary engine, a 12-inch horizontal engine and an 8hp portable engine. In addition there was a 12 x 5-inch Hall jaw crusher, a Hall patent pulveriser, a jig, crushing rolls, three buddles and a large amount of sundry equipment.[22] The Bell Vean sett later became a part of Tresavean Mine.

The remains of the mine may be seen at Rough Street, about 100 metres before the tramway bridge on the left hand side. Although the area is very overgrown, the truncated remains of an engine house, which has been robbed of much of its worked granite blocks, can be seen, along with portions of a boiler house and the loadings for stamps. Perhaps the most interesting feature on the mine is the entrance to the Bell Vean Adit which is clearly visible, and can be entered, although on no account should this be attempted without proper equipment and supervision.

Carvannel (SW 712 391)

Situated on the south side of Penstruthal, Carvannel was a small and unsuccessful mine, which commenced operations in about 1831. Its early history is inextricably tied up with that of Penstruthal; one of the earliest references, of 1835, noted that it was worked with its larger neighbour.[23] In 1840–41, the mine was reported by the *West Briton* to have been worked by a company in 64 or 84 shares.[24] The year 1850 saw the mine reopened on the initiative of a very well known and successful mine promoter, Captain J. Lyle.

The new company was in 132 shares, with £12 paid on each, which was later increased to 1056, and the first meetings were held at the Penstruthal Count House.[25] In May 1850, it was reported that a new copper lode had been cut and shares were fetching £40 each, but that there were very few sellers.[26] By September 1851, the mine was 56 fathoms deep, the 46 and 32 fathom levels were active, and a new shaft was to be collared at the surface, and a steam-winder was being erected.

In 1852, 12 tributers were at work in five pitches, and the 76 fathom level was reached. Four-hundred-and-seventy-four tons of good grade copper ore was sold in 1855 which realised £3868 in revenue, but did not cover the cost of mining operations, and calls (requests to investors for more money to keep going) were made regularly. In May 1854, it was decided to dewater the Western Shaft and by the following year, Engine Shaft was down to the 118 fathom level. In 1856, the mine was reported to have been employing 22 tributers. By 1857, Engine Shaft reached the 130 fathom level, and levels were active on the 118, 106, 96, 86 and 76.

Carvannel, in common with many small Cornish copper mines, found that it could not make its output balance the cost of operations, resulting in an endless series of calls, even though its ore was of a good grade. Investment in the mine was calculated to have been in the region of £29 124 to 1861.[27] Shaft sinking was halted, work abandoned on the deeper levels, and 48 tons of copper ore, the mine's last, were sold in 1860. The following year the mine's machinery was advertised for sale by public auction, and included a pumping engine with two boilers, a drawing engine with a boiler, a capstan and shears, and about 200 fathoms of pitwork.[28] Total recorded output between 1851–60, was 2766 tons of 7.25 per cent copper ore, 222 tons of tinstone in 1860–61, and 5 tons of pyrite in 1857.

Pennance Consols (SW 7128 4055)

It is not known for certain when the mine was started, but it is likely to have been in about 1836. The area which was to become Pennance Consols had seen a considerable amount of disturbance from tin bounders, as evidenced by scrutiny of Thomas' map of 1819. Situated on the southern flank of Carn Marth, the sett (area of ground leased for mining) runs east-west for about three quarters of a mile, following a lode which also crosses Ting Tang Mine near Carharrack. The 1845 Symons Map shows a series of shafts, which mark the course of a copper lode, indicating that it ran through a sett called Wheal Amelia, the original name of the mine. In the years 1836–8, Wheal Amelia was reported to have been employing four people.[29] The *Mining Journal* of January 1841, carried a notice of shares for sale in Gwennap, which were to be sold by public auction at the Red Lion Hotel in Truro. Nine 64th shares were offered for sale at Wheal Amelia.

By the 1850s, a company calling themselves The Pennance Consols Mining Company had emerged to work the mine. In 1850, Lord Clinton had leased a sett of a part of Pennance Common for a term of 21 years to William Williams, Esq. The dues payable were 3/4 of 1/15 until a steam engine was erected, after which the dues were to be 3/4 of 1/18.[30] The name 'Pennance' was taken from the name of the settlement nearby, but the choice of 'Consols' is interesting, D.B. Barton asserting that the term coincides with the name of a Government stock, regarded as of unimpeachable worth.[31] 'Consols' for this reason, proliferated in the South West mining regions, and even ridiculously small mines such as Pennance were elevated to consolidated status in the hope of attracting 'up country' investment. The company operated under the cost book system, the secretary being resident at Gracechurch Street, London. The main workings were above adit level, operating on a small scale for the recovery of copper ore. In June 1853, a call of ten shillings a share was made on the adventurers, and the committee was requested to examine the propriety of sinking a new shaft, and installing a new engine.

Lord Clinton had stipulated in the 1850 lease that an engine house had to be erected on the sett within two years of the commencement of the lease, but this appears to have been delayed. Later, in 1853, it was reported that work was continuing on driving the adit west, the end being some 93 fathoms from Williams' Shaft. The lode had improved, and was perceived as a good speculation. The *Mining Journal* reports in September 1860 that Pennance Consols 'is at present working by Messrs Williams, but only by an adit, where there is a very strong lode in the granite of Carn Marth – supposed to be the Ting Tang lode.'[32]

There are no recorded production figures for the early workings. In 1864–45, T. Spargo reported that the adit was 75 fathoms deep, and that there were no workings below it. The mine employed three men and three boys. It was further noted that the operators, the Williams' of Scorrier had been driving the adit for about 30 years regularly, but had met with very little metallic material. The report concluded with the remark 'This is a remarkable instance of perseverance in mining on a small scale. The present adit end is not far from Wheal Beauchamp.'[33]

The mine acquired the unusual sobriquet of 'Wheal Bloody Nose' locally, which might suggest that those who had invested in it could have had some cause for disappointment. A.K. Hamilton Jenkin, however, noted that this strange name for Pennance Consols came about after a vicious fight between the miners who worked there and those of Penstruthal Mine across the valley.[34]

Around 1865 it became apparent that to proceed to greater depths, it would prove necessary to dewater the mine with a steam engine. It was noted in 1864 that there was no mine machinery except a whim in use, but as already indicated, the idea of erecting an engine on the mine had been mooted several times in the past, the *Mining Journal* of 1860 mentioning the possibility.[35]

The engine house, the only one built on the mine, dates from about 1866. Constructed of granite and killas, it accommodated a 50-inch cylinder engine, constructed above the main shaft, namely Baronet's Engine Shaft, which was situated some 100 yards south of the margin of Carn Marth granite. (There were a further two shafts to the east of this - Williams' and Amelia's.). A boiler house attached to the north-western side of the building housed a ten ton Cornish boiler. This new machinery allowed workings to a depth of twenty five fathoms below adit.

Opposite the rather fine engine house for such a small mine was the count house, where the mine's business was transacted. Like the engine house, this has also survived, having been converted to a dwelling house, for many years the home of the Jewell Family, and renovated during the mid 1980s. Various auxiliary buildings appear on plans of the mine dating from the late 1860s, which probably included stores, a carpenter's shop and the smithy. The 1880 OS Map

(1:2500), shows the position of a circular magazine which lay to the south-west of the mine, similar to the remains of one which can still be seen on Penstruthal Farm, where the blasting powder was stored, and which has long since vanished. Coal to power the steam engine was delivered to the mine by the Redruth & Chasewater Railway which ran close by.

Following the installation of the pumping engine, production figures become available. Surviving documentation indicates that between 1866 and 1872, the mine is reported to have produced 590 tons of 6 per cent copper ore, and a little tin. In 1866, it was reported that the company was in 264 shares, the purser was Hugh Sims of Scorrier, the Manager, John Richards of Trefula, the agent, James Higgins of Pennance and the clerk, Martin Skinner of Carharrack. The landowner was Lord Clinton, and pay day was the third Saturday after the first Wednesday in the month.[36]

At a meeting in December 1869, the accounts for the six months ending in October showed a loss of £964. The costs were £1062 which included bills of £275. The ores sold fetched £97. Baronet's Shaft was down 12 fathoms under the 30 and the lode was reported to have been three feet wide. The price for sinking was £20 per fathom, and it was intended to sink three fathoms further in the engine shaft, then to drive east, where Captain J. Richards felt the ground offered favourable prospects of meeting with a good course of ore.[37] By 1870 Pennance Consols was employing 40 people, the main workings being at the 15 and 30 fathom levels. However, the mine continued making calls right through 1870, and in August of that year, Captain Richards resigned.

Just when all work at the mine was about to be suspended, in the summer of 1871, a splendid new copper lode was cut on the 45 fathom level west, although by this time Pennance Consols had become increasingly reliant on tin which was fetching better prices on the international market.

The mid 1860s had witnessed the disastrous collapse of the copper mining industry in Cornwall, as competition from foreign producers such as Cuba, South Australia and Chile translated into falling prices, compounded by the failure of the banking giant, Overend, Gurney and Co. Ltd.[38] Many mines went over to tin production to avoid closure, and Pennance produced some tin in the boom years of 1870–72, but the rising cost of coal which fuelled the pumping engine, and the vagaries of the tin market which crashed in 1874, sounded the death knell for marginal mines such as Pennance Consols.

On 7 February 1874, the *Royal Cornwall Gazette* and the *Mining Journal* advertised a sale of the mine's machinery, to be held at the site on the twelfth of the month. Among the items for sale, were the 50-inch cylinder pumping engine, a ten ton boiler, balance bob, pumps, capstan, a horse whim and even the blacksmith's bellows and anvil.

The late Miss Esther Polkinghorne of Carn Marth (1863–1951) remembered the mine working in her early childhood. She recollected that when the beam engine was being dismantled, an accident occurred which resulted in a man losing his life.

It seems ironic that of all the mines which worked in the parish of Lanner, among them the mighty Tresavean and the highly prolific Penstruthal, the only substantial remains of an engine house stands on the windswept southern flank of Carn Marth, marking the site of one of the smallest mines - the largely unsuccessful Pennance Consols.

The large waste tip which betrayed Pennance Consol's working past, and which could be seen for much of this century, has been removed in recent years, and Baronet's Engine shaft has collapsed and is therefore dangerous. Access to the workings is not possible.

A dominant landmark which can be seen for many miles, the ivy-clad engine house is a Grade II listed building, and is the most visible and significant reminder of Lanner's mining heritage (Fig. 3.1- page 48). In 1990, the *West Briton* reported that the owner had offered it for sale, as concern mounted about its rapidly deteriorating condition. For this reason, plans were set into motion to preserve it as a fitting memorial to the area's industrial history. The purchase of the building was approved in principle by English Partnerships in 1996. The engine house will be stabilised, and plans also include the purchase of the surrounding land, a shaft capping scheme and landscaping project. Work commenced just as this book was being completed, thus ensuring the survival of Lanner's most visible mining relic.

Penstruthal (SW 707 398)

Penstruthal Mine lies a mile east-south-east of Four Lanes, the Redruth to Stithians road running across the west end of the mine, half a mile after leaving the Redruth-Helston road. Little remains to be seen at the mine, the oldest workings of which date back to the mid eighteenth century. According to Thomas in 1819, 'Bestruthal' had been idle for many years, an unsuccessful attempt having been made to work the mine in the 1790s.[39]

In 1819 the mine was reopened in 64 shares, and two years' work produced 221 tons of copper ore.[40] For some unexplained reason, little was done until 1822 when production recommenced by a company which appeared to have been held in 60 shares which were subdivided in 1824. A rapid increase in output followed, from 78 tons in 1822 to 11 842 tons in 1827. The latter figure accounted for 9.35 per cent of the whole copper ore production of Cornwall in that year; the only other mines in the area to exceed this figure in a single year were Wheal Buller and Tresavean.[41] After producing 50 000 tons of ore between 1825 and 1835, production declined and the mine ceased production in 1837. A 40-inch pumping engine, a 22 inch steam winder and five horse whims were among the items listed for sale in 1836.[42]

It was noted by Watson that most of the ore mined was at the 60 fathom level, and that this period of working produced dividends of £100 000 (probably a grossly exaggerated figure), but that mismanagement had precipitated the mine's demise.[43] Returns show that the maximum revenue obtained from ore in any one year was £66 242 in 1827.

A company worked the mine in the 1840s with a 36-inch engine and four horse whims, producing 1688 tons of ore between 1842 and 1846. The workings were reported to have been chiefly confined to one lode, although parallel lodes were known to have existed.[44] The concern was abandoned in 1848 during the depression in Cornish mining because of the low price of copper caused by revolutions on the Continent. A 36-inch engine had still not sold by the autumn of 1849 in this severe economic recession.

However, a new company in 120 shares, with a subscribed capital of £6000, was formed by Mr Little of Redruth, who reopened the mine in 1855.[45] Taking heart from the success of the neighbouring mine, Tresavean, the company planned to deepen Penstruthal, which was between 60 and 70 fathoms deep, in the hope of finding ore at greater depths, as had occurred at Tresavean, and to exploit the parallel lodes noted above. A 60-inch pumping engine was put to work on Hodge's Shaft to dewater the mine, and there was also a 24-inch crushing and winding engine.

Two years' work saw the mine attain a depth of 110 fathoms, but no ore was produced and constant calls were made on the shareholders. The company had concentrated efforts in driving the 90 and 110 fathom levels, the 60 and 70 fathom levels were active, and by 1858 William's Shaft had been sunk to a depth of 130 fathoms, a parallel lode had been cut on the 60, and a new north lode developed. However, after the 60 fathom level the mine was found to have been hard and poor, and failure to find significant amounts of ore resulted in the mine's closure in 1859.[46]

An enormous amount of machinery was advertised in the *Mining Journal* which included the 60-inch engine, two boilers about 10 tons each, a 24-inch steam-whim and crusher with an 8-ton boiler, 2 horse whims and shaft pulleys, 2 balance bobs, 2 capstans, 2 shears, a variety of pumps, whim chain, H-pieces and wind bores, the blacksmith's 40-inch bellows, two tram wagons, one 4-wheel skip, an excellent miners' dial and the account house furniture.[47]

The boom in the tin market of the early 1870s inevitably led to Penstruthal's reopening. The Penstruthal Consols Tin and Copper Mines Co. Ltd. was formed in 1872 in 50 000 £2 shares. The mine was bought for £50 000, and the new sett was extended to take in East Buller, Lannarth and Bell. The directors were Messrs J. B. Freeman, F. Richardson and J. Little, with J. Kendall of Redruth acting as consultant engineer. The secretary was M. Greene and the company's offices were situated in Old Broad Street, London.[48]

Highburrow Shaft was cleared out and sinking began; Bell Vean Engine Shaft, Simmon's Shaft and Boundary Shaft were reopened and Little's Shaft was selected for hoisting and renamed Greene's Shaft, operated at first by a horse whim, but later an engine house was erected. A tremendous amount of development was carried out by this company, who appeared to have sunk no less than six new shafts or trial pits. A horse whim was erected on one of these new shafts, named Richardson's. With prospects looking favourable, good tin having been found in the old workings, in 1872 it was decided to purchase a stamps engine and the following year, dressing floors were built. Total production in 1873 was 4 tons of black tin and 143 tons of lower grade tinstone. In order to raise share prices, working capital was paid out in dividends.[49] In the spring of 1874 steam stamps were erected, which by summer numbered 32, and treatment of the ores began in May.

Production figures for 1874 amounted to 37 tons of black tin worth £2070, and yet again working capital was paid out.[50] Two new shafts were sunk the following year and production rose to 98 tons, which sold for £50.14s a ton, and £1450 was divided amongst the shareholders that year. By 1877, with tin prices falling, the inherent weakness of the company was shown all too clearly. The huge expense of rehabilitation and development of the mine at a time when tin prices were declining undermined the company, which had paid out £6500 from a gross ore revenue of £7900. Matters were made worse with the discovery, in 1877, that there were 4035 more shares than there should have been. Financial impropriety on behalf of the secretary, Mr Greene, who had forged 4000 shares and siphoned off £15 000 of the company's money into a personal bank account, placed the company on a precarious footing.[51]

Work was concentrated on Highburrow Shaft which reached 88 fathoms (528 feet) in 1878. The slump in tin prices resulted in only tribute labour being employed at the mine. By 1879 just six men worked there and production figures were lower than the previous year. The company was losing £155 a month and calls were £1000 in arrears. Owing to a series of repeated management blunders, Penstruthal Consols had lost over £8000 a year for six years, producing just 500 tons of copper ore and 500 tons of black tin, and as a result, went into liquidation.[52] A plan to sell off the south part of the sett to a company for £3000 came to nought. The machinery advertised for sale included a 50-inch engine, a 31-inch stamps engine and 32 head of stamps. Claims that the company mined £20 000 worth of tin within 60 fathoms of grass (i.e. the surface) have since been proven to be entirely false. Assertions that a new ore zone had been discovered below the barren 50-60 fathom levels has never been proved or disproved; perhaps this fact, coupled with rising tin prices after the disastrous collapse of 1874, once more focused attention on Penstruthal's potential.

In late 1879, two cost book companies, in 6000 shares apiece, emerged to work the two halves of the sett.[53] North Penstruthal purchased the area of the sett centred on Highburrow Shaft for £1700, occupied by an ancient working named Wheal Gallish. The South Penstruthal Company acquired the old Penstruthal Mine which had been reopened by Penstruthal Consols. The North Penstruthal Company continued the sinking of Highburrow Shaft under the supervision of Captain W. Polkinghorne. Difficulties were encountered with hard rock which made drilling arduous and ventilation poor when driving the 88, 58, 46 and 34 fathom levels. (This mine made use of the new technology then on offer, utilising a variety of rock drills).

By early 1880 £786 had been expended on labour, and a further £379 paid out in merchants' bills. In summer of 1880 a steam winder was erected on Highburrow, and a skip road constructed. By June 1880, a call was made and the debit balance was £1200. Great expense had been incurred on the installation of machinery and buildings on the mine.

Fifty people were employed in the spring of 1881 and Highburrow reached the 120 fathom level. However, the operation cost £525 a month, but tin production amounted to just £90 a month. By the spring of 1882, 40 shares were surrendered and calls were in arrears by £266, which rose to £377 by the end of the year. Hopes of finding the rich ore ground which the previous company had claimed existed appeared to diminish as Highburrow was sunk to the 165 fathom level in 1884. Here the lode beyond a crosscut was found to be poor, and prospects did not improve with subsequent development.[54]

By spring of 1884, liabilities exceeded assets by £1009 and over 650 shares had been surrendered. In its five year history, the North Penstruthal Company had produced 57 tons of black tin. The mine was therefore abandoned and the machinery (a 50-inch pumping engine, a 23 inch horizontal engine, two 18 x 6-inch compressors, a 31 x 9-inch stamps engine with 32 head of stamps, ten buddles, plus boilers and a variety of rock drills) was advertised for sale.[55] Further work was done on this sett in 1901–2 and 1910–11, but only 45 tons of tinstone (a low purity product) was produced.

The South Penstruthal cost book company was also a failure. In 1880 a 60-inch pumping engine was erected in the old engine house which was rebuilt to dewater the mine and the adit was cleared, as Boundary Shaft had collapsed and a stream of water was running into the workings, and work began on rehabilitating the shaft. The water level fell during 1881 enough to allow the sinking of Walton's Shaft to commence, and the engine house, built in 1872 (on this shaft then named Greene's), was being done up. This shaft was sunk from the 70 fathom level to the 126 level. However, by the summer of 1881, the company was already £720 in arrears, and by mid 1883, 577 shares had been surrendered.[56]

The mine was down to the 170 fathom level in Flat Rod Shaft by 1885, when tragedy struck the operators who hit a cross course which threw water from the bottom of Walton's Shaft into Flat Rod Shaft, flooding it to the 150 level.[57] This calamity appears to have precipitated the company's collapse. A bed of mundic (iron pyrites) came in after the copper died out, but the tin-bearing zone which the management hoped to encounter was not found. After great investment, the total production during the five years of working was 20 tons of raw tinstone in 1880. The plant went up for sale in July 1885, and included the 60-inch engine, a 25-inch winder, steel rope and various rock drills.[58] No further development occurred on this sett.

Shaft capping was carried out by Kerrier District Council on the Penstruthal sett in 1992, and the engine house at Hodge's Shaft was uncovered, but little of archaeological interest remains to be seen at the mine, apart from the old Count House, which is now the farmhouse in the occupation of Mr and Mrs Alan Pascoe, and the circular powder house (now unfortunately ruinous) in the field beyond the farmhouse, which would have been used to store the gunpowder, and later dynamite (Fig. 3.2).

Fig.3.2. *Circular Powder House, Penstruthal Mine, 1995.* (photo. S.P.Schwartz).

The Penstruthal adit forms the major part of the leat which formerly ran uncovered through Lanner, and a metal grille on the left, opposite the old Bell Vean workings, covers the entrance to a tunnel which leads into the mine. Water to supply the town of Redruth was taken from the Penstruthal adit at the end of the nineteenth century.

Trethellan (SW 717 390)
West Trethellan and Wheal Brewer (SW 716 390)

Trethellan lay to the south of Tresavean, and was not mentioned by Thomas in 1819. According to William Francis, Trethellan commenced operations in about 1836; it was held in 120 shares. He mentions that the mine first made returns in April 1837. He adds that between 1837 to the end of 1843, Trethellan produced 20 870 tons of copper ore, yielding £87 159 and a profit of £37 535 to the adventurers.[59] Morrison's figures for the period 1839–1860 show that about 35 000 tons of copper ore was produced, providing dividends of about £48 900.

Trethellan was held entirely by a group of the Tresavean adventurers. Operating costs were kept down by the Tresavean engine working flat rods in the Trethellan Shaft keeping the mine dewatered, and for which the Trethellan adventurers paid a portion of the water charge. In 1836, considerable controversy surrounded an attempt by some of the local adventurers in Tresavean Mine, with the complicity of the mineral lords, to exclude the London out-adventurers from participation in obtaining shares in the other mines adjoining Tresavean, which appeared to offer the same favourable prospects for dividends as Tresavean had. Teague, the purser of Tresavean Mine, took up 13/60ths of the shares in Trethellan, Trethellan Barrier, Wheal Brewer and other setts, whilst the remaining 47/60ths went to interested local 'worthies', which included the Williams' of Scorrier, the

Harveys of St Day, Benjamin Sampson and others, who thought they had pulled a fast one on their London co-adventurers. This resulted in a case being brought against them at the Rolls Court which considerably tarnished the reputation of Captain Teague.[60]

However, the prosperity of Trethellan was of short duration. From April 1837 to November 1842, Watson reported that the adventurers received £27,000 in dividends from a gross ore revenue of £70,693 tons of copper ore.[61] The average price of the copper ore was £4.150 per ton. Profits reached nearly £1000 a month in late 1840, but declined thereafter. By September 1843, the *Mining Journal* reported that 'this mine, except in a winze, is but poor - Brewer particularly so. Two levels are already through and into West Trethellan and are very poor'.[62] The following year the mine was reported to have been mining out its reserves without making any fresh discoveries. Dividends ceased in 1848 with the exception of £900 paid in 1850–51, and calls commenced in 1853.[63] The price received for copper ore was not very high, well below the west country average. In November 1859 the plant was put up for sale, which included a 22-inch steam whim engine with boiler and crusher attached, plus six tons of railroad iron. Trethellan was eventually taken into the Tresavean sett. The greatest depth of the mine was 74 fathoms below adit, which was 64 fathoms from surface, the whole depth being 139 fathoms.

Wheal Brewer was a piece of ground south-west of Tresavean and north-west of Trethellan, and was intermittently worked in tandem with either Tresavean or Trethellan. Tredinnick claims that Wheal Brewer produced £10 600 in dividends, but the only surviving records of production are 4500 tons of copper ore in 1841–49 and 1852–53.[64] Spargo notes that the mine was worked to a depth of about 70 fathoms under adit, which was 40 fathoms from surface. West Trethellan was worked in tandem with Trethellan and was reported to have produced 1334 tons of copper ore between 1844 and 1850.

Wheal Trefusis (SW 707410)

Situated half way down South Downs and straddling both sides of the A393, the Wheal Trefusis sett lies partly inside the Lanner Parish boundary, in the metamorphosed killas which overlies the western flank of Carn Marth. The south-east part of the mine was formerly known as Wheal Gordon, the name appearing on a tin bounds map by Thomas Towan, dated 1806. Wheal Trefusis was first active from 1824 to 1831. Two 120th shares in the mine were advertised for sale by mine broker William Trenery of Redruth in 1828. A second period of development under the same name occurred between 1840 and 1845, but the mine was abandoned once more. In 1850 a company in 512 shares had emerged to work the mine. A part of the sett was severed and called East Trefusis, which continued under the same management. The Captain was Z. Carkeek, the Chief Agent, John Jope Junior (later J. Tregonning) and the Secretary, Thomas Richards.[65] From its inception, the mine was a 'calling' one. In August 1850 the accounts showed a balance against the mine of £647 10s 8d, necessitating a call of 25s.3d per share.[66] In September 1851, a further call of £1 per share was made, but because £195.10s was in arrears, the purser was requested to take proceedings in the Vice-Warden's Court for the recovery of the calls so due.[67]

The tinstuff raised in July and August 1851 was valued at £150. In January 1854, the balance against the adventurers stood at £656.10s.7d. A call of £1 per share was made but Thomas Richards reported that he believed that the sett would ultimately show promise.[68]

In 1855 there was a 30-inch pumping engine on the mine and the workings were down to 44 fathoms.[69] A new shaft was sunk on the boundary with Clijah and Wentworth Mine, aptly called the Boundary Shaft. From this, the Clijah Lode was cut. By February 1855, the Boundary Shaft was sunk 15 fathoms below adit, a plat was cut and it was estimated that another 10 fathoms sinking would hit the lode, which was soon realising 2 tons of copper ore per fathom, at £8 per fathom. However, when Boundary Shaft was developed below the 15 fathom level, the management were obliged to suspend the sinking operations due to a large amount of surface water which had flooded the shaft.[70] In April it was decided to set eight men to work on deepening Reynold's Flat-rod Shaft on the Gordon Lode below the 10 fathom level. Eight men were employed in the task and were paid £12 per fathom.

A new shaft east of Boundary was being sunk by four men who were reported to have been down eight fathoms below the surface (48 feet).[71] By mid June the 44, 34 west and 24 fathom levels were active on Engine Lode. Reynold's Shaft was down five fathoms below the 10 fathom level, and development work on Nicholl's Shaft had begun, progress of three fathoms from surface being made. The tribute pitches were reported not to have looked so good of late.

In the years since Wheal Trefusis had commenced operations up until mid 1855, exclusive of the copper ore sold (some £3000-4000), about £10 000-12 000 had been spent upon it, yet the mine did not attain a depth greater than 44 fathoms. The mine was said to have been well laid out, with adequate machinery and pumping equipment, and some of the London shareholders thought that they should have been seeing their investments in the mine show dividends. A letter appeared in the *Mining Journal* in May 1855 from one shareholder who questioned the wisdom of the delay in deciding to sink the Boundary Shaft, when neighbouring Clijah and Wentworth Mine had proven the existence of a rich copper lode undoubtedly passing through the Wheal Trefusis sett. The suspension due to flooding which had delayed sinking the shaft further was thought to be unacceptable.

Some 30 to 40 tons of undressed black and yellow ore had been hauled to surface from the Field's Lode, and a small quantity of it had been dressed. It was noted that pitches set on the back of the lode were reported to have been doing well, but not an ounce of ore had been sampled. 'One would suppose that a point of so much interest would be referred to now and again, for the satisfaction of distant shareholders, whose only business, one might infer, was to pay calls.' In March 1855, a £1 call per share (£512) was made, yet almost immediately afterwards about £400 worth of tin was sold, a picture repeated the following month, in both cases the monthly meeting being called about a fortnight early.[72] This particular London shareholder found it most suspicious that a mine which appeared to offer such promise should have been making constant calls.

Laid open to unlimited yet legally binding demands on their pocket, which were often levied without their foreknowledge or consent at a meeting of shareholders from which they were absent, distant shareholders found to their dismay that cost book companies were sometimes effective vehicles for fraud. The early Cornish mines were largely financed from within the county, but the need for heavier investment and the rising commercial power of London and the Midlands meant that capital for mining ventures was increasingly sought from would-be investors resident outside the county. Being abused in this way, the cost book system came to be discredited among English investors.

In 1858, 58 tons of copper ore was sold realising £160.7s.1d, but the mine increasingly became a tin producer, raising over 27 tons of black tin in 1860, the peak year for tin production, which sold for £2066.20s. Between 1853–63 Wheal Trefusis sold 205 tons of black tin and 350 tons of 6.5 per cent copper ore.[73] With copper production on the wane, the decline in the market price of tin put paid to losing mines such as Wheal Trefusis. The workings were abandoned in 1863, but were afterwards combined with those of neighbouring Clijah by Messrs Crawshay of Gloucester, under the name Wheal Perseverance, which was worked with limited success between 1875 and 1877.[74] The workings had reached a depth in excess of 67 fathoms by the time of closure.

Wheal Beauchamp

The Wheal Beauchamp sett lies at the top of Lanner Hill behind the garage, and was a very old mine, dating from the eighteenth century. The site included a couple of rich tin bounds, Wheal Fatt and Wheal Zawsen, the adits of these two old workings being mentioned in a cost book of Wheal Sparnon, 1765–66. The history of Wheal Beauchamp is inextricably mixed up with that of Wheal Buller, especially after the mid nineteenth century, so by necessity, this history will only cover the early working of the mine.

In 1799 a Government report on the British Copper Industry indicated that a continual loss had been borne by the adventurers of Wheal Beauchamp, from the early 1790s, in their attempt to reopen the mine.[75] A further attempt was made at the turn of the nineteenth century. In 1810 some copper ore was sold but production ceased soon after. Two years later the reports appeared very favourable, but Wheal Beauchamp was worked only above adit, which discharged on the west side of the Turnpike Road at South Downs, and eventually ran into the shaft at Pedn-an-Drea Mine at Redruth. However, the eighteenth century workings had gone far below adit level, but the deeper levels were flooded and little appears to had been done on them for years. In 1819 it was noted that the mine was 16 fathoms from surface. It was worked by the Taylors and others very profitably in the following years. Collins states that the early working of Wheal Beauchamp with Wheal Buller realised a profit of £80 000.[76]

Lean's Engine Report of 1821 gives some figures for the 36-inch, 7-foot stroke 9-inch cylinder Western Engine, which was of an inverted design, with the beam at ground level. During that year it was drawing water from 110 fathoms below the adit at an average 92 gallons per minute, and consumed 320 tons of coal.[77] In 1828 the same engine was drawing water from 72 fathoms below adit at an average of just under 118 gallons per minute, and had consumed 1860 tons of coal.[78] By 1835, Lean's report noted that a second engine had been erected on Wheal Beauchamp, named Eastern Engine, which later became known as 'Pownings'. The new engine was a 36-inch cylinder with a stroke of 8 feet. Both engines were drawing water from the 74 level below adit, the Western Engine burning 375 tons of coal and delivering an average 125 gallons of water per minute; the Eastern Engine consumed 276 tons of coal and delivered 142 gallons per minute.[79] From the above engine reports, it appears that the lower levels in the mine were abandoned sometime between 1821 and 1828.

Morrison mentions two companies, Wheal Beauchamp and South Buller, and West Wheal Beauchamp, which were probably flotations of the mining boom of 1824–25.[80] By 1836, Wheal Buller and Wheal Beauchamp were regarded as one concern. Production ended in 1840 and efforts to sell the combined plant of Wheal Buller and Wheal Beauchamp in 1845 continued for over two years in the depressed economic climate of the mid to late 1840s.[81] It included the two 36-inch engines, and an 18-inch winder which was offered for sale with Powning's Engine. There were also horse whims, 2600 feet of iron rails, and 600 feet of iron flat rods. The total recorded output of Wheal Beauchamp, as far as can be ascertained, was about 7743 tons of copper ore between 1821 and 1840.[82]

East Wheal Buller (SW 713 406)

The ground in which this mine lay has been referred to by Morrison as being in an area which 'underwent a more confusing series of changes of name and ownership than any other in the district'.[83] In 1853, East Wheal Buller took over the area centred on the old Wheal Beauchamp workings. The old Engine Shaft (which was probably originally a shaft on Wheal Beauchamp) was reported to have been down beneath the 60 below adit, and was being drained. Crosscuts were being driven towards the Wheal Buller lodes, the sections in this easterly part of the mine being dewatered by the Wheal Buller and Copper Hill engine. However, a failure to negotiate correctly with the Copper Hill management concerning the draining of the water from the mine, led to them damming up their 70 fathom level, allowing the water to rise to adit level in neighbouring East Wheal Buller.[84]

For much of the 1850s it was touch and go whether the mine would continue working. The 60 and 80 fathom levels were declared unproductive, and the mine was nearly abandoned. In 1865, Spargo reported that operations had been recommenced a little over twelve months previously, by a company, in 2000 shares, on a new part of the Company's sett, northward of their first workings which had been abandoned. (Apparently this was a part of the old Wheal Beauchamp.). The Engine Shaft was being sunk, work was continuing in readying the 50-inch pumping engine and the 10-inch winding engine for service. The depth was one fathom below adit, which was 20 fathoms. The Purser and Manager was Captain Thomas Richards of Redruth and the dues were 1/18.[85]

Morrison believes the mine was probably abandoned during the depression of 1866–67. The only recorded production figure is that of 20 tons of copper ore in 1855. Some further work was done under the name East Wheal Buller in the early 1880s on a piece of unworked ground between Wheal Buller and Ting Tang. An old shaft was reopened and some work was done on driving the 40 fathom level, but without much success, and the concern was abandoned.[86]

Wheal Comford (SW 718 395)

Wheal Comford was a narrow sett squeezed between Bell Vean and Tresavean. The mine was originally named Bell Veor, and was opened on the North Lode of Tresavean in about 1841–42.[87] In 1842, the first recorded output of copper ore amounted to 119 tons. Early meetings were held in the Wheal Buller Count House, Messrs S. and R. Davey, of Wheal Buller Mine, being prominent shareholders in Wheal Comford which was held in 128 shares.[88]

Output from the mine increased steadily throughout the 1840s, but in spite of the tonnages raised, the grade was not of a high quality. In May 1847, a 36-foot x 23-inch water wheel was advertised for sale along with a number of pumps, which could indicate that the mine was drained through a new connection with Tresavean.[89] The best period of production was obtained in 1849–50, allowing £2112 to be divided among the shareholders, but by 1851, the mine slipped back into a losing position, and by 1853 the Daveys had relinquished their holdings in the company, and F. Pryor became the purser, and Captain R. R. Mitchell the agent.[90] The new company appeared to have been held in 256 shares.

In 1856 the mine's plant was offered for sale to the mineral owners, failing which it was to be sold at public auction. The total outlay had been £19 968, but the total dividends had amounted to a paltry £2304. The materials were taken by the mineral owners at a valuation of £1314, and the company was wound up. However, for some inexplicable reason, the mine continued to work for a further two years after this date, when in 1858 an advertisement for a 24-inch pumping engine and an 18-inch winder and crusher heralded the 'knacking' of the mine.[91]

In 1872 the mine was reopened in 400 shares which were quickly subdivided into 6000. The agent was Captain J. James.[92] In 1880 the mine became known as Wheal

Fig.3.3. *Wheal Comford Engine House. Behind are the arsenic stack and assay lab, Tresavean, and on the left is Harvey's Engine Shaft, Tresavean.* (© Royal Institution of Cornwall).

Comford and North Tresavean, the company having secured a large slice of the ground known as the Old Tresavean Mine and added it to their sett (Fig. 3.3).

There were no water charges for pumping, the mine being drained free of cost by the pumping engine on the adjoining Tresavean Mines.[93] In autumn of 1880, stamps were erected and the old workings were cleared out. Peter's Shaft was deepened in November, by the summer of 1881 being down 20 fathoms below the adit. By January 1883, James's Shaft was 15 fathoms below adit, and stoping was continued apace in the 15 fathom level where the lode was 8 feet wide and worth, for the width, £16 per fathom. In the spring of 1884 Morcom's Shaft was cleared out and the following February North Shaft had been cleared and timbered to a depth of 75 fathoms below adit. The mine did not produce much in this period of working, and was abandoned in about 1885. The sett was later incorporated into Tresavean. Copper ore tonnages 1842–85 amounted to 18 426, black tin, 92 tons and tinstone about 1100 tons.

East Tresavean (Treviskey) (SW 727 396) and Barrier

Treviskey was situated directly east of and adjoining Tresavean and south of the Turnpike Road (A393). It was also known as East Tresavean, and absorbed a piece of ground known as the Barrier. East Tresavean was referred to by Thomas in 1819 as having not worked recently, but was restarted in the early 1840s under the name Treviskey. The mine produced 159 tons of good grade copper ore in 1844, and continued to increase until 1850, reaching a maximum of 2884 tons. The mine was down to below the 272 fathom level in the mid 1840s, and the workings were dewatered by the Tresavean Engine to which the Treviskey adventurers contributed. However, after the peak year of 1850, when the mine employed 66 tutworkers and 34 tributers, production declined, and the mine stopped in 1855. It had clearly reached quite a depth, a shaft named Diagonal was sinking below the 248 fathom level in 1851.[94]

Total output of ore was estimated as 17 979 tons of copper and 1 ton of black tin. The plant put up for sale included a 24-inch winder and a 30-foot by 2-foot water wheel, driving a crusher and a sawmill.[95] In 1865, Spargo noted that the mine was once again active, having taken the old name of East Tresavean, and was worked by a company in 5000 shares, 10 shillings per share paid. The secretary was Mr Adam Murray of Charing Cross and the manager, Captain Gilbert of St Day, but the venture seems to have enjoyed limited success and Treviskey was ultimately absorbed into the Tresavean sett.[96]

The Barrier was described by Watson as a piece of ground around Tresavean sett, 5 fathoms in width and on the east, joining Treviskey, 4.5–5 fathoms in length on the course of the lode.[97] The ground was held by 120 shareholders who wished to work it through Tresavean, as there seemed little point of going to the expense of sinking a shaft from surface. The Barrier might well be described as a party or boundary wall, and in 1843 the deepest levels in Tresavean were driven up to the Barrier. In 1844 the Barrier produced 529 tons of copper ore, continued to rise to a peak of 874 tons in 1845, and then declined rapidly, ceasing in 1848, which Morrison has concluded represented the exhaustion of the minute lode which ran through the Barrier.[98] Total output of copper ore was 2882 tons. Dividends amounted to £2120. In early 1850, it was reported in the *Mining Journal* that nothing was being done in the Barrier, which was absorbed into the Tresavean sett thereafter.

Tresavean Mine (SW 717 397)

Tin in this district is found in irregular deposits on the backs of lodes, but more abundantly in the elvan patches embedded in the granite. It was on one of these that the only traces of any extensive tin workings in the Tresavean sett were noted by a Tresavean adventurer writing in 1867, and which he considered to have been of great antiquity.[99] (Ancient workings for tin to the north-east of Boyes Shaft are indicated on a Tresavean Mine plan.). He noted that the old men probably discovered the Tresavean lode where it cropped out at surface, at which point it was principally composed of oxide of iron and quartz (constituting a very fine gossan), interspersed with occasional leaders of rich black and grey ore, traceable for about four fathoms in length. It was at this spot that the working of Tresavean Mine may be properly said to have commenced, and large copper deposits were soon found.

There is considerable doubt as to the date of the original working, with two authorities giving the dates 1737 and 1745. C.C. James states that Mr Williams of Burncoose was reputed to have been the discoverer, and to have received £14 000 in his share of the profits in 1752. Mr Rogers of Penrose, the Mineral Lord, gained so much from the land dues that he built a gallery in Gwennap church which survived there for many years, bearing the date 1752.[100] In 1755 the first printed reference is to 'Tregevaen', and a steam engine, presumably an atmospheric one, was noted at 'Trejeuvyan' by Borlase in 1758, suggesting that the mine must have been fairly rich to have employed such a costly and largely inefficient piece of machinery.

The strings of ore met with led to the discovery of a rich deposit extending from above the shallow adit to the 60 fathom level (about 120 fathoms from surface), where in consequence of its easterly dip, it abutted against the killas, where the lode in this mine was invariably unproductive. In 1766 a Hornblower engine had been installed at the mine to facilitate development below adit.[101] However, a recession in Cornish copper mining, finally made disastrous by the competition from Parys Mountain, probably contributed to Tresavean's closure in the early 1770s. The total profit for this working is estimated to have been in the region of £96 000.

After being discontinued for some time, the workings were again resumed under the 'judicious' direction of John Williams, of Scorrier House, a 'son or grandson of Mr Williams of Burncoose,' and large profits were initially made. A 30-inch x 8-foot single-acting Boulton and Watt engine was installed on the mine in 1779 followed by a 30/36 Hornblower and Winwood compound in 1793.[102] (Fragments of the arch heads of a wooden bob engine were recovered from the burrows during shaft capping a few years ago, plus an 11-foot length of arch head chain which might have come from one of these early engines. They are now stored at King Edward Mine, Camborne).[103]

The explorations were extended, with only moderately remunerative results (a figure thought to be approximately £48 000), to the 100 fathom level, when the mine was again abandoned in about 1808 after being in small and unprofitable production for much of the 1790s.[104] The ground in one particular 'end' was so hard and troublesome that a group of men were employed from Derbyshire in about 1780 to drive it. These men worked with expanding drills, but succeeded no better than the Cornishmen and after a prolonged trial, admitted defeat. The end was never driven through, but the level was known as 'the Derbyshire Level' up to the stoppage of the mine in 1858.[105]

In about the year 1812 an engine was again put on the old shaft by Captain Teague, and flat rods extended to work two nearly parallel lodes lying to the north (perhaps Michell's and Caddy's Lodes), which were profitably worked till the eastern dip of the ore ground carried it against the killas, and the lodes became poor under the same circumstances, and at about the same depth as that first worked. The operations on the north lodes were then suspended, and had not been resumed by 1867.[106]

In 1816, Thomas Teague had, on behalf of himself and his co-adventurers in Tresavean mine, taken the lease of the Lane Stamps, the Lower Stamps and the Bell Stamps, together with their watercourses, leats, bye-leats and buddles for a term of 14 years, from John Rogers of Penrose, at a yearly rental of £31.10 shillings. These stamping mills had formerly been in the tenure and occupation of John Williams Esquire and his co-adventurers in Tresavean.[107]

In 1819, the mine was taken up from R. Magor and J. J. Borlase (who had mainly reworked some of the old workings above adit), by Mr Mancur, Captains J. and William Martin and J. Michell. One of the principal shareholders was Captain T. Teague.[108]

William Martin's name will long be remembered in the annals of Cornish mining history, and the following account is the very stuff of legend, illustrating the speculative genius which occasionally manifested itself among our Cornish ancestors and which led to mineral bonanzas and great fortunes for the adventurers and mineral owners.

William Martin had worked at Tresavean as a barrow boy sometime after the beginning of the nineteenth century. He was working on the 96 fathom level on the old lode when convenience had required he rest his barrow at a point near a winze which had been sunk to the 110 level, the deepest part of the mine. What Martin saw, a part of the lode on the south or hanging wall, which he believed to be the main part containing some rich ore, convinced him that Tresavean Mine had a most promising future. The mine continued working above adit only shortly after his discovery and the deep levels then flooded.

Martin became a successful tributer and by 1812 obtained his first position as a Mine Captain in a lead mine near Bodmin. In 1817, he applied for and obtained the sett of Tresavean, and was made the Lord's Agent.

Work was continued on a south lode (Magor's) to the 100 fathom level in the early 1820s, which soon gave an immediate but short-lived profit (the ores yielded 30 per cent produce). By 1824-5, Martin realised that the time had come to either drain the old mine, or abandon the concern. He therefore recommended the drawing of the old mine, to a chorus of opposing voices, which so alarmed many of the shareholders that the shares, by the numerous relinquishments, became reduced. The company had initially been in 64 shares, but by 1826, a quarter of these had been surrendered leaving 48. (These were later subdivided into 96.). Cap'n Teague, not only one of the major shareholders but also the mine purser, persevered in carrying out Martin's plan to dewater the old mine, although encumbered with debt. This was in spite of the considerable aid he derived from Wheal Trumpet, a tin mine in Wendron which was then rich, and of which he was the principal owner, keeping the men there at work the day before the monthly pay at Tresavean, so that he could take the tin to the smelter that day to get his cash.

On clearing up the deepest level, the mine was found to be almost without a trace of ore, except at one place in the bottom of the old 100 fathom level, where there was a great 'splat' about two feet long, as noticed by Martin when he was a barrow boy. On this, considered by many as a forlorn hope, a sink was put down and the ore was found to lengthen rapidly, so that on winzes being put down and a level extended, the mine became able to pay. In the 166 fathom level, the lode was 1200 feet long and 10 feet wide, valued at £200 per fathom. Cap'n Martin was thus vindicated.[109]

The further prosecution of this bunch opened the great deposit which lasted, with varying value, to the depths of 310 fathoms under adit, or a total depth from surface of 370 fathoms (approximately 2220 feet), with every probability of the lode becoming further productive at a still greater depth. This deposit evidently occurred on the junction of one of the north lodes, which, in consequence of its greater underlie south, was carried under the lode first wrought and formed a junction with it, dipping west. From the junction of the granite and killas dipping east, the ore course appeared to follow this direction, but it was believed that further extension of the deep levels west would no doubt prove that the ore deposit continued on the intersection of the lodes. An extension of the shallower levels west led to the discovery of a second deposit on a junction with a caunter lode. This second deposit continued into the adjoining setts, dipping west as it passed through the crest of the hill, the whole forming one almost continuous mass of yellow copper ore, extending for above a mile long, through the setts of Brewer, Trethellan, Tresavean and Treviskey.[110]

Output increased rapidly and exceeded 10 000 tons a year for the first time in 1833, a year which saw maximum dividends of £60 480. A present of 50 guineas was given to each agent. In 1836, operating costs were noted as being £3600 per month, while income from ore, after dues, was estimated at £8650 a month, leaving a monthly profit of a sum in excess of £5000 divisible between 96 shareholders, attaining a maximum value of £4000 each (in today's money, a tax free income of well over half a million each year).[111]

These were the golden days of Tresavean Mine, which had increased its work force from a monthly average of 100 people in 1819, to 1354 people by 1836–37. This led to rapid population growth and the subsequent development of Lanner as people gravitated towards the area seeking work at the mine.[112] The ore was very rich considering the tonnages mined; in 1832 Tresavean ore commanded £8.110 a ton when the Cornish average price was £6.011.

The whole operation was enormous, as can be seen by the list of materials put out to tender in the *West Briton* in September 1839. In 1834, two engines, a 60-inch and a 63-inch, dewatered the workings and in addition there were a three 20-inch x 4-foot winders on the mine. The adventurers bought another 80-inch x 10-foot engine from Pembroke Mine near St Austell in 1839, and might have attempted to fix up this engine to suit their requirements.[113] However, in 1840 an 85-inch x 12-foot engine was built by Perran Foundry to replace the engine from St Austell.[114] This 85-inch engine was erected on a new engine shaft which had been excavated to a depth of 276 fathoms between 1840–43.

There are still families in Lanner today who remember being told that their grandfathers or great-grandfathers were contracted to work on this marvellous feat of engineering (Fig. 3.4). The shaft, named 'Harveys', was vertical until the 286 fathom level and kept 120 men busy in 24 crews, 12 sinking and 12 raising, completing on average, 63.5 feet of shaft each month. It was said a lighted candle at the 286 level could be seen from the surface.

The cost of the operation was in excess of £20 000, and the engine and the pitwork cost £4185 delivered at the mine. The nine lift of pumps moved 8130 gallons of water at each stroke.[115] In 1842, the celebrated man engine was installed in the mine at an estimated cost of £2601 (see below), marking the mine's technical apogee.

However, by 1843, the first signs of decline began to show. Output of copper ore had fallen from the 11 030 tons of 1842, to 8682 the following year, and thereafter continued to decline. The old books show that the course of copper was shortening considerably around the Old East Shaft (a whim shaft). Therefore development on the Engine Shaft and other shafts were suspended and Old East Shaft was sunk down in the root of copper, 24 fathoms below the Engine Shaft, at a fearful expense and inconvenience.[116] By autumn 1850 this shaft was down to below the 300 fathom level. However, the copper lode did not improve with depth, so the materials were pulled back to the 248 fathom level.

Fig.3.4. *Harvey's Engine House, Tresavean Mine, after 1909.* (© Royal Institution of Cornwall, Truro)

There were however numerous tin capels (stone composed of quartz and hornblende usually occurring on one or both walls of a lode, and normally accompanying tin) noted from the 260 level down.

Tributers were working pitches which were let at 5s in the pound (the average tribute appears to have been about 4s in the pound), when tin was fetching £42 per ton, and selling their tinstone to bargain buyers with good profits).[117] A new lode of copper was finally discovered on a side lode, and a shaft, named Devonshire, was sunk on this and which was down below the 20 by August 1850.

In September 1843, the *Mining Journal* had sounded an ominous note by reporting that the mine was poor in her lower levels, with the exception of the 260 west of Harvey's Engine Shaft which was seeing some improvement. Although the mine broke even throughout the 1840s, the last dividend came in 1847, followed by the first call in 1851, amounting to a £10 share, to cover a debit balance of £323 plus estimated operating costs for the near future. Another call came in the following year, but the mine appeared to break even for the remainder of the 1850s after the operating costs were significantly trimmed.

The 1840s at Tresavean were characterised by steadily declining production; the revolutions of 1848 in Europe caused the price of copper to plummet with the result of widespread unemployment coming at a time of crisis,

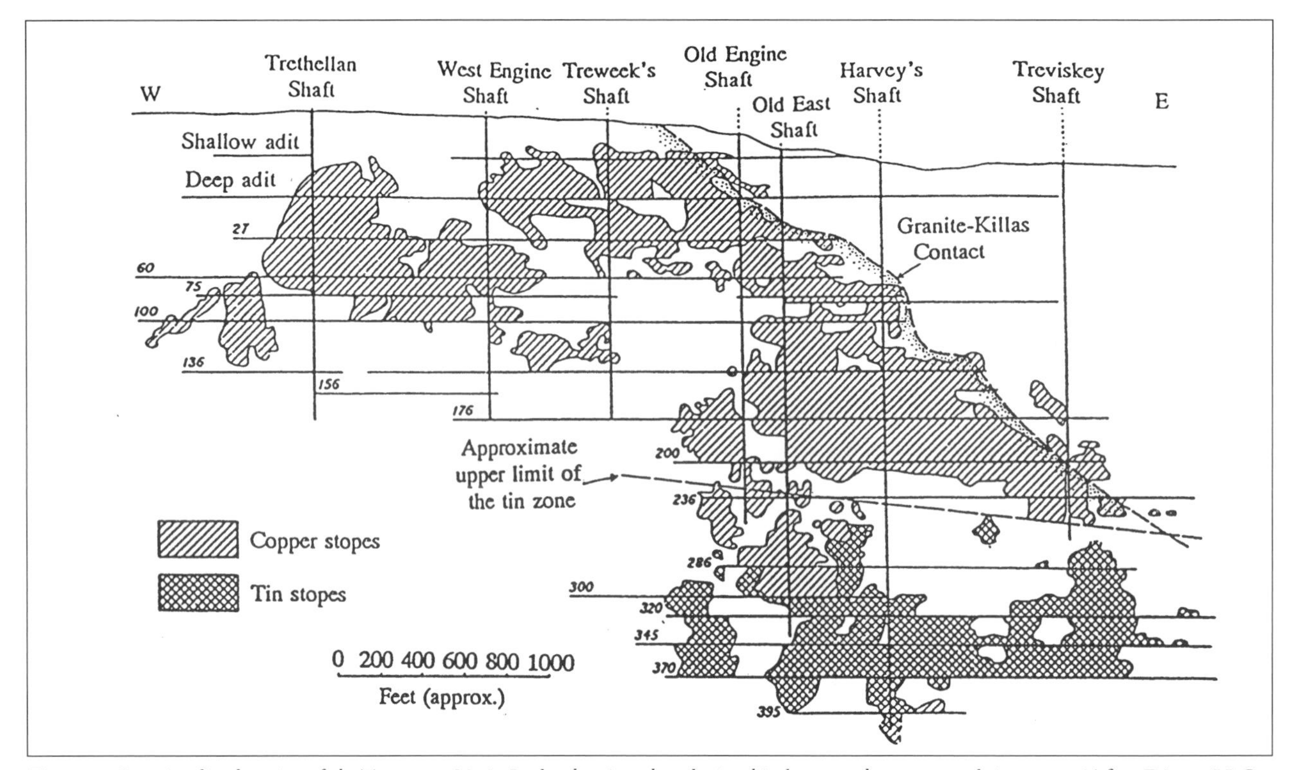

Fig.3.5. *Longitudinal section of the Tresavean Main Lode, showing the relationship between the copper and tin zones.* (After Dines, H.G., HMSO, London, 1956)

compounded by the failure of the potato crop. The above were aggregate factors in the beginnings of the mass migration which characterised the period from the mid nineteenth century in Lanner. By this time the mine was working below the 300 fathom level, Old East Shaft was sinking below the 300 in 1851, and by 1854 New Shaft was sinking below the 112 level and the 112, 100 and 88 fathom levels were being driven from it.[118] (Fig.3.5).

By 1857, with tonnages of copper ore falling below 2000 for the year, it became apparent that Tresavean's golden days were over. The mine had been worked almost exclusively by tributers for over a decade, who had 'picked the eyes out of the mine' to suit their immediate purposes. When a request for a remission in dues, late in 1857, was not forthcoming, early in 1858 the company folded and the plant went up for sale in May that year. This included 85- and 36-inch pumping engines, a 20-inch winding and crushing engine, 24-, 20- and 18-inch winding engines, two 30-foot diameter water wheels driving crushing plant, a 30-foot diameter water wheel driving the mine sawmill, and a 40-foot diameter water wheel driving tin stamps, in addition to several massive ropes, some of which were manufactured locally in the rope walk at Tolgullow, St Day.[119] The 85-inch engine on Harvey's shaft was sold and taken to Harvey's Shaft of West Wheal Seton.

However, it appears that there was more behind the mine's closure at this time besides the falling tonnages of copper ore. During the sinking of Treviskey's Shaft, 'deads' were trammed back into the mine and dumped into the ground which ought to have been left open for future working. This resulted in some of the stopes being closed. The Lord of Tresavean complained of this and much ill feeling was caused.[120]

The lessees had also worked the Barrier and beyond it on both the eastern and western sides of the Royalty. In 1837, the *Royal Cornwall Gazette* had printed a warning to Captain Teague, Michael Williams, Benjamin Sampson and their co-adventurers, from John Rogers, the Mineral Lord, not to allow operations to exceed the five fathoms of land known as the Trethellan Barrier granted to them in 1836.[121] In the late 1850s, the adjoining Lord came down on the Tresavean adventurers with a heavy penalty for exceeding the eastern boundary of the royalty which they refused to pay. After this event and the ill feeling caused previously, John M. Williams was alleged to have ordered the pumps to be withdrawn and the mine was allowed to fill with water so that the trespass could not be ascertained.[122]

Tributers continued to work the levels above adit, raising small tonnages of tin ore. Captain Martin attempted to form a new company to work the mine in 1858, with the intention of taking in the setts of Tresavean, Tretharrup (which had been a part of Tresavean), Trethellan, Wheal Brewer, Wheal Comford, West Treviskey and the area of the boundary pillars between the mines. Entitled the Tresavean United Mines, Martin sought to raise £25 000 in 1250 shares at £20 apiece, with an initial subscription of £4. A twenty-one year lease was secured from Rogers of Penrose with dues at 1/20 on ore mined at and above the 100 fathom level and 1/30 on ore mined beneath this.[123] Brewer was worked without a shaft, and Treviskey by means of a single shaft sunk through barren ground to a depth of 212 fathoms. The water in this run of fine old mines was remarkably small in quantity, and the whole (except where it was interrupted by cross-courses) drained to the bottom, whence it was raised by a single 80-inch engine in Tresavean, through a single column of 8- and 12-inch pumps,[124] but the venture proved unsuccessful and Tresavean became idle yet again.

In about 1860, a company was formed named Tresavean and Tretharrup, with the sett of Treviskey added later. The company was in 512 shares, with a lease of 1/24 from James Wentworth Buller and J. J. Rogers. The directors were E. Michell and Son, of Tresavean Farm, and the Captain was Joseph Odgers.[125] The intention of the company was to extend the deep adit which was 60 fathoms from surface on the north lode, where it was believed a gossan (the soft weathered zone of ore where a lode has been near the surface) might have been met with. This would have led to the same favourable results as had been discovered in the parallel workings.

A new shaft named Curnack's was sunk from surface on a pipe of gossan and crystallised ore, thought to be an indicator of a large mass of copper ore.[126] In 1865 Spargo noted that there were just 15 men, 1 female and 5 boys employed on the mine, which serves to illustrate that Tresavean had become a mere shadow compared to the concern once employing over 1500 people in the 1830s. Even in 1870, when it employed 70 people, this figure did not amount to more than just over 19 per cent of the workforce employed during the mine's heyday. This helps to place the large emigration from the village of Lanner in perspective.

Sales of copper ore never went over 150 tons in the late 1860s and early 1870s, tin ore sales were negligible, the mine was constantly making calls, and 24 shares were relinquished. Due to the higher price of tin in the boom of the early 1870s, Tresavean attempted to capitalise on the rising tin prices by installing a battery of Willoughby's patent steam stamps and building tin dressing floors.

In September 1871, it was reported that about 8 tons of tin were ready for dressing, which by November had risen to 12, as new tin bearing lodes were discovered. In 1871, 943 tons of tinstone (a low purity product) was sold, probably from fossicking about the dumps and ripping out the old stopes. By December, the steam stamps were operational, and it was intended to increase the number of heads until the engine was fully loaded. The old copper dressing floors were full of tin awaiting stamping. 'The copper miners of the district say the stuff is worthless,' reported the *Cornubian* on 22 December 1871, adding that many 'have persuaded their friends to go out [cease work], while the West Country tinners say the issue may be safely left with the stamps, and advise their friends to go in.' (Fig. 3.6).

In 1872 the adventurers decided to erect an 80-inch engine with the intention of draining the mine to the bottom. But the debate as to whether the mine should go

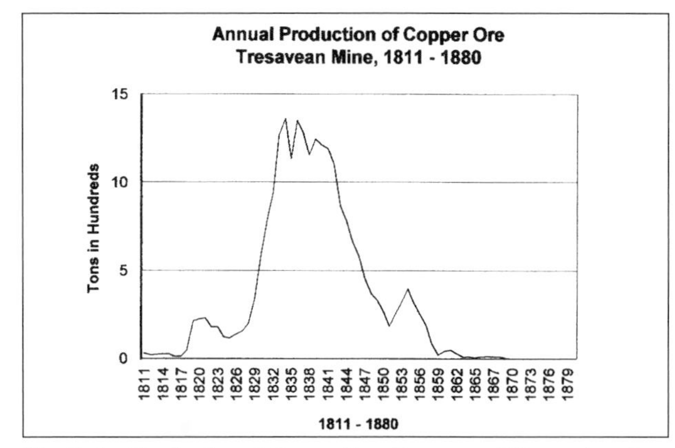

Fig.3.6. *Production of Copper Ore, Tresavean Mine, taken from T.A. Morrison's data in* Cornwall's Central Mines.

over to tin production became increasingly rancorous, with many of the old captains and agents doggedly opposed to the development of the property for tin and who persisted with their efforts in seeking out and working profitable copper lodes.[127] An acrimonious dispute between the adventurers in the summer of 1872 saw the resignation of one of the directors, E. Michell, share prices plummeted and all activity ceased. There was more than a hint in the local press that the former mine management and agents were incompetent. An unsuccessful attempt to reopen some of the old workings by a company named East Tresavean in 5000 shares was made in 1876.[128]

Much excitement was occasioned in the area in the early 1880s when it transpired that there were plans afoot to rework this famous old mine for its tin reserves. According to a report made by Captain Joseph Odgers, the agent of Tresavean when the mine closed in 1872, the mine was rich in tin in her lower levels:

Tin capels made their appearance in Tresavean at the 236 and gradually increased in size as we got deeper, until at the bottom they were from 5 to 6 feet wide, with rich solid branches of tin. Some of the richest of them were taken away by tributers down to the 280 fathom level in Old Sump Shaft for a short length, and we sold £12 000 worth from this place. I have no doubt the capels will be found extending away east of Harvey's Shaft and west beyond the Old Sump Shaft for a great length, as no proper search was made for tin for any period of its working. There are hundreds of fathoms where the capels are not touched.'

He mentioned in his report that in the 310 east, just before the mine stopped working, a vug, or cavity in the lode, was cut from which the water boiled up and drained that part of the mine:

I was so much impressed with the indications that I at once went to one of the largest shareholders and begged to be allowed to sink another 20 fathoms, as I was confident there was another 'shoot' of ore close at hand, but I was told that it was determined to stop the mine, and that she would not go on if she was pumping ore.[129]

James Opie, described as a practical miner and one of the sub agents during the working of the 1870s, stated that when the miners heard the mine was to stop, they were all much surprised: 'they could not understand why attention was not paid to the great tin lode. I remember many working up to their waists in water at 3/4 in the pound tribute and making good wages at that.'

In a comparatively short time over £12 000 worth of tin was produced, showing clearly the richness of the lode for tin.[130] Captain Odgers stated that 'at this time tin was not much regarded, the price being often low, and the mine agents in copper mines had little acquaintance with it.' It was far more costly and complicated to dress tin ore, adding to the financial debt with which the mine was already encumbered. 'Tin capels were much harder than copper ground, and the captains used to be vexed and say, "we don't want to hear about that old hard tin,"' stated James Opie, but noted that on a tin lode opened for nearly 100 fathoms in length between Old East and Man Engine, and about 80 fathoms in height, 'almost any amount of tin stuff could be broken from this ground worth from 30 to 40 lbs of tin to the ton of stuff.'[131]

A similar scenario was repeated on the 10 fathom level east of Boyes Shaft, where a copper lode was crossed by a tin lode. 'Those old tin capels have come in, covered the bottom of the shaft, cutting out every blink of copper,' one of the mine agents was reported to have said in frustration. 'Where they do come from, I'm sure I don't knaw.'[132]

Yet again we have evidence of the over specialisation and over dependence on copper mining, to the clear detriment of Tresavean Mine and the community of Lanner with it. The argument over whether the mine should seek its future as a copper or tin producer ultimately tore the company apart. Sadly, the mine could have been profitably worked for tin at this time instead of being allowed to flood. Shortly before the mine was closed it was inspected by Captain Charles Thomas of Dolcoath Mine. Afterwards, in the mine count-house, Captain Joseph Odgers asked him what he thought of Tresavean. Captain Thomas noted the similarity between Dolcoath and Tresavean, which were both worked well into granite. 'I feel sure that Tresavean is not done, and it is my opinion that the tin lode will master the copper in depth,' stated Captain Odgers. Captain Thomas persevered at Dolcoath with spectacular results, and was later reported to have said that old Cap'n Joe was right, and that Tresavean should never have been stopped.[133]

Tresavean Mine was the third largest copper producing mine in Cornwall. Its total recorded output of copper ore was 233 372 tons, a figure bettered only by Dolcoath in the Camborne–Redruth area in the nineteenth century, although many of the earlier records of production at Tresavean have not survived, so we might speculate that the figure was in reality much higher. A relatively shallow tin lode was encountered beneath a deep copper deposit, and the decline in the price of copper and the virtual collapse of the local copper mining industry caused more attention to be focused on Tresavean's tin potential during the 1880s, when tin prices were high. A company called Tresavean Mines Ltd, was formed in the summer of 1881 with a capital of 100 000 £1 shares.[134] The company was certain that vast quantities of tin would be encountered beneath the copper zone and planned to work the areas missed or neglected by the previous management.

The new sett included Tretharrup, Trethellan, West Trethellan, Wheal Brewer and Treviskey. The directors were Sir G. Innes, G. Forman, J. V. Gooch, F. Tamblyn, T. Saunders, A. N. Sherson and J. V. Smedley. A new engine house was constructed on the remains of a former engine house on Harvey's Shaft, and a 90-inch engine was bought that had been built in 1873 by Harvey & Co. of Hayle for a colliery in South Wales, but which had never been erected, and had lain instead in Harvey's yard. In 1881 it was fitted with an extra long beam to fit the old Tresavean engine house, originally built for a long-stroke 85-inch engine.[135] With this new engine, it was hoped the mine would be dewatered within 18 months. The engine house for the two 24-inch engines, for winding at Harvey's Engine and Old East Shafts, was in the course of erection in May 1883. A 32-inch stamps engine was purchased which operated a battery of 48 stamps, the engine house of which overlooked the dressing floors, and although ruinous in 1998, is the only Cornish engine house to survive at Tresavean Mine. Williams', Old East Shaft and Wheal Boys Shaft were chosen for rock hoisting and a half-mile tramway was constructed from the latter to the stamps in early 1882.[136]

Other equipment installed included a crusher and a weigh bridge. (It is suggested that a little known Tresavean engine, a double-cylinder capstan engine built by Harveys in 1881, to accompany the 90-inch engine, is stored at King Edward Mine.).[137] The 90-inch engine commenced work in April 1882, and by the end of the year, 36 of the 48 stamps were working. The expenditure had been £14 350 on equipment and supplies and £18 814 on labour.[138] In 1883, 60 slime frames were constructed, but blockages in Harvey's Shaft (which was vertical until the 286 fathom level) frustrated efforts to dewater the mine which was only drained to the 156 fathom level by the summer of 1885 at considerable expense, illustrating the extreme difficulty with which an abandoned mine can be entered.

In 1885, the books were showing a deficit of £29 571. With bills outstanding and calls in arrears, serious cash flow problems led to the company being restructured. The amalgamation of Tresavean Mines Ltd with the Old Shepherds Mines Ltd, East Wheal Rose Ltd and Mounts Bay Consols Ltd, was a spectacular failure.[139] By mid 1886 calls were £1582 in arrears and the Company owed £16 169. A large sale of equipment in 1886 heralded the 'knacking' of Tresavean yet again, after it had produced a mere 54 tons of black tin in the three years between 1883–86.[140]

The price of black tin had risen to a peak of £57.350 per ton in 1882, but had fallen back to £44.250 two years later. Morrison has commented that if tin prices fell below £45 per ton, marginal or inefficient mines were in trouble.[141] The Tresavean management had spent heavily on dewatering and modernising the mine, but had been disadvantaged by the instability of tin prices. The 90-inch engine went to Fortescue's Shaft at Wheal Grenville near Troon. It eventually ended its life at Cook's Shaft at South Crofty, where the beam broke in 1950, resulting in its being scrapped.

The mine was resurrected yet again in the twentieth century, solely as a tin producer. Copper precipitate was merely a by-product of tin production. In 1905 a mining engineer named Thomas Blandford, of Corbridge on Tyne, journeyed to Cornwall to inspect Tresavean Mine. He had obtained a 21-year license to search for tin and other minerals from John P. Rogers in 1904.[142] He set about putting the shafts in order and clearing the adit level so that he could inspect the several lodes on the property, which he considered offered excellent prospects.

Numerous lodes traversed the sett (which took in Treviskey, Barrier, Tresavean, Trethellan, Tretharrup, Comford and Bell) in a north-east and south-west direction, the principal of these being the Tresavean Main Lode, Mitchell Lode, Bell Lode, Major's Lode, Boyes' Lode, Comfort Lode, Caddy's Lode and Treviskey Lode. Much of the work of the nineteenth century was done on the Tresavean Main Lode which had been exploited for a total length of 3516 feet to a depth of 1060 feet. The depth of the main shafts were: Harvey's Main Engine Shaft 1716 feet, Old East Shaft 1860 feet, and Man Engine Shaft 1600 feet. Blandford had noted that some good ore remained in the stopes over the back of the deep adit, which it was thought would furnish an appreciable asset, and believed there to be a fine tin lode from Boyes' Shaft (a side shaft on a parallel lode) which he had noticed continuing downwards below the waterline in the flooded workings. Blandford, writing to a colleague in 1905, could barely conceal his excitement. 'This to you will seem scarcely credible, it is so much like a fairy tale, and I must confess it does to me, so much so, that I dare tell scarcely anyone... I believe that there is more tin in her than there ever was copper taken out.'[143] The Tresavean Mines Ltd was registered on 29 January 1908, in Edinburgh. The consideration was £5000 in fully paid £1 ordinary shares.[144] (Fig.3.7.).

The biggest question facing the new operators was how to dewater the mine. Several ideas were mooted including the installation of a Cornish pumping engine, as the engine house was in good repair and the pitwork, bearers, cisterns and main rods which remained from the previous reworking were at first thought to be in reasonable condition from a depth of 20 fathoms below adit. (This was later shown to be incorrect.). It was also suggested that the Cornish beam engine could be replaced by a Hathorn Davey Engine, or three Worthington Centrifugal Pumps could be placed at convenient levels so that they could deliver one to the other, with one acting as a sinking pump.

The question of the motive power required for pumping purposes was the most important; the operators were faced with three choices: steam, compressed air or electricity.[145] (Fig.3.8.).

Fig.3.7. *View of Tresavean Mine before 1914, by Govier. The Count House is on the extreme right, and in the field to the left of it, what appears to be a circular Powder House. The open arsenic calciner and stack are centre right, and the mill has not yet been constructed.* (© Susan Gribble, Trevarth)

Fig.3.8. *Harvey's Engine House, Tresavean mine, c.1914. Note the chimney of the stamps engine house on the extreme right.* (© The Paddy Bradley Collection)

In the end three high pressure Lancashire boilers were installed to steam three Bellis and Morcom high-speed pressure-lubricated compound engines driving an alternator accommodated in the old stamps engine house, which powered electric turbine pumps. This was by far the cheapest option available, the cost of machinery and dewatering to the bottom estimated at £12 000 as opposed to the £40–50 000 quoted by Hathorn Davey's of Leeds.[146] The boilers were housed in a low building, standing by the side of the engine house, whose stack was extended to 150 feet to provide adequate draught for the boilers, making it the tallest stack in Cornwall. Tresavean thus became the first Cornish mine to be dewatered by electric turbine pumps. The company later took an electric power supply from the public mains and the engine was cleverly converted to an air compressor by changing the steam cylinders for new air compression cylinders and substituting an electric motor for the alternator.[147]

Preliminary work consisted of clearing Harvey's Shaft to adit level, erecting the headgear, repairing old buildings and putting up new ones, getting the reservoir into shape and bringing in a new water supply, and attending to any foundation work that could be decided upon before the final plans for the plant were made. The adit was found to be in a bad condition and it was cleaned out and repaired from Williams' Shaft to the mouth, a distance of about 4500 feet, before pumping started. After that it was repaired from Williams' Shaft northerly to Comford Lode along Caddy's Lode to Boyes' Shaft and westerly of Williams' to the extreme end, an additional length of 4000 feet, making a total of about 8500 feet, or more than one-and-a-half miles. A 4-inch iron pipe carrying the water supply came through the fields and over the dumps for a distance of about 5100 feet, and an additional water supply came through a 7-inch stoneware pipe, laid in the same trench as the iron pipe, for a distance of about 3850 feet.[148]

Work began on excavating the area around Harvey's Shaft, where a solid choke was found at 46 feet from the surface. A windlass was erected over the shaft and the work of clearing out proved successful. The dimensions of the old shaft were about 12 feet x 6 feet within the old timbers. A concrete lining was inserted from solid rock (about 40 feet down), to surface to secure the shaft. The headgear foundation was built of reinforced concrete resting on rough masonry covering a large base. This headgear, designed with dewatering and regular mine work in mind, was erected very cheaply and was constructed of timbers 12 x 12 inches, with the exception of two old timbers which were 15 x 15 inch.[149]

A temporary rock-bin and shoot was constructed on the headgear to take all the material discharged from the temporary skip during the dewatering operations, and a small tram line was built in a northerly direction from the rock-chute to the dumps in one direction, while a second smaller line led in a southerly direction from the skipway, taking the old pit work and other bulky material brought up from the shaft. A powerful winding engine and one large, duplex horizontal engine were installed at surface. The remains of the house and the massive concrete foundation plinths with the deep pit between, where the two drums for the wire rope revolved, are still visible at the mine in an overgrown corner behind Harvey's Shaft. (Fig. 3.9.).

Fig.3.9. *Harvey's Engine House, Tresavean Mine, c.1915.* (c. Royal Institution of Cornwall).

Fig.3.10. *Harvey's Engine Shaft, Tresavean Mine, c.1914, centre. Extreme left, blacksmith's shop (with air vent), and next, carpenter's shop. The white building is the boiler house, and on the right, is the winder house. The old stamps engine house is on the left, and housed the transformer during the last working.* (© Royal Institution of Cornwall).

Rehabilitating Harvey's Shaft was a difficult and time-consuming operation, fraught with problems. The chief engineer was a talented man named Cyril Brackenbury, an Englishman, who devised many ingenious ways of overcoming the various engineering problems. The first 80 feet from surface was cleared using a hand windlass and kibble, and from this depth to the water level, 150 feet from surface, the work was carried out with the aid of a small steam winch and tip bucket and a small temporary headgear erected on a platform over the excavation. The shaft was cleared and secured from surface to adit in about three months.[150]

Men were taken away to open up another lode on the property while waiting for the pumping plant to be installed. Two independent ladder-ways in different parts of the mine were erected from surface to adit and numerous excavations were made on the main lode and in other parts of the mine. Before pumping operations began, severe chokages were encountered all the way down to the 27 fathom level (168 feet from surface). Regular pumping was commenced at about 1pm on 26 April 1909.[151]

Great difficulties were caused during pumping by the discovery of old mine equipment, such as occurred at the 27 fathom level where a large amount of old pump work was discovered. This had to be removed, including a cistern, H-piece, plunger barrel and supporting timber. Similar equipment was discovered at the 75 fathom level (427.5 feet below adit). Brackenbury devised a special skip which operated inside a rider frame thus facilitating the easy removal of pieces of equipment and other debris from the shaft. The suction pipe ran the risk of becoming blocked with the large amounts grit, gravel, crushed timber and broken rock found in the chokages, and finding a way to prevent this happening called for much ingenuity. The suction pipe was cleverly adapted to break through the chokages. A conical device was welded on to the end of the suction pipe, with a special valve box on the upper end containing a strainer made of copper sheeting with 1-inch punched holes. The point of this improvised suction pipe was made of mild steel and was employed to punch through the deep solid chokes.

In September 1909 the sinking pump failed, requiring it to be hauled to surface and replaced.[152] Tresavean had six such sinking pumps, but never more than three were used at any one time, showing the importance of having spares. Attempting to dewater Tresavean Mine without spares would probably have resulted in failure.

Plans to fix up the first pumping station at the 100 fathom level were thwarted due to the heavy inflow of water there. It was decided to install a duplicate set of horizontal pumps at the 75 fathom level instead, which were set to work on 4 February 1910.[153]

From March 1910, the station pump also received its supply of water from the sinking pump, as well as from the 75 fathom level, and the figures quoted by Brackenbury confirm the good progress made in the ten weeks following the installation of the pumping station – 35 feet per week, or 5 feet each day.

A lot of work had to be done at the 166 station, where a cross course was encountered, to make it suitable to receive two station pumps and a cistern.[154] The number two sinking pump took the water down to 1035 feet below adit. Delivery of the two new horizontal pumps for the 166 station was delayed and they were not put to work until after September 1910. A good deal of exploration work was carried out on the mine, and a new dam was built at the 75 level to cope with the large amount of incoming water collecting there. Unduly heavy rainfall hampered efforts to lower the water level in December 1910, and the pump was driven back 133 feet. The bottom of the mine (286 fathoms below adit) was reached in 1911.[155] (Fig. 3.10.).

The successful dewatering of Tresavean Mine, using centrifugal pumps, marked a watershed in Cornish engineering. The Cornish pumping engine (which had proven to be inadequate and expensive during the attempt to dewater Tresavean in the 1880s) was shown to have had its day. Mines elsewhere in the world, such as on the Rand in South Africa, in Northern America and at Pachuca, Mexico, were already making good use of electrically driven pumps. The golden era of the Cornish pumping engine, developed and constructed in the great foundries of Cornwall had passed. This further added to Cornwall's industrial decline and paralysis.

In 1914, it was reported that the section around the Old East Shaft was proving most promising. In February of the same year a new Hathorn Davey three-throw pump, of 450 gallons per minute capacity against 1850 vertical head of water, was installed in the 248 fathom level.[156] On the 300 fathom level west, a 'shoot' of ore was being developed and at the 320 fathom level, the deepest on the mine, results exceeded expectations. Harvey's Shaft was being sunk with all expedition to the 320 fathom level, and preparatory stoping was being continued apace. At the surface, the mill buildings were being constructed from galvanised iron sheeting, but building had been severely delayed in mid March due to storms and gale force winds. Cap'n Walter Langford of Lanner Green was one contractor overseeing the construction of the mill. (Fig.3.11 and Fig.3.12.).

The power supply to the mine from the Hayle Power Station failed during this inclement weather, causing the pumping in Harvey's Shaft to cease temporarily. A new miners' dry (the building where the miners changed their clothing and washed themselves), with accommodation for 300 men, to replace the one which had burnt down in January 1914, was nearing completion by May.[157]

About 40 new employees joined the workforce that spring, and the Captain was John Faull, a former mine manager in the Transvaal. He decided to move the mine offices closer to Harvey's Shaft, and the old count house at the end of the tramway terminus was abandoned, leaving

Fig.3.11. Erection of stamping mill and tin dressing plant at Tresavean, under the supervision of W.H. Langford, in 1914. The arsenic stack on the left was being built by Henry Thomas, father of Edwin Thomas, the founder of E.Thomas & Co Ltd. (© Arthur Langford, Redruth)

Fig.3.12. *The construction team for the Tresavean Mill, 1914. Middle Row: 6th from left, W. Allen; 7th, J.H.Langford. Second from left behind Middle Row, ? Knowles; Front Row, third from left, Le Roy Gumma; extreme right, Henry Goldsworthy.* (© Arthur Langford, Redruth).

only the main coal yard and the assay lab some distance from Harvey's. By the summer of 1914, with the mill almost complete, Tresavean sold its first tin resulting from the boom-driven ventures of the pre-war mining boom, and was in fact the only mine of the boom-driven ventures of 1906-13 to survive.

The new plant was accommodated in a battery house, a table house, a vanning house, a tin yard and a crushing station, the latter being situated near to Harvey's Shaft (Fig. 3.13). Eight Nissen Stamps were employed to crush the ore, at first on the day shift only, until the table adjustments had been done. Village residents once again became used to the constant pounding of the stamps which echoed around the valley. Mrs Martin of Bell Veor remembers her father, Captain W. Langford, telling her how even at night he would immediately awake and hurry to Tresavean if the stamps stopped, as the sudden silence was eerie.

The starting of the tin yard in 1914 was a little delayed on account of the Merton calciner furnace (one of only a handful in Cornwall) not having been completed (Fig. 3.14).

Top: Fig.3.13. *Mill at Tresavean Mine, c.1914. Note the construction of the calciner on the right.* (© Lanner Historical Society)
Above: Fig.3.14. *Erecting the 'Merton' calciner at Tresavean, 1914.* (© Lanner Historical Society)

The rock from the mine was hoisted in 3-ton skips and passed over a grizzly in order to separate the fine from the coarse. The coarse was then passed through a 20 x 10-inch Hadfield rock-breaker; the stuff from the headgear bins was filled into 1-ton trucks and hoisted up a gantry to the mill ore bin. From there the stuff was fed into the Nissen stamps by Challenge feeders. After classification the sands were treated on six James tables, and the slimes on nine James tables.[158] Boyes Shaft was restarted in July 1914. A report made in 1915 stated that Caddy's Lode was a strong and well-defined body of ore, which below deep adit had received little attention and could be considered 'virgin ground'. About £5500 was required to develop that part of the property.

Tresavean Mine in a buoyant state was a heartening sight to the people of Lanner, described in the *Cornubian* as 'a boon and a blessing,' an old timer from the village commenting upon the sight of smoke issuing from a chimney on the mine, 'That es a sight that hasn't been seen there for a passel of 'ears, and et's a welcome one I can tell 'ee.'[159] A great percentage of the men who worked at Tresavean at that time were from Lanner.

The year 1915 was one which saw periodic stoppages at the mine due to labour shortages, caused by men being conscripted into the armed forces. In October about 72 men were judged to have left the workforce (representing 75 per cent of the skilled labour force). By May 1916 this had risen to 95 men. John Faull, the Manager, attempted to get as many men as possible attested under the Scheduled Trades List D, 'Occupations of Cardinal Importance for the Maintenance of some other Branches of Trade and Industry', to prevent them being conscripted. However, the men were reported to have been exceedingly suspicious about this, and work at the mine suffered greatly from a lack of experienced labour.[160]

Unskilled labourers were drafted in to assist the miners underground, but mistakes were made occasionally due to their inexperience. At one point, too much ore was pulled out of the stopes, making it impossible to reach the backs, and the sinking of Harvey's Shaft to the 345 fathom level was retarded. Fortunately the mine had sufficient supplies of coal for its requirements. Work continued on the sinking of Old East Shaft, and the driving of winzes from the east of Harvey's Shaft to the 320 fathom level west of Old East Shaft. The working of the new lode in the 320 west of Old East Shaft was proving satisfactory.

However, the black tin produced had been of low quality as it was combined with many other minerals, particularly copper, at about 1 per cent, which had increased milling costs. The low price at the fortnightly Ticketings and the inability of the Cornish smelters to separate the minerals, led to the Tresavean Management's decision to sell their tin privately. Arrangements were made with the Thames Metal Company Ltd to purchase the 'witts' (undressed tin nearest the stamps after reduction) on a returning charge basis, with payment for the copper as well as the tin content. The by-products were shipped in barrels via Penryn to their works, owned in one-third shares by Messrs Henry Merton and Co., on the banks of the River Thames.[161]

Merton's process enabled the profitable recovery of the copper, and consequently the Tresavean shareholders benefited from the increased value of both tin and copper. Between 1914 and 1919, 1678 tons of black tin were sold. Tresavean installed a Record Table (of the kind used by tin streamers), where the re-concentrated tailings from the sands' tables were treated to recover the tin.

The mine management had encountered problems with their calciner due to the hot noxious gases blighting crops and fields surrounding the property which had led to claims for damages by local farmers. Apparently, the calciner did not have a long enough flue to cool the heated gases, which were hotter than usual due to the presence of a high percentage of sulphur pyrites in the ore. Plans to lengthen the flue by linking with the old one and the construction of a new chimney at the top of the hill, costing £380, were mooted during the war, as it was feared Merton would demand the arsenic be removed before the witts were treated.[162] The plan went ahead, and the old count house at the top of the hill, at the tramway terminus, was demolished to make way for the new arsenic stack just after the war.

In January 1917, the Lanner Syndicate Ltd had exercised an option to acquire the assets and liabilities of the company, the consideration being £10 000 in fully paid £1 shares. The capital was £200 000 in 80 000 10 per cent non-cumulative participating preference, 80 000 8 per cent cumulative prior participating preference, and 40 000 ordinary shares of £1 each. For the 14 months ended 23 February 1917, accounts in Glasgow showed that Lanner Syndicate Ltd had expended £187 042 on erecting plant and buildings, and in the development of the property.[163] But the end of the First World War brought economic difficulties to Cornwall's mines as the price of tin plummeted on the international market, and Tresavean and other local mines faced closure without Government intervention.

Problems were compounded in 1918; the mine was affected by strike action by the workforce. With few exceptions, the employees at the mine were members of the Workers' Union, but some had fallen in arrears with their subscriptions and the mine owners were warned that unless the defaulters paid their arrears, or were dismissed and the non-union men became union members, all work would cease, a matter which had long been a cause for friction. John Faull attempted to defuse the situation, to no avail. Fortunately the strike was short lived, as non-union men at Tresavean quickly agreed to join the Workers' Union and the employees returned to work immediately.[164]

Having overcome the problem of strike action, the management then faced a sterner test, as the price of tin continued on a downward spiral. In 1920 a deputation of Cornish miners went to the Board of Trade in London to ask for a grant or loan of £200 000 to support development at Dolcoath, Grenville United, Tresavean (which required £30 000), Tincroft and Wheal Kitty. By 1921 the tin price had fallen from £396 to £156 per ton. This, coupled with the high and fixed price of coal, meant that Cornwall could not compete with the cheap alluvial tin production of South East Asia without massive Government subsidies.

In order to keep the mine open until working costs fell, or tin rose in price to a point which would enable the company to once again assume responsibility for operations, the Tresavean adventurers were prepared to allow the Government to work the mine and take the proceeds of any mineral raised, on condition that it paid the wages of the miners. This would have obviated the need to pay dole to hundreds of workers, but the Government flatly refused to vote financial assistance in this way, although it had helped the coal mines at this time, This perhaps illustrates the weakness of Cornwall's business lobby.

In February 1921 came the news everybody dreaded. 'Tresavean gives notice' read the headlines in the *Cornubian*, reproducing the poster which had been displayed at the mine.

> *In view of the very serious and unexpected fall in tin and the consequent heavy monthly loss to the mine, it is as a precautionary measure deemed advisable to give the above company's employees formal notice. All contractors', other underground workers' and all surface workers' agreements will therefore terminate on Saturday, February 5, 1921.*[165]

A skeletal staff was kept on at the mine and the pumps were not turned off, in the hope that Tresavean could weather the economic storm. The cost of keeping the pumps running was estimated to have been about £1500 per month. Three-hundred-and-forty men were working there at the time, and as there was no other industry in the district to absorb the men, great hardship prevailed (see Chapter 11).

The local press was highly critical of the Government, claiming it had 'played no small part in the present crisis', by keeping the price of tin low after the war by price controls.

> *Had the mines been permitted to sell their tin at a price commensurate with the cost of production, they would not be in their present plight, for it is their custom to bank reserve funds to meet eventualities. But they were forced to the wall by a conscienceless control...the disastrous fruit of the Government's policy is to be seen in the sufferings of these last few months.*[166]

The blame was laid squarely with the Government, The *Cornish Post* and *Mining News* being critical of the Government's decision not to allow unemployment dole of 7s.6d to be paid to the workers as a part of their wages had Tresavean remained open, stating that the Government was therefore 'subsidising idleness by paying men to walk the streets'. All this sounds very familiar in the light of the history of Cornish tin since the collapse of the tin price in 1985.

'The mines,' declared the Prime Minster, Lloyd George, 'are the interest of the nation as a whole; they are the interest of the community as a whole; they are the most valuable property of the nation.'[167] So in 1922, the Government belatedly gave South Crofty a loan of £30 000, the first official assistance of its kind in Cornwall. Tresavean then received a loan of £25 000 from the Trade Facilities Committee, an amount which was only a fraction of the total raised by the adventurers.[168] This allowed work to re-start and Harvey's Shaft was sunk to the 395 fathom level.

Production ran at 500 tons of tin per year between 1924 and 1927 after a recovery in the price of tin in 1923. In 1926, 500 tons of black tin, 28 tons of copper precipitate, and 75 tons of arsenic were produced. With level and cross-cutting, new lodes were discovered, a new vertical shaft sunk, but the lodes proved to be of insufficiently high value to encourage further development. In 1927 the lodes of Bell Vean and Comford Sections were re-examined, but without encouraging results and men were laid off.[169]

By March 1928, the price of tin had dropped to £230 per ton and thereafter, the gradual falling off in the produce of the stopes 2660 feet from the surface conspired to cause the closure of Cornwall's second deepest mine. A continuous loss could not be borne by private enterprise for an unlimited time. With the mine's closure, the Company lost its entire capital, as the Tresavean property stood as a Government mortgage on the whole of the mine's assets due to the loan of 1922. 'The shareholders will have the sympathy of all who have admired their pluck and shared the benefit of the outlay of their capital', reported the local press.[170]

The remainder of 1928 was spent on cleaning out the property and selling anything of value. The mill, slime pit and calciner flue were cleared out, the table house and ore bin leavings, plus the low grade concentrate, were sold to Tolgus Tin and Wickett and Rodda. The dumps of Bell Vean and South Penstruthal were worked over, the former by James Uren and Richard Hichens who, on 19 September 1928, took out a three month lease from the Lanner Syndicate to work the dump on James's Shaft, Bell Vean, at 6s.8d in every pound for the value of all ore which was sold.[171] The three Lancashire boilers were taken away with a traction engine by Will Carlyon. With this final closure of Tresavean, apart from a little tin streaming at Penponds by Rodda and Sons, Lanner, a Cornish mining parish, had ceased to be.

At one time there were estimated to have been as many as 13 engine houses on the Tresavean sett of the late nineteenth century (which included the old setts of Bell Vean, Comford, Wheal Brewer, West Trethellan, Trethellan, Treviskey etc.). The chimney of Harvey's Engine House was dynamited in 1936 by Captain W. Langford and his son Arthur, assisted by Tommy Benbow and Gordon Drew, their employees, who drilled the holes for the charges (Fig.3.15 and Fig.3.16). The chimney at this time stood at 140 feet.

Apart from a couple of pieces of worked granite blocks, little remains of the engine house. A small, shabby concrete bollard with a ventilation hole marks Harvey's Shaft, which has been capped. The truncated remains of the stamps engine house, which overlooked the dressing floors of the 1880s, and which was converted to house a transformer during the final reworking, is the only remains of a Cornish engine house to have survived at the mine. Substantial remains of the engine house, constructed to house the horizontal winder during the final phase of development, have survived.

A good proportion of the mortared stone walling exists, with the eastern wall having two portholes with brick surrounds, leading to two boiler ponds to the rear which are overgrown, but well preserved. Inside the structure are the massive concrete plinths for the cylinders which occupy the centre of the site. Their dimensions are as follows: 2m wide x 14m long x 4m high).[172]

Fig.3.15. Setting the charges on Harvey's engine house. Arthur Langford on left, W.H.Langford on right, 1936. (© Arthur Langford, Redruth)

Fig.3.16. *The remains of the Tresavean stack, after its demolition by the Langfords, 1936.* (© Jack Evans, Camborne).

Although several water wheels were known to have existed at Tresavean Mine, no remains of a water wheel pit have been found.

The tin dressing floors which were installed in the 1870s and 80s were virtually destroyed when the mill was constructed in the last working of the mine 1907–28. Numerous features on a number of levels covered the area of this extensive new mill. A few round buddles were concentrated in the north-east corner of the site, plus a further 2.5m diameter convex-centred buddle, one small concave-centred buddle, a large convex buddle some 5m in diameter, and a further two large concave-centred buddles, described as battered and very overgrown, were located at the south-west corner of the mill. A 1.6m diameter concrete-built, circular thickening tank, with its buttonhole launder still complete, was in situ in the north -east corner of the mill area. Two large circular features, probably the plinths for Cornish round frames, with their concrete square-section plinths in the centre of each to 0.6m high, the bases of shaking tables surrounded by stone revetting walls up to 3.0m high, plus rapidly decaying remains of the concrete terraces for other mill machinery, were also sited in the area.[173]

The concrete base for 5 or 6 crushing plant and the distinctive slab plinths for shaking tables dating from the twentieth century, considered as of 'low archaeological value', remained until 1990 when they were bulldozed to create a football pitch.[174] For over 20 years there had been local efforts to get the area 'improved', but land ownership could not be ascertained. The principal owners turned out to be the National Trust. The landscaping was carried out by Kerrier Council with a large grant from the Department of the Environment.[175] All that appears to remain of the 1880s phase of working are stretches of the long calciner flue which runs uphill. The calciner and labyrinth which this flue served, and the chimney which once stood on the hill above, have vanished. At the time of writing, much of what does remain at the mine by way of industrial archaeological interest, surprisingly comes from the earlier workings of Tresavean, when it was a copper producer.

At Caddy's Shaft, a horse whim plat has survived, although the circular mellior stone is not visible, but at Trethellan mine, a mellior stone was visible in the 1960s (Fig.3.17). Remains of horse whims, which were once very common on all local mines, are rare in this part of the county. Just to the south of the shaft is a cobbled area, the remains of a dressing floor, where the copper ore was dressed by hand labour, as described below. A similar area may be seen directly below Highburrow Shaft at the end of the tramway terminus. Several rectangular reservoirs remain at the site; one north of Magor's Shaft is filled with slimes, and

Fig.3.17. *A.K. Hamilton Jenkin inspecting a circular mellior stone at Trethellan Mine.* (© Royal Institution of Cornwall)

another one is distinguishable nearby. To the east and downhill from Treweeke's Shaft lie two very large reservoirs, one of which is 10m x 25m x 1.25m deep at the front face with a roughly flat base. A leat appears to be running east from the Man Engine Shaft. The other reservoir is three metres deep.

A rather interesting feature was noted by the Cornwall Archaeological Unit. This is aligned approximately SW-NE on a line between Mitchell's and Highburrow Shaft. About five metres deep and originally thought to have been about 20 metres wide, it has been surmised that this might have been a small open-work or a Gerrard Type 1 Lode back working. It has been partially in-filled with rubbish.[176] Man Engine Shaft was made safe in 1990–91.

A balance bob pit is visible on the north-east corner of the shaft, as are two stub walls. The shaft now has a metal grille over it, but peering down into its blackness gives one a good impression of the level of skill and engineering possessed by our Cornish ancestors who worked on sinking this shaft over 150 years ago. Many of the mine's other shafts were capped and made safe during the landscaping project of 1990–91.

The rise and subsequent decline of metalliferous mining in the Central Mining District had enormous consequences for the towns and villages which grew up in the shadow of the Cornish engine houses and the vast heaps of 'deads' which lay scattered around them. For the rapid industrialisation connected to mining made the area what it was: 'The mines, Sir, the mines'. Here was the golden key, the solution of all the comfort, and the source of all the wealth, prosperity, and happiness of which Redruth Market was such palpable and convincing evidence.[177] The decline in mining and slow de-industrialisation caused many problems, the effects of which are arguably still discernible today.

Mineral Tramways

On either side of Lanner's valley lie the remains of two mineral railways built in the nineteenth century to convey coal and minerals to and from the once mighty mines of the area. On the slopes of Carn Marth running from the top of Lanner Hill parallel to Pennance Road, are the very scanty remains of the former track bed of the Redruth & Chasewater Railway which ran from the Wheal Basset coal yard and Pedn-an-Drea Mine down to Devoran. On the opposite side of the valley, the bed of the Tresavean Branch of the Hayle Railway is far better preserved, and can be followed from the top of Lanner Hill, swinging east to skirt the south side of the village, terminating at the site of Tresavean Mine.

The mines of Gwennap were developing very rapidly in the early nineteenth century, and in common with many other areas in Cornwall, a more satisfactory way of conveying materials to and from the mines than teams of mules was required. This had become apparent to the adventurers of Tresavean Mine as far back as 1797, when one of the copper companies refused to buy any more ore from the mine on account of the cost of transporting it to the coast. The arrival of the two railways in the parish provided yet another visible reminder of the area's rapid industrialisation.

The Redruth & Chasewater Railway

In 1824 the mining entrepreneur, John Taylor, obtained Parliamentary authorisation to build a railway or tram road from Pendandrea in Redruth to Point Quay at Devoran. The gauge was 4 feet, a width then common in the collieries of Wales (but less than the future standard gauge of 4 feet 8.5 inches), with wrought iron edge-rails for use with flanged wheels, set in cast iron chairs, bolted to granite sleeper blocks spaced three feet apart. The Redruth & Chasewater was the first proper railway in Cornwall, since the early plate ways, such as the Portreath tram-road, used an L-section rail and the wagon wheels were flangeless. Much of the granite for the sleepers along the length of track which traversed Lanner Parish came from the Carn Marth Quarries. Some of these granite sleepers can be seen at Tram Lane which runs off Pennance Lane at the Redruth end.

The path of the railway through Lanner can still be traced in places, although it has been built over in many locations. From its terminus in Redruth, which adjoined Pedn-an-Drea Mine, it ran in a straight line past Wheal Sparnon towards the flank of Carn Marth on a raised embankment, to the saddle formed above Lanner between the Carn and the uplands of Carnmenellis to the west. At Carn Marth Lane the line ran under a wooden bridge. In 1915 this bridge was reported to have been in need of repair and was considered quite dangerous. Just below the bridge, the line met the short branch that came across from Buller Downs (which always carried more traffic than the main line to Redruth) and crossed the main road (A393) by means of a level crossing just below the brow of Lanner Hill. For many years prior to the line's closure, this crossing point was manned by gatekeeper, Annie Blewett, who appeared from a little hut as the train approached sounding its shrill whistle, to lower the gates over the road.[178] A section of rebuilt wall may be seen on the left as the road descends towards Lanner, with the overgrown track bed behind still intact.

The Basset branch of the railway continued between stone walls on the opposite side of the road (which now form the boundary of a bungalow drive), to the crossing with the rival Tresavean Branch of the Hayle Railway. The point where the Redruth and Buller branches met was the highest point on the line, some 570 feet above sea level. From this point the line ran downhill (1-in-35), following the slopes of Carn Marth just below Pennance Road. At the top of Pennance Lane was another crossing and a coal yard, opposite the Pennance Brick Works, into which a siding ran. At Trevarth the line turned sharply left to head towards Carharrack, crossing as it did, the minor road that links Pennance Road with Trevarth Road. As the line progressed towards Carharrack, it ran below Wheal Damsel and close to Ting Tang Mine where there was a yard and a loop for the use of the surrounding mines. From here, the line ran straight into Carharrack, running under the iron footbridge which is still visible today. The line was not intended for passengers, but local people often hitched a ride on the buffers. John Arthur Bray of Wheal Buller did so every week when he wanted to visit his relatives in Carharrack.[179]

The line was opened on 30 January 1826.[180] A special train ran by gravity from Wheal Buller to Devoran in just over an hour, the return being horse drawn and taking one-and-a-half hours. From the outset until 1854, horses were used on all traffic. It was at one time intended to work by gravity in the down direction but this was never done, one horse and one wagon being the normal form of operation. Private operators ran on the line, using their own horses and wagons, for which tolls were payable for the quantity carried and the distance covered.

In 1839 the standard gauge Hayle Railway which ran from Hayle to Redruth, with branches to Portreath and Tresavean, provided the first direct competition to the Redruth & Chasewater operators, John Taylor expressing his concern for this at a company meeting of 1840. Dramatic cuts were made in the levies on the Consols traffic and profits dropped by 20 per cent in 1840 alone.[181] By 1846 coal was the largest single item being transported. As the mines became deeper, more coal was required to steam the engines which dewatered them. Coal was also gaining in popularity for domestic use, and the granite-walled coal yard at Pennance (still partly visible) often received deliveries for this purpose. This posed a dilemma for the operators, because more coal deliveries inwards meant that the coal ships had to pass Portreath (the port used by the opposition), round Lands End and travel up the River Fal before reaching Devoran. The railway had to become more efficient to offset the challenge posed by the Hayle Railway.

In 1854 the locomotives 'Miner' and 'Smelter' arrived from the builders Neilson and Co. of Glasgow.[182] Initially the locomotives only ran up to Ting Tang, the rest of the line being horse drawn, but from 1857 heavier, more durable track was laid beyond Ting Tang and the engines worked the entire line. 'Spitfire' was deployed in 1859 from the same builders, but was a slightly more advanced engine.[183] This locomotive was evidently well named, as the two previous engines labouring up the incline towards Lanner Hill periodically threw a lot of cinders and sparks on to the thatched roof of W. H. Tregoning, a shareholder and customer of the railway company, who resided at West Trevarth Farm. With the roof being in imminent danger of a conflagration, threatening to completely destroy his residence, in about 1857 the operators were prevailed upon to pay the cost of £200 to rebuild his house further up the hill, including the replacement of the thatch with slates.[184]

The onset of the collapse of the local copper mining industry was not at first disastrous to the Redruth & Chasewater Railway which was kept busy transporting coal at 2s.6d per ton. The 1867 closure of a part of the Clifford Amalgamated Mines, a huge concern, severely rocked the company which found that in the years following the gradual demise of the local mines, traffic was increasingly one way. By 1870 the Clifford Amalgamated Mine had closed completely and the railway lost, in one fell swoop, a large source of its income.

Several mines in the Lanner area used the railway, including Wheal Buller, Tresavean, Penstruthal, Trethellan, Wheal Comford, Treviskey and Pennance Consols which all saw limited success as the nineteenth century wore on. The Redruth & Chasewater Railway Company passed into the hands of a receiver in 1879.[185]

The company tried to recover from this blow by diversifying into conveying other freight. The china clay pits at Trevarth and Pennance were ideally situated to use the line for transporting bricks and china clay, but the Trevarth works closed less than two years after it began production, and the Pennance Brick Works was not the huge enterprise the operators would have liked, bricks from here being far fewer in number than those produced at the rival St Day works. Grain was sometimes delivered to the coal yard at Pennance, being ground in a mill situated on the opposite side of Pennance Lane, close to the site of the brick works. This, it appears, was a short lived affair.

Plans to transport granite quarried at Carn Marth came to naught as it became obvious that the stone there was not of commercial value outside the district, the cost of transportation by rail to Devoran was prohibitive, and the quarry operators had neither the resources or business potential to fulfil large scale orders.

The failure to find new and lucrative freight contracts again provides clear evidence of the detrimental effects of over dependence on the local copper mining industry. Throughout the 1880s one engine was found sufficient for the traffic carried. The Basset Mines were now the mainstay of the operation, consuming over 15 000 tons of coal annually. Apart from the Basset and Seleggan Smelting Works' order for coal, some busy periods when it was impossible to unload coal at Portreath due to inclement weather, and the conveyance of stone chippings from Devoran to create roads in the Lanner-Redruth district, the line would probably have closed long before it did.[186]

In the last 20 years of operation the condition of the track and the general standard of safety was cause for some concern, but there was little money for repairs, and derailments and accidents became more frequent. In 1891, Francis Faull, a lad of seven years old was killed, and his brother had his leg severed. The train was on the downward trip to Devoran with nine trucks and had just left the brick works when some bullocks strayed on to the line. The guardsman, William Cleer, immediately applied the brake to allow them to cross safely. When he released the brake, the coupling on one of the wagons broke and three wagons began to run away out of control, striking first one of the bullocks, and then the two boys who were standing at the unmanned crossing gate at the top of Pennance Lane.[187]

In 1902, what might have been a very serious accident occurred at Carn Marth whilst the engine 'Spitfire' was on her way to Wheal Buller with about six trucks of coal. A rail was broken in two and displaced from its saddles. The engine fortunately escaped without damage. In 1903 Mr Samuel Cock, a Pennance coal merchant, had a narrow escape when one of the locomotives came upon him unawares as he left the coal yard at the top of Pennance Lane. The engine collided with his coal wagon, damaging it somewhat, and it was only his presence of mind in quickly stepping aside which saved his life.[188]

In about 1910 three wagons left un-braked at the Lanner junction suddenly began to move off. Tom Lavin, the assistant brakesman, jumped aboard to attempt to stop them, but to no avail. They began to gather speed rapidly as they thundered down the gradient towards Pennance and Carharrack, Lavin all the while frantically blowing his whistle to alert several men who were ballasting a section of line near the Pennance coal yard. Fortunately the runaway wagons never reached Carharrack, for they struck the crossing gates at Ting Tang and were derailed down the slope to the right. Lavin, crouching on the last of the wagons, threw himself free on the left but remembered seeing the tin ingots 'flying through the air like a flock of seagulls'.[189]

The death knell for this unique mineral railway was the announcement in 1915 from the Basset Mines that they would in future be having their coal supply delivered at the collieries' expense over the Portreath and Great Western Branch from Portreath, an option which was 6d per ton cheaper.[190] The decision to close the railway was inevitable. The last train to operate over the line was ironically 'Miner' on 25 September 1915.[191]

In July 1916 a Board of Trade enquiry was held at Truro to consider an application to abandon the railway and on 19 April 1918, a certificate authorising abandonment was issued. The rails were taken up for their scrap metal value and the granite sleepers were gradually pillaged by farmers and others.

The Hayle Railway

The growing importance of Hayle as a mining port led to the incorporation of the Hayle Railway Company by an Act of 27 June 1834. With a capital of £64 000, the line was opened on 23 December 1837 in direct competition to the Redruth & Chasewater Railway, and ran from the Hayle Foundry to Pool and Portreath, with a further two branches to Roskear and North Crofty. In 1838 the sections to Portreath Junction on to Redruth, and from Redruth Junction to Tresavean Mine were opened, making some 17 miles of track in total.[192] The line to Tresavean from Redruth Junction provided an important link with the extensive mining area around Gwennap, but although it crossed the rival Redruth & Chasewater Railway, no exchange of traffic was known to have taken place.

The Tresavean line ran from Redruth, from the junction with the main Great Western Railway (GWR) line south of the old Redruth Hospital, to Churchtown, up past Wheal Uny, across Buckett's Hill, then swung east to pass the present site of the water tank on the top of Lanner Hill. There

Fig.3.18. *G.W.R.Hayle Railway. Tresavean Mines end of branch, on 10 June 1933. Assay house behind arsenic stack; centre right, horses' stables.* (Locomotive & General Railway Photographs, No. 11473 © Derek Reynolds Collection)

it crossed the track of the Redruth & Chasewater Railway just behind the present site of P. Williams Motors, and ran first south, then east, skirting the southern edge of the village to reach the terminal at Tresavean Mine just below the modern electricity sub-station (Fig. 3.18). Hayle to Tresavean was a distance of 12 miles 5 chains. Until the Hayle line was taken over by the West Cornwall Railway in 1846, the line from Hayle to Tresavean was the main line.

Construction of the Tresavean Branch line beyond the Tresavean Incline was by means of granite block sleepers, to which rails were bolted, with a 4 ft-8.5-inch gauge. Two bridges were built to take the line, the one at Rough Street being the better known of the two, having been granted the status of a Grade II listed building; the other crosses a minor track leading up from Lanner Green. A cutting had to be negotiated before the bridge at Rough Street and embankments were created in places (Fig. 3.19). The half mile long Tresavean Incline (1-in-15) was rope-worked, but by counter-balance. The engine proceeded up the incline first, and then the coal trucks ascended at the same time as the wagons of ore descended. The length of line from Buckett's Hill into Tresavean was entirely horse worked, as the engines were not allowed to travel along the track from this point.

Lanner man, Jack Evans, remembers that the track on the Redruth side of the incline was of a far higher quality, built to carry the heavy locomotives, and that the sleepers were wooden, not granite. The last operators of Tresavean Mine reached an agreement with the GWR (which had acquired the line completely in 1878 from the West Cornwall

Fig.3.19 *'Tresavean Tramway' of the GWR Hayle Railway, taken before 1936, when the rails were removed. View through the cutting, from Rough Street Bridge.* (© Lanner Historical Society)

Railway) for an annual rental of £10 and a payment of 1d per ton, the tenancy to be terminable at short notice.[193]

During the last working of Tresavean Mine (1907–28), Jack Evans's father, John, had the contract with the mine to haul coal. Coal for Tresavean was unloaded at Portreath and delivered to the coal yard at West End which is now the area covered by the car park. Wagons of coal were taken to the Tresavean Incline by locomotives, and upon reaching the top, the engine would nudge the wagons across the road at Buckett's Hill where there was a coal yard, and John Evans would then couple each wagon to one of his four horses, Trooper, Rose, Dandy or Victor. The single axle, wooden frame coal wagons were painted black with the name CANNOP COLLIERIES in white lettering displayed on the sides, and had a capacity of 10 tons. The weight of the load was also indicated on the wagon sides in gross and tare. Jack Evans recollected that they looked like black boxes on wheels but were easily pulled along the track by one horse. The coal was then hauled to the main coal yard at Tresavean which was in front of the assay house and mine lab, where Will Trethewy and Willy Gay worked, and the stables, able to accommodate about six horses, lay just behind. John Evans transported the coal from the tramway terminal coal yard to the mine coal bunkers at Tresavean by horse and cart.

There was also a light tramway at the mine to facilitate the transportation of coal which ran from the mine coal bunkers to the Lancashire boilers. The wagons were pushed by men and carried about 3–4 cwt of coal at a time. Jack Evans stated that in his father's day no tin ore came back along the Tresavean Tramway, but was transported by road on a horse and cart to the Seleggan or Redruth Tin Smelting Works. Conveying the ore by road reduced the amount of times the heavy sacks had to be handled.[194]

Tresavean Mine ceased production in 1928, and the route finally closed in 1936. Soon after, the rails were taken for scrap metal (Fig. 3.20). Lanner Parish Council purchased the tramway in the 1980s from British Rail which had taken over the line from the GWR, and a part from the Beauchamp family, for the recreational use of local residents.

The track bed of this mineral tramway has been mutilated in places, particularly the section over which South West Water laid a water main, but much remains to be seen. The section which runs from Chapel Hill into Tresavean Mine is particularly well preserved, and plans have been set into motion to include the clearance of vegetation to expose the granite sleepers and a possible re-laying of a section of rail to provide visitors with an idea of how the tram looked when it was working.

With the closure of first the Redruth & Chasewater mineral railway with its noisy and unique engines, and the stopping of Tresavean Mine and subsequent closure of its attendant tramway, the process of de-industrialisation was becoming ever more evident to the people of Lanner, and the closure of these tramways heralded the total demise of heavy industry in Lanner's valley.

Conclusion

The only mine in Lanner which could be said to have been really successful was Tresavean, and even then, it has to be remembered that this success was punctuated by periods when the mine lost considerable capital, in the 1880s for example. The only other concern to enjoy success and outstanding profits was Penstruthal, and this was for a short period only. Millions were invested in Lanner's mines, but millions were also lost in speculative ventures with little chance of long term success. Mining was always a precarious

Fig.3.20. *Tresavean Branch line. The removal of the sleepers from the Copper Hill Section, at the top of Lanner Hill.* (© Cornish Studies Library, Redruth)

affair, subject to the vagaries of metal prices, particularly that of tin on the international market. This created a boom bust type of local economy, which affected things as diverse as numbers of people marrying, chapel building and extensions, and even revivals.

As the nineteenth century progressed, local adventurers gave way to investors who lived beyond the Tamar, as investment was increasingly sought outside the county, in cities such as London, Birmingham and Manchester. This sometimes made it easier to defraud distant adventurers, many of whom must have lost a fortune. Mismanagement at mines such as Wheal Trefusis and Penstruthal were all too common occurrences on Cornish mines, and led to the discrediting of the cost book system of management.

The big winners in the local mining industry were often not the distant adventurers, or the men and women who toiled on them, but the mineral lords, such as the Rogers of Penrose, who owned the land through which the lodes ran, and the in-adventurers with vested interests, the likes of the Williams of Scorrier. Such families often supplied the mine with materials and even if paying calls, were still creaming off enormous profits from the sale of commodities to various mines like Tresavean.

For the local population the mine became the centre of everything. Gone were the days when the independent tinner could work his tin bound relatively free from interference from the Lord's Agent. The changing nature of work in the local mines by the mid nineteenth century, with less tribute and more contract work, resulted in the rise of a formal wage economy, which made the local population increasingly dependent on the mine for their livelihood. In many ways they could be said to have become enslaved to it. This made it the more difficult when the local copper mining industry collapsed. The overspecialised copper miner was ill-equipped to undertake work of a different nature.

With the demise of the mining industry, Gwennap eventually returned to a rural backwater. In the eighteenth and nineteenth centuries, Gwennap and its villages, such as Lanner, were places well known to investors and speculators far outside the county. But by 1948 Gwennap had sunk back into obscurity, as illustrated at the House of Commons debate on the structure of Parliamentary Constituencies. This once important and prosperous mining parish was recognised as 'a small place of some historical importance, especially in the field of Cornish Methodism'.[195] Its mining history had seemingly faded into insignificance.

REFERENCES

1 Henwood, George, *Cornwall's Mines and Miners*, ed. Roger Burt, Bradford Barton, Truro, 1972, p.181.
2 Bristow, Colin M., *Cornwall's Geology and Scenery*, Cornish Hillside Publications, St Austell, 1996,p.102.
3 James, C.C., *History of Gwennap*, Privately Published, 1944, p. 189.
4 Pennington, R.R., *Stannary Law*, David & Charles, Newton Abbot, 1973, pp. 74-80.
5 X 293/9, Eighteenth Century Tin Bounds Book, CRO, Truro.
6 WH/3988 CRO.
7 WH 3987/3988/3989/2, CRO.
8 Tresavean lease in private collection.
9 Brooke, Justin, 'Wheal Buller', *Trevithick Society Journal* no. 4., 1976, p. 69.
10 Berg, Maxine, *The Age of Manufactures, 1700-1820*, Routedge, London, 1994, (Second Edition), p.5.
11 Pollard, Sidney, *Peaceful Conquest: The Industrialisation of Europe 1760-1970*, Oxford, 1981, p. 14.
12 Henwood, W.J., *The Metalliferous Deposits of Devon and Cornwall*, J. Pope Vibert, Penzance, 1843, p. 471.
13 CF/1347, CRO.
14 BRA 846/50, CRO.
15 *West Briton*, 16/12/1836; 23/3/1849.
16 *Mining Journal*, 7/1/1854.
17 *Mining Journal*, 1/10/1859.
18 *Mining Journal*, 22/3/1873.
19 *Mining Journal*, 20/12/1879; Morrison, T.A., *Cornwall's Central Mines, The Southern District, 1810-1895*, Alison Hodge, Penzance, 1983, pp. 354-5.
20 X234/122, CRO.
21 Ibid.
22 *Mining Journal*, 10/3/1883.
23 *West Briton*, 6/2/1833.
24 *West Briton*, 4/12/1840.
25 *West Briton*, 14/3/1851.
26 *Mining Journal*, 15/5/1850.
27 Morrison, T.A., *Cornwall's Central Mines, The Southern District*, p. 373.
28 *West Briton*, 4/4/1861.
29 Henwood, W.J., *The Metalliferous Deposits of Devon and Cornwall*, p. 471.
30 BRA/833/363, CRO.

31 Barton, D.B., *Essays in Cornish Mining History: 1*, Bradford Barton, Truro, 1968, p. 102.
32 *Mining Journal*, 22/9/1860.
33 Spargo, T., *The Mines of Cornwall, IV, The Redruth Area*, Bradford Barton, Truro, 1961, p. 25.
34 Notes by Hamilton Jenkin contained with Collins 'Observations', held at the Cornwall Studies Library, Redruth.
35 *Mining Journal*, 22/9/1860.
36 *Kelly's Directory* of Redruth, 1866.
37 *Cornubian*, 14/1/1870.
38 Jenks, L.H., *The Migration of British Capital to 1875*, Nelson & Sons Ltd., London, 1971, p. 261.
39 Thomas, R., *Report on a Survey of the Mining District from Chacewater to Camborne,* London, 1819.
40 *West Briton*, 20/8/1819.
41 Morrison, T.A., *Cornwall's Central Mines, The Southern District*, p. 359.
42 *West Briton*, 16/9/1836.
43 Watson, Joseph Yelloly, *A Compendium of British Mining*, London, 1843, p. 28.
44 *Tredinnick*, 1857, p.50.
45 *Mining Journal*, 25/11/1854.
46 *Mining Journal*, 8/10/1859.
47 *Mining Journal*, 19/10/1859.
48 *Mining Journal*, 20/4/1872.
49 *Mining Journal*, 3/1/1874.
50 *Mining Journal*, 28/11/1874.
51 *Mining Journal*, 21/7/1877; 28/7/1877.
52 Morisson, T.A., *Cornwall's Central Mines, The Southern District*, pp. 363-4.
53 *Mining Journal*, 25/10/1879.
54 *Mining Journal*, 25/11/1882.
55 *Mining Journal*, ?/10/1884.
56 *Mining Journal*, 23/7/1881; 2/6/1883.
57 *Mining Journal*, 11/4/1885.
58 *Mining Journal*, 19/9/1885.
59 Francis, William, *Gwennap, A Descriptive Poem in V Cantos*, 1845, p. 18.
60 HJ/1/17, RIC, Truro, *Mining Journal*, 12/5/1838.
61 Watson, Joseph Yelloly, *A Compendium of British Mining*, p. 29.
62 *Mining Journal*, 30/9/1843.
63 *Mining Journal*, 20/8/1853.
64 *Mining Journal*, 15/3/1856.
65 Burt, Roger, *Cornish Mines, Metalliferous and Associated Minerals, 1845-1913*, University of Exeter, 1987, pp. 491-492.
66 *Mining Journal*, 10/8/1850.
67 *Mining Journal*, 20/9/1851.
68 *Mining Journal*, 29/1/1853.
69 *Mining Journal*, 13/1/1855; 20/1/1855.
70 *Mining Journal*, 10/3/1855.
71 *Mining Journal*, 14/4/1855; 28/4/1855.
72 *Mining Journal*, 12/5/1855.
73 Burt, Roger et al, *Cornish Mines, Metalliferous and Associated Minerals, 1845-1913*, University of Exeter, 1987, p. 492.
74 Morrison, T.A., *Cornwall's Central Mines, The Southern District,* p.455.
75 Ibid, p. 336.
76 Collins, J.H., *Observations of the West of England Mining Region, Cornish Mining Classics*, Lamborne, 1988, p. 428.
77 Lean, T., *On the Steam Engines in Cornwall*, Bradford Barton, Truro, 1969, p. 36.
78 Ibid. p. 64.
79 Ibid. p. 103.
80 Morrison, T.A., *Cornwall's Central Mines, The Southern District*, p. 337.
81 *West Briton*, 4/4/1845; 18/9/1846; 15/10/1847.
82 Morrison, T.A., *Cornwall's Central Mines, The Southern District*, p. 347.
83 Ibid, p. 351.
84 *Mining Journal*, 11/4/1857.
85 Spargo, T., *The Mines of Cornwall, IV, The Redruth Area,* Bradford Barton, Truro, 1961, p. 25.
86 *Mining Journal,* 31/1/1880; see also Morrison, *Cornwall's Central Mines, The Southern District*, p.353.

87 Watson, Joseph Yelloly, *A Compendium of British Mining*, London, 1843, p. 30.
88 *West Briton*, 30/6/1848.
89 *Mining Journal*, 14/5/1847.
90 *Mining Journal*, 8/1/1853.
91 *Mining Journal*, 30/10/1858; see also Morrison, *Cornwall's Central Mines, The Southern District*, pp. 374-5.
92 *Mining Journal*, 4/5/1872.
93 *Mining Journal*, 27/1/1883.
94 *Mining Journal*, 27/9/1851.
95 *Mining Journal*, 25/8/1855.
96 Spargo,T., *The Mines of Cornwall, IV, The Redruth Area*, Bradford Barton, Truro, 1961, pp. 23-24.
97 Watson, Joseph Yelloly, *A Compendium of British Mining*, London, 1843, p. 30.
98 Morrison T.A., *Cornwall's Central Mines, The Southern District*, p. 393.
99 *West Briton*, 4/10/1867.
100 James, C.C., *History of Gwennap*, Privately Published, 1944, p. 216.
101 Barton, D.B., *The Cornish Beam Engine*, Bradford Barton, Truro, 1965, p. 138.
102 Ibid., pp. 271-2.
103 Kenneth Brown information sheet, 'Tresavean Mine and Railway', 28/7/1996.
104 Morrison, T.A., *Cornwall's Central Mines, The Southern District*, Government Report on British Copper Industry, p. 378.
105 Hamilton Jenkin annotated O.S. maps, held at CSL. Jenkin claims this was called the 'Lancashire Level', but old mine plans appear to indicate that it was known as the 'Derbyshire Level'.
106 *West Briton*, 4/10/1867.
107 Lease in private collection.
108 *West Briton*, 17/1/1851.
109 *West Briton*, 4/10/1867; Mining Journal, 13/8/1861.
110 *West Briton*, 4/10/1867.
111 *Mining Journal*, 16/10/1858; see also Morrison, *Cornwall's Central Mines, The Southern District*, p. 381.
112 De la Beche, *Report on the Geology of Cornwall, Devon and West Somerset*, London, 1839, Longman, Orme, Brown & Green, p. 622.
113 Barton, D.B., *The Cornish Beam Engine*, Bradford Barton, Truro, 1965, p.58.
114 *West Briton*, 21/11/1840.
115 Morrison, T.A., *Cornwall's Central Mines, The Southern District*, P. 383.
116 Tresavean MSS, CRO, Thomas Doidge's Report, 1892.
117 Ibid.
118 *Mining Journal*, 7/10/1854.
119 *Mining Journal*, 8/5/1858.
120 Tresavean MSS, CRO.
121 *Royal Cornwall Gazette*, 20/1/1837.
122 Tresavean MSS, CRO.
123 *Mining Journal*, 16/10/1858.
124 *West Briton*, 4/10/1867.
125 Spargo,T., *The Mines of Cornwall, IV, The Redruth Area,* Bradford Barton, Truro, 1961, pp. 22-3.
126 *West Briton*, 4/10/1867.
127 *Mining Journal*, 20/4/1872.
128 *Mining Journal*, 23/9/1876.
129 Tresavean MSS, CRO.
130 Ibid.
131 Ibid.
132 Ibid.
133 Ibid.
134 *Mining Journal*, 28/5/1881.
135 Kenneth Brown information sheet, 'Tresavean Mine and Railway', 28/7/1996.
136 *Mining Journal*, 28/5/1881.
137 Kenneth Brown information sheet, 'Tresavean Mine and Railway', 28/7/1996.
138 *Mining Journal*, 13/12/1882.
139 *Mining Journal*, 29/5/1886.
140 *Mining Journal*, 5/2/1887.

141 Morrison, T.A., *Cornwall's Central Mines, The Southern District*, p. 19.
142 Tresavean, MSS, X/91/2, CRO.
143 Ibid.
144 Tresavean MSS, X/91/2, CRO.
145 Tresavean MSS, CRO.
146 Ibid.
147 Ibid.
148 Brackenbury, C., Unwatering Tresavean Mine, *Institute of Mining & Metallurgy*, 1912, pp. 258-9.
149 Ibid., pp. 253, 255.
150 Ibid., p. 259.
151 Ibid.
152 Ibid., p. 263.
153 Ibid., p.265.
154 Ibid., p. 267.
155 Ibid., p. 268.
156 *Cornubian*, 12/2/1914.
157 *Cornubian*, 21/5/1914.
158 *Cornubian*, 2/7/1914.
159 *Cornubian*, 9/7/1914.
160 Tresavean MSS, CRO, X234.
161 Tresavean MSS, CRO, X234. See also Barton, D.B., *A History of Tin Mining and Smelting in Cornwall*, Cornwall Books, 1989, p. 265.
162 Tresavean MSS, CRO, X234/17.
163 *The Cornish Post and Mining News*, March, 1928.
164 *West Briton*, 22/4/1918.
165 *Cornubian*, 3/2/1921.
166 *Cornubian*, 12/4/1921.
167 Ibid.
168 Barton, D.B., *A History of Tin Mining and Smelting in Cornwall,* Cornwall Books, 1989, p. 260.
169 *West Briton*, 9/2/1928; 15/3/1928.
170 *The Cornish Post and Mining News*, March, 1928.
171 Tresavean MSS.
172 Cornwall Archaeological Unit, Report on Tresavean Mine, Undated. Courtesy of Rob Gibson.
173 Ibid.
174 Ibid.
175 *West Briton*, 6/12/1990.
176 Cornwall Archaeological Unit, Report on Tresavean Mine, Undated. Courtesy of Rob Gibson.
177 Henwood, G., *Cornwall's Mines and Miners*, Burt, R. (ed.), Bradford Barton, Truro, 1972, p.175.
178 Information from the late Mr J. Sleeman, son of the late Annie Blewett.
179 Information from the late Mr Frankie Bray, son of the late John Arthur Bray, Wheal Buller.
180 Barton D.B., *The Redruth & Chasewater Railway 1824-1915*, Bradford Barton, Truro, 1978, pp. 23-4.
181 Ibid., pp. 37-38.
182 Ibid., p.49.
183 Ibid., p. 56.
184 Ibid., p.54.
185 Ibid., p.68.
186 Ibid., pp. 71-2.
187 *Cornubian*, 30/1/1891.
188 *Cornubian*, 19/6/1903.
189 Barton, D.B., *The Redruth & Chasewater Railway 1824-1915*, Bradford Barton, Truro, 1978, pp. 76-7.
190 Ibid., p. 80.
191 Ibid.
192 Fairclough, T., *Cornwall's Railways*, Tor Mark Press, Penryn, 1990. p. 15.
193 Tresavean MSS, CRO.
194 Information from Jack Evans, son of the late John Evans.
195 *West Briton*, 29/4/1948

Fig.4.1. *A Cornish miner poses for the camera, complete with resin-coated hat, candle fixed into a lump or 'tob' of clay, spare candles and coil of safety fuse.* (© Royal Institution of Cornwall).

Chapter 4
The Work and Social Conditions of Lanner's Mines

There has been much discussion about the general conditions prevailing in the various mining districts within Cornwall in the nineteenth century, by mining journalist George Henwood, and historians Hamilton Jenkin and Bradford Barton. For the purpose of this study, we shall concentrate on the work and social circumstances which were characteristic within the mines of Lanner and District. By the mid nineteenth century, there was mounting concern about conditions on the mines of Britain, especially as regards child labour, but also the overall state of health and working quality of Britain's miners. To this end, in 1841, a Children's Employment Commission was formed, followed by a Commission on the Condition of all the Mines in Great Britain, in 1864. Both commissions published their findings, which contained some very interesting information. Unless stated otherwise, the information given below refers to the mines and people of Lanner.

For the average Cornish family during the last century, the mine was of prime importance, as D. B. Barton has stated, 'life was the bal, and the bal was life'.[1] It provided employment for the head of the household, his sons, as well as his daughters. A boy's mother was likely to be a former bal maiden, herself the daughter of a miner and would in turn have married a miner. In 1836–37, De La Beche estimated that Tresavean Mine's monthly employment average was 1354 people. This was for one mine alone; other mines nearby, such as Trethellan, employed in excess of 150 people, and the great Gwennap mines, United and Consols, employed many thousands, clearly showing the importance of and the community's dependence on the local copper mining industry. Work on the mines may be divided into two categories: that which took place at the surface, and that which took place underground.

Juvenile Surface Workers

Surrounding the mine would be the cobbled dressing floors where the material won from the ground would be processed to separate the value material from its matrix of waste rock (gangue). Most of the mines in the Lanner area were copper producers, and the methods of dressing copper ores in readiness for dispatching to the Welsh smelters were labour intensive, employing men, women and youths in great numbers. Hours of work for those at the surface at Tresavean in 1841 were from 7am–5.30pm during the summer months, but in the winter they began and ended with the daylight. A quarter of an hour was allowed for 'crowst' (a mid morning break for refreshment) at 10.00am, and half an hour for dinner at Tresavean Mine, which was eaten in an open shed. On Saturdays, it was common practice for the mine to close an hour earlier than usual and on setting days (when the manager read out the working places available for tributing, and bids for contracts were invited), little work was done. Sunday was the only day off in the week, and there were no holidays except those at Christmas and Good Friday. Tresavean might have formerly allowed its workers a day off for the Midsummer celebration and Gwennap Feast, but this custom had died out by the mid nineteenth century.

Child labour was very much a fact of life in the middle of the last century, when a child's wage could make up a vital part of a household's total earnings. It was common in the early nineteenth century to find children as young as seven or eight working on the surface at the mine. A great cause for concern was the rise in the numbers of children seeking work at Tresavean, and other mines in the area, after the introduction of the New Poor Law in 1834. Mr Jennings, Agent at Tresavean in 1841, remarked that 'in the course of one month we send back many, thinking them too small for the work, being from 7 to 8 or 9; they are brought by their mothers who complain that they cannot get bread for them.'[2] Doubtless, there were some children who lied about their ages to secure work at the mines, and we can speculate that there were probably children as young as 6 working on the dressing floors.

Surface work in the Cornish mines was hierarchically organised, structured as much by age and sex as by skill.[3] At the bottom were the youngest boys and girls who were usually set the task of 'picking' (hand sorting) the ore to separate it from the waste, so that milling costs would not be incurred on the treatment of low grades. This task followed 'washing up' and was done at a table at which the youngest boys and little girls sat 'haunched' over a small pile of mineral which was periodically thrown before them. This they sorted into 'prills' which were lumps of pure value mineral which did not require further concentration, which they placed into baskets. 'Drague' lumps of value mineral mixed with gangue were thrown into the 'boxes', which the bal boys wheeled to a large heap called the 'shambles' which was subjected to further scrutiny by the youngest children on the mine. This task, which involved further hand sorting, often made youngsters' hands very sore, and must have been thoroughly unpleasant in cold weather, as the mineral was wet from the washing process. In very cold weather it was sometimes impossible to do this job.

John Henry Martin, aged 12, related how during the early months of 1841, the inclement weather had prevented him from working some days. He 'came up to the floors and found the tables covered with snow, and the pickers could not work.'[4] He was forced to return home and his wages were only 10 shillings (50p) that month as opposed to the twelve he usually earned. The shed or 'hutch' at which the children worked, picking and washing up at Trethellan, was very primitive and was open on both sides, so that when it rained, the wind often blew the rain directly on to the children. Twelve year old Mary Ann Rescorle did this job at Tresavean, and Martha Williams, aged 11, at Trethellan.

For children, the sexual division of labour began at about the age of 12, when the girls were sent off to the dressing sheds and the boys given the task of wheeling heavy barrows of ore, which doubtless built up their strength for their future career underground. Tresavean employed 58 boys under 13 years of age, and 68 aged 13–18 in 1841. Eleven under 13-year-olds worked at nearby Trethellan.

We have already described 'picking', work done by the youngest children. Those a little older were given the task of 'washing up'. During this process, the copper ore at times underwent two or three washings; the first process being that of washing the slime and earthy particles from the rougher and large pieces of ore. Richard Uren, 11 years old in 1841, had been employed at this dirty task since 1839 at Tresavean Mine. John Henry Martin did the same job at Trethellan Mine.

Work at the 'slimes' was also a wet and filthy job, at which the boys' clothes would become stained red with the iron oxide in the mud. Some of these children were fortunate if they received a change of socks for the next day. For this job at Trethellan in 1840, Samuel Tippett, aged 9, was paid seven shillings (35p) a month. Young surface workers were also expected to be able to 'wheel stuff', a task which was done at 'sampling', and occurred about twice a month. Here the ore was placed into 'doles', or heaps, which were divided for the convenience of the purchaser. The young boys were expected to take turns at filling the barrows and conveying them to the doles. Other jobs, including the transport of barrows of matrix to and from the crusher were done by the bal boys.

'Jigging' was considered the toughest surface job for the young boys. The powder from the bucking sheds was placed in a 'griddle' or wire sieve, which the boys moved up and down in water contained in large tubs. The heavier substances passed through the lower part of the sieve, and the lighter substances, remaining on the upper part, were skimmed off with a 'limp', a half circle of wood, and put by for 'halvans'. (The halvans were ores which were not rich enough for sale until more of the impurities with which they were mixed had been removed, by crushing and further water operations.). The agent of Trethellan Mine, Mr Sprague, had the following to say concerning jigging in 1841: 'It is perhaps the most irksome; the position is constantly stooping forwards, and the exertion strains the back, which often aches. The jiggers are rather small boys, because they can stoop better.' Another agent at Trethellan also added that he had known of several instances in other mines in the area, when the jigging was continued for many days in succession by the same boys, they had brought up blood.[5] At Trethellan, it was the custom for this work to be taken by 'pairs' (in relays).

Joseph Odgers, aged 14, a jigger for three years who had been employed at Tresavean since 1839, commented to the commissioner that this work often caused him pain in the 'chines' (legs) and he heard most of the boys complain of this after working some hours.[6] On some of the larger mines, jigging machines, worked by hand levers, were introduced, but Trethellan and Tresavean Mines seemed to have persisted with the old method of hand labour. Another surface task was that of 'griddling', work not dissimilar to jigging, involving the washing of the bigger pieces of ore in a larger 'riddle' or sieve to expose waste material. For this job, William Harris, a 15 year old, received 15 shillings a month at Tresavean in 1841.

The Bal Maidens

Next in the hierarchy came the women. In 1841, Tresavean Mine employed 326 females. Of this number, 143 were adults, 136 were aged between 13 and 18, and 57 were younger than 13. At Trethellan, the number of young females was 8 girls under 13, and 36 aged 13–18. The female workers only ever worked at the mine's surface and were known as 'bal maidens', and it was normal for them to continue to work at the mine until such time as they were married. However, there were exceptions. Some married women, the impoverished wives of sick or incapacitated miners, those who never married or who found themselves widows, had to work as bal maidens well past middle age.

The 1851 Census for Lanner lists several such cases; widow Phillippa Jose, aged 49, who worked at the mine with her two daughters; Ann Crougey, 54, also a widow who worked on the dressing floors with her four daughters, aged between 14 and 25. Ann Rogers, an unmarried 47 year old, who lived alone at Pennance, and the three Crougey sisters, spinsters Jane, 59, Elizabeth, 50, and Rebecca, 49, who lived together at Lanner. Perhaps the widows were looked upon with sympathy by the community, but as to whether the spinsters or married women who worked as bal maidens past middle age were classed as failures by their contemporaries we can only speculate.

As many as 30–40 bal maidens worked together on one of the 'floors' at Tresavean. 'Spalling' and 'cobbing' the ore was generally done by young women, after the stones had been 'ragged' by men using 10lb hammers. 'Spalling' consisted of the breaking of large stones with a long-handled hammer, a

Fig.4.2. *Bal maidens busy 'cobbing' ore. Note the characteristic 'gook', the hat worn by the maiden on the left.* (J. Henderson etching. © Royal Institution of Cornwall)

task which was usually performed in a standing or rather stooping posture in the open air. 'Cobbing' broke off as much as possible of the waste material from the ore fragments, done using a short-handled hammer, with the aid of an anvil type device; the girls sat at this work, often surrounded by a large heap of wet, broken stones, by which the lower extremities were apt to be chilled, even though this was usually performed under cover (Fig. 4.2).

'Bucking', considered the hardest work for bal maidens, was the term applied to the last reduction of the mineral by hand. Requiring a degree of manual dexterity and skill, it was a bruising process performed on anvils, a series of which were placed along a table at which the girls stood with a short hammer which had a piece of iron, about three inches square and about two to three pounds in weight, at its striking end. This hammer was used with a half striking, half rubbing movement by one hand, the other engaged in sweeping the stones in upon the anvil. Occasionally, their work involved the wheeling of barrows.

In order to draw any conclusions about the true life and nature of work for bal maidens, such as those who worked on the mines of Lanner and district, we have to consider the divergent views of people who wrote about them. Much of what has been recorded about their work on Cornish mines in the nineteenth century has been written to suit the object of the author, who sought to either champion, romanticise, trivialise, moralise or condemn them. To the best of our knowledge, no memoirs or diaries of bal maidens have been found which would allow them a voice, and photographs taken of bal maidens towards the end of the nineteenth century are very much 'posed' shots, showing them assembled in groups in their tidy bonnets and clean aprons. For present generations too young to remember the bal maiden, she has taken on something of an aura of mystique and remoteness which she scarcely bore in her own day.

One of the predominant perceptions of the nature of the work of Cornwall's bal maidens and their aptitude to it, is well illustrated by Lucy Fitzgerald, writing to Lady Sophia Fitzgerald from Falmouth in 1825:

> *We went off on Wednesday to the mines (in the Gwennap vicinity), which were quite a new scene to me and the whole process is very curious and interesting, the boys pushing little carts full of ore on rails. The little girls washing and picking out the best parts, the bigger ones beating it with hammers all the time, thirty nine in a row, was a very pretty thing. They were all singing hymns which sounded beautiful, and they looked so blooming and healthy from being so much in the air, so different from the appearance of the manufacturing classes in Glasgow. I did not go down a mine, much as I wished to, for fear of catching cold.*[7]

This very romantic image of a healthy, happy bal maiden is also hinted at in Barham's report. Grace Bawden, aged 17 years and 9 months, worked at Trethellan Mine in 1841. She was formerly employed as a straw bonnet maker, until failing health forced her to give it up. Working in the fresh air at the mine seemed to agree with her, and when asked about her tasks there, remarked that, 'she'd just as soon do one as the other'.[8]

A similar romantic impression of the dress of the average bal maiden may also be detected. Bal maidens wore very characteristic clothing to work, consisting of a white apron, changed upon arrival at the mine for an old 'towser', a coarse hessian apron, which soon became muddy and soiled. Upon leaving, the clean white one would be put on again. Traditional white hats called 'gooks' were worn, which had large brims and side flaps, and were tied under the chin. They offered some degree of protection to the face from flying stones, and also helped to keep off the rain and sunshine. There are numerous descriptions of them as being all neatness and prettiness in their snowy white bonnets and aprons, one lady commentator stating that there was 'not a cleaner, nattier girl in England than the bal maiden'.[9]

Yet their cleanliness and pristine appearance does not seem somehow compatible when analysing Barham's Report, in which he describes the bal boys at Trethellan and Tresavean with wet, dirty clothing and stockings. Anyone remotely familiar with a mine environment will be aware that the areas for the treatment of ore would be stained red from the iron oxide in the mineral, and it was probably impossible to avoid clothing from becoming stained the ubiquitous rusty red colour.

Many women were accustomed to tie a handkerchief across their mouths, to prevent the inhalation of mineral dust, and with their heavy boots, strapped legs (see below) and dirty towsers, would have looked anything but the pretty and pristine worker spoken of by many Victorian commentators. By contrast, there are very few favourable descriptions of other female industrial workers, such as colliery women, who were invariably described as grimy and blackened with coal dust, with the intimation that they had been in some way sullied through their labour, thus presenting a negative view of womanhood. For many in the nineteenth century, blackness was synonymous with dirt and depravity, what Burke has dubbed 'the "underside" of respectable white Victorian society'.[10]

The North of England, with its 'dark satanic mills and mines', contrasted with a view of the West Country whose people were commonly distinguished from those in the rest of English society, as being a 'religious, courteous, peace loving race'.[11] This far gentler, more civilised image, included Cornwall's metal mines and perhaps accounts for the idealised reports of bal maidens' working attire and cleanliness. And doubtless on a Cornish summer's day, a bal maiden's work in the warm open air would have seemed pleasant, unlike the insalubrious environment endured by their more unfortunate counterparts in the mines and factories of the North of England.

However, it would also be fair to say that the work of the average bal maiden was laborious, and in bad weather, very unpleasant. Cyril Noall's description of the bal maiden as an 'ill-used drudge'[12] is a far cry from the blooming, hymn-singing image presented by Lucy Fitzgerald above. And not all found their work pleasurable, as much of it took place in the open air, particularly spalling. Mary Johns, aged 14, was employed at Tresavean at this task. She related how she daily worked in all winds and weathers, and regularly got soaked through, but was fortunate not to take a chill.

However, Martha Buckingham, aged 14, who had always worked on Gwennap's mines, commented that she had been kept at home a full fortnight by catching cold, chiefly by getting her feet wet in coming to work, and having to stand out in the cold in damp footwear all day. 'The girls cannot get a pair of shoes to change when they come to the mine; it is hard enough to get one pair to wear,' she complained to the Commissioner in 1841.[13] Sally Fall, aged 19, who had worked at Gwennap's Mines since the age of 11, suffered greatly from a pain in her left side, palpitations and shortness of breath. Employed at bucking, she considered that she had overstrained herself some months previously in lifting a heavy weight. This had aggravated a weakness in her stomach, caused by inflammation in her side when she was 13.

Girls who were set to work at 'cobbing', where their legs were in constant contact with wet, cold lumps of mineral, were accustomed to wrap woollen bands of material around their legs in winter, and cotton ones in summer, in order to protect them. Some mines, such as Trethellan, introduced steam-driven crushers which lessened the amount of bucking the women had to do, but they were then exposed to mineral dust created by the crusher. The agent at Trethellan stated that the inconvenience at the mine was much less, as it was only necessary to use the machine once a week, but he knew of some mines on which the machine, driven by a water wheel, was constantly at work and the dust was then very hurtful.[14] Yet strangely, by 1841, Tresavean was still persisting with the hand reduction of mineral, demanding of women a physical endurance many today would find difficult to contemplate.

Bal maidens appeared to have enjoyed a certain amount of independence at the local mines, with respect to their wages, and in as much as they were free to go when they had completed the task set them for the day. Elizabeth Karkeek, aged 18, had been employed at Tresavean Mine for five months during 1841, engaged at bucking, and was expected to buck eight barrows a day for one shilling (5p). She commented that the quota had recently gone up from six a day, but that she usually finished the job by four, and was free to go.

Wages varied greatly, but the random earnings for those employed at Trethellan Mine for the year March 1840–March 1841 reveals that most of the girls' wages did not usually rise above a shilling a day, the eldest of whom seldom earned over a pound a month on average.

Grace Bawden, who found accommodation two miles away from Trethellan Mine in 1841, lived in very uncomfortable lodgings for which she paid 6d a week, cooking and victuals included. She received 9d a day for her work at the mine, which, after the deduction for her rent, would nevertheless have left her with a tidy sum to herself each week. This disposable income was the woman's to spend in whatever way she chose. Her wages therefore gave her a degree of independence not found in many classes of Victorian females, providing the opportunity of emancipation from the male-dominated household.

However, there were limits to this independence; at times it was necessary to work overtime. This occurred about once a month at Tresavean during 'sampling', and sometimes in winter when the days were short. Girls under 16 were seldom asked to remain behind to do bucking unless they were particularly strong. Bucking was done about four times a month on average, and was generally continued until about 8.30pm by candlelight in the winter. The work was considered voluntary, but an agent on the mine commented 'a girl might be considered lazy and lose her place if she declined'.[15] As far as wages were concerned, although their earnings allowed them a degree of economic and social freedom, compared to the unskilled male surface workers whose wages were double that of the bal maidens, women's employment in the local mines can be defined as being of low status, 'acknowledged by low wages and lack of any recognition that acquiring skill could lead to promotion'.[16]

Indeed Valenze has challenged the perception that work in mines or factories opened up new possibilities for higher wages and independence for female labour.[17] Yet one woman who did rise to a managerial position appears to have been from Lanner: Miss Lidgey, of Rough Street, who managed the Magdalen Mine (pronounced Maudlin) near Ponsanooth, although this was in the early twentieth century, long after the golden era of the bal maiden had passed.[18]

Independent 'Amazons'?

The independent spirit and apparent ability to compete successfully in a man's world, which manifested itself among the bal maidens of mines such as Gwennap, ultimately led to condemnation by some observers. Doubtless many of them at their work appeared to be quite masculine, swinging their long-handled hammers as they broke up the ore and carted the mineral around in wooden wheelbarrows. They hardly appeared to be the model of genteel womanhood, so prized by middle class Victorian England, so much so, that Henwood, in the *Mining Journal*, described them as 'Amazons'. Confirming this observation is the following rhyme, reputed to have been sung by Gwennap's bal maidens:

I can buddy and I can rocky,
And I can walk like a man.
I can lobby and shaky,
And please the Old Jan.[19]

Henwood was to go a step further in his 'observations' about Cornwall's bal maidens, particularly in their 'out of core time', echoing the fears of typical middle class professional men. 'Their being associated in such numbers and before men, a spirit of rivalry in dress... is soon engendered... . To see the 'bal maidens' on Sunday would astonish a stranger; whilst at their work the pendant earrings and showy bead necklaces excite the pity as well as the surprise of the thoughtful. All desire to save a few shillings for after life is discarded, and nothing but display is thought of. This is carried on to an incredible extent and all the preaching in the world will never interfere with the wearing of a fine bonnet'.[20] Bal maidens were noted for their brightly coloured and often pretentious display of clothing, a feature well commented on in the Victorian press.

Moreover, Henwood's attack on the bal maidens' attire had important class connotations. Working class women who were well dressed were becoming indistinguishable from the class above them, so much so, that a clergyman unacquainted with 'Cornish ways' was totally unaware that his congregation in a mining district was completely that of the labouring class. To him, they appeared to be the very epitome of ladies and gentlemen.[21] This extravagant love of clothes amongst bal maidens challenged the social order, as it threatened to erode accepted class divisions.

There were also important implications for gender relationships. Over time, bal maidens who worked at the mines alongside men, probably lost some of their deference to them, and were seen to be increasingly offering the very model of a free woman, mistress of herself, who was not to be destined to a life of duty and obedience centred on her husband and home. In proto-industrial (pre-industrial era) Lanner women had worked, but usually at home, and were employed at a variety of traditional handicrafts such as spinning, knitting, bonnet making and basket weaving, bringing some form of payment, either reciprocal, in kind, or financial. However, with the advent of industrialisation and the rise of a formal wage economy, these women were made increasingly dependent on a wage earned outside the home for their livelihood, and this began to challenge and break down an accepted maxim in society, that a woman's place was in the home. Clarke has argued that the migration of women from the domestic sphere to places of industry – mines and factories, created a fear among men of the potential for female labour to undercut their economic privileges and skills.[22]

It was possibly this belief of the threat posed by female mine labour which led to men like Henwood arguing that the logical end of the continuing association of the sexes at the mines, coupled with the bal maidens' financial independence, to be the cause of much degeneracy, and by implication, immorality. (Cases of rape by workmen and agents on the mines were not uncommon.). But underlying all this was really the burning issue of whether women should undertake paid labour at all, and whether this should be in the industrial sphere – at a metal mine – a thing which evidently did not entirely please all their men folk.

This sentiment may be detected in the following comment by James Harper, of Gwennap: 'I have four daughters, but if I had fifty I would never allow one of them to go on to a mine; they are exposed to be corrupted by bad conversation'.[23] Yet it appears that this was not in fact the case on all the mines, as an agent who had been employed on the Gwennap mines remarked: 'there is a great improvement with regard to decency in this neighbourhood, both old and young; they take example from the agents, and where they hear an agent using oaths they do the same. I take care to check swearing or bad language in this mine, threatening discharge if the offence is repeated. The result is, I hear very little of it'.[24]

The era of the bal maiden, coming as it did during a period of transition from a proto-industrial society to one which manifested many of the features associated with other industrial regions, inevitably called for an evaluation of women's role in an industrialising society. Clarke has argued that at this time a new kind of masculinist working class politics emerged, supporting an ideal of separate spheres – domestic for women, whilst men alone should play the role of the family breadwinner. This perhaps explains the attitude of local men such as James Harper, quoted above.[25]

Whether 'Amazons', dangerously free spirited, or hymn singing, blushing and modest, the 1851 Census shows that Lanner's women chose work on the local mines over any other form of employment, as shown in Fig.2.8. However, although the process of industrialisation in Lanner at first increased work opportunities for women, in mining in particular, the gain was not to be long term. With the copper mining collapse, job opportunities for women became more restricted (see Chapter 2).

Yet paradoxically, Lanner, at the beginning of the twentieth century, was showing definite signs of becoming a matriarchal society. The 'independence' many of these women enjoyed in their youth probably equipped them well to deal with the task of decision making and bringing up a family alone, as their men were forced to migrate in search of work later in the nineteenth century. But although women then had control over the whole family budget, many had also become isolated (financially and economically) within the domestic sphere.

Fig.4.3. *The carpenters at Tresavean Mine, c.1914; Joe Moyle third from left.* (© Lanner Historical Society).

Male Workers 'at Grass'

Two groups of men worked at the mine's surface: the first group, who by accident, age or ill health were precluded from work below grass, were unskilled labourers. They were employed at 'ragging', the breaking of large stones into more manageable sizes, pushing wagons, operating whims, minding the stamps machinery and watching the pumps. Their pay was above that of the bal maidens. The second group was the class of skilled artisans, carpenters, smiths and masons, who maintained, repaired and oversaw the smooth operation of the mine's plant and equipment. Skilled as they were, their wages were not on a par with the tributers who worked underground (Fig.4.3).

At the top of the hierarchy were the mining captains, known as 'grass captains', who oversaw the efficient operation of the dressing floors, pumping machinery and stamps, and were also responsible for organising and disciplining the workforce. They were very characteristic in their billycock hats and white duck coats, and commanded respect, as did their counterparts underground.

The Agent, or Managerial Captain, was the man who had ultimate control over the whole mine operation, a position of great responsibility. His decisions could either ensure the future success of the mine, or wreck its chances. He decided the ground to be mined, oversaw the discipline of the workers, negotiated with the adventurers and tributers, and attended the ticketings. Many of the Mining Captains achieved legendary status in their lifetimes, among whom might be mentioned Tresavean's Captains Martin, Teague and Odgers.

A man who became a Captain was always addressed as such, and was expected to play an important role in local society, perhaps as a Chapel trustee, local preacher, chairman of a village committee, or fund-raiser for worthy causes.

Juvenile Underground Workers

In 1841, forty-two 13–18 year olds and 481 adult men were employed underground at Tresavean Mine. Boys proceeded underground usually with their fathers or older brothers at about 12–13 years of age. However, many families were eager for their sons to proceed underground where they could command a higher wage. This is borne out by the report of a child of eight, killed in 1831 at Consols Mine in Gwennap. Thomas Martin was working in Morcom's Shaft, four fathoms above the back of the 120 fathom level, when 4–5 tons of earth and rock fell on him.[26] We learn too of the death in 1829 of 10-year-old William Benbow, who was descending a shaft in Tresavean Mine with his father and another man, when he fell about 20 fathoms down an unnoticed shaft before him. He was so injured from this fall that he died the following day.[27] The Gwennap Vestry Book of the 1830s and 40s contains numerous entries of requests by poor parents, which were subsequently granted, for items of clothing and footwear to enable their children to begin work underground on the mines. 'Selina Dunstone, underground suit for second boy, and for shoes to put him underground'.[28]

One of the first tasks set a boy below surface might be 'blowing air', to improve the air quality in the tunnels by means of a large hydraulic bellows. This device consisted of two boxes or cisterns, one moving inverted upon the other, which was filled with water. The moving power was applied at the end of a lever, closely resembling the handle of a common pump. This was the job that John Henry Martin first did at age 11, in 1840 at Wheal Brewer, 60 fathoms below adit, 120 fathoms from surface.

Captain Walter Harold Langford, a well known Methodist lay preacher, went underground before he was 14 to work the air machine at Unity Wood Mine near St Day, in the early 1880s, the mine captain, John Penhall, 'taking the risk' of employing a boy who should really have been at school. The work was tedious but not difficult, and was very necessary as the air in some of the local mines was poor (see below).

As they progressed and grew stronger, youngsters underground would be employed holding, turning or beating the 'boryer', within a pare (a group of miners who worked together during the period of a contract; an average size pare would have been about 5–6 in number) to make the holes into which the gunpowder was lodged for blasting. In 1841, teenagers Henry Francis and James Orby were employed in turning and beating the 'boryer' at the 74 fathom level at Tresavean. Other jobs included filling kibbles (large metal buckets), and loading, pushing and emptying wagons. Apprenticed to their experienced elders, 'taken into concern', boys rapidly acquired the skills which they in turn would pass on to their own sons. To be 'taken into concern' was a sort of promotion for the boy, who was now considered a partner with the men, holding a half, or three-quarters of the share allotted to each man.

Most boys underground were expected to work an eight-hour core. James Orby, aged 18, working as a tributer at Tresavean, sometimes did a double core of 16 hours in total, but James Stevens, a tributer employed in 'stoping' (excavating the lode), explained that the boys did not remain behind to work overtime unless they were asked.

The exception to the 8-hour core was for those who worked in the sump (the pit at the bottom of the engine shaft), whose shift was for six hours. There were only four sump workers at Tresavean, and this job was unpleasant, in the wet atmosphere, where there was a strong draught which chilled the body. Boys employed at 'tutwork' very seldom exceeded eight hours. (Tutwork was different from tribute work, in that the miner was paid so much a fathom for his work of sinking or driving a shaft.). The tributers, who were considerably fewer, sometimes worked overtime when their pitch looked promising. Boys of the former class were recommended to the miners by the agents.

Captain Jennings of Tresavean explained that the tributer chose his own boys and was not interfered with, unless it was noticed that he was employing a very small or weakly boy, when he would probably have been advised to get a stronger one in his place.[29] Surface workers were paid separately at the end of each month, but complaints of non payment to boys working in a 'pare' underground were sometimes received. At Trethellan, the agent commented that he had 'recently checked a man's pay who had come here from another mine where he had not paid the boy hired by him. When such complaints are made against a man who continues to work in our mine, we pay the boy ourselves, and deduct the sum from the man's pay'.[30] Boys' wages within a pare usually averaged anywhere from 3–8 shillings a month.

Men Underground

Men's work underground was very much the same as that of teenage boys; beating and turning the borer, setting charges, tramming, stoping, and filling skips and kibbles with rock, most of which were extremely laborious jobs. Tributing formed a system which in modern terms might be likened to sub-contracting. A small portion of the mine, the 'pitch', was 'rented' by public competition among the pares of miners on 'setting day' (contract day). The pare agreed to prepare the ore for market, breaking it from the surrounding rock, and raising it 'to grass' (surface), but were free to work it as they chose. They received their tribute either weekly or monthly, tribute being the proportion agreed upon with the mine captain to take for every pound's worth of 'stuff' brought to grass. As tributers were paid a certain amount of the value of the ores they raised, tributing provided an added incentive to work. The harder and more economically the pare drove a level, and the more skilfully they followed and stoped the lode, and the quicker they got the ore to grass, the more money they earned.

Added to this, there was always the bonus of making a 'sturt', happening upon an unsuspected very rich part of the lode, when much money could be earned. Things could go either way; some months the earnings would be so slight that the pare would end up owing money to the mine from which the tributers had to buy all their candles, powder, safety fuse, clay, etc.. Miners would then have to rely on 'subsist', an advance on earnings paid by the mining company to see them through to their next pay-day, or 'tick', putting things bought in the local shops 'on the slate', to be paid when the miner received his next wages. This was a common feature in the mining districts.

We can see how much money Tresavean and Tretharrup Mine made through the sale of gunpowder and candles in the early 1860's. There were 2952 pounds of candles purchased at £73.16 shillings, realising a profit for the mine of £24.12 shillings. One pound of candles cost the mine £6, but they sold them to the miners for £8 a pound. Likewise with blasting powder; 3000lbs of powder purchased for £75, made the mine a profit of £25. A pound of gunpowder cost Tresavean and Tretharrup £6 to buy, but it was again sold for £8 a pound.[31] Tribute pay varied widely; at Wheal Comford and North Tresavean Mine in 1883, nine men were working a stope for tin where the lode was 8 feet wide and worth for the width, £16 per fathom. Their rate was 5s.6d per ton of stuff. In a different part of the same mine, a copper lode was being developed, and 3 men were working a winze in a tribute of 10 shillings in £1.[32]. Below we can analyse the typical earnings for underground workers employed at Trethellan Mine in early 1884. (Fig. 4.4)

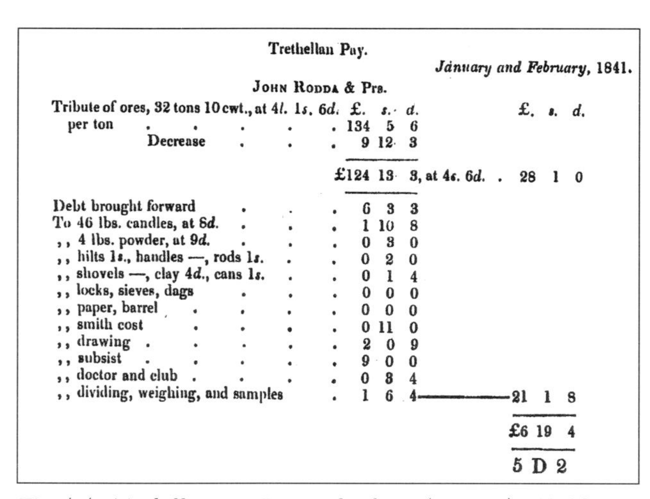

Trethellan Pay.

January and February, 1841.

JOHN RODDA & Prs.

	£.	s.	d.		£.	s.	d.
Tribute of ores, 32 tons 10 cwt., at 4*l*. 1*s*. 6*d*. per ton	134	5	6				
Decrease	9	12	3				
	£124	13	3,	at 4*s*. 6*d*.	28	1	0
Debt brought forward	6	3	3				
To 46 lbs. candles, at 8*d*.	1	10	8				
,, 4 lbs. powder, at 9*d*.	0	3	0				
,, hilts 1*s*., handles —, rods 1*s*.	0	2	0				
,, shovels —, clay 4*d*., cans 1*s*.	0	1	4				
,, locks, sieves, dags	0	0	0				
,, paper, barrel	0	0	0				
,, smith cost	0	11	0				
,, drawing	2	0	9				
,, subsist	9	0	0				
,, doctor and club	0	8	4				
,, dividing, weighing, and samples	1	6	4		21	1	8
					£6	19	4
					5	D	2

Fig.4.4. *Trethellan pay, Jan. and Feb. 1841.* (1841 Children's Employment Commission, British Parliamentary Papers).

Conditions Underground

Conditions underground at Tresavean and many of its satellite mines were often poor and sometimes appalling. Hot, wet and humid with poor air, Tresavean in particular eventually sapped the strength of the most hardy miner. The hard nature of the ground, chiefly granite, required the use of a large quantity of gunpowder. In the 1860s, Tresavean and Tretharrup Mines, a mere shadow of the former industrial giant of the 1830s and 40s, consumed 3000 lbs of powder per year.[33] Captain Sprague of Trethellan, when asked in 1841 about frequency of blasting and conditions underground, replied:

> *Our ground is very hard, and we are almost always "shooting". We use about a ton of gunpowder a month; the air may be tolerably clear for a time in the mornings before the first "shooting", but it is afterwards mostly very thick with powder smoke often so that you can hardly see your hand.*[34]

In Tresavean Mine, an air sample was recorded in 1841 at the 156 fathom level, 936 feet from surface. The two men working their core directly after firing a hole were 65 fathoms (almost 390 feet) from a winze or shaft. The air sample was: specific gravity .993; nitrogen 83.52 per cent; oxygen 16.35 per cent; carbolic acid 0.13 per cent; a slight trace of sulphuretted hydrogen.[35] This air sample was quite poor (the normal atmospheric oxygen content is about 20 per cent), but the worst air in Tresavean Mine was said to be that in the 146 fathom level.

Imagine the conditions for men working in a dark winze or drive, a cul-de-sac, where the ventilation was likely to be poor, and the air made worse by the burning of 'miners' dips', crude tallow candles. The acrid stench of gunpowder fumes from blasting, on average every 2–3 hours, created noxious black smoke which added to the carbon given off by the candles. This reduced the amount of oxygen in the dust and smoke-filled air, so at times the light from a guttering candle provided illumination scarcely adequate to see the shining end of the drill bit. Often the air would be fouled by the smell of human excrement. There were no adequate sanitary provisions underground in the nineteenth century, and it was only after the outbreak of ankylostomiasis, an infection which thrived in the warm conditions underground causing anaemia and blotches on the skin, that new measures were introduced to improve the sanitary conditions in mines. This disease was caused by skin contact with a parasitic worm which lived in human faeces, and led to mines such as Dolcoath introducing pails underground in 1904. Even after such a measure, it was not uncommon to find one or two miners in most mines suffering from the disease.[36]

In 1837 Captain Oates of Tresavean took a series of rock and air temperatures which appeared in the *Mining Journal*: 200 fathoms from surface, the temperature was 77.2°F; 250 fathoms, 83.2°F, and at the 262 level, 85.5°F.[37] Miners climbing to grass would therefore experience a drastic change of temperature, sometimes during winter exceeding 40°F, from the hot, 80°F depths of the mine to the cold, damp atmosphere of a Cornish winter. Indeed, the *West Briton* of 22 February 1867 made reference to the plight of men who worked in high temperatures like those of Tresavean, and then had to walk a quarter of a mile or more in wet clothing, in the cold, to reach the changing house. 'If we were to subject a horse to such a change, we should kill it,' the paper commented.

Heat and poor ventilation made work at Tresavean very arduous, particularly in the deeper levels, making it necessary to dispense with top garments. Flannel trousers, heavy boots without socks and a strong resin-coated felt hat with a convex crown, usually from one to two pounds in weight, were all that most miners could suffer to wear. A thick lump of clay into which a candle was secured was stuck on to the front of the hat (see Fig.4.1, page 84). In certain localities, some 200 fathoms from surface, the water was so hot that the workmen of the 1830s and 40s were obliged to withdraw their feet from it until, by repeated attempts, they became inured to the temperature.

In 1843, water issuing from rock on the 264 fathom level was recorded at 84.50°F, and on the lode at 85°F.[38] In 1855 Henwood recorded that on the 208 level, which had been extended east and west nearly 100 fathoms on the course of the lode, the water issuing from a cross cut was at a temperature of 114°F. 'The men work nearly naked and it is necessary to bring cold water down in pipes to pour over them while working.'[39] Miners who worked there at the last working (1907–29) remembered rigging up galvanised sheeting when drilling, because the water issuing from the fissures in the rock was so hot, it often burnt those stripped to the waist in the stifling heat of the narrow drives. The water was hot enough to warm up a pasty inside a dinner pail in minutes.[40] By the 1920s, Tresavean was approaching the 395 fathom level, the deepest part of the mine, 2370 feet from the surface, where the water was several degrees hotter.

Even more dangerous, were 'air blasts' or 'ground bursting' which commonly resulted in injuries such as broken legs. Air entering cracks in the rock would expand and blow the rock to pieces. In 1874, it was reported that one Tresavean miner had been off work for twelve months because of this phenomenon.[41]

One of the greatest evils on the local mines was the necessity of climbing many hundreds of feet of ladders each shift, particularly for those miners who were suffering from the early stages of phthisis. Henry Vincent, aged 18, reckoned it took him about half an hour climbing to reach the 200 fathom level at Tresavean, where he was employed in 'tramming', pushing a tram wagon along a rail, a job he had been doing for four years. This was 1500 feet from the surface. It took him about an hour's climbing to reach the surface, but he said that he did not feel much tired on 'coming to grass'.

Thomas Dunstan, aged 16, working at the 136 fathom level, 'wheeling stuff', in a type of narrow wheelbarrow, said he liked to come up the ladders 'brave fast', but that he sometimes felt out of breath. James Orby, aged 16, commented that he 'did not think much of the climbing', but that he found it more of an exertion after a core employed at 'rolling' or wheeling stuff.[42]

Older men found the climb far more strenuous. Captain Jennings of Tresavean said that he had come to the mine in 1835, after having been the agent of Cathedral Mine for seven years. His health was good, but had deteriorated over the last two years, and he had suffered in the throat and chest. 'I feel much from climbing the ladders, especially since I had an attack of indigestion, attended with a rash upon the skin, which came on after I took a glass of beer while heated and fatigued with climbing.' Dr Barham's opinion was that the Captain had suffered an attack of urticaria, or 'nettle rash'. He noted that he carried some of the usual signs of dyspepsia about him.[43] Great concern had been expressed over the miners' habits of repairing to a 'wink' (beer shop), immediately on finishing their core, as it was considered to be very injurious to health, as evidenced above.

Climbing ladders involved a certain amount of risk, and there are numerous obituaries in local newspapers of miners who had fallen from ladders on their long climb to grass. In the year 1838–39, four miners were killed by falling in Tresavean. By 1841, the agents at Trethellan and Tresavean had attempted to make the climbing as easy as possible by installing ladders with 10-inch staves, as opposed to the former distance of one foot apart. The new ladders at Trethellan were all of this kind, inclined nearly 2 feet in a fathom, and were five fathoms in length. A platform was supplied at the foot of each, but there was no penthouse over the head of the ladder below. 'The miner would travel 200 fathoms as easily as he would 150 before; there is a great difference in the ease of climbing between the 10 inch and the one foot stave, but it must be adopted on all the ladders alike,' commented Captain Sprague, describing the ladders at Trethellan in 1841. 'Nothing is worse in climbing than to find at one time that you have not lifted your foot far enough, and at another to bang it down upon the bar from having lifted it too high,' he added. 'No accident that I can recollect has happened on our footway.'[44]

In 1841 Trethellan Mine was only 75 fathoms below adit, or 139 fathoms from surface, so it was not difficult to dispense with the old one foot stave, but Tresavean, far deeper, had begun installing the new 10-inch stave ladders by 1841, inclined one foot nine inches in the fathom. 'This is found to be the best inclination for dividing the weight of the body between hands and feet', remarked Captain Joseph Jennings in 1841. 'The miners will go many fathoms out of their way, in order to come up by these ladders,' he added.[45]

In the early days of mining in the area, a variety of means of descent were employed, from lowering miners by rope attached to a windlass, or within a kibble. A windlass was found in recent years in a shaft at Wheal Beauchamp.

The Man Engine

As mines grew deeper, the amount of ladder climbing began to take a toll on the miners' health and output. Tresavean was one of the deepest mines in the county at this period, which meant that the miners, 'had to perform the equivalent of a stiff mountaineering climb in addition to their arduous core.'[46] A drop in earnings for the miners also spelt a fall in the profitability of the mine. In order to solve this problem a prize was offered by the Royal Cornwall Polytechnic Society and Mr C. Fox, in 1834, for the design of a machine which would convey miners up and down the shaft of a mine. Michael Loam and the adventurers of Tresavean Mine won the coveted prize for the first 'man engine' in 1841, even though there was evidence that such a device had been in use in the Hartz Mountains in Germany prior to its 'invention' by Loam. It was however, the first of its kind in Britain. The man engine was based on the traditional Cornish beam pumping engine, and could have been thus easily installed and maintained without incurring heavy expense or changes in working methods. Its original design consisted of two parallel wooden rods which were set up in the shaft, each being fitted with a series of steps or platforms, set 12 feet apart; this was the stroke of the 36-inch beam engine installed at Tresavean.

By the beginning of 1842, the device was installed to a depth of 27 fathoms (powered by a waterwheel, but this arrangement was soon after superseded by the 36-inch steam engine) and the first public trial of the man engine was undertaken. By September 1843 the 264 fathom level had been reached, and the device was finally completed to the 288 fathom level at the bottom of the mine, at a cost of £2601, £500 of which was a gift from the Royal Cornwall Polytechnic Society.[47]

To demonstrate the man engine's safety, pupils from Trevarth Grammar School were taken down 100 fathoms. The shaft was vertical for 70 fathoms, and then followed the lode. The rods moved in contrary directions, the steps on the rods coming opposite to each other at the top and bottom of every stroke. A miner stepping from one side or the other could be carried up or down the shaft in 12 feet stages, facilitating a much safer and speedier ascent and descent in the shaft. William Francis lauded the philanthropy of the adventurers of Tresavean Mine and The Royal Polytechnic Society in his 1845 poem, for installing the man engine:

The engine by which he is raised from below
Now supersedes climbing, health's deadliest foe –
Were such means provided on all our deep mines
The lamented effects of climbing would cease,
Nor exhaustion produce the miners' disease. [48]

However, the celebration which heralded the machine's arrival at Tresavean was to be short lived. Just after the final extension had been completed, the device's safety record was blotted with the death of a 14-year-old boy named Peter Williams. At the changing of the afternoon core, Williams was ascending by the man engine, when, making a false step, he fell a depth of 28 fathoms and was so much injured that he died a short time after having been brought to grass.[49] In mining, one could never eliminate accidents.

Life was the bal, but was the bal life?

From these cavern'd depths, with great labour and pain,
Is drawn the material of commerce and gain;
Ninety thousand carts loads of work, rich and coarse,
Our lodes yearly supply, amazing resource
Of various employment! these honey-comb'd cells
Are pregnant with labour!
... That our mining promotes the general good
Of men, and these arguments can't be withstood.[50]

When reading the lofty verse of poet William Francis, one obtains an essentially idealised view of mining – that which bestowed wealth and prosperity; 'blessed industry', for which the inhabitants of the mining districts were eternally grateful, taking an immense pride in their work of winning and processing the minerals which nature had provided. But this romantic view of the local mineral industry obscures the harsh reality of life for many of those who worked on Gwennap's mines, where disease, accident, death, hunger and monotony at some point touched the lives of the majority of mine workers.

Most people who work long hours relish the opportunity to take a break for something to eat and drink. At most industrial places of work today, a canteen is provided for workers to do so. Not so on the mines in Lanner in the nineteenth century. There were no proper facilities for washing beforehand, and surface workers ate their dinner in an open shed. At Trethellan Mine there was no provision for warming dinners or supplying any warm drinks. Cold water was brought to the surface workers in an 'anker', a small wooden barrel. The bal boys and maidens carried their dinner with them, sometimes a pasty, or more commonly a 'hobban', a coarse kind of cake, prepared by mixing pieces of potato, or sometimes 'figs' (raisins), with a sheet of dough, which was

Fig.4.5. *The blacksmiths at Tresavean mine, c.1925. Harry Polkinghorne, far right.* (© Sylvia Kessell, Redruth).

then rolled up and baked. It was uncommon for a pasty to contain much meat, and if it did, it was usually pork. Since the workers commonly gathered in groups for their dinner, one agent at Trethellan had noticed some of the bal maidens 'steal away' at times to eat their meal behind a hedge, ashamed of the meanness of their fare.[51] He had also noted the faintness of young women at their work, which was, he believed, a consequence of insufficient sustenance. Some workers who lived nearby might have been fortunate to have had a warm pasty brought to the mine for them by a relation, but this only became common at the last working (1907–28).

Miners took their 'crowst' and dinner underground with them, usually the same type of fare as that brought to the mine by the bal boys and maidens at grass, and was eaten if and when it was possible, as no regular time was allowed. Water was taken underground in wooden 'kegs', but at times miners found it impossible to find them. James Orby, who had commenced work at 6am, and completed an eight hour shift beating the borer, and Thomas Dunstan, also underground since 6am 'rolling', had received no water and were very thirsty on coming to grass. Henry Vincent admitted to sweating freely underground at Tresavean.

One can only imagine the discomfort of a dry throat in the choking atmosphere of a narrow drive, with an unquenchable thirst made worse by profuse sweating. Doubtless, this chronic lack of water wrought injurious long-term effects on the inner organs such as the kidneys. Plus, it was often difficult to eat a dry hobban or pasty without a drink of water, as noted by James Orby.

There is no doubt that many workers at the local mines were poorly nourished, as many of the mining families in Lanner lived on or below subsistence level. This makes sad reading when the subject is a child. The amount of food a child received both at work and at home was dependent upon the size and condition of the family. Some children ate well, as in the case of Martha Williams, aged 11, who was described as 'hale and hearty'. Her father had died when she was two, but her resourceful mother had found useful employ in taking in washing. She received wheat and barley bread with milk (probably 'sky blue and sinker'), as much as she could eat for breakfast, pasty with meat in for dinner, and tea and potatoes for supper.[52] However, Tresavean miner James Stevens, aged 15, lived at Redruth and found the walk to his home tiresome. He did not always receive breakfast before departing for his eight hour core, and only took a little bread and butter with him for crowst. He did not eat again until he arrived home, and as there were nine children in his family, did not always eat as much as he would have liked.

After a hard day's work, the walk to and from the mine would not seem quite as tiring for one who enjoyed a good diet. But teenage miners were sometimes required to work a double core, which occurred about once a week on average. Eighteen year old John Tresidder, who lived four miles away at Wendron, admitted to being tired with the walk home after such overtime. And it was not unusual for many children to be expected to help with chores upon their arrival home after a long day at the mine.

With the miner-smallholder existence being very much a feature of life in around Lanner, it is hardly surprising to discover John Henry Martin, 12, and William Harris, 15, in common with many of the local men, working at tasks such as harrowing, weeding and harvesting on the smallholdings which were their homes in their 'out of core time'.

On coming to grass, the provision in the 1840s at Tresavean and Trethellan for the miners to wash and change into dry clothes were quite primitive, although the latter mine did have a crude miners' dry. Miners commonly left their good clothes in the engine house, and most attempted to wash off the worst of the grime in the warm water of the engine pool. A decent miners' dry only came to Tresavean during the last working in the early twentieth century. Consequently, the miners were forced to return home in wet, dirty clothing, and the distances some had to travel were great. It seems barely conceivable today that people worked under such brutal conditions, especially children of such tender years, who were forced by necessity to rise at an hour commonly from 5am, to go to work. Often a walk of several miles had to be taken to reach the mine, through the well walked winding lanes and bridleways of the countryside, and in all winds and weathers. In the winter, this would have been in darkness; fortunate children might have had the soft glow of a lamp to light their way.

After eight hours, the same walk had to be undertaken to return home. Children commonly went to bed at 7 or 8pm, leaving little free time for themselves in what must have appeared a seemingly never-ending cycle of bed-to-work, work-to-bed, punctuated only by the brief respite of the Sabbath. Moreover, some of the children who worked in the mine were scarcely fit to do so. Twelve year John Henry Martin was half lame, having suffered from scrofulous affection of the right hip-joint when he was but six months old. It is heart-rending to read of his proud announcement to the Commissioner in 1841 that 'he could "travel" and play with the other boys', adding that he did not feel any more in that leg than the other. His father died when he was 10, leaving his mother with 12 children to care for, so the poor lad was put to work underground and was expected to climb the ladders, just like the able-bodied boys, his wages of 12 shillings a month doubtless vital to the family's maintenance.[53]

Yet many of the local children who worked on the mines around Lanner in 1841 had similar tragic backgrounds which necessitated them having to work. Sally Fall who began work at age 11, was one of six children, all of whom worked in the mining industry. Her father had died of cancer, and 'his death had obliged them to go to work early'. Richard Jeffrey started work when scarcely eight years old. His father died of cholera in Mexico, leaving his mother with four children. Richard Uren began work at age 9, a year after his father had died of 'a galloping consumption'. William Harris' father died of a 'hurt' when he was three; his mother was left with five children. Mary Ann Rescorle was brought up in the Redruth Workhouse, as her mother could not provide for her. At 12, she considered herself very fortunate to have received board and lodgings with a man called Reed, 'who was kind to her'.[54] These life stories, all tinged with sadness, illustrate the harshness of life for Lanners' labouring poor in the mid nineteenth century. The onus of responsibility often fell on young shoulders and as a result we see children who were, in essence, cheated out of a childhood, forced into premature adulthood and denied access to regular education, as we shall discuss in Chapter 10.

The average age for the 41 miners who worked at Tresavean and Tretharrup in the early 1860s was calculated to be 22.80 years.[55] Miners were old men by their mid forties, as can be seen by the following cases of former Tresavean miners, whilst many never lived long enough to even reach mid life. A 59-year-old from Penventon, who had begun work underground at Tresavean Mine when aged 19, was examined in 1862. He stated that he had worked in the 250 fathom level of the mine for 22 years. He remembered that the air was 'hot, but quite good'. Nevertheless, he was diagnosed as suffering from chronic bronchitis and emphysema, pleuritic effusion, and disease of the stomach. He added that he often worked naked to the waist, and his boots used to be wet through with perspiration.[56]

A 58-year-old miner from Halwin, Wendron, diagnosed with advanced miner's asthma in 1862, also worked at Tresavean in the 250 fathom level. He attributed his illness to a lifetime of climbing the ladders from the hot, wet depths of the mine, and then having to walk four and a half miles home in damp, dirty clothing in all winds and weathers after an eight hour core. His health was so bad that he could not have continued to work there, and for the past four years he had been unable to work at all owing to his condition.[57]

Another miner from Halwin, suffering from miners' asthma, partial paraplegia and commencing general paralysis at 49, was a former Tresavean miner and had a three mile walk to the mine. He attributed his illness to working in poor air, 86 fathoms from adit.[58] A miner from Porkellis was in dire health by 41 years of age, after 21 years' work at

Tresavean. He also had a four mile walk to work each day, and attributed his illness, miners' asthma (phthisis), to working in cold, damp and poor air.[59] In 1841, James Stevens, described as 'worn and exhausted' and looking much older than his 40 years, found he seldom had the strength to work double cores anymore.

The Health of Towns Association returns for 1841 showed that the average age of all who died in the Redruth district was 28 years, four months, the lowest of any district in Cornwall. Undoubtedly this was due to the high proportion of the population employed in mining in that district.

Mining – A Dangerous Trade

Local mid nineteenth century society was completely dominated by the copper mining industry, which made widows and fatherless children indiscriminately. The Gwennap Vestry Book of 1836 noted this fact with the entry: 'Now from the nature of the mines' occupation the average duration of male lives is from accidents and other causes, very materially shortened and in consequence, the number of widows with young families is very large'.[60] The 1851 Census for Lanner, provides further evidence of this. One hundred and fifty three widows were listed, which constituted 19.5 per cent of the adult female population. By contrast only 17 widowers were noted. In one year alone, 1838–39, there were seven deaths at Tresavean. One occurred at surface, the unfortunate victim entangled in machinery. Six more fatalities were recorded underground; two died during blasting, and four from falling.

The children of incapacitated or deceased miners were always given precedence when jobs at the local mines were allocated, to help provide some degree of financial relief for the unfortunate wife. This contributed to the growth of child labour. As we have seen above, local children perished in the great mines of Cornwall's 'Copper Kingdom', but blame never seemed to be apportioned to the mine management. When Lanner boy Thomas Henry Bosanko, aged 9, died at Copper Hill Mine near Redruth in 1861, in consequence of some boards tied to a crushing machine falling on him, an inquest held at Lanner typically returned a verdict of accidental death.[61]

Walking funerals were a common sight in the last century, and were events which united a community in grief. In 1857, more than 3000 people attended the putting to rest of a Lanner miner killed at West Basset Mine.[62] Henwood describes a similar funeral at Stithians of a miner, Nicholas Hill, killed by a rock fall in Tresavean mine. Married a year, and with one child, the young widow was sent a sovereign by Michael Williams (who was one of the chief adventurers in Tresavean, and a well known local landowner), and two sovereigns by Billy Martin, the Mine Captain. Several thousand men and women were in the procession, led by a Methodist minister, who gave out hymns sung by the choirs of several local chapels, over 80 male and female voices. He was followed by Cap'n Billy Martin, and other agents of the mine, in deep mourning, the bearers and the family. They walked three miles to the church, and after the service the choirs repaired to the various public houses to sing their hymns over again.[63]

In 1828 two fatal accidents occurred at Penstruthal Mine; the first involved a miner named Spargo who suffocated to death after a large quantity of earth fell on him when a stull collapsed. Hitchens, his colleague, remembered his friend's last words, 'God have mercy on me!' as he ran off to find a shovel to dig him out.

John Moyle, speaking at the inquest into the death of Anthony Cock, related how he had been ascending at the end of his core, and upon reaching the 20 fathom level, the deceased had asked for his assistance in freeing a kibble which had become hitched in the shaft. Moyle recalled that Cock suddenly became pale and was heard to exclaim, 'O Lord, O Lord'. Moyle had no sooner uttered, 'Don't faint!' when he saw the man fall away into the shaft.

In 1839, an old man named Benbow met his death at Tresavean whilst adjusting the machinery of a whim, the crank wheel of which struck him and literally severed his head from his body.[64]

Even the improved safety standards of the twentieth century could not eradicate accidents. In 1915 John Richard Benny was blown up in an explosion whilst sinking Old East Shaft, due, it was believed, to a miscalculation of the burning rate of a fuse.[65] On 23 August 1917, three Tresavean miners working in Harvey's Shaft met their untimely end by drilling into an unexploded charge which had been left in situ when sinking the shaft. John Henry Vickers Curnow, a well known local preacher, aged 37, John Moyle, a past Grand Master of the Lannarth Lodge of Oddfellows, aged 37 and Francis Gluyas Pryor Collins aged 16, were the victims.

When Mr Curnow was buried at Gwennap Churchyard, about 2000 people walked in procession to attend his interment, and the route to the church was thronged with people who solemnly paid their respects. Shops in the village were closed and curtains drawn in deference to the three victims.

In 1921, another sad fatality occurred at Tresavean when Mr Richard Ripper, a 33-year-old married man with a young child, fell from the 75 fathom level to the bottom of Harvey's Shaft, a distance of 1500 feet. An act of clearing some guttering had, it was thought, caused him to overbalance and fall to his death. A verdict of 'accidental death' was recorded at the inquest.[66]

The price in human terms of extracting Cornwall's mineral wealth from the ground was high. As well as deaths, accidents which blinded, maimed, disfigured, or led to long-term injuries were also frequent. If a job 'at grass' was not secured, the miner found himself cast on to parochial relief, unless he was resourceful or fortunate enough to forge a new 'career' hawking sand, vegetables, furze or some other commodity from a barrow or cart. 'Blind Stephen' Moyle, of Rough Street, who lost his sight in a mine accident abroad became a well known tea dealer in the Lanner area, whilst blinded 'Billy Sandman' of St Day hawked sand for cottage floors in the Gwennap area.

In 1841, Elisha Williams aged 27, was reported to have 'recently caught a hurt' in beating the borer, and as a consequence, had been unable to do any hard work at Tresavean since. John Crougy, 44 in 1841, was employed as captain over the trammers at Tresavean. He had been underground since age 15, and spent 20 years at the mine. He had received a blow to his side from a wagon, aggravating an old wound, resulting in his being employed only on light tasks.[67]

		£.	s.	d.	
Constance, 21 years old, earns	.	0	15	0	per month.
John, 19 „	.	2	0	0	„
Richard, 17 „	.	1	6	0	„
James, 14 „	.	0	16	0	„
Elizabeth, 12 „	.	0	2	0	„
Total with his own wages		£7	10	0	

The monthly expenses are these:—

	£	s.	d.
"Shop," i. e. flour, barley, soap, starch, tea, butter, &c.	3	10	0
Coals and candles	0	8	0
Market, (meat, &c.)	1	0	0
Shoes, and clothes	1	5	0
Sundries	0	15	0
	£6	18	0

Fig.4.6 *Typical earnings of a Gwennap family, 1841.* (1841 Children's Employment Commission, British Parliamentary Papers)

In 1915, shift Boss James Paull was thrown out of the cage at Tresavean, which instead of being lowered, was hoisted up towards the headgear where his right arm was smashed against the grizzly bars, due to the forgetfulness of the engine driver. He fell 20 feet, and his badly mangled arm had to be amputated.[68]

Miners were required to pay 'doctor's pence', and club money; the latter, a weekly levy, was supposed to ensure, in the absence of any type of public welfare, that a few shillings were paid to the family of a man killed, injured or incapacitated. At Trethellan in 1841, the deduction of doctor's pence amounted to about 2d of John Henry Martin's wages of 12 shillings a month. A pare might pay over five shillings for 'doctor and club', as can be seen in the examples of Trethellan pay in 1841 (Fig.4.4). Often, the sum of these funds realised a considerable amount. Doctor's pence usually provided surgical assistance only, and the bal surgeon it must be noted, never ventured underground however serious the accident. The injured miner would have to have been moved as carefully as possible and hoisted to surface, often in a kibble or skip, resulting in a significant and often fatal delay in the giving of initial treatment.

The following scene occurred at Tresavean in 1833. Richard Prisk and his partner William Dower were working on the 166 fathom level, when 40 year old Prisk was killed by the belated discharge of a missed hole (a charge which had failed to ignite at the correct time). Dower escaped unhurt. As Prisk's remains were being fastened in a kibble to be hauled to grass, a stone fell away from the upper part of the shaft and struck Thomas Odgers on the head, placing his life in considerable jeopardy. Odgers had been assisting in the gruesome task of placing his dead comrade into the kibble. The corpse was thereupon removed, and Odgers, about to die, was placed in the kibble instead to be hoisted to grass where the bal surgeon could attend to him.[69]

Life at Subsistence Level

That life was undoubtedly harsh for a high percentage of Lanners' miners is evident. Many families lived just above subsistence level, requiring the whole family to work to provide a reasonable standard of living, as can be seen by the example of a 'respectable' Gwennap mining family of 1841 (Fig.4.6). The miner's age was 47, his wife was 45. They had been married 26 years and had 12 children. Of those, four had died, and one had married. Rent for this family was formerly paid at £4 per year, but a neat substantial house was reported to have been built on lease, with a good garden, and almost paid for. The whole family were said to be 'comfortable and respectable'. However, it would have been impossible to have had over a pound left after expenses every month, had the eldest children not worked on the mines. The head of the household's highest wages had been 55 shillings a month, and the whole 'gettings' of the family in 1841 are shown in Fig.4.6.

By contrast, mine count houses were often very sumptuous, especially those on the larger and more successful mines such as Tresavean, which was reputed to have displayed considerable opulence. Henwood, writing in the *Mining Journal*, commented on that of Wheal Basset, which boasted magnificent oak furniture and walls hung with impressive charts, plans and drawings of the mine workings. He considered it to be little short of a miniature hotel with its air of opulence, stables, servants, fine food and refreshment, but remarked that Tresavean's count house was 'still more handsome than Basset's.'[70]

The Counting House at Tresavean was an L-shaped building with a hipped roof and was situated directly behind a coal yard at the end of the tramway. Here, the mine captains and adventurers, interested visitors, and other local socialites were entertained at the mine's expense, and banquets and dinners, of a kind beyond the imagination of the poor miners who sweated out a living in the hellish subterranean world beneath the count house, were regularly held. (Fig.4.7).

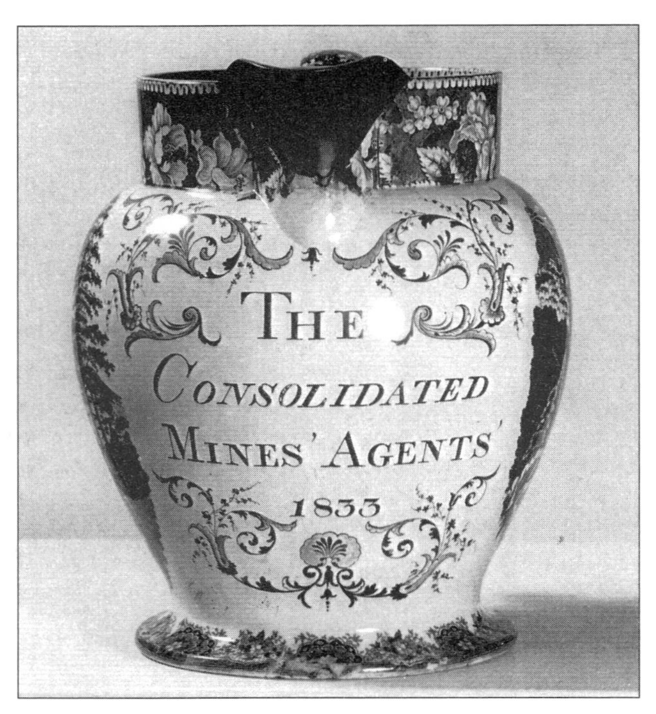

Fig.4.7. *Fine chinaware graced the tables of many local count houses. This example comes from Consolidated Mines, Gwennap, 1833.* (© Royal Institution of Cornwall).

But the tendency to cast the mine in a wholly unfavourable light must however be tempered. On the whole, it would seem that the miners were intensely proud of their work at the mines, and valued the independence it gave them when working as tributers, lamenting the loss of this independence when contract work became more the norm towards the mid nineteenth century. And the rapport between miner and management was often very good, as evidenced by the above example of charity on behalf of the Tresavean Management on the occasion of Nicholas Hill's funeral. In many ways, the large mine replaced the normal country village as a social focus, and it is probably true that the focus of Lanner as a village decreased in significance as the mines collapsed and mining was no longer the main source of employment, as we shall analyse in Chapter 11. In bad times, such as those at the end of the eighteenth century, starving miners at mines like Tresavean were given barley and fish by the mine, and the accounts for this were noted in the cost book. Mineral lords were known to forego their dues, and to pay dole to the starving poor.

It is certain Lanner would not have developed into the thriving community it was in the nineteenth century, had it not been for the wealth which was wrought below ground, nor benefited from the improvement to many hundreds of acres of non productive wasteland. The following description of 1844, aptly sums up that development:

The external features of these mining districts are peculiar - for, although occasionally we see the machinery and rubbish of a mine in the centre of a fertile spot, sterility in general marks the surface which covers mineral treasures; moors, enlivened only by the furze and heath, or granite hills, bare of vegetation, are most commonly the scenes of mining operations. The landscape, as Nature left it, is one of desolation - but a productive mine is discovered, and the scene is changed. White-washed cottages thickly cover the soil - the transforming effects of industry; and the vegetables for use, and flowers for ornament, grow in these cottage gardens. In the centre of this scene of life, the tall house, and its taller chimney, of the steam engine are seen.[71]

Legislature and Change in Working Conditions

The results of the two commissions of 1841 and 1864, eventually led to Government legislation. In 1872, the Metalliferous Mines Regulation Act introduced official mines inspections and important safety regulations, and prevented boys under twelve from working underground, while those under sixteen were not allowed to work for more than ten hours a day. The Factory and Workshop Act of 1878 prevented women and children from working at surface, chiefly in ore dressing, for more than twelve hours a day, including an hour-and-a-half for meals. For young persons, there was a maximum 30-hour working week and no night work. Conditions were improving, but this was at a time when the availability of employment for local people was diminishing as the process of de-industrialisation in the area began. The 'Copper Kingdom' that was Gwennap, had, since the 1860's, entered a period of terminal decline and great concern was expressed as bal after bal was 'knacked' in the Lanner area. The tin mining industry did not require the large female workforce which the copper mines had. People were faced with the threat of unemployment resulting from over specialisation and over dependence on the copper mining industry, promoting a huge emigration as we shall see in Chapter 8.

When Tresavean Mine obtained a new lease of life in the twentieth century it was as a tin producer. This did not require the labour-intensive methods of ore refinement which had characterised its years as a copper producer, thus limiting the opportunity of employment, for women in particular. The era of the bal maiden had passed in Lanner, as had the very worst abuses of child labour. Improvements in safety and social conditions had occurred at Tresavean for those employed there during the last working (Fig.4.8). A miners' dry for example, had been built which was able to accommodate 300 miners who could wash and change into clean, dry clothing before returning home. However, men daily worked in the calciners at the surface, shovelling arsenic powder, obtained as a by product from the roasting of the tin ore, with only plugs of cotton wool inside the nose and a damp handkerchief over the mouth to prevent inhalation of the arsenic dust. The job would not be carried out today under such circumstances, but was viewed with no great alarm then. Wilfred Bray junior, working in the calciner in the 1920s, nonchalantly commented, 'Did you ever hear of anyone dying of arsenic poisoning on a Cornish mine?'[72]

Fig.4.8 Group of men at Tresavean Mine c.1914. (© The Paddy Bradley Collection).

For our Victorian forbears, life without the bal seemed barely conceivable to those who for generations had relied on it for their livelihood.

It seems appropriate here to let William Francis, describing Lanner's wide valley in 1845, have the last word, as he so aptly summed up the attitude of the contemporary mining generation, to whom for better or worse, the bal was life:

The prospect of riches may flatter the hope
That the mines which are found along this wide slope
Will long call for labour above and below,
Which duly rewarded will comfort bestow.
A vast population increasing around
Depend for subsistence on work underground;
'Mines are not productive of fruit or of grain.'
True - but they yield work and do myriads maintain.[73]

REFERENCES

1 Barton, D.B., *Essays in Cornish Mining History: 1*, Bradford Barton, Truro, 1968, p. 14.
2 Children's Employment Commission, Report by Charles Barham, Esq., M.D., 1841, pp. 823-4
3 Burke G., The Decline of the Independent Bâl Maiden, Angela John, ed., *Unequal Opportunities*, Blackwell, 1986, p.183.
4 Children's Employment Commission, Report by Charles Barham, Esq., M.D., 1841, p. 822
5 Ibid, p. 821
6 Ibid., p. 827
7 Barton, D.B., *Essays in Cornish Mining History: 1*, Bradford Barton, Truro, 1968, p. 56.
8 Children's Employment Commission, Report by Charles Barham, Esq., M.D., 1841, p. 823.
9 *Ladies Journal of the Court, Fashion and Society, Volume 2*, no. 29, 2/10/1872. The Work Done by Women in the British Isles: The Bâl Maiden.
10 Burke G., The Decline of the Independent Bâl Maiden, Angela John, ed., *Unequal Opportunities*, Blackwell, 1986, p. 186.
11 *Ladies Journal*, 1 2/10/1872.
12 Noall, Cyril, 'The Cornish Bal Maiden', *Cornish Magazine, Vol. 4*, part 6, 1961, p. 179.
13 Children's Employment Commission, Report by Charles Barham, Esq., M.D., 1841, p. 845.
14 Ibid. p. 822.
15 Ibid., p. 824.
16 Burke G., The Decline of the Independent Bâl Maiden, Angela John, ed., *Unequal Opportunities*, Blackwell, 1986, p. 184.
17 Valenze, Deborah, *First Industrial Woman*, Oxford University Press, New York, 1995; see also Koditschek, Theodore, The Gendering of the British Working Class, *Gender and History, Vol 9, No. 2*, August 1997, p. 342
18 Private Communication from Mr Walter Langford, Redruth, 1998.
19 James, C.C., *History of Gwennap*, Privately Published, 1944, p. 242. To 'lobby' means to toss.
20 Henwood, G., *Cornwall's Mines and Miners*, Burt, R. (ed.), Bradford Barton, Truro, 1972, p.120.
21 *West Briton*, 30/6/1870.
22 Clarke, Anna, *The Struggle for the Breeches: Gender and the Making of the British Working Class*, Univ. of Carolina Press, Berkeley, 1995, pp. 11-88.

23 Children's Employment Commission, Report by Charles Barham, Esq., M.D., 1841, p. 829.
24 Ibid., p. 833.
25 Clarke, Anna, *The Struggle for the Breeches: Gender and the Making of the British Working Class*, University of Carolina Press, Berkeley, 1995, pp. 220-63.
26 *West Briton*, 25/11/1831.
27 *West Briton*, 6/2/1829.
28 P 79/8/1, Vestry Meeting, 17/7/1839, CRO.
29 Children's Employment Commission, Report by Charles Barham, Esq., M.D., 1841, p. 824.
30 Ibid., p. 821.
31 Report of the Commissioners into the Conditions of all the Mines in Great Britain, 1864, G.E. Eyre and W. Spottiswoode, pp. 821-822.
32 *Mining Journal*, 27/1/1883.
33 Report of the Commissioners into the Conditions of all the Mines in Great Britain, 1864, G.E. Eyre and W. Spottiswoode, p. 439.
34 Children's Employment Commission, Report by Charles Barham, Esq., M.D., 1841, pp. 821-822.
35 Children's Employment Commission, Report by Charles Barham, Esq., M.D., 1841, p. 737
36 Second Report of the Royal Commission on Metalliferous Mines and Quarries, 1914, pp. 128-133.
37 *Mining Journal*, 26/7/1856, p. 495.
38 Henwood, J., *Transactions of the Royal Geological Society of Cornwall, Vol V.*
39 Tresavean MSS, CRO.
40 Private Communication with Mr Rodney Nute, 1997.
41 *Cornubian*, 10/7/1874.
42 Children's Employment Commission, Report by Charles Barham, Esq., M.D., 1841, pp. 825 & 842.
43 Ibid., p. 824.
44 Ibid., p. 821.
45 Ibid., p. 824.
46 Noall, Cyril., *Cornish Mine Disasters*, Dyllansow Truran, Redruth, 1989, p. 33.
47 *Mining Journal*, 22/6/1844, p. 211.
48 Francis, William, *Gwennap, A Descriptive Poem in Seven Cantos*, J. May, Redruth, 1845, pp. 17-18.
49 *Mining Journal*, 30/9/1843.
50 Francis, William, *Gwennap, A Descriptive Poem in Seven Cantos*, J. May, Redruth, 1845, pp. 60-61.
51 Children's Employment Commission, Report by Charles Barham, Esq., M.D., 1841, p. 821.
52 Ibid., p. 823.
53 Ibid., p. 822.
54 Ibid., pp. 822,826, 827, 828, 846.
55 Report of the Commissioners into the Conditions of all the Mines in Great Britain, 1864, G.E. Eyre and W. Spottiswoode, p. 432.
56 Ibid., pp. 104-5
57 Ibid., pp. 46-47.
58 Ibid.
59 Ibid., pp., 48-49.
60 P 79/8/1, CRO.
61 *West Briton*, 2/8/1861.
62 *Mining Journal*, 12/12/1857.
63 Henwood, G., *Cornwall's Mines and Miners*, Burt, R. (ed.), Bradford Barton, Truro, 1972, pp. 12-14.
64 *Royal Cornwall Gazette*, 31/5/1828; *West Briton*, 4/10/1839.
65 *Cornubian*, 23/9/1915.
66 *Cornubian*, 24/11/1921.
67 Children's Employment Commission, Report by Charles Barham, Esq., M.D., 1841, p. 822.
68 *Cornubian*, 30/9/1915.
69 *West Briton*, 8/3/1833.
70 Henwood, G., *Cornwall's Mines and Miners*, Burt, R. (ed.), Bradford Barton, Truro, 1972, p. 21.
71 *Mining Journal*, 22/6/1844.
72 Private Communication with Mr John Bray, Redruth, 1996.
73 Francis, William, *Gwennap, A Descriptive Poem in Seven Cantos*, J. May, Redruth, 1845, p. 19.

Chapter 5
Quarrying

In Cornwall there are five large bodies or 'plutons' of granite, the Isles of Scilly, Land's End, Carnmenellis, St Austell and Bodmin. In addition to these larger granites, there are numerous smaller bodies, including Tregonning Hill, Carn Brea, Carn Marth, St Agnes, Cligga Head, Kit Hill and Gunnislake. These granites rise from a large parent body, the Cornubian Batholith, which extends from the Isles of Scilly to Dartmoor.

Granite was formed from the melting of rocks deep within the earth's crust between 300 and 270 million years ago. The granite magma was of a low density and rose through the crust to a relatively high level and crystallised during slow cooling. The granites of Cornwall are composed of the minerals quartz, feldspar and mica, generally with a little tourmaline, and vary considerably in appearance from one locality to another, fine grained equigranular types contrasting with the coarsely grained varieties in which large individual feldspar crystals are scattered. It is not uncommon to find dykes or veins of a fine-grained granitic rock usually of a pale grey colour, locally known as 'grey elvan', within the granite which can occur up to several metres in size.[1] These were produced by an injection of granite magma up a subvertical crack, which cooled the magma quickly.

The exploitation of 'moorstone'

In the Lanner area, there are two granite regions, those of Carn Marth and the north-eastern section of the Carnmenellis granite, which ends in the area of Tresavean and Tretharrup. The southern margin of the Carn Marth granite approaches within thirty yards of the Carnmenellis granite at Pennance at the surface. Surrounding the granite intrusions of Carn Marth and Carnmenellis the sedimentary rocks, known locally as 'killas', have been metamorphosed, or altered, producing a hard slate type rock ideal for building. Granite has probably been quarried in the Lanner area long before written records begin.

Prehistoric man realised the value of granite as a good building material, utilising the attractive stone with its flecks of shiny mica set in quartz and feldspar for the building of chambered tombs such as those found at Penwith. From the beginning of the Christian era, early stone masons had learned how to exploit the naturally occurring 'moorstones' (large granite boulders) which lay strewn across the upland regions of the peninsula from Lands End to Dartmoor as clitter (the geological term for moorstone), to craft the wayside crosses which can still be seen in various locations, and some churchyards. Later, masons in the Middle Ages worked the same moorstone into blocks to build churches such as Gwennap and St Euny, Redruth. William Francis comments on the arches of Gwennap Church in his poem of 1845: 'fairly proportion'd in granite are seen, and freestone, with Gothic wide arches between. The columns all granite and fluted convey to the mind what effect if polished they would doubtless produce...'[2]

Here in Cornwall, the granite industry began to gather momentum around the beginning of the nineteenth century. Stone for the Eddystone Lighthouse had been taken from the Constantine area in 1759, placing Cornwall on the map as a granite producing region. Until 1809 all gunpowder, the explosive used to quarry stone, had to be imported into Cornwall, but the opening of the Cosawes Wood Gunpowder Works in 1809, and the larger Kennall Vale Works in 1812, near Ponsanooth, meant that the quarry industry could really take off. (The word quarry comes from the Latin 'quadraria' meaning a place where squared stones are cut.).[3]

By the middle of the nineteenth century much of the local moorstone had already been taken for field hedges, cottages and farm buildings, millstones, stiles, drinking troughs and gate posts. These surface stones, which were in many cases partly decomposed, were not really suitable for large-scale engineering and commercial projects. A better quality granite was needed, which could resist heavy pressure or wear.

The easier procurement of blasting powder coincided with the Industrial Revolution which was gathering momentum all over Britain, creating a demand for stone for civil and engineering projects. Quarries could now be excavated into the sides of hills, making the large-scale recovery of good quality stone possible, and the decades after 1810 saw quarries opened all over the granite regions of the county.

Cornish granite is in general much coarser in texture than that found in other parts of the British Isles, and its unique formation gives it the advantage of being found in larger and more regular masses or beds. Its composition also allowed it to be cheaply worked by masons into the various shaped blocks required for large-scale works, such as the creation of docks, harbours, breakwaters, civil buildings, engineering works and monuments, and also for 'casting stones' – moulds supplied to the South Wales smelters for casting the ingots of copper. The granite industry in Cornwall was to become extremely important, especially in the latter half of the nineteenth century, in engineering and construction, and valuable as a labour factor, but an industry often overshadowed by mining.

At Lower Tretharrup, a part of the Carnmenellis outcrop, an intrusive granite of a very fine-grained type, occurring within the predominant coarser-grained stone, had been quarried from the middle of the nineteenth century. This vein was about 15 yards wide, thinning in a south-westerly direction.[4] It was quarried for stone for local building purposes, and had ceased production by the turn of the century. Another quarry was worked in the early nineteenth century for 'killas' (metamorphosed clay), seen on the OS Map to the north-west of Highburrow Shaft, and was opened possibly to supply the stone needed to construct the engine houses on Penstruthal Mine.

But Carn Marth was by far the more important of the stone producing areas of Lanner Parish, and here commercial quarrying was carried on for almost 200 years. From whatever direction one views this distinctive hill (which forms an irregular intrusion between two and three square miles in size), several disused quarries, some of which fall inside Lanner Parish boundary, stand out on its surface as gaping scars. In years gone by, tons of granite have been removed from the hill for use in construction and engineering projects, both locally and further afield.

That Carn Marth was a location where granite was readily available, was realised by the residents of Redruth and district in the eighteenth century. The area had seen a large influx of people seeking work in the mines around the town, and in order to accommodate the rising population, many existing houses were enlarged and extended, and new cottages built. Doubtless, many of the lines of miners' cottages constructed in the villages of Lanner, Trevarth St Day and Carharrack, as well as those at neighbouring Redruth, were built using worked moorstone.

The walls of many dwellings in the district are constructed of irregularly shaped stones, in all likelihood carried away from Carn Marth. For years people had been illegally taking moorstone from the hill, an abuse which became so obvious, that William Jenkin of Trewirgie House, Redruth, had to pay 6d in 1776 for publishing and displaying a notice in the town forbidding people from, 'cutting stones in Carn Marth.'[5]

Commercial stone cutting was going on at Carn Marth in 1813, as James Buller Esq., landowner, was erecting 'landmarks' to delineate the boundaries of his land; the markers were of Carn Marth granite and a bill showed that he paid a driver, one Benjamin Nicholls, 10 shillings a day for the rental of a cart to go to Carn Marth to collect and convey the boundary stones.[6] Again in 1824, granite was taken from the carn for use as sleepers in the construction of the Redruth & Chasewater Railway. The operators were buying granite sleepers for the generous sum of one shilling apiece.[7]

Five shallow quarries on the southern flank of Carn Marth, producing granite and killas, probably date from the latter part of the eighteenth century, are shown on a map produced by Richard Carveth for the Edgcumbe Estate in 1827.[8] Three of them are deeper than the others and show a north rock face, formed as they were cut horizontally deeper into the gradient of the hill. The largest of these quarries was approximately 40 yards north-to-south, and 33 yards east-to-west, and was shown on the map as being about 95 yards from Pennance Road, and directly above Ting Tang's West Adit shaft.

Two quarries situated at Carn Marth Cove, near Carharrack, are about 70 yards from Pennance Road, and their dimensions are 33 yards north-to-south, by 22 yards east-to-west, and 30 yards north-to-south by 23 yards east-to-west. The deepest of these quarries is located in the centre of the carn's southern flank, 130 yards from Pennance Road, being approximately 50 yards north-to-south, by 22 yards east-to-west.

These shallow predecessors bear little resemblance to the larger quarries which were to be excavated on the carn in the mid nineteenth century, but provide excellent examples of the type of limited working for stone which occurred before the local quarry industry really took off. It is possible that one of the quarries supplied a limited amount of granite for the sleepers for the Redruth & Chasewater Railway, the track of which ran close by. Since those nearest Pennance Road also produced killas, it is possible that stone for building some of the new dwellings, being erected in the rapidly developing village of Carharrack, came from them, as well as road stone and the granite and killas used to build the engine houses which once stood on Ting Tang Mine, situated on the downs just below Carn Marth. Today, these early 'quarries' are difficult to determine, being but shallow depressions in the hillside, much in-filled with vegetation.

Francis remarks that granite was also required for the installation of the steam engines at work on Gwennaps' mines: 'next the cylinder's bed of granite composed, well cut for the purpose, and skilfully clos'd where the cylinder rests...'[9] Granite was also required for the base stones for the Cornish stamps of which there were many in the area, ensuring a local demand for granite from the beginnings of the industrialisation of Gwennap Parish.

In the late 1700s and the early 1800s, Redruth lay at the heartland of Cornish Methodism, the impact of which left its mark on the physical appearance of the town. In November of 1825, an agreement was drawn up for the building of the Wesley Chapel at the top of Station Hill. The front wall of this imposing structure was to be of 'the finest Carn Marth granite.'[10] It was opened on 31 December 1826.

Chapels were springing up all over the area in the nineteenth century, and those built at the beginning of the century were at intervals enlarged and extended, each subsequent design to be more imposing, and grander than the places of worship of rival denominations. The majority of these alterations used granite as a building material.

During the 1840's, several such improvements and renovations were made to Lanner Wesley Chapel. Numerous references were made to stone being conveyed from Carn Marth for building purposes: 'Samuel Gray, bill for men raising moorstone, 6d,' 'Lord Clinton, land lief for moorstone, £1.14,' 'John Greeg, rising stone, 350 perches, 11 perch, £16.0.10,' 'Thomas Cornish, carriage of moorstone, 8s,' 'William Michell, carriage of stone from Carn Marth, £1.0.0.'[11]

It seems likely that the members of the congregation had decided on the use of moorstone, as it was far cheaper than purchasing dressed stone. Some of the more irregular blocks from which Lanner Wesley is built appear to be of moorstone, and Lord Clinton was paid for stone taken from his land. Likewise the 1903 renovation used granite from Carn Marth to construct the new front given by Mr J. Davey, formerly of Tocopilla, and the granite ball at the front end of the roof was crafted by Harry Blight, a local stonemason.[12]

In 1900 a memorial was erected in Lanner Square by Miss Pascoe in memory of her deceased sister Maud, in the form of a public fountain. 'The fountain will be of chaste design and of Carn Marth granite,' reported a local newspaper.[13] Without a doubt, granite was one of the chief building materials in the parish for much of the nineteenth century, and the primary source of both moorstone and dressed blocks was Carn Marth.

The growing quarry industry provided jobs for many local men; John Tregoning of 'Gwennap Moors' (Lanner Moor) was described as a 40-year-old moorstone cutter on the 1841 Census, and details contained within the 1851 and 1861 Census returns for the Parish of Gwennap show that several families were dependent on the industry at Carn Marth, with the head of the household being employed as a stone cutter or mason. The granite quarries of Lanner were to become a very important labour factor, particularly when the mining industry went into decline. Furthermore, these families had moved into the area from elsewhere in Cornwall, doubtless attracted to a rapidly industrialising region, requiring increasing amounts of granite and leading to the opening of new quarries. Francis, in his descriptive poem of Gwennap (1845), remarks that Carn Marth's granite was, 'for strength and for corners renowned,' and that it had often, 'been exported the country around,'[14] providing evidence that granite quarrying had clearly been going on for some time.

The Cornish Granite and Freestone Company

By the 1880s, Carn Marth was well established locally as a quarrying area, and its stone had acquired its own name. 'Quarries have been opened on Carn Marth Hill near Redruth, and from the few samples of the stone we saw, it appears to be a good material. It is known as Redruth Granite, and is much used locally'.[15] The area near the summit of the carn was worked for granite from around the 1850s. The *West Briton* of 9 January 1868 reported on a memorandum it had received, detailing the registration of a new company, The Carn Marth Cornish Granite Quarries Company, to acquire the leasehold interest in the Carn Marth Granite Quarries, with a capital of £6000. Two thousand shares were offered at £3 per share and the company was granted full right to acquire and erect machinery and to sell usable granite and stone. Interestingly, the memorandum was signed by men exclusively from Manchester: William Herbert, grocer; Lester Jeffery, merchant; John Tinling, commercial clerk; James Pontey, inn-keeper; William Burrows, currier; Thomas Dunning, corn-factor and Joseph Davis, warehouse-man. Again we have evidence of the rising commercial power of distant cities, whose residents were keen to put up money for distant ventures. Perhaps the company hoped to market their Carn Marth granite in Manchester. It is not clear which quarries this company planned to work, but it is likely to have been two quarries at the summit (Grid reference number SW 7164 4082).

However, it appears the enterprise was not long lived, for by the 1880s those two quarries (which were eventually blasted into one large one, now flooded), were being worked by the Cornish Granite and Freestone Company (CGFC), of 77 Fore Street, Redruth (Map. B). This company also exploited the surface moorstone (hence the word 'freestone'), and ran the quarry facing Pennance, which was not quarried extensively for stone until the close of the nineteenth century, and about which more will be discussed below.

By far the most successful and commercial enterprise operating on the carn, this company supplied granite for some of the most ambitious, prestigious and elegant buildings in Redruth and district, and elsewhere in England. The Director was James Hicks, FRIBA, MSA (Fig. 5.1). A lease

Fig.5.1. *James Hicks, major shareholder and director of the Cornish Granite & Freestone Company, Redruth.* (© Frank Chappell, Redruth)

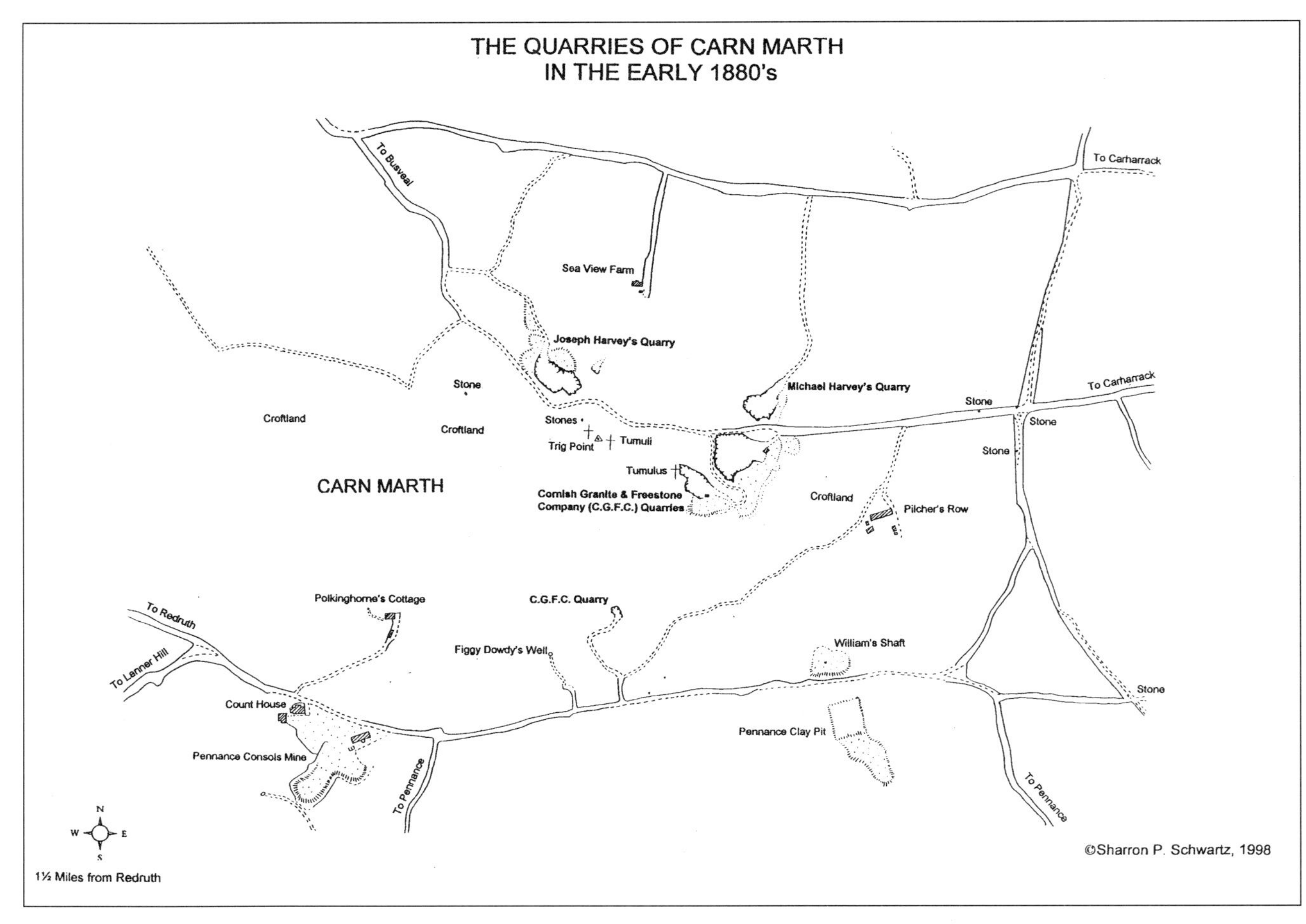

Map B. The Carn Marth Quarries in the early 1880s (based on the 1880 O.S.Map).

dated 24 June 1883 was made between Sir Redvers Buller, and James Hicks, architect, granting the lessee full and free liberty to operate quarries on Carn Marth; an indenture between the same dated 18 April 1887 for a term of 21 years, empowered Hicks, his agents, workmen and servants, 'to use, work, dig and so extend the quarries, rock beds and pits situate at Pennance, in the Parish of Gwennap'. The dues were one fourth of a sixpence on every ton of granite raised. (A similar lease would have been obtained from Lord Clinton, as the land was held jointly. His dues would have been three fourths of a sixpence on every ton raised, as he was the chief landowner.). The lease granted permission to erect machinery and workshops, but Hicks had to keep accurate records of granite sales, which could be subject to scrutiny by Buller or his agent(s) at any time. This also applied to the premises.[16]

Born in Redruth on November 10, 1846, James Hicks was the youngest son of John Hicks, the surveyor of Redruth Parish. He was educated at the prestigious Trevarth School, and was afterwards articled with John Watson of Torquay, an architect and surveyor. On his return to Cornwall, Hicks rapidly became a success, one of his first local projects being the extension and redesign of imposing shop premises of brick, granite and Bath stone at Fore Street (which later

Fig.5.2. *John Hicks (elder brother of James), manager of the Cornish Granite & Freestone Company, Redruth.* (© Frank Chappell, Redruth)

became Woolworths) in 1870 for Messrs Trounsons, prominent and wealthy Redruth merchants. In the same year he redesigned Tolvean House at West End, Redruth, for a very powerful Redruth businessman, Alfred Lanyon. Lanyon proved a good contact for the aspiring Hicks who designed, rebuilt, or extended the houses of several of his wealthy associates. These commissions included Trevarno, for William Bickford-Smith, owner of the Tuckingmill fuse factory and MP for Truro; Treliske, for William Teague, mining entrepreneur and Director of the Cornish Bank; and Mellingey, at Perranarworthal, for a Lanner man, John Jose, who had made a fortune in Latin American mines and smelting works.

Hicks went on to design numerous buildings of note in Cornwall, including The Coffee Tavern and Masonic Hall at Redruth, the Passmore Edwards Art Gallery at Newlyn, the new City Bank at Truro (now Barclays Bank) and numerous chapels such as Plain an Gwarry Methodist Chapel, St Day Primitive Methodist Chapel, the Wesleyan Memorial Hall and Baptist Chapel at Redruth, Lanreath Wesley Chapel and the Free Methodist Chapel at Truro.

Hicks also designed various Board Schools following the 1870 Education Act, including those at Treleigh, East End, Tuckingmill, Camborne, Kehelland and Penponds. He was the architect responsible for the design of the office buildings at Bickford Smith's Fuse Factory at Tuckingmill, the biscuit factory of Messrs Hosken, Trevithick, Polkinhorn & Co. at Hayle, and the restoration of St Euny Church, Redruth, to which he gave a granite font. Many of these buildings incorporated granite, some of which came from his quarries.

Hicks enjoyed a high and widespread reputation as an architect, becoming the Vice President of the Society of Architects in London in 1889–90, his designs and illustrations appearing in various architectural papers, among them a sketch design for the proposed Truro Cathedral, and a sketch elevation of the upper arcade of the south transept of Westminster Abbey, both published in *The Building News*.

Designs for buildings throughout England were made by him, including plans for a Wesleyan Chapel at Sherborne, Dorset, a residence in Chippingham, and a Methodist Chapel at Brentwood, London. But the crowning achievement of his career must surely have been the design of the Wesley Memorial Chapel at Epworth, Lincolnshire in 1887, the birthplace of Wesley. The *Cornish Telegraph* of 28 April 1887, reported that from hundreds of architects' plans submitted in a nationwide competition, a short list of 10 was decided upon, and Hick's design was finally chosen as the winning entry.

A forthright and opinionated man, renowned for his outspokenness and pertinacity, he was also a regular contributor to *The Builder* journal, the spokesman for the Redruth Rate Payers' Association, and a director of the Cornubian Manufacturing Company, Redruth. In 1895 he became a councillor on the new Redruth Urban District Council and was elected Chairman of the Sanitary and Highways Committee. He also owned a tin streaming works near Redruth, and was a major shareholder in numerous local mines.

Hicks' association with Lanyon served him well, for he soon attracted the attention of Charles Henry Rolle Hepburn Stuart Forbes, the Twentieth Lord Clinton, an important landowner with large estates in Devon and Cornwall. Lord Clinton appointed him chief agent of his Treruffe Estate, Redruth, and Trefusis Estate, Flushing; Trefusis House being redesigned by Hicks. Lord Clinton also owned the land on which the Carn Marth quarries were situated. Hicks, seeing a chance to profit from the exploitation of the granite there during the building boom of the 1880s, formed the Cornish Granite and Freestone Company, being its principal shareholder, and the Director and promoter of the company's three quarries on Carn Marth. The secretary of the company was Edwin Bond of Sparnon Terrace, Redruth, and the junior secretary, S. Jones.

The quarries were managed by Hicks' older brother John, engineer of Sparnonville, Redruth, also a prominent member of the Redruth Urban District Council (Fig.5.2). Besides being a shrewd businessman, James Hicks was without a doubt one of the county's finest architects, who left the town of Redruth a wonderful legacy and growing civic pride with its fine new buildings, a far cry from the dull and dingy mining town described by a traveller earlier in the century. It is regrettable that his work is not given the recognition it rightly deserves. Clinton and Messrs Hicks were responsible for various construction projects in Redruth which were instrumental in shaping the town we know today. Indeed, a terrace of five houses at Sparnon Hill was built by the Hicks Family using granite from Carn Marth.

In 1878 Lord Clinton gave the land on which a new road was to be constructed, providing an alternative southerly route into the town. Clinton Road was thus created in 1878–79, and elegant new villas were gradually built along what became a highly fashionable tree-lined avenue. Many of these modern dwellings incorporated granite into their elaborate facades, and also as quoins, ashlars, sills and transoms. Additional neat, rectangular blocks of housing quickly sprang up around Clinton Road on ground reclaimed from the former dressing floors of Pedn-an-Drea and Wheal Sparnon Mines, creating a demand for stone to build Redruth's late Victorian middle class 'suburb'.

By 1888, it was estimated that about 136 houses had been built since 1879–80 on Lord Clinton's property close to the town, for the most part residences for professional men and tradesmen, or at any rate for classes considerably above miners.[17] This perhaps gives some idea of the wealth accumulated by the growing middle class of Redruth, in many instances money which had been made through, and because of, the local mining industry when it was at its zenith, or remitted from abroad, particularly from South Africa.

Clinton Road boasted some of the most architecturally beautiful buildings in the town, many designed by Hicks and built of Carn Marth granite. Most notable were the Science and Art School, opened in 1882, the Church, dedicated to St Andrew, constructed in 1883 (of which he was joint architect of the western portion with architect Mr Sedding, and to which he gave his proportion of fees, a sum in excess of £100, to the building fund), the Robert Hunt Memorial Museum, opened in 1891, and the Free Library (now the Public Library), costing £2000, and opened in 1895. And it was in Clinton Road that Hicks resided, at 'Penarth', the elegant villa next to St Andrew's Church, built and designed by him as his family home in the early 1880s.

In other parts of the town, Hicks designed several industrial and commercial buildings of note. The Devon and Cornwall Bank, (now the National Westminster Bank) with its elegant granite facade, in Fore Street, and the Old Bacon Factory, constructed in 1892 using granite from his company's quarries, as did the restoration of the new Tabb's Hotel, a year after the disastrous fire of 1894.

Hicks' quarries also provided some of the granite for the laying out of Clinton Road, a scheme which provided valuable employment for out-of-work miners. The Redruth Local Board Reports of 1889 indicate that 96 feet of channelling was ordered at 6d per foot from the Cornish Granite and Freestone Company.[18] Moreover, the Urban District Ledgers for Redruth contain numerous entries for the payment of cheques to the CGFC for street works and improvements, main and other roads, and water channelling.

The 1895 Tolgus Hill improvement used stone from the CGFC, which was paid £17.11.6 for the contract. The sums involved in raising the standard of municipal services within Redruth were huge, and Hick's company received by far the lion's share of payments made to local granite operators.[19] So much so, that a 'ratepayer' wrote the following letter to the *Cornubian* of 16 April 1897:

> *...it is to be hoped that the Council will take care not to elect members Chairmen of Committees who are financially interested in what they have to pass and sanction... is it legal for a member of a Council who is also a large shareholder in a Cornish Granite Company to supply granite to such Council and who at the same time has to certify that the granite supplied is according to order, by virtue of his being a member of the Highways Committee?* (Both John and James Hicks had served on the Redruth UDC in this capacity).

Stone was also supplied for monumental work, and many local gravestones are of Carn Marth granite. One at St Day churchyard has the company's name in lead lettering clearly displayed (Fig. 5.3).

But by far the most visible and ambitious project in Victorian Redruth was the construction of the new railway viaduct, replacing the rather rickety old wooden one designed by Brunel. Work on the new viaduct was started in 1885, and took three years to complete. A marvel of Victorian engineering, it was built by Stephens of Ashburton, at a cost of about £25 000, and was to have been about 600 feet long, 28 feet wide, with the line of rails some 60 feet above the principal street, and was to consist of seven

Fig.5.3. *Granite headstone at St Day churchyard with 'Cornish Granite Co. Redruth' clearly displayed.* (photo S.P. Schwartz)

arches of 57 feet span, and one arch of 61 feet open. The viaduct was built entirely of granite. Much of the stone was supplied by the Cornish Granite and Freestone Company, from its Carn Marth Quarries.[20] (Carn Brea Quarry also supplied granite.). Whilst quarrying for the stone for the viaduct, a block of Carn Marth granite in excess of 200 tons was dislodged in one of the quarries, which was later split into smaller pieces.

Working flat out to produce the granite for these projects, 40 to 50 men were employed by Hicks in cutting and raising the stone to fill the orders, giving valuable work to men in an area hard hit by the closure of its copper and tin mines. The two quarries at the summit were at this time blasted into one, as tons of granite were recovered for the viaduct. Two men working in one of these quarries in 1886 had alone returned over £25 for dues, providing a fine profit for the landowners.[21] The Cornish Granite and Freestone Company also occasionally exported granite from Carn Marth. In England, the construction of harbours, breakwaters, bridges and embankments created a huge demand. Granite from CGFC Quarries went into the construction of the Thames Embankment in London, and at Cardiff and Chatham Docks.

The CGFC were insured in the Employer's Liability Corporation which covered the company in cases of industrial accidents. In 1896 a quarryman named John Pooley had a hand and part of an arm blown off whilst in Messrs Hicks' employ, caused by the failed ignition of a charge. And 39 - year-old Edward Dunstan of Carharrack, a father of three, had his skull crushed when the arm of a crane broke off and killed him in 1887. In times of accidents such as these, the quarryman's family would receive some financial recompense. Dunstan's family received the amount of one years' wages.[22] This treatment compares quite favourably with that of the miners, who were supposed to receive a few shillings for a man who was killed, injured or incapacitated. This payment was made from the fund deducted from their wages in the form of club money (see Chapter 4).

With so much industrial activity on the carn, it seems hardly surprising that several residents had reason to complain to an estate agent, Mr Letcher of St Day, who acted for several landowners in the area in 1886. Various problems were caused by the quarrying operations of the CGFC in particular. Carn Marth was home to many people who found their lives disrupted by the granite industry. One resident, Mr Prisk, complained about Messrs Hicks and Co. encroaching upon his croftland to exploit surface stone without his permission. His neighbour, Mrs Williams, complained that her croft hedges had been deliberately breached to facilitate the transport of granite by cart, causing her cattle to stray.[23] By the mid 1890s, the main building boom in the area was drawing to a close, and the workforce in the Hicks Brothers' quarries by 1895 had shrunk to 18 men. In January 1896, James Hicks died unexpectedly at age 50. He had attended a funeral at Treleigh Church from which he had returned home wet through. He was taken ill with a fever and died less than 48 hours later.

The company's office was moved to the Redruth County Court buildings in Penryn Street, and Hicks was succeeded in his practice by Horace Collins (who had been trained by Hicks). The company was dealt a further blow with the death of John Hicks in 1897 from cancer. But the heyday of the Cornish Granite and Freestone Company had by this time passed; the demand for granite diminished and a depression in the granite industry began (see below). Matters were made worse by operational difficulties encountered when the quarry near the summit was being deepened; flooding occurred as the water table was hit. This quarry was probably abandoned sometime before the First World War, as the granite industry nationwide had been hit hard by cheap imported stone from Scandinavia in the years after 1905. This resulted in the loss of the lucrative markets such as London and other industrial towns, and many of the larger commercial quarries were amalgamated or closed, and smaller quarries gradually went out of business in the years leading up to the Great War.

In 1903, the operator of this particular quarry was Mr Harris (possibly James Hicks' nephew), who was requested by the trustees of Lanner Wesley Chapel to submit a price for new granite posts and curbing for the chapel entrance. He continued to lease the quarry until at least 1917, but it seems unlikely that he was working it at this time. At first there was only water in one of the back corners of the quarry, but in time it became completely flooded and is now a favourite spot for fishing. Sadly, it was also used as a convenient place to dump unwanted rubbish, the deepest part being about 40 feet. During the 1950s the police force used it for a time to train their divers, and a cache of jewellery was recovered from its depths, along with a motorbike stolen years before.

On a more sombre note, a baby's body was found floating in its cold waters, and several people have drowned there. In recent years, the quarry has been purchased by the environmentally conscious Carn Marth Protection Group, which oversaw the clearing out of the debris dumped there. Three rusty old cars were thus removed, and the quarry made safe for people to enjoy.

The Quarry Industry and People Power.
The Carn Marth Protection Group

By far the best known of Carn Marth's quarries is the one overlooking Lanner on the southern slope (SW 7152 4068), by virtue of the fact that it has been much in the news during the 1980s. This was one of the last quarries to be opened on the carn, and the last to work commercially. The 1880 OS map shows it as a pea-sized concern, dwarfed by its sister quarries near the summit, also operated by the Cornish Granite and Freestone Company. A schedule in 1895 of all the quarries operating under the Quarries act of 1894, lists it as being unworked, and in 1893, John Hicks, manager of the CGFC Quarries, noted it as being disused and containing a pool of water into which all manner of rubbish had been dumped.[24] Although small, according to the 1894 Quarries' Act, to qualify as a quarry it had to have an entrance over 20 feet deep in order to be included on the schedule. It saw an astonishing expansion in the years between the first OS map of 1880 and the 1906 edition, the latter showing it had mushroomed in size, probably as a result of the decline of the larger quarry experiencing water problems.

A new road along which to transport the granite had to be opened up through croftland, belonging to the Polkinghornes, who charged the quarry operators half a crown a year for the privilege of using the road. They were also expected to maintain it.[25] This is the road which leads to the top of the carn from the engine house today.

The quarry worked in the early decades of the twentieth century, but lay idle for a number of years. In 1954, planning permission was granted to the owner, valid until 2042.[26] A company called The Lanner Moor Roadstone Company was operating the quarry during the late 1950s and early 1960s. Stone was taken from the quarry to the Penventon Quarry near Trevince, where a crusher was situated. The company supplied stone for aggregates, but also a finely crushed gravel called 'Layers Granny Grit' which was used for fowls to scrabble in. This was taken up country by Tony Vale Transport, and later Bolitho Redruth Ltd, by eight-wheeler trucks. There was an enormous ready market for the product, but only as long as the granite was white. When the colour deteriorated, the orders dried up and the business ended.[27]

By 1965, The Lanner Roadstone Company had been succeeded by Bell and Pascoe Ltd which also produced aggregates at the Penventon crushing plant near Treviskey. This enterprise had ceased by the late 1960s and the quarry lay idle until planning permission was granted by Kerrier District Council, in 1976, for the quarry to be operated by an established local company called Penventon Concrete, one of the partners in this enterprise being the well known businessman, Ellis Moses. Again the quarry was worked in tandem with Penventon Quarry where the aggregates were produced. It was never really all that successful, with much of the ¾inch aggregate (chippings) being brought in from another quarry at Longdowns, and the company ceased production in 1977. During Penventon Concrete's ownership of the quarry, much of the overburden (surface earth, grass and loose rock) was removed to locations nearby, creating the tips which are still visible today. It was a difficult quarry to work because much of the mother stone lay near the surface, making blasting awkward and sometimes dangerous.

The first blast detonated by the company was unlikely to have been forgotten by residents. Fourteen charges were set off simultaneously, completely filling the entrance to the quarry with rubble, and sending rocks and stones showering down all over the hill as far away as Pennance. Lanner people remember the constant thunder of the lorries passing through the village en route to the concrete works at Penventon, and people living in Treviskey Lane were prompted to complain to the Council during the summer of 1976 about the dust and noise nuisance.[28]

People also worried about damage to their properties by the blasting which occurred daily at 10.00am, 12 noon and 3.00pm, so many were only too happy to learn of the quarry's closure. During the 14 years of Penventon Concrete, the company had supplied materials for the manufacture of concrete which had gone into the construction of Goonhilly's satellite dishes, Leo's Superstore at Falmouth, and the new Tesco's Supermarket at Truro.[29]

When local people came to know about the new proposals to reopen the quarry in 1986 by a company called Mineral Contract Services of Bissoe, which had identified possible markets for 100 000 tons of stone a year, they raised clear objections. The Bissoe company, working ten-hour shifts, would have recovered 200 tons of stone a day, to be carried by 14-ton capacity lorries. Blasting would have occurred twice a week, the whole enterprise creating less than six jobs. The company sought planning permission in 1986 for the erection of a crusher, a screening plant, weighbridge, site offices, and an explosives store at the quarry.[30] In a remarkable show of people power, the residents of Lanner and district engineered a public outcry. Meetings were held in Lanner Village Hall and the TV and press were involved to maximise publicity. A 300-strong protest march was held from the Village Hall to the summit of Carn Marth and a 22-page report was compiled, including illustrations, and was dispatched to every member of the Council outlining the reasons for their opposition. Local MP David Mudd wrote to the Department of the Environment stressing the overwhelming public opposition. About 214 letters from concerned individuals were received before the 1986 site meeting, as were four petitions containing 463 signatures.[31]

During the publicity mêlée, the Carn Marth Protection Group was born, with the aim of thwarting further quarrying operations and to preserve the natural beauty and wildlife of the carn for future generations to enjoy. Graham Davies was elected Chairman. The objectors were delighted to learn that the owners, Penventon Concrete, went into voluntary liquidation two weeks before Christmas of 1986.[32] However, the battle was won but not the war and the Carn Marth Protection Group, aware that planning permission for quarrying still existed, decided to attempt to raise the

Fig.5.4. *Pennance Quarry, Carn Marth. Now converted to form an open-air theatre.* (photo. R.H.Parker)

necessary capital to purchase the site and several acres of land at the summit of the carn, including the flooded quarry. The protection group were fortunate to secure a grant of £10 000 at an early stage from Cornwall County Council, and a grant of £1000 from Lanner Parish Council. Further money was donated from other councils, both local and from as far away as the Isle of Skye. A sum of £19 000 was raised to buy 18 acres of land in 1986 and a trust of four people was formed to legally own the site; in addition a committee was set up to run it.[33] The Carn Marth Protection Group undertook the clearing away of rusty old machinery, and men worked on making the newly purchased quarry safe on a Kerrier Groundwork Trust Project, funded by a Department of the Environment reclamation grant.[34] The quarry was landscaped and turned into an amphitheatre where performances are held annually by local theatre groups, the money raised by these summer performances helping to finance the running of the protection group (Fig. 5.4).

The first play was 'The Three Musketeers', performed by the Shiva Theatre in 1987, watched by an audience of about 400 by the light of car headlamps.[35] More recently, stone benches have been created to seat the audience, and an electricity supply has been installed. The Carn Marth Protection Group has relinquished all planning permission for the extraction of stone, so it seems unlikely that quarrying will ever be carried out on this side of the carn again. In 1996, the group celebrated its ten year anniversary with a splendid programme of summer performances, including the Kneehigh Theatre's production of 'Tregeagle'.

The Harvey Quarries

Behind the trigonometry point are two disused quarries, facing Busveal. These were leased and later owned by members of the Harvey Family who, for over 80 years, were well known locally in the industry as granite merchants, running a family business spanning four generations. The largest quarry on the carn today, known as North Quarry, Harvey's, or Holman's Quarry (SW 7148 4088), has one of the longest histories, being worked for well over a century and has gone through several great changes in the granite industry. Stone was first quarried in this location sometime around the mid nineteenth century, when a working was opened in commonland lying in the Manor of Tolcarne. The land was deemed useless for agriculture, but yielded good stone, and the quarry became noted for the diversity and variety of its rock composition, producing granite and blue and grey elvan. In 1921, when the quarry was being enlarged, two exceptional rock specimens known as pegmatites were found by James Harvey, who saved them. The specimens were mentioned in an article of The Royal Cornwall Geological Survey of the same year.[36]

The Harvey Family came to Carn Marth in the late 1820s from the St Austell area. Michael Harvey (1796–1870), was attracted to the area by the prospect of employment caused by the flood of people pouring into the region to work in the mines. Demand for granite to build the rows of miners' cottages which line the village of Lanner and elsewhere saw an expansion in the local quarry industry. Men such as Michael Harvey often ran farms or smallholdings as well as working the granite on their land. His two sons, Michael, born in 1829, and Joseph, in 1841, followed their father into the quarryman's trade. Michael junior worked the quarry (SW 7166 4087) directly behind the flooded quarry. It was quite large by 1880 and had probably provided work for upwards of twenty men, but by 1895 was only employing one man.[37] Today this quarry is very overgrown, and probably ceased working during the pre World War One granite depression.

Michael Harvey junior was a strange character, a childless widower who lived alone on Carn Marth in a four-roomed cottage, and liked to play the violin to an audience of rats. Apart from working at his quarry, he lived the life of a virtual hermit. Joseph was the more successful of the two, running the quarry closer to the trigonometry point which eventually bore his family's name. On the 1895 schedule of quarries operating under the Quarries Act of 1894, Joseph was named as the owner and employer of six men. By now the building frenzy of the previous decade was slowing down, so Joseph had cut his workforce back from nearly 40 men.

Harvey's Quarry was not in the same league as Hicks' Quarries nearby, being more a family run affair, with cousins, nephews and brothers-in-law all finding jobs there. At Messrs Hicks' Quarries, John Hicks, the manager, probably acted as a 'ganger', hiring stone cutters who were paid on a piece work basis, and was probably kept busy enough overseeing the running of the quarries to have time to work as a stonemason himself. But Joseph Harvey worked with his men and did all his own smithy work in a shed situated on the croftland, to the right of the quarry entrance.

The lot of the stone cutter was often poor, as he was only paid for quality stone, even if a block was rejected because of a naturally occurring flaw. Work took place more often than not outside, and at best in an open shed, and workers earned on average anywhere between 17 to 30 shillings per week, less than miners, but more than agricultural labourers.[38]

Fig.5.5. *Joseph Harvey, manager of Harvey's Quarry, Carn Marth, with his wife, Martha (née Inch).* (© Gwen Skewes, Redruth)

Joseph Harvey used to go into Redruth by pony and trap each Friday to the bank to draw out the money to pay his workers. A strong, well-built, distinguished looking gentleman with a long white beard, he was remembered as being 'a hard case' with a very quick temper, although fair to his employees (Fig. 5.5).

During Joseph's ownership of the quarry, all work was effected by hand with the aid of hammers, jumpers (long iron rods, weighing in excess of 200 pounds, with a pear-shaped iron ball welded into the centre and a sharp cutting edge at each end), and chisels. Horses and carts conveyed the stone to the customer via the unmade quarry road on the Cal Hill side of the carn. Moving the stone to be worked was managed with the aid of a hoist, a type of home-made crane, comprising a sturdy central mast of wood, hand-operated using a wheel, to which was attached strong rope or chains. Grappling claws called 'dogs' connected to the chains gripped the rock which could be swung into whichever position was necessary for working, or loaded into carts for transportation.

The CGFC quarries had several larger cranes within, which are plotted on the 1904 OS map. Some of them might have been steam operated, as the quarry at Carn Brea did contain such a crane, although for the most part, Victorian masons had to rely on their own strength for shifting large blocks of granite with a system of crowbars, jacks and rollers.

Joseph Harvey was a small-time granite merchant, providing local needs for stone to be used in monumental masonry, and as setts, quoins, kerb stones, coping, transoms, and blocks for use in general building. Blasting with Davey's powder (gunpowder) was only carried out about once a week, as Victorian masons usually ensured that enough stone was brought down in one blast to keep them busy for many days. Gunpowder was the preferred explosive for nineteenth century operators, as the stone was 'lifted' from its horizontal 'bed' often in huge blocks, and not shattered as would be the case with dynamite. Only a fraction of the granite brought down in a blast was actually used by Victorian masons, and much debris was created when dressing the stone at the site. Sometimes this was used to back fill the excavated area, and later was used for road construction. Harveys' explosives were stored outside the quarry in a shack, well away from the workings. Joseph's son James was always careful to guard the store around Guy Fawkes Night, fearing someone would break in to steal the explosives, as the practice of throwing around dynamite and other explosive material was still widespread among the local mining community.

Joseph Harvey's five sons all became involved in the family business. The eldest son, Joseph, was to inherit his father's business, but tragically died in 1895 at the age of 31. Working alone late one Friday night at the quarry to fulfil a large order for granite blocks, he suffered an epileptic fit and, falling face downwards into a pool of shallow water, quickly drowned. James (Jim), born in 1876, was using a 15 pound hammer and cutting granite quoins at age 12, and it was he who bought the quarry in 1914 and took over the operation of it from his sister, Emma Bray, after his father had retired in about 1912 and sold it to her.[39] Just back from Ironwood, Michigan, Jim, a pensive man of few words, continued to run the quarry along much the same lines as his father had done (Fig.5.6).

Fig.5.6. *James Harvey took over the operation of Harvey's Quarry about 1914. Here he is with his wife Emily Ann, daughter Minnie and son, Leonard.* (© The Late Mrs Minnie Haughton).

The quarry had provided the local council with granite for paving and kerb stones at Station Hill, Redruth, some road stone and also had a share in the lucrative contract for providing the same materials for Clinton Road, as the Redruth Urban District ledgers of 1895 indicate. The making of the footpath from the New Church at New Road to South Gate, Redruth, was carried out by Joseph Harvey and his sons in 1884, at a rate of 11d per foot, including fixings, at a total cost of £27 10s.

Chasewater also has Harvey's granite along its streets, delivery of the stone being made by Jim with a horse and cart. Monumental masons such as Jack Pascoe in St Day Road regularly purchased granite from the Harveys, and Redruth Grammar School (1907), and the West End Drapery stores (1915), were supplied with granite blocks from their Carn Marth Quarry. Until recent years, a block of public lavatories stood at Fish Cross, Redruth. The fine granite 'Ladies and Gentlemen' sign over the building was crafted by Jim Harvey and polished by his brother Tom. And the base of the Mill's Monument in the town of St Day came from Harvey's Quarry, made by Jim and his son Leonard, as were many local headstones, but being an unpretentious man, Jim never signed his name. Many of the headstones in the style of a scroll are examples of his work.

Occasionally, Harvey's Quarry exported granite to London for paving and monumental use. The stone was conveyed by horse and cart to Redruth Railway Station, where it was loaded onto a train bound for the capital.[40]

Accurately reading the market's increasing demand for aggregates, Jim decided to install a small crusher in the early 1930s, ushering in a new era for Harvey's Quarry, and making it the most modern of the quarries on the carn. During the 1930s the Camborne and Redruth Urban District Council (CRUDC) was carrying out numerous road improvements to accommodate the increase in motor vehicles travelling on poor and overburdened routes. Road resurfacing and construction required tons of aggregates, and the Council was constantly searching for sources of local road stone. In 1935 stone was being taken from the burrows of Tresavean and Comford Mines for road building, and available quarries in the area were urgently required, as was the purchase or hire of a crusher.[41] Jim Harvey now found that the Council, besides buying granite for paving and kerb stones, also purchased aggregates and orders flowed in.

Jim's daughter Minnie remembers how each morning her brother Leonard would leave their home in Pennance early, in order to arrive at the quarry half an hour before his work mates, to 'fire up' the crusher with special fuel cartridges. The engine ran on diesel, and was easier to start if warm, by cranking it up with a handle. It's familiar 'chug chug' sound could be heard some distance away. Safety was always foremost, and Jim was remembered as a good boss who looked after his men well, always sensitive to their working and personal needs, a sensitivity borne of the numerous setbacks and grief he had endured in his own life. No one was ever killed or seriously injured in the quarry. A system of coloured flags alerted residents when blasting was in progress. A red flag showed that it was about to commence, and a green flag signalled the all clear. This system was also used by other operators on the carn.

The CRUDC era

In 1934, Jim decided to retire. His son Leonard, who had worked with his father since leaving school at age 14, had other plans for his working life and had no interest in running the quarry. Thus ended the Harvey Family era of the quarry. The thriving business was sold to Jack Johns, a local man with several business interests in Redruth.[42] Jack Johns cemented the close relationship begun by Jim Harvey and leased the quarry to the CRUDC until 31 June 1961. The council, which had an annual requirement for about 5000 yards of stone, now took over operation of the quarry, paying the new owner a set amount for every yard of stone recovered, as well as paying the workers their wages.[43] During the ensuing years, the quarry became a very modern and efficient place of work for the supply of aggregates, using compressed air and powered by electricity. The crusher was situated just outside the quarry entrance on the right and a ramp ran up to it, where wagons loaded with stone were brought by tramway from within the quarry and dumped into the crusher, which was constantly fed by two men. The crushed rocks were then carried by half-moon-shaped buckets on a conveyor belt up to a trommel which had various sized holes along its length. Constantly rotating, this device graded the stone into five sizes. The graded material was then stored in concrete bins with doors on the front, enabling lorries to drive underneath and load the stone quickly with the aid of small chutes. The aggregates were used mainly for road building and concrete manufacture.

The use of wagons and rails was an ingenious idea, obviating the need for cranes to move the stone which could now be rapidly and easily transported to the crusher. The rails of the tramway could be moved to wherever they were required within the quarry, and a turntable enabled the loaded wagons to be rotated in whichever direction was needed. Drilling was effected using compressed air. The quarry was now operated in a completely modern fashion, far removed from the Victorian methods employed during most of the Harvey era. During the 1940s and 50s, about 15 men worked there. A machine man was hired to drill the holes for blasting and there were usually several men engaged in 'tramming', that is loading the wagons with stone for the crusher, which was fed by two men. There were also a foreman and a blacksmith (Fig.5.7). During the late 1950s, the workforce shrank to about ten men. James (Jimmy) Opie of St Day remembers working there in the late 50s, and early 60s. Blasting with dynamite took place daily, unlike the policy employed by the Harveys and other nineteenth century operators. Sometimes there were three blasts in one day, of the deep hole type, to bring down huge quantities of shattered rock and subsequent blasts known as 'pops' to break large stones into smaller pieces.

Fig.5.7. *Camborne-Redruth Urban District Council workers at Harvey's Quarry, 1947–48.* Back row, left to right: *Alfie Hitchens, Leslie Dunstan, Ronnie Seddan, Joe Heard, Chris Pedley, a visitor, Frank Matthews, Leonard Pedley, Bill Webb (foreman).* Front row, l-r: *Dick Hall, Stanley Whitford, a visitor, Henry Light, Dickie Delves.* (© Jimmy Opie, St Day)

Being worked in this way the quarry expanded rapidly. In 1948 F.V. Rolfe, planning officer for the Cornwall Western Area Planning Sub-committee, stated that an application for 4.5 acres to expand the quarry was to be granted. It was specified that no excavating operations were to take place outside the limits granted without further consent of the planning authority, or within 50 feet from the centre of the road, and that, as far as possible, all waste material was to be dumped and levelled in existing hollows, or tipped in such a form as would fit 'the configuration of the landscape'. The above specifications had to be adhered to, as Carn Marth was considered to be a place 'of considerable amenity value'.[44] Jimmy Opie remembers it being enlarged. The 'overburden' would be knocked down into the quarry by the work force and was taken away by horse and cart by local man John Thomas.

Constant checks were made by inspectors to ensure that the rock face was safe and the men were ordered to wear safety hats of the type miners wore at the turn of the twentieth century. Overalls were not supplied to the trammers, and conditions were often harsh for the workers who were exposed to the elements all year round. It was sometimes insufferably hot in summer, and bitterly cold in the winter when the wind tore into the quarry which faced directly into the north and east winds. In this respect, conditions for quarry men had not changed much in a hundred years. Local men were, however, glad to have the opportunity of work in this and other quarries, and the pay was better than that collected by road workers.

For much of the 1950s the quarry was in a losing position. In the month of November, 1951, a deficit of £74 10s 1d had to be met from the Council's reserve fund. About 388 hours had been lost by the company's employees due to sickness, and the hire of a mechanical digger, for the removal of overburden, at a cost of £63 8s 8d had resulted in a further financial setback.[45] In 1956 employees were warned that unless production was improved, the council would be forced to consider abandoning the quarry. The deficit for the last quarter stood at £143. It was noted that the severe weather was partly to blame for the poor production figures, along with the failure of the granulator bearings.[46]

In November 1960 the Highways Committee of the CRUDC asked Mr Barrett, Chief surveyor, to prepare a statement as to whether the quarry should continue to be worked. The lease of the quarry was due to expire the following year, and a financial report for the past quarter showed that the production of stone and dust, estimated at £1154. 9s. 6d., had cost £1493. 17s. 9d., resulting in a deficit of £339. 8s. 3d.[47]

In February 1961 the Highways Committee of the District Council resolved to discontinue the working of this quarry, as it was now in an uneconomical position. Furthermore, it was nearly worked out at its present level, and had reached the limits of expansion.[48] On the east it ran up to the boundary of Sea View Farm and in the centre and on the south-west, was worked to within feet of the pathway running over the carn. No more land could be purchased for quarrying, which brought to a close over a century of continuous working. The workers were offered alternative employment in other departments of the Council.

Although no more quarrying occurred, during the 1970s the quarry did attract the attention of Holmans, a local engineering company, who tested their experimental drills on the quarry's rock face, the 'Swiss cheese' effect left by this experimentation so obvious today. Now the largest of the disused quarries in Lanner Parish, plans were implemented by Kerrier District Council for the purchase of the site, to ensure that the quarry should not attract the attention of potential rubbish dumpers. In 1987, the conservationists narrowly won the day in their fight to prevent more debris being deposited there.

Once purchased by Kerrier, the site was transferred to Lanner Parish Council, which was also instrumental in securing the necessary finance to purchase the site. Management has passed to the Carn Marth Protection Group, already caring for the other disused quarries nearby. English Partnerships agreed in principle to a grant of £30 000 towards the proposed clearance of the site, and stone steps have been created on the northern face of the quarry to facilitate easier access to the bottom.[49]

Martin's Quarry

On the Trevarth side of the carn are two more disused quarries. Although it lies just outside the Lanner Parish boundary, the one nearest the village (SW 7236 4091) was operated by the Martin Family of Grove House, Pennance, and is of interest as it is little changed since it ceased production, and preserves its nineteenth century characteristics which the quarries already mentioned have lost. It was probably opened in the 1850s, and supplied stone for local mines and buildings in and around the villages of Trevarth, Lanner and Carharrack. With his sons, Mr James Martin, who originated in Mabe, ran the granite and elvan producing quarry, from the latter half of the nineteenth century, on land owned by the Beauchamps. The 1895 schedule of the quarries operating under the Quarry Act shows Jim Martin as the owner employing eight men. Martin's Quarry was run in much the same fashion as their rival company, Harvey and Sons, prior to the installation of the crusher. The business was taken over by James Martin junior sometime at the close of the nineteenth century.

The late Mr Tommy Martin, born in Lanner in 1910, remembered working in his father's quarry earlier this century. He recollected huge holes being bored by hand, with one man hitting the drill (jumper) with a large hammer, while a second man guided the drill giving it half a turn between blows. Blasting happened only once a week, and the stone brought down from its 'bed' was set upon by stone cutters who 'scappled' the block to the required size, for building and monumental masonry. Tommy well remembered how his father split blocks of granite by the 'plug and feather' method. This involved boring three-inch holes into the surface of the stone, about three inches apart. Plugs and feathers (thin, semi-circular strips of metal) were then inserted into the holes and every other one tapped in succession until the block split. He also remembered the sound made by the jumper, once familiar on the carn. When hit it let out a sonorous metallic sound not unlike the peal of a bell.

In the centre of Martin's Quarry was a crane with a wooden mast, about 40 feet in height, supported by wooden stays at the quarry rim. The anchor stone, which took the iron-tipped end of the wooden mast, can still be seen today. The angle of the wooden jib was fixed and a hand-winch was attached to the mast, allowing the crane to be swivelled round with ease to move large blocks of granite, either on to a cart, or placed on two large pieces of granite for working. The crane was made by the blacksmith whose shed was situated outside the quarry entrance.

Tommy's father used to travel regularly to Truro with a load of granite which was bought by Trevails, a business located behind the Cathedral, to make headstones, Setting off in the early hours of the morning, Jimmy seldom returned the same day, as the journey with a full load of stone was a painfully slow one. Besides supplying Trevails, Jack Pascoe, another monumental mason at Redruth, purchased Martin's granite. The Redruth Drapery Stores at West End bought granite from Jimmy Martin after the shop's disastrous fire of 1915, and the construction of the steam house floor in Redruth Brewery incorporated stone from this quarry.

Martin, in common with rival granite merchants of Carn Marth, supplied stone for municipal improvements in the 1890s, as the Redruth Urban District ledgers show. In 1903 he was asked to supply a price for new granite posts for the Lanner Wesley Chapel entrance and secured the order at £17.16.0.[50] When the Primitive Methodist Chapel at Lanner Moor was extended in 1904, some 'spalls' for the yard were also obtained from his quarry.[51]

In 1928 Martin supplied the granite posts for the entrance to the new Lanner playing field at Lanner Moor. The business was operating until the Second World War; *Kelly's Directory* entry for 1939 reads, 'James Martin and Sons, quarry owners'. When James died, he left the quarry to his son Sylvester, who bequeathed it to his son, a United Reform Minister, who had no interest in operating it and subsequently sold it in 1962, soon after his father's death.[52]

Today, partially flooded and unspoiled, it provides a good example of the size and type of family-owned and operated quarry which was quite common throughout the granite areas of Cornwall. There are plans afoot for the purchase of this quarry, control of which would then pass to the Carn Marth Protection Group.

Conclusion

Although Carn Marth did produce many thousands of tons of stone for construction projects in Redruth and other local towns and villages, the quarrying operations there were dwarfed in comparison with other granite producing areas of the county. Operators such as James Hicks or Joseph Harvey could never have hoped to have been as wealthy and famous as the likes of John Freeman who managed almost a hundred granite quarries throughout Cornwall, particularly in the Mabe and Constantine area. Carn Marth was disadvantaged in two ways. Firstly, although its stone was a good building material, it was commercially inferior to the granite recovered in the Freeman quarries, which fetched a good price and was of a fine grained matrix and a far stronger stone, without the large crystals of feldspar which marred the appearance of Carn Marth granite.

Secondly, the geographical location of the carn severely disadvantaged the operators. Freeman's quarries were no further than four miles from the port of Penryn which kept transportation costs down (granite was transported by sea to other parts of Britain).

The operators of the Redruth & Chasewater Railway had hoped to replace the falling tonnage of copper ore over its tracks in the 1870s with Carn Marth granite, only to discover that there was insufficient demand for its stone outside the immediate area. By comparison, Freeman's quarries were thriving and in 1863 were employing about a thousand men. Stone from them had regularly been exported to London and elsewhere to create prestigious monuments such as the Carlo Alberto, Waterloo Bridge and the Wellington Memorial at Strathfieldsaye. A block of granite weighing 35 tons was sent to The Great Exhibition of 1851, establishing Freeman's enterprise as the flagship of the Cornish granite industry.[53]

The collapse of the Cornish mining industry in the late nineteenth century resulted in a contraction of the local building trade, as the area called the Mining Division (the Camborne-Redruth area and the constellation of mining villages surrounding this conurbation) was subjected to the slow process of de-industrialisation. With a limited market for dressed granite outside the immediate area, and the cost of transportation by rail to port prohibitive, it was only the demand for aggregate in the 1930s which saved the industry on Carn Marth and ensured its survival, long after many of the other local industries, resulting from the copper mining boom of the mid nineteenth century, had foundered. Even after the granite market saw a recovery during the First World War, the Carn Marth Quarries, reported to have 'never faced brighter prospects', could not take advantage of accepting contracts of magnitude. Restrictive resources and a shortage of labour was blamed for the limitations placed on the quarry operators.[54]

In February 1998 safety posts were placed around the top of Harvey's Quarry on Carn Marth, as a part of the £1.1 million Mining Villages Regeneration Project. These posts were of granite – from Portugal. Cornish granite was judged to have been twice the price of Portuguese stone, and even if it was raised in Cornish quarries, the local granite industry had witnessed such a severe decline that the local press reported that the stone would in all likelihood have to had been cut and dressed in South Wales. 'We have to look at the cost and at the end of the day we can do almost twice as much as than if we used local granite', explained Austin Green, principal engineer and regeneration manager.[55] The Portuguese posts ringing the most successful of the carn's quarries present a sad reminder of the death of a once thriving local industry, and one which looks to be increasingly threatened within the remainder of the county.

For over a century and a half the various quarries in Lanner Parish provided the granite required by the demands of our local commercial and industrial society. Major engineering and construction projects in Victorian Redruth and district utilised the moderately priced stone from Carn Marth, creating buildings which form the skyline of the town and villages we know today. Even Redruth's impressive timepiece was heightened and beautified with stone from the carn in 1904. Many of the roads we travel and the pavements we daily walk are constructed of granite from Lanner's quarries.

Quarrying provided many local jobs, often offering work when other employment was scarce. During the building boom of the 1880s, it is possible that the quarries mentioned above, together employed well over 120 men. But twentieth century quarrying for aggregates has brought quarry operators into conflict with local residents far more than the methods employed by Victorian masons ever did, and has proved to be a most contentious issue with the ability to divide a community, as we shall discuss in Chapter 11. However, it must be remembered that Lanner was a working parish and without the granite industry there would not be the amenities and infrastructure upon which modern society has become reliant. The summit of the Carn, now included in the County Council's draft structure as an area of outstanding natural beauty, is open to the public for recreational use, and the emphasis, as in many other sites of former industry in Cornwall, is on recreation and conservation, with Carn Marth vital as a lung for the Parish of Lanner.

REFERENCES

1 Cornwall County Council Minerals Local Plan, Consultation Draft, Dec. 1994, C.G. Ceriffin, p.7.
2 Francis, William, *Gwennap, A Descriptive Poem in Seven Cantos*, J. May, Redruth, 1845, p. 75.
3 Stanier, Peter, *Quarries and Quarrying*, Shire Books, 1985.
4 James, C.C., *A History of Gwennap*, undated, p.153.
5 Michell, Frank, *Annals of an Ancient Cornish Town, Redruth*, Dyllansow Truran, Redruth, (1978), p.51.
6 WH/4132 & WH/4133, Notes From Pennance Lands, CRO, Truro.
7 Barton, D.B., *The Redruth & Chasewater Railway*, Bradford Barton, Truro, 1978, p.22
8 ME/2386, CRO, Truro.
9 Francis, William, *Gwennap, A Descriptive Poem in Seven Cantos*, p. 45.
10 Private Communication: Mr J.C.C. Probert.
11 MR/R/395, Lanner Wesley Account Book, May-August, 1844, CRO, Truro.
12 Private Communication: Mrs Rhona Blatchford, Lanner.
13 *Cornubian*, 27/7/1900.
14 Francis, William, *Gwennap, A Descriptive Poem*, p. 115.
15 Harris, G.F., *Granite and Our Granite Industries*, 1888, p. 49.
16 WH/4541, CRO, Truro.
17 *Cornubian*, 27/7/1888.
18 Michel, Frank, *Annals of an Ancient Cornish Town, Redruth*, 1978, p. 191.
19 DC/CR/120, 1894-1897; DC/CR/121, 1897-1899, Urban District Ledgers, CRO, Truro.
20 *Cornubian*, 25/3/1887; 27/2/1888.
21 WH/4132 & WH/4133, CRO.
22 *Cornubian*, 10/4/1885.
23 WH/4133, CRO.
24 1895 Schedule of the quarries operating under the Quarry Act of 1894 in Cornwall, RIC.
25 Private communication: Mr & Mrs J. Craze, Redruth.
26 *West Briton*, 13/5/1986.
27 Private Communication: Mr J. Craze, Redruth.
28 H352, Minutes of Kerrier District Council, April, 1976.
29 *Camborne & Redruth Packet*, 4/12/1986.
30 *West Briton*, 6/3/1986.
31 *West Briton*, 3/4/1986.
32 *Camborne & Redruth Packet*, 4/12/1986.
33 *West Briton*, 16/4/1987.
34 *West Briton*, 22/2/1990.
35 *West Briton*, 27/8/1987.
36 E.H. Dawson, Note on a Pegmatite from Carn Marth, Royal Cornwall Geological Survey, 1921, p.p.133-135, RIC.
37 1895 Schedule of the quarries operating under the Quarry Act of 1894 in Cornwall, RIC.
38 Stanier, Peter, *Quarries and Quarrying*, Shire Books, 1985, p. 6.
39 Private communication: the late Mrs Minnie Haughton, interviewed when 80 in 1995.
40 Ibid.
41 *West Briton*, 31/1/1935.
42 Private Communication: the late Mrs Minnie Haughton.
43 Private Communcation: Mr James Opie of St Day.
44 *West Briton*, 25/11/1948
45 *West Briton*, 4/1/1951
46 *West Briton*, 3/5/1956
47 *West Briton*, 10/11/1960
48 *West Briton*, 2/2/1961
49 *West Briton*, 7/12/1995, Cornish Voice, March, 1996.
50 MR/R/399, Lanner Wesley Trustee Minutes, 20/2/1907, CRO.
51 Probert, J. C. C. *Primitive Methodism in Cornwall*, privately published, undated, p. 31.
52 Private Communcation: the late Mr Tommy Martin, interviewed when 85 in 1995.
53 *West Briton*, 30/1/1863.
54 *Royal Cornwall Gazette*, 7/1/1915
55 *West Briton*, 12/2/1998

Chapter 6
China Clay and Brick Manufacture

When we think of clay, the St Austell area springs immediately to mind, but in the nineteenth century a number of districts in Cornwall (and Devon) produced clay in significant quantities, and Lanner was one of them. China clay, we must remember, had a multitude of uses during the nineteenth century, and was used not just for the manufacture of common and fire bricks, various other fire-clay products, pottery and ceramics, but also had less obvious uses, such as for lining cupolas and furnaces. It was also widely employed underground for 'claying' a hole prior to blasting, helping to ensure that the hole to receive the charge was as moisture-free as possible. Nineteenth century housewives often bought a bucket of 'growder', soft decomposed granite, which was used for scouring pots and pans and for scrubbing the kitchen table and wooden floorboards.

Great interest was shown in the manufacture of china clay in the Victorian period, the *Mining Journal* of 1 August 1874 commenting:

> *The extraction of China Clay from the hills has never been attended with any of those sudden jumps of fortune that more particularly belong to mining, but has gradually worked its way until it has become one of the soundest speculations, paying steady and high interest on invested capital.*

Local Sources of China Clay

China clay (or kaolin) is formed when the feldspar in granite decomposes, a process taking millions of years. Kaolin had originally been discovered in China, and was known in Europe, at Meissen, Saxony, from about 1710.[1] During the eighteenth century, the first china clay deposits were prospected in Cornwall, most notably by a Quaker, William Cookworthy, who discovered the Tregonning Hill deposits in the Parish of Germoe in 1746, an event which was to herald the birth of the china clay industry within the county.

The late eighteenth century saw the involvement of Josiah Wedgewood, who was reported to have taken samples of clay from locations within Gwennap, reputedly finding 'growan clay' (see below) 'in great abundance, and of a very fine white colour',[2] but it was later reported by John Penderhill-Church, that the samples proved to be clay of a very inferior quality, and the deposits were not immediately worked.[3] It seems likely that the location in which this clay was prospected was in the St Day vicinity.

Within the Lanner area, growan clay ('growan' in the Cornish language meaning 'gravel,' which refers typically to a soil type characterised by its gravel and clay content) occurs most notably on the southern slope of Carn Marth and at Trevarth. Here, clay was recovered for use in the manufacture of pottery, pipes, tiles and bricks, and dispatched as china clay. However, it is possible that several other sites were exploited for clay within the area in former times, clay having value as a building material for cob cottages which were springing up all over the Lanner area from the late eighteenth century, as well as for more obvious uses in the making of domestic earthenware, and in the growing mining industry. At Penstruthal Common, records of eighteenth century and early nineteenth century tin bounds mention the existence of a 'Wheal Clay Bound': 'The south east corner under Penstruthal Hedge to the south of the clay pits.'[4] Mention is also made of a 'Wheal Growan Bound,' at Penstruthal.[5]

In 1921 a company prospecting for tin deposits on the moors above Four Lanes had located large deposits of good quality china clay, small quantities of which had been used for making fire bricks, floors and mortar for building walls. It was felt that about 35 000 tons of exploitable clay was located in a three mile area between Four Lanes and Lanner.[6] Similarly, C.C. James notes the existence of clay deposits at South Downs, at a location named 'Pits Spry', 'pry' in Cornish meaning clay.[7] It was also the name of a tin bound which appeared on a map, dated 1806, and intersected the Turnpike Road below Wheal Gordon, so it is possible that the clay pit was situated on the rough croftland near Clijah.

It appears this old clay-pit was mentioned in the *Royal Cornwall Gazette* in 1896, and described as being 'a considerable distance from the road and partially flooded'.[8] Another clay deposit at Bell Vean, probably of decomposed elvan, occasioned interest in the 1860s, a lease being taken out on 25 March 1868, between John Jope Rogers, Esq. of Penrose, in the County of Cornwall, and John Truscott Paul of Ruan Lanihorne, a merchant, and Edmund Michell the Younger of Carharrack, a mine agent. The lease was to run for 21 years, with an annual rental of £10.10.0. The dues payable on minerals yielded were, 'one shilling and six pence per ton for china clay and china stone, and one shilling for fire clay,' on all those minerals 'which shall be raised and gotten and made merchantable.'[9] Scrutiny of the 1880 OS Map 1:2500, shows no tangible trace of a working for clay in the Bell Vean area, which suggests that the enterprise was unsuccessful, perhaps only consisting of a trial pit. The manufacture of china clay saw only limited success within the Lanner area, its works being unable to compete successfully with the larger clay companies of the St Austell region.

Brick Manufacture

In a granite region like Cornwall, brick manufacture has never been as essential as in regions where indigenous stone is lacking. Nonetheless, research suggests that in the nineteenth century there were as many as 50 commercial brickmaking sites noted in the county.[10] Yet the production of bricks in Cornwall was small scale and localised compared to the rest of Britain, and for a parish as small as Lanner, it was surprising to find two brick works. But as the *Royal Cornwall Gazette* pointed out in 1874, the works were 'situated in the centre of a large mining district, where there exists a constant demand and ready sale for high class fire and other bricks, such as may be manufactured from this clay.'[11]

Cornwall's mining industry was the main user of bricks of the fire or 'refractory' type; less were used in house construction or civil engineering projects in the early to mid nineteenth century, although the first use of brick in the county had been for construction purposes as, for instance, in the building of Tehidy Mansion in 1734.[12] The central mining areas of Camborne, Redruth and Gwennap were, on the whole, slow to acquire their own facilities for brick making, one of the earliest commercial works being the establishment of the St Day works in the early 1860s.[13]

However, William Francis in his work 'Gwennap, A Descriptive Poem' mentions an early use of bricks, undoubtedly made in the area, for the installation of steam engines on local mining sites.[14] In earlier periods, bricks would have been burnt in clamps rather than re-usable kilns, or by itinerant brickmakers using faggots of furze, and some of the probable sites for such early brick manufacture appear to have been mentioned in the 1843 Tithe Map for Gwennap (see below).

A reference in Richard Thomas's *Survey of the Mining District of Cornwall from Chasewater to Camborne*, of 1819, confirms this. He states that the superficial parts of various decomposed elvan courses in the area had been used as clay for burning into bricks. C. C. James notes the existence of a bed of decomposed elvan at Ting Tang which was worked for the manufacture of fire-brick in about 1840.[15] Two elvan courses are noted as the sources of this fire-clay in 1839. The first of these could be traced almost to the granite of Carn Marth, on the north of Roach's Engine at Ting Tang Mine, and thence across the common to the White Works north of Poldory. This contained decomposed portions, 'which have been removed for the manufacture of a coarse but useful kind of fire-brick and employed as a fire-clay for lining furnaces and setting the fire places.'

The second it was stated 'appears at Trevarth, and is met with in the workings of Ting Tang Mine, south of which, and near the road from Carharrack to Comford, the decomposed superficial parts are used for the manufacture of fire-brick.'[16] The 1843 Tithe Map for the Parish of Gwennap mentions a 'brick meadow' (field number 3085 in the Manor of Trevarth), which might have been the site of the manufacture of early crude fire-brick. An unnamed clay pit appears on both the 1880 and 1906 OS maps, and has been identified as the probable site from which the clay came to manufacture some of these early bricks. It can be seen in the woods at Ting Tang, near the Carharrack Sports Club football pitch, and measures 30–40 feet in width, by 80–90 feet in length, and is in the region of 4–5 feet deep.[17]

The Trevarth Enterprise (SW 7290 4085)

At Trevarth, a brick works was created in the early 1870s by a company called The Trevarth Fire Brick and Clay Company. In order to set up the company, a sum of £30 000 was necessary, so shares were offered for £3 apiece.[18] (This was a considerable sum of money, equivalent to almost £1million today.). A clue to the setting up of the company at this particular time was probably due to the revival in the fortunes of the Cornish tin industry, with tin fetching 'fabulous prices... tin has in one or two instances realised near £100 a ton. There is a mining mania. The mining speculators have run wild'.[19]

The clay setts, comprising about 20 acres, were held under leases from Lord Clinton, The Earl of Mount Edgcumbe, Edmund Beauchamp Tucker and others, for a term of 21 years, from 9 February 1872. The total minimum rent was £40 per annum, merging into royalty, which was 6d. per ton.[20] The Trevarth Fire Brick and Clay Company was registered on 24 December 1872, the purchase of the clay sett made by Messrs John and Frank Savage of Gwennap, on the one part, and Mr C.L. Eatenton of the other, with £15 000 in cash, and the other half in fully paid up shares. There were to be no less than three, or more than seven, directors of the company, and it appears that potential investors were targeted from outside of the county.

Indeed, the *West Briton* of 13 January 1873 reported that several people from London had placed a considerable amount of money into the enterprise. Captain P.H. Elliot of the Army and Navy Club, Pall Mall and Messrs J.G. Fraser of Westminster purchased 50 shares each, as did Mr Hamerton Cramp of Hanover Square, Mr A.D. Thornton of Brompton Crescent, London, and Mr Charles Thomas of Buckhurst Hill, Essex. These were the company's first directors. The offices were at 18 Coleman Street, London, and the Secretary was C.L. Eatenton. In addition, many more people from the South East brought shares in the company, including accountants, stockbrokers and solicitors resident in London. The manager of the brickworks, John Savage of Clinton Villa, was also a shareholder.

It was the company's intention to target the market for fire clay products in the form of fire bricks, gas retorts and crucibles, as well as brick arches and common red brick. It was also planned to exploit the clay, which had been prospected by Messrs. E. and H. Ensor of the Pool Works, Woodville, in 1871. They stated that it was of the very best quality, in their estimation superior to the finest Stourbridge clay, having the peculiar characteristic that, while taking great heat to vitrify, when it was brought to that point it was suitable for the purposes of sanitary ware of all kinds. It was also reported to take a high salt glaze, producing the white glazed bricks then in great demand, which were selling for £20 to £22 per thousand.

The clay was abundant less than two feet from the surface; this superficial clay, usually of poorer quality, was found to the astonishment of the prospectors to produce a most superior blue ware. Large quantities of the clay were expected to have been shipped via the Devoran Railway in its raw form, there being such a demand for clay both at home and abroad.[21]

The company hoped to make a good profit on the sale of fire bricks, those of the finest quality for furnaces were at that time fetching £5.10s per thousand. To remain competitive, the Trevarth operators estimated selling for £3.10s per thousand, the cost of manufacture being about £1.5s per thousand, thus yielding a profit upon the bare manufacture of over 150 per cent. The company published a table of their probable results for one year, calculated to show the value of investment in their undertaking:

Cost and expenses of manufacture of each 1000 bricks at £1:5s, and cost of carriage by rail to port, at 2s per ton on 10 million bricks	*£15 000*
Management, working, and current office expenses	*£1500*
	£17 000
Surplus balance receipts	*£18 000*
	£35 000
Taking the income returns for the manufacture of 10 000 fire bricks per annum, at the price only of £3:10s per 1000 being about £2 less than the selling price of fire bricks.	
Revenue	*£35 000*

The net profit was an estimation on a dividend upwards of 50 per cent upon the total capital of the company, even taking the selling price of the bricks at the most moderate estimate of profit. This of course did not take into account the proceeds of the sale of the clay itself, or the large profits which were expected to have been realised by the manufacture and sale of 'gas retorts, fire-lumps, crucibles and ordinary building bricks, for which there is a very large demand in the neighbourhood of the works.'[22]

Moreover, the proprietors had handed over to the company a contract for the supply of 150 000 fire bricks, to have been delivered to London at 85s per thousand, and future large orders were reported to have been in the offing.

Several eminent persons connected with the brick and mining industry gave very favourable reports on the clay sampled in order to attract investors; Messrs Candy and Luckin (Devon brick makers), had no doubt as to the value of the property. Mr W. Sara of the Town Mill Foundry, Redruth commented 'I have used fire clay during the last 20 years for the lining of our "cupolas" in which we smelt large quantities of iron for heavy castings, and where it is exposed to immense heat; and I have no hesitation in saying that the clay from Trevarth is superior to any I have ever used, and we shall be glad to have a further supply.'[23] Similar favourable reports were received from James Pope, Mining Engineer, and Thomas Williams, the superintendent of the Devon Great Consols Foundry, who believed the Trevarth bricks to be equal or superior to those of Stourbridge.[24]

By the following year, the proprietor was reported to have opened one pit, 100 feet by 50 feet, and the depth of the clay was found to have been 36 feet. According to the analysis of Dr Taylor Rowe in 1874, the clay 'was of the best quality, containing less than 3 per cent of iron waste.'[25] The bricks manufactured at the works bore the name TREVARTH set in a 'frog' (the indentation in which mortar is placed). Susan Gribble of Trevarth has an almost complete part of a brick manufactured at the works; Joy Hadfield, also of Trevarth, has an example incorporated into her fireplace, while another is reputed to be set in a cottage wall at Carharrack, but they are rare. The reason is obvious. By January of the following year, the works was advertised for sale in the *Redruth Times and Camborne Advertiser*, and the *Mining Journal*. A total of 92 000 fire and red bricks, plus arch bricks, a grey mare (three years old), a cart and some railroad iron, were advertised for sale in four lots, to be sold at public auction on Tuesday 20 January, at twelve o'clock at the works.

In addition, a further sale was to be held at five o'clock the same day at the Steam-Engine Inn, Carharrack for the sale of the clay setts, and brick making plant. The latter was reported to have comprised one new horse upright pug mill, with two holes, manufactured by Clayton; one new hand press, also by Clayton; moulds and barrows; pallet boards; 400 reed covers or hats; 54 sheets of iron, 5 feet by 22 feet, suitable for roofing; one new double-acting pump, with 15 feet 32-inch lead tubing, and picks, shovels, fire-bars, mats and other materials for use in brick making. Two kilns were offered for sale, one capable of holding 40 000 bricks, and the other, capable of containing 25 000. Also included in the sale were a moulding shed, an open shed and offices. It was further noted that, 'The whole of the plant is new, and in good working order. The clay beds only require to be worked with spirit to prove a most lucrative investment, and will be sold in consequence of the proprietor leaving the country through ill health.'[26] This description of the works and its equipment suggests an enterprise much larger than the scarcity of the bricks locally leads one to believe.

The works could have continued to operate, but six months later a further notice appeared in the *Royal Cornwall*

Gazette dated the 9 July 1874, advertising the works for sale by tender. This sale notice again advertised the two new stone built, iron-bound kilns, plus crushing rollers, a pug mill, hack grounds, sheds, offices and other plant, which could suggest that some of the equipment advertised for sale earlier that year had failed to sell. The clay sett was described as extending for upwards of half a mile in length over a bed of high quality elvan clay. Supplies were delivered by the Redruth-Chasewater Railway which ran close by, and an ample supply of water was guaranteed the year around. It is highly doubtful that the enterprise worked after this sale.

The story of the Trevarth venture raises a number of important points, both about Lanner and about the state of the English investment market. In the first place we note the heavy dependence on the London market to raise a sum in excess of £1million at today's values. Of course the Gwennap area would not have been unknown to London investors, which had been until recent years, a world centre of copper mining. In the heyday of mining, would not local adventurers have put up the money? Now it was left to outsiders, many of whom were financially severely stung in the speculative mining mania of 1872, in which numerous enterprises, only ever likely to enjoy but limited success, such as the Trevarth Brickworks, were set up. Another interesting feature was that the success or failure of the venture seemed to hinge on a single contract to deliver a large number of bricks to London (a city which was well supplied with brick works) with several more large contracts expected. The promise of a large dividend on a rosy-sounding project and a rapid failure was a feature of much speculation at the time.

The reason the Trevarth works foundered was probably in part due to the decline in the local tin mining industry, which after the mania of 1872, was the following year reported to have been very gloomy, crashing in 1874. Also, stiff local competition from the more robust works at St Day and new competition from Messrs Beer and Musgrave's operations at Pennance, established in 1874 and situated less than half a mile away (see below), probably did not help either.

We might speculate as to whether the Pennance enterprise bought up the Trevarth equipment at rock bottom prices and carried on at a profit? This type of operation was not unknown in local industry. The fact that the company was held in shares might also have precipitated its decline, or the fact that the large London orders promised had failed to materialise. Cornish brick works found that despite the high quality of their products, they could not successfully compete with brick works situated closer to the rapidly expanding industrial towns and cities of England. Cornwall was too remote and the costs of transportation were therefore prohibitive.

By the time of the survey of the OS map in 1878, the works are noted as disused, although buildings remained to betray the site's working past. The size of the clay pit (approximately 50 feet wide by 100 feet long and some five feet in depth), suggests a very rapid exploitation of the clay within a couple of years, which lends even stronger evidence to a short-term large-scale enterprise. Furthermore, a newspaper article of July 1878 relates how a 19-year-old man, Alfred Ernest Sampson, drowned whilst swimming out of his depth in an abandoned clay pit between Carharrack and Trevarth. Three or four of his friends present could not prevent the tragedy after joining hands in a vain attempt to save their comrade, who it was reported sank into a deep kind of hole from which the clay had been dug, and his body disappeared for over an hour.[27] It is likely that this deep hole was a 'trial pit,' probably dug in 1871 when the clay was prospected, and which could be in the region of 30–40 feet deep. (The clay was reported to have extended to 36 feet in depth.). Nothing of industrial archaeological interest remains to be seen at the site, except the flooded clay pit, which more closely resembles a duck pond than a site of former industry.

The Pennance Enterprise (SW 7180 4040)

It is not known when clay was first extracted for use from the southern flank of Carn Marth, but an interesting clue can be gleaned from the 1843 Tithe Map for the Parish of Gwennap.[28] Listings for the Manor of Pennance include a field named 'Park Bussa' which was situated close to where the clay pit at Pennance was to later appear. Since 'bussa' is the Cornish word for a large ceramic salting pot, it could be surmised that clay was once recovered from this field (given as number 4038 on the Tithe Map), and used in the manufacture of such earthenware.[29] It is also likely that a number of cob cottages, some since demolished, at Pennance and on the carn, were built using clay recovered from the southern flank of Carn Marth.

The first documented excavation for clay at Carn Marth was in the 1870s. A lease for the Pennance works was granted for a term of 21 years, dated 24 March 1874 to Mr Thomas Beer of Falmouth, ship owner and merchant, and Mr John Musgrave of Falmouth, merchant, together with their co-adventurers, executors, and administrators, assignors etc., by James H. Buller Esq. of Downes in the County of Devon. (A similar lease would have been obtained from Lord Clinton, as the land at Pennance was held jointly)..

The lease stipulated that the lessees could excavate for clay on an area of land covering 32 acres, 3 rods and 7 perches, to a depth not exceeding 20 fathoms below the surface. Full and free liberty was granted to the lessees to erect buildings and create up to fourteen pits at one time. The use of an existing watercourse was guaranteed but permission to restrict the flow of this and other sources of water was not. Provision was made in the agreement that the works was to be securely fenced off from surrounding land and that the workings should not come to within 20 feet of any dwelling house. A sum of one hundred pounds was to be paid to Buller for all agricultural land permanently damaged from the recovery of clay, and fifty pounds per acre for all crofts or wastelands destroyed. The lessees were to, as far as possible, restore the land to its former appearance. The annual

PENNANCE
FIRE-CLAY & BRICK COMPANY
NEAR REDRUTH, CORNWALL,
Are now selling Fire Goods of superior quality, manufactured from clay which has been subjected to the strongest tests, and proved to resist a greater amount of heat than any yet offered in the market.
Samples and prices on application at the Works; or of
BEER, MUSGRAVE, AND CO.,
MERCHANTS,
FALMOUTH.

Fig.6.1. *Advertisement for Messrs. Beer and Musgrave's new company, 1875.* (from the *Mining Journal*)

minimum rent was £12.10.0., and for the rental of the watercourses, £1.5.0. The dues to Buller were one-fourth of one shilling per ton for all china clay, and one-fourth of one shilling for every ton of fire bricks, tiles, drainpipes, chimney pots and like materials. One-fourth of one sixpence was due for every ton of common brick produced.[30]

In February of the following year, Beer and Musgrave placed an advertisement in the *Redruth Times and Camborne Advertiser*, for 'superior quality fire bricks and tiles,' manufactured by the 'Pennance Clay and Fire Brick Company,' near Redruth.[31] Another advertisement was placed in the prestigious *Mining Journal*, pushing the fire clay products manufactured at the works (Fig.6.1). The advertisements ran in both publications for a period of six months, but there seems to be no evidence that the company placed further notices in local or national newspapers; unlike the St Day brick works, which orchestrated a vigorous advertising campaign, appearing in the *West Briton* and other county newspapers each week for many years. Business nevertheless appeared to flourish; a counterpart lease was drawn up dated 18 April 1887 between Buller and the same lessees, which was to run for 60 years.[32] The annual rent had increased to £20. Mention was also made of Lord Clinton, who was to receive three-fourths undivided parts in dues for the operations carried out on the land held jointly with Buller. China clay for the manufacture of pottery and fire clay good for brick manufacture was recovered from a clay pit which had been opened in pasture land on Carn Marth South. On the 1880 OS map, it appears as a neat square section, which could be indicative of an area in which dry clay has been worked by hand. The area immediately to the south of the pit is characterised by a waste heap covering the majority of the area marked on the OS map as 2050. (The manufacturing process of china clay resulted in about seven tons of waste for every ton of clay produced. This and the removal of overburden resulted in large tips, although some of the gravel from the clay making process was likely to have been incorporated into brick production.).

To the south-west of the waste heap is what might have been a 'sun pan,' or large reservoir for settling clay, the area marked 2085.[33] The first edition OS map, surveyed in 1877, shows this feature in blue, strengthening the case for supposing it to be a sun pan. Nearby were two more features in blue which appear to be mica drags (described below).

On the opposite side of Pennance Road a clay and brick works grew up, established in a former goat field, marked 3347, which had formerly been leased by Messrs Williams and Martin. The 1880 OS map revealed that the works had two thickening pits ahead of three kiln tanks. The long building between the tanks and the railway was a pan kiln and linhay, with a chimney at its east end. A siding from the Redruth & Chasewater Railway ran alongside the linhay, where the blocks of dried clay thrown off the pan kiln were stored to await shipment by rail to Devoran. Two beehive brick kilns are also indicated on the map, adjoining a building, and in front of them is shown what appears to be a heated dry with its chimney. The clay dug from the clay pit was loaded into wagons running on a tramway passing through a tunnel, not shown on the 1880 OS map, and was probably excavated during the 1880s, appearing on the 1906 edition.

This tunnel connected the pit with the brick works situated opposite and ran under Pennance Road. China clay was mixed with water obtained from a source which lay to the west of the present day dwelling 'Bolivar House', called the Carn Marth Chute. This suspension of raw china clay in water was run through a series of launders known as mica drags where the larger particles of waste could settle out. The clay in suspension passed on to the two settling pits, where, after standing undisturbed for a time, it would settle, allowing clear water to be run off at the top. After the clay in the bottom of the two pits had reached the thickness of cream, it was transferred to one or other of the three kiln tanks to further thicken. By settling and by evaporation, it reached the consistency of soft butter and was then ready to be taken into the 'dry'. It was ladled into wagons, taken into the dry building and spread onto the 'pan'.[34] In the early days of china clay production, this took place in a 'sun pan' and 'air dry' but was later replaced by drying in a pan kiln. The floor of the pan kiln was tiled, under which ran flues carrying heated air. The clay was finally cut from the pan kiln in blocks and thrown into the adjacent linhay. The coarse remains left in the mica drags at the start of the clay process would have been ideal for brickmaking, either on its own, or mixed with raw matrix from Pennance Pit, perhaps explaining the inclusion of the two beehive kilns to manufacture brick as an auxiliary industry.

Fire clay for brick manufacture was mixed with coarse sand and water in a pug mill until it was of a plastic consistency. This machine ground and kneaded the clay inside a chamber where the material was pushed straight downwards by an Archimedes' screw, and out through an opening of specific size at the bottom. The blocks of clay were then cut to the required size, usually larger than the finished product to allow for shrinkage during firing, and finally, a brick press stamped the company's name on to the surface of each brick, sometimes within a 'frog' or mortar key. The bricks were then pre-dried in a shed to a leather hardness. These 'green' bricks were then loaded on to pallets, and taken to the kilns for firing.[35]

Pennance brick and clay works, under the management of John Thomas, seemed to have had quite a good sized work-force in the 1880s (the larger rival works at St Day employed anywhere upwards of 24 men), enough to cause Mr Gray to complain to Mr Letcher, acting as an estate agent for Clinton and Buller. He was concerned about men from the clay works walking through his fields on their way to and from work, and also wanted a fence erected to prevent encroach-ment on his improved land, in accordance with the terms of the lease.[36]

Clay and brick workers were quite poorly paid and were probably on a par with quarrymen, towards the bottom of the wages hierarchy, earning on average 2s 6d for a day of 7½ hours in the late 1870s.[37] The 1891 Census for Gwennap lists 16-year-old William Carvolth and 47-year-old William Martin, who lived at 'Lannarth', as brick works labourers, and 21-year-old Edward Holman, as a fire man at the works.

By the mid 1880s, the works had phased out the produc-tion of china clay, raising the question of why this should have been so. It must be remembered that world demand for clay was shooting up by leaps and bounds, not just for pottery but for the new and expanding pharmaceutical and chemical industries. Cornwall enjoyed a near monopoly of output and should have made big profits but production was fragmented between 70 or more small companies engaged in cut-throat competition, and marginal firms were often forced into bankruptcy. This might have been the case with the Pennance Pit which turned to brick making for local markets as a 'better proposition', the latest brick machines and mech-anised pug mills facilitating rapid production. Mr Tonkin also considers it likely that the Pennance enterprise could not compete with clay of a similar quality produced at St Austell, once the St Austell clay area's shipping arrangements were well organised. The price per ton, a good percentage being the cost of transportation by 'delivered cart' to the customer, from Pennance was probably too high.

J.R. Smith includes a graph which shows that the years 1870–1890 were the peak years for the opening in Cornwall of new brick works, and this is the period which saw the opening of the Pennance enterprise.[38] The reason for the expansion of the brick making industry at a time when the local mining industry was entering a period of decline could be due to the repeal of the brick tax in 1850. But although mining was the most important aspect of the local economy, it was not alone in providing an expanding market for bricks at this time; the launch of the Pennance works coincided with a local building boom, which saw the construction of new terraces of housing to accommodate the increasing numbers of miners, quarrymen and other people who had moved into the industrial areas of Cornwall such as Camborne, Redruth, Lanner and St Day. Some of these new rows of housing incorporated local bricks, if not within the body of the structure, then certainly for chimneys and window surrounds. An example in the village is Woodlands Terrace, built during the 1880s, which has ornamental brick window surrounds.

Bricks were also required for lining railway tunnels and water culverts, such as would have been needed in the Redruth district during municipal improvements in the 1880s and 90s. (However, the relatively small number of brick dwellings in Lanner, and nearby towns and villages, points to the continued economic advantage of the local quarry industry for building materials, a picture repeated throughout most of the county. This makes the importance of the Cornish brick making industry small in comparison with that of much of England.).

The clay settling tanks and pits disappeared, and in their place were constructed three more beehive kilns. In 1885, the business was reorganised, and the company took a new name, the Carn Marth Fire Brick and Clay Company Limited. This was an enterprise in 5000 shares at £2 apiece with a nominal capital of £10 000.[39] The affair was short lived, as another business was formed only a few years later named the Vulcan Clay and Fire Brick Company, under the management of Thomas Fisher, who hailed from Brixham, Devon. His name appears in the Harrod's *County Directory* in 1878, as Captain Fisher of 'The Amelia Clay Works'. In 1873, a John Netting had appeared in *Kelly's Directory* as a china clay merchant of the Amelia Clay Works. This name could have been used in error for the Pennance works, the name 'Amelia' having previously been used for the mining sett which later became Pennance Consols (Chapter 3, above).

In 1889, the Vulcan Fire-Brick Company Ltd was award-ed a bronze medal at the Paris Exhibition for the excellence of its fire clay products, and the local press reported that the clay at Pennance was said to have produced the best fire brick in Europe.[40] However, in September of 1892, the *Cornubian* newspaper contained an advertisement for the Vulcan Fire-Brick Works, Carn Marth near Redruth, Cornwall, to be sold as a going concern.[41] The public auction was to have taken place at Tabb's Hotel, Redruth, on 14 September, at 6pm.

Several valuable insights into the operation of the works can be gleaned from this advertisement. The property was held under two leases dated 1887, from Lord Clinton, and Sir Redvers Buller, for a term of 60 years from 25 December 1886. On the property were five kilns for burning, each with a capacity of 20 000 bricks, a 12-inch horizontal engine, a 10-ton boiler, with heavy clay-crushing elevator and two brick machines attached, capable of turning out 10 000 bricks a day. Also listed was a vertical engine of 42-inch cylinder, 8-inch stroke, with a boiler, a pug mill (manufactured locally, by Sara & Co. Penryn), and an addi-tional complete horse pug mill, two brick presses, about 120 fathoms of tram iron, tram wagons, and 100 fathoms of 4-inch air pipes. Other items mentioned were a spur wheel, drums, shafting, chain, barrows, picks, shovels and hilts. On the site, there were carpenters' and other shops with corrugated iron roofs, and an office inclusive of furniture. This sale notice points towards an organised and modern mechanised enterprise capable of producing substantial numbers of bricks per week, and doubtless was a valuable labour factor in the local economy. The advertisement claimed that the bricks made and sent out had been, 'used and well reported on by the leading tin smelters, mining engineers, gas companies, founders, assayers and others.'

Some eight months later, another notice announcing the sale by auction of the Vulcan works appeared in the local press.[42] The list of the machinery is similar, but two brick presses are advertised as practically new. This and the inclusion of 15 000 burnt bricks, and 18 000 green bricks, points towards an unsuccessful attempt to restart the works after the previous sale. This time the contents of the office went under the auctioneer's gavel, and a list of sundry equipment, including rakes, pokers, oil cans, brick moulds, timber, corrugated iron roofing, drawing knives and spanners, point towards the intended total closure of the works.

With increased brick production consuming large quantities of clay, it is not surprising to find that. at the turn of the century, the clay pit on Carn Marth had doubled in size. On the 1906 OS map (surveyed in 1904), it appears as 'the old clay pit', which seems to indicate that at the time of survey, the works were closed. The five circular, down draught beehive kilns, each about the size of the width of Pennance Road, were a very visible landmark. The fuel used for firing the bricks was coal, delivered to the works by the Redruth & Chasewater Railway. The siding which ran into the site where the china clay was once loaded, was also used for the delivery of coal, and the dispatch of bricks. Protruding fireplaces were situated at the base of each kiln into which coal was fed gradually until the correct temperature for firing the bricks was achieved. It could take a day to stack a kiln, as the bricks had to be arranged within to allow hot air to circulate and to ensure an even firing. This took in the region of four days, followed by a period of five to eight cooling days. The coal used was a long flame variety full of volatiles, giving a flame tens of feet long under ideal conditions. The hot gases produced by the coal circulated through the kiln which fired the bricks at a temperature of about 1000°C. (Fig.6.2). The amount of coal used on average was ten hundredweight to 1000 bricks.[43]

The fire bricks were used locally for the lining of chimneys or fire places, furnaces, fire boxes and the installation of Cornish ranges. Calciners and boilers in the mining industry also used fire bricks. The Redruth Tin Smelting Company, established in 1862 below the junction of the Falmouth and Helston road at Southgate, used Pennance bricks in their reverberatory furnaces.[44] Common bricks were used in agriculture, and for lining graves and culverts, and in house construction. With the Redruth & Chasewater Railway running down to the Port of Devoran, it is highly likely that a good many bricks manufactured at Pennance found their way to South Wales where the coal to power the Cornish pumping engines was obtained, and where a large copper smelting industry was situated, refractory bricks acting as an inexpensive ballast once the loads of copper ore being shipped there from Cornwall declined. These bricks were consumed in great number by Welsh metal smelting businesses.

Bricks marked PENNANCE REDRUTH were found by Lanner builder John Thomas, when renovating the former post office (now the Londis shop), in 1990, and by Nigel Pender in the chimney flue of 8 Grays Terrace. During renovation of the back of a shop at 83 Fore Street, Redruth, in February 1997, a large quantity of common Pennance bricks was found by local builder Ryan Medlyn. VULCAN bricks were discovered in a toilet block by builder Barrie Kessell in 1995 at Agar Road, Illogan Highway. (Inspection of these samples appears to reveal that these bricks might have been recycled from a smelting works, traces of molten metal being evident on their surfaces.). Interestingly, Charles Thurlow has found bricks bearing the name B.M. & Co., within the Lanner area, and in April 1998, a brick bearing this mark was found in a field close to Lanner Green by 'Chicky' Richards. It could be that these bricks repre-

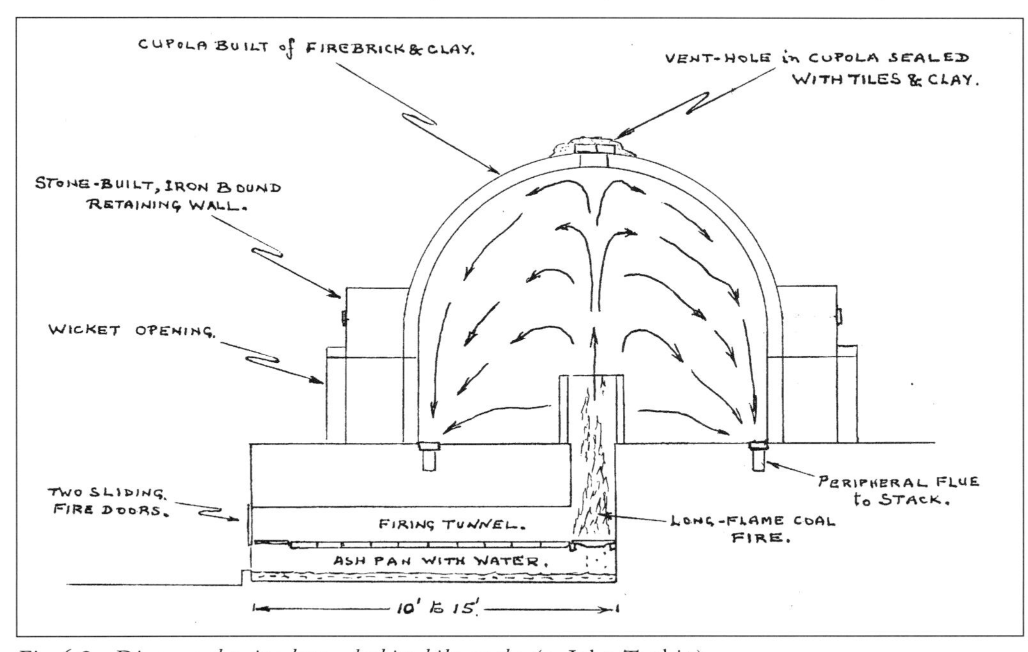

Fig.6.2. *Diagram showing how a beehive kiln works.* (c. John Tonkin)

Fig.6.3. *Carn Marth hill, showing the three chimneys and five beehive kilns of Pennance Brickworks centre-right. September 1919.* (© Royal Institution of Cornwall, Truro)

sent the very early years of the Pennance enterprise, under the management of Beer, Musgrave & Company. Bricks bearing the mark 'Pennance Redruth' are far more common than those marked 'Vulcan', which is understandable, since the latter enterprise was probably of only about five years' duration.

The bricks vary considerably in colour, from a creamy white, through a light salmon colour, to pink, depending on the amount of iron oxide in the clay. The clay for common brick was sometimes deliberately dyed red.

The rival brick works at nearby St Day was capable of producing upwards of 20 000 bricks per day. Pennance found it hard to compete with its successful neighbour. It appears that for the mid to late 1890s, the site was idle (the trade directories for Lannarth do not list the works after 1889), but it worked briefly again in 1902, perhaps following the end of the Boer War and the brighter economic conditions this fostered.

A lease dated 1906 indicates that an attempt to revive the enterprise was tried. At this time the *Royal Cornwall Gazette* reported that the pit was reputed to have been producing 15 tons a day for 'tramming,' but was capable of producing 40 to 50 tons if the demand arose.[45] The *Cornish Post and Mining News* further reported in August that the enterprise was not employing many people, and that the demand was only for limited quantities, even though 'better clay is rarely met and is not wished for'.[46] The workers at this time opted for the more progressive method of clay extraction, 'stoping' the pit rather than terracing, as it was thought to yield better clay by this method. It is not clear whether at this time any brick manufacture was carried out. It appears that this restart was short lived, no further mention to it being made in the local press.

By the beginning of the twentieth century, there were only about 25 brick works active in Cornwall. The Pennance works probably closed before 1910. In a photograph taken in 1919, which shows a view over Lanner towards Carn Marth, the disused brick works can be made out right of centre, with the five beehive kilns and the three chimneys of the works clearly visible (Fig.6.3). In 1924, the *Cornubian* mentioned that the East Pool Mining Company, which had recently purchased the chimneys and kilns, was reported to have been demolishing them for their brick and stone.[47] Mrs Joan Craze, formerly of Carn Marth, remembers seeing at least three of the five kilns in the 1940s, and recalls they had become somewhat ruinous.

An aerial photograph taken over Lanner in 1946 shows the circular outline of five kilns, three of which appear clearly. The site was finally cleared for the construction of bungalows in the 1950s and 60s.

The boundary of the brick works is still evident, as the old hedges of Pennance Road remain, on either side of the new bungalow walls made of concrete blocks, where the works were situated. At the rear of the bungalow named 'Alvern', the remains of the siding which ran into the works can just be detected through the undergrowth.

The clay pit, although overgrown, is still visible. Site visits were made by author and china clay historian John Tonkin and local historian Paul Annear in 1995. Calculations showed that the pit measured about 75 yards in length from east-to-west, and was in the region of 50 yards wide. On the gradient of Carn Marth, the pit measures on the top (north) side about 45 feet high, and 30 feet at the opposite southern end. John Tonkin has found some evidence of terracing as a 'working bench', probably dating from the original workings, plus what might well have been a 'wharf' from the sidings of which barrows of 'matrix' (clay soil) were loaded into hand-wagons and transported by rail into the tunnel cut into the wall base, near the south-south-west of the pit, now closed and inaccessible.[48]

Conclusion

By the turn of the twentieth century, Cornwall's brick works were suffering from several factors, resulting the closure of many. The mining industry had witnessed a steady decline from the 1860s onwards, and by the twentieth century this decline was very evident. Mining used far fewer bricks than is at first realised, with the exception of calciners and boiler houses. The main demand in this industry came from the processing sectors of smelting and refining, which were few in number locally.[49] The collapse of the mining industry in Cornwall, and the gradual cessation of smelting enterprises both within the county and further afield (Swansea, which was for much of the nineteenth century the world's copper smelting centre, had seen the industry dwindle to near extinction by the First World War), sounded a death knell for small brick works such as Pennance. This further points up the result of over-specialisation in, and over-dependence on, the local mining industry. And the market for brick within the building industry suffered a set back with the arrival of the standard gauge railway in 1892, allowing cheap bricks to be transported directly from England into Cornwall.

The building boom in the Redruth area was of relatively short duration, as the underlying somnolence of the local economy became apparent in the late 1890s. Smaller Cornish brick works found it difficult to compete in a more vigorous market, which had also witnessed, at the beginning of the twentieth century, the increased use of concrete as a cheaper and alternative material for construction and the installation of heavy machinery. These factors, combined with the rising cost of coal, the fuel used for firing the bricks, meant that brick works increasingly struggled to remain competitive, especially when cheaper bricks were produced in brick works closer to the expanding cities of England. By 1914 few Cornish works remained open, and within Gwennap, once the heartland of Cornwall's mining industry, the brick works were all closed; St Day, the most important enterprise, had ceased production in 1912.

Certainly, the Pennance brick works was one of the leading brick making establishments in West Cornwall. But the failure of the Trevarth enterprise illustrates the dangers of the speculative madness, manifesting itself in the local mining industry and related industries. The mere mention of the name 'Gwennap' was sufficient to relieve men of their money, which was foolishly invested in shares on the promise of fabulous profits contained within lofty prospectuses, such as that of the Trevarth Clay and Fire-brick Company. If intended to be the mainstay of these Victorian enterprises, the refinement of china clay soon became less important than brickmaking. Lanner's china clay could never have hoped to compete with the larger enterprises of the St Austell area, which produced clay of a very high quality. Yet some local houses, and sites of former industry, contain bricks made in Lanner Parish's two brick works, and it is possible that more examples will come to light in future as older buildings are renovated or demolished.

REFERENCES

1 Thurlow, Charles, *China Clay*, Tor Mark Press, 1996.

2 Wills, Geoffrey, *Proceedings of the Wedgewood Society, Josiah Wedgewood's Journey into Cornwall*, 1956.

3 Penderhill-Church, John, *China Clay in West Cornwall.* ECC International, St Austell. (Undated). We acknowledge Paul Annear for this information.

4 X293\9, Tin Bounds 1760-1810, CRO, Truro.

5 Ibid

6 *West Briton*, 14/10/1948.

7 James, C.C., *A History of Gwennap*, (undated), p. 113.

8 *Royal Cornwall Gazettte*, 26/11/1896.

9 Lease in private collection.

10 Smith, J.R., *Cornish Bricks and Brick Making*, 1991, p.1.

11 *Royal Cornwall Gazette*, 25/7/1874.

12 Tangye, Michael, *Tehidy and the Bassets*, Dyllansow Truran, Redruth, 1984, p.14.

13 Smith, J.R., *Cornish Bricks and Brick Making*, 1991, p.7.

14 Francis, William, *Gwennap, A Descriptive Poem*, 1845.

15 James, C.C., *A History of Gwennap*, (undated), p.156.

16 Henwood, William Jory, *The Metalliferous Deposits of Cornwall and Devon*, J. Pope Vibert, Penzance, 1843, pp 84, 85; *West Briton*, 20/9/1839.

17 Personal communication, Paul Annear.

18 *Mining Journal*, 18/1/1873.

19 Townsend, Elizabeth Kendall, *The Journal of John James, 1822-1885*, transcribed 1984, not published.

20 *Mining Journal*, 10/1/1874.

21 *Mining Journal*, 18/1/1873.

22 Ibid.

23 Ibid

24 Ibid
25 *Mining Journal*, 10/1/1874.
26 Ibid.
27 *Royal Cornwall Gazette*, 1/12/1873.
28 1843 Tithe Map of Gwennap Parish, CRO, CSL.
29 Annear, Paul, *Brick Making in Gwennap, Part Two, Echoes of the Past*, Lanner Historical Society, Edition 3, 1997.
30 DD1 WH 4542\1, CRO.
31 *The Redruth Times and Camborne Advertiser*, 16/4/1875, and *Mining Journal*, 13/2/1875.
32 WH 4543, CRO.
33 Personal communication, Paul Annear.
34 Methods of china clay production as explained by John Tonkin, 1997.
35 Methods of Brick Manufacture, as explained during a conversation with Charles Thurlow in 1996.
36 WH\4143, WH\4133, Notes from Pennance Lands, Part 1. CRO.
37 Mingay, G.E., *Rural Life in Victorian England*, Sutton Publishing Ltd., Stroud, 1998, pp.119-120
38 Smith J.R., *Cornish Bricks and Brick Making*, 1991, p.6.
39 *Mining Journal*, 9/1/1886, p.53.
40 *Cornish Post and Mining News*, 5/10/1889.
41 *Cornubian*, 2/9/1892.
42 *Cornish Post and Mining News*, 5/5/1893.
43 Methods of brick firing, as explained during a conversation with Charles Thurlow, 1996.
44 Michell, Frank, *Annals of an Ancient Cornish Town, Redruth*, 1978, Truran, p.236.
45 *Royal Cornwall Gazette*, 23/8/1906.
46 *The Cornish Post and Mining News*, 30/8/1906.
47 *Cornubian*, 20/3/1924.
48 Personal communication, Paul Annear.
49 Smith, J.R., *Cornish Bricks and Brick Making*, 1991, p. 11.

Chapter 7
Agriculture

In many history books, agriculture always seems to play the passive partner in discussions of the relationships between industry and manufacturing. Indeed, Rowe has commented that agriculture in Cornwall was viewed as 'the Cinderella of the economic order'.[1] But recent scholarship has cast a new light on the interdependence of agriculture and industry. Berg has pointed out that in mineral areas (such as Gwennap), agriculture and industry were ancient by-employments and it was difficult to say which started first.[2]

Agriculture in fact played a dynamic role in the wider economy. Inexpensive agricultural improvements in the eighteenth century, increased labour productivity, and a smaller percentage of the labour force engaged in agriculture had freed more labour into mining and related industries. It therefore became much easier to produce more food at lower costs, which in turn, except in years of exceptionally bad harvests, sustained a steady demographic rise.

The population explosion in Gwennap meant that much of the remaining commonland was enclosed and improved from the late eighteenth century onwards, in order to produce enough grain to feed the mining workforce. This saw an increase in the number of farms. Lanner, in common with many areas west of Truro, contains small farms and moderate to poor soils. Most comprise 10 acres or less and might be better described as smallholdings. Overton has shown that of Cornwall's 13 542 farms in 1870, by far the greatest percentage were those of 5 acres or less at 30 per cent and between 5 to 20 acres, also 30 per cent. Only 10 per cent were over 100 acres and just 2 per cent over 300 acres.[3] In fact the Smallholdings Act of 1894 defined a smallholding as over one acre and not more than 50 acres; or if exceeding 50 acres, not valued at more than £50 per annum for purposes of income tax.[4] Therefore in the Lanner area, the larger farms would have been found on the boundary with Gwennap Parish, such as Trevarth Farm (57 acres), Govorrow Farm (70 acres), or Trebowland Farm (100 acres) .

During the early decades of the nineteenth century, arable farming expanded rapidly in Lanner, as a large influx of miners ensured a ready market for grain crops. In Lanner, as in many other rural areas subjected to rapid industrialisation due to mining, farm workers lived next to miners and switched from one occupation to another from season to season or even day to day. The miner's smallholding achieved a position of great importance, as it subsidised the production costs of mining by reducing real labour costs. And families who were able to raise their own crops on their smallholding were able to maintain a degree of independence from the mine and did not become 'wage slaves', as did many of their contemporary workers in the mills and manufactories of industrial England.

But as Deacon has shown, this independent, mutually beneficial way of life to both mine and smallholder was disrupted by the calamitous potato blight of the late 1840s.[5] The access to land formerly enjoyed by mine workers was lost, and the opportunity of leasing a smallholding was on the wane by the mid nineteenth century. Mine workers were increasingly to be found residing in a terraced cottage and had become more dependant on a formal wage economy. Women, who had contributed to the household economy in pre-industrial times through gleaning, petty trading at local markets and with a variety of domestic handicrafts, were especially hard hit and forced on to the mines to work. For those out of work and divorced from the land, the last resort was the charity of the Guardians of the Poor, the ultimate grave of independence.

The decline of the mining industry from the mid nineteenth century meant that local farmers were forced to change their methods of farming in order to keep their farms commercially viable. Mining collapse coincided with a massive influx of cheap food, especially grain, resulting in agriculturists having to diversify into mixed farming with more emphasis on permanent pasture, animal husbandry and dairy farming. By the twentieth century horticulture featured strongly in Lanner.

The advent of industrialisation also had important repercussions for agriculturists. The agricultural revolution, more accurately described as the industrialisation of farming, witnessed increased mechanisation and the introduction of food processing and strict quality controls. This was viewed as responsible for dismantling a much-treasured rural way of life. Farmers lamented the decline of their independence as farms were forced to operate more like factories, striving to produce top quality produce, in standard quantities and fixed deliveries, for a fickle and ever-changing consumer market. By the twentieth century, the need to meet the strict criteria of quality control in the production and marketing of pigs, cows and other livestock, has witnessed a drastic decline in farming in Lanner Parish, with many of the once popular smallholdings no longer economically viable, and a large percentage of the bigger farms being sold or broken up, with many acres of former farm land being taken for building.

Agriculture and Proto-industrialisation

Before the advent of lode mining in the last quarter of the eighteenth century Gwennap Parish had been a predominantly rural community, and agriculture had been an important industry in the area probably since the Iron Age, place names with first elements 'tre' (Tresavean, Tretharrup, Trevarth, Trethellan), denoting a farming settlement or homestead (see Chapter 1).

In proto-industrial Gwennap (the period which preceded and paved the way for industrialism proper), families engaged in tin streaming or working of superficial moorstone, had for generations derived many of the necessities of life from the soil and the resources of the countryside, and the whole emphasis was on independence and self sufficiency. The countryman relied on established rights to pasture for his animals to graze upon local commonland, and his wife and children worked at home, or from home, engaged in a variety of proto-industrial pursuits (typically cottage industries, i.e., spinning, knitting, etc.), which supplemented the family income.

Numbers of women were once engaged in spinning, as the Gwennap Vestry book of the late eighteenth century makes many references to 'cards' and 'turns', the former used for combing wool and the latter being the spinning wheel. Other handicrafts included knitting, basket making and straw bonnet making, occupations which occasionally crop up on the 1841 census for Gwennap, and any surplus wares were sold at the local markets of St. Day or Redruth.

Dairying was very much a woman's domain, and they were usefully employed in dung spreading. They also helped at harvest time, in early times, by reaping with a hook, and later by binding the sheaves, with a binding made from straw, and performed winnowing, a useful winter chore. With their children they gleaned for seasonal fruits to supplement the table, collected 'gloys' (dried cow pats, a valuable fuel), and 'stubs' (sticks) in the hedges and woods for firewood. They also helped to gather furze and turf on commonland, also for fuel, thus exercising their ancient rights of turbary, which many eighteenth century leases mention, an exemple being an indenture of 1750 between William Painter of Gwennap, carpenter, with William James of Gwinear, tinner: '...the right of common of pasture and turbary in and upon Crook-Glaze Commons...', near Bell Veor.[6] (Local cottagers regularly cut peat and 'tashes' of furze on Carn Marth for fuel. The latter was harvested in the early spring and dried during the summer.). In 1734, women loading dung were paid about 4d per day and those carrying faggots earned about 1d per day, wages which formed an important part of the collective family income.

The men who cut furze had to wear thick leather gloves and a long leather protector on their right leg. About four tashes made up a faggot. Most households burnt an average 1000 faggots in the course of a winter, the ash of which was a valuable source of manure, used to enrich the land for growing potatoes, and was therefore a very important component of proto-industrial farming, as we shall discuss below. Even after the use of coal became more widespread, a furze rick was still to be found stacked neatly outside many cottages in the area in the early nineteenth century, from which a few faggots were periodically removed with a furze hook to the 'ookener', or wood corner, near the fire.[7]

Turf was also dried and stored in a rick and was valued more than furze, since it burnt slowly and retained the heat for cooking over an open fire far better than furze. The late Mrs Minnie Haughton can remember seeing the men cutting furze on Carn Marth when she was a child, in the depression years of the 1920s. And the level of self sufficiency exercised by many local cottagers extended to the brewing of their own ale, using barley, or cider from fermented apple juice. Noted among the chattels of Edward Reed in 1762 were two 'ceivfs' or keeves, vats or tubs commonly used for brewing, indicating that he probably brewed his own ale.[8] At Penventon Farm the remains of a cider press have been discovered. As many of the local water sources were impure, from the medieval period it had become common for people to brew their own beverages.

Until the mid 1700s Cornwall was virtually self sufficient in grain. However, a large population increase, particularly in the mining districts such as Gwennap, caused periodic shortages which in some instances led to rioting in local towns. The steward of James Buller of Shillingham, a local landowner, reported this to his Lord in 1757: 'The times are realy bad here, for the farmers are affraid of Tinners taking it, (their corn) away if they carry it to Markett... all the corn in Redruth Markett has been plundered.'[9] In 1801, the spectacle was repeated, Mr Jenkin of Trewirgie House reporting upon:

> *the disgusting sight of a riotous assemblage of Tinners from Gwennap who broke into the Market and are compelling the people to sell at the prices they choose... I would willingly hope that as the Farmers feel themselves so powerfully protected both by the Civil and Military power, they would be so grateful as to lower the price of corn within the bounds of reason and humanity, and not to hold it up at such prices as to starve a numerous class of subjects of the Government.*[10]

We have seen in Chapter 2 that such food riots in the eighteenth and early nineteenth centuries marked the struggle for the defence of customary rights which were being eroded by increasing industrialisation, and the rise of a wage economy, at a time when the thrift of the self sufficient countryman was being gradually replaced by commercial thrift. The need to produce more grain led to the enclosure of marginal land – the commonland many local families depended on for their livelihood – and which meant the difference between self sufficiency and subsistence.

Enclosure

Periodic shortages of grain in the Redruth area were only compounded by the Napoleonic Wars of 1776-1812, and the Government's passing of the Corn Laws, keeping corn prices abnormally high. The net result of such a shortage and the demographic explosion in areas such as Gwennap, meant that more land had to be brought into cultivation. Recent research by Chapman[11] has shown that the bulk of enclosure was of marginal land, or land reclamation, and Hudson claims that the period of enclosure coinciding with industrial change was 'merely the tail-end of a long process which had been going on since medieval times'.[12]

Enclosure in Gwennap became more pronounced in the mid eighteenth century, and was actively encouraged by the landowners, as evidenced by the terms of a 99-year lease from James Buller of Shillingham to James Munday, a tinner of Gwennap, in 1742. 'The lessee is, within two years, to enclose the premises and build a dwelling house'. The area was some two acres of waste land on Pennance Downs, with a rental value of one shilling a year.

In the neighbouring Parish of Illogan, on the Basset Estate, from 1798–1842, around 400 acres were brought into cultivation, providing homes for two thousand persons.[13] And much the same picture is repeated for the Lanner area of Gwennap. The rough, wild slopes of Carn Marth, strewn with moorstone, and the open downs at South Downs, Pennance, Lanner Beacon, Penstruthal and Trevarth were gradually enclosed and cultivated. Indeed, Richard Thomas of Falmouth, the Chief Mine Surveyor in West Cornwall wrote in 1819, that 'Thousands of acres of downs, commons and wastes, have been enclosed by the miners and others on a small scale, generally from three to six acres in a tenement on each of which one or two cottages are erected.' He mentioned the difficulty encountered in clearing the land in order to prepare it for ploughing, and makes a specific reference to Carn Marth, stating:

> *This has been particularly so on the south west slope of Carn Marth where the enclosing tenants (chiefly miners and labourers) have had to blow the rocks in pieces with gunpowder before they could be collected and heaped up to form fences to their little plots. Two or three thousand tons per acre are thus removed from some spots before the ground is cleared.*[14]

The Government had been actively encouraging enclosure since the 1770s, and this process was hastened in the years following the Napoleonic Wars. In the Gwennap area much land which had previously been uncultivated went under the plough. In all, Mr Thomas estimated that, by 1819, some 30 tenements of the kind he had mentioned had brought into cultivation about 150 acres of land on Carn Marth. He also stated that many more tenements would have been enclosed had the land not been divided among so many landowners. 'The cost of so many leases which the tenants have to pay, amounts to more than the freehold of the surface is worth'.[15] Pennance Downs in the mid nineteenth century for example, was held jointly by Lord Clinton and James Buller Esquire, of Downes in Devon; the former held the lion's share.

Landowners were willing to rent small parcels of land to labourers and miners under the three lives system, upon which they could build a home and improve the land at their own expense for the payment of a moderate rent. The land and cottage eventually reverted back to the landowner. Landlords, whose main source of income was through rents, were keen for land to be enclosed because it was worth much more than commonland, and in this period the latest research has shown that rents rose by about 30 per cent.[16]

It is clear how this system of land tenure certainly benefited the landowner, but it also gave the miner/smallholder an independence from total reliance on the mine for his living. For those who were industrious and resourceful could raise their own crop of barley, oats, corn or potatoes, rear their own livestock and poultry, and produce their own dairy products. This kept large mining families above subsistence level, but also subsidised the mining industry by reducing the production costs, as workers' wages could be kept lower. Therefore mining and agriculture in early nineteenth century Lanner coexisted harmoniously. In 1812 several tenements situated at Lannarth Common (the newly enclosed southern flank of Carn Marth), the property of Henry Mitchell, came up for sale by auction, most consisting of a house and about six acres of land, with a rental value of 2s 6d per year, typical of the type of homesteads sought by mining families arriving in the area as the local mines began to boom.

But Carn Marth was in places still a harsh, forbidding, rocky wilderness in the early nineteenth century, as evidenced by the refusal of the local militia to train there. In 1805, one hundred privates, five sergeants, four corporals and two drummers of the Redruth Royal Infantry were exercised there by General Dunlop in readiness for the Napoleonic Wars. The majority of them were tough local miners, but showed such great apprehension in participating in future manoeuvres on the steep windswept slopes of Carn Marth, that nearby Carn Brea was chosen instead.[17]

The Polkinghorne Family who settled on the carn in the mid 1860s cleared some of the of the croftland near the summit of the south-west flank of the hill in order to plant potatoes on their eight acre smallholding. Even after attempts to remove stones with explosives and crow bars, some of the pieces of moorstone stubbornly refused to move. These and the roots of the 'furze' (gorse) bushes made ploughing difficult, but miner, John Polkinghorne, used to go around the stones with a pick axe instead of a plough to prepare the ground to 'teel' his potatoes.[18] Brambles, gorse and fern quickly grew back on to ploughed land which had to be carefully tended to produce crops, one reason why potatoes were preferred, as they helped to keep down weeds. So it was hardly surprising that it was a local custom to clear a plot of land, take a couple of crops from it and then allow it to revert back to croft. But this was no longer practicable when pressure was placed on the finite land supply as the population grew, and better methods of increasing the fertility of previously cultivated land were sought (see below).

The clearance of croftland at Carn Marth continued periodically up to the turn of the century with unemployed miners put to work there in 1870 and 1896. The dry stone 'hedges', with their angular granite rocks enclosing the plots made by our eighteenth and nineteenth century forbears, can still be seen on Carn Marth, and have stood the regular buffeting of the Atlantic gales well. Many of the enclosures in and around Lanner were very stony and, in the late nineteenth century, T.C. Knuckey remembered his peers at school used to help out their families on Saturdays and during holidays by picking stones from the fields for local farmers. This helped to achieve the fine 'tilth' required for planting, for which they were paid 2½ pence a day. Yet even after careful management and improvement over many years, in the 1960s much of the area about Penstruthal and Rough Street was described as, at best, rather precarious grazing land.

Although enclosure meant that more land was cultivable, and the output of grain to feed the mining population increased, there were big losers in the countryside. The contribution of women's work – gleaning, the manufacture of domestic based handicrafts, petty market trading and seasonal piece work, so central in traditional pre-industrial society, was either relegated to the principle of the invisibility of domestic housework, or exploited in jobs of low status, acknowledged by lack of any recognition that acquiring skill could lead to promotion, and at wages below their economic value. This Valenze classes as the 'ideological devaluation of women's labour'.[19]

For Lanner's women, the main option of employment became that of bal maiden, which, as we have argued in Chapter 4, was perhaps not the model of female independence once thought. And the loss of a domestic based economy also witnessed the evil of children working on the mines, as the rise of a wage economy led to a magnification of child labour to keep working class families above subsistence level. The enclosure of land in Gwennap led to the start of a breakdown in the ancient rhythm of rural life which began to move to a different beat, 'the hollow jarring of the distant steam engines'.[20]

Agrarian Change

To produce high-yielding arable crops to feed a rapidly expanding population of miners, it was necessary to maintain the fertility of the soil, which in the Lanner area was predominantly that of 'growan', a light, black, peat-like soil, interspersed with grit, not very fertile and attaining no great depth. By the nineteenth century, local farmers were aware of the advantages of integrating grass and grain in rotation, the benefits of certain nitrogen fixing crops, and the application of dung to achieve better results. The value attached to a dung heap was exemplified upon farmer Edward Reed's death in 1762. The dung on his farm was estimated to have been worth £2. Many farmers in Cornwall applied ash, soot, putrefying fish, crushed bone, seaweed and a variety of other less orthodox manures on to the soil. But to increase the fertility of the local soils, in areas which were very acidic, farmers had to devise ways of increasing the rate at which organic nitrogen decays into mineral nitrogen to be more readily taken up by the roots of crops. One way to do this was through the application of lime (imported into Cornwall); probably an expensive option for local farmers who perhaps utilised the proximity of the North Coast to apply sea sand, with its high lime content.

But careful examination of nineteenth century maps provides clues indicating that another type of fertiliser was used; one which was cheap because it existed nearby, therefore reducing transportation costs and which was also easily accessible. This was a fossil earth known locally as 'marl'; and two large marl pits have been identified in the Lanner area. Worgan gives the definition of 'marl' as 'a brown or yellow ochreous earth, which is slightly cohesive and becomes friable upon exposure to the atmosphere, breaking and crumbling into gritty particles. Among its constituent parts there is a large quantity of yellow mica'.[21]

One such pit lies behind Trevarth House, and was indicated on a map of the Edgcumbe Estates by Richard Carveth, dated 1827.[22] The pit does not appear on the 1843 Tithe Map for Gwennap, but the area in which it appeared on the Carveth Map is shown on the 1880 OS Map. Inspection of the site in 1997 showed no trace of it, the ground having been disturbed by heavy machinery. Another pit shown on the 1843 Tithe Map for Gwennap was located in the Trebowland vicinity.[23]

Improving the land with dung, sand, marl, or later, imported Peruvian guano, was of prime importance before the advent of artificial fertilisers. For by the application of fertiliser and careful management, much marginal land could be made capable of producing good harvests. In his poem of 1845, William Francis notes the change :

This beautiful hill, once so rugged and bare,
What may be effected by tillage and care
Delightfully proves, green and fair are the fields,
Cheering hopes of rich harvest the scenery yields. [24]

While changes were being adopted to increase the productivity of the local soil, farmers' homes were also undergoing improvements. Many of the early farmhouses in our area were constructed of cob with a moorstone base. 'The lower divisions consist of a kitchen and an apartment dignified with the name of parlour, commonly the larger side, a cellar and dairy room; (but these latter) are frequently under a lean-to roof; the rooms are very low, not ceiled and two bed chambers over; the floor of the chamber are of oak plank, the ground floor – earth, lime-ash or flagstone,'[25] and the roofs of these long houses were usually thatched.

An old thatched cottage of this type, home of the Martin Family, formerly existed on southern Carn Marth, dating in

Fig.7.1 *A thatch and cob cottage at Carn Marth, ca. 1905. Home of the Martin family; the little boy is Sylvester Martin.* (© Joan Martin, Lanner)

all likelihood, from the seventeenth century, or even earlier (Fig.7.1). One can still be seen at Rough Street. Lannarth Farm, known locally as Peter's Farm, an ancient homestead opposite the old Church Green, has been 'raised up' a storey, and has had the thatch replaced with slate, but the wide chimney and the animal quarters attached to the house are still visible.

But Worgan, writing in 1811 commented that 'more modern houses are built upon a more liberal plan; the walls of stone, and roofs of slate'. He noted that things were often still 'thrown under one roof, chall-barns, ox and cow challs being under the chamber for thrashing the corn'.[26] The advent of some of these new buildings in and around Gwennap were described by Francis:

> *...the march of improvement behold,*
> *In handsome buildings that supersede old*
> *And long-decayed houses, with cov'rings of thatch,*
> *With low doors, and rooms, and small windows, to match'.*[27]

Changes in the management and housing of farm animals had led to more being stall-fed, particularly cattle. Instead of being allowed to roam freely, the advantage offered by stall-feeding animals meant that their dung could be collected and used as a fertiliser exactly where the farmer wanted it. However, the improvement in soil fertility and living conditions probably distorts the reality of life for many farmers and smallholders. The advent of industrialisation and enclosure was followed by a breakdown of a customary rural way of life, in which every hour of a countryman's work now had a monetary value. Unemployment became a disaster, for there was a limited amount of land the wage earner could turn to, as was shown all too clearly in the late 1840s.

The Mechanisation of Farming

The power of steam which drove the Cornish engines on the local mines was adapted to drive agricultural machinery by the late eighteenth century, thus introducing mechanisation to the farming world. Cornish engineer, Richard Trevithick, had experimented with the application of steam technology to agricultural implements, successfully making a threshing machine before 1812. Although the spread of threshers was halted after the Napoleonic Wars, when there was no longer

Fig.7.2. *Sid Carlyon's threshing machine.* (© Cornish Studies Library, Redruth)

a labour shortage, they began to reappear in our area in the 1830s–40s, and were a common sight on all farms in and around Gwennap before the Second World War (Fig.7.2). Other mechanised farm implements of the 1830s included winnowing machines and chaff cutters.

Mechanisation enabled certain tasks to be carried out more efficiently and allowed the replacement of human labour. In Cornwall, where the transportation of copper ore to the coast for dispatch to Swansea had been performed by mules, the advantage of taking these animals from labour on the land to transport ore was obvious, in the days before the use of mineral railways became widespread. Threshing machines were estimated to have saved about 70 per cent of labour in the threshing of wheat, and slightly less for oats and barley.[28]

But the introduction of threshing machines was much resented by farm labourers across Britain because they were perceived to deprive men and women of useful winter employment, and some parts of Southern England witnessed rioting. Mechanisation was slow to catch on in the Gwennap area, as evidenced by the comments of a correspondent for the *Royal Cornwall Gazette* writing about the harvest of 1896:

> *About Portreath and Lanner the fields with the cheery harvesters wielding the scythe or superintending the building of the sheaves, present a most businesslike appearance. The use of machinery to facilitate the gathering in of the corn is not yet become general. Unfortunately farmers in this part of Cornwall do not mind being stigmatised as old fashioned and consequently they work according to the methods of their grandfather.*[29]

The collapse of the local copper mining industry probably resulted in a pool of cheap, surplus labour, readily available at harvest time.

Moreover, the suspicion and hostility shown towards increased mechanisation in the local farming world did not diminish. Farmers fiercely defended their independence and viewed increased mechanisation as a threat to their traditional way of life. This attitude was exemplified when Mr Harris of Devis Farm purchased a Hornsby Binder in 1902. The 'contraption' was met with dismay and apprehension by the other local farmers who thought it would create unemployment. However, upon seeing the machine in operation they were slowly won over by its efficiency and eventually it became sought after on all the neighbouring farms. And this suspicious attitude persisted into more recent times. Michael Veall of Gwennap remembers local people harbouring a similar resentment when he took delivery of the first dung spreader, in about 1948. When the machine arrived at Redruth Railway Station the men there refused to unload it, claiming it would do local men out of a job.[30]

The reduction of numbers on the land through enclosure and mechanisation did not seriously affect Gwennap while the mines were at their zenith and employing thousands of people. But in times of economic depression, such as the late 1840s, the danger of divorcing people from the land was made apparent, with many families of the labouring poor reduced to near starvation.

Give us this day, Our Daily Bread – The Preponderance of Arable Farming

When analysing the type of farming prevalent from about 1760–1840, one is struck by the fact that few cattle were kept before the mid nineteenth century in Lanner, or indeed in the Redruth district. Dairying and the rearing of livestock was in its infancy. In 1793, Sir Francis Basset of the Tehidy Estate, a wealthy local landowner with extensive estates throughout Cornwall, only had 35 head of cattle on his 750 acre 'Home Farm', and 15 of these were draught oxen and only one a milch cow.[31] However, there was some local sheep rearing; William Francis in his poem of 1845 remarks that, 'at Devis in past times the sheep, in the crofts rang'd at large and through every creep, midst the dense and high furze with rabbits and hares...'[32] These sheep were probably a native variety, kept outdoors through the mild Cornish winter, with little fodder except that on which they grazed. Their fleece was so coarse, it was named 'Cornish Hair', but was homespun into wool on hand-crafted spinning wheels or 'turns', for making coarse garments. Large scale pig farming was almost unheard of. Instead, farmers concentrated their efforts mainly on the production of grain to sustain the mining community.

That arable farming was once predominant in our area can be seen by analysing some of the wills of local farmers from the eighteenth and nineteenth centuries. We find that their equipment and livestock was perfectly suited to the production of grain. An inventory of one Edward Reed of Gwennap, who died in 1762, shows that he owned 10 mules and furniture for working, to the value of £45, two mares and furniture, priced at £4, and 3 horses and furniture, with a value of £4. Farmers depended on beasts of burden, mules and oxen, to help to plough the land, bring in the harvest and transport goods. In addition, Reed's inventory gives a list of farming equipment including 'a plow share and

Fig.7.3. *Horses 'Trooper' and 'Captain', belonging to the Reed family, plough the fields at Trevarth, looking down towards Treviskey. Early twentieth century.* (© The Paddy Bradley Collection).

coulter,' 'three harrows and harrow tines,' 'a butt and wheels,' 'yokes and chains,' 'two pair of dung potts,' ' one barrow and one slide,' 'two pair turf crooks,' 'a barn floor' and 'a horse rack.'[33] (Fig.7.3). There is no mention of any cattle, sheep or poultry, the overwhelming emphasis being on the equipment and beasts of burden necessary for the careful preparation of the land for the production of arable crops.

The Diocesan Agricultural Returns of 1801 noted that in Gwennap that year the wheat crop was average, the barley and turnips slight, but that oats were good and potatoes very good, although it was impossible to be totally accurate with these figures, for as it was noted 'farmers think that no one has the right to be let into the secret of their traffic, and of course will conceal as much as they can'.[34]

One of the most important crops grown in Lanner was that of oats. From the little surviving documentation concerning agriculture in the area, oats feature prominently. A notice to quit Lannarth was issued on September 16, 1841 to Messrs Job and Job for non payment of rent. A list of the goods distrained from their smallholding included a milk cow and a yearling heifer, plus two small arish mows of oats (a specially constructed pyramid-shaped pile of sheaves) and two plots of oats standing which were impounded on the premises to the value of eight pounds and four pence, the amount outstanding to the landowners.[35]

William Francis notes the growing of fields of oats near Gwennap Churchtown in 1845, and oats were also grown at West Trevarth Farm, which was farmed in a small way by the Tregonings, one of the new middle class families to make a considerable amount of money through the local mining industry. In 1852, William Henry Tregoning of the Bissoe Tin Smelting Co., wrote a letter to his nephew in which he described the summer harvest. 'We took up the little field of oats yesterday. It was, notwithstanding the wet weather, in good condition and we have had the produce put up into two Arish Mows in the Mowhay to prevent them killing the grass in the field. The Western field of oats has not been cut, but it is not fit to be put under bind'.[36]

Lanner farmer and butcher James Davey also worked some land at Trevarth, where in 1870 he sold 15 arish mows (covering about 1.5 acres) of prime black oats, which were sold at auction for the sum of £28.6s. (a rate of £19.8s. per acre). In 1887, 16 mows of oats, the property of Philip Blamey (a butcher/farmer who succeeded the Tregonings at West Trevarth) were advertised for sale by auction.[37]

Also of great importance was barley, one of the main staples of the labouring classes for centuries. A barley loaf was the poor man's bread, being half the price of wheaten bread, and was widely consumed in Gwennap and neighbouring parishes. Local families in former times consumed a daily mixture of barley sops in skimmed milk – 'sky blue and sinker.' Many farmers grew a combination crop of oats and barley, known as 'dredge corn' and used as an animal feed. Michael Veall of Gwennap remembers this crop being widely grown when he was a boy and, as a combination crop, it was harvested together. The fields of dredge corn could be mowed when the barley was ripe and put up into 'shocks'. While it was standing in the fields, usually for ten 'dews', the oats would ripen, after which the sheaves could be carried in. Not a lot of wheat was grown in the Lanner area, as the topography of the land was not suited to wheat growing, the small fields on the downs above the valley being too exposed to the wind. Wheat growing on a large scale was more likely to have occurred in lowland areas in the east of the county, where the fields were larger and more sheltered.

The Diocesan Agricultural Returns of 1801 observed that the reason for the proliferation of oats over corn was due to the huge number of mules being taken off the land to engage in carrying copper ore. Furthermore, the nature of the thin layer of growan soil on many of the high exposed downs was unsuited to wheat growing.

Potato Blight,
the Final Blow to Proto-industrialism

Growan soils were, however, perfectly suited to growing potatoes, a crop which had acquired great importance in the Gwennap area from the eighteenth century. The poet William Francis, commented in 1845 on the custom of farmers depending on a successful potato harvest to pay off their rent. In many other districts, paying off the rent would have been done with wheat.

The humble potato was to have a profound effect on the future development of Gwennap Parish; failure of the crop in the 1840s was to have far reaching consequences for this mining parish, with social and economic relations shifting from what has been interpreted as proto-industrialism (a merchant-dominated, family wage economy, where workers had significant access to non-commodity production, i.e. gleaning for fuel), to a more 'modern' industrial form.

By the 1840s, the areas being enclosed and brought into cultivation was slowing down. This could be in part due to the lack of available land for enclosure, but also the restructuring of the mining industry. Less tribute and more contract work resulted in men having less time at their disposal to work the plots of land surrounding their houses. In the neighbouring Parish of Redruth, Tremenheere, in his report on the 'State of Education in the Mining Districts of Cornwall', found that a significantly smaller number of miners than expected had rented land (on which to build a cottage), on the three lives system, thus suggesting this method of leasehold had witnessed a significant decline.

From the 1840s, people in Lanner increasingly lived in terraced cottages (albeit with large gardens), in common with their proletarian counterparts in the industrial towns and villages elsewhere in England. The early to mid nineteenth century saw gradual changes in the lifestyle of the miner–smallholder, with less opportunity to engage in activities to supplement their income, for instance small scale farming. In short, wage relations had begun to oust the customary relations of non-commodity production. However, Tremenheere does draw attention to a form of collateral aid which remained open to miners by the 1830s – the cultivation of potatoes.

Among the most important is the opportunity of cultivating potatoes in the fields of neighbouring farmers. A natural allotment system has thus sprung up, which proves mutually beneficial to both parties. The miner obtains a stock of potatoes, without, in general, any money payment; the farmer in that case allotting a perch of land for each load of manure furnished by the miner. The latter plants and draws the crop, the farmer preparing the land and carting the manure, of which he has the benefit for the corn crop the following year. The number of perches which a miner can thus secure depends upon the quantity of manure he can collect; and this again greatly depends on his facilities for cutting turf or furze for fuel, of which the ashes form the staple of the manure.[38]

This symbiotic relationship between miner and farmer enabled the farmer to prepare the land for the most important crops, in Lanner, those of barley or oats, while the potato harvest enabled the miner to support his family for several months, and often a pig as well. This it appears, was the chief way in which families in rural-industrial Cornwall maintained access to land, even if they could not aspire to the actual lease of a few acres.[39] In an area such as Lanner, where the difference between miner and farmer was often blurred, this made the provision of allotments much easier.

Deacon argues that, as the population increased in the mining districts, so the availability of land began to decrease, thus placing pressure on the finite resource of land supply, with the result that families became more reliant on collateral aid in the form of the informal potato plot. In Lanner we find that even the new rows of cottages had long gardens used for growing potatoes (for example those at Lanner Moor), reflecting the practice of customary access, which as well as insulating the miners from economic troughs, also helped to maintain a partial independence from landlords who alone decided who could have access to land.[40]

Smallholders and miners alike relied on the potato as their main staple, and suffered dreadfully from the potato blight of 1845–47. This event it can be argued, was as calamitous for the labouring poor in Gwennap as the 1866 copper crash. The terrible blight made the allotment system unworkable and cast working class families back on to parochial relief in the form of bread. In 1847 the *Royal Cornwall Gazette* commented on the effects of the failed potato crop: 'in past seasons, the industrious cottager or miner could rely on his potato crop in aid of wages... his winter comforts secured; but his crops have failed, and he has nothing but his wages to rely on, with bread nearly double its usual price'.[41] The Gwennap Vestry book noted in February, 1847 that certain paupers in possession of smallholdings had been compelled to sell their property because they could not pay the rates.[42] This scenario was not unique to Gwennap, but affected the whole country, and was one of the unfortunate outcomes of enclosure.

Hudson states that the 'logic of enclosure' was the shift towards larger farms, and many small farmers sold up at or shortly after enclosure. 'Small plots carried a heavy burden because they were disproportionately costly to enclose. They were also too small to support families without the aid of customary use rights for grazing, hunting and gleaning which had been integral to the ancient usage of the common lands'.[43] In times of agricultural depression, such as the catastrophic potato blight, small farmers found themselves vulnerable to being bought out by larger farmers. The potato blight, coupled with the detrimental effects of enclosure disrupting the traditional way of life, was the chief factor in the beginnings of the huge migration from Gwennap Parish, a rational response to ease the pressure on collateral aids, and actively encouraged by the Gwennap Vestry.

Contrary to orthodox history, therefore, mass migration began while mining was still doing well. But those who remained in Gwennap became gradually proletarianised and made increasingly dependent on the mine and their wage packet. When the copper mining industry collapsed in the 1860s, a return to making a living from the land, at times other than harvest, seemed little more than a remote hope for many miners. The opportunity of leasing a smallholding was more limited, mechanisation had decreased the amount of labour needed on local farms, and farm work was mainly seasonal and characterised by low wages. In short, to make an independent living solely from the land was becoming impossible for many large families. The only answer to long-term unemployment and the dole, an affront to the pride of the fiercely independent local miner, lay in migration.

Changing Patterns of Farming

Changes in the type of farming carried out in Gwennap and Lanner are closely interconnected with the fortunes of the local mining industry. The de-industrialisation and subsequent depopulation of the area, following the collapse of the copper mining industry, meant that farmers lost a large percentage of the market for their barley, oats and corn. The Government lifted the ban on imported grain at precisely the time that the large-scale migration from Cornwall had begun. Cheap imported grain caused severe competition to Cornish farmers. Michael Veall recalls that locally grown wheat was considered to be of inferior quality, and imported hard-grained American wheat was preferred in the twentieth century. He also remembers cheap imported 'Azov' barley from the Ukraine, which was ground locally, decreasing the amount of home-grown barley finding its way to the mills. The arrival of the standard gauge railway in 1892 further compounded the problem by ensuring that grain from the Eastern wheat growing areas of England could be transported directly to Cornish markets.

Their local market for grain having collapsed, Lanner's farmers found themselves unable to compete in the wider market and were made to realise the price of their dependence on the mining community for their livelihood. They too had become indirect victims of over-specialisation in the copper mining industry. By concentrating their efforts on arable farming they therefore suffered equally from the effects of the painful process of local de-industrialisation. Furthermore, the increase in real wages and rising standard of living amongst the working classes, who were now able to afford to consume more dairy products and meat, produced a decrease in the proportion of bread consumed, again leading to a shift away from large-scale grain production. Moreover, a series of wet summers and disastrous harvests in the late 1870s meant that some farmers, who had borrowed money too freely during the good years to buy new equipment, now found themselves over-stretched.

In the Lanner area there were numerous examples of families quitting farming altogether in the late nineteenth century, such as John Vine of Buller Downs, who sold his farm and equipment in October 1870, including livestock, ploughs, harrows, a corn-crushing machine, a patent churn and butter slab and hay, oats, cabbages, mangolds and turnips. F. Richards of Bell Farm left farming in 1871, selling his 6 prime young bullocks, 3 dairy cows, and one cow fit for the butcher, as well as 2 fat heifers, 2 slip pigs and farm equipment.[44] T. Trengove, of Bowling, near Trethellan, did the same the following month. His stock consisted of 7 dairy cows, 2 heifers, a brood sow and 4 slips, a horse, 2 carts, a light wain, a chaffing machine, ploughs, harrows and rollers.[45] William Barrett of Trevarth Farm, put his farm up for auction in 1885, the Kemps of Carn Marth ceased farming in the late 1880s because their smallholding could not be made to pay, while Mr Skinner of Lanner Hill sold his farm in 1897 before he emigrated.

Local farmers had to change their methods of farming to survive and many had already begun to practise mixed farming from around the 1870s. The fall in cereal prices cut the cost of animal feeding stuffs, so that homebred meat, being cheaper to produce and of better quality than imported meat, held its prices. Cattle, poultry and pigs were introduced in greater numbers on some local farms, and small scale dairying became more prevalent in the area. By changing their emphasis from large-scale grain production to mixed farming and animal husbandry, many local farmers were able to survive the calamity of the collapse of the copper mining industry. In 1885 the livestock on Trevarth Farm included 20 good breeding ewes, 10 lambs, one cross bred bull, 17 fat and 'growthy' steers, 2 good labour horses, a pony and a colt, plus a variety of poultry.

In 1894, Thomas Kneebone's farm of 14 acres at Lanner Hill contained 3½ acres of good hay, plus two acres of oats, two fields of grass and a quantity of potatoes. He had 10 bullocks and about 40 fowls, a good example of small scale mixed farming. The equipment on his farm consisted of a Johnston combined mower and reaper with platform, an iron roller and shafts, plough harrows and an American hay rake. The annual rental on his five-bedroomed farm was £25.5s.[46] Michael Veall estimates that by the 1940s only about one quarter of the total acreage on most local farms was arable. The remainder was pasture land, which had favoured the rise of small scale dairying.

The Rise of Dairying

On most nineteenth and early twentieth century smallholdings it was common to find one or more milch cows providing milk to be made into cream, butter and cheese. In 1897, the stock on Mr Skinner's dairy farm at Lanner Hill comprised five dairy cows, of which four were well seasoned in calf, 1 yearling, and a useful amount of dairy equipment and implements (as well as a store sow, and about 120 good laying hens).[47]

Easier rail access from the 1890s, however, brought real problems to farmers who tried to sell their produce in local markets. Small-scale family farms like those in Lanner, following traditional methods, used to store their produce for some time before they had enough to make it worth while taking it to market and, in the process, as Hamilton Jenkin has described, butter acquired a greyish tinge, while other items were 'tinctured with a variety of flavours'.[48] To their horror, local farmers found that the Cornish housewife would pay a premium for Danish and Dutch butter, bacon, eggs and cheese, standardised and graded for quality, size and colour. To save the Cornish farmer from disaster, food processing factories were needed, and Cornwall's modernising bourgeoisie of industrialists, merchants and bankers rallied round to finance them.

Erecting the factories was one thing, getting farmers to deliver a standard output of uniform quality at regular times was quite another. Although farmers were realistic and practical, they were 'men of the soil' as Rowe called them, temperamentally opposed to becoming – as they saw it – slaves to a factory system. The result was some spectacular failures. One dairy-processing factory at Truro closed because farmers, in open carts in warm weather, delivered cream that went sour before it arrived. Another, in Helston, collapsed partly because the quality of milk was poor, partly because in times of drought, farmers switched to supplying the growing tourist industry.[49]

Yet despite these problems, Lanner farmers continued in the dairy trade. Mrs James' smallholding of nine enclosures of fertile pasture land at Bell, containing about 6½ acres, was stocked with 4 dairy cows, in calf and in milk, 8 fat bullocks, 2 yearlings, plus all the implements and utensils necessary to carry on the small-scale dairying prevalent in Lanner at the time.[50] The Nicholas family, who farmed Tregiffian before and during the Second World War, were well known locally; Dora Nicholas demonstrated butter making and dairying all over the county and later inspected farm premises for the Ministry and the Milk Marketing Board (see below), to create and maintain hygienic standards.

G. Blamey remembers the dairy at West Trevarth Farm in the early 1920s with its hand-operated milk separator with various fitments and funnels through which the milk passed. The separated milk was fed to the calves. Earlier this century at Carn Wartha and Rockfield, smallholdings at Carn

Marth, were dairies with flagstone floors. The Kellows, who farmed Tregiffian after the Second World War kept two or three Jersey cows, and the Whears also had a few milking cows. The milk, cream and butter produced by such small-holdings was for the immediate use of family and close neighbours, while any surplus was sold locally at markets or by running a milk round in the area.

Some of the larger farms sold their milk for about 4d a quart around the time of the First World War. Lanner people would go to the farm nearest their place of residence for their daily dairy produce. In the early 1920s and 30s, Joan Martin of Bell Veor can remember going to Bell Farm each day for eggs, milk and cream. The farm was kept by the Nicholls. 'I would go there twice a day, for a quart in the morning and a quart in the evening, except on a Saturday. My father was a strict Methodist and did not believe in doing on a Sunday what could be done on a Saturday or Monday, so I had to collect two quarts on my Saturday visits'.

Joan Martin also remembers the large dairy herd of Jersey cows kept at the Harris's farm which was later farmed by George Moyle. This farm was where Lanner School is now situated and covered much of Lanmoor Estate. The high walls surrounding the farm's garden can still be seen. The Moyles also grew and sold vegetables from the farm, as well as selling eggs.

William Peters, who kept Lannarth Farm at Rough Street, opposite the Church Green, used to sell his milk door-to-door, from a cart laden with a milk can, from the rim of which hung half pint and one pint measures. Irene Williams remembers the milk still being warm when delivered. On Sundays, Irene would be sent for a quarter of cream for tea, and Mrs Peters would weigh the glass dish first before putting the cream in. 'She would cover it with a milk filter pad so we kids couldn't dip our fingers in before we got the cream home'.

Michael Veall remembers other milkmen delivering with a pony and trap, in the Lanner area, were Mr Knuckey and Mr Berryman. Larger producers included the Pearce's at West Trevarth Farm, with 20 cows, and James Mewton of Tresavean Farm with a herd of 25 milking cows (as well as 22 other cattle).

E.A. Ellacott, at Carn View, Lanner Hill, with a good sized dairy cattle herd, produced 30 pounds of cream each week which his wife sold for two shillings a quarter. Surplus milk was sent to milk processing factories, at Trenheer, and the Primrose Dairy at St Erth.

However, by the early twentieth century, small farms across the nation were suffering from competition with the large-scale enterprises nearer to the growing towns and cities, and could not compete with their prices for dairy products. Cornwall was severely disadvantaged because of the high cost of transportation by road or rail to distant markets. The Milk Marketing Board, set up in 1933, helped farmers from places such as Cornwall to compete in a competitive market. The Board fixed milk prices which meant that Cornish farmers were not hampered by peripherality – remoteness from the large towns and cities of England. James Mewton was one Lanner farmer whose farm produced a milk surplus for his local dairy round, but some milk was collected by the Treswithian Milk Marketing Factory at Camborne. And Mrs Ivor Pearce, formerly of West Trevarth Farm, remembers the length of Pennance Road had churns filled with milk placed ready for collection by the Milk Marketing Board. The churns were later returned to the farms containing the separated milk.

Yet those farmers who remained in dairying faced another change when refrigerated bulk tanks replaced churns in the 1970s. Susan Gribble of Trevarth Farm decided to finish milking and to go over solely to beef cattle, as the change to bulk-tank delivery would have entailed modernisation of the milking parlour, an expense she was not prepared to meet.

However, on most of Lanner's farms earlier this century there were not enough milking cows per holding to make the farm pay by undertaking dairying alone, and it was therefore carried on in tandem with the rearing of pigs.

Pig Production and the Industrialisation of Farming

Pig farming became an important feature on many Cornish farms from the late nineteenth century, and was often also connected with horticulture in Lanner, as we shall see below. Lanner man, C. Andrew, was a dealer in the carcass pig trade for much of the 1870s and 80s, and bought and sold the carcasses at Plymouth Market, travelling there three times a week to superintend the sale. He transacted business in the Redruth Market every Friday.[51] Redruth weekly market was once alive with the grunts and squeals of hundreds of pigs and weaner pigs awaiting purchasers each Friday. Many local farmers made good money before and just after the Second World War by beginning with a sow producing a litter of piglets which were sold at a small profit.

Lance Bray estimates that his uncle, horticulturist Bill Harnden, usually kept 2–3 sows in the 1930s and 40s. At times there could be in the region of 30–40 piglets which were sold to local farmers such as James Mewton or Michael Veall, providing an important additional source of income.

Simeon Gribble at Trevarth Farm kept about 40 pigs in the 1940s, and the Banfields also kept pigs on their farm at West Trevarth, Michael Banfield being responsible for rearing the piglets which were fattened and sold to the Cornish Meat and Provision Co., Redruth, or to C.&T. Harris, Redruth. Probably one of the largest pig farmers in the parish, just after the Second World War, was James Mewton at Tresavean Farm, who kept at least 600 pigs. During the 50s and 60s E.A. Ellacott of Lanner Hill also kept pigs, as did John Kellow of Ivy House, Penstruthal, Mr Peters of Lannarth Farm, Mrs R. Whear, and Ivor Pearce of West Trevarth Farm.

In fact Michael Veall remembers that there was hardly a farm which did not have pigs, and that pig farming and dairying, so prevalent in Lanner, was carried on in a symbiotic cycle. Milk produced by the dairy herd was sold to the Milk Marketing Board, where the cream was separated. The skimmed milk, returned in churns, was then mixed with barley and used as a feed for pigs. The pigs were fattened and sold, for either pork or bacon, at the Redruth bacon factories. The manure produced by the pigs was utilised as a fertiliser, 'skidded' over the fields to increase the fertility of the grass upon which the dairy herd grazed, or to enrich the soil for the barley crop which formed a part of the pigs' feed. When fattened sufficiently, pigs were sold for slaughter at local factories, or, at five score deadweight (the carcass weight of 100lbs, after removal of the intestines etc., but including the head and tail), were dispatched by train to Smithfield Market.

The West of England Bacon Factory at Redruth, financed by a list of shareholders that read like a roll call of West Cornwall society, offered a striking example of the reluctance of farmers to engage in standardised, industrialised systems that removed independence and control over their lives. Farmers produced two types of pig – that for pork, once very popular amongst Cornish housewives – the smallholder's pig. It was raised and fattened for pork and lard on home-produced food and slaughtered at a lighter weight than the second type – the bacon pig. This was leaner and of a far higher quality. The Redruth factory attracted pigs from as far east as St Austell and as far west as Penzance, but the farmers complained that the management rejected too many pigs as too fat, or too short. After a decade of loss-making, the owners sold out for a song to the Wiltshire firm of C.&T. Harris of Calne, who made farmers toe the line and breed their pigs from standard boars.[52]

In the post war period, pig production in Cornwall became a very important industry, with the South West region third in importance nationwide. At many local farms, such as West Trevarth, Tresavean, and Govorrow (just outside the Lanner Parish boundary, but which employed Lanner men), pigs were the largest enterprises. Before 1950, the Danes led the market in lean bacon production, an industry subsidised by their Government. Britain had to match the quality of Danish produced bacon if the British bacon industry was to survive without any subsidy.

The rise of the bacon pig was the first factor in the decline of pig farming in Lanner. Coupled with changes in the consumer market, came problems connected to the modernity and fabric of many local farms, which did not favour large-scale, intensive farming. The Government encouraged farmers to borrow money to modernise their holdings, as the trend towards bigger, more efficient units gathered pace, but grants were only in the region of one-third of the total cost. Therefore, only the bigger farmers could afford the two-thirds necessary to secure the Government grant.[53] In Lanner, there were not many farmers large enough to consider this option. Smaller local farmers were therefore pushed out by the bigger, more efficient, and modern farms in the county and beyond.

In the years following the Second World War, a new breed of pig was introduced into Cornwall from Denmark and Sweden which soon replaced local breeds such as the Cornish White. This Scandinavian newcomer was called the Landrace Pig, and was bred for the bacon market.

This animal improved the quality of local stock, but hand in hand with this improvement came a seemingly never-ending battle to meet the stringent new requirements for top quality in an increasingly competitive market. Housewives, used to high quality Danish bacon, now demanded leaner home-produced bacon, and local farmers had to reach set standards of excellence for lean carcasses. A study undertaken by the Department of Economics at Bristol University in 1958 concluded that for mainly homebred pigs in 1956–57, every £100 spent on food produced on average £142 of pig output; where pigs were mainly purchased the corresponding figure was £132. A difference of £10 on either side of these averages was likely to mean a good profit, or none at all.[53] And on top of this, Cornish pig producers were disadvantaged in the national market. They had to market their pigs at the highest possible price, which meant meeting the strict criteria of quality control, because the cost of pig production in Cornwall was amongst the highest in the country due to transport difficulties and distance from urban markets.

In about 1960 the Cornwall Quality Pig Association (CQPA) was formed. This organisation and others like it, were formed by the bacon factories with the object of improving the quality of the pigs supplied to them.[54] They set rigid quality controls which many Lanner farmers were unable to meet, and so were gradually squeezed out of the market, leaving only a couple of local producers maintaining top quality pigs – Michael Veall at Govorrow, and Michael Banfield at West Trevarth Farm. This highly competitive market hit local pig farmers very hard and those who remained in pig production found they were forced to co-operate with other pig producers in order to exert some influence over the price of the product they hoped to market. This was set by the Fat Stock Marketing Corporation (FMC), an industrial Leviathan which bought pigs at the price they chose from local producers.

Due to this pressure in the economic hard times of the late 196's, Michael Veall and a handful of other Cornish pig farmers were forced to set up an independent co-operative named the Western Quality Pig Producers (WQPP) in order to survive in pig production. This co-operative aimed to successfully market and sell locally-produced pigs at fair prices. Challenged by the monopolistic Fatstock Marketing Corporation, the co-operative created a limited company in 1000 £1 shares. Members promised to market 90 per cent of their produce to the company for the next three years, and the company then marketed these pigs to various bacon factories, bargaining for the best deal and concessions, and thus breaking the monopoly of the FMP. The WQPP saw their grading for pigs improved from 50 per cent to over 80 per cent (the top quality) in the space of a few years even though the standard of grading pigs tightened considerably. Only producers who were likely to meet the strict requirements were accepted as members.[55]

In 1975, Cornish producers of the WQPP opened the first producer-controlled bacon factory in the South West, at the Redruth premises of the old Cornish Meat and Provision Company. The co-operative contained between 30–40 Cornish pig farmers, including Michael Veall, who was its Vice-Chairman. The success of the co-operative was underlined in its yearly bonuses awarded to members, something they could never have achieved as individual producers. In the Lanner area, the only pig producer who managed to remain in the competitive market for pigs was Michael Veall, after the tragic death of Michael Banfield of West Trevarth. Michael has since retired from farming, and pig farming in Lanner has completely died out.[56]

Other Livestock, Poultry and Eggs

It was not until the twentieth century that large herds of beef cattle were introduced to some of Lanner's farms, but this was never to be as important as pig farming. Leonard Winn of Sea View Farm, Carn Marth, had about 40 head of cattle in the mid 1900s which were sold for beef, and in the 1940s, Simeon James Gribble of Trevarth kept about 40 beef cattle. Herds of cattle were once driven to markets; John Arthur Bray of Buller Downs formerly drove cattle from Busveal to Helston market on a regular basis, and Simeon Gribble drove his beef cattle to Truro market, but by the mid twentieth century, this job was being done with the aid of cattle trucks.

The Stephens family, originally from Chasewater, came to Lanner in 1955. Harold Stephens married the daughter of haulier, Joe Dunstan, of Bell Farm, and took over the haulage business which he built up by securing contracts for haulage with FMC Meats, the West of England Bacon Factory and the Cornish Bacon Factory, based in Redruth. He also regularly transported animals for many farmers both to markets and to local abattoirs. He owned three lorries, and employed four men as drivers; Joe Combellack, Clifford Stevens, Henry Holland and later, John Sobey. The business thrived until the 1990s, when new EEC laws governing the transportation of livestock and the closure of local abattoirs, meant that the Stephens' had to compete for longer haulage contracts which became uneconomic. In 1994 Calvin Stephens pulled out of the business thus ending one of Lanner's more successful enterprises.

Sheep rearing never made much of an impact in Lanner. One of the only farmers to keep sheep was Mr E.A. Ellacott, who sold his dairy herd in 1965 and replaced this with a flock of pedigree South Devon Sheep. Susan Gribble has experimented with flocks of sheep, but commented that it is a specialist job, and a farmer has to keep a large flock for it to be lucrative. The sheep market is financially precarious, and the use of increasingly controversial organo-phosphates in the sheep dip has made many farmers think twice before going into sheep farming.

The appearance of more livestock on Lanner's farms and smallholdings led to an increase in demand for veterinary surgeons. Most farmers could not afford to call a vet when an animal required medical attention, but farmer Philip Bray acquired a reputation as a kind of 'cattle doctor', and people from far and wide relied on him to effect a cure for their animals. 'Never passed for 'veterinary', but had a gift', recalled his daughter, the late Mrs Mary Job. 'I used to help him make his 'drenchin's' with stale beer mixed with various powders'.[57] Today, the procedures for treating animals are very complicated, with all medicines administered having to be strictly recorded in a log book. Susan Gribble commented that she often spends more time in the kitchen measuring out the doses, than working on the farm.

Many local farms raised poultry before the war, and Mary Job was frequently asked to kill, pluck, draw and dress poultry, a job she did at home to earn extra money, charging three pence for a chicken, sixpence for a duck and a shilling for a goose. She hung the birds upside down by their legs from the trees in her orchard and then slit their throats. After they had been left to bleed, she brought them in to be plucked and drawn. During the busy season at Christmas and Easter, the floor would be covered with a thick layer of feathers each day.

Older people of the village might remember 'Sick 'in (hen) Moyle', a village character who used to visit various local farms buying up 'wisht' hens for a few coppers. These he would try to sell on to people who were bed-ridden or sick!

The local production of eggs had reached quite a substantial level by the twentieth century. Many farms and smallholdings in Lanner had chickens. By the late nineteenth century the Opies, a Lanner family, established themselves both locally and further afield as successful entrepreneurs in the collection and marketing of eggs. Their business in locally produced free range eggs proved so successful, that Bennett Opie went to London in 1879 and founded a firm to sell Cornish eggs. At times quality was questionable, as small farms kept eggs for many days before there were sufficient numbers to be collected by Opie's local agents. And these were often not dispatched immediately.

Opie's company soon dominated the local egg market and began to dictate the price of eggs. In 1898, local producers were angered by the appearance of an association affiliated to the London firm, which held meetings at Comford and Redruth. 'Let supply and demand govern the price of the egg commodity as any other business', commented a local farmer, who drew attention to the fact that this association, which folded soon after its inception, had been responsible for driving the price of eggs down to 7d a dozen, with the price looking set to take a further nose dive.[58] Farmers feared that they would be squeezed out of the market as the cost of keeping the chickens was outweighed by the price they received for their eggs.

Opie's company continued to enjoy the virtual monopoly well into the twentieth century, collecting eggs from large farms, such as James Mewton of Tresavean Farm who had 300–400 fowls, and also smallholders like Wilfred Bray junior, who had about 200 deep-litter fowls in his large gardens at Winn's Terrace, Carn Marth. Wilfred's wife tended them while he worked at Falmouth Docks. The Opie Egg business was carried on by Ewart Opie until recent years from a shed behind his house at Woodlands Terrace. Ewart and two or three employees (Bert Graham, Willie Treloar and Cecil Knuckey) collected the eggs from local farms by van, which were then graded on an electrically-driven grader and boxed for market.

Yet free range egg production has declined to virtual extinction in Lanner, with just a handful of farms producing an egg surplus. In common with pig production, the poultry and egg industry became a victim of industrial food processing, with hens increasingly housed in batteries, lowering the cost of egg production and pushing free range egg farmers out of the market. And after the salmonella scare in the 1980s, farmers lost the confidence of the public, and by law are unable to sell eggs which have not passed the strictest quality controls.

Flower Power – the Rise of Horticulture

By the early twentieth century, a new form of farming had arisen in Lanner's sheltered valley – market gardening. In many cases this was supplemented by the raising of a few pigs which supplied the manure necessary to fertilise the land for this form of intensive agriculture. Horticulture had increased in importance in Cornwall ever since the main line railway had made it possible to send quantities of fresh produce in the form of vegetables, fruit and flowers by rail to markets in London and further afield. Lanner as a flower growing area hardly springs immediately to mind, the 'golden crescent' around Mount's Bay, the Isles of Scilly and the Tamar Valley being by far the better known locations for this industry. But Lanner's sheltered valley meant that it was possible to produce high-quality flowers, and some vegetables, as important cash crops on many local farms.

The Dowers, nurserymen from Carn Marth, grew roses for wedding bouquets and sold flowers at Redruth market each Friday. They also grew a large amount of tomatoes in their long glass greenhouses. Bill Harnden had market gardens at Pennance, which covered two fields and were about 4–5 acres in extent. He had four large greenhouses in which he grew tomatoes, cucumbers, freesias, carnations, and a variety of pot flowers, such as geraniums, and bedding plants. He sent anemones up country to Covent Garden by train from Redruth. Many of his flowers went into wedding bouquets and wreaths.

As a child, Sylvia Kessell and her cousin Lance Bray, Bill Harnden's nephew, often gathered moss from one of the Carn Marth quarries for the wreaths. He also grew violets, pittisporum and statice, plus a variety of outdoor vegetables such as cabbages, peas, beans, turnips and some potatoes which he sold in his flower and vegetable shops at Penryn and Falmouth. He also had a wheelbarrow-round in the Lanner area. The manure to fertilise the ground came from the pigs he kept. He also kept chickens and ducks, and occasionally pruned people's shrubs and fruit trees, such as the apple trees at Treviskey House. Lance Bray remembers

Fig.7.4. *Banfield's Flower Farm, after the Second World War.* (© Prudence Danby, Trevarth).

that his uncle made a living, but that the market garden business was not very lucrative, especially in the more competitive market following the Second World War. In about 1962 Bill Harnden sold the land and shortly afterwards bungalows were built on the two fields.

By far the largest and most successful commercial business in flower production was that of Banfield's at West Trevarth Farm. Jack and Barbara Banfield came to West Trevarth House in 1925 from the Isles of Scilly, where horticulture was an established business, and where Jack and Barbara had been flower growers. West Trevarth Farm contained about 40 acres. The business, known locally as 'Banfields', grew flowers for export to the English markets, particularly Covent Garden, and was incredibly well run. The farm employed six or seven men and two women, most of the time, and during the height of the spring and summer flower-growing season, many more would be hired on a piecework basis. A wide variety of flowers were grown all year round, the busiest time being the daffodil season. Numerous varieties of daffodils were grown, including Princeps, Spur, Ornatis, Sunrise, Flame, King Alfred, Scilly Whites, Magnificence and Soleil d'Or (Fig.7.4.).

The daffodils were picked by perhaps five or six men and placed into wooden boxes, then brought into the greenhouse where the women bunched them into 12s. They were potted and next day packed into wooden boxes (later metal trays), lashed into pairs and sent, in early years, by horse and wagon to Redruth Railway Station where they were destined for Paddington Station. Later, a lorry, or car and trailer, were used to transport the flowers. At the height of the daffodil season as many as 200–300 boxes a day were sent to London on the 4.30pm flower train from Penzance. Flowers thus dispatched were on sale in Covent Garden by 6am the following morning. Later on the business also sent flowers to Birmingham to two suppliers, A.W. Carey and George Monroe. The boxes were sent back to West Trevarth and in the winter months the employees, even the women, were put to work mending any which were becoming dilapidated.

Other flowers were sent to Covent Garden throughout the year. 'Governor Herrick', a large violet, was a very popular flower, much sought after in the large industrial towns of England and once worn by Edwardian hunting ladies as buttonholes. Many of the south-facing smallholdings in the area formerly grew these violets for local markets. Narcissi and irises were also successfully grown, as were 'scillas', a cross between a bluebell and a hyacinth. This particular flower is no longer fashionable and shows how tastes have changed over the years. Marigolds, arum lilies, acidanthera (gladioli), Kaffir lilies, alstromeria and freesias, grown under cloches, were dispatched throughout the spring and summer months. Pittisporum was grown for foliage and packed in large hessian containers.

Every three years the daffodil bulbs would be lifted and sterilised at the end of the summer and replanted by the autumn in rows of six. Dutch salesmen called frequently at West Trevarth; Mrs Todd, the daughter of Jack and Barbara Banfield, remembers their interest was in the bulbs, and that two such visitors were named Martin Kruff and Jon de Vries.

Margaret Sedgley of Carharrack was a full time employee at Banfields for 34 years. She remembers packing the flowers in the long greenhouses to the rear of the farm. She recollects that there was a 'pecking order' among the employees; because she was one of the longest serving workers there, she had the privilege of standing next to Barbara Banfield when packing. The Banfields were producing flowers for the top end of the market, King Alfred daffodils being an expensive variety with a price in Covent Garden of 1–2 shillings a bunch in 1948. 'Governor Herrick' violets commanded on average about 1 shilling a bunch, arum lilies 1–2 shillings per bunch and Wedgewood irises up to 5 shillings per bunch. During the Second World War, much of the acreage was broken up for vegetable growing, the soil enriched by pig manure, and the farm produced runner beans, peas, potatoes, carrots and lettuce for the home market. Two Land Army Girls worked at the farm at this time. The flower business ended with the death of Jack Banfield in 1980, and the farm eventually reverted back to pasture for cattle, farmed by the Andrew family.[59]

Michael Veall grew broccoli and potatoes on his farm after the Second World War as cash crops. Farmers benefited, as they had done at the time of the First World War, from high prices. And even after the war many basic foods remained rationed, so in order to stimulate production, the Government offered attractive incentives to farmers to produce crops at the time they wanted. An example was the Ministry of Food's decree that if potatoes were harvested by 1 June, local farmers would be paid £40 a ton. The price dropped daily by £1 thereafter. Lanner farmers competed to take their potatoes to the Ministry of Food depot at Drump Road Station on, or as near to 1 June as possible, where Rowe & Co. of Redruth acted as local Government agents. And as it was imperative to harvest the potato crop at the very beginning of June, local schoolchildren were often allowed time off school to help with the harvest. The Government ended this practice in about 1950, and farmers then had to sell to potato wholesalers at the prices they chose to pay, which made potato farming a less attractive proposition, and it became uneconomic in the long run.[60]

Broccoli was planted immediately after the early potatoes had been cropped. But the price fetched by broccoli and cauliflower in the London markets often made it uneconomical to send them up country. A newspaper report related how a Cornish grown cauliflower on sale at Covent Garden was on average 6d in 1948, but could be found on sale in the London shops for as little as 2d. The report noted that Cornish producers of these vegetables found the cost of transportation to the London markets prohibitive as they had to pay a duty of 3 shillings a hundredweight, plus heavy freight charges, which eventually priced them out of the market. Moreover, cheap imported Italian and French broccoli decimated the Cornish farmers' market in the large cities and a combination of both led Michael Veall to abandon broccoli and potato production in about 1955 as uneconomical.[61]

Flower growers found themselves subject to much the same economic factors and were hard hit by cheap imported flowers from the Continent. Small producers such as Bill Harnden could not compete in such a competitive market and it was only the large producers such as the Banfields who managed to remain in the market long term. The brief flowering of horticulture was not to be long lived in Lanner and has all but died out.

Bringing in the Sheaves

There can be few scenes as evocative of an idyllic rural way of life as that of harvest time. Artists have tried to capture the essence of harvest on canvas and it has featured in countless novels. It tends to be this scene which springs to mind when we think about agriculture, not pig farming with its smells, muck and slaughterhouses. Arable farming, embodied in harvest home, was glamorous – pig farming and food production was not.

Bringing in the sheaves was the most important event in the farmer's calendar, as his whole livelihood depended on a successful harvest. As harvest home was something in which the majority of the population participated in some capacity,

Fig.7.5. *Harvest at West Trethellan Farm, early 1900s. Note three pikes, hay mow and croust!* (© Derek Reynolds Collection).

it therefore embodied a real community spirit which has inevitably diminished in an age where mass produced foodstuffs are readily available in supermarkets all year around. Therefore the Harvest Festivals and suppers of yesteryear were events of far greater importance and significance in the rural calendar than those of today, and Church and Chapel congregations went to great lengths to beautify the interior of their respective places of worship.

Earlier this century, Rhona Blatchford remembers the altar of the Lanner Wesleyan Chapel being painstakingly decorated by Maud Nichols and Alice Langford with heather bells, flowers, fruit and vegetables, whilst a prettily decorated shield bore the legend 'The Earth is full of Thy Riches'. At the end of a harvest service, it was customary to share out the harvest gifts to members of the community who were old, sick or poor, a form of community aid. To a population which lived much closer to the soil and relied directly on the earth's bounty far more than do today's generations, the successful Harvest-home meant so much more, immortalised in the words of the harvest hymns which resounded around the Church or Chapel walls.[62]

Michael Veall, whose family has held numerous farms in the area for generations, well remembers harvest time (see photo below). When a farmer was ready to harvest his crop, the word went around the community. Labourers from neighbouring farms (and local men out of work, known as 'slingers'), would come to help the Harvest-home and the courtesy was always repaid by a reciprocal gesture of help. Neighbours often lent their farm equipment during harvesting. Jack Evans remembers how his father John always helped the Polkinghornes of Carn Marth bring in their hay by loaning them his cart.

Reaping in the days before combine harvesters was hard work, performed by a team of men who mowed the fields with a sickle and stick for grain crops and a scythe for hay. They began at dawn and their work lasted until dusk. Women worked in the fields too, in the old days, reaping alongside the men, but latterly binding the sheaves cut by the men with 'hand twine', made from straw.

Tea was taken in the field, provided by the farmer's wife. Irene Veall remembers working hard over the stove for hours on end preparing the substantial repast with which the harvesters working on their farm were provided.

On average, Michael Veall estimated that a team of four reapers could mow about an acre a day in the era before the advent of mechanised binders, and later, combine harvesters. The custom of 'crying the neck', a ceremonial event performed whilst binding the last sheaf, had all but died out in the Gwennap area by the twentieth century, but the end of the mowing was always keenly awaited, as it was possible to catch the many rabbits trapped in the small area of crop remaining to be cut.

A Lanner correspondent for the *Royal Cornwall Gazette* had this to say in 1906: 'When the long day's work is over and the harvesters tramp home to the village, there is not a man or boy amongst them who has not a bundle of dead rabbits to carry. When one considers how little of butcher's meat can ever find its way into a cottage when the average-earner's

Fig.7.6. *The Veall family at Trebowland Farm, Gwennap, c.1909. The ricks are only partially thatched, requiring trimming and strengthening. In the foreground are William Veall (he later owned a shop in Lanner Square), with a dog, and Mrs Veall. The man on the wagon is unknown, John Veall is building the rick, Henry Veall (who died in 1922) is on the rick in the centre, and the young lad is Henry Veall.* (© C. Veall, Stithians).

income is 13–15 shillings a week, one can understand the value of these rabbits at harvest-time'.[63]

Shooting for rabbits was a lucrative side line for many people in the past and the rabbits were taken to various Redruth butchers who sold them in their shops. Michael Veall remembers that his father often took 40–50 rabbits there each week. Trapping moles was also another pursuit which earned people extra money. Classed as a nuisance by local farmers, moles were caught and skinned, and the pelts taken to Redruth, where a retailer in Alma Place would buy them. Michael Veall remembers moleskins were still in great demand when he was a boy, for making into soft, durable clothing.

Once the sheaves were cut, they had to dry. In Western Cornwall, the traditional method of drying oats, barley or wheat was in an arish mow. This was a pyramid-shaped pile of sheaves, constructed with the butt ends of the sheaf sloping outwards to the 'dryth,' or wind, so ensuring that the sheaves received little damage from the elements.[64] The arish mow was still the preferred method of drying the sheaves locally in the nineteenth century, as evidenced by William Tregoning's account of the harvest at West Trevarth Farm. However, by the twentieth century this had been superseded by two new types of mow – the hand mow and the knee mow, although the latter closely resembled the arish mow.

Once dry, the sheaves were carried in by mule, and latterly on wagons, to the mowhay (a loft or chamber in an enclosed courtyard, used for the storage of grain and hay). A good example of a mowhay still exists on Carn Marth on the smallholding 'Rockfield'.

The rick was then carefully constructed on a wooden framework covered with furze, standing above a circular base of wooden posts or 'staddle stones' (mushroom-shaped granite pillars with a stone cap to prevent vermin from getting into the sheaves). In former times a thatched roof covered the precious sheaves, but in more recent times, a tarpaulin sufficed (T. L. Richards of Lanner Moor sold such rubber covers in the 1880s).

During the months following the harvest home, the sheaves would be thrashed. For over a thousand years, this job was done with a flail on an oaken barn floor. Noted amongst the chattels of Edward Reed of Gwennap who died in 1762, was a 'barn floor' (a frame of planks on three beams, which had gaps in between for grain to fall through when being threshed with flails). Proto-industrial farm labourers were grateful for the opportunity of work this job afforded when there was little else to do, as most threshing took place in the winter months. Winnowing, an onerous task, was usually performed by women, who would take a basket of grain to an area most exposed to the wind, and toss the grain in the basket to separate it from the chaff.

But such labour intensive methods of farming were under increasing threat from the late eighteenth century, as mechanisation gradually entered the farming world, and farming began to be increasingly industrialised, with threshing machines, and by the mid twentieth century, tractor driven grist mills and later, combine harvesters. By the 1930s most of the threshing in the Gwennap area was done by Sid Carlyon of Unity Wood, who went from farm to farm with his pale red coloured Marshall machine towed by a powerful traction engine. Other threshing machine operators of the time included Ted Moore and Stanley Prowse.

'It was always a thrill to see the thresher arrive when I was a boy', remarked Michael Veall, 'threshing day was good fun'. Carlyon's thresher roamed the countryside with its two attendants, Bert Hocking and Lonzo Harvey, who arrived on the specified day at the farm for 'steam up' at eight o'clock prompt. Since the work was under contract, both parties were eager to ensure that they were ready on time. The engine and the thresher would pull in between the ricks. The traction engine was connected to the thresher by a long leather belt and had to be carefully balanced to ensure that the drum of the thresher would rotate correctly.

About ten men were required to operate the threshing machine. Two minded the machine, one of whom controlled the steam engine, and the other, the trusser, at the back of the machine. Another man fed the grain into the machine as his colleague cut the binds, while two more would be carrying away the threshed grain to the barn in sacks, each one weighing in the region of 130 pounds. Another man would be kept busy clearing away the 'douse' from beneath the revolving drum.

Michael Veall remembers this job well, as he did it as a boy on several occasions. 'It was the job which nobody else wanted because it was so dusty and dirty, and it always fell to the youngest person'. A further two men took away the trussed straw which was used for animal feed or bedding. In addition, three men were required to constantly fork the sheaves to the feeder from the rick. As the end of the rick was reached, people in their 'yorks' (trousers securely tied below the knees with binder twine) would gather around brandishing sticks and stones, often accompanied by their dogs, to engage in a little 'ratting'. Despite the farmer's best attempts to prevent rodents getting into the rick, it was impossible to stop them. All present enjoyed the ribald fun and horseplay which occurred; Michael Veall can remember his dog once caught over 100 rats from a single rick! Ratting was a popular pastime in former times, with 'rat weeks' being sponsored by the Redruth Urban District Council's Sanitary Committee. In 1921, 1d per tail was offered to anybody for rats caught in the Redruth Urban District.[65]

After the grain had been threshed it was ground into flour, or rough ground for cattle feed. In past times, landowners would stipulate in the leaseholds granted to tenant farmers that all grain grown had to be ground at their manorial mill, where a certain percentage of the grain would be taken by the landlord for the 'privilege' of using his mill. Such a manorial mill was that of Pensignance, Court Grist Mill, upstream from Comford.

Much of the grain grown in the area in the late nineteenth and early twentieth centuries was ground in the mill at Trethellan Water by the miller, John Spargo (Fig.7.7). The

Fig.7.7. *The Mill at Trethellan Water, with the miller, John Spargo.* (© Irene Veall, Gwennap)

mill had an overshot waterwheel, which was dismantled and sold to Tolgus Tin in about 1953.[66] Another mill was situated where the Tresavean adit discharges, at Penventon Farm, which was formerly the site of an ancient crazing mill (see Chapter 3). Many of the millstones are still visible.

A more modern grist mill stood at the top of Pennance Lane on the right. The present occupant of the site believes it might have had an undershot waterwheel, the water being conveyed in a channel from the Carn Marth Chute nearby. But it appears this mill had disappeared by the 1940s. Nowadays, any locally produced grain is sent up country for processing, and the old mills stand ruined and silent.

Farm Work and Wages

It is argued that farming is a way of life, that family farms were inherited, one generation merely the custodian of the land which passed to the next in a cycle spanning generations.[67] Therefore the farming way of life is one which is conservative and fiercely independent. Farms were places of work from which families had to earn a living and traditionally employed the whole family in some capacity. Indeed, most of Lanner's farms were not large, but were family run affairs, small indeed alongside those of Eastern England.

The farm which Philip Bray worked at Lannarth in the nineteenth century was about 18 acres in size, and his daughter, the late Mrs Mary Job, remembered as a child helping her father to plant potatoes as he ploughed the fields. In 1851, at Penstruthal, William Henry Richards farmed 24 acres with the help of his wife, son and brother-in-law, whilst a nearby 10-acre farm, worked by Robert Keast, was managed with the aid of his four children, his wife, plus two members of her family.

Some farmers employed casual labour, such as the 10-acre farm worked in 1851 by Henry Jenkin who employed one boy, but was also helped by his son, daughter, two step daughters and his wife. The 7 acres farmed by widow Martha Andrews was worked with the aid of two married couples who lodged with her at the farmhouse.[68]

Many widows continued to run the family farms, but were usually forced to take on extra labour to cope with the heavy work of ploughing, and reaping, carting, rick building and the soul destroying job of 'skidding' dung. Nineteenth-century women usually performed the mundane jobs – looking after the animals, performing milking and egg collecting, plus keeping house, but also helping with cropping, dung spreading, at the annual harvest and winter threshing. And this was much the same picture a hundred years later, in the 1950s, as Perry has noted:

> *Farming was very much a family affair in which all members of the household, male or female, had to pull their weight. Wives and daughters controlled the interior of the farmhouse, looked after small livestock, did the hand milking, helped with outside work on demand and increasingly did the mounting paperwork generated by officialdom. The farmer (95 per cent of farm proprietors were men) and his sons did the heavy work, operated and maintained the machinery and did the buying and selling as well as working for other farmers or in the towns to make ends meet.*[69]

For those employed by farmers before the Second World War, wages in the agricultural world were well below those which could have been earned in the mining industry. Farm workers' wages had not risen much at all during the nineteenth century; their work was characterised as of low skill, with little prospect of advancement, the stereotype of the 'country bumpkin' portraying contemporary opinion of agricultural labourers as of limited intelligence and ambition. In 1885 a local farm labourer's pay was reported to have been 16s per week, but this also included his daughter's wage as a milkmaid. Without her income, his wage would have been but 14s 6d.[70] Yet wages in mining were on average three times higher. Even by 1920, W. J. Vincent of Trevarth, who began work for farmer Charles H. Stephens, could only command £1.16s. per week. The following year his wage increased to just £2.6s.[71] But in 1923, mill fitters at Tresavean were earning over £7, a sum which most considered inadequate enough to prompt thoughts of migration. And if for some reason a farm labourer was dismissed, he was likely to lose his home if he lived in a cottage belonging to the farmer who hired him, and was unlikely to have ever found employ in the area again. Therefore his welfare, and that of his entire family, depended very much on the goodwill and cordial relationship between him and his employer.

Although statistical analysis of the 1851 Census clearly shows that mining was the chief occupation for both men and women in Lanner, agriculture was jointly the next most important employment category for men at 6.44 per cent. For women it amounted to 4.44 per cent, and appeared of less importance, but this figure might be misleading, as many women, farmers' wives and daughters for example, worked on their family farms but this was not indicated by the enumerator on the Census returns.

By 1891, the percentage of females employed on the land had fallen to 3.4 per cent, but the male figure had doubled to 12.6 per cent. The male increase can probably be explained by the decline in the area's mining industry. With less employment on offer in the mines, men who had formerly combined their work as miners and smallholders were forced to rely solely on the land for their income. This was common throughout the old mining districts, and it must be remembered that miners often lived cheek-by-jowl with farmers, and switched occupation seasonally or even day-to-day. The female decrease is interesting, and enforces the argument that before the decline of proto-industrialism, more women were usefully employed on the land, and their payment, although subsumed within a framework of traditional domestic patriarchy, was nevertheless a valuable contribution to the family economy.

But enclosure had led to the decline of customary practices, and drove women out of field service, whilst increased mechanisation in dairying, planting, and harvesting, further reduced their role. Wages offered to women on the land were no incentive to stay there, and many turned their attention to securing work as a bal maiden, said to have offered wages a third higher than those of agriculture. And this move away from the land appeared to be permanent.

When mining declined, Lanner's women did not return to farms for their livelihood, but worked instead in manufacturing and domestic service, or worse still, became dependent on a banker's draft from their husbands or sons in distant mining camps. However, it must be noted that there was still likely to have been many more women who worked on the area's farms than the figure suggests, much of their work being invisible by its seasonal nature, or piecetime basis.

But the male rise perhaps strengthens the case for the masculinization of agriculture, even in such tasks as dairying, which had been seen for generations as a mainstay of women's work. For it was men who operated the farm machinery, applied new fertilisers and sold the produce at the market, while women were left with the less popular, onerous, and more mundane tasks.

The Decline of Farming in Lanner

Many factors have contributed to the decline of farming in Lanner. The constant drive to meet ever-strict criteria for quality control of farm produce, as we have shown above in egg and pig production, have placed severe restraints on how farmers farmed their land. And despite farmers being fiercely independent, farming is, paradoxically, more controlled than almost any other industry. And the peripherality of Cornwall hampers its ability to compete in an open market. For example, the closure of local abattoirs meant that Calvin Stephens had to compete for longer haulage contracts which became uneconomic, with the result that he pulled out of the business in 1994.

Competition from cheap foreign producers has killed off the horticulture industry in Lanner. Nationwide, the trend is away from unprofitable small farms, to larger, more efficient units. This underlines the case for arguing that farming has become less a way of life, and more a business, which has to make a profit to be viable. Unlike during the heyday of mining, Lanner's smallholdings no longer need to feed their occupants, who have the option of buying relatively cheap, mass-produced milk, meat and vegetables at local supermarkets. In terms of labour time, it is not worth the effort to raise home grown crops, and there is not the financial necessity to do so in a country which has a welfare system.

The sale and break-up of the Penrose Estate in the 1950s meant that many Lanner families were able to buy parcels of land or small farms after this time. This sale came at a time when farmers were increasingly feeling the chill winds of competition from foreign producers – for example Danish produced bacon, and were being squeezed out of the market. This coincided with the Government's post-war reconstruction package, to encourage in-migration to depopulated areas of the county in order to stimulate the local economy. Large areas of Lanner were earmarked by the local council for potential large scale building developments in the late 1950s and 60s.

For many small-scale, disillusioned farmers who faced financial ruin, the option to sell their land for building proved irresistible. Numerous farmers sold off fields on which new bungalow estates were built. Lanmoor Estate, formerly a part of the estate of the Rogers family of Penrose, Lanner's biggest development, was built over land belonging to Bell Farm. This began a trend of land sales. Bill Harnden's market gardening fields at Pennance were sold for bungalows. Penmayne Parc, May Gardens and Valley View Estate were also developed on farmland. But farming remains one of Lanner's most important and enduring industries. It is also highly visible. Farmers are in essence the custodians of the landscape, a fact which has become increasingly important in Lanner as fears about sub-urbanisation have been heightened and intensified since the late 1960s. It is farmers who maintain the landscape, and who often keep public footpaths clear, thus making the countryside a safe and accessible place for all to enjoy.

In recent years, heightened bureaucracy has resulted in a mountain of paperwork for farmers, who are subject to checks by Ministry of Agriculture officials and Health and Safety officers. Many aspects of farming are now subsidised and heavily controlled by the EEC; for example, farmers in Lanner who grow flax receive a subsidy in the region of £240 per acre. But the paperwork which comes with the subsidy puts smaller farmers off, for mistakes in the forms carry a heavy penalty, and according to Susan Gribble, makes it very much akin to taking an exam. And the criteria for gaining subsidies are constantly changing. The latest bureaucratic nightmare for farmers has broken in the wake of the BSE crisis in cattle, which scientists claim is transferable to humans. Paperwork is now in triplicate for the movement of animals to help eliminate BSE.

Susan Gribble saw 17 of her prime beef cattle taken away to St Merryn Meat, Probus, for incineration because they were over 30 months of age. 'It was soul destroying,' she commented, even though she was fully compensated. 'There was nothing wrong with those animals. It makes you wonder why on earth you bothered to work so hard to rear them. They didn't even take the hides, which could have fetched £28 apiece.' She had never had an incidence of BSE on her farm, her herd was not a dairy herd, in which BSE is most commonly found, but nevertheless, any animal over 30 months old had to be slaughtered by law. And the price of beef has fallen dramatically since the crisis. For bullocks, Susan has seen the price per kilo plummet from £1.34 to just 73p. 'We've lost consumer confidence now,' she commented, 'but all we can do is hang on in there and hope things will improve in the long run. We have to stick with what we know.' Moreover, BSE is not the only transferable disease to worry scientists and bureaucrats. There are 27 others. Susan's animals are regularly checked for tuberculosis and brucellosis. It is little wonder then, that in the heightened tension surrounding EEC subsidies, the BSE crisis, mounting paperwork and falling prices, many families are quitting farming, whilst 16 farmers in Cornwall have committed suicide in recent years. Susan Gribble captures the essence of the farming way of life with her motto 'Live as if you were to live forever; farm as if you were to die tomorrow'.

Not surprisingly, today very few smallholdings keep livestock, but many do accommodate horses, as smallholding has become a hobby for those who want to live the good life, and enjoy a healthy way of living. Farmers like Susan Gribble agree that mechanisation and careful use of fertilisers have undoubtedly improved many aspects of farming, but at what cost? Susan feels that many of the old ways of doing things were far better for the environment, and in spite of modern technology, farming is still heavily dependent on nature to provide the rains and the sunshine for the growth of grain, hay and silage. And the following poem, by an unknown composer, set to the harvest hymn 'We Plough the Seeds and Scatter', captures the message many farmers are keen to get across in an age of technological advances in farming methods which should have resulted in a cheap surplus:

Then why are people starving
When we have it so good?
When then in cities' garbage
Must men still search for food?
Because we've been too selfish
To share what God has given,
And so life is for millions
More like a Hell than Heaven.

But all is not gloomy. Several farms in the parish – Alan and Doreen Pascoe at Penstruthal, Susan Gribble and her mother at Trevarth, and Jason Andrew and his mother at West Trevarth, for whom farming is a way of life and not just a business, doggedly refuse to be worn down by the bureaucratic 'meddling' of the Government and the EEC, mounting paperwork and the BSE crisis. They will hopefully ensure the continued presence of the farming industry in Lanner in the twenty-first century.

REFERENCES

1 Rowe, John, *Cornwall in the Age of the Industrial Revolution*, Cornish Hillside Publications, St. Austell, 1993, p. 208.
2 Berg, Maxine, *The Age of Manufactures 1700-1820*, Routledge, London, 1994 (2nd. ed.), p. 90.
3 Overton, Mark, *Agricultural Revolution in England*, Cambridge Studies in Historical Geography, Cambridge University Press, 1996, p. 175.
4 *Cornubian*, 8/4/1894.
5 See Deacon, Bernard, 'Proto-industrialisation and Potatoes', *Cornish Studies 5*, Philip Payton (ed.), University of Exeter Press, 1997.
6 AD 299/2, CRO, Truro.
7 Hamilton Jenkin, A.K., *Cornwall and Its People*, David & Charles, Newton Abott, 1970, p. 353.
8 The will of Edward Reed, Courtesy of Michael Veall, Gwennap.
9 Notes on the Buller Family, RIC, Truro.
10 Michell, Frank, *Annals of an Ancient Cornish Town, Redruth*, Dyllansow Truran, Redruth, 1972, p. 66.
11 Chapman, J., 'The Extent and Nature of Parliamentary Enclosure', *Agricultural History Review 35*, (1987).
12 Hudson, Pat, *The Industrial Revolution*, Edward Arnold, London, 1992, p. 73.
13 Tangye, Michael, *Tehidy and the Bassets*, Dyllansow Truran, Redruth, 1984, p. 48.
14 Michell, Frank, *Annals of an Ancient Cornish Town, Redruth*, Dyllansow Truran, Redruth, 1972, p. 83.
15 Ibid.
16 Overton, M., *Agricultural Revolution in England, Cambridge Studies in Historical Geography*, Camb.Univ. Press, 1996, p. 162.
17 Michell, Frank, *Annals of an Ancient Cornish Town, Redruth*, Dyllansow Truran, Redruth, 1972, p. 71.
18 Private Research on the Polkinghorne Family by S.P. Schwartz.
19 See Valenze, Deborah, *The First Industrial Woman*, Oxford University Press, New York, 1995.
20 Maton, William, *Observations on the Western Counties of England, Vol 1*, Salisbury: J.Easton, 1797, as quoted by Deacon, in Ella Westland (ed.) *Cornwall, The Cultural Construction of Place*, Patten Press, 1997, p. 16.
21 Worgan, George B., *A General View of the Agriculture of the County of Cornwall*, McMillan, London, 1811, p. 129.

22 ME 2386, CRO, Truro.
23 Gwennap Tithe Map, copy held at the Cornish Studies Library, Redruth.
24 Francis, William, Gwennap, *A Descriptive Poem in Seven Cantos*, J. May, Redruth, 1845, p. 80.
25 Worgan, George B., *A General View of the Agriculture of the County of Cornwall*, McMillan, London, 1811, p. 23.
26 Ibid., p. 24.
27 Francis, William, *Gwennap, A Descriptive Poem in Seven Cantos*, J. May, Redruth, 1845, p.120.
28 *Royal Cornwall Gazette*, 30/7/1896.
29 *Royal Cornwall Gazette*, 30/7/1896.
30 Information courtesy of Michael Veall, retired farmer.
31 Annals of Agriculture, Vol. XXII, 1794, p.146.
32 Francis William, *Gwennap, A Descriptive Poem in Seven Cantos*, J. May, Redruth, 1845, p. 81
33 The 1762 will of Edward Reed, courtesy of Michael Veall. Horses and furniture = horses with saddles, bridles and all necessary equipment ready fore use; butt = cart; dung-pots = a pair of wooden pots with hatches which were slung over back of horse or mule for spreading dung; slide = sledge; turf-crooks = similar to dung pots, but with spikes instead of pots for holding turf; barn floor = frame of planks on 3 beams, with gaps in between planks for grain to fall through when being threshed with flails.
34 PS 3/975/1 Diocesan Agricultural Returns, 1801. CRO, Truro.
35 D/6/1138, CRO, Truro.
36 Tregoning, E.A., *Two Centuries of a Cornish Family*, Edgar Backus, Leicester, 1950, p 23.
37 *Redruth Independent*, 12/8/1887.
38 Tremenheere, Seymour, *The State of Education in the Mining Districts of Cornwall*, BPP, 1840, p. 88.
39 Deacon, Bernard, 'Proto-industrialisation and Potatoes', *Cornish Studies 5*, Philip Payton (ed.), University of Exeter Press, 1997, p. 70.
40 Ibid., p. 71.
41 *Royal Cornwall Gazette*, 1/1/1847.
42 P 79/81/1, CRO, Truro.
43 Hudson, Pat, *The Industrial Revolution*, Edward Arnold, London, 1992, pp. 74-5.
44 *Cornubian*, 18/9/1871..
45 *Cornubian*, 20/10/1871.
46 *Cornubian*, 18/5/1894.
47 *Royal Cornwall Gazette*, 23/9/1897.
48 Hamilton Jenkin, A.K., *Cornwall and Its People*, David & Charles, Newton Abott, 1970, p. 402.
49 Rowe, John, 'Bringing Home the Sheaves', *Journal of the Royal Institute of Cornwall*, Truro, 1990.
50 *Royal Cornwall Gazette*, 4/11/1915.
51 *Cornubian*, 21/3/1890.
52 Perry, Ronald, Regenerating Cornwall, Cornwall Focus Seminar, Plymouth, unpublished, 1998.
53 Interview with Michael Veall, former pig farmer.
54 Burnside E, and Rickard, R.C., *An Economic Study of Pig Production in South West England*. 1953-57, University of Bristol, Report no. 105, p. 45.
55 Interview with Michael Veall, former pig farmer.
56 Ibid.
57 Information concerning the life of the late Mrs Mary Job, taken from an interview with her in 1991, aged 101.
58 *Cornubian*, 11/3/1898.
59 Information courtesy of Mrs Todd, daughter of Jack and Barbara Banfield; also Prudence Danby.
60 Interview with Michael Veall, 1998.
61 *Cornubian*, 14/10/1948.
62 Schwartz, S.P., 'Bringing in the Sheaves, Memories of Harvest Time', *Echoes of the Past, Issue 2*, 1996.
63 *Royal Cornwall Gazette*, 23/8/1906.
64 Schwartz, S.P., 'Bringing in the Sheaves, Memories of Harvest Time', *Echoes of the Past, Issue 2*, 1996.
65 *Cornubian*, 17/11/1921.
66 Courtesy Mrs Irene Veall, 1996
67 Blunden, Cathy, In the Field With Forty Farmers, Cornwall Focus Seminar, Plymouth, unpublished, 1998
68 Census Returns for Gwennap, 1851, 1861, 1871 and 1881
69 Perry, Ronald, *Cornwall circa 1950*, *Cornwall Since the War*, Philip Payton, (ed.), Dyllansow Truran, 1993, p. 37
70 *Cornubian*, 4/9/1885
71 *Cornubian*, 28/4/1921

Chapter 8
Emigration from the Parish

The Cornish are distinguished as both a mining and an emigrating people.[1]

That the men and women of such a small, impoverished peninsula in one of the remotest parts of Britain should be noted as having left a very tangible mark upon many countries in the world is remarkable. Nineteenth-century emigration was a phenomenon common to Northern Europe, and it has been estimated that in the one hundred years, between 1814 and 1914, approximately 35 million people left European shores. Britain was the leading migratory country for the period 1840–1950, recording around 11.4 million; Italy records 9.9 million and Ireland 7.3 million.[2] But Cornwall, with a far smaller population than Ireland, a country whose contribution to the European exodus is more marked worldwide, must have lost a larger percentage of its total population through emigration than is at first apparent. Indeed, the Registrar General in his report on the 1881 census concluded that the population of Cornwall had decreased by 8.9 per cent in the last ten years, and he thought it highly likely that the percentage of miners who had departed was as much as 24 per cent of the total.[3]

Dudley Baines has shown that, as a rural region, the South West of England lost (net of returns) around a third of a million migrants between 1861–1900 and that emigration from Dorset, Devon, Somerset and Cornwall was exceptionally high. But Cornwall alone is estimated to have lost 118 500 people through overseas emigration, a staggering figure, comprising over 40 per cent of its young adult males, and over 25 per cent of its young adult females. These percentages, when analysed within the broader context of England and Wales, make it possible that gross emigration could have included about 20 per cent of the male Cornish born population in each ten year period, and about 20 per cent of the female. This would make the Cornish male by far the largest group of native migrants to leave English shores, and the Cornish female a close second.[4] Further estimates claim that gross out-migration from Cornwall over the 60 years 1841–1901 could have been as high as 460 000 split roughly 50/50 between those moving overseas and those moving to other parts of Britain.[5]

The Cornish therefore played an important and often overlooked role in the building of evolving nations throughout the world. Their presence in the United States and Australia, (particularly Southern Australia) was very strong. It is also evident in South Africa, Canada and New Zealand, and can be detected in less obvious places such as Mexico and Chile.

The Cornish were in the vanguard of mining technology. Pryce in his *Mineralogia Cornubiensis* (1778), mentions that Cornishmen had been sent to the area around Lake Superior to inspect mineral deposits during the eighteenth century,[6] and the most knowledgeable and skilled miners, engineers, carpenters and masons, had been recruited, from the 1820s, by British-owned mining companies investing considerable capital to develop mines in South America. These miners took with them the technology and equipment to deepen and dewater foreign mines, attracted to do so by offers of good pay. By the 1840s, a thriving Cornish community had sprung up at Mineral Point, Wisconsin. Added to this steady trickle of people leaving the county from the early nineteenth century, were numerous disillusioned and dispossessed agriculturists, attracted overseas to new lives as farmers in America and the British Colonies, as well as people seeking religious and political freedom.

The conventional picture of Cornish history in the nineteenth century is of mining collapse in the 1860s, followed by mass emigration. But as Deacon has shown, the first signs of mass migration from Cornwall came during the late 1840s, when the failure of the potato crop, compounded by a temporary depression in the mining industry, drove thousands out of the county. A migratory trend was thus established which became firmly ingrained in the Cornish imagination.[7]

The exodus of the 1840s was heightened by what was to come in the 1860s. Until this time, Cornwall had been the world's chief supplier of copper ore, with Gwennap accounting for 30.1 per cent of the total production for Great Britain between 1823–32. However, after the mid nineteenth century, Gwennap's pre-eminent position was slowly eroded, due to competition from new copper producers in the Americas and Australasia. By the mid 60s, copper prices began to plummet with disastrous effects on local economies throughout the county. Mine after mine was abandoned, including some which had turned to tin production, as this industry was also hit by the vagaries of the international tin market and competition from Malaysian, Australian and Bolivian sources. Most of the mines in the Lanner area and those in the neighbouring parishes of Gwennap and Redruth were copper producers. Tresavean had already seen its heyday and provided sporadic work for the last half of the nineteenth century (see Chapter 3). In 1866 alone, three mines in Gwennap Parish, Wheal Busy, St Day United and the Clifford Amalgamated closed, causing great concern.

The burden of unemployment fell heavily on Lanner. Unable to find work locally, the only answer to long term-unemployment, and therefore hardship, with the threat of admission to the workhouse, lay outside the county. Some parishioners left to seek work in other parts of Britain, but the majority by far went overseas. It is a common misconception to think that all the people who emigrated were miners; they were not. Tradesmen such as masons, carpenters, wheelwrights, quarrymen, blacksmiths and rope makers migrated, as did those who serviced the developing communities abroad; cordwainers, tailors, shopkeepers, bakers, butchers, barbers, domestic servants and hoteliers. And the importance of farmers as migrants should not be marginalised. Cornish agriculturists were every bit as much pioneers as the county's miners, and played a valid part in the forging of new economies worldwide.

In this mass exodus, termed 'The Great Migration' by Philip Payton, which began in the mid 1800s and spanned about one hundred years, thousands of 'Cousin Jacks' left their native towns and villages to destinations worldwide, often in less than ideal conditions. Emigration became an phenomenon accepted as necessary and intricately bound up in the Cornish psyche, reaching its height by the turn of the twentieth century. Indeed, architect James Hicks, writing to the *Cornubian* in January 1891, commented 'it would be difficult to drop down on any part of the mining world without finding a Lanner boy.'

The report went on to describe how, in his estimation, 90 per cent of the houses in the village were supported by foreign money. Village institutions had benefited enormously from the remittances of expatriates, and over 600 letters from abroad were delivered by postman Harry Folley each week. The report concluded with the comment 'Lanner may be truly reckoned to be the richest village in Cornwall according to its size; and men who have travelled in various parts tell me that the impression among foreigners is that Lanner is not a village, not a town, but a city; everybody they say, comes from Lanner.'[8]

Although we can allow a little for artistic licence, there is truth in this statement. Irene Veall remembers her grandmother, who had been a long term resident of Grays Terrace, recalling how for much of the late nineteenth century the terrace was entirely inhabited by women, the men were all away working. Indeed, the *Cornubian* commented in 1892 that 'if the women and children emigrated to the same extent as the men, it would be "Good night" to Lanner.'[9]

Hundreds of local women found themselves the head of a large family, some entirely dependent on the remittances of an absent husband; money which could be delayed, or irregularly sent, if at all. A tough matriarchal resilience entered the working class of Lanner and villages like it. These were the heady days of emigration from the parish, when a ticket direct to a faraway place such as Virginia City, Nevada (Fig.8.1), or a passage aboard a ship to New Zealand or

Fig.8.1. *Virginia City, Nevada., USA, in 1868. It was here that young Richard Jose arrived in 1877.* (© The Joe Curtis Collection, Virginia City).

Australia, could be purchased in Lanner from one of several emigration agents. Indeed, when it was decided to set up a YMCA branch outside the main towns in Cornwall, Lanner, noted for the large numbers of its youth which migrated, was chosen to be the test location.

Lanner parishioners were not at all insular in the nineteenth century, and although few had much schooling, people nonetheless had a good understanding of the wider world, an interest which was fostered by letters home from absent family and friends, and colourful stories of those who returned. A unique link with settlements abroad was thus forged and places such as Moonta, Bendigo, Ballarat, Tocopilla, Real del Monte, Pachuca, Grass Valley, Butte, Calumet, Ironwood, Johannesburg and Randfontein became household names. From the few surviving names of houses and cottages in the village chosen by returning migrants, one can imagine the impact emigration had on Lanner.

The old adage, 'wherever you happen to find a pit, there'll be a Cornishman working in the bottom of it,' bears testimony to Cornish mining expertise. In time, the beam engine, housed in the engine houses so characteristic of the Cornish landscape even today, came to mark stranger and more exotic landscapes, from Moonta to Mexico. By the close of the nineteenth century, there was barely anyone in mining villages such as Lanner who did not have a relative or friend who had not emigrated, or at least worked in a mining settlement overseas. This has prompted historians such as A.L. Rowse to conclude that the Cornish were distinguished as both a mining and an emigrating people.

For the purpose of this study, various sources were consulted, which when analysed collectively, enable a more complete picture of Lanner's migratory experience to emerge. Foremost of these sources are the ten-year census returns, and local newspapers, the *Cornubian*, *West Briton*, *Cornish Post and Mining News* and *Royal Cornwall Gazette*. The Exiles' List of the Memorial Scheme, compiled over many years and held at the Royal Institute of Cornwall, Truro, provides intriguing personal details and some shipping records. The Cornish American Connection, based at Murdoch House, Redruth, holds a biographical index, which documents over 32 000 names of Cornish migrants to the USA, and the Cornwall Family History Society also hold valuable genealogical information charting the movements overseas of individuals and families. But even when collated, the information these sources reveal is far from complete, and by their very nature the sources possess inherent weaknesses. As far as the newspapers are concerned, the majority of the entries only appear after 1880, by which time a considerable amount of migration had already occurred from the parish. For the earlier mass movements, such as those to the Antipodes, one is reliant upon shipping records, which, sadly, are incomplete. However, in the absence of any other research material of a like nature, and when used collectively, it has to be assumed that these sources provide a reasonable sample on which to base an investigation of Lanner's migratory experience.

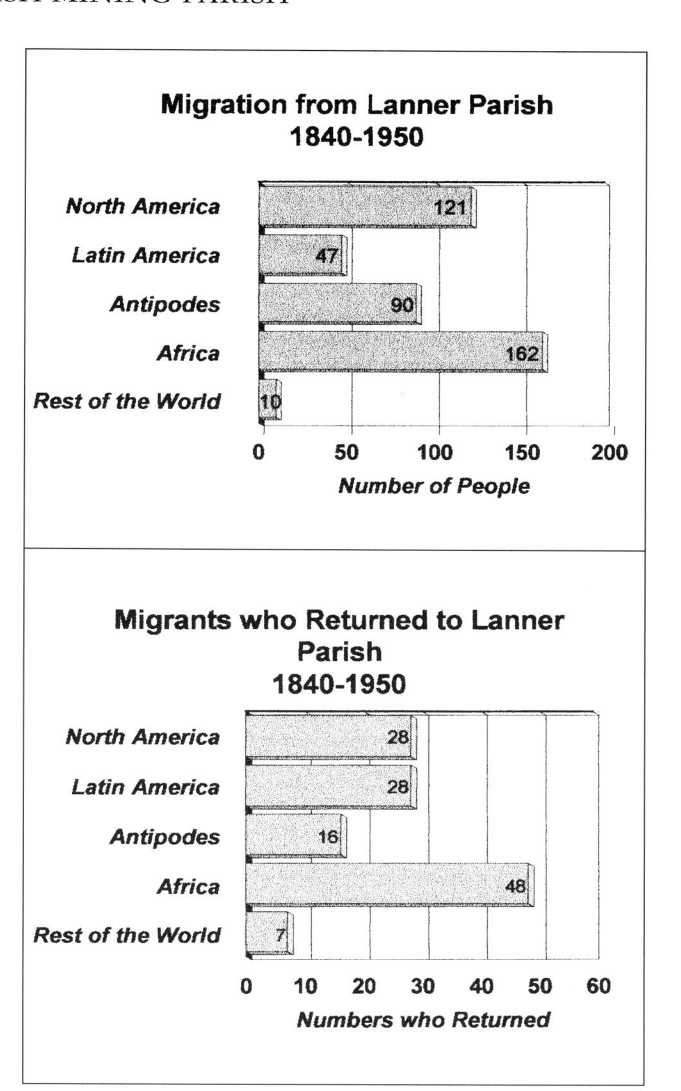

Fig.8.2. *Migration from Lanner Parish, 1840–1950.*
Fig.8.3. *Migrants who returned to Lanner Parish, 1840–1950.*

Our sample consists of 430 men, women and children. The results for departures and returns are presented statistically (Fig.8.2 and Fig.8.3) and for convenience are grouped into five categories: North America, including Canada and the USA; Latin America, including Mexico, the Caribbean and the countries of South America; the Antipodes, inclusive of Australia and New Zealand; Africa, encompassing all the African continent, and finally the countries comprising the Rest of the World. In the following pages, some of the stories of Lanner folk abroad will be related, among them the well known, but also those whose sacrifice has gone unrecognised.

It is beyond the scope of this book to account for the movement of all those persons who left the parish, but by recording the exploits of some Lanner people abroad, examining their motives for migration and the effect it had on the community, a picture of nineteenth century emigration from Lanner can be established, indeed one which was repeated in mining communities throughout Cornwall.

Potato Famine, Revolution, and the Demise of 'the Copper Kingdom'

In the first third of the nineteenth century, Lanner was characterised by large scale immigration, not emigration. There had been some migration from the parish, of miners and artisans who had been recruited by local agents for British companies operating in the newly independent countries of Latin America in the Post Napoleonic Period. This followed the collapse of the Spanish Empire and the opening of Brazilian ports to direct English trade in 1808, and the Independence of Brazil from Portugal in 1825. The mines were sited across the South American continent, in Mexico, Colombia, Venezuela, Chile, Peru, Bolivia, Brazil, and Cuba.

One such miner was Captain Davies Trebilcock, who went to the mines of Cerro de Pasco, in the Peruvian Andes, in 1825, with 50 other men from the district. They were to attempt to dewater the silver mines there which had so interested Richard Trevithick a few years before.

The numbers travelling to Latin America were relatively few, for in the first third of the nineteenth century Lanner lay at the heartland of an industrialised area dominated by copper mining. Lanner had witnessed an enormous influx of people, especially from the rural parishes of the county, as men and their families poured into the area seeking work in the mines, the majority from neighbouring parishes.

In 1801, the population of Gwennap sprang from 4594 to 10 794, just 40 years later,[10] and Lanner and it satellite hamlets was home to about a quarter of that number. Such migration within the county was sustainable as long as the employment levels in the local mines held up. Tresavean Mine was, for the first third of the nineteenth century, extremely productive. In 1819, Richard Thomas, Surveyor and Engineer, noted that Tresavean Mine was employing a monthly average of 100 people,[11] but by 1836–37, De La Beche's quote for monthly employment figures at Tresavean Mine shows a startling increase to 1354 people.[12] This famous mine was the village's main employer, the confidence the local people had in the mine reflected in the rows of miners' cottages built along the course of the Turnpike Road which snaked its way through the valley beneath its labouring engine houses.

The area was one of relative stability and growth from the 1820s up to the mid 1840s, as evidenced by the opening of Lanner's Anglican Chapel of Ease in 1840, and the rebuilding of both the Bible Christian and Wesleyan Chapels in Lanner during 1844; other chapels were also opened in the district, including those at South Downs, Ponsanooth and St Day.

However, by the late 1840s the picture began to change somewhat, as the prosperous Gwennap area witnessed a considerable degree of hardship. There had been plenty of work in the local mines, but unemployment was beginning to make its presence felt by 1847–48 'in consequence of the depressed state of the mines of this parish (Gwennap) owing to the low price of copper and tin caused by the troubled state of the Continent, a great many men, boys and women are thrown out of employ and those that are at work are so, at very reduced wages'.[13]

A series of poor harvests and the failure of the potato crop at this time only added to the misery by creating inflated prices (barley flour was retailing at £2 per bag of 240 lb, and wheat flour £4 per bag of 280 lb.[14] In the Gwennap mines, the average monthly man's wage was calculated to have been in the region of £2).[15]

As we have shown in Chapter 2, the depression of the 1840s was made the more acute due to the rise of a formal wage economy, coupled with reduced opportunity for customary access to land for food and fuel. Redruth erupted into violence on 4 June 1847, as hundreds of miners and their womenfolk mobbed the town market demanding grain at a fair price (see Chapter 2). Food riots were repeated in other local towns such as Camborne, Helston and St Austell.[16] But the labouring poor of Lanner were dealt a further and more severe blow when Tresavean ceased production, in 1858, after a decade of steadily declining production. Although it was reopened in the following decades, the golden days of Tresavean were over.

There seems to have been no large exodus from Lanner, particularly of miners, who formed the bulk of the parish's workforce, until the local economic situation became uncertain. The 1841 Children's Commission estimated that those in mining were on average likely to receive wages over one-third higher than those in farming, so whilst the mines were flourishing and wages sufficient, there seemed little reason to contemplate a change of residence or occupation.[17]

But Gwennap was over dependent on copper mining, and as a consequence, over-specialised in this particular industry, as can be seen quite clearly from the graphs depicting the occupations of men and women resident in Lanner in 1851, shown in Figs.2.6 and 2.8. Herein lay the root of the problem. Those formerly employed in the copper industry now found themselves unable or unsuitable to find work in other fields. Even industries which grew up in the area following the decline of the mining industry, such as the brick works at Pennance and Trevarth, relied too much on mines and foundries for the greater part of their income, and foundered as a result. For those who were unemployed the only solution seemed to be emigration, which was becoming a fairly accurate barometer of economic failure and uncertainty. And people employed in the agricultural world fared little better, for as the miners left the parish, so their main market for wheat, oats and barley diminished. They too had, in effect, become dependent on the copper industry, and were either forced to change their patterns and methods of farming to survive, or emigrate. The over-reliance on arable farming with its attendant uncertainties, exemplified during the period of poor harvests during the late 1840s, saw a gradual shift towards mixed farming, with more emphasis on dairy farming, sheep breeding, permanent pasture and, later, horticulture.[18]

We can go some way towards appreciating the extent of migration from Lanner between the years 1851–1891, by using a longitudinal cohort analysis. All the children shown as aged between 0–9 years old on the 1851 Census were recorded, and this cohort of 826 individuals was then followed through to adulthood to determine how many persisted and how many moved away from the area. A greater degree of accuracy was achieved by noting marriages of the females, occurring in either Lanner or Gwennap Parish churches, to obtain their married names.

Year	1861	1871	1881	1891
Age of Cohort Group	9-19	19-29	19-39	39-49
Total	369	118	51	37
Percentage Persisted	44.67%	14.29%	6.17%	4.48%

As can be seen by the above table of results, in 1861, 44.67 per cent persisted from 1851, and only 14.29 per cent in 1871. By 1891, only 37 individuals, or just over 4 per cent of those who lived in Lanner when aged 0-9, persisted. But the biggest loss of individuals from the cohort occurred from 1851–1861 (a loss of 55 per cent). Between 1861 and 1871, a further 30 per cent left the parish. This supports the proto-industrial thesis of migration on a significant scale before mining collapsed in the 1860s and 70s. Remember that children aged 9 in 1851 would be 19 by 1861 and capable of leaving.

As we will see below, many of the migrants in the 1850s were young people, most of them married with infant children. Migration by occupation shows little difference, with miners and farmers appearing to have been equally affected by migration. The results for Lanner are not surprising, and are similar to those found in other mining parishes in Cornwall. What the results do not reveal of course, is to where the people migrated. Undoubtedly, many would have moved to nearby parishes, but there were a large number who migrated to other areas of Britain and overseas, continuing a migratory trend which was already well established.

Push/Pull Factors

From the late 1840s, there were regular movements from the parish as people sought new beginnings, many of these first migrants making use of various assisted passage schemes. In 1826, a Select Committee on Emigration from the United Kingdom published its first report, articulating the need to encourage an excess of population to migrate to the colonies. This was to some extent prompted by the fear concerning the nation's ability to feed an increasing population, in accordance with Malthusian principles. It was thought that such migration would avoid ultimate dependence on parochial relief.

The Colonies, sparsely populated and struggling to create viable economic bases, were keen to attract able-bodied immigrants. As a result, there was official support both at home and abroad for the poor to migrate, and Government assisted passage schemes to the British Colonies of South Australia, Canada, Van Diemen's Land (which became Tasmania), and New Zealand, helped to attract numbers of people to their shores in the nineteenth century, making emigration much easier.

South Australia, which operated an assisted passage scheme from 1836–1886, was a very popular destination for would-be migrants from Cornwall. Between the years 1846 and 1850, Cornwall sent by far the highest number of Government emigrants to the colony, 4775 people in all. This was about a quarter of the total of 17 750 for all the United Kingdom.[19]

Public meetings were held extolling the virtues of migration to South Australia, and posters appeared in the district advertising free and assisted passages, most notably those of Isaac Latimer of Truro. Applicants had to fulfil certain criteria, usually dependent on age and occupation. Local parishes saw in this scheme a chance to rid themselves of many poor families who regularly sought relief, as numerous entries in the Vestry Book for Gwennap illustrate. In 1836, it was written that 'The overseers are desired to inquire whether any of the young women who occasionally infest the work house will volunteer to go to Australia'.[20]

In 1840, another item was recorded, adopting a rather more stern and urgent message: 'That the list of paupers sent from the Union House be received and the recommendation of sending the parties named therein to Australia be adopted and that the overseers take such steps as are necessary for carrying out the same immediately.'[21]

An added incentive for migration to Australia came with the discovery of copper at Kapunda in 1843, and then at Burra Burra in 1845. Mining families from Lanner then began to take the opportunity of carving out for themselves a new life in the Southern Hemisphere. It must be noted however, that not all migrants were assisted passengers, many paying their own fares.

One of the first Lanner families to sail to Australia was tin miner William Jose, his wife Mary, and their three children, who sailed out to Adelaide in 1846 (see below).[22] Another miner, William Lawn, his wife and seven children, his sister Elizabeth and her husband William Spargo, were successful applicants for migration to South Australia and the hope of a better life. The Gwennap Vestry Book notes that William Lawn was granted, in total, £26.2s.10d by the parish to emigrate in 1847.[23] The Lawns sailed to Adelaide with about fourteen other families from Gwennap, not all of them travelling as assisted passengers. By 1849, the policy of sending the able-bodied poor to South Australia had involved considerable expense to the parish and it was suggested that 'a sum of £135 be raised to defray the expenses of the emigration of poor persons having settlement in this parish and being willing to emigrate, be paid out of the rates raised for the Relief of the Poor of this Parish.'[24] More Lanner families followed these first pioneering groups to Australia, some of whom travelled on to other parts of that continent as minerals were found in neighbouring states.

Fig.8.4. *Lanner emigrants aboard RMS* Walmer Castle *en route to Capetown, 1915.* Middle Row. *5th Lady from Left, Mrs Rowe; 7th Lady, Marion Blight.* Front Row. *5th from Left, Mrs Rowe's son; 6th from left, Harry Blight (Marion's son).* (© Mrs R. Blatchford, Lanner)

Among such families were copper miner James Bray and his wife Mary (née Francis), and four children who left Lanner in 1848 sailing aboard the *Aurora* from Plymouth for Geelong, Victoria. Philip Bray and his wife Mary (née Bullen), and their five children migrated in 1849 aboard the *Thesis*. Thomas Job, a miner from Lanner Moor sailed out to Melbourne in 1854 on the William Money and once settled in the gold fields of Ballarat, sent for his wife Mary (née Barnett) and the eldest four of their five children. They sailed to Melbourne on the *Undaunted*, arriving on 5 June 1857, joining Thomas in the gold mining town of Ballarat.

The Vincent family from Trevarth were connected to the Jobs through the marriage of Thomas and Mary's youngest daughter, Amelia, to Richard Vincent. Nicholas Vincent was joined by his brother Richard and wife Amelia and all three migrated, arriving at Adelaide on 13 November 1855 aboard the *Victoria Regia*. They headed to Ballarat to join the Jobs already resident there. Thomas Job did not live long, dying of phthisis in 1858. Richard and Amelia Vincent bought some land just outside Ballarat, at Warrenheip, which they farmed. They eventually died at Ballarat, Victoria. Thomas Pascoe, another villager, his wife Lena (née Dickman), Atwell Berryman and his wife Elizabeth, Thomas Pascoe's sister, all sailed to Melbourne aboard the *Blue Jacket* in 1859. On the same voyage was John Lean of Lanner, his wife Eliza and their children.[25]

The majority of the migrants who left Lanner for the Antipodes in the years 1840–1886 were people with young families; the average age for migrating males being 22 and the average age for females being 20. These migrations represented people whose expectations of return were probably, on the whole, minimal.

The fortunes of the local mining economy acted as a catalyst, largely determining the ebb and flow of migration from the Gwennap district, and reflecting the overwhelming importance of the mining industry to the area. This, coupled with the Government encouraging people to move abroad as we have discussed above, constituted the 'push' factor in the migration phenomenon. But of equal importance was the 'pull' factor, characterised by numerous mineral strikes worldwide, the discovery of gold in the Transvaal in the 1880s for example. Another important attraction was the expansion of agricultural lands, such as the wheat frontier in South Australia in the last quarter of the nineteenth century, in which Lanner man William Rowe Manuel played a part, and the expansion of farming land in Canada at the turn of

Fig.8.5. *A reunion of the Knuckey Family in 1951 in Lanner Wesley Sunday School. This was a family gathering (mainly of the Knuckeys, Pryors and Griggs), on the occasion of the visit, lasting six months, of Dick Knuckey and his wife, Mary, from Australia. Dick had emigrated from Lanner many years previously.* Back row, from the left: *Carrie Knuckey, Tom Grigg, Frank Coppin, Harry Grigg, Arthur Harris, Harold Lapham, Cyril Williams, Ellen Knuckey.* Second row from back: *Mabel Knuckey, Clara Holman, Laura Grigg, Gracie Coppin, Nellie Holman, Kathleen Macgrath, Betty Pryor, Olive Pryor.* Third row from back: *Willie Pryor, Joan Harris, Eniss Grigg, Tom Knuckey, Willie Knuckey, Lynn Lapham, Dorothy Williams, Joan Grigg, Norman Pryor.* Seated: *Artie Knuckey (Gail Knuckey on knee), Annie Knuckey, Janie Knuckey, Tom (T.C.) Knuckey (Elizabeth Williams on knee), Mary Knuckey, Dick Knuckey, Joanna Pryor, Joseph Pryor, Mabel Pryor.* Front row: *Roger Pryor, Kathryn Knuckey, Alan Grigg, Anne Grigg, Angela Knuckey, Edmund Harris, Anthony Grigg.* (© Mrs Anne Martin, formerly Anne Grigg, Mawnan Smith).

the twentieth century, with the Government of Saskatchewan guaranteeing 'situations for farm hands in 1914'.[26] In 1902, T.H. Kneebone of South Downs migrated with his son Thomas John to Winnipeg, Manitoba where here, in common with many other Canadian states, rich virgin soil that only 'needed to be scratched twice with a light plough to yield 20 bushels of wheat to the acre', could have been 'had for the asking'.[27]

The prospect of better wages was by far the most tangible factor in pushing people overseas when the mines in Gwennap and District had either closed, or were paying poor wages (£2–3 per month on average). For example, wages in the Transvaal mines, before the Jameson Raid of 1895, were reported to have been in the region of £40–50 per month for miners; a machine man's monthly wage was about £90–95, a small fortune, but that was for extremely hard work. A blacksmith prepared to work overtime could also have picked up about £90 a month.[28] Although these wages were to decline after the Boer War, wages paid in the South African mines were far above those of Cornwall; in 1923 a mill fitter at Tresavean was lucky to earn £8.14s. a month, and a miner £4.4s.[29] In the American mines during the early twentieth century, miners earned anywhere between $3.50 and $4.00 a day, employees at the Empire, North Star and Idaho Maryland mines in California, successfully striking for a $1.00 wage increase in 1918.[30]

In the early twentieth century, it also became difficult to resist the lure of new forms of employment offering high wages, and some Cornish people were willing to sacrifice their independence to work on the factory production lines of the Ford, Chevrolet and General Motors plants of Michigan's Lower Peninsula. At $5 a day, these were jobs which could be learnt relatively quickly, and which required little or no skill. Furthermore, this form of employment, although exhausting, was less dangerous than mining and infinitely more salubrious. Powell brothers, William Gordon and John Henry, both miners, and two Winn brothers, Abraham and Claude, formerly quarrymen, migrated to Michigan specifically to work in such car factories prior to the outbreak of the First World War.[31]

Wilfred Harvey of Carn Marth did the same, but he joined a steady flow of Cornish miners who had migrated to the Upper Peninsula copper and iron mines, only to discover that they were to suffer the same fate as their Cornish counterparts in the inter-war period. In one month, about 600 people of Cornish descent left their homes in the Keweenaw towns of Houghton, Calumet and Laurium to settle around Detroit and Flint, seeking work in the new factories.[32] It was unusual for these migrants to return to Lanner; their imaginations were captivated by the 'American Dream' and many became naturalised, Wilfred Harvey becoming an American citizen in 1928 after six years in the US.[33] (Fig.8.11.).

Once overseas, the new immigrants added to the 'pull' factor, by encouraging family and friends who remained in Cornwall to join them. The improving standard of literacy in the nineteenth century meant that favourable reports in letters sent home were read by increasing numbers of people. These letters relating to life in the new communities overseas were often deliberately published by local newspapers and this doubtless inspired people to take the decision to migrate. Papers such as the *Royal Cornwall Gazette*, the *West Briton* and the *Cornubian* kept Lanner people in touch with events abroad. The *Cornubian* was a permanent feature in the lounge of Blake's Hotel in New York, a business operated by a Cornishman from St Austell for Cornish people migrating to and from the USA. Blake's weekly letter to the *Cornubian* in the early decades of the twentieth century was often the only way local people knew what had happened to a friend or relative in America, emphasising the importance of modern communication to the migratory experience.

Reports of men striking it rich and being set up for life further added to the fascination of a new life overseas and did much to inspire those seeking to improve their lot in life to migrate. In 1877, the extraordinary story of a Lanner man named Hosking who had migrated to South Africa with the intention of working at the Kimberley diamond mines in the early 1870s was printed in the *Cornubian*. He was lucky enough to have found a gold nugget weighing 123 ounces in the veldt, which he sent home to his wife via a colleague who was returning to the village due to ill health. The fortunate recipient dutifully put it in a Redruth bank for safety.[34]

Methods of Migration

The Cornish abroad were famous for their clannishness and exclusivity, living in close-knit communities bound together by shared traditions peculiar to their place of origin. Their allegiance to Methodism and their strange fashion of speech set them apart. But their cultural exclusivity was not the only facet of their clannishness, for to be Cornish became synonymous with mining skill and excellence, so it was in the best interests of migrants to emphasise their Cornish roots, giving them a distinct advantage in the job market.

The Cornish became fabled for their adeptness at helping their fellow countrymen to migrate, the fare for the ocean passage often sent home by a relative or friend, and a job and lodgings for 'Cousin Jack' found upon arrival in his new community. Some of the South African mines were managed by Lanner men; J. Richards, former head of Lanner School, supplied work for many Lanner lads on the Rand in his capacity as a mine manager. Another example is that of the Henry Nourse Gold Mine, captained by John Veall Inch in the post Boer War era, which had numerous village boys on its pay roll. The Tregoning Family, of West Trevarth, industrialists and entrepreneurs, helped Gwennap men to find employment within the companies in which they had an interest in England.[35] One such example is John Evans of Lambriggan House, Lanner, who worked as a copper sampling agent for Nevill, Dulce & Co., of Llanelly, South Wales.

It was usual for migrants to travel with family members or friends. 'Messrs. W. Ball, J. Webster, W. Tucker, C. Job and C. Richards departed for South Africa recently. All but Tucker had been before,' read a typical report in a local newspaper.[36] Martin Tresidder, who died in Utah, USA in 1901, was reported to have 'left Lanner in company with his eldest brother James,' eighteen months before his death.[37] William Trewin migrated to Montana 1911 to live with his cousin, William J. Dunstan, who resided in Butte along with seven other cousins from Lanner.[38]

The Cornish were highly visible in their affiliation with Friendly and Masonic societies, as most towns and many villages in Cornwall had such organisations. Lanner had two friendly societies in the nineteenth century, the Loyal Lannarth Lodge of Oddfellows and the Lanner Philanthropic Society. Many Cornishmen joined or formed such societies in the new mining towns worldwide; one of the first buildings constructed in the predominantly Cornish town of Gold Hill, on Nevada's famous Comstock Lode, was the Masonic Lodge.

The majority of Cornish burials in the public cemeteries of the United States will be found today in the sections reserved for the Oddfellows or Freemasons. Carn Marth miner Joseph Kemp, buried at the Glenwood Cemetery in Park City, Utah, has Masonic insignia on his headstone.[39] Richard Jose, Lanner's best-known migrant, was a member of the Ancient Arabic Order of the Mystic Shrine in San Francisco.

The continuance of the Masonic tradition abroad, particularly in the USA, must have served the Cousin Jacks well, with its expressed aims of social philanthropy and welfare, strengthening the kin network and providing a degree of security for the families of those who were Masonic members. Kin networks were an important feature of migration to places such as the United States, Mexico and Chile where there were no assisted passage schemes.

In some areas special emigration societies were formed, such as that of Breage in 1850. The capital was all locally subscribed, and it was created for the purpose of sending eight men to the gold diggings in California. This scheme was the first of its kind in Cornwall.[40] There is no evidence of such a society in Lanner, but during the 1890s in the Camborne and Redruth District, the Mining Unemployment Relief Committee displayed posters in the area advertising that in Calumet, Michigan, USA, 100–500 miners and underground men were wanted immediately.[41]

The nineteenth century saw the development of regular shipping lines, while transport at home was also improving, enabling the population to achieve a far greater mobility than had before been possible. Fares aboard transatlantic ships, particularly steerage or third class tickets, became more affordable as the century wore on and emigration evolved into an organised industry, with agents, shipping rebates and propaganda offices. We have already mentioned Isaac Latimer of Truro.

RAILWAY FARE

PAID TO LONDON.

T. L. RICHARDS is authorised by Messrs. Donald Currie and Co. to take passengers for their line of Mail Steamers to the Cape, Natal, and intermediate ports. Persons engaging their passage with the above will be allowed 3rd class fare from any Railway Station in Cornwall to London or Dartmouth. Apply to

T. L. RICHARDS,

Emigration Agent and Mineral Specimen Dealer

Lanner Moor, Gwennap.

Fig.8.6. *Emigration evolved into an organised industry by the late 19th Century, and South Africa was one of the main migratory destinations for Lanner people. Advertisement by T.L.Richards , of Lanner Moor.*

In Lanner, two emigration agents were noted in *Kelly's Directory* of 1873: Thomas L. Richards of Lanner Moor, agent for the Allan and White Star Lines, was also a boot maker and mineral specimen dealer (Fig8.6), and John Secombe Tonkin, a cordwainer, was agent for the White Star Line. In 1869 Tonkin was reported to have been the first agent in the Redruth District to have sent an emigrant to Liverpool, some 18 years before (Fig.8.7).

EMIGRATION TO ALL PARTS OF THE WORLD.

AMERICA AND AUSTRALIA (By steam and sailing ships); free and assisted passages to CANTERBURY, OTAGO and NEW ZEALAND; Free and assisted passages to QUEENSLAND; passages to BRAZILS, LISBON, &c.

Persons about to emigrate would do well to call on Mr J. S. Tonkin, emigration agent, Lanner, near Redruth, who will afford any necessary information.

The S.S. "Great Britain" will sail for Melbourne on October 1.

Fig.8.7. *J.S.Tonkin advertises as an emigration agent. (The* Cornubian, *25 Nov 1870).*

In 1874 Tonkin arranged the embarkation orders for 50 of the 520 passengers aboard the *Eastern Monarch*, en route to New Zealand, and in 1876 the local press alerted prospective migrants to South Australia to obtain free handbooks on Adelaide from Tonkin of Lanner. These contained maps, illustrations and information on the climate around Adelaide, and details about the vast mineral resources of the Colony of South Australia, lists of wages for artisans, miners, labourers and female domestic servants and advice as to what would be needed on the long voyage. These handbooks were indispensable to all those about to migrate from the Lanner District.

In the 1880s, John Evans Junior, tailor and draper, advertised in *Doidge's Almanack* as an agent for numerous navigation companies and advertised passages to America, the Antipodes, South Africa, Mexico, Chile and Peru. By 1886 T.J. Scoble, a miner born in the State of Hidalgo, Mexico, whose wife was born in Minas Gerais, Brazil, and who had worked in Nova Scotia, Canada, was for many years, an agent for the Allan Line of Royal Mail Steamers, operating between Liverpool and the USA and Canada.[42]

In most villages a moneylender was on hand to arrange a deal to help prospective migrants find their fare. Sometimes mining companies offered to pay the fares of migrating miners; this form of migration was quite usual among South American, South African and North American mining companies, the money for the fare being deducted from the miners' wages over the ensuing months. Cornish miners were grateful for the opportunity of work these large companies offered at a time of dearth at home, as expressed in the words of a local miner Peter Varker, who travelled to the Great Dome Mines in Northern Canada with 108 other Cornish miners in 1920: 'We'll do our best for the Company, who have done so much for we.'[43] The convenience of these schemes made emigration so much easier.

Changing Migratory Patterns

Patterns of migration from Lanner Parish changed over the years, and varied according to destination. Research of our sample shows that in the mid nineteenth century, the Antipodes were very popular destinations for migrants; by the 1880s these had been superseded by migration to the USA, Chile and Mexico. By the turn of the century, the USA and South Africa were the main destinations, with the latter being of greater importance. New areas of migration such as India, Burma and Malaysia only attracted small numbers of migrants in the twentieth century.

As already seen, the majority of the migrations to the Antipodes, particularly those who migrated under the assisted passage schemes, were of the extended family kind. After the free fare schemes came to an end in 1886, the numbers migrating to Australia and New Zealand fell away sharply. Those who did migrate after this period were more likely to have been single men and not families. Two mine engine drivers, William Knuckey and Ernest Steward Martin left Lanner in 1900 and 1919 respectively, the former for the gold mining fields of Kalgoorlie, Western Australia and the latter for Melbourne. They were both younger than 25, and unmarried. The percentage of returns to Lanner from the Antipodes was very small.

In the early days of migration to the USA, when placer gold (alluvial gold) was being exploited, and the first tentative attempts at deep lode mining were being tried, it was unusual to find many women in the early mining camps which sprang up haphazardly around the workings. The very nature of the placer miner's existence, often licentious as well as solitary, nomadic and harsh, precluded family involvement.[44] It was only when lode mining took off in Wisconsin, the Western US, and later in Michigan and Montana, that permanent towns such as Mineral Point, Grass Valley, Virginia City, Butte and Calumet developed. For example, Cornish miners found mines so rich and going to such depths in the hills of the Sierra Nevada, that they and their descendants were employed to the third and fourth generation.[45]

With a more sedentary existence, men now found it possible to send for their wives and children. By the 1870s, among those migrating to America from Lanner were women and children, as the USA increased in popularity for family-type migration. Thomas Davies, who migrated from the village to Cheevor, USA, in 1871, was followed by his wife and family a couple of years after.[46]

Analysis of Fig.8.2 shows that North America was second only to Africa in popularity as a migratory destination. In the twentieth century more of those who migrated chose to remain in the USA. Research of our sample of 430 people concludes that about a third of those who migrated to North America were women and children, and nearly a quarter of the total number of people known to have migrated there returned home, as shown in Fig.8.3. Roughly a third of the lone males remained in their new communities.

Mexico and Latin America, particularly Chile, were popular destinations for both lone male and family-type migration in the mid to late nineteenth century. However, the War of the Pacific, 1879–1883, disrupted migratory patterns, and this, followed by the outbreak of the First World War, effectively ended migrations to Bolivia and Peru. The installation of a Marxist government in Chile in the 1920s, and a series of military coups, dissuaded people from settling there. The revolutionary holocaust which broke out in Mexico in 1910, and the troubled years which followed, saw the gradual abandonment of migration to one of the most popular migratory destinations in Latin America.

Over half of the people who migrated to Latin America appear to have returned to Lanner. In Chile, a large expatriate community was situated in the northern town of Tocopilla (part of the Republic of Bolivia until it was annexed by Chile after the War of the Pacific), where people from the village were involved in both the industry and commerce of the town, William Lean for example, operating two copper mining companies and large merchandise stores.

The Jose Family, brothers William, Henry and John (sons of William and Elizabeth Jose, née Roberts), also made a significant contribution to the Tocopillan economy in the industrial sphere, being the owners of several copper companies. John Jose left the Lanner area in 1853, at 17 years of age, and went to the silver mines in the district of Chañarcillo, Chile. After two years, he travelled to Bolivia, where copper mining was in its infancy. Jose introduced the Cornish pumping engine to Bolivian mines and founded the Tocopilla Copper Mining and Smelting Company, and was the managing director until 1881 when he returned to Cornwall to reside at Mellingey. John Jose & Co. occasionally placed orders for mining equipment with Harvey's of Hayle. In 1880, a request for two dozen miners' hammers and twenty car wheels was received by the Hayle foundry from this Lanner man's Bolivian company.[47] In 1875, James Davey, a Lanner butcher who resided at Pennance House, was prompted to sail to Chile on account of his health. He sold up his shop and household effects and migrated to Tocopilla, where his sister and brothers in law, the Knuckeys, were resident, and they helped to set him up as a butcher, a business he operated there for several years, returning to Lanner when his health was restored.[48]

The smallest category, the Rest of the World, comprised such countries as India, Malaysia, Burma and other parts of Europe; over half those people who worked in these countries returned to Lanner. Both graphs clearly show the importance of Africa as a migratory destination. In this category, more than any other, adult males dominate, and over a third of all those who emigrated to Africa came home. From this we can conclude that Africa was not viewed as a permanent home in the same way that Australia or New Zealand were, but as a place in which to work for a given period of time, with return to Lanner the main objective.

Men who migrated solely to gain employment, with the intention of returning to Cornwall as soon as the job situation improved, became known as 'birds of passage'. This type of lone male migration from the parish became more prevalent towards the end of the nineteenth century, probably as a result of cheaper passages aboard ocean liners, and a society which had increasingly come to view temporary migration as a normal consequence of economic depression, or a welcome opportunity to do better financially. About a third of the men who travelled to America from Lanner could be defined as birds of passage, but the best example is, without a doubt, South Africa.

At the turn of the twentieth century, there were probably more Lanner men working on the Rand than at any other place in the world, and Africa was a word on everyone's lips. The Transvaal, in effect, became almost the parish next door. Where formerly men had travelled to a district such as South Caradon when the mines around Lanner had declined and closed, they now migrated to the Transvaal in huge numbers to keep their families clothed and fed. Unlike most other migratory destinations, few women travelled out with the men, as Africa was not just unhealthy, as we shall discuss below, but also a dangerous place in which to work, with the political situation there always precarious. In 1895, it was reported in the local press that in the Transvaal, 'There are frequent attempted outrages by Kaffirs on defenceless women. In Pretoria and Johannesburg women are learning the use of a revolver.'[49]

It became necessary for European men to carry a gun at all times, as the native workforce was under the impression that white men, who usually held the positions of Captain or Shift Boss on the mines, carried large sums of money around with them. To do so would have been to invite murder. Men who worked on the Rand for any length of time were always careful not to flash money around, even upon their return to Lanner. Minnie Haughton could clearly remember her father, James Harvey, disappearing on numerous occasions into a shop doorway in Redruth street to avoid drawing attention to the fact that he had taken out his wallet to give her some money; a legacy of his South African days.[50] Vicious murders in the mining towns and camps were not infrequent, miners even being attacked for the contents of their dinner pail, the poverty amongst the natives being so acute. Thomas Job, working in Randfontein, was once attacked on his way to work and would probably have been murdered had he not been carrying his treasured banjo, with which he intended to entertain his colleagues at the mine. He used it to fend off his assailant.[51]

There were some intrepid Lanner ladies who, with their children, followed their husbands out. They were every bit as much pioneers as their menfolk. These included Marion Blight and her son Harry, and Mrs Rowe and her son, who travelled out together on the RMS *Walmer Castle* in 1915.[52] The late Mary Job, who lived in Randfontein from 1913–1916, remembered how all her family saw her off on the train at Redruth Station. She had received a cable from her husband telling her to sell up and ship out to join him. Emma Jane Harvey of Pennance also sold up her home and belongings to join her husband, and operated a boarding house in Johannesburg during the 1890s after his untimely death, but they were the exception rather than the rule. Weekly newspaper columns confirm the predominantly lone male migratory pattern, with reports of South African departures and arrivals, as men commuted to and from the Rand. 'W. R. Pascoe of Lanner is leaving for an appointment at the Robinson Deep G.M.C. Johannesburg today', reported the *Cornubian*, adding 'this is Mr Pascoe's third visit to the Transvaal'.[53]

The extent to which economic necessity had driven the young men of the village to the Transvaal is illustrated when reports appeared in the local press of the funeral in Johannesburg, 1903, of Lanner man Sidney Andrew. Over 200 mourners, chiefly Cornish, attended the funeral, and in the obituary appeared the names of no less than 31 Lanner men.[54]

Old World Culture, New World Ideas

Once abroad, the Cornish deliberately sought to retain their distinctive cultural identity, particularly their allegiance to Methodism. Familiar chapel choirs and Glee Clubs were formed; W.J. Phillips was singing first bass in the Grass Valley Glee Club in 1915, and Captain Thomas Edwards was the treasurer of the Pachuca Glee Club in Mexico in 1896.[55] Sunday Schools were started, with their popular anniversaries keenly awaited. In Roodeporte, South Africa, two Lanner brothers, F.J. and W. Scoble participated in the Wesleyan Chapel's seventh anniversary, the former conducting the Chapel's musicians, and the latter being one of the singers in the choir.[56]

Cornish societies became popular, especially in the early twentieth century. The Southern California Cornish Association's annual 'Down Along Social' in 1934 was attended by the society's oldest member, 83-year-old James Lawn of Lanner, who had hair 'the hue of St. Austell's china clay'.[57] Also prevalent were 'Dinners', the *Cornubian* remarking in 1892 that 'It has come to be recognised that wherever 3 or 4 Cornishmen dwell, in that place there will be an annual Cornish dinner.' Lanner men J. Bray, W.A. Hocking, Thomas Tyacke and Joe Trewern attended the dinner at Kimberley of that year.[58] That of 1906 was attended by J. Lean.

Methodism, with its twin pillars of revival and evangelism was a potent force in the mining communities overseas where the Cornish dwelt in large numbers, and Methodist preachers from Cornwall often continued their evangelistic crusades abroad. William Henry Chapman, born in Lanner in 1852, was attached to the Bible Christian Chapel from his youth, and at only fifteen years of age received his first ticket of membership. Only two years later he began to preach, the beginning of a life-long ministry. In 1870, he migrated on board the *Allumbagh* to Australia where two years later, he began work as a home missionary with the United Methodist Free Church, and was received into regular ministry two years after this. He achieved prominence in the church, holding various offices, including Conference President and Secretary. After Methodist Union in Australia in 1902, he became a circuit minister until his retirement in 1918.[59] Several more Lanner preachers were active in the USA in the nineteenth and early twentieth century. The Reverend George Tippet was a Methodist preacher at Butte and Meaderville in Montana, the Reverend J. Jeffrey Martin preached in San Francisco in the 1890s and William Thomas Hosking, who left Lanner in 1922 as a mine engine driver, became a Congregational minister in California.[60] Lanner-born Reverend Thomas L. Burden gave the following invocation to the Southern California Association in 1934 on the occasion of their annual Christmas 'Down Along Social':

> *We have joined hands we Cornish Folk across the main!*
> *Hail One and All, Old Cornwall!*[61]

It is hardly surprising to discover that Methodist ministers from Lanner were active overseas, since they originated in an area so obviously 'Nonconformist', but it is interesting to note, particularly in the above example of the Reverend Burden's address, that there seems to be a certain fusing of Methodism with a perceived sense of Cornish identity and international belonging.

But perhaps the greatest expression of Cornishness came in less happy circumstances, namely the outpouring of grief at the loss of a friend. Cornish funerals were always sombre, strictly organised, well attended affairs. Local papers usually included comprehensive obituaries of former parishioners who had died abroad. Hymns such as 'Rock of Ages', 'Lead Kindly Light', 'A Few More Years Shall Roll' and 'The Old Rugged Cross', were among the favourites, the deceased being laid to rest to the morbid strains of the Dead March in 'Saul', as the black clad mourners bade farewell to their comrade; a scene repeated in chapels all over Cornwall. When young Lanner man W.J. Trewin died, aged 24, at the Mountain View Mine in Centerville, Montana, the pall bearers were reported to have been 'chosen from among his boyhood friends in far away England,' and a large chorus of young men, the deceased's former associates, sang 'Nearer My God to Thee' with great feeling.[62] The Cornish loved 'a good buryin' and these walking funerals were a major part of the Cornish miner's life, and the preoccupation with death, doom and gloom often seemed to set them apart in their new communities.

'Out of core time' was spent in much the same way as at home, with rugby and football being popular sports in Cornish communities. Friendly rivalries between neighbouring towns such as Grass Valley and Nevada City in California echoed the rivalry, for example, between Camborne and Redruth back home in Cornwall. Mr Allen of the area remarked in 1915, that he 'liked it in Arizona, and Miami was a fine town to be in. They have all kinds of sports there, such as cricket, football etc., and the natural little rivalries for supremacy with Globe, which is only ten miles away, makes the sports very interesting.'[63]

And wrestling, a sport which was typically Cornish, became as popular abroad as it once was at home. In 1906, a Cornish wrestling match, for which £30 of competition prizes were put up, was reported to have taken place at Fordsburg, South Africa, the venue being the prestigious Port Elizabeth Hotel. On the committee responsible for organising the event was Tom Goldsworthy of Lanner; the referee was fellow villager William Oliver. Not surprisingly, the first and second prizes were awarded to James Triggs and William Goldsworthy, both from Lanner![64] Later that year at the same place, Lanner man 'Tit Wills' won the coveted belt, and was reported to have 'shewd great pluck and skill.'[65]

Area and street names in the new mining settlements – the Redruth suburb at Burra, South Australia, Uren Street in Nevada City, Hocking Street in Grass Valley, California, Clinton Road in New Redruth, Alberton (South Africa), Falmouth Road at Mowbray, Cape Town, and Cornwall Street, Turffontein, in Johannesburg – find an echo in their counterparts, such as Californian Moor at Four Lanes, Australia Terrace at Drump Lane, Redruth, Akankoo Place at South Gate Street, Redruth, Zimapan near Tolgullow and Chili Road at Illogan Highway. And house names chosen by returning migrants were often named after the area or mine in which they had worked abroad. The mining district of Camborne and Redruth provides numerous examples, some of which are still visible: 'Mysore Villa', 'Robinson Deep', 'Kimberley', 'Langlaagte', 'Huasco House', 'Central Villa', 'Wemmer Villa', 'Peru House', 'Malabar', 'Phoenix Villa', 'Ferreira House', 'Reefton', 'Silver Bow', 'Bendigo', 'Huelva', 'Inca Villa', 'Benoni', 'Kolar Villa', 'Nevada House', 'Globe Villa' and 'Eureka Villas'. In Lanner and at South Downs there are the following: 'Reno', 'O'Okiep House', 'Buena Vista', 'Jeppe Villa', 'The Kloof', 'Santa Cruz', 'The Rockies', 'Calabar', 'Simmer Farm', 'Virginia Cottage', 'Talana House', 'Pioche House', 'Bolivar House', 'Balaghat House', 'Denver House', 'Wisconsin' and 'Calumet Villa'.

A curious copper badge bearing the inscription 'Junction Shaft, C.A. Mine, Bisbee, Arizona' (a badge of the Calumet and Atlanta Mining Company), was found several years ago at Tresavean Mine by Yvonne Reynolds, and serves as a further reminder that many miners who returned to work at Tresavean had worked in metalliferous mines worldwide.[66]

Moreover, returning migrants had a preference for certain items and styles of clothing which soon found their way into village shops. John Evans Junior, tailor, draper and emigration agent in the early to mid 1880s, catered to the taste of those who had returned home yet wanted to be able to buy 'Yankee Trousers' which were found to be more durable and comfortable than the usual Cornish ones, and he even kept customers' sizes, so he could continue to make their clothes and mail them overseas.[67]

Many of the miners who returned from foreign mining fields brought with them the politics, as well as the new ideas and techniques in mining and engineering, which challenged the old social order. The 1885 election success of C.A.V. Conybeare, a Radical MP in the Mining Division (of which Lanner was a part), has been linked to the vote of miners, enfranchised in 1884, who had recently returned to the Camborne–Redruth area from the mines of Chile, Australia and Nevada, where profitable mining had been undertaken without the miners having to pay for tools or explosives, or wait for wages.[68] Such men had become increasingly unwilling to be exploited at home. The 'Rand Miners' Vote' was considered responsible for unseating Arthur Strauss, the Unionist MP for the Mining Division, in the 1900 General Election[69] and the growth in the popularity of trade unionism in Cornish mines was aided by the return of expatriate miners who had worked in America and South Africa in particular.

By 1918 the entire work force of Tresavean Mine was affiliated to the Workers' Union, after a successful strike to demand that non-affiliated Tresavean employees become members.[70] Cost book companies gave way to limited liability companies and some local mines began to introduce rock drills in greater numbers. By the early twentieth century these were being widely used abroad, particularly the One-man Drill.[71] North and South Penstruthal utilised new rock drills in the period following the late 1880s, and Tresavean used One-man Drills in the last working. When the latter mine reopened in 1907, it was decided to dewater the mine with electrically-driven centrifugal pumps. Electrically-powered machinery and pumping equipment reflected a technology then widely available in foreign mines. The Golden Gate Mine in Mercur, Utah, USA, was the first in the world to be powered by long-distance alternating electricity, in the 1890s, and mines in South Africa and in Pachuca, Mexico, used electrically-driven pumping equipment instead of the old Cornish pumping engine, considered to be both costly and inefficient.[72] Indeed, the man appointed as mine manager at Tresavean, John Faull, had gained his mining experience in the Transvaal, South Africa.

In Cornwall, still recognised as a great world mining region, a large rift opened up between theory and practice. Camborne School of Mines was a world leader in the field of mining technology and many Camborne/Redruth firms were world class, exporting mining equipment around the globe. Yet paradoxically, mining methods and practices remained antiquated here. For in terms of practical mining skills, Cornwall was becoming increasingly marginalised and therefore peripheralised in the emerging international mining market.

Living on the Backs of the Rand

The collapse of the Cornish copper and then tin mining industries created deep recessions, punctuated by very brief periods of economic growth. Thus money which came from overseas was vital to the local economy. Families waited anxiously for the arrival of the monthly or annual remittance from a family member overseas. Tweedy's Bank at Redruth regularly received money sent from Mexico to miners' families living in this area, and in the early 1880s received the princely sum of £44 pounds, sent to Lanner man Joseph Eastwick from his son, John, in Real del Monte. One list of remittances for 16 March 1867, shows that Williams & Company, Redruth bankers, had received £4619 from expatriate miners in Mexico,[73] much needed currency in an area experiencing great poverty. This was a year which, according to a Methodist minister at Redruth, witnessed a terrible depression. 'I helped to relieve 600 persons twice a week in this district,' he commented, further adding 'I pray that this neighbourhood may never be called to pass through such sufferings again as was experienced in 1866 and 1867.'[74]

By the end of the nineteenth century, Cornwall had become almost totally dependent on money sent from the Rand, a situation which the *Cornubian* summed up with the terse statement 'We are living on South Africa'.[75] That many village men sought to make their money on the Rand is exemplified by the comment made in the *Cornubian* of 12 June 1903: 'As in other Cornish towns and villages, the population of Lanner is decreasing weekly by the departure of residents for South Africa. Messrs Cyrus Southey and J. Tregellas left on Friday'.

The arrival of the South African Mail, the main delivery from Johannesburg, Kimberley and other South African cities, was keenly awaited and the dispatch of the post was soon followed by a rush to the banks to cash drafts sent home. The local shops and market always did a roaring trade after this. In 1896 it was estimated that each week a sum exceeding £1000 (over £33 000 at today's values) was received, in Redruth alone, from the Rand.[76]

Richard Blewett, the former headmaster of St Day school, provides a vivid description of the effects of South African remittances upon the Gwennap area in a paper given to a group of teachers assembled at a course in Cambridge, in 1935:

> *Here is a picture of St Day, and many another Cornish mining village from 1890–1910. A large village, half denuded of its men. Monday, the great day of the week, for the Africa mail comes in. Wives, hitherto used to a domestic economy based upon a pound a week or less, suddenly blazing in the glory of £20-30 a month. A Bank Draft headed with the magic words 'Standard Bank of South Africa'... miserly saving or mad spending; new furniture, a piano... Methodist Chapels a tournament of fashion... ostrich plumes floating from head and neck, gold mounted lions' claw brooches... .*[77]

This dependency culture was shown up for its inadequacies towards the end of the nineteenth century, as anxiety set in when the political situation in the Transvaal began to look ominous. Even in the early years, the political situation had been precarious. The Witwatersrand lay in one of the two Boer Republics, the Transvaal, a region populated mainly by descendants of Dutch settlers, a farming people who resented the interference of 'Uitlanders,' and who were keen to remain independent of Crown intervention in their affairs. Britain cast a covetous eye at the fantastic mineral prospects of this region, and after years of securing Imperial sentiment amongst the largely English-speaking community on the Rand, and following the ill-fated Jameson Raid of 1895, war was inevitable.[78]

A good many Lanner men, seeing that war was the most likely outcome of the highly-charged political situation, had already packed up and left. Those who left South Africa, among them some Lanner men, suffered the indignation of being hissed and spat at by the English sympathisers in the country, and were branded cowards, something many of them never forgot. Jenifer Lawn of Prisk's Terrace, writing in 1897, commented that 'there are a great many men coming home from South Africa as the mines are closing, which is worrying, since there are so few jobs here for them.' The Second Boer War began on 12 October 1899 and lasted until May 1902. The Wesleyans and Bible Christians noted that the donations received at their annual anniversaries of 1900 were down from the previous year, 'the war having driven most of the young men home.'[79]

These were indeed worrying times, as there was little work in the village and most miners hoped to be able to return as soon as the situation improved so important were South African remittances to the local economy. Before the war, W.S. Caine MP, estimated that those working in South Africa were remitting money yearly to their families in Cornwall to the amount of £220 000 (several million pounds in today's money). 'That money was lost last year,' he remarked in the *Cornubian* of January 1901, continuing, 'The effect upon the county may easily be imagined.'[80]

On a local level, George S. Bray, chairman of the Lanner Lamp Committee, also expressed his regret at the war preventing subscriptions from South Africa, and hoped that it would prove unnecessary to touch the reserve funds.[81]

Living was very expensive in South Africa as food prices were high, few mines remained opened, and men were unable to remit money in the amounts to which their families had become accustomed. And many of those who returned to their families in Lanner found that the money which had been remitted had been wantonly spent, leaving the family yet again in penury.

A good many Cornishmen were stranded on the Rand, as they had purchased a one-way ticket to the Cape and did not have sufficient money to return home. The *West Briton,* of 27 January 1899, carried the story of some Cousin Jacks who had managed to leave South Africa: 'The only inducement to stop was to carry a rifle, for which remuneration was made at five shillings a day,' commented one Cornishman. He did not wish to fight, as he explained 'I had nothing to complain of at the hands of the Government [of the Boer Republic], and was asked, or ordered by the manager to either get a rifle or leave the property. I could find no reason to fight, so came away. The manager said, "get a gun, or clear out".' Whether the British Government was justified in starting the Boer War was a question which divided the Cornish community both at home and abroad.

This was a particularly bleak time in South Africa's history, and one stranded Cornishman wrote the following letter to the *Cornubian* in May 1902, just before the war ended: 'The town I am in is short of water and full of mosquitoes and the bush fires at night light up the surrounding hills and give the country a weird aspect with the historic background of the war. During the day there are fearful dust storms.'

Cornish miners now found themselves guarding the mines and railways, or fighting the Boers at the front. One Lanner man caught up in the war was James Harvey of Carn Marth, who could not afford to go home. He enlisted in the South African Rifles, and whilst in uniform, met the young Winston Churchill who was engaged as a war correspondent.[82] Wallace Curnow, who left Lanner before the war, volunteered to join The Imperial Light Infantry and, by July of 1901, was promoted to Lance Corporal.[83]

Some villagers were injured during the fighting, including a Mr Edwards, who volunteered to guard the Natal Railway. After serving a good while in South Africa, he was shot through the leg and underwent three operations in a Government hospital. He was extremely upset that he received no commendation for his bravery, remarking in the *Cornubian* of 7 June 1901: 'It was unkind and inconsistent treatment of the Government and those who rule affairs which disgusted me.' He was permanently disabled. Less fortunate was John Hocking who died at the front. Beethoven's funeral march was played at Lanner Bible Christian Chapel in February of 1901 as a mark of respect at the loss of this former member of the congregation.[84]

With events as poignant as this, the Boer War could not have passed unnoticed in Lanner. Indeed, the Teacher's Log Book for Lanner School notes that in March 1900, a whole holiday was granted by the Board 'to imprint on the minds of the children the importance of the Relief of Ladysmith'. The end of the Boer War was marked with a half-day holiday in June 1902.[85] (Fig. 8.8.).

Fig.8.8. *Ceremony in Lanner Square, c.1902. This could have been on the occasion of the end of the Boer war, or the Coronation of Edward VII. Tom Knuckey is third from the left of the group of four immediately behind the horse in the foreground. Note that Lanner Wesley Schoolroom has not been built, but the water fountain is there, without its 'moon'. The building at the back of the Commercial Inn was the skittle alley.* (© Mr and Mrs C. Williams, Lanner)

The war in Africa severely disrupted migration patterns, and was in effect a precursor of the World War which was to come. Fortunately, the mines of Michigan were still buoyant, and many Lanner men switched their destination to the copper mines there to avoid unemployment, a *Copper Country* newspaper commenting that the miners in Keweenaw had been awaiting the chance to return to the Rand.[86] The onset of the Boer War did, however, severely shake the confidence of Lanner and similar villages dependent on the bright prospects of foreign mining fields, at a time when their own were so bleak. Several projects which had been mooted in the village in the early to mid 1890s, such as the plans for a Lecture Hall and Literary Institute, involving the construction of a building costing £500, designed by James Hicks, were dropped. Similarly the plans for a public subscription to initiate an improved sewerage system for the village were shelved, in part due to the collapse of mining at Tresavean, but chiefly because of the uncertainty created both before and during the Boer War.

However, after the war had ended, many building propositions devised by the chapels were begun, culminating in the construction of new Sunday School rooms for Lanner Wesley Chapel and South Downs Wesley, the extension of the Primitive Methodist Chapel at Lanner Moor, a new Sunday School for the Bryanites and the reconstruction and refurbishment of Lanner Wesley Chapel.

Some of those who returned from foreign mining fields had done very well. Indeed, it was the hope of many to save enough to purchase the leasehold of a cottage and some land upon their return home. The 1891 census for Lanner shows several retired gold miners, one a 37-year-old married man, who had obviously secured a favourable future for his family. Various properties were built in the village with money earned abroad, an example being Grays Terrace, constructed by Captain Gray, who made his money in the goldfields of Australia in the 1840s and 50s.[87]

David Polkinghorne, of Carn Marth, built the house 'Carn Wartha' during the First World War with his savings, made in the USA as a miner.[88] William Taylor, the proprietor of the public house in the Square, the Commercial Hotel (which he named the 'Taylor's Hotel'), had returned to Cornwall from Colorado in the late 1880s where he had made his money, perhaps as a miner, and he used this to buy the business.[89] The late Mary Job and her husband were able to purchase a cottage called 'Windy Heights', at Pennance, with the money they had accumulated in Africa.[90] Likewise, James H. Phillips of Lanner Moor came home in 1911 from the Transvaal with £106 he had saved from his wages as a miner, and used it to set up his own grocery shop in the village.[91] Mr and Mrs Stewart Morrish who arrived home from America in 1931–32 used their savings to buy the village fish and chip business from Mr and Mrs R. A. Minson.

Village institutions benefited enormously from expatriates worldwide. Methodist places of worship regularly received donations from former members resident in mining towns all over the world. Taking 1907 as an example, Lanner Wesley Chapel received £5.10s. from men on the Rand, 30 shillings from men in the USA and £1 from a former parishioner in Mexico. In the same year the Trevarth Wesleyan Sunday School received 10 shillings from both H. Webster and W. Bolt in the Transvaal. Donations later that year of £2 from F. and C. Job, further swelled the coffers of the chapel's funds.[92] The same pattern emerges for the other Chapels.

Mrs Eddy of Colorado was a long term benefactor to Christ Church, giving in 1899 the beautiful east stained-glass window in memory of her husband Edward. Over the ensuing years she gave many gifts at great expense, most extraordinary of these being the presentation in 1902 of a half sovereign each to the choir members, organ blower and church cleaner in appreciation of their contribution to the continuance of the spiritual life of the Church.[93]

IMPORTANT NOTICE.

Agency for the North Atlantic Express Company.

PARCELS OF ALL SIZES

Sent to and From

Europe to all Parts of America

AT THE LOWEST POSSIBLE RATES.

For Tariff of Rates & Further Particulars, apply to

T. L. RICHARDS,

LANNER MOOR, GWENNAP.

The Authorized Agent for Cornwall.

Fig.8.9. *T.L. Richards, of Lanner Moor, advertises his parcel service from Lanner to America in the 1870s.*

When renovations or new buildings were planned for these places of worship, money was sent from men working overseas, particularly those on the Rand. When the Lanner Wesleyan Chapel was raising funds to build a new school room, it was stated in the *Cornubian* that, 'Lanner boys the wide world over will undoubtedly desire to subscribe to this scheme, which will supply a long felt want.'[94] James Davey and his sister, Mrs Knuckey, former residents of Tocopilla, Chile, were responsible for giving a considerable amount of money that they had made in Chile towards the Wesleyan Chapel refurbishment of 1903, Davey providing the whole amount for the new granite facade.[95] The Lanner Lamp Committee, in February of 1903, received the huge sum of £45 from Lanner men in the Transvaal, the amount being collected by H. Nicholls. The Boer War had ended and no doubt this giant sum was intended to make up for the period in which it had been impossible to send gifts of money. The Lamp Committee found it, 'most encouraging that they still had friends at a distance who not only had not forgotten the effort they were making, but were willing and able to help.'[96]

In July 1903, the Gwennap Cottage Garden, Horticultural and Poultry Society was sent the sum of £26.10s. from men who were working in South Africa towards the funds for the society's annual show.[97] In 1928 it was reported that Granville 'Bill' Blatchford had sent a £1 donation from Kuantan, Malaysia, to Frank Trethowan, towards the fund for supplying a playing field for the village. He was not alone, for several other people were mentioned in connection with the fund; Bennett Opie sent a cheque for £2.2s. from London, Arthur James of South Africa donated £1 and Reginald Treloar remitted £5 from Rangoon, Burma.[98]

The teacher's log book of Lanner School mentions that, on 28 December 1921, the Cornish Association in South Africa had sent a gift of money to enable all the children in the distressed area of Redruth to have a memorable Christmas. Pupils at Lanner School were regaled with roast beef and potatoes, bread and plum pudding, and each received an apple, an orange and some nuts. Upon leaving, every infant was given a toy from a Christmas tree.[99] Clearly, those who had emigrated had not forgotten their roots and their benevolence to their one-time community was truly touching.

The Poverty of Dependency

With wealth flowing back into the village, it is easy to fall into the trap of viewing emigration in a wholly favourable light. We have already touched on the negative aspects of Lanner's late nineteenth century dependency culture. Migration was no panacea, and probably created just as many problems as it claimed to solve. Firstly it was a traumatic event in a family's history, involving painful decisions and considerable anxiety. Sales of furniture, livestock and other chattels were advertised on a regular basis as people broke up their homes to raise money to migrate. Tearful and distressing farewells were regular occurrences for Chapel and Church congregations who assembled to sing the poignant hymn 'God be With You Till We Meet Again,' for those about to migrate; absent friends were also remembered in hymns; 'keep our loved ones, now far distant, 'neath thy care'.

Family, (and also extended family) migrations constituted a considerable loss to the community; we will note in the following chapter the grave repercussions for small chapel congregations such as Trevarth Wesley or the Carn Marth Primitive Methodist, both of which ultimately closed due to the effects of migration.

Lanner was gradually afflicted by cultural poverty, as organisations such as the brass band, rugby club and Odd Fellows suffered a paucity of members due to emigration and therefore ceased. And the departure of several 'core families' from a community would seriously affect the neighbourhood; people with individual talents or skills were often irreplaceable.

Weekly scenes at Redruth Railway Station witnessed large numbers of migrants assembled on the platform with their trunks labelled for worldwide destinations (Fig.8.10). Imagine the feelings of those assembled to bid farewell, as

Fig.8.10. *Redruth Railway Station. The weekly exodus to South Africa (early 1900s).* (© Cornish Studies Library, Redruth)

Fig.8.11. *Carn Marth man, Wilfred Harvey* (Front row, fourth from left), *among fellow employees of the Tamarack Iron Mine, Ironwood, Michigan, c.1923.* (© I.M.Staat, Michigan, USA)

they watched the train leave the station in a cloud of steam and haunting whistles, to disappear abruptly into the blackness of the tunnel underneath the Wesleyan Chapel, taking with it their loved ones in whom was embodied all the hopes and ambitions of their family. Some never saw their relatives again. The late Minnie Haughton remembered when she was 7 years old the day she stood next to her father at Redruth Station to say good bye to her eldest brother, Wilfred Harvey, leaving for Ironwood, Michigan. She recalled her father did not shed a tear, but she knew he was broken by his son's departure, whom he was never to see again. 'It was the saddest day in my life,' she remarked, adding, 'I was an old woman the next time I saw my brother. We had been parted for over 50 years.' (Fig.8.11.).

Moreover, people often disappeared without a trace, one such was Richard E. Williams of Penstruthal, who left home in 1868 for Grass Valley. He then travelled on to the Comstock in neighbouring Nevada, and vanished.[100] Years later, anxious relatives were still trying to find him. The disappearance of people often had grave repercussions. The three-lives system of lease meant that it was crucial to know if the lives named on the leasehold deeds were still extant, as inability to do so could result in the payment of a heavy heriot (a fine), or complete loss of the leased property. In 1915 a local newspaper contained a request for information concerning Joseph Thomas, son of Joseph Thomas, who lived in Gwennap in 1835, afterwards migrating to Australia, and was the remaining 'name' on a lease. It was imperative the solicitors in question establish if or when he had died.[101]

Some women, abandoned by their husbands, found themselves heading large families not even knowing whether they were widows, receiving no remittances and being forced to apply for parochial relief. The following tragic case of a Lanner family appeared in the local press: 'A miner of this neighbourhood who recently went to South America died two days after reaching Panama. Now his widow and 10 children are being aided by the parish.'[102] In 1928, Mrs E. M. Symons of Brays Terrace was forced to contact the South African Cornish Association with a request for help to find her husband Thomas. He had gone to South Africa in 1920, and had last remitted money in 1924. He was traced to the Finsbury Gold Field, where a court order for a £2 weekly remittance was delivered to him.[103]

Men sometimes ran abroad to escape family responsibilities. Such an example was reported in 1883: 'A young girl of Lanner under 19 years of age, came forward and said she was 'enceinte', the father of the child being a young man of Lanner who had left the country, and was now in Mexico or Africa – she scarcely knew which part of the globe.' It was further suggested that this particular man had been encouraged to flee by his family and friends, leaving the pregnant girl at the mercy of the authorities.[104]

Some village men overseas were known to have had second and even third families, creating complex triangles of secrecy and deceit. The image of the Cornish miner as a deceiver is well illustrated in the 'Emigrant's Song', collected by S. Baring Gould in 1891:

Oh some say that I am rakish
And some do call me wild
Some say that I am rakish
And many maids beguiled
But to prove that I am loyal
Come on sweet love with me
I'll take you to America
My darling you shall be.[105]

Moreover, migration robbed the community of many of its brightest and best; the *West Briton* of 23 January 1879 cruelly calls those left behind 'half-men,' remarking that, 'the real men are away... the 'half-men' remain to perpetuate the race of the weak, the sickly, the mentally and physically good for little'. This theme was taken up by Richard Blewett of St Day, who, quoting A.H. Cherrill (HMI of Schools who inspected St Day in 1911), wrote scathingly about the Gwennap mining district. 'The majority (of the men) were unenterprising, unadventurous and satisfied with things as they were... the decay in local industries and consequent migration of much of the vigorous element of the population may be accountable for the apparently large proportion of the children of limited intellectual power.'[106]

This state of affairs only added to the somnolence of the local economy, which helped to hasten Cornwall's peripheral status, a point which has been argued convincingly by Philip Payton in his book *The Making of Modern Cornwall*.[107]

Furthermore, it must be noted that on the whole, by the latter decades of the nineteenth century, Cornish mines lacked the capital and modern equipment to remain competitive. This is a big issue requiring some explanation. The technology and capital were available locally, but why were they not applied? It could be that potential investors thought that there were likely to be better rewards in the growing local tourist industry; indeed, towards the end of the nineteenth century many new hotels were built around the county and newly-rich Lanner man, John Jose, formerly of Tocopilla, invested in a Cornish hotel. Internationally, there were big opportunities for investment in developing new mining fields in places such as Malaya, hence the formation of the Gopeng Tin Mining Company Ltd in 1891, with its head offices at Station Hill, Redruth. Alternatively, other fields of industry, such as the production of china clay, could have been viewed as offering better prospects of a return on capital.

Lack of investment in Cornish mines limited the opportunity for the application of innovative machinery, and by the early twentieth century the loss of many experienced miners to foreign parts meant that local mines lacked even the skilled labour which had been responsible for training the next generation of Cornish miners. Numerous examples can be found of top mining and engineering men from Lanner and district engaged in positions abroad and within the British Isles. Lanner men seeking work in mines, particularly those overseas, would have found it much easier to rise higher in the mining hierarchy, where the opportunity for personal achievement was greater, than they would had they remained in Cornwall. In the mid nineteenth century most of those who were native to the new metalliferous areas of the world had little or no experience and were employed to do the most arduous labour. Cousin Jacks who left Cornwall, after hearing reports of the rich mines overseas, and the success of their fellow countrymen in such mines, hoped in turn to find themselves in well paid positions of authority and responsibility as shift bosses, engineers and Mine Captains.

James Martin of Stithians, hailed as the 'Father of Gawler' in South Australia in his day, as a boy was apprenticed as an engineer at Tresavean. Whilst there, in about 1841, Martin was instructed by Loam, the engineer of Tresavean, to construct a model from one of his drawings of the famous 'man engine'. The contrivance was accepted, and Loam won a prize for its invention. Martin's model was exhibited in the Polytechnic Hall in Falmouth (see Chapter 4). Martin later emigrated to South Australia and started a very successful foundry business.

In South Australia, Henry Roach formerly employed at Tresavean, became the superintendent of the Burra Burra Mine in 1847. In 1865, the South Australian Mineral Agency appointed Captain Isaac Killicoat to review the Burra Burra Mine's ore dressing plant, by virtue of the fact that he had a good reputation, earned at Tresavean where he had been a 'Grass Captain'.[108] John Tregoning, of West Trevarth, founded the firm of Clint, Tregoning & Co., metal and ship brokers, in Liverpool in 1844, and later the Llanelly Tinplate Works in South Wales.[109]

In 1863, Thomas Gray, who died in his fiftieth year, was described as having been a long serving, zealous and faithful servant of the Imperial Brazilian Mining Association at their mines in Minas Gerais, Brazil. Captain Blamey of Lanner Moor was a manager at the Real del Monte Mines in Mexico, and Thomas Edward Morcom of Trevarth, a former engineer at the Gwennap United Mines, worked first as an engineer at the Birmingham Waterworks, leaving his position there for Mexico in 1895, following his profession at Real del Monte for over 20 years.[110] William Jose, another skilled mining engineer, migrated to Tocopilla, Bolivia (which became a part of Chile), where he resided for over 40 years.[111]

Captain A.E. Doidge was a manager of the Mikado GMC, Canada, and Joseph Winn emigrated to Ironwood, Michigan in 1911, to work as an iron miner at the Newport Mine until 1929. He was then transferred to Wakefield as mine captain of the Sunday Lake Mine, which position he held until his death in 1953.[112] Captain John Veall Inch was a captain at one of the Pachuca mines in Mexico and, after 1903, with the Henry Nourse Gold Mining Company in the Transvaal; Captain William Edwards, formerly of Tresavean Mine, proceeded to the Sheba Mine, Transvaal, as Mine Manager in 1887, and Mr J. Vigus took a five-year appointment in 1901 as a captain at Okiep, Namaqualand.[113] William Whitburn, who drowned in the Usutu River in 1892, was the manager of the Forbes Reef Gold Mining Company, South Africa.[114]

Sometime after the close of Tresavean Mine, in 1929, Bennett Moyle took a position as engineer to the Mawchi Tin and Wolfram Mines in Burma, later working for the North Africa Company as an engineer in their palm oil plants in Nigeria and the Gold Coast. Also in 1929, Granville W. Blatchford, a former employee of Tresavean Mine, was working as an electrical engineer for the Pahang Consolidated Company, in Malaysia.[116]

Added to those who were high profile in the mining and engineering world were numerous artisans and people of commercial backgrounds, and some who made important contributions to public life. Lanner man, Thomas Bosanko, was the proprietor of the Northern Saloon in Grass Valley, prior to the First World War.[117] Edward Coombe, who migrated from Trevarth in the 1850s, ran a successful cold drinks business in Castlemaine, Victoria, Australia.[118] John Tresidder became a blacksmith to the City of Seattle in the 1930s (Fig. 11.9), and John James Willoughby, who started his working life as an errand boy for S. & J. Trounson of Redruth, went to America in the 1920s, becoming a manager for the Martha Washington Chain Stores. T.H. Kneebone, a printer, took a position in a Government Post Office in Canada in 1915.

In 1898, the local press noted that F. Moore, who went to London 18 years before, had been for the past seven years an employee of the late G.E. Streat, as clerk of the works of the new Law Courts, being the superintendent in charge of the erection of the Palace of Justice. Also in 1898, the success of traveller J.H. Scoble was noted; this Lanner man was the representative in the South and West of England for Thomas Cooke, a clothing firm based in Tamworth in Staffordshire.[119]

T.L. Skewes was elected Mayor of Wareham, Dorsetshire, in 1874 and Bennett Opie, egg merchant, left Lanner for London in 1879 to found a successful business marketing eggs produced in Cornwall. The loss of people such as these deprived the Lanner area of their energy and vision.[120]

However, not all those migrants who returned were successful. Some people did not find their 'pot of gold' at the end of a South African or American rainbow, and came home either no better, or indeed worse off, than before their departure. Often men who had been away many years returned to their community to find things much altered, and themselves treated as total strangers. J.H. Harris paints such a scene in his fictional short story *Cousin Jacky* set at the turn of the century, but doubtless drawn from true-life experience:

A miner returned from Chile to a village just outside Redruth to discover that his father was dead, his brothers had migrated to South Africa and his old sweetheart had married and moved away. 'Now that he had returned with his welcome in his hand, there was no one to rejoice with him'. Everybody he met was a stranger and as he walked through the street of his native village, of which he knew every stone, many of the houses were empty and the gardens overgrown, including those of his father, his boyhood friend and his former sweetheart. The gate of her house was hanging on one hinge. 'He wandered as one living amongst ghostly memories, and no one in the deserted village in which he was born to say 'How are 'ee?' His dream of a joyous homecoming was thus wiped out and he once again went into voluntary exile.[121] Often those who had been away found it difficult to reintegrate into local society, and consequently could not settle in their former home. William Lean is one such man, who undertook a long and arduous voyage from Chile and 'wasn't home five minutes before leaving again'.[122]

This was particularly hard on the families of those who were married. Catherine 'Kate' Bray, (née Harvey) of Carn

Fig.8.12. *Carn Marth men, employees of the Calumet and Hecla Mine, Michigan, USA, pose at Herman's Studio, Calumet, about 1905.* Left to right: *Wilfred Bray, Thomas Harvey and Bill Harvey. Bill lost his life in Dreifontein Mine, Transvaal, in 1907.* (© Mrs V. Greenwood, Lanner).

Marth, spent most of her 15 years of married life apart from her husband, Wilfred, who was working in mining camps in the USA and South Africa, and then served in the 1914–18 War.[123] Many children did not know who their father was when he returned home from overseas after several years' absence, which inevitably strained family relationships. Some women who took in male lodgers entered into adulterous relationships, or were forced to entertain gentlemen to eke out a living which, when discovered, sometimes led to further family complications and even divorce. Scrutiny of the 1851 and 1891 Census returns for Lanner reveals a number of lone parent families headed by the mother or grandmother and many extended families, for example sisters and their children living together. In 1891, over one eighth of the 500 homes in the parish were headed by married women whose husbands were absent. The matriarchal nature of Lanner strengthened as the nineteenth century wore on, and probably only diminished after the Great War of 1914-18.

Disease and Death

The same industrial hazards existed abroad as were common in Cornwall and in the case of phthisis the danger was magnified, particularly for those who worked on the Rand. Indeed, Hamilton Jenkin commented, 'The name "South Africa" is cut deep in the heart of mining Cornwall, not so much engraved with an instrument of steel as jagged and ghastly with the malignant quartz that hid the gold and filled the lungs of the Cornish pioneers.'[124] Very old residents of the village can still remember the dry cough of the sick miners as they fought in vain for breath, and the thick phlegm on the pavements spat up by men with choked lungs. Drilling through the hard quartz rock made a lot of fine dust, the crystals of which quickly ravaged the lung cavities and also led to heart complications.

Cornishmen were accustomed to dry rock drilling, a practice they claimed was faster than wet drilling. The drill used on the Rand became known as the 'Widow Maker' since premature death among the men who operated it became so common. Many miners returned home to end their days in familiar surroundings, and as Lanner was situated in a sheltered valley, its climate was claimed to be gentler on those of fragile health.[125]

T.J. Curnow of Prisk's Terrace died in 1915, aged just 37. He had spent 17 years in Africa, and left a wife and two children to mourn his premature death from phthisis. He was remembered as a keen footballer and sportsman in his youth.[126] We read too of the death of Sam Job in 1906 from phthisis, the *Cornubian* of 6 September, stating that he had played for the mines on the Rand in the football arena. Tom Job died in 1896, at age 58 from heart and lung disease brought on by the years he had spent underground in African mines.[127] T.H. Osborne, a former employee of the Simmer and Jack Gold Mine, Transvaal, had done three spells in Africa and died at age 30 from lung disease.[128] 'The men emigrate to South Africa in search of gold to return with death written on their faces', commented Lanner's Reverend Oliver R. Walkey to his congregation in 1915, as obituaries such as the above had become depressingly common in the local papers.[129] By the time of the First World War people began to seriously question the wisdom of a long stay in the Transvaal Mines.

'The men are coming home from Africa, but not laden with gold. Some have not been gone long, but have decided to return quicker than they otherwise would have done owing to the sickness prevailing in that climate.'[130] Enteric fever, or typhoid, flourished in the hot unsanitary conditions of the mining towns on the Rand and diamond diggings. In 1884 21-year-old William Phillips died at the diamond fields after fighting fever for nine days. In 1902, news of the death of Samuel Magor reached Lanner, and in 1906, that of Alfred Vincent. John Michael Harvey of Carn Marth succumbed to fever at the Randfontein Hospital in February 1907, aged 35, leaving a wife and two children to mourn him. In 1915, the death of 27-year-old Joseph Dower was reported in the local press, the only son of John Dower of Pennance. A commemorative headstone recording his untimely demise was erected in Lanner Churchyard.[131] When Rhona Blatchford's brother Harry became ill with fever, the family was advised to return to Cornwall for the sake of his health. Rhona's father, Harry Blight, an assayer, decided to stay on in Africa for a little longer but sent his family home. Tragically, he fell ill with fever himself and died not long after.[132] More fortunate was Samuel Osborne, who contracted the illness on the way home to Britain aboard the SS *Moor* in 1896. He survived, but had to postpone his wedding, the reason for his return to the village.[133] In our sample of those Lanner people known to have worked in South Africa, 35 per cent died out there, the majority through disease and phthisis.

Indeed, migration was a risky business which sometimes ended in disaster. The *Cornish Post and Mining News* of 23 July 1892, for example, provided dismal reading for Lanner people, reporting the deaths of three former residents of the village in that one edition. William Annear had been killed in or near Butte, by a train running over him and severing his head from his body; William Reed had died of inflammation of the lungs at the Black Hills, Dakota and William John Chapman had died at the Blue Mine, Negaunee, Michigan, from injuries he had received underground. Such industrial and freak accidents occurred with distressing regularity in mining fields worldwide, as they had done in Cornwall.

In 1843, young miner Richard Job was killed at the Calpeana Mines, Carthapena, Spain, in an accident whilst preparing a blast, and in 1874 Thomas Davies was killed at Cheevor, USA, from injuries he sustained whilst 'tamping' a hole.[134] Penrose brothers, Alfred and Edwin, aged 24 and 22 respectively, died in 1882 in an explosion caused by the accidental ignition of dynamite at the Kimberley Diamond Mines.[135]

In the pine-scented English Cemetery above Real del Monte in Mexico lie the Eastwick brothers, both casualties of mining accidents. Joseph died in 1886, aged 24, and John in 1887, aged 27.[136] James Martin, who had lost a brother months previously in Chile, was killed in an explosion at Terraville, Dakota in 1888. Sixty-six-year-old John Gluyas died on a voyage home from Chile in 1888, and a memorial stands in Gwennap churchyard. John Uren was killed at Granite Mountain Mine in Montana when caught between the timbers of the shaft in 1888 and in 1890, Edmond Harvey was being winched to the surface at the end of a shift in the Ferreira Gold Mine, Transvaal, when the rope broke. The bucket in which he was travelling fell some 230 feet.[137]

Thomas Martin was drowned in a Californian river whilst responding to a cousin's plea for him to come to a mine some eight miles away, where his brother James had just died in an explosion. Their mother Mary back home in Lanner, dependent on her sons for remittances, was said to be distraught.[138] William James Pryor was accidentally shot at age 19 at the Moonta Mines in South Australia in 1892. Tristam B. Vivian, an experienced miner, had left home in

February 1901 for Western Australia, where he worked at the Coolgardie and Kalgoorlie gold fields. In 1906 he was killed by the collapse of ground in a West African gold mine at the age of 33. This young man had certainly courted danger in his life before he was killed in this freak accident, having previously seen active service in the Rhodesian Campaign and was at the short siege of Bulawayo, for which he received the Queen's Medal with two clasps.[139] In 1908, John Harris Clemo, of Trevarth, was killed in an underground accident in the Mysore Mine, India. William Inch Harvey, a former shift boss at the Calumet and Hecla Mine, Michigan, died in a dreadful explosion which claimed the lives of three other white men and 50 natives at the Dreifontein Gold Mine, Eastern Transvaal, in March 1907 (Fig.8.12). There was suspicion that some native workers had tampered with the explosives to cause the blast.[140] William left a pregnant wife and four children at Carn Marth, plus his heartbroken parents Joseph and Martha (Fig.5.5), who must have felt the blow keenly in view of the fact that they had lost another son, John, to fever in South Africa the previous month. William Norman James was accidentally killed at Number 8 Shaft at Randfontein Mine in 1915, aged 22. He had served as a trooper in Botha's Horse in the war with German South Africa, returning to mining when the fighting ceased.[141]

Furthermore, the mining camps of the world were often turbulent, dangerous places. In 1869, 35-year-old Lanner man Isaac Pearce, nephew of John Secombe Tonkin, migration agent, was brutally murdered by an Italian who split his skull in two with a hatchet in a Californian mining town. These awful accidents often spelt ruin for a family, especially those abroad, who found themselves dependent on the charity of family and friends. Those at home who were forced to apply for parochial relief saw this as a dreadful affront to their pride, going against the philosophy of independence, self help and improvement, so dear to Cornish hearts and minds. They had, after all, sent their men overseas to avoid that very occurrence. Again, the inherent weakness of the dependency culture is shown clearly.

'And Did Those Feet...' Stories of Lanner Migrants

At this point it would be useful to examine a selection of the colourful life stories of some Lanner migrants, many tinged with sadness and tragedy, but also with courage and unfailing energy in pursuit of self improvement. Some of the accounts below clearly illustrate how the Cornish had become international nomads, drifting from one mining field to another hoping for a 'sturt' to ensure a comfortable future.

Tin miner William Jose, born in 1814, married Mary Tippett in 1842 at Gwennap Church. Four years later, the family decided to emigrate to the Colony of South Australia, making use of the assisted passage scheme. With their three children, they sailed from Plymouth for Adelaide on 15 November 1846 aboard the *Princess Royal*. Their daughter Mary Ann, aged 22, died en route due to the poor conditions on board ship, and was buried at sea. On reaching Adelaide, the family travelled on to the Burra Burra Mines, where three more children were eventually to be born. At Burra, the Jose Family were forced to live in the squalid conditions of the unsanitary 'dug outs' – makeshift homes of holes carved out of the banks of the Burra River.

Maybe the deplorable state of their living conditions, or the lure of gold, led them to the goldfields in the neighbouring state of Victoria, where they settled at Forest Creek. It was here that William's wife, Mary, tragically died in a mine wagon accident in 1853, leaving her husband to care for five small children. As a solution to his plight, William left Forest Creek after hearing the words of a charismatic preacher, a Mormon named Elder Frost, who had been sent to Australia by Brigham Young to recruit 'saints'. Seventy-two such candidates, including the Joses, gathered in Melbourne and set sail for San Francisco on 27 April 1855 aboard the *Tarquenia*. The ship had to be landed in Honolulu as it was not seaworthy, and the journey to the USA was completed aboard the *Willamartic*, arriving at San Francisco in August, thus completing a gruelling four-month voyage at sea. A further difficult journey awaited the Lanner family, as they travelled, first by boat to San Pedro, then on to Los Angeles, which was at the time 'no more than a cactus patch', and thence to San Bernadino where there was a Latter Day Saints' Church.

After resting, the party headed for Washington County, Utah, finally arriving before Christmas 1855. William married again in 1857, and found employment, firstly as a farmer, then a teamster. The Mormons were an agrarian people, at this time opposed to mining, which ended Jose's chances of following his trade. His daughter Jennie Jose remembered how her father would gather them around in the evening and nostalgically tell them stories of Cornwall. But William became disillusioned with the Church of Latter Day Saints and left its ranks; perhaps his heart was never truly Mormon, and his affiliation with the Church only served as a vehicle to aid his migration to the US.

In 1870, the Joses moved to Pioche, Nevada, where William purchased mining claim number 8 on 22 September, for $100, from Howard Livingston of New York. The claim was in the Meadow Valley Mining District, Utah Territory, which is now in the State of Nevada. In 1872 William tried to shoot his wife, and an attempt on his life was made by his son-in-law, James Stevens, who tried to stab him for refusing a drink. William never returned to Cornwall; he was declared destitute in 1895, and died the following year. His gravestone in the Pioche Public Cemetery states that he was born in 'Red Ruth', Cornwall, England.[142]

William Lean, born in 1832, was the youngest of six sons of John and Jane Lean. His parents died when he was a child, and he lived with his brother and cousin. When a young man, he became a copper miner at Tresavean, and whilst employed there he was engaged in sinking Harvey's Shaft. At age 19, he married Ellen Gray of Pennance. In 1854, with his wife expecting their first baby, William left home to sail to Australia aboard the *Magdelena*, arriving in Adelaide in January 1855. It is likely that he joined members of his wife's family resident in the goldfields of neighbouring Victoria. William returned to Cornwall in May 1857 with a little money. Yet things were still very depressed in Lanner and Tresavean closed the following year. William could see little future in the Gwennap area, so in about 1858 he migrated to South America, where he began work in an area, once a part of Bolivia, in the north of modern day Chile, on the British-owned nitrate railways. Here he eventually found congenial ground for his many capabilities, becoming a valued and esteemed member of the expatriate community in Tocopilla, Bolivia, which was seized by Chile in the War of the Pacific 1879–1883. There he became co-owner of two copper mining companies, a business in the export of guano, several steamships, and large merchandise stores.

He also worked under licence as a prospector to the Chilean Government. Most of his life was spent in Bolivia and Chile, but his wife, Ellen Gray, and his three children remained behind in Lanner. Mr David Lean, a descendant, remembers being told that Ellen would not accompany William to Chile on account of her being afraid of sea travel, but he thinks it more likely that she remained behind in Lanner to manage her family property, Gray's Terrace.

As the family grew up, they too migrated to join their father in Chile. John, who was also a miner, after a period in Chile, sailed to South Africa where he lost his life in 1890. William James, William's other son, gave up his job as a cabinet maker to become a miner at Tresavean, after which he migrated to Chile to help his father run the family business, returning after 16 years' absence. William Lean returned to Redruth and died in 1915. Perhaps this event, and the disruption caused by the First World War, prompted the family to sell the mining companies in Tocopilla in 1919, ending over 60 years of the Leans' involvement with South America.[143]

Two pioneering Lawn brothers, the sons of James and Jenefer Lawn (née Webster) of Pennance, had worked since their childhood in the mines around Lanner. John and James left the village in the early 1850s for British Columbia, then heard of the success of the copper mines of Southern Australia; a relative William Lawn had migrated there in 1848, so they headed for Adelaide via Panama. They settled at Moonta in the Yorke Peninsula, known as Australia's little Cornwall, so pronounced was its Cornishness. John Lawn took the opportunity of bettering himself, and whilst a pupil at the Moonta School of Mines, he gained a first class mine manager's certificate. When gold was discovered in the neighbouring state of Victoria, a lot of miners rushed there, hoping to get rich quick. In this exodus were James and John who worked at the diggings of Ballarat and Bendigo. In the years following the rising at the Eureka Stockade in 1854, they felt compelled to move again, this time leaving for New Zealand aboard the *Aurefira*, which arrived at Port Chalmers on 20 September 1861.

The voyage to New Zealand was one unlikely to have been forgotten by the Lawns, who survived a mutiny. The captain was planning to wreck the ship for insurance purposes, but his evil scheme was thwarted by the first mate who enlisted the aid of the passengers in locking him in a cabin. The ship eventually arrived safely at port, and the crew deserted to the diggings at Gabriel's Gully, where gold had been discovered in 1861. They were joined there by the Lawns. The indomitable spirit of these two Lanner men was tremendous. They pushed a collapsible handcart, heavily laden with stores, tents and mining equipment, for miles inland over difficult terrain. They did well for a while, but in true Cousin Jack style, forever roving after the proverbial pot of gold, wanderlust gripped them yet again when they heard of the West Coast gold strike of 1864. On returning to Dunedin, they sold their trusty handcart, and took a passage to the wild West Coast, where dense bush came right down to the beaches, streams quickly and unpredictably became raging torrents, and men were forced to eat wild pigeon boiled with fern tops, as there was a total absence of fresh meat.

John and James obtained a claim to sluice for gold at Murray Creek. Unfortunately, it turned out to be less rich than they had hoped, so they returned to Australia for a few years, John marrying a Cornish girl in Moonta in 1873. Their younger brother Henry, no doubt captivated by the stories of his brothers' exploits relayed in letters home, also emigrated to Blackspoint near Reefton, New Zealand, in 1873, from Dalton-in-Furness, where he had migrated from Cornwall. The New Zealand Government was hoping to attract emigrants to its shores, with the offer of free passages to eligible persons. Henry's two wandering brothers and their families eventually settled in New Zealand, as did two Lanner cousins, Thomas and Edmund Lawn, who emigrated in 1869 and 1871 respectively. They also made their homes at Reefton, where fantastic gold-bearing quartz reefs had been discovered in 1870 (Fig. 8.13).

Fig.8.13. *Thomas Lawn (1842-1902) migrated to New Zealand in 1869, and settled at the gold mining town of Reefton. He died of phthisis.* (© Helen and Ross Lawn, New Zealand)

Sadly, as in a picture repeated so often in the gold reefs of South Africa, both fell victim to 'miner's complaint' – phthisis. Edmund died of the dreaded disease in 1894, and Thomas in 1902. The Lawns of Lanner in so many respects typify the Cousin Jacks who travelled the world in search of that rich strike that would set them up for life, a wealth earned in the only way they knew how. The dream of discovering a rich mineral strike did however come to fruition for the Lawn family, through the genius of James's grandson, Harry Evans OBE, a geologist who found the world's largest deposit of bauxite at Weipa, Australia in 1954. The wife of this celebrated geologist, the grandson of a Cousin Jack from Lanner, very aptly commented that, 'geology was in her husband's blood.'[144]

In 1894, the *Cornubian* carried an article written by architect, James Hicks, describing the exploits of Lanner men, James and William Job, who went to the Kimberley diamond fields in the late 1870s. The output of diamonds became so great, and the diggings so overcrowded, that the Job Brothers decided to strike for the 'Land of Ophir' in search of gold in about 1881. They bought a wagon drawn by 18 oxen, hired 'boys' (African natives) and in company with two Americans, loaded the wagon with three years' supply of all sorts of provisions, including powder and rifles. The journey cost £900 (in today's money, a sum close to £300 000) and took the party through a part of Mashonoland and then up to Bulawayo in Matebeleland, a journey lasting three months. Here they lived in the kraal belonging to the Matebele Chief, Lobengula, whom the Cornishmen nicknamed 'Old Ben'. Trekking through the bush was perilous, and fraught with all manner of dangers; fever, heat fatigue, and the rivers were full of crocodiles. The Job Brothers remembered guarding their camps under the purple African skies, bright with stars, 'rifle to shoulder', listening to the terrible roar of the lions in the dead of night.

Lobengula received them warmly, and although described as a bully to his own people, and a tyrant and an oppressor of his neighbours, he treated the white men well, showing them where to hunt and providing escorts on such trips. However, he would not allow them to search for gold. 'If we were to pick up a stone and examine it, one of the 'boys' would bolt away to the king and it would not be very long before a messenger would be back summoning us to the kraal at Buluwayo to give us a warning not to search for gold.' For, as Lobengula knew 'if we found gold, we should write home to England to our brothers and cousins for them to come out, and they would multiply and take the land from us'. As a result, the Jobs were never allowed to approach the Zambesi River, and were reduced to gazing upon this mighty torrent from distant hills, so 'Old Ben's' land would not be made a track for the 'Land of Ophir'. After 18 months, somewhat dejected and £900 out of pocket, the Jobs returned to diamond mining in Kimberley, and eventually came home to Lanner.[145]

Josiah Kemp was born in 1884 on the north facing slope of Carn Marth on a small farm of about eight acres. His father, Joseph, a stationary engineer (a man who maintained the steam engine at the mine's surface), died when he was just six weeks old. His mother, Catherine Jane, was left with ten children to rear alone, with only the income from the farm to support the family. After some time, it was realised that this was not sufficient, as times in the agricultural world were very depressed, so the farm was sold and the family moved to a house in Redruth where the eldest boys could be closer to the mines in which they had started work. By the time Josiah was thirteen, the family, now much reduced in numbers, had again moved, this time to Hayle and he began work as a barber's apprentice to his brother, as there was little opportunity of work in the mining industry. He was then his mother's sole means of support. During the 1890s, three of his older brothers had migrated to Utah where two had found jobs as miners at the Golden Gate Mine, in the mining town of Mercur.

In 1904, owing to the closure of the shipbuilding yard in Hayle, which crippled local business, Josiah decided to follow them out, spending his small savings on a second class ticket aboard the Cunard ocean liner, the *Etruria*. After a brief stay in New York with Cornish friends, he travelled across America by train to Mercur, where his brothers financed him to set up as a barber, and his business did well (Fig.8.14).

Fig.8.14. *Not all migrants were miners. Josiah Kemp (left) outside his barber's shop in Utah. His brothers helped him to start his business when he migrated in 1903.* (© Janeen Nelson-Watkins, Lehi, Utah).

Fig.8.15. *Carn Marth man Josiah Kemp (front, right) became the fire chief at Pleasant Grove, Utah, USA.* (© Janeen Nelson-Watkins, Lehi, Utah)

Josiah later joined the Mercur Fire Department and, finding the fire service to his liking, eventually became the Fire Chief at Pleasant Grove, a town near Utah Lake (Fig.8.15).

A lover of music, Josiah's brother Harry set up a brass band, aptly named the 'Kemp Band', which entertained the residents of Mercur. His other brother Joseph, who worked as a miner in Park City, Utah, was a colourful character, an abstemious man who had been reformed by his wife. Whilst working at Tresavean Mine in the early 1880s, he was fond of a tipple or two at the ale house after his shift had ended, and would come home late and drunk to their home at Carn Marth. His wife, not liking his expensive drinking habit, decided to do something about it. Once, after she had been chastising him severely, he was heard to say 'I'm the King of this house, and I shall do as I please!' Her reply was swift, 'Well, if you're the King, then I'll crown 'ee!'

When Joseph next went to work at Tresavean, little did he know that the tasty looking pasty in his dinner pail did not contain the usual 'meat and tatties,' but a collection of 'cherts,' - smashed up saucers! When Joseph broke open his pasty, they all fell out, much to the amusement of his colleagues. Needless to say, he never lived that down, but it did cure his drinking! The story is still told in the village today, but even more surprising, it is often told in Lehi, Utah, where his descendants gather to remember their colourful ancestor, and the strange sounding places in which he lived and worked in the 'Old Country'. Joseph and Emily Kemp are buried in the Glenwood Cemetery, Park City, Utah; Josiah at Pleasant Grove, Utah. None of the Kemp brothers ever returned to Cornwall, but did send money to their mother occasionally, to allay her fears of ending up in the Union House.[146]

'The Phenomenal Alto'

Lanner's most famous son is undoubtedly Richard James Jose (1862–1941), one of the world's greatest counter-tenors (Fig.8.16). His life story is truly extraordinary, and although much has been written about him, unfortunately many basic facts about his life have been distorted and sensationalised.

He was born on 5 June 1862, the eldest child of Richard Jose, a Carn Marth miner. His father died in December 1876 when he was 14 years old (not nine years old as some sources quote), leaving his mother, Elizabeth, to head a family of five on a limited income. Hard as the decision must have been, she agreed to the offer made by an uncle, Alfred Jose (the son of Thomas and Mary Jose, baptised at Lanner Bible Christian Chapel in 1845), to have her eldest son Richard reside with him. This was probably in the hope that Richard would find a job and remit money to help maintain his surviving brothers and sisters, Emily, Henry, Almond and Elizabeth, and his mother, who began work as a charwoman (a further two brothers, Thomas and William, had died in infancy).

This in itself was not unusual; what made the circumstance exceptional was the fact that Dick's uncle, Alf, lived 4500 miles away in a mining camp called Virginia City, in Nevada, USA (see Fig.8.1). By 1877, his uncle had sent the fare for him to purchase his fourth class ticket, taking him from Redruth Station, where the bewildered teenager stood with Alfred's American address attached to his jacket, to the other side of the world. He probably had little or no conception of the enormous distance he was about to travel, but must surely have wondered whether he would ever see his mother and siblings again as he stepped on to the steam train to Plymouth. Here began one of the most extraordinary rags to riches stories.

Dubbed 'the singing kid' by fellow passengers on the unpleasant winter Atlantic crossing, his ability to charm with his singing was evident from the start. Upon arrival in New York, after surviving a shipwreck, the young lad was penniless, but was befriended and fed by a Swiss family on the gruelling overland train journey across the vast American continent. Finally, he arrived in the rough mining town of Virginia City, recently rebuilt after the great fire of 1875. This settlement, surrounded by smoking mills and mining headgear, crept up the rocky desert hillside of Mount Davidson, above the fabulously rich silver and gold mines of the Comstock Lode. Here awaited the very worst news imaginable. His uncle had disappeared, and was thought to be dead, whilst other sources believed he had moved on to another mining camp at Butte, Montana. Thankfully Richard was resourceful, and managed to fend for himself for about a year, selling bread to the miners by driving a bakery wagon, managing in this way to buy a bed in the back of a dingy second-rate boarding house each night.

Tired of Virginia City, whose wooden sidewalks were 'thronged with motley crowds – broadcloth elbowed by greasy flannel and diamonds and dirt in glaring contrast,'[147] the boy decided to move to Carson City. 'Virginia City set in a desert, had something prison-like in its encircling wall of barren hills, and few thought of venturing outside its circle of lights.'[148] But this did not deter Jose. He walked the twenty miles to Carson City virtually barefoot, where he agreed to sing for his supper in a saloon – his audience, a selection of gamblers and drunkards who rubbed shoulders with card sharps, prostitutes, hawkers, idlers and desperados. He instantly became a hit, finding a friendly welcome among a group of hard-working, gambling, heavy-drinking Cornish miners, who were deeply moved by the sight and sound of young Jose singing the hymns and carols of their distant homeland. So popular was he, that years later, a ballad writer commemorated the Lanner boy with the words:

Youthful minstrel of the Comstock,
Carson's barefoot ballad boy,
Who filled saloons with Cornish tunes,
And miner's hearts with leaping joy.[149]

Worried as to the effect the undesirable environment of the saloon might have on an impressionable teenager, the Women's Temperance League had him moved to Reno, where fate finally smiled on the boy, who discovered a relative there, a blacksmith called Bill Luke.

Whilst serving his apprenticeship with Luke, Dick, nicknamed 'Reno's Blacksmith Balladeer', attracted the attention of one of his customers, the head of the Bishop Whitaker's School for Girls, who arranged for him to have singing lessons. Dick thereafter began to appear at local churches and public gatherings, stunning audiences with his unique voice. In 1884, a friend became the manager of a Californian touring minstrel troupe, and introduced him to Charles Reed, a booking agent.

Jose joined a Reed group in Sacramento receiving a salary of $12 per week, and from that day forward his future success was ensured. Very soon he found himself earning $100 a week and regularly appeared on stage in San Francisco. An appointment with the famous Lew Dockstader's Minstrels followed at a salary of $150 per week, culminating in Jose being given an engagement on Broadway in New York, billed as 'the Phenomenal Alto.'

After winning a gold medal for ballad singing at Carnegie Hall, he was given a contract to appear in the musical 'The Old Homestead', with tours and recordings following. For thirty years he appeared in vaudeville at Madison Square Garden, and travelled all over the world, singing for many crowned heads of state. During one tour of South Africa, Cecil Rhodes was reputed to have closed down the diamond mines so his men and their families, many of whom were probably Cornish, could attend his concerts. In Montreal, Canada, an organist was said to have stopped in mid phrase, awe-struck by the man's voice. In 1898, he was chosen to bid a musical farewell to Teddy Roosevelt who was setting off for Cuba during the Spanish-American War. On this occasion, he entertained the audience with 'Goodbye, Dolly Gray.'

Jose is perhaps best remembered for his ballad, 'Silver Threads Among the Gold,' a song written by H. R. Danks for the World Fair at Philadelphia in 1876, and thereafter forgotten, until Jose rediscovered it. He persuaded the Victor Talking Machine Company, a fledgling enterprise, proud to have signed 'the most popular minstrel and vaudeville singer of the day', to allow him to record this song in 1903. In 1906, Jose's rendition of the song was the biggest ever seller the American recording industry had seen at the time. Ever aware of the hardships he had endured in his own youth, he sought out the composer, who was ill and living in poverty. He saw to it that the man was paid royalties by the publisher.

Around the turn of the twentieth century, motion pictures were in their infancy and sound to accompany such pictures was yet to be invented. Jose once stood in the wings at Madison Square Garden, capable of seating 12 000 people, and sang the theme song to the film which was showing, synchronising his singing with the movements of the actor's lips on the big screen and filling the immense theatre with

Fig.8.16. *Juan Ricardo José (Richard Jose), arguably Lanner's most famous son, found fame and fortune in the USA with his unique counter-tenor voice. Photograph c1900.* (© Joe Pengelly, Plymouth).

his voice. He might well have claim to being the first ever 'talkie'.

Jose was a clean living man who neither smoked nor drank liquor, a pledge he was alleged to have made to his dying father years before, but probably because as a teenager he had witnessed the misery created by drink in the saloons of Nevada. He was a devoted mason of the Ancient Arabic Order of the Mystic Shrine in San Francisco. From their members, he formed 'The Joseans', a choir which appeared on parades at the Hollywood Bowl, at State Conventions and in the streets of the city, singing Cornish carols at Christmas time.[150]

Jose did return to Lanner, in August 1891. Tradition somewhat sentimentally has it that he was met at the railway station at Redruth by one of his brothers, the two then walking home together by moonlight, their way lit by the tallow candles burning in his honour in every cottage along the road. But there is no doubting the fact that his return was an event which occasioned great excitement in the area, and the venues at which he entertained were packed, with people being turned away. Dickie Jose, the little boy 'with a bird in his throat', who had entertained the villagers with the hymn 'We Shall Meet at the Fountain,' and who had left the village over 15 years before, was reported to have taken his old seat in the choir of Lanner Wesley Chapel and to have sung several solos. A correspondent for the *Cornubian* wrote: 'Mr Jose possesses a wonderfully flexible and well cultivated voice, and is one of the leading professional singers of New York. He selected some simple melodies, and his exquisite rendering of them almost entranced those present.'[151] Jose also performed in a concert to raise funds for the Lanner Band of Hope at the Bryanite Chapel. His name appeared in the programme for the last eight items.

Tradition has it that while he was performing one of his songs to a packed audience 'Where Is My Wandering Boy Tonight?' he was remembered as breaking down and unable to continue, being overwhelmed with sorrow for the years of separation which had deprived him of his mother and his family, and the realisation that soon he would have to say farewell again. It is said that Dick could not bear to tell his mother that he was planning to return to the USA, but stole away in the early hours of one morning, after looking in on her one last time, while she was asleep. He never saw her again; she died in 1918 at Lanner Hill.

Dick's younger brother, Almond Jose, a miner, also migrated to America, where he worked first of all at Butte, Montana, before going to Grass Valley, California, where he was seriously injured by falling down a mine chute in 1903.

Richard Jose was certainly well respected both in Lanner and abroad for his genuine good nature and charitable ways. He often acknowledged an acquaintance or friend from his childhood having recognised them amongst the audience, and during a tour of Bridgeport in 1893, it was recorded in the *Cornubian* that 'friends from his native place greet him cheerfully.' He often performed at events organised by Cornish expatriates in America, such as that given at the St George Hall at Centerville, Montana, in 1900, at which he sang 'The Blind Mother', 'Belle Brandon' and 'With All Her Faults I Love Her Still'.[152]

During his 1891 visit to Lanner, he heard of an old neighbour who was laid low with a broken leg at the Women's Hospital at Redruth. He paid her a visit, and at her request, sang to the inmates who highly appreciated the treat. He was also hugely popular amongst the residents of the American Hispanic community who knew him as Juan Ricardo José by virtue of his name, Jose, which was widely thought to have been of Spanish origin. This is due mainly to the stories of his ancestry broadcast in interviews given by his wife, Sophie Therese, which were probably designed to curry favour with the large Hispanic community in states such as California. In America, Dick was appointed Deputy Commissioner of the Real Estate Commission to help raise the professional standards of brokers and agents. He held this position until his death in 1941, aged 79, leaving a widow who then married the publisher of *The Pony Express*, Herbert Hamlin.

It is claimed that Jose had one of the finest voices Cornwall has ever known. He was a true counter-tenor, possessing a voice which resembles a boy soprano, but with the power and brightness of an adult. With the limited technology then available, acoustic recordings depended upon the sheer clarity of the voice to give presence and dynamics to the wax recordings. Even the famous tenor, Enrico Caruso, was enough moved by the strength and purity of Jose's voice to exclaim 'Ricardo, you are the world's greatest ballad singer!'

No new Jose records were issued after 1909, but there was an historical reissue in 1927, and another in the 1940s, his work having been popular on early radio. In 1988, Joe Pengelly, a sound archivist resident at Plymouth, released a selection of some of Dick's recordings on cassette. These were digitally re-mastered from the originals, recorded between 1904 and 1905, and the distinct Cornish vowel sounds in Dick's voice can be clearly heard; Joe Pengelly's dream of enabling the Lanner man's unique voice to be heard again in Cornwall was realised. Dick Jose's records are in the collection of the Library of Congress in Washington, USA.[153]

In 1966 Jose was remembered with pride at Lanner Village Hall, when Dr A.C. Todd, resident tutor in the South West for Exeter University, and author of the book *The Cornish Miner in America* presented the extraordinary story of Richard Jose's life. Musical tributes were played by Lanner and District Silver Band conducted by Tommy Martin, and various members of the audience gave their recollections of the famous counter-tenor. His only known surviving niece was present, Gwen Irvine, a former member of Lanner Wesley Choir, who had given the Richard Jose silver cup to the Cornwall Music Festival.[154]

Conclusion

Just how many people left Lanner for worldwide destinations in the period in question is impossible to substantiate. Those mentioned here are only a fraction of the total. The emigration phenomenon has never ended, and some of the parish's brightest and best are still forced out of the county to seek better lives. What drove thousands of Lanner parishioners to England and abroad during the period in question is a subject far more complex than at first appears. It was something more than mere speculation as to the state of the Cornish mining industry, although this was the most obvious reason. The Government did much in the mid nineteenth century to foster an interest in migration, which was viewed rightly or wrongly, as an elixir to cure some of the problems of Victorian society, as the poor were off-loaded to the colonies. As the century wore on, assisted passage family migrations gave way to expedient or 'commuter' migrants, usually single men whom the Cornish called 'birds of passage', the majority of whom returned to their place of origin. How many people migrated intending to return is difficult to assess, but we can safely conclude that the majority of people who went to South Africa intended to come home after making some money. The same appears to be the case with Latin America and to a lesser extent with the USA, although we find more people willing to settle in America as the nineteenth century came to a close. With the Antipodes, the return was small, owing to the remoteness of Australia and New Zealand, and also because so many people were assisted migrants who had no money to return to Lanner.

But on a far more subtle level, the emigration phenomenon was a case of 'because everybody else is going, then so too shall I.'[155] And as Payton and Deacon have shown, Cornishmen, including those from Lanner, left their homes in large numbers even when the mines were still doing well in the 1840s and 50s, many seeking better wages and increased independence. By the late nineteenth century, Transatlantic fares aboard the ocean liners became more affordable and greater numbers of people who had the money to migrate did so. Migration became as much a feature of Cornish life as Methodism, inextricably bound up in a sense of Cornish identity. Sadly, many of the mines in which the exiled worked suffered the same fate as their Cornish counterparts. As a result the Cornish, in common with the workers from other mining regions of the world, became pawns in the hands of an international mining labour market, part of the international mining economy that had emerged in which market forces sped the Cousin Jacks from one area to the next as the relative fortunes of the different mines and different countries waxed and waned.[156]

The communities in which the miners lived and worked became fragmented and gradually the people dispersed, as was the case in Michigan's Copper Country. The Boer War, followed by the First World War, caused disruptions in migratory patterns which were never fully reinstated, factors limiting the opportunities for prospective migrants from Lanner.

By the inter-war period, it had become apparent that the mining and engineering expertise, long perceived to be the domain and preserve of the Cornish, had passed from Cornish hands to people who were native to the new metalliferous areas of the world. There was no longer such a demand for the Cornish miner or engineer, or indeed, Cornish technology. The depression which had been avoided in the 1860s and 70s, the result of industrial collapse and stagnation caused by over-specialisation in the Cornish copper and tin mining industry, was only temporarily ameliorated by migration overseas. Even the new political ideas, innovative methods of mine management and technological advancements in mining and engineering, which expatriate miners brought back with them from Africa and America, in particular at the turn of the twentieth century, came too late to save the terminally ill Cornish mining industry.

The years following the 1914-18 War threw the Cornish economy into a deep slump, further compounded by the worldwide depression of the 1930s. Migration from Lanner in this period continued, but the numbers of those departing were few in comparison with those at the turn of the twentieth century. The resulting 'Great Paralysis' as Dr Payton refers to it,[157] posed a very grave problem in the mid twentieth century for Cornish towns and villages such as Lanner.

In the heyday of emigration, the imagination of whole communities was gripped by the stories which reached home from mining settlements all over the world, where the grass must have seemed much greener to the impressionable. Indeed there were those who were only too glad to get away from the narrowness and constraint of family commitments, and a society perceived by them to have been dominated by Methodism. These people eagerly sought the chance of fleeing overseas, many seeking to 'improve' themselves through the opportunity of earning better wages. Men at Redruth Station were known to have changed their destination at the last moment to travel with a fellow Cousin Jack on the promise of work where his compatriot was headed. Most of these pioneers had little or no idea of what to expect, and their departure sometimes created more problems than they solved.

Abandoned women, fatherless children, several generations of whom did not know what it was to have a father living within the family unit, grew up in a matriarchal society which must surely have had long term negative effects. And it is somewhat ironic that the Cornish should have so much pride in the migration phenomenon, because by fostering emigration, the Cornish merely hastened their own industrial decline, and helped nurture the dependency culture so detrimental to the county's development in the twentieth century.

Lanner has made its contribution to the emigration phenomenon. This is no surprise, since Lanner's very *raison d'être* was the mining operations and related industries within the parish boundaries. It therefore follows that large numbers of people chose to emigrate when these industries fell into serious decline. Lanner's sons and daughters have fanned out all over the world, and despite the negative aspects of the migratory experience, they left us a proud legacy, for the life of each one of the Cousin Jacks who left the parish has left a colourful stitch, a bright spot on an enormous tapestry, the whole of which tells the story of a proud, pioneering, peninsula people.

REFERENCES

1 Rowse, A.L., *The Cornish in America*, Dyllansow Truran, 1967, p. 6.

2 Baines, Dudley, *Emigration From Europe, 1815-1930*, Macmillan, 1991, pp. 7 & 9.

3 Jenkin, A.K. Hamilton, *The Cornish Miner*, Allen & Unwin, 1927, p. 322.

4 Baines, Dudley, *Migration in a Mature Economy and Internal Migration in England and Wales, 1861-1900*, Cambridge University Press, 1985, pp. 145 & 150-155.

5 Mitchell, Peter, *The Demographic Revolution, Cornwall Since the War, Institute of Cornish Studies*, Dyllansow Truran, 1993, p. 136.

6 Pryce, William, *Mineralogia Cornubiensis, A Treatise on Minerals, Mines and Mining*, 1778, Reprinted, Bradford Barton, Truro, 1972, p. 61.

7 Deacon, Bernard, 'Proto-Industrialisation and Potatoes', *Cornish Studies 5*, University of Exeter Press, 1997, pp. 73-75.

8 *Cornubian*, 30/1/1891.

9 *Cornubian*, 2/9/1892.

10 James, C.C., *History of Gwennap*, privately published, undated, p.129.

11 Thomas, R., Report on a Survey of the Mining District of Cornwall from Chasewater to Camborne, London, 1819, p. 74.

12 De la Beche, Report on the Geology of Cornwall, Devon and West Somerset, London, 1839, Longman, Orme, Brown & Green, p. 622.

13 P 79/81/1, Vestry Book for Gwennap Parish, 7/6/1848, CRO, Truro.

14 Jenkin, A.K.H., *The Cornish Miner*, Allen & Unwin, London, 1927, p. 251.

15 Ibid, p. 252.

16 Rowe, John, *Changing Times and Fortunes, A Cornish Farmer's Life 1828-1904*, Cornish Hillside Publications, 1996, p.87-91.

17 The Children's Employment Commission, A report by Charles Barham, Esq. M.D., 1841, p.108.

18 Payton, Philip, *The Making of Modern Cornwall*, Dyllansow Truran, 1992, p.105

19 James-Korany, Margaret, 'Blue Books' As Sources for Cornish Emigration, *Cornish Studies I*, University of Exeter Press, 1993, p. 38.

20 P 79/81/1, CRO.

21 P 79/81/1, CRO.

22 Holbrook-Adams, Caroline, *The Jose Family, Utah, By Way of Australia*, Herrington Publishing Company, Texas, 1995.

23 P 79/81/1, CRO.

24 Ibid.

25 Memorial Scheme List, nos. 3352, 6297, 7114, RIC, Truro; Cornish Settlers Arrivals' Dates, compiled by the Cornish Association of Victoria, Australia. CFHS, Truro.

26 *Cornubian*, 1/1/1914.

27 *Cornubian*, 26/9/1902.

28 *Cornubian*, 24/1/1924.
29 *Royal Cornwall Gazette*, 31/10/1923.
30 Lescohier, Roger, *Gold Giants of Grass Valley, History of the Empire and North Star Mines, 1850-1956*, Empire Mine Park Association, 1995, p.98.
31 Emigrants' List, no. 3160, RIC, Truro.
32 Acknowledge Mr C. Harvey of Alexandria, Virginia; private communication in 1996.
33 Information from the US Certificate of Naturalisation no. 2435255, of Wilfred Harvey, courtesy of Mrs I.M. Staat, Flint MI.
34 *Cornubian*, 20/4/1877.
35 Tregoning, E.A., *Two Centuries of a Cornish Family*, Edgar Backus, Leicester, 1950, pp. 6-7.
36 *Cornubian*, 5/1/1907.
37 *Cornubian*, 30/8/1901.
38 *Cornubian*, 5/2/1914
39 Noted at a visit to the Glenwood Cemetery, Park City, Utah, in October 1996 by Sharron Schwartz. The idea of using friendly societies as a means of promoting and aiding migration to the US was mentioned by Sid Blake, Proprietor of the Cornish Arms Hotel, NYC, in a letter to the *Cornubian* in 1929.
40 *West Briton*, 30/8/1850.
41 Poster Courtesy of Keweenaw Kernewek, MI.
42 1871 Census Return for Gwennap Parish; RG/10, 2313/F. 49, 58; *Cornubian*, 15/5/1874; 29/9/1876.
43 The Collected Poems of P. Varker Snr. & P.J. Varker Jnr., Unpublished, courtesy of Mrs Jean Ball, Lanner.
44 *The Old West*, with text by R. Wallace, 'The Miners', Time Life Books, New York, 1976, pp 148-158.
45 Calhoon, F.D., *Coolies, Kanakas and Cousin Jacks*, Privately Published, 1995, p. 290.
46 *Royal Cornwall Gazette*, 31/1/1873.
47 Polglase, J.R., *South American Demand Expressed in Cornwall, 1810-1920.* Privately Published, 1986.
48 *Cornubian*, 9/5/1907.
49 *Cornubian*, 1/3/1895.
50 Private communication with the late Mrs Minnie Haughton, interviewed when 80 in 1995.
51 Information concerning the life of the late Mrs Mary Job, taken from an interview with her in 1991, aged 101.
52 *Royal Cornwall Gazette*, 11/2/1915; information from Mrs Rhona Blatchford (née Blight).
53 *Cornubian*, 7/3/1902.
54 *Cornubian*, 2/10/1903.
55 *Royal Cornwall Gazette*, 19/3/1896; 29/4/1915.
56 *Cornubian*, 31/10/1903.
57 *West Briton*, 25/1/1935.
58 *Cornubian*, 12/2/1892.
59 Menhenott, David, *Gwennap Parish, A Local Profile*, Privately Published, 1996, p. 50.
60 *Cornubian*, 3/2/1906; Memorial Scheme Emigrants' List, no. 3337, RIC, Truro.
61 *West Briton*, 25/1/1935.
62 *Cornubian*, 5/2/1914.
63 *Cornubian*, 3/4/1915.
64 *Cornubian*, 27/1/1906.
65 *Cornubian*, 18/10/1906.
66 Lanner Historical Society, *Echoes of the Past, Issue 3*, 1997, p. 24.
67 *Doidge's Almanack*, Redruth, 1885, p. 28.
68 Burke, G.M., *The Cornish Miner and the Cornish Mining Industry 1870-1921*, Ph.D. Thesis, University of London, 1981, p.108.
69 Ibid., p. 141.
70 *Cornubian*, 25/4/1918.
71 *Cornubian*, 9/7/1914.
72 Blackenbury, Cyril, 'The Unwatering of Tresavean Mine', Paper presented on 18/1/1912, Institute of Mining and Metallurgy, London, pp. 286, 289. Reference to the Golden Gate Mine, courtesy of Janeen N.Watkins, Lehi, Utah.
73 List of Remittances to Tweedy's Bank, Redruth, from Real del Monte, RE 7, List of Remittances to Williams & Co., Redruth from Real del Monte, B1, courtesy of L & T. Dudley, Newport, Gwent.
74 Probert, John C.C., *Primitive Methodism in Cornwall*, Privately Published, Redruth, 1966, p.19.
75 *Cornubian*, 31/1/1902.
76 *West Briton*, 24/9/1896.

77 Blewett, R., 'The Village of St. Day in the Parish of Gwennap'. Paper presented to the Board of Education Short Course for teachers in Public Elementary Schools on 'The Citizen in the Modern World' held at Selwyn College, Cambridge, July 13-27, 1935, as quoted in Burke, G.M., Ph.D Thesis, University of London 1981, p. 142.
78 Chilvers, H. A., *Out of the Crucible*, Cassel & Co. Ltd., London, 1929, 3rd Edition, 1934, pp. 79- 16.
79 *Cornubian*, 11/5/1900.
80 *Cornubian*, 4/1/1901.
81 *Cornubian*, 18/1/1901.
82 Information from the late Mrs Minnie Haughton.
83 *Cornubian*, 1/2/1901.
84 *Cornubian*, 15/2/1901.
85 Teacher's Log Book, Lanner School, SR/GWE.4/2, CRO, Truro.
86 *Cornubian*, 31/10/1902.
87 Communication from Mr David Lean, Redruth, in 1996, a descendant.
88 Communication from Mrs J. Craze, Redruth, in 1996, granddaughter of David Polkinghorne.
89 1891 Census Return for the Parish of Gwennap, RG/12, 1845, f. 14-66.
90 Information concerning the life of the late Mrs Mary Job, taken from an interview with her in 1991, aged 101.
91 *Royal Cornwall Gazette*, 31/10/1923.
92 *Cornubian*, 9/5/1907; 23/5/1907; 30/3/1907; 6/6/1907. *Cornish Post and Mining News*, 6/1/1898, lists remittances from 10s to £2 from the following men in connection with a bazaar to raise funds for the Lanner Wesley organ rennovation fund: Hugh Nicholls; Sam Osborne; A.J. Osborne; Joseph Billing; Fred Scoble; James Whitburn; John Phillips (all in the USA) and James Tresidder; Thomas Opie; James Harris; John Dunstan; James Dunstan; James Rogers; Sam Job; Fred Lawn; Joseph Curnow; James Lawn; James H. Chapman; S.J. Reed and James Phillips, in South Africa.
93 *Cornubian*, 25/7/1902.
94 *Cornubian*, 6/9/1901.
95 *Cornish Post and Mining News*, 30/6/1904; *Cornubian*, 1/7/1903.
96 *Cornubian*, 13/2/1903.
97 *Cornish Post and Mining News*, 30/7/1903.
98 *West Briton*, 14/6/1928; 19/7/1928.
99 SR/GWE. 4/2, CRO, Truro.
100 *Nevada Daily Morning Miner*, 16/3/1904.
101 *Cornubian*, 23/12/1915.
102 *Cornubian*, 11/5/1883.
103 *West Briton*, 12/4/1928.
104 *Cornubian*, 28/3/1883.
105 Hitchcock, G., *Folk Songs of the West Country Collected by S. Baring Gould*, Newton Abbot, 1974, p. 34-5.
106 Blewett, R., *These Things Have Been, 54 th Installment*, 1968, p. 214.
107 Payton, Philip, *The Making of Modern Cornwall*, Dyllansow Truran, 1992, p.p. 99-114.
108 Payton, Philip, *The Cornish Farmer in Australia*, Dyllansow Truran, 1987, p.p. 60-64; *The Cornish Miner in Australia*, Dyllansow Truran, 1984, p. 35 & 40.
109 Tregoning, E.A., *Two Centuries of a Cornish Family*, Edgar Backus, Liecester, 1950, pp. 6-7.
110 *Cornubian*, 26/1/1907.
111 *The Daily Union of Grass Valley*, 23/6/1907.
112 Unidentified newspaper clipping from Michigan, courtesy of Mrs S. Albrant, Fenton, MI.
113 *Cornubian*, 14/3/1902; 27/5/1887; 5/7/1901.
114 *Cornubian*, 22/1/1892.
115 Schwartz, S. P., Life and Times, *Echoes of the Past, Issue 1*, Lanner Historical Society, 1996.
116 Interview with Rhona Blatchford in 1997.
117 *Cornubian*, 29/4/1915.
118 Private communication with Mr R. L. Mann, Duncraig, Western Australia, a descendant, in 1997.
119 *Cornubian*, 15/12/1898; Cornish Post and Mining News, 4/4/1898.
120 Michell, F., *Annals of An Ancient Cornish Town*, Redruth, Dyllansow Truran, Redruth, 1978, p.180; *Cornubian*, 2/10/1874.
121 Harris, J.H., *The Luck of Wheal Veor and Other Stories*, Joseph Pollard, Truro, 1901, pp. 85-91.
122 Communication from David Lean, a descendant, in 1996.
123 Communication from Mrs S. Kessell and Mrs J. Kellow, granddaughters, in 1995.
124 Jenkin, A. K. Hamilton, *The Cornish Miner*, Allen & Unwin, 1927, p. 330.
125 Communicated by Mr J .C. C. Probert in 1996.

126 *Cornubian*, 14/1/1915.
127 *Royal Cornwall Gazette*, 27/8/1896.
128 *Cornubian*, 24/8/1900.
129 *Royal Cornwall Gazette*, 28/1/1915.
130 *Royal Cornwall Gazette*, 19/5/1904.
131 *Cornubian*, 14/4/1906; 21/2/1907; 14/1/1915.
132 Communication from Mrs Rhona Blatchford in 1997.
133 *Cornubian*, 10/4/1896.
134 *Royal Cornwall Gazette*, 26/6/1843
135 Dickason, Graham B., Cornish Immigrants to South Africa, Balkema, Cape Town, S.A. 1978, p. 102
136 Dudley, Laura & Terry, British Cemetery, Panteon de Los Ingleses, Real del Monte, Unpublished, 1987-1989.
137 Interview with Mrs Irene Veall, Gwennap, in 1996, a descendant.
138 *Cornubian*, 20/3/1891.
139 *Cornubian*, 30/8/1906; 8.2.1901.
140 *West Briton*, 4/4/1907; *Cornubian*, 25/4/1907.
141 *Cornubian*, 23/12/1915.
142 Holbrook-Adams, Caroline, *The Jose Family Utah, by Way of Australia*. Herrington Publishing Company, Texas, 1995.
143 *Cornubian*, 6/5/1915; information courtesy of Mr David Lean, Redruth, 1995.
144 Lawn, Helen, 'The Lawns of Lanner', unpublished, undated; Christchurch Star, June 1989; The Aus IMM Bulletin & Proceedings, Vol. 293, no. 8, 12/1988.
145 *Cornubian*, 19/1/1894. Lobengula married a Cornishwoman named Miss Jewel, who apparently bolted a short time after their marriage, *Cornish Post and Mining News*, 15/2/1900.
146 'The biography of Josiah Kemp', unpublished, courtesy of Mrs J. N. Watkins, Lehi, Utah., plus additional interview in 1996.
147 Lord, Eliot, *Comstock Mining and Miners*, Nevada Publications, Las Vegas, 1959, p.199.
148 Ibid, p. 200.
149 Todd, A. C., *The Cornish Miner in America*, The Arthur H. Clark Co., Spokane, Washington, 1967, p. 106.
150 Ibid., p. 200; Nevada Historical Society Journal, Number 35, March 1985.
151 *Cornubian*, 21/8/1891.
152 *Cornubian*, 3/2/1893, 15/6/1900.
153 *C.F.H.S. Journal, No. 35*, March 1985, 'Dick Jose of Lanner 1862-1941, Cornwall's Greatest Singer', Joe Pengelly; The *Western Morning News*, 22/4/1988; *C.F.H.S. Journal, No.48*, June 1988.
154 *Cornishman*, 6/10/1966.
155 *Cornubian*, 24/4/1891.
156 Payton, Philip, *The Making of Modern Cornwall*, p.113.
157 Ibid., pp. 119-163.

Fig.9.1. *Lanner Bible Christian Chapel , which became the United Methodists Chapel after the 1907 Union. This building is now the Village Hall.* (© The Paddy Bradley Collection).

Chapter 9
Religious Institutions

It seems almost inconceivable that in the last third of the nineteenth century, Lanner, a parish which covered only a few square miles, had no less than six chapels and a parish church. Its situation on the outskirts of Redruth, an important market town serving a large mining district, coupled with its position at the heartland of Gwennap's 'Copper Kingdom', created a dramatic rise in population for Lanner. In common with many other local villages, a spate of chapel building followed.

In Lanner we see the Wesleyan and Bible Christian Chapels in the heart of the village close to the Square, and the Primitive Methodist Chapel at Lanner Moor, the Trevarth Wesleyan, and the South Downs chapels of the Wesleyans and the United Methodist Free Church answering the demand for worshippers living, on the whole, in the immediate vicinity of these places of worship. There was even a Primitive Methodist chapel built at Carn Marth. An Anglican Chapel of Ease was erected in Lanner which became Lanner Christ Church.

This chapter will seek to examine the reasons why Methodism came to enjoy a position of hegemony in Lanner. Although Methodism may be perceived to be essentially a working class movement, this chapter challenges this hypothesis by examining the extent and influence of the new middle class in the running of the Methodist chapels in Lanner. But the strength of Methodism lay also in its acceptance by the working classes, and its incorporation into their everyday lives. What factors led to this? We will also explore the reasons for the antipathy against the Church of England in Lanner, fuelled by Popery, Ritualism and a succession of bad clergymen, aggregate factors in its poor following amongst Lanner's population until the inter-war period. Much interdenominational competition followed the building of the parish's chapels, resulting in periodic enlargements and renovations to these places of worship. We will examine the legacy of such intense church building as the painful process of de-industrialisation and over dependence on the local mining industry prompted a large migration from the area. This inevitably led to dwindling membership, smaller congregations and surplus church provision, the outcome of which was increasing financial headaches.

Mining and Methodism were inextricably intertwined, so much so that it was difficult to escape the all-pervading influence of the local chapel. The local Mine Captain was often a Methodist lay preacher, and would exert his influence over a prospective employee to attend chapel. If he or she did not turn up, he would want to know why. Socially, the chapels often provided the basic needs of the community in the days before the Welfare State, and also in the provision of basic education, which we shall discuss in the following chapter. As far as leisure was concerned, the chapels provided many of the spare time activities which gave nineteenth century Lanner its characteristic identity, and this will be discussed in Chapter 12. For over 150 years, culturally and socially, Methodism was the very heartbeat of Lanner, a Cornish mining parish.

Post Reformation Religious Affairs and the Rise of Methodism

Little can be substantiated about religious affairs and provision, prior to the nineteenth century, within Lanner Valley and the vicinity, although there is a tradition that a chapel with a baptismal well was once sited at Chapel Hill, a continuation of Bell Lane, on the south side of Lanner. However, other than the discovery of two old crosses thought to have originally come from this ancient chapel, nothing is known of it. These two crosses, of worked moorstone, were re-erected near the entrance to Christ Church. The chapel may have been used by pilgrims on their way from the famous St Day shrine (closed in the sixteenth century) to that of St Michael's Mount (see Chapter 1). James concludes that, like St Day, it probably shared the fate of other confiscated chapels during the reign of Elizabeth I.[1] Another school of thought claims that Chapel Hill might be so named because the early followers of Wesley held their services in that area. But there is no conclusive proof for either. There is also a tradition that there was a chapel at Skyburrier, West Trevarth. This may have been a private chapel used by the occupants of Trevarth Manor before the Reformation. James describes very old buildings surrounding the farmhouse, and two worked stones in the hedges, one of which may have been the shaft of a cross.[2]

A Religious Census of Cornwall in 1676 showed that in the Parish of Gwinnapp, Decanat Kerriar, there were 800 Conformists and 7 Nonconformists.[3] However by the time of the 1851 Census (see below), Methodism had become the popular religious choice. Methodism was originally founded as a revivalist movement within the Established Church.

People worshipped at the parish church at usual services, and attended additional prayer meetings and services at meeting houses. Eventually those Christians who 'dissented' from the established church set up their own modes of worship. Methodism was rooted in the dedication of the everyday life of its adherents to its cause, rather than a religion perceived as separate from the people, and the revivalist preaching of the Wesleys moved the working class people of Cornwall deeply.

In particular, the involvement of lay persons in the activities of the church, and the development of the hymn book (Methodists developed their own new hymns), were in tune with the feelings of the people at that time. The Sunday School movement, which developed rapidly after 1780, was one of the first systematic attempts to give education to the bulk of the working people, and contributed strongly to the growth of the Methodist Church in Cornwall.

Rule argues that the strength and appeal of Methodism was the relationship of Methodism to pre-existing beliefs and attitudes.[4] Luker also explores this theme and concludes that Methodism was dependent for its spread at the popular level on indigenous folk religion which persisted into the nineteenth century. Methodist practice was in many ways congruent with the older superstitions, with for example, a belief in the healing qualities of holy wells, the power of 'white' witches and the use of prayers, replacing charms and chants to dispel evil. This symbiosis of Methodist spirituality and indigenous popular religion helped it to overcome 'opposition accorded to "external" influences in general, and to become an established part of west Cornish communities.'[5]

Also of great importance to the success of Methodism in the Lanner area in the nineteenth century was the emergence of a new social class. Although perceived to be essentially working class, the Methodist churches were not, on the whole, working class led. (The baptismal registers for the chapels and the Church of England of Lanner show little difference in the parents' occupation.). The main difference was one of leadership. Organising meetings, sitting on committees, managing chapel finances or making crucial decisions would have been beyond the capabilities of the majority of ordinary, poorly-educated working class men. The Church of England leaders were usually to be found among the squirearchy, some bigger farmers and professional people, whereas the Methodist leadership was composed mainly of the new aspiring middle class of independent industrialists, small farmers, shopkeepers and self employed tradesmen, which had arisen through, and because of, the local mining industry.

Munson has included numerous examples of leading English Nonconformist, wealthy, middle class businessmen who made enormous contributions to Victorian religious and cultural life, among whom might be mentioned W.H. Smith, H.V. Mackintosh, Jesse Boot, Sir Christopher Furness and William Hartley.[6] In nearby Redruth we can see a greatly scaled down example of the national pattern: Sir Arthur Carkeek (constructional engineer and Chairman of Cornwall County Council), Alfred Lanyon (owner of the town's gas-works, market and Cornish Tin Smelting Works), James Wickett (dealer in shares), the Trounsons (merchants) and Harry Rich (Mine Agent).[7] And in Lanner, middle class involvement in religious life had also begun to have an effect. This is aptly portrayed upon examination of the trustees for the Trevarth Wesleyan Chapel of 1862 – John Whitburn, William Reed and Richard Goldsworthy, Mine Agents; John Barnett, Draper and Grocer; John Williams, Builder; John Nicholls, Butcher; Vincent Sarah, Merchant and William Martyn, Farmer. The list of the trustees for Lanner Bible Christian Chapel in the early twentieth century further reflects this new middle class involvement, featuring the names of engineers, mine agents, greengrocers and butchers; and the same picture emerges for the South Downs Wesleyan Chapel, which has mine agents, purveyors, provision merchants, commercial travellers, builders, plumbers and chandlers named among its trustees.

Such self-managed Methodist chapels came to embody 'the community', providing social and spiritual support for all. This helped to limit the effect of rural class divisions and provided the resources necessary for families (especially working class families) to cope with the increasing pressures of a rapidly industrialising society, fostering the element of independence which came to be so associated with Methodism, and with the Cornish. Moreover, the knots which bound the community to the church had, during the nineteenth century, been considerably loosened. The tithe system (in which land users had to pay money, or one-tenth of their produce, to the local church, even if they were not members of that church) was relieved by stopping payment in kind, and tithes became a rent on land, eventually by 1891 only payable by landowners. The Marriage Act of 1836 permitted marriage ceremonies in Methodist churches to be legally binding if notified to the Registrar of Births, Deaths and Marriages, although many Methodists continued to use the Church of England for the rites of life. Thus, the strong ties of the people to the Established Church were considerably loosened, and the Methodists were even more strongly encouraged. By the mid nineteenth century in Lanner they had become the dominant religious force.

THE DISSENTERS: CHAPEL HISTORY IN LANNER

John Wesley (1703–1791), the evangelist and founder of Methodism, made thirty-two journeys into Cornwall, and Richard Williams and Elizabeth Williams of Trevarth were among those who entertained him. He gave his strength to working class neighbourhoods, particularly to mining communities like those in Cornwall. In the Lanner area, Wesley often preached at Gwennap, including sometimes at Gwennap Pit, to thousands of people at a time, and his journals record that he once preached to twenty-thousand people at Gwennap. Pearce has argued that one of the reasons for the success of Methodism in the county is because

Fig.9.2. *John Dower (1864–1931), seated on the left, with his parents. John was a joiner at Tresavean Mine, and a local preacher at Lanner Wesley. Photo c.1904.* (© Mr J.J.D. Eastman, Redruth)

Fig.9.3. *Mr Walter Langford, a Methodist local preacher, on his 80th birthday in 1951. Immaculately turned out in the Sunday best dress of a Cornish Mining Captain.* (© Joan Martin, Lanner)

the Wesleys and their itinerants restored heart, religion and religious fellowship to Cornwall. Cornish preachers who had passed rigorous training were usually picked by Wesley himself, or his brother, and these sympathetic local men appealed more to the Cornish than did the parish priests, who were usually English outsiders.[8]

Many local men became respected lay preachers, well loved and followed on the circuit. Thomas C. Knuckey (1881–1981), a member of Lanner Wesley, became a fully accredited lay preacher at the age of 21, and thus began a career which spanned 60 years (Fig.10.12). John Dower of 6 Pennance Terrace, a pit joiner at Tresavean and then at Basset Mine, was taught to read and write by his wife and then became a local preacher, until his death in 1931, aged 67 (Fig. 9.2).

J. Vivian, a butcher of Fairfield House, Lanner, was noted as a popular local preacher in 1948 and Walter Harold Langford, of Lanner Green House, had conducted over 2000 services at his 80th birthday in 1951, having been accepted as a fully-credited lay preacher in 1894. This venerable white-bearded gentleman was remembered in Lanner Wesley where he often preached, as being immaculately turned out in the Sunday-best dress of a Cornish Mining Captain: black trousers, frock-tail coat and a tall black silk hat (Fig.9.3).

In 1764, Wesley's first Cornwall Circuit was divided into Cornwall West and Cornwall East. A page of the Cornwall West Circuit Book for 1767 gives the names of the members living in the Lanner area.[9] It should be remembered that Lanner had not yet developed into a settlement of any size, and was part of the Parish of Gwennap. In addition to the tinner, Richard Williams of Trevarth, and his wife Elizabeth, the following are among those listed: William Wats, tinner of Tresavean, and his wife Sarah; William Morcom, tinner of Carnmarth, and his wife Elizabeth; Richard Fransis, tinner of Lanner, and his wife Blanch; Richard Renfrey, tinner and his wife Alice; and Grace Blackler and Jane Tregilgas. The members of the Gwennap Society living at Lanner soon formed their own local society and sometime afterwards built a small chapel (in what is now known as Church Road) in 1828, which became known as the Lanner Wesleyan Chapel.

Five other chapels, of three different denominations and in two different circuits before the Methodist Union, were eventually set up in Lanner Parish. These were the Lanner Moor Primitive, the Lanner Hill Bible Christian ('Bryanites'), the South Downs Wesleyan, the South Downs United Free Methodist, and the Trevarth Methodist chapels.

Although it was strictly outside the present Lanner Parish boundary, there was a Primitive Methodist chapel on the north-west slope of Carn Marth, which would undoubtedly have been used by Lanner people residing on Carn Marth. According to *Wesleyan Methodist Chapels and Preaching Places in Cornwall*, 31 December 1876, Lanner Wesley had 700 'sittings' and 244 members of the Society in that year. South Downs Wesley had 150 sittings and 69 Members. Trevarth was 'a small chapel in connection with larger ones', had 50 sittings, but no membership numbers were quoted.

Before Methodist Union in 1932, when the traditional modes of organisation characteristic of each was wound up and restructured as a single organisation, there were many Methodist organisations as we shall see below. After 1932, the Redruth Methodist Circuit was established to include Lanner's chapels. For example, the last quarterly meeting of the Wesleyan Circuit was held at 'Lanner Wesley' in 1934. Eventually all the Lanner chapels joined together in Lanner Methodist Church, the building still in use being that of the Lanner Wesley, in Church Road, proving, as the Reverend Thomas Shaw has commented, that 'six into one will go!'.

Lanner Bible Christian Chapel

A chapel was built in 1817 on Lanner Hill, a few hundred yards on the right above the present Square, by the followers of John Boyle. The Memoirs of John Blewett, 1843, note the existence of this early Chapel, with the entry, 'it is a fact beyond dispute that there was a society there, and a Chapel erected previous to the union, as the date of 1817, engraved in the arch stone over the original door testifies.'[10] This was probably one of the first chapels in Lanner built by 'Nonconformists'.

Boyle was an itinerant preacher who had travelled on the Redruth circuit and then left the Wesleyans to form his own circuit. William Bryant of Luxulyan founded the Bible Christians, an evangelical off shoot of Wesleyan Methodism, in Devon during 1815. He was later known as 'O'Bryan', and the Bible Christians were often known as the 'Bryanites'. This sect was a revivalist one, best known for their spontaneous outbursts of religious passion, resulting in much laughing, dancing, clapping and outpouring of spirit, and appealed to the less sophisticated working class. The Bible Christians showed a particular strength in rural areas such as Lanner.

In 1817, the Lanner Hill Chapel was taken over by the Bible Christians, who had united with Boyle's followers. By 1844, their chapel had been rebuilt twice, materially altering its original shape, and in 1866 it was rebuilt once again. The Bible Christians were omitted from the returns of the 1851 Religious Census which research has shown to have been somewhat unreliable, similar omissions having been recorded for various denominations in other areas. T. P. Oliver reported in 1867, that for some years it had been contemplated to build a new chapel, but the task seemed insurmountable. However, at length it became imperative, due to the large congregations pressing into the 'feeble old chapel' each Sabbath. Trustees were found, and the chapel was made over to the connexion. 'They were determined to make the chapel as large as the ground would admit, which is 50 feet long by 38 wide outside, and 24 feet from floor to ceiling, with side ends and galleries,' he commented, adding that the foundation stone was laid at half past two on 14 June 1866 by W.J. Sheehan, who placed £5 upon it, on behalf of Captain R. Manuell.

The Wesleyans had kindly lent their chapel for the occasion of a sermon, preached by W.B. Lark of Exeter, and a spirited public meeting took place afterwards, followed by a tea, the proceeds of which realised £53. When the building had progressed so far as the flooring and the galleries, it was decided to hold Midway Opening Services, which added £9.1s. to the chapel's funds. The reason for opening the uncompleted chapel two days before Christmas Day was given by T.P. Oliver as being because of 'the coldness and smallness of the place where we were worshipping'. Combining the Christmas services with the chapel's opening was, however, a fine way to increase the buoyancy of its financial position, particularly during the economic downswing of the mid 1860s!

The opening and subsequent services at which a number of well known local preachers from various denominations presided, were successful. 'The congregations were large, the influence solemn, deep and powerful.' The amount received at these services, by collections, profits of tea and a Christmas tree, was a little more than £24, T.P. Oliver adding that 'We thought this very good, considering the depressed state of mining, and the great poverty prevailing in this neighbourhood'. Presumably the chapel building had begun before the calamitous crash of the local copper mining industry. The total cost of the chapel was estimated to have been about £500, towards which it was hoped to raise £200.[11]

In 1891, a considerable proportion of the cost of £150 to renovate the chapel yet again was raised at a Bazaar; in all, £147.5s. being collected by means of a harvest festival, the sale of wood, reopening services and book collections, which left just £12 more to raise. It was hoped that items left over from the bazaar would soon be disposed of, thus realising the outstanding amount.[12] Extensive alterations were made, including a new pitch-pine rostrum, new seats of the same material in the body of the chapel, new side seats with back rails, and a new choir gallery with two vestries underneath. T. Willoughby was contracted to do the work, his tender of £119 being accepted, but extras were expected to increase that sum to £160. The late Mary Job recalled that her father, Philip Bray, brought sand in a horse and cart to help construct the new chapel front. The opening took place on the 14 and 15 December.

In 1904, plans were drawn up by Mr Horace Collins, MSA, for a new schoolroom, including heating, a vestry, furnace house, a chamber for apparatus and earth closets. 'The building will be a commodious structure, and built of random coarse granite, with pointed facings of the same material at a cost of about £400. The contractors are Messrs. J. Tiddy and T. Willoughby', reported the local paper. The stone-laying ceremony was presided over by the Reverend Pascoe in June 1904, when the following stones were laid: number one by John Jeffery, on behalf of the Sunday School, a donation of £10 being placed on it. The second was laid by Miss E.J. Hocking with a donation of £5; number three, by Mrs Job on behalf of her daughter Miss May Job, also with a £5 donation. Stone number four followed, laid by Mrs Hitchens on behalf of her daughter Miss Eileen Hitchens, with a further £5 donation; the fifth stone was placed by

Miss Ferkins on behalf of her deceased father, a tireless worker for the Bryanites, also with a £5 donation (see Fig. 9.1, page 176).

The final stone was laid by Thomas Eastman on behalf of the trustees, with donations amounting to £7.5s. The day's proceedings realised £55, but prior to this the treasurer had received £200 towards the building funds. The new schoolroom was opened in 1904.[13] In 1907, the Bible Christians amalgamated with the United Methodist Free Church (UMFC), and the chapel became the place of worship of the United Methodists. In 1912, there were 21 teachers, 51 adult scholars, 36 scripture scholars, and 52 infants. The total congregation was 167 people; a large decrease in numbers had occurred due to emigration (Fig.9.4).

Readers who are familiar with the Village Hall will be interested to know that the chapel occupied the site of the present Men's Institute, built over the body of the former chapel (Fig.9.5). The main Village Hall is where the schoolroom was located, with the vestry and boiler room built on to the end. Chapel trustees of the early twentieth century were: Thomas Eastman, greengrocer; Edward Dower, miner; John Henry Blewett (of Waltham Abbey, Essex), engineer; James Job, retired miner; Thomas Ferkin, engineer; Henry Spargo, butcher; Edward Uren, miner; John Martin Uren, miner; Stephen Moyle, miner; Bennett Treloar, miner; William James Dower, miner; William James Job (London), draper's assistant; Francis Thomas Job, accountant; and Thomas Williams, retired miner. The Pastor of the circuit was S. Pascoe, who lived in Clinton Road, Redruth, and

Fig.9.5. *Interior of United Methodist Church, Lanner ('Bryanites'), before 1908.* (© The Paddy Bradley Collection)

Thomas Eastman was the Trustee Steward. Regular services ceased before 1940, but there was one last service in 1945 to celebrate the return of Charlie Job from a Japanese prisoner of war camp. The chapel was sold on 12 January 1946 for £301.13s.9d, to become the Lanner Village Hall.

Lanner Wesleyan Chapel

James Francis, a miner of Gwennap, had secured a lease dated 1820 from John Rogers of Penrose for a parcel of a croft in the tenement of Bell. On 16 July 1828, he assigned this area containing about 15 lace, to a group of 12 local miners, 'to have and to hold the aforesaid plot or piece of land upon

Fig.9.4. *Lanner's United Methodist Church Sunday School officers and teachers, c.1907–14. Note the fine china ware and elaborate tea pots, and the predominance of women over men, probably due to migration.* (© The Paddy Bradley Collection)

which to build a Wesleyan Methodist Chapel which is to be built by subscriptions and collections raised for that express purpose'.[14] The annual rent was 10 shillings.

The Wesleyan Chapel Department's Committee for granting permission to build chapels, records entry 502 as being a request to construct a chapel at Rough Street in 1828. It is interesting to note that Lanner as a place is not mentioned, being obviously an insignificant, minor settlement at that time. The estimated expenditure for the building was expected to have been £300, subscriptions £100, and the probable income was estimated to have been about £20 per annum, probably from seat rents.[15] The 12 trustees were all described as 'miners', but the term is misleading and it is highly likely that some of this number were mine captains, as only two were unable to sign their name. Lanner Wesley had been on the circuit plan long before the building of the chapel in 1828, and a meeting place or chapel of some description definitely existed at Rough Street before this date.

Lanner Wesley Chapel in 1828 would have followed the usual pattern, as at Carharrack, with a central pulpit standing in front of the Communion area. Parts of the Commandment tables can still be seen on the wall behind the rostrum. The building was enlarged in 1844 to accommodate the ever-increasing population resulting from the growth of mining within the area, thus altering the original chapel beyond recognition. The entrance to the chapel was formerly on the eastern side, but was moved to the northern wall during the 1844 rebuild (Fig.9.6). All the carpentry work was done by Henry Strick of Trevarth, carpenter and undertaker. He made and glazed the windows for the sum of £36, and was paid a further £97 for fixing the gallery.

Fig.9.6. *Lanner Wesley chapel, originally built in 1828, and renovated and rebuilt in 1844. This photograph, taken before the 1903 renovation, shows the 1844 façade.* (© Paul Annear, Probus).

Various members of the congregation helped in the building of the chapel, raising and carrying moorstone from Carn Marth, and conveying sand by cart from St Agnes, but the work was not voluntary. Everybody who in any way contributed in the task was paid, even the children who cleaned the chapel before the opening service.

The work cost £691.11s.8d, and the money raised at the opening ceremony was £82. The entrance door was now in the centre of the northern wall with three arched windows above. A further two windows stood on either side of the doorway. Enclosed in a circle below the apex of the building were the words 'Wesleyan Chapel, 1844'.

Fig.9.7. *The Wesleyan Chapel and the new Sunday school building (right), after the 1903 rebuild. The money for the stone to build the new granite façade of the chapel was given by James Davey, formerly of Tocopilla, Chile.* (© Paul Annear, Probus)

In 1875 a rostrum was erected to the plans drawn up by architect James Hicks, replacing the pulpit at a cost of £172. In 1876, we have seen that Lanner Wesley had 244 members, and a thriving Mutual Improvement Class was set up in the late nineteenth century. A Band of Hope was established in the 1890s and Richard Jose, the Lanner lad who found fame with his counter-tenor voice in the USA, sang in the chapel in 1891. In 1894, the chapel was licensed for the solemnisation of marriages, and Messrs Chapell and Osborne were married there.

In 1903, the front of the chapel again underwent alterations to harmonise with the new chapel schoolroom, which had been built across the road (Fig.9.7). The new Gothic front of granite and Bath stone was constructed at a cost of about £350; the whole of the amount was met by James Davey, a butcher, formerly of Tocopilla, Chile, a society member and the treasurer of the Sunday School. He also promised to provide iron railings for the chapel entrance at a further cost of over £60, which, with his gifts to the new Sunday School amounted to about £500 (about £165 000 in today's money). Mrs Knuckey, James Davey's sister, who had also lived in Chile, gave £400. These were enormous amounts of money, and the local press felt compelled to reprint the amounts in a later edition, as the news was met with incredulity locally. One local paper commented, 'The gifts are almost unique in Cornish village Methodism.'[16]

Two entrance porches were also added at this time. The builder involved with both the new chapel front and the schoolroom was Richard Jacob. The windows were of 'cathedral glass', and the new front extended the building by six feet. New staircases and four separate entrances were provided, two in the porches and two opening on to the gallery stairs. Inside, the old seats, both at ground level and in the gallery, were replaced by a uniform design in pitch pine. The Choir Gallery was enlarged to seat 45 persons and the newly installed pipe organ was brought forward three feet from the organ chamber. The whole of the interior was redecorated, 'making it one of the handsomest buildings in the neighbourhood'. The total cost was £850.

At the reopening ceremony, a hymn was sung outside the building, the Revd H.C. Bassett offered a prayer, and R. Johns gave a short address. The Revd W. Humphries then presented James Davey with 'a richly chased silver key' (supplied by Chandlers of Redruth) and requested him to open the building. James Davey said as he let the people in, 'The Chapel at Lanner brings many a recollection to my memory. It is in this building that 38 years ago I consecrated myself to God's service. I have witnessed many revivals here and I trust these old-fashioned Methodist revivals will continue'. Mr Dennis, organist of Redruth Wesley Chapel, then gave an organ recital and 'drew out the capabilities of the instrument, to the delight of the listeners'. Sacred solos were contributed by Mrs Joseph Rich, Mrs Harry Rich of Redruth, and A.E. Old, of Camborne. A well-attended tea followed in the schoolroom, the provisions being contributed by Mesdames Edwin Hosking, J. Spargo, J. Trewern, W. W. Teague, M. Curnow, S. Lavin, Messrs W. Martin, C. Opie and the Misses Opie of Bell. James Wickett (a prominent Redruth Wesleyan, and mine stockbroker) presided at the evening meeting.[17]

The year 1903 was a very successful one for Lanner Wesleyans, a year which had witnessed the building of a new Sunday School and renovation of the Chapel, at a cost of £1740, (over half a million in today's money) of which £1575 had been generously met, leaving a small deficiency of £165. This was a remarkable achievement, and provides an indication of the wealth in the village at that time, a great deal of which came from money remitted from Lanner miners working overseas. In 1977, the most recent alteration to the Lanner Methodist Church front combined the entrance porches to make a single entrance. The chapel was reopened by Miss 'Janie' Langford, supported by Revd S.E.A. Underhill. In the early 1980s, the Lanner Methodist Church's collection of silver and pewter ware was 'rescued' by Alice Opie from being abandoned in the cupboard under the rostrum. It was cleaned by Ken Minson, and put on display in a cabinet provided by Mrs C. Kellow, lined in red velvet by Elsie Mitchell, and lit by John Tredrea. On March 26, 1995, the church was rededicated after further renovations carried out by volunteers from the membership (Fig. 9.8).

Fig.9.8. *Lanner Wesley Chapel Harvest Thanksgiving. The rostrum has been painstakingly decorated by Alice Langford and Maud Nicholls, c.1930s.* (© Rhona Blatchford, Lanner).

The membership of the Wesleyan Chapel in former times generally thought themselves more 'well to do' than the congregations of the other village chapels and the Church. Elderly residents can remember some of the strict and almost pretentious chapel-goers in the old days. One member always arrived last to take his seat in the front of the chapel, 'so everybody would glaaze at 'n as 'ee traapsed up front in 'is Sunday toggery'. He always wore kid gloves and never went out without a spare one. 'Ow 'ee come carry a spare glove weth 'ee all the time?' asked a female member of the congregation. 'You ought to knaw,' he said in a grand voice, 'I do 'ave two to wear and one to flinkey!'[18]

Lanner Wesley Sunday School

The present Sunday School of the Lanner Methodists was first formed in 1828, and a book 'Rules of Lanner Wesleyan Sunday School (new edition 1899)' is in existence. The 'Objects of the School' were the religious instruction of the scholars on the Sabbath Day, and the last rule was that the rules should be read out to the teachers and scholars once a quarter. Prizes were awarded for good attendance; W. D. Holman was presented with *The Bristol Tune Book* in September 1900 for regular attendance.

The new schoolroom was built by Richard Jacob in 1902, and was 62 feet by 24 feet, and in addition to the main room there were six classrooms, which, by the removal of partitions could have been thrown into one room.[19] The building was able to accommodate 300 children, so it was certainly a thriving organisation. Mrs Knuckey, formerly of Tocopilla, gave £170 towards the total cost of £1000 for the building. There were separate entrances for boys and girls.

At the Stone-laying Ceremony, the importance of Sunday School work was stressed. Presiding as Chairman of the District, the Revd E.J. Brailsford said, 'To plant a Sunday School is an important work, for it may be the means of keeping many souls from darkness'. This theme was taken up at much greater length by Sir George Smith presiding at the public meeting held in the evening. 'I feel that England is stronger for every Sunday School in our midst... in this county with so many leaving for foreign countries we are sowing for future ripening. Many encouragement's have come to me from across the Atlantic.'[20]

At a bazaar held in Lanner in late 1902 to raise money to help the building funds, it was stated by Mrs J.H. Tregonning that some of the stone from the only chapel in the Parish in which John Wesley was known to have preached was being used in the construction of the new Wesleyan Sunday School.[21] It is possible that the 'chapel' referred to could have been the Octagon Chapel at Carharrack, or alternatively, one of the early cottage meeting houses mentioned above, whose location is now lost to us.

The importance attached to the opening of the new building, in May 1903, is revealed in the teacher's Log Book of Lanner School. The entry notes that lunch was cut by fifteen minutes, and the School closed fifteen minutes early on a Thursday morning 'to give the children (who wished to go) time to prepare themselves for attending the opening ceremony of the new Wesleyan Sunday School'.

On Sunday mornings, pupils were expected to sit through the service in a group, in the charge of the Superintendent and one or two teachers. A 'Children's Address' might brighten up the proceedings, and perhaps a hymn appropriate to their youth was sung. Moving into the schoolroom for the afternoon session, the procedure would have followed a similar pattern.

In quite early times, a 'Methodist Catechism' was introduced. It was issued to each scholar in the form of a booklet, and contained a lengthy series of questions and answers. A certain number to be learnt would be set each week as a sort of homework, and tested orally by the teacher the following Sunday. This was not necessarily compulsory, but it earned an extra mark if one participated. Star cards were issued at the beginning of each new school year, and were used to record attendance. They grew grubbier and more tattered week by week! By the late 1930s, the Junior and Senior Guild had an outing to Newquay each year. Five Marigold buses, owned by Newton Trewern, who lived in what is now the Manse, took them to the seaside with baskets of food, pasties, meat and apples and cream. This 'feast' was washed down with 'herby beer', a non-alcoholic beverage made in a bath, with Masons extract and yeast, and sold for a penny a bottle.

Gradually, despite the Children's Address and the occasional outing to somewhere like Perranporth, arranged by Ewart Opie to reward 'the Sunday morning regulars', numbers attending the Sunday School dwindled. By the mid 1950s, it was evident that it was the only children attending were those with parents who were regular chapel-goers, and who perhaps brought along a friend or a relative. Alice Opie then started the 'Morning Stars', taking the children below the age of about ten years into the Vestry after the second hymn. Activities, such as 'colouring in' of illustrated Bible texts and Christmas Cards, supplemented short stories.

'Mothering Sunday' celebrations became a major Sunday School event within the morning service, with musical items and readings provided by the children, and the presentation of gifts for mothers. Attendance at afternoon school was dwindling significantly, and eventually the afternoon sessions ceased. The general pattern of life was changing, with alternative ways of spending a Sunday afternoon competing very successfully with the old Sunday School sessions. The 'Morning Stars' disappeared, replaced by Morning Sunday School for all ages of children, after the second hymn. Alice Opie was the Superintendent, and different age groups were taught in separate places in the chapel and school buildings.

One product of the 'Morning Stars' was a playgroup for pre-school children, held in the Lower Vestry on Thursday afternoons. This eventually developed into a full playgroup, run in the Schoolroom. Barbara Minson, Maureen Thompson and later, Ruby Penglase, provided musical accompaniment. Mrs Underhill also played a great part in the activities when she came to the village with her husband, the Minister. The playgroup developed into a 'Mother and Toddler' session, and there is a record, in July 1987, of Barbara Minson leading a trip to Portreath. Gillian Langford took over as leader from Barbara, and the group still runs, complementing the pre-school playgroup, which developed separately from the church, and is run in the Village Hall.

'Lanner Hill' Wesleyan Association

In the 1851 Religious Census for Lanner, there is mention of a Lanner Wesleyan Association, which had a chapel able to accommodate a large congregation, with 510 free seats, and 460 paid for. To house a congregation of this size, a substantial building would have existed. There are references to this being in the Lanner Hill area, and the date of consecration of the chapel is reputed to have been 1828, likely to be an error for 1838–39. There appears to have been a good following for this denomination, which split with the Wesleyan Church in the early 1830s; the 1851 census reports that, during the day, 600 worshippers and 240 Sunday School pupils attended the chapel. There is considerable confusion as to where the chapel was located, but it seems likely that 'Lanner Hill' referred to South Downs, where in 1837, the foundation for the Wesleyan Methodist Association Chapel had been laid. It opened two years later, and was capable of seating 200 people.

This chapel closed because few people attended, but reopened on Sunday 14 October 1849, after repairs had been made, in the aftermath of a cholera epidemic which swept the district. Such crowds attended the opening services, at which Mr Ellery preached two sermons, that hundreds were unable to gain admission. It was reported that the chapel was afterwards well attended, being mostly full, even on the weekday evenings. A class was formed which promised well, and a Sunday school of 70 scholars was thriving.[22] This chapel stood on the site of the southern end of Chapel Terrace.

In 1857 the Wesleyan Association merged with the Wesleyan Reform Society to become the United Methodist Free Church (UMFC). A further union came in 1907, when the UMFC merged with the Bryanites to become the United Methodist Church. The chapel was known as Hancock's, perhaps after the society steward, J. Hancock of Mount Pleasant, Redruth, and was closed in 1905 and subsequently demolished in 1908–9. The stone from this place of worship was used to build two more houses of a terrace which has perpetuated the memory of the existence of this former chapel – Chapel Terrace.

Lanner Moor Primitive Methodist Chapel

In 1825, William Clowes (founder of Primitive Methodism from Staffordshire) came to Redruth to speak to a congregation of breakaway Wesleyans, led by William Turner, one of O'Bryan's helpers. This led to a rapid development of Primitive Methodism in Cornwall, and the first society in Lanner was at Rough Street in 1831–34. The Society had three names in this period – 'Lanner', 'Rough Street', and 'Lanner Downs'. The most members it had at any one time was 13, and the rent at Rough Street in 1833 was five shillings a year.[23] It would be interesting to know where the meetings were held as there were few houses in Rough Street, according to the 1843 Tithe Map, and Church Row had not been built by that date.

It was common for meetings to be held in cottages, or farm out-buildings in the days before a chapel was built to accommodate a growing congregation. Most of Cornwall's Methodist churches derive from simple 'house churches'. Joseph Morcom, born in 1805, who worked as an engine man at Ting Tang Mine, was one young man attracted by the Primitive Methodists, becoming a member and a class leader at Rough Street in 1831, at South Downs in 1832, and later the Superintendent at Carn Marth Primitive Methodist Chapel.

The organisation in Lanner appeared to peter out, which was not unusual, since Primitive Methodism was stronger in the towns and found it more difficult to establish a strength in rural areas such as Lanner. It did reappear again, and at the second attempt the Primitive Methodists were holding cottage meetings at Lanner Moor in 1857, after Robert Tuffin had come and preached by the roadside. In 1858, a blacksmith's shop was secured for services, and number 9 Tresavean Terrace was rented from William Jory for 30 shillings a year to be used as a Sunday school. A relative of William Jory, Johanna Evans, was an early member of the chapel, and arranged the rental from him. The chapel was built in 1859–61 for £179, half the size of the present building.

Josiah Bawden, born in Breage in 1855, came to Lanner at the age of four. Converted to the church in 1875, he became a local preacher for 32 years.[24]

An 80-year lease was signed on 29 July 1884, between The Right Honourable Charles Henry Rolle, Baron Clinton, of Heanton Satchville, in Devon, and Joshua Williams, of Lanner. For a yearly rent of £3, Joshua Williams obtained the shop and premises on the land at Lanner Moor, in the Manor of Trevarth, together with the Lanner Moor Primitive Methodist Chapel which had been built in 1859–61. A further 90-year lease, still at a yearly rent of £3, was signed between Lord Clinton and Joshua Williams on 18 October 1897. This also covered Mr Williams' shop, the Lanner Moor Chapel, and the land on which they were built.

On 30 June 1876, the *Cornubian* mentioned the Lanner Loyal Philanthropic Association, which comprised members from 'Valley of Hope' Lodge No 34. Divine service followed the meeting, and was held in the Lanner Moor Primitive Methodist Chapel. William Knuckey was Treasurer and preached the sermon.

The chapel was extended in 1903–04, by 20 feet, by builders John Tiddy & Son, of Lanner, at the cost of £300. A new granite front was added, two extra windows installed and a boundary wall built around the chapel for safety. The chapel was re-seated to double the capacity to over 200

Fig.9.9. *Lanner Moor Primitive Methodist Chapel, after the extension in 1903. Note the 'leat' to the left of the lamp post, and the shops on either side of the chapel, which is now the Lanner Silver Band Room.* (Postcard by Bragg. © Royal Institution of Cornwall)

persons and the door was moved to its present position.[25] (Fig.9.9.). The door had formerly opened out on to the road and had a little porch built on to it for added safety as the road traffic increased through the village. The pulpit of the old chapel was on the east side with the choir on one side; on the other side was what was termed 'the Leader's Square'.

On 15 November 1921, the property leased to Joshua Williams was sold by the heirs of Lord Clinton to Joshua Williams, Miss Lilian Mary Williams, Miss Elsie Williams and Mrs Elizabeth Charlotte Blight. In 1937, the personal representatives of Joshua Williams, who had died in 1935, were Miss Lillian Williams, Mrs Elizabeth Trezona (née Williams) and Mrs Elizabeth Charlotte Blight. On 24 November 1937, these three ladies sold the chapel and the land on which it was built to the Trustees of the Lanner Moor Methodist Church. The house (formerly the shop) was sold to William Norman Dunstan and Kathleen Phyllis Dunstan on 12 July 1948. The Primitive Methodists came into the body of the Methodist Church at Union in 1932, and there were barely more than 800 Primitive Methodists in Cornwall at the time of Union.

Lanner Moor Sunday School started in Tresavean Terrace in 1858. Children went to Trevarth Wesleyan School in the morning, and Lanner Moor in the afternoon. In the early days, they had an alphabet class, which was in no way religious, and was aimed at teaching them to read. In later years, five Hitchens brothers in South Africa regularly sent donations home to the Sunday School. A new heating system was installed in 1946, and in 1951–54, there were further enlargements, a new vestry being added entirely by voluntary labour (Fig. 9.10).

Fig.9.10. *Interior of the Lanner Moor Primitive Methodist Chapel, after the 1903 renovation. Note the pull-down seats on the right.* (© Jack Evans, Camborne).

The first wedding was in 1957, between Leslie Goodland and Margaret Collins, who were married by the Revd Martin, and their daughter Linda was the last child to be baptised there, in the 1970s. The chapel celebrated its centenary in 1959, but dwindling numbers and increasing expense saw its closure in the 1970s, and in 1983, it was bought by Lanner and District Silver Band at the cost of £13 500. After improvements and repairs bringing the total cost to £16 000, it was declared open as their new band headquarters.

South Downs Wesleyan Chapel

There was a new chapel built on the site of the old South Downs chapel which had been built in about 1857. It was described as 'a very plain building', which was thatched and felt to be inadequate to the requirements of the place, and a larger building was rebuilt on a part of the site of the old chapel during 1887. It was opened in November of that year at a cost of £247, with a seating capacity of 150 people, £167.5s.6d having already been raised prior to opening services. A portion of the old chapel was retained and fitted up for a schoolroom at a cost of £19.7s.10d.[26] The memorial stone laying ceremony took place in June, four stones being laid by S. Chellew, R. Thomas, Tom Moore and Master S. G. Chellew, which realised £1.7s.6d. The front was described as being Gothic in design, an architectural style then very *en vogue,* with dressing of granite and facing of local stone (Fig.11.22). The roof in the interior was open with chamfered timbers, picked out in bright red. The walls were pointed to imitate stonework and were described as being of a salmon tint. The pews and communion rail were of pitch-pine, the former being without doors. The rostrum was comprised of pitch-pine, white wood and mahogany. The contractor for the masonry was J. Odgers, from whose design the Chapel was built, the carpenter, Mr Lee and the painter, Joseph James of Redruth.[27]

In December of 1887, it was reported that several concerts and teas to raise money for the Chapel's rebuilding had realised £43.10s., leaving about £40 to be raised.[28] However, the opening services were likely to have been remembered for some time afterwards by the congregation, for the scenes of impropriety which occurred during the lecture given by the Revd T. Clarke, entitled 'My Trip to America'. This was duly interrupted by Mr Wilton, a chapel member and trustee, who apparently did not understand some of the finer points in the Reverend Clarke's talk, and considered him to have been getting too political. He stood up and voiced his opinion much to the consternation of the appreciative audience who began to stamp and hiss, and shouts of 'turn him out!' resounded around the new chapel, described as the disgraceful scenes of a 'lynch mob' by one local newspaper!

In July 1893, it was recorded that substantial help had been received by the Chapel from former Sunday School Pupils. Master W.C. Sweet and Miss M.J. Sweet, aged 14 and 12, were among the donors. They acknowledged their obligation to South Downs school, and now lived five miles away from any place of worship, in Montana, USA.

In 1894, a Harvest Thanksgiving Platform Meeting is reported, which bear the hallmarks of proximity to Redruth Town, with a scaled down version of what had recently occurred in the Wesleyan Chapel there:

The Reverend Carvosso Spencer and Richard Penna delivered two earnest speeches, both calculated to draw the attention of the young to the necessity of a fair amount of well-directed labour to secure a healthy condition of body and soul as well as to ensure a bountiful corn harvest. The chapel was prettily decorated, the most striking features being two archways, one spanning each path, composed of corn and sunflowers, similar in design to one which appeared in the town chapel some weeks previously. Tomatoes, pears, apples and grapes were in abundance, while a large loaf of bread occupied a conspicuous position. This together with the fruit and vegetables were sold in the vestry at the conclusion of the service'.[29]

In 1902, proposals to build a new Sunday School room were put forward by Horace Collins, MSA.[30] The Chapel celebrated its Jubilee in 1937 with reunion services, an old fashioned Love Feast and high teas. In 1943, there was a presentation of a hymn book and certificate to J.H. Richards to celebrate 68 years in the choir. His son Henry Richards had been organist for 60 years, and had played the American Organ, whilst his father and Mr W. Richards on the violin, together accompanied the choir every Sunday. Alan Opie, the famous opera singer, sang as a young boy in the Sunday School choir at South Downs during the 1950s.

The building ceased to function as a Wesleyan Chapel in the early 1980s, briefly became an undertaker's 'Chapel of Rest', and is presently the Kingdom Hall of Jehovah's Witnesses, a thriving church with a large congregation drawn from Redruth and District.

Trevarth Wesleyan Methodist Chapel

On 3 February 1862, Lord Clinton leased to Thomas Bawden, a yeoman, 'all that piece or plot of land in which a school house had then lately been erected, at Trevarth', for a term of 99 years from 4 June 1861.[31] Thomas Bawden then sold the schoolroom and land for £25, to a group of men acting as trustees for what became the Trevarth Wesleyan Chapel, and the Reverend James Mitchell of the Parish of Gwennap, superintendent preacher of the circuit in the Methodist Connexion. The yearly rent was 10 shillings. There were 25 trustees, most being merchants, farmers, artisans and mine agents.

It is probable that the Wesleyan schoolroom had served as a temporary meeting house prior to its becoming a chapel included in the Gwennap Methodist Circuit. (We have seen that it was functional in 1858 when scholars from the Primitive Methodists came to use it on Sundays.). The chapel had 60 sittings, all free. In 1875 the chapel had 351 scholars, but the congregation gradually dwindled away, suffering greatly at the close of the nineteenth century from declining membership due to emigration.

Indeed, the Gwennap Circuit register of 1890 stated, 'This was formerly the most flourishing mining district in Cornwall. Not a single mine is at work, and the foundry [at Perranwell] is abandoned. The population has decreased by

Fig.9.11. *The Trevarth Wesleyan Chapel (1950), after it was no longer in use as a place of worship, but before conversion to a private residence, with two storeys.* (© Paul Annear, Probus)

near 50 per cent, and many of the members are aged women. There is great difficulty to get circuit stewards, and chapel debts mount. At nearby Carharrack, there is a great deficiency of men.'[32] In March 1909, the Society Steward was J. Taylor, from Carharrack, and one of the preachers was F. Austice, of Trevarth, but the declining congregation and membership numbers eventually conspired to close the chapel. In 1929, permission to sell the building and surrounding land, 66 square yards in extent, was granted by the President of the Methodist Conference.[33] Planning permission to turn the former chapel into a private residence was given in 1951. The single storey structure was converted into a two storey house, and may be seen on the right side of the road opposite the house named 'Clinton Villa', just after the sharp bend in the road from Lanner to Carharrack through Trevarth (Fig.9.11).

Carn Marth Primitive Methodist Chapel

According to Probert, there were two societies at Carn Marth. The first was in existence by 1830, and lasted until about 1839. Among the membership was Joseph Morcom, who was the Superintendent of the Sunday School. The second lasted from 1852 to 1877. A chapel was built on the slopes of Carn Marth in 1858 (and possibly opened in 1859). It was registered as a place of worship on 7 December 1860, the minister noted as the Reverend Joseph Best of Redruth.

The remains of this chapel lie at the back of a house above Sandy Lane, where two footpaths join, one going west to Sandy Lane, the other north to join the Busveal Road. The chapel was built at a cost of £29, and seated 56 (12 pews being 'paid-for'). By 1866 it had been enlarged, and new pews were installed. Membership in 1836 was 17, and in 1865, 26. The Sunday School Anniversary of 12 July 1868 was held in the South Downs Wesleyan Chapel, kindly lent for the occasion. But the membership declined through emigration, and in 1879, the chapel was sold. There was another Primitive Methodist society nearby at South Downs from 1834 to 1839, and in 1836 it had 14 members.[34]

Chapel organs and organists

Prior to the era of the harmonium, and later the organ, the various chapels and also the parish church, had to rely on a group of musicians playing violins, violas, cellos, basses, ophicleides, bassoons, and the curious 'serpent', to provide musical accompaniment for the choir and congregation. The orchestra was often housed in a gallery, which were taken down after the arrival of harmoniums and organs. In 1846, various new instruments were purchased for the Wesleyan Chapel at a cost of £3. The account for the serpent (a wooden reed-instrument) in 1847 was noted as £1.5s.[35] Joseph Pryor, a village blacksmith (1810–1880), was a leader of such an orchestra, being an expert player on the cello and violin, and was well acquainted with the serpent. He was a prolific composer of carols, anthems and hymn tunes, which, although never published, were well known and loved in the neighbourhood, being handed around in manuscript. Some Pryor tunes eventually found their way into the 'old' Methodist hymn book. A contemporary of Aaron Woolf and Thomas Broad, Joseph Pryor did not compose on ordinary staves but recorded his ideas on paper by means of figures. The tunes were fugal in style, the most well known carol being 'The Moon's Pale Beams Were Shining'. His funeral anthem, written in a minor key, 'Blessed are the Dead', and his Easter hymn were also very popular. Christmas in Lanner would not have passed without the strains of a party of glee singers singing one of Pryor's tunes.

In 1869, the harmonium player at Lanner Wesley, Miss Trebilcock, was paid £2 for playing the instrument that year. In 1889, the Wesleyan Chapel was closed for three months, to undergo extensive renovations, including the opening of the end of the chapel to build an organ chamber. This space was spanned by a bold and effective arch, moulded and supported by Ionic pilasters. The recess was taken out of the vestry at the back, which was then divided into two rooms.[36] The whole chapel was redecorated and the entrance lobby was renovated in anticipation of the arrival of the organ. Permission was granted by the Wesleyan Chapel Committee in 1890, for the organ to be installed in the Lanner Wesley Chapel, the original makers being Messrs Fleetwood of Camborne.

In 1903, the instrument, now in situ, was brought forward three feet from the organ chamber. It needed little attention until 1924–25, when it was overhauled by a Plymouth firm.

In 1939, a ten thousand shilling scheme was inaugurated as an Organ Renovation Fund, but due to the outbreak of war, the rebuilding did not start until October 1947. The loft was extended by three feet into the Choir Vestry, giving better access for tuning and repair. Thomas Born presented an electric blower to the church. Walter H. Langford and a band of helpers gave many hours' voluntary labour to the extension of the organ chamber, as well as constructing a new stairway to the choir vestry. The work was estimated to have exceeded £800, a sum raised by the members, while reopening services realised another £63. The organ at Lanner

Methodist Church today presents a stunning spectacle in all its ornate Baroque splendour, displaying much gold and pastel pink and blue, and puts one in mind of the Marenghi and Gaviolli organs which graced the fairgrounds earlier this century (Fig.9.8).

A good organist was highly valued, and often the ability of the player helped to determine the size of a congregation. Lanner people were known to have changed their allegiance from one denomination to another, purely to follow a good organist. In 1883, an interesting case involving a village organist made the press. Entitled, 'Lanner Methodees and Bryanites', the report brought to light some interesting skulduggery. 'The Methodees had a harmonium player and I suppose he was not up to much; at any rate, the choir and the congregation did not speak very favourably of his playing', began the report. 'The Bryanites had a player also, and one able to play pretty well, and if he was as strong in other points as in that, things would have gone on differently.'

Apparently, the Wesleyans had set out to obtain the Bryanites' organist at all costs. It appeared that the organist concerned, a timid man, was bullied by the Captain of Tresavean Mine into accepting the offer to play instead at the Wesleyan Chapel. The report concluded with the statement, 'Still, one must not be too hard in this direction, for it won't do for a man that a wife dependent on him has, to run so great a risk, so as to get heaved out of the bal (mine).'[37] Here we have direct evidence of the influence exerted over the community by a Methodist Mine Captain.

Lanner Wesley has had a succession of organists, including Mrs Bessie Tregonning, who played the American Organ until the installation of the pipe organ in 1890. Her sister Miss Kate Mitchell was her deputy, and her husband, J.H. Tregonning was choirmaster at the same time. James Bailey was the first organist of the new instrument. He was followed by Mr Thomas until 1904, when Harry Veall, proprietor of the local bakery, operating in Lanner Square, took over for many years, until he eventually moved to St Austell.

John Ivan Gill was appointed about 1919, and served for 28 years. He kept a smallholding at Cox Hill (Twelveheads), and cycled from there to a weekly choir practice, and two, sometimes three, Sunday services. He also gave piano and organ lessons. Mr Gill is remembered as never being punctual, affording much humour among the waiting congregation, who speculated audibly as to which cow or calf would provide an excuse for his being late. He was a very robust organist, 'literally belting out the music when emphasis was required', and the hymn 'Eternal Father, Strong to Save' always gave him the opportunity to thunder out the storm effects. Much consternation was caused in Lanner when he announced, in 1947, that he wanted to leave, to become organist at Copperhouse, Hayle.

A young man from Troon came to the rescue. One day in 1947, Reverend Frank White and Ewart Opie, representing the Chapel, called at the house of Donald Bennetts, an electrician who was carrying out major alterations in his own house. After much discussion, Donald was persuaded to take on the position of organist and choirmaster at Lanner Wesley for a couple of weeks, to help out. He stayed on, but rebuilding of the pipe organ meant that he had to improvise for twelve months on the American Organ. He persevered, the old tracker action organ was remodelled in 1948, and in 1972, his 25 years' service was marked by a presentation of a gift to buy a picture. In 1987, Donald Bennetts' fortieth anniversary saw him presented with a leather music case.

Remarkably, at the time of writing, Donald is still there. Among his achievements was the introduction of oratorios and cantatas for the choir to perform, and perhaps the most ambitious was 'The Darkest Hour', with orchestral accompaniment. Apart from his musical contributions, he is a good photographer, always ready to help in recording church events, and giving slide shows. He also made two new hymn boards for the chapel.

Although there were only two organists at the chapel in 75 years, a number of deputies have come and gone. Stephen Andrew helped J. Ivan Gill before moving to Pencoys. Miss Mabel Pryor or Joseph Pryor could be relied upon in emergencies, and Willie Knuckey (son of T. C. Knuckey), one of Mr Gill's pupils, was appointed Official Deputy from the age of twelve. When Ivan Gill left, Willie took over until a temporary organist, Mr Swayne, was appointed, then Donald Bennetts eventually took over.

For many years, Willie Bray was the Organ Blower at Lanner Wesley. He operated the wooden hand pump in the Choir Vestry, and was a well-liked comic character, known as the 'snorter' because of the noise he made when he was pumping. His high hat, quaint ways and mode of speech caused him to be the victim of much good-humoured leg-pulling and practical jokes. When the minister announced a certain hymn, Willie was once heard to say to the organist, 'You can play what you like, but I'm goin' to blaw "Lead Kindly Light"!' He lived with his mother, and for years did not work. For a time, in the 1930's, he was kept by the 'Parish Pay', just a few shillings a week. His passing marked the end of an era; the organ is now blown electrically.

Wilfred Bray junior, of Carn Marth was, during the 1930s, the organist at the 'Bryanites' or United Methodists' Chapel (UMC). He also did spells at Lanner Moor Methodist Chapel, and he was well followed on the circuit as an extremely skilled organist. He learned to play at six years old, and composed music for local choirs and brass bands (Fig.9.12). The UMC Choir were expected to rehearse in his small cottage at Pilcher's Row on Carn Marth. Those who had been absent had to pay a fine of one penny into a wooden box, the contents of which went to chapel funds. When Wilfred Bray was the regular organist, the congregation at the U.M.C. was swelled, as were the funds! In 1958 a new pipe organ from Adjewhella Chapel was installed at the Lanner Moor Chapel. Mrs Kate Penglase served as organist for 27 years, teaching music. One of her pupils, Mrs Elsie Mitchell, succeeded her as organist. Some time later, the

Fig.9.12. *The choir of the 'Bryanite' or United Methodist Chapel, c.1934. Wilfred Bray, organist, is in the middle row, seventh from the left.* (© Lance Bray, Lanner)

present organist at St. Day, George Evans, did quite a spell. Paul and Dorothy Langford and just before the chapel closed, Christine Langford and Nancy Treloar, were organists.

In 1973, a 100 year-old single-manual organ was installed in South Downs Chapel which replaced a harmonium. For 50 years, it had been used at Twelveheads chapel, and was then bought by Mr Dower, a nurseryman at Pennance, Lanner, who had a bedroom floor cut away at his cottage so that the organ could stand in the kitchen. It stayed there for 40 years, until 1960, when it was bought for Wheal Busy Chapel. When that chapel closed in 1973, the organ was acquired by South Downs. It was 'opened' by Ethel Odgers, at 86 years, the oldest member of the church. This story illustrates the value placed on the organs in the chapels, and the care with which they were preserved and passed on from one chapel to another. (Fig. 9.13)

Fig.9.13. *The Dedication of the new organ at the South Downs Methodist (former Wesleyan) Church in 1973. This organ stood for many years at the Carn Marth home of Mr Dower.* (© Mr and Mrs Paul Langford, Lanner).

The Manses and their Residents.

In the original Redruth Wesleyan Circuit, the Minister in charge of Lanner Wesley was housed in the 'manse' at 15 Trewirgie Road, Redruth. This continued until the restructuring programme for Methodist Union began. Following the Revd J.W. Garforth in the early 1920s, Revd and Mrs Joseph Coombs kept up the general welcome for members of the church in the manse, as did W.H. Noble, Frank T. Copplestone and George Merritt. With Methodist Union, it became necessary to bring the Minister to the centre of his area, and a semi-detached house was purchased in Lanner.

Number 2, Glen View had just been constructed by C.W. Langford, and was the Lanner Manse for many years. The first residents at 2, Glen View were the Reverend and Mrs Geoffrey Parrinder, and Geoffrey Parrinder was a member of the Lanner Civil Defence Corps during the Second World War, while his wife walked to and from Redruth Hospital where she was a wartime nurse.

They were followed by the Reverend E.C. Nicholls, and his wife, who founded the Lanner Amateur Dramatic Society, for which she was the producer. The Reverend Frank and Mrs Maud White followed, then the Reverend Alan and Mrs Freeman. The latter had young children and Alan had a very active ministry, dashing about on his moped to at least nine churches. He was involved in the Lanner Moor chapel extension scheme.

Newly ordained, Jack Mitchell had been upgraded from the role of Pastor, and had already ministered to three churches in the Stithians area – Hendra, Penmenor and Penmarth. He came to Lanner in 1954, and combined the two sections, becoming very popular with the young people in the area. The Reverend Mitchell remarked that 'the manse at Lanner was a great improvement, having all the facilities: running water, indoor toilet, bathroom and the good old Cornish range in the kitchen'.[38] He married 'Sister Lily' while he lived at 2, Glen View.

The Reverend and Mrs K.A.J. Martin came into this enlarged ministry, and were followed by Ian and Margaret Haile, and then Malcolm and Tricia Adams. Margaret Haile inaugurated the Young Wives Group, which is still running today, albeit not as the young wives group! Ian eventually became Chairman of the Cornwall District. In 1966, Number 10, Lanmoor, a bungalow, was built and purchased as the new Manse during Michael Adams' ministry. The Reverend G.W. Griffiths, Superintendent Minister, conducted a dedication ceremony one Saturday afternoon. Ivor and Maureen Thompson, Edgar and Kathleen Roberts, and Stanley and Lillian Underhill followed Michael Adams. The accommodation in the Manse was still not totally suitable, and 'Epworth', a much larger house in Lanner Square, was bought during the Underhills' ministry. This house had been constructed by Newton Trewern on the site of the old Miners' Arms alehouse, belonging to the Gray family. The site had been a dump for some years, after the alehouse was demolished.

The manse was named 'Epworth' after the rectory in the town of that name, in which the Wesley brothers were brought up by their High Church father.

'Epworth' is still the Lanner Manse today, and the Underhills were followed by Colin and Lorraine Allen, who spent a long period there, before the Keast family replaced them in 1993. The Reverend A. Keast was a strong supporter of 'Christian Zionism' and had spent much time in Israel. In 1997, the Reverend and Mrs Anthony Keast left the Methodist Circuit to set up a Christian Guest House at Portreath called 'Fountain Springs'. The Revd A. Keast was succeeded by the Reverend David Bolton.

Financial Support

When the early followers of John Wesley broke away from the Church of England, they set themselves and generations of their successors upon a never-ending series of fund raising activities. Each new breakaway among their ranks, and there were many of them, added to the trail of financial dilemmas. The minutes of very early meetings provide a picture of this struggle. At Lanner Wesley, total income for the Michaelmas Quarter of 1858 was £14.13s.11d. Disbursements for the Quarter were Quarter Board £13.3s.2d, Steward's Book 1s.6d, Debt payment £1.9s.3d. This left a 'remaining debt' of £1.7s.4d. By the end of the Christmas Quarter, the debt was 4s.6d, and by the Lady Day Quarter of the following year, there was a balance in hand of 16 shillings. The balance fluctuated over the years, but by February 1879, it was still only 6d.

One of the main ways in which money was raised in the last century was through seat rents, recorded as 20 shillings per year at Lanner Wesley in 1884. On average, the Wesleyans could expect to realise anywhere between £20–30 per year in this way. By comparison, the Lanner Moor Primitive Chapel with a far smaller congregation, was fortunate to collect £9 per annum. This money, although vital, was never enough, and so the Churches were always devising ingenious ways of meeting costs, and continued initiating new projects undaunted.

We have seen above the ingenuity shown by the Bryanites in holding three services during the course of the reopening of their chapel in 1866, collections at which helped to reduce the debt on the building. Weekly collections at all services which came into fashion around the 1880s, and eventually an 'envelope' scheme involving a weekly commitment independent of attendance, became the mainstay of fund raising.

The self-help contribution of church members to schemes like building alterations and decorating was significant. Bazaars were first mentioned in Lanner in the 1860s, after they had become fashionable in the nearby towns. The 1875 bazaar of the Wesleyan Chapel, held in a field, raised almost £150 from five stalls, and saw the sale of a washing machine, a sewing machine, an ottoman, a case of minerals, a walnut table, a gipsy crock, picks and shovels, as well as a variety of clothing and other household goods and refreshments. This was a new method of fund raising, and church organisers were not permitted to use the Lanner Schoolrooms for bazaars until the 1890s. A two-day event, beginning on Boxing Day, became a major activity for Lanner Wesley in the early years of this century. A Souvenir Booklet for this Bazaar of 26 and 27 December 1911 was full of quaint and nonsensical quotations, including:

They say that men have sprung from apes,
But cannot tell us how, or when,
Or why some apes retain their shapes
While others develop into men.

Charles Corfield contributed: 'He that stayeth in the valley will never get over the hill'. Of course, bazaars were held at other times in the year, such as the one held in Lanner School, in aid of the building of a new Sunday School, on Easter Monday, 1896. About £50 was raised. Direct giving started in 1908, when it was decided to raise at least £165 over the following twelve months. The Reverend Hicks offered to devote three days in the Spring Quarter to a canvass of all members. Money subscriptions were invited to cover costs before embarking on a project. Tea Treats, Harvest Suppers and especially Anniversaries were real money-spinners, the sale of programmes for concerts and entertainments, and charges for food and drinks raising much needed money.

The collections for the 1888 Wesleyan Sunday School Anniversary raised over £10 through the collection during the service, but a breakdown of the collection immediately shows us that it was a mere handful of individuals which gave the lion's share of the total. Nine hundred and seventy halfpennies, 697 pennies, 225 three penny pieces, 36 six penny pieces, 13 shillings and a half sovereign made up the total.[39] Most of the money raised for the chapels and the church in this way came from a small number of regular better-off members of the congregation drawn mainly from the village middle class.

Among other money-making schemes mentioned in chapel records are: Treasure Hunts, Mile of Pennies, 'Buy a Brick' in building undertakings, Ten Thousand Shilling Scheme, Flower Festivals, Interest Free Loans, Pickled Onion Sales, Waste Paper Collections, Jumble Sales, Chopped wood sales, and Bring-and-Buy stalls. Thomas Knuckey of Melrose House even bagged the conkers which fell off his horse chestnut trees to sell for Chapel funds! Earlier this century, Lanner Wesley entertained the community with the film 'The Guv'nor', with George Arliss, shown in the Lanner Wesley schoolroom, in aid of the Junior Guild Outing Fund, 'Adults 6d, Children 3d. One night Only'. The 1994 '100 Years of Lanner' Exhibition was just one in a long line of these events, which added to the colour of social life in the village, as well as boosting the funds supporting the Lanner Methodist Church.

Lanner acquired quite a reputation for its vigorous fund-raising capabilities, a local paper remarking in 1903, 'Of all Cornish villages, Lanner should undoubtedly be given the cake for wealth.'[40] This comment was in connection with the spate of building activities which followed the end of the Boer War, and optimism about the possible reworking of Tresavean Mine.

Revivals and Missions

Periodic revivals were common features of nineteenth century Methodism, and were the means through which the various chapels gained members. Such revivals often lasted for several days and even weeks, until the religious zeal had burnt itself out. Central to Cornish Methodism was evangelism, the aim of which was to save souls by bringing them to the Lord through conversion. Methodism won for itself a leading position in Cornish popular culture from the late eighteenth century to the early nineteenth century by strongly establishing itself in communities, particularly in industrial areas. It came to provide such industrial communities with a special identity, and was noted for its brand of local control within its chapels.

The most effective method of such control was through revivals, which recruited members by initiating mass-conversions. The early nineteenth century witnessed scores of revivals, particularly in the mining towns and villages, which swept through the neighbourhood from chapel to chapel, such as those reported in the Redruth area in 1849 and 1874.

The 1849 Revival began before the outbreak of cholera in the Redruth area, and reached its peak during the epidemic; the class of persons converted were mainly those of the working or labouring classes, chiefly miners. The revival was noted for its degree of decorum, 'with less noise and vociferation than usual, the order has been remarkable'.[41] South Downs Wesleyan Association Chapel was said to have taken an active part in this revival, and many people were added to the congregation. In 1882, the local press noted religious revivals in almost every village in the district, and in 1888, the *Cornubian* carried the report of a large revival at Lanner Wesley Chapel, where it was thought 60 more people had been added to the congregation.

It is interesting to note that revivals often occurred during economic upswings. The 1849 Revival came at the time of the Californian Gold Rush, and the revivals of the 1880s coincided with a period of relative prosperity during the building boom in the Redruth area. In Lanner, hopes for a new period of economic greatness were stimulated by the reopening of Tresavean Mine in the early 1880s, thus suggesting a direct relationship between religious revivals and upturns in the local economy. Emigration would slow down and chapel congregations would not be so depleted, thus creating a feel good factor. Often the gain was quickly lost and membership numbers were seldom stable, but rose and fell regularly, bearing a resemblance to the swings in the local economy which was closely governed by the prices of copper and tin. The latter mineral was particularly subject to huge fluctuations. We also find that chapel buildings or extensions, often begun in good times, were not completed before the unstable local economy took a nose dive, creating financial headaches.

In 1901, the Primitive Methodists at Lanner Moor reported such old style revivals which resulted in an increase in membership numbers, but by the twentieth century, revivals were being superseded by 'missions'. The decline in the revivalist approach to Methodism can be attributed to the growing influence of the Wesleyan Conference which preferred a steadier and less volatile form of management, recruitment and expansion. This new evangelistic approach saw charismatic local preachers, agents or even ministers from other denominations travelling widely throughout the

Fig.9.14. *The visit to Lanner of Pastor Yates was marked by a gathering in Lanner village square, about 1936. Ewart Opie is on the right of the front row.* (photo by Tom Roskrow, Truro. © Royal Institution of Cornwall, Truro)

district initiating mass conversions. Such a mission was recorded in Lanner about 60 years ago, when the famous orator Pastor Yates visited the village (Fig.9.14). His coming was heralded by the sight of a large banner in the square, which read: 'Great Evangelistic Mission and Young Life Campaign, Now Proceeding Nightly. Christ For All, All For Christ'. The tedium and monotony of life was lifted through such evangelism, which did much to characterise Cornish Chapel life for so long.

Chapel Anniversaries

To celebrate the anniversary of their founding, each chapel held an annual celebration. At Lanner Wesley, the first 'Anniversary' was held on Sunday 5 March 1904, and on the following Thursday. This probably celebrated the anniversary of the chapel's reopening, rather than its original opening. A Special Anniversary was held at Lanner Wesley on Sunday, 29 October 1978, to celebrate 150 years of Methodism in Lanner. In later years, the celebrations switched to the present timing of a Sunday in late March, often coinciding with Holy Week, and until very recently also on the Thursday following. In former years, the morning and evening services would probably have had visiting preachers, such as the current Chairman of the District. In the afternoons, programmes of sacred music were given, with the Chapel Choirs giving of their best, often with guest soloists. These concerts would attract large congregations, including people from outside the Church. Events during the week were aimed at fund-raising for the upkeep of the buildings. The Trevarth Wesleyan Chapel Anniversary was held on the first Sunday in December. But far greater occasions were those of the Sunday Schools.

Sunday School Anniversaries

In the first half of this century, the Sunday School Anniversaries were great events in the life of the village. Congregations were large, sometimes overflowing, and were a real 'gathering of the clans', attracting former scholars and friends from far and wide, and were yet another manifestation of Lanner's distinctive village identity (Fig.9.15).

On the first Sunday in May, the Lanner Wesley Sunday School Anniversary was held. Known as the 'Top Dogs', they attracted the practical jokes and other spoofs played by non attendees, members of other chapels, and even the Church, as they approached their chapel. The Lanner Wesley anniversary became known facetiously as the 'Lanner Show Fair' because of the display of new clothing worn by the participants. One resident of Grays Terrace who remembered the ladies coming up through the village on their way to the chapel in the 1950s, in all their finery, commented 'the hats were outrageous, rivalling anything seen at Royal Ascot!' One visitor to the Bryanite Chapel in 1882 commented in the local press that he had never before seen such elegant clothing, particularly the scores of women's black velvet dresses.[42] The ladies in particular went to great lengths to outdo each other with their hats and costumes, and if someone arrived looking better than the rest, it was said 'you could see the other women in a grubby, whisperin' and tisperin', and geking down their nawses at 'er. They'd 'ave cut tha throat weth a oiled feather!'[43]

Lanner Wesleyan Sunday School Anniversary always brought huge crowds to the village; a local reporter at the turn of the century believed that many friends would be taking their accustomed walk to Lanner on May Sunday, 'just to have a peep at the smiling faces and the profusion of new costumes which are displayed there on that day. It is certainly a red letter day for Lanner. The Wesley Chapel is not large enough to hold nearly the number of people.'[44]

The fame of the event often aroused jealousy amongst those of a different denomination, or those who never attended chapel, and it is perhaps to one such person that we owe the following slightly malicious report of the May Sunday proceedings: 'the previous week's parade had not been up to the usual form. In ladies' dresses there was a distinct reminder of the jumble sale. One belle was very smart, but wore second hand boots a size too large. Another was very gay but wore odd gloves, which were worn at the fingers. The 'Prince's' trousers were gone at the knees, and the cigarettes were very cheap.' The 'Grand Swell' and the 'Prayer Boss' were also not up to standard; the report continued that the latter, who should have had his hat ironed gave the whole show away, 'yet he looked as contented as a calf chewing a dishcloth'.[45]

Earlier this century a group of seven to eight friends, heavy drinkers who frequented pubs far and wide, earned themselves the nickname of 'The Lanner Oil Brigade'. One of the group was Frank Trethowan, a Churchgoer, and the 'book man' at Tresavean Mine. Every year this group continued the customary pranks which had been carried out on Anniversary Sunday for years, hanging signs on the lamp posts and placing white arrows on walls directing people to the anniversary. One year they painted a huge whitewashed

Fig.9.15. *The Serpentine Dance in Lanner Square in 1909, a well known part of the Lanner Wesleyan Sunday School Anniversary. Note Knuckey's grocery store, and the 'stannins' and roundabout (far right) at the end of Prisk's Terrace.* (© Royal Institution of Cornwall, Truro)

sign in the middle of the road which stated 'this way to Lanner Show Fair'. People thought that this was going too far, and a court case was brought against them at Penryn. It was said that Mr Morrish, one of the group, was reduced to a nervous wreck with worry![46]

It was probably The Lanner Oil Brigade who were responsible for placing a banner in the square on the occasion of a visit to the anniversary of a preacher named Joseph Coombes. The banner read 'HELLO JO, COME TO THE SHOW' which really angered the chapel-goers. Likewise, a person with a rather wicked sense of humour was responsible for defacing a privy wall which stood in a garden of a cottage going up Lanner Hill. Being somewhat civic minded, the person who lived in this particular cottage had placed a sign, 'LANNER SHOW FAIR' on the whitewashed wall, indicating that people attending the Anniversary could use the toilet. The prankster had carefully scrawled underneath, 'PENNY A S ----'! Needless to say, the writing caused considerable offence among the visitors and chapel members, most of whom did not see the funny side of it at all.

On the second Sunday in May, the 'Dog and Poultry Show' of the Lanner Moor Primitive Methodists' Sunday School Anniversary took place. This great rivalry between the various church groups was continued by the 'Wild Beasts' of the Bible Christians of Lanner Hill:

Then down through the village would come the cheldurn, two wallopen g'eat bands strampen way in front. When they was on the stage you never heard such a hubbedullion! They was hollen and hooten to their mawthers an' faathers who was sittin' grizzlen all awver their chacks – some proud they was! Then the cheldurn was gallivantin up an' down, haelen and draggin' till their clothes was in lerrups – so you can see how twas called the 'Wild Beast Show!'"[47]

On the first Sunday in July, the South Downs Methodists had their anniversary (Fig.9.16).

SOUTH DOWNS
UNITED METHODIST FREE CHURCH
SUNDAY SCHOOL
ANNIVERSARY.

ON SUNDAY, JUNE 4TH, 1882,
Three Sermons will be Preached: In the Morning at 10-30, by
REV. F. CLEMENTS,
In the Afternoon at half-past 2, by
REV. E. T. HARRIS,
And in the Evening at 6 o'clock, by
MR. GEORGE SARA.

ON MONDAY EVENING, JUNE 5TH,
A PUBLIC MEETING
Will be held, when Addresses will be given by Revs. E. T. Harris, F. Clements, Mr. W. Wasley, and other Friends.
Chair to be taken at 7 o'clock by Mr. J. S. Hill.
The Children will give Recitations and sing the following Hymns during the Services.

REDRUTH:
J. S. DOIDGE, STEAM PRINTER, ETC., FORE STREET.

Fig.9.16. *The United Methodist Free Church, South Downs. Anniversary Programme for 1882.* (MR/R/59/A Cornwall Record Office © reserved)

Inside the various chapels, the Superintendent would announce the donations sent by people abroad and old members too distant to attend, and the scholars and teachers were sat in a prominent position. A set of special hymns was chosen for the service, and much effort went into practising them beforehand. New spring clothes were regarded as essential for these great occasions, especially for the choir. Besides the two regular morning and evening services, there was an afternoon event, also attracting a large congregation to a programme of miscellaneous items presented by the scholars, sometimes described as a 'demonstration'. This replaced a public meeting addressed by a speaker in the early days. In the 1970s, these events changed into plays and even a musical show. Irene Williams, of Tresavean Estate, recalls the Anniversary at Lanner Wesley in the 1930s.

The Lanner Show Fair, as the very dressy Lanner Wesley Anniversary was called, was on the first Sunday in May. It was out of this world, and we wouldn't dare tell anyone at school what colour or what style we were going to wear. The chapel would be full, with people sitting in the windows and on the stairs. People would arrive for evening service at five o'clock, as if you were not there before half past, you had to sit sideways downstairs on a form brought from the schoolroom. I remember my first dress was pale pink, all frills and bows with a white straw bonnet and white buckskin ankle strap shoes, and a tiny white handbag. We would all sing our hearts out, especially for the Choral March which usually had long choruses to every verse. Everybody gave it 'Bell Tink', as we used to call such strong singing! Then on Monday we would give a play in the schoolroom. The place would be packed and we would be all dressed up again, in crepe paper and green, white and yellow ribbons as it was usually something to do with Easter. By the time we had finished, we were glad to go home to bed. An old lady, Miss Lidgey, lived up by the church, and she used to take a photograph of all the children who lived in Church Row.

Tea Treats and other Sunday School Treats

Children attending Sunday School were given a reward from very early times, in the form of 'Tea Treats' and Prize-giving, usually taking the form of books. Children were given 'a saffron bun and pop' at some suitable field. Lanner Wesley held their Tea Treat in the grounds of Melrose House, and recently, a Tea Treat Pitcher – a tall terracotta jug for dishing out the 'pop' – was found in an overgrown corner of the field. An alternative site was in Peters' field opposite the chapel.

Sunday School scholars would all meet in the Square, and march in a long procession from one end of the village to the other, and back to the Square. This was usually to the accompaniment of a local brass band; in 1891 Lanner Wesleyan Sunday School Tea Treat had invited the Redruth Independent Band and the visiting Hungarian Band which livened up proceedings and made the village quite gay.[48] (Fig.9.17.).

Fig.9.17. *Tea Treat in 1908, possibly Lanner Wesley. Note the old Post Office, now the Londis Shop, on the left, and Veall's bakery sign, centre right. In between the two sets of houses is the small blacksmith's shop of Willoughby.* (© Royal Institution of Cornwall)

Fig.9.18. *Famous old local 'character', 'Lizzie Sherdy' (Elizabeth Dunstan), who frequented all the local fairs, chapel anniversaries and other town and village events, early in the twentieth century.* (© Lance Bray, Lanner)

The older men would proudly carry the embroidered, highly coloured silk and velvet Sunday School banners, and a serpentine dance was usually performed in the village square, where stalls would be set up either side of Prisk's Terrace. A 'trigg stannin' selling shell fish such as limpets and cockles and a 'nicey stannin' displaying sweets such as 'Tom Trot', 'Clidgey' humbugs and rock, were always popular as were the vendors selling ice cream and mazzards (cherries).

Always present at village tea treats in the early years of the century was Elizabeth Dunstan, an old character locally known as 'Lizzie Sherdy', who would attempt to make people part with their pennies to buy a few limpets, which she served on broken sherds of 'cloam' (chinaware), and jelly babies, which she hawked as 'baabies that went screech', which were produced from her large wicker basket. By selling such 'delicacies', she managed to keep herself and her 'tired' (lazy) husband for 36 years![49] (Fig. 9.18.).

Earlier this century, Jack Cox and the Moyles were among those with a stall, and Mr Woodley from Carharrack would bring his fish and chip van. Frank Trethowan and his pals – the Lanner Oil Brigade – would put up flags and banners in the Square, to make fun of the Wesleyans. The rivalry between church groups even spilled over into these events! The children would have their tea treat bun and a cup of tea in the field, and the older people would have tea all laid out in the schoolroom. Somebody would usually spoil their lovely white dress by falling in a cow pat! In the evening, the stalls would light up their Naphtha Flare Lamps, or gas lights, and the square would be alive with people for hours, with the young ones playing games like 'Three Old Bachelors' (a form of 'Kiss in the Ring') played in the field until it became dark. Entertainment was sometimes provided by Birchall's Steam Driven Dobbies (a roundabout) which usually set up at the end of Prisk's Terrace in the village square earlier this century.[50] The Wesleyan Band of Hope, set up in 1893, also held an annual parade with banners and a brass band, followed by tea in a local field, as described in Chapter 12.

The Bible Christians would hold their Tea Treats in the fields below Job's Buildings, and the Primitive Methodists also used fields near their chapel. Leaving their chapel at Lanner Moor, the members formed a procession, led by a local brass band and Banner Bearers. They walked up to the old poster hoarding, into Bell Lane; at Job's Buildings, they would turn and make their way back to Bray's Terrace, past the chapel, up into Tresavean Estate, emerging on the main road just below 'Glenmoor' for the final effort back to the field (later used as the Playing Field) for buns and games.

On 8 July 1886, the Ponsanooth Band attended the Lanner Moor tea treat. In the same month, the South Downs Wesleyan Sunday School tea treat was held in a field near their chapel. Redruth Town Band was in attendance, and the Member of Parliament for the Mining Division, C.A.V. Conybeare, called for tea with the teachers in the chapel, on his way to Lanner. A Radical, Conybeare had won the seat in the election of 1885.

The members of the South Downs Wesleyan Chapel used to march through the streets of Redruth, but the custom was dropped towards the end of the nineteenth century, as this circuitous route was thought to be too much for the younger children. The Trevarth Wesleyans would normally meet in their chapel at around half past one, and form a procession which marched behind a brass band, sometimes from Ponsanooth, towards Lanner House, the residence of 'Lawyer' Bray. Afterwards, the march went through Lanner Village, Penponds and back to Trevarth, where the group often assembled in a field lent for the occasion by Mr Davey, to be regaled with tea and buns (Fig.9.19).

From the 1950s there was a switch to seaside outings. Coaches would be hired, and if the railway was convenient, that was used instead. Perranporth, Carbis Bay and St Ives were popular destinations, with Carbis Bay in 1951 providing the first great venture for teachers used to the older style event. Buns travelled with them, so the old traditions were not entirely lost. Evening outings to Godrevy, and barbecues at Gwennap Pit were more for the older children and eventually, more and more people travelled in their own cars to various outings, which meant the community atmosphere

Fig.9.19. *Tea Treat procession at Lanner Moor, c.1905. This might have been that of the Trevarth Wesleyan Chapel, as their route took them in the direction of Treviskey, on the right.* (© Derek Reynolds Collection)

diminished. Today, the village-based Sunday School Anniversaries in the old style are sadly just a fast fading memory.

Sunday School Burial Clubs

In the nineteenth century many deaths were the result of poverty, especially among young people. It was an accepted fact of life that the mining industry was dangerous, and men daily courted death deep underground, where a fall from a ladder, the collapse of a 'stull' or the unexpected explosion of a charge could end a man's life in an instant. During the late 1840s, rising food prices, the failure of the potato crop, the main staple of mining families, and the crash in the price of tin and copper, caused much misery throughout the mining districts and people found it difficult to make ends meet. It was during this atmosphere of gloom that the Lanner Wesleyans formed the Sunday School Burial Club, in 1846, to ensure for its members a decent Christian funeral and interment.

The Cornish were great believers in self help, and the formation of burial clubs was a strategy devised by working class people in response to the changes wrought by a rapidly industrialising economy. To the Cornish 'a proper send off' was of vital importance. Nothing could be worse than the indignity and shame of a pauper's funeral, as evidenced by the following story. One bedridden elderly woman who lived in the area in the 1890s was given half a crown by a philanthropic lady visitor. The recipient was so grateful upon accepting the gift that the visitor was curious to know what she intended spending it on. 'It will help nicely towards the money I am saving for my coffin', came the reply, the old woman further adding 'I could not bear to be buried by the parish'.[51]

All chapels had a burial club; members of the South Downs UMFC of 1862 had to pay a halfpenny for a copy of the rules, and upon the death of an adult member, a sum of £2.15s. was paid to the deceased's family or friends. A smaller amount was paid upon a child's death.[52] There was a burial club in connection with the school of the Primitive Methodist Chapel at Lanner Moor (one penny a month up to the age of 14, then two pence over that age). Payments on death were £2 for children, £4 for adults. The club was wound up before Methodist Union. The revised rules of 1902 for Lanner Wesley show that the club was open to all, from 4 to 30 years, who were in any way engaged in the school, whether as teachers or scholars. Membership cost one penny per month. No benefit was payable if payments were more than three months in arrears. On the death of a member, four pounds was paid to the family 'for the purpose of decently interring the said deceased member'. The club was wound up in 1927.

THE ANGLICANS: LANNER CHRIST CHURCH

The increasing popularity of Methodism and the erection of numerous chapels in newly industrialised places such as Lanner prompted the Anglicans to fight back. Parliamentary measures and internal measures in the period 1836–40 were taken to create new parishes in industrial districts such as Lanner, and to spread out funds more evenly to attract parsons to these new livings. It was during this era that a church in Lanner was established as an offshoot of Gwennap Parish Church, as part of the Church's great effort to recover the ground which seemed to have been lost. It has been argued that this was based on the assumption that the Church only needed to provide church accommodation and staff adequate to the population, for that accommodation to be made use of and that staff to be kept busy.[53] This was not to be, in the case of Lanner, and the Anglicans had to swallow the hard lesson that the people had not absented themselves from the Church of England because there were no seats for them, but for more deep-rooted reasons.

The Erection of Lanner Church and the Creation of Lanner Parish

In the first half of the nineteenth century there was a lack of Established church accommodation in the Parish of Gwennap, which had had a church since the thirteenth century. By 1841, the population of Gwennap had risen to 10 974, from 4594 in 1802, reflecting the significant growth of mining in the parish. At nearby St Day, a church was founded in 1826, but the rapidly growing population of Lanner was isolated from the Anglican Church at Gwennap, about a mile and a half away, or St Euny, Redruth, over two miles in distance from Lanner, and over a mile and a half from South Downs, an expanding settlement along the course of the Redruth–Penryn Turnpike Road. In 1818, £1million had been set aside by Parliament, ostensibly as a thanksgiving for victory at the Battle of Waterloo, but more importantly, for the building of churches in places where the population had grown substantially, and where it was necessary to re-impose the Church of England's position within society, particularly within the newly industrialised areas.

Lanner is mentioned in a letter from Gwennap Vicarage on 25 October 1838 to the National Society, which channelled Government funds for Church schools. The letter was in connection with proposals to build an Episcopal Chapel in Lanner. A piece of ground had already been granted by the

Reverend Canon Rogers; on part of this a National Schoolroom had been erected within the previous two years, and already this had more than double its planned number of pupils. The letter justified the building of a new chapel in Lanner on these grounds alone, but also pointed out that there were a large number of aged and infirm people in the neighbourhood, who were 'excluded, by the distance, from the ministrations of the Church'. The chapel and school would be at the 'centre of a district with a large and rapidly-increasing population consisting almost entirely of miners'. There was to be a schoolroom attached to the chapel, with residence for a mistress.

The Chapel of Ease at Lanner was not built with money from the Million Fund, but 'in consequence of a grant from the Incorporated Society for promoting the enlargement, building and repairing of churches and chapels', noted the Gwennap Vestry Book, adding that 'The whole of the sittings are hereby declared to be free and unappropriated for ever'.

The Incorporated Building Society developed out of deepening concerns felt by laymen and clergymen alike, that the apparent defection towards sectarianism and Methodism, particularly by the working classes, was the result of a lack of places for public worship and that it was essential to attempt to draw the growing populace back to the Church of England. [54]

A contemporary newspaper cutting describes the laying of the first stone of Christ Church Chapel, Lanner by the Venerable Archdeacon Sheepshanks, with a procession, preceded by music, formed of the children of Lanner School, the principal inhabitants, and the neighbouring clergy. The weather was particularly fine, and the proceedings afforded great delight to the persons assembled. After Archdeacon Sheepshanks had addressed the assembly upon the importance of the work, the Reverend Canon Rogers and the Revd J. P. Keigwin also delivered impressive addresses. It was estimated that the building cost £550.[55]

At the opening service in the new chapel on Ascension Day, 28 June 1840, the *West Briton* noted that the Christ Church Chapel of Ease at Lanner was calculated to hold 400 persons, and the attendance, especially of the working classes for whose benefit the chapel was more immediately built, was very gratifying. The service was read by the Vicar, the Revd T. Phillpotts, assisted by the Curate, the Revd J. Flamank. The *West Briton* could not conclude without expressing its admiration of the building itself, which afforded another proof of the taste and skill of that eminent architect, Mr G. Wightwick, of Plymouth.

The architect of Christ Church, George Wightwick, and his work on the building in 1840, are described by Pearson.[56] Wightwick was a well-known architect in the South West, and in the Camborne-Redruth area, he designed St Mary's Church, Portreath and St John's, Treslothan, the chapel to Pendarves House, near Camborne (both built in 1841).

On 3 December 1844, the Ecclesiastical Parish of Lanner was gazetted out of the old Parish of Gwennap, following the same path as neighbouring St Day, which had previously become a parish in its own right. James describes Lanner's Christ Church as a plain stuccoed building, consecrated in 1845 on St. Swithin's Day (15 July).[57] He wrongly states that it was built in 1845, whereas we have seen above that it was erected as a Chapel of Ease in 1840. The 1845 date was the consecration as a full church, following the gazetting of Lanner as a new parish out of Gwennap.

Lanner Christ Church has seldom received any flattering remarks. The celebrated poet, John Betjeman, in 1963, described Christ Church, Lanner as 'usually locked, a very plain 1840 Italianate building, with nave, shallow chancel, and transepts and some clear glass – it looks like a small mission church of 1920'. We might speculate that the plain design of Christ Church was deliberate, an attempt to attract the poor, who would not go to a smart place of worship, but might more readily go to a humble one.[58] (Fig.9.20.).

The Church Interior

Internally, the Church comprises a chancel, nave, vestry, north porch, and a western turret containing one bell. Behind the altar are four wooden tablets which display the Lord's Prayer, the Decalogue and the Creed in gold lettering. Polsue mentions the marble tablet installed in memory of Alicia Maria, daughter of Eliza and the Revd John Tucker, who died in 1861, aged 22. There are three further tablets in brass in memory of former church members; one is dedicated to the memory of Theodora, the wife of the Revd J.B.D. Hopgood, who died on 4 September 1877, aged 35. Another was given by Charlotte, the wife of Sergeant Major John Eddy of the Royal Engineers, a Crimean War Veteran, who died 16 December 1906. Eddy had been a former Churchwarden, and had given the pulpit in 1902, which can still be seen in the church today. The most recent is a tablet commemorating the life of John Michael Job, and records that the clergy and choir vestries were dedicated by the Arch Deacon of Cornwall on St Luke's Day, 1932 in his memory. A lectern was given in memory of former churchwarden, George Skewes Bray, 1850–1930.

Christ Church has undergone many changes in its 150 year history, reflecting changing times and attitudes. The church's gallery was taken down during the Reverend J.B.D. Hopgood's ministry in the 1870s, and a chancel and screen with ornate arches was formed. Many alterations and improvements were made to the interior during the ministry of the Revd G.J. Scott, who came to Lanner in October, 1881. These went a long way 'towards beautifying the somewhat unornamental building,' and included the addition of a south aisle in 1883.[59]

In the same year, a new Ascension window was installed in the church above the altar, and was the work of Gibbs of Bloomsbury Street, London. 'Lannarth Ascension window will compare, it is said, with any modern window in the County,' reported the local press, and it was given by Mrs Mary Andrew of Pennance in memory of her husband Thomas, a former Churchwarden.[60]

Fig.9.20. *Lanner Christ Church, c.1905. Note the schoolmistress's residence on the far right, and,between that and the church, the schoolroom, built in the 1830s. This is now the Parish Hall. The cemetery, across the road from the church, had not yet been opened.* (© Royal Institution of Cornwall, Truro).

In 1899, a stained glass window was given by Mrs Edward Eddy of Colorado, USA, in memory of her husband, indicating the strong overseas ties which exist between Lanner and its former inhabitants. Mrs Eddy presented many gifts of money and furnishings over several years, such as sanctuary fittings, chancel carpets, and a clergyman's stole, as did other benefactors, but there have never been benefactions from the landed gentry, as was the case with the churches in Redruth, St Day and Gwennap. This perhaps explains the rather stark interior of the building. There is a further stained glass window on the northern side of the church depicting St James. This was erected in 1930, following the bequest from the will of the late Reverend Dr. J. Walker of £50, and was given by Ann Elizabeth Manders Walker, in memory of her husband James.

In 1884, the church was reopened by the Bishop of Truro, after having been partially restored. In 1890, the ceiling was renewed, at a cost of £70. The octagonal font, whose age is uncertain but may have been sixteenth century, with a winged female figure on each face, was formerly in the Church of St Dunstan, Fleet Street, London. It was presented by the Rector of that church to the Reverend Francis Thomas, Curate-in-Charge of Lanner between 1892 and 1897. It replaced a font, described as 'of good modern workmanship' with a marble bowl and resting on a shaft of Portland stone, which had previously been in use in Gwennap Church. This was buried beneath the chancel when the present one was erected.[61]

The twentieth century saw the arrival of more 'modern' lighting, when a tender of £25 for the installation of acetylene gas lighting was received in September 1925, and was afterwards further improved by a change to oil lighting. Discussions took place in 1926–27 about replacement of the old pews, but there was a dispute about the finish. Cornish bench ends were to be used, but the Church Council 'would not put their money into deal, nor into anything stained brown or green'. It took until 1930 to pay off the debt for the new seating. It was agreed in 1935 to melt down the two old bells and to recast them as a single bell, at a cost of £12. However, this was not carried out, and in 1938 the two old bells were replaced by a bell purchased from Portreath Church.

Again, in 1935, the church lighting was further improved, changing from oil to electricity, and a Litany desk was provided as a memorial to R. Rendle, who had been a churchwarden and tireless worker for the Church. In 1938, A.E. Douglas arranged the digging out and replastering the whole of the exterior of the church, at his own expense. Eight tons of cement and twenty tons of sand were used. The building has always suffered from problems with damp, making redecorating an all too regular event. In 1997, night storage heaters replaced the inadequate wall heaters. In 1950, Miss E. Barkworth left the parish, and presented a clock for the church vestry. A new church gate, black with gold rays of the sun, was installed in 1960.

In 1947, a proposal to purchase a secondhand American organ was passed by the parochial church council, as the church's original organ, a one manual tracker organ by Hele and Company, was in a bad state. It was later agreed to purchase a new organ, and a new two-manual Compton organ was dedicated in the church on 5 June 1949 by the Bishop of Truro. It cost £1000, and a plate was attached, stating 'In affectionate memory of Eleanor Laura Parr (née Millbank) of Lanner House, who died on the 25 September

1948. One stop and organ stool were provided by her family'. In 1951, it was reported that the organ had unfortunately broken down more than once, and had to be repaired. Damp conditions had taken its toll on the Compton organ, which by 1989 was in a dilapidated and dangerous state. A new organ was offered for sale by Lance Foy, originally made for St Michael's Mission Church at Ponsanooth by Brewer of Truro. The purchase price was £1150.00. The work was completed in 1990, and the new organ was placed in the same position as the former one. The memorial plates from the old organ were placed on a nearby wall.

The Churchyard and Vicarage

The original churchyard surrounding the church and containing few headstones, was closed by order of the Privy Council in 1854, and a new cemetery was opened across the road from the church. On 18 August 1911, the Local Government Board gave approval for an extension to this burial ground after a petition from George Skewes Bray. Almost an acre in size and at a cost about £100, it was consecrated on 15 January 1914. Pupils from Lanner Board School were given a half day off to attend the consecration ceremony. With a large influx of people to the parish since the Second World War, by 1975 this ground was nearly full, reflecting the growth of Lanner in the previous 30 years to become one of the county's largest villages. It was recommended by the Medical Officer of Health that no more burials be allowed, but that this would not apply to the reopening of graves.

This act caused considerable anguish amongst Lanner parishioners, particularly when people who were not from Lanner had been buried there. Locals felt aggrieved at being denied a final resting place in their own parish, as no more ground could be obtained for burial near the churchyard. Interments had to take place at Trewirgie, a thing very much resented. In view of this, in 1996 Lanner Parish Council were considering extension of the burial ground to right this wrong. The extension will take place before the year 2000.

Lanner's connection with countries across the world due to emigration, particularly to South Africa and the United States, can be detected by the inscriptions on some of the monuments. There is also a monumental inscription to Joseph Henry Geach, who died at Tresavean Mine in 1925, yet another link to Lanner's mining past. Many more examples can be seen at Gwennap Churchyard. There are very few elaborate or expensive headstones within, and many plots are unmarked, reflecting the lack of wealth in the parish in former times.

Polsue states in his *Lake's Parochial History* that the perpetual curacy of Lannarth was constituted by an order of Her Majesty Queen Victoria in Council, dated 28 November 1844.[62] The patronage was at first vested in the Crown and the Bishop alternately. Then an order of Her Majesty in Council, dated 9 September 1865, assigned the advowson, or right of perpetual patronage, to the Revd John Tucker, the first incumbent, who had been instituted on 14 February 1845. In 1873, the living and vicarage had a yearly value of £184, and were in the gift of Mrs Tucker of Falmouth.[63] The foundation stone of the vicarage, 'a substantial and commodious parsonage house', was laid in February 1847. 'Besides a liberal donation, this site, containing little more than half an acre of land adjoining the churchyard was given by the Reverend Canon Rogers. The Parsonage is to be built by public subscription, aided by a grant from Queen Anne's Bounty'.[64] It was sold by the Diocese to John and Mary Anson in 1978, for use as a private dwelling. In 1893, *Kelly's Directory* quotes the living as a vicarage, net yearly value £180, with three-quarters of an acre of glebe and residence, in the gift of trustees. In later years, the patronage was in the hands of the Martyrs' Memorial and Church of England Patronage Trust Company.

The Challenge of Methodism and the 1851 Religious Census

The Anglican Church in Lanner had much ground to make up if it was to hope to win back souls from the Methodist Chapels which had already strongly established themselves in the new mining village of Lanner. But Christ Church was not to be well supported and always lived in the shadows cast by Methodism. Indeed this is aptly portrayed when we read Francis' poem of 1845:

Two chapels at Lanner at noon and at eve,
Two hundred and fifty instruction receive
at each of these places...

By comparison, he writes the following concerning Christ Church:

Next to Lanner new church our steps we direct:
From the large population 'twas fair to expect
Many more would attend, for the number is small,
Scarce eighty grown persons attend there at all.[65]

The relatively small number of worshippers at Christ Church is further elucidated by analysis of the 1851 Religious Census.[66] The aim of this census, conducted right across the country, was to determine two points: How many people attended a place of religious worship, and which denominations were the most popular. Held on Sunday 30 March, the returns for Lanner were: Christ Church Lanner 150; Lanner Wesley 680; Lanner Wesleyan Association 840.

Here we have further evidence that Lanner was overwhelmingly a Methodist community. Although 1670 people from the parish attended church or chapel that Sunday, the figures also reveal that of a total population of 2710, 1040 people did not attend a place of worship at all, indicating that over a third of the community escaped the ministrations of a place of worship. We must also remember that the figures contained within the Census possess an inherent weakness, in that they do not reveal how many people attended church or chapel more than once that day, so the overall figure was in reality much lower. Indeed, William Francis had noticed the large numbers of people who did not attend church or chapel, commenting:

> *...yet, must we submit,*
> *That nearly two thirds of the people around*
> *Meet seldom, or never, on hallowed ground;*
> *...yet it is too plain,*
> *That hundreds, or thousands, still careless remain.*[67]

It is very easy to fall into the trap of viewing Victorian Lanner as being an overwhelmingly religious place when reading local newspapers, dominated by reports of tea treats, anniversaries, harvest festivals, church and chapel bazaars and concerts. The reality was somewhat different in what was essentially a rough, working class mining village, many of whose inhabitants were too busy trying to survive the day-to-day drudgery of their miserable lives to be greatly concerned about the life to come. John Probert has argued that what we are witnessing with the 1851 Census is an index of secularisation, the results of which shocked and appalled the Victorians, since it revealed a society far less religious than they would have liked.[68] Yet today, the Lanner churches would be most happy to have even a half of those 1670 Christians attending their services.

For the Anglicans, the above returns must have been very embarrassing, in effect reducing them to just another denomination. A hard lesson had to be learnt, one that was to teach them that they could take little for granted. To help combat the popularity of Methodism, the Church ran evangelistic mission services, which had proved very effective in recruiting souls for the Methodists. Such a mission was held in the Lannarth Old School in 1888, led by Mr Day of London, and was conducted under the supervision of the Minister of the Church. The local press commented, 'It is hoped that these services will be of a real good to many'.[69] Yet affairs at Christ Church in the late nineteenth century present the picture of a church often on the verge of extinction, one under threat from the encroaching Revivalist waves of Methodism, and a Church at war with itself, not helped by the ineptitude of many of its incumbents.

Clergy and 'Popery'

The lack of wealthy benefactors, and the relatively small congregation, have always left Christ Church in a state of poverty. Yet it seemed impossible to add members to the congregation or to attract donations for parishioners to maintain the fabric of the Church. In the *Royal Cornwall Gazette* of 23 January 1875, the deplorable state of the church had forced the Vicar of Lanner, the Reverend J.B.D. Hopgood, to write the following:

> *Will you kindly allow me a small space in your columns to plead a most pressing case? Our church is thoroughly saturated with rain, the aisle and vestry being so completely swamped that they cannot be used. Consequently, I am obliged to put on my surplice in church, as there is not an inch of dry ground in the vestry. Since my arrival here I have had several repairs done, and also a new chancel formed, and the gallery removed.*
>
> *This is a very poor parish, consisting totally of miners and as they cannot afford to give much, the offertories are exceedingly small, not more than 6d or 8d a Sunday. There are no funds for lighting, heating or cleaning the church, or ringing the bell, consequently the expense falls very heavy upon me. It is very important that something be done immediately: £10 must be got this week. There is a debt of £60 under these pressing circumstances. May I ask each of your readers to send me a few stamps towards making the church water proof? I shall be thankful also to receive contributions (if only a few stamps) to help clear off the debt. I appeal to the Christian sympathy and liberality of Cornishmen.'*

Less than a month later it was reported that, 'On Sunday night, some person, or persons broke into the church of Lanner and took away about 2lb of candles which were placed about the church, and dressed up an image and placed it on the altar with a surplice and skull cap on. At present, no one has been suspected'.[70] (Presumably the altar was dry!) The candles were later found scattered in the churchyard.

Lanner's Reverend Joseph Bartholemew Davy Hopgood arrived in the village in 1871, a young man aged about 28, and lodged with Edward and Nanny Lean at the village Post Office until the Vicarage was vacated by his predecessor. He was a most controversial figure, and was not much liked within the village, particularly by the Methodists, because he was a High Churchman. In 1874 a newspaper article appeared in the *Church Times* describing the changes made at Lanner Christ Church, including a new chancel, screen, vesper lights, cruets for wine and water, and a processional cross and banners, as 'another step in the march of true religion'. But the pro-Methodist *Cornubian* saw it rather differently, and attacked the *Church Times* as 'a stupid advocate of full-blown popery', and Hopgood was accused of disgusting the majority of his parishioners.[71] In 1875 he was openly accused of being a supporter of Romish practices, which prompted a denial from him to the *Royal Cornwall Gazette*: 'If there is anything at Lannarth Church which is strictly Romish, and not allowed and authorised by the English Church, I will forthwith abandon it'.[72]

But Hopgood was not noted for his tact and only added to the controversy surrounding him by circulating a rumour about a prominent and respected Lanner Methodist. John Lean, a former resident of the village then living at 42 King Square, Goswell Road, London EC, had felt sufficiently incensed to write to the *Cornubian*, which published his letter on 16 March 1877. He was referring to an anonymous letter, but one suspected to have been written by the Reverend Hopgood, to the *Royal Cornwall Gazette* of 8 February 1877, in which Mr Hopgood appeared to suggest that the Late Captain Trebilcock, a respected Methodist, one of the first men to travel to the Andean mines of Cerro de

Pasco, and a former South American mine manager, had committed suicide by stuffing his head down his lavatory. Mr Lean, (and a number of other letter-writers), refuted the insinuation that Captain Trebilcock had committed suicide, and were most indignant and dismissive of the erroneous comment which stated that his body had been found with his head down a WC. Mr Lean continued:

The deceased was not a Jesuit, I know. He did not worship the Virgin Mary, he had no confidence in the advocacy of the defunct, crusading, yet canonised King Louis IX of France; nor had he any faith in the virtue and saving merits of St Peter's fishing hooks, nor in any of the paraphernalia and relics of Popery; but he grounded his hope of salvation solely on the merits of the atonement of his Lord and Saviour Jesus Christ.

Mr Lean concluded his long letter:

Up to the time that Mr Hopgood's shop was opened, the pure gospel which – time out of mind – had been preached in the neighbourhood – a neighbourhood which I can but respect, for it was there that I was born, cradled and bred – had remained uncorrupted, not even the semblance of mummery was seen in the parish. But times are altered, as well as things, and Mr Hopgood is there, and there may he shake his bell until the sound thereof reaches the clouds, and his arm sink under the effort.

He may adorn all the gewgaws, and exhibit all the dolls that human ingenuity can devise – may burn candles at mid-day, either of three feet long or six, as may best suit his fancy; may elevate both the cross and crosier, swing the smoking censer until the fumes thereof darken the air; turn to the east, west, north or south; may mutter and peep until he is both dumb and blind, and preach to his congregation, composed of himself, his wife and servant, all to no avail. Like the prophets of Baal, in the presence of Elijah, no response will come – the sacrifice will remain unconsumed on the altar. 'I will not hear thee'. I trust that Mr Hopgood will see the error of his ways, and, by sincere application to the proper source, obtain a more benevolent and feeling heart, and a better and more charitable Christian spirit; for surely the malice manifested by the letter to which I have referred, was never surpassed, and is almost, if not altogether, unparalleled'.

Religious sectarian feelings were running high in Lanner, but surely they were stirred up by their tactless vicar. The vicar of a church seen as an island set in a sea of Methodism. In fact, relations became so strained between the Methodists and Hopgood, that the vicar became totally paranoid and convinced that the village Methodists were conspiring to murder him. On 5 November 1877 he wrote a sensational letter to the *West Briton* accusing the Methodists of attempting to kill him. He claimed that the church gates had been unhinged and placed so as to fall on him, but providentially he put out his hand and prevented this until assistance arrived.

Thus foiled, the Methodists once more showed the cloven hoof by attempting to stone him during a service. During the 'Magnificat' a crash of glass was heard when a huge quarry boulder was hurled against the window above him, which fortunately struck the casement and rebounded into the churchyard. He claimed he had prior knowledge of a plot to stone him to death, which he had not treated seriously until the above events. He also stated that the churchgoers in Lanner were subjected to constant threats, conspiracies, persecution, and in some cases, starvation and house expulsions, to force them to give up going to church and agree to attend the 'schismatic meeting-houses, set up by the Devil in opposition to God's Church'. But the Methodists fiercely countered Hopgood's claim of a murder conspiracy as nonsense, a letter of 12 November to the *West Briton* stating that 'the Wesleyans neither care about him, nor would they trouble if a pilchard seine full of such priests were landed on the Cornish coast tomorrow'.

Yet Hopgood continued to stoke the fires of animosity. In 1878 John Lean of London again attacked him, after Hopgood had placed an article in the *West Briton* insinuating that the Methodist places of worship were not sacred as they permitted the use of their chapels for all manner of secular uses – teetotal lectures for example. To enter one, Mr Hopgood intimated, was to 'contaminate oneself'. Mr Lean invited the reader to ask the question 'Why such a feeling of animosity against the Wesleyans?' He proceeded to answer it thus:

Long, long ere Mr Hopgood saw the light of the sun's rays, there was a Wesleyan Chapel at Lanner, where from the beginning, up to the present day, the gospel of Christ has regularly been preached in its purity... the services are attended by overflowing numbers of worshippers, whereas Mr Hopgood's establishment, but as of yesterday, stuck up within a stone's-cast of the Wesleyan Chapel, is left cold, comfortless and empty. No one wants either Mr Hopgood, his church or his doctrine.

He continued his attack on Mr Hopgood's 'House of Popery' by adding:

The people are all Wesleyans, as were their fathers before them... a few years ago they cut off a few acres from the N.W. corner of Gwennap, and called it the Parish of Lannarth. On this they stuck up the fabric which no one desires nor ever did desire, and which has been, and still is, an eye-sore.[73]

Extraordinary Doings at Lanner Church

But Hopgood continued to remain controversial, and even the way in which he left the parish was subject to much talk, as evidenced by the following sensational article, printed in the *West Briton* of 21 October 1880.

Extraordinary Doings at Lannarth Church, Gwennap

The Reverend John Tucker was formerly the respected vicar of the village church of Lannarth, Gwennap. He was succeeded by his son, and afterwards by the Reverend J.G.D. Hopgood, who married Mr Tucker's daughter. Mr Hopgood was a Ritualistic or High Church clergyman, and after a time he thought it desirable to exchange livings with Mr Wallace, of Whitehaven, who was consequently inducted into the Lanner living; but Mr Hopgood was not so fortunate, for it appears that the Bishop refused to appoint him as Mr Wallace's successor at Whitehaven. Then the public heard of county court actions in reference to various things at Lannarth vicarage, but Mr Wallace seemed to get the better of the matter, and there was quietness until the last few weeks. A few weeks ago Mr Wallace married his servant, who has now left him, and it appears there is a great deal of feeling against him in the village. Mr Wallace has utterly failed of late to attract people to the church, and sometimes on a Sunday no service has been held, the vicar's practice being to wait and see if three persons should assemble; if so, then to go into the belfry, ring the bell, and go through the service, and if none came the church doors remained firmly closed. This was contrary to the practice of Mr Hopgood, who, while he was vicar, after having himself rung the bell, was accustomed to go through service daily whether he had a congregation or not.

On Sunday last the village was thrown into a state of excitement by the strange news that the late vicar had returned on Saturday evening, had entered the church by the belfry window on Sunday morning, and intended to conduct services during the day. This, of course, was sufficient to draw a congregation, and the excitement was intense when both vicars attempted to 'do duty' in the church. Mr Hopgood preached on Sunday morning at eight o'clock, and at eleven he again performed the service to a crowded congregation. Mr Wallace, however, was soon on the spot, and told Mr Hopgood that he had no right there, as he (Mr Wallace) was the vicar of the parish. Mr Hopgood said he had an authority for what he was doing, and that he was the vicar of the parish of Lannarth. Some hard words were used on both sides in the church before the congregation, and Mr Wallace threatened legal proceedings. When Mr Hopgood gave out a hymn the congregation 'one and all' sang most heartily, but when Mr Wallace uttered a word he was hissed.

In the afternoon Mr Hopgood preached again, and Mr Wallace, attended by his solicitor, urged the congregation to take no notice of him; but this had little effect, for during the service held by Mr Hopgood the congregation joined in hearty response, but when after he had finished Mr Wallace began his service most of the congregation left. In the evening the church was literally crammed, and Mr Wallace did not appear. The singing was most hearty. Mr Hopgood preached extempore, as he is accustomed to do, from the text, 'As thou sowest so shalt thou reap'. Four services were held by Mr Hopgood during the day; he was in the church from morning till night, and was evidently more popular than Mr Wallace, refreshments being supplied him by people between the services. During the service disgraceful proceedings were carried on by some roughs from the village of Carharrack. They were beating each other with their hats, making all sorts of noises, and causing quite a disturbance. All this was done in the sight of a policeman, who was quietly looking on. In answer to a question, the policeman stated that he had no power to deal with them.

At the conclusion of the sermon Mr Hopgood said that the congregation might sing or not, as they pleased, 'Hold the Fort'. This was immediately begun, and a noise at a village inn in olden times was no comparison to it. All sorts of digressions were made in the tune, the chorus being repeatedly sung in a most idiotic and offensive way whilst the people were leaving the church. Mr Hopgood was standing inside the altar, and the policeman at the door, both seeming powerless. Mr Hopgood, no doubt, did not wish to offend the people, as they had in a certain sense welcomed him back, and he did not say a word to them. It is fair, however, to state, on the testimony of several, that the brawling and bad conduct in the church was caused by the rough gang from Carharrack; the villagers apparently were more devotional and sincere. Mr Hopgood stated that it was a great pleasure for him to come amongst them again, and in the future he would do everything in his power to please them, and if any member of the church should object to any part of the service, by mentioning it to him he would remove that which appeared offensive. He raised the tunes himself, and apologised for having only two or three pieces of candles stuck about, and said that before next Sunday he would have the church cleaned and made decent. It is thought that Bishop Benson will try to cure such strange and disorderly church proceedings in his diocese.

Mr Hopgood writes to say that in 1878, when Mr Wallace agreed to exchange livings with him, he took care to see that Mr Wallace was duly nominated, but Mr Wallace did not take the same care as to his (Mr Hopgood's) nomination to Moresby, and consequently some one else was appointed. He has since discovered that he is legally entitled to return to his own benefice. The noise in the church on Sunday, he says, was not so great as described - simply a confusion of so many getting out.

This was no doubt an occasion which provided great entertainment for residents of the village and beyond (news of the event spread as far away as Plymouth, where it found its way into the *Western Daily Mercury*), an almost farcical event which was talked about for many a year afterwards. An acrimonious court case did follow, and when Hopgood eventually took up a new position as the vicar of Tolland Royal, Wiltshire, he was greeted with shouts of 'No Popery here!' and 'objectionable' objects were removed. In the light of all these goings-on in 1880, it is interesting to examine the list of incumbents of Christ Church, Lanner:

Revd John Tucker. First Vicar and Patron 1845-1870
Revd George William Tucker. Son of above 1870-1871
Revd Joseph Bartholemew Davy Hopgood. Vicar 1871-1878
Revd William Baillie Wallace. Vicar 1878-1904
Revd Arthur James Mason. Canon Truro Cathedral 1880-81
Revd George James Scott. Curate in Charge 1881-1887
Revd William Fox. Curate in Charge 1887-1889
Revd Charles Henry Shaw. Curate in Charge 1889-1892

Revd Francis Thomas. Curate in Charge 1892-1897
Revd Alfred Darnell. Curate in Charge 1897-1900
Revd Henry Wright. Curate in Charge 1900-1904
Revd Lyttleton Fitzgerald. Curate in Charge 1904-1905
Revd Frank Buckler. Vicar, nephew of First Patron 1905-10
Revd Charles Salmon Paddon. Vicar 1910-1916
Revd William Harry Castell Malton. Vicar 1916-1922
Revd Edward Wyvill Stuart. Vicar 1922-1924
Revd Fenton Ernest Bury. Vicar 1924-1928
Revd Oliver Roland Walkey. Vicar 1929-1930
Revd Percy Edward Henthorne Stott. Vicar 1930-1933
Revd Clement Thomas Walker. Vicar 1933-1937
Revd George Frederick Sandfield. Vicar 1938-1940
Revd William Henry Greening. Vicar 1940-1944
Revd Leslie Evan Glascott. Vicar 1944-1947
Revd Colin de Clonet Craven-Sands. Vicar 1947-1950
Revd John Vernon Shaw. Vicar 1951-1961
Revd W.H. Greening. Priest in Charge 1961-1962
Revd W. Fitkin. Priest in Charge 1962-1964
Revd W.H. Greening. Priest in Charge 1964-1969
Revd D.E. Knight. Vicar 1969-1975

Mr Hopgood did not get his parish back in 1880, and it was deemed necessary for the Canon of Truro Cathedral, followed by seven Curates-in-Charge, to assist Mr Wallace with the Parish, or was it to stand between him and his parishioners? According to the *Cornubian* of 8 April 1892, out of the value of the living of £175 per annum, £100 went to Mr Wallace, the 'absentee holder of the living'. In 1892, the Bishop paid the balance of the full stipend to the new curate, out of his own pocket.

It could not have been easy for Church of England ministers to reside in an area so strongly Methodist, and many found, no matter how hard they tried, that they could do little right. Some vicars went to great lengths to foster good relations with the village chapels and their members. In 1887, the Reverend W. Fox, Curate-in-Charge, attempted to bridge the gap between the Dissenters and the Church on the occasion of Queen Victoria's Jubilee. He invited the Reverend J. Hender, a Bryanite Minister to preach during the service, an event which, 'caused great interest, because it was the first occasion that a Nonconformist minister was allowed to preach there. The church was filled to overflowing, and everyone was delighted to witness the recognition of brotherly love and fellowship.'[74] Special Mission Services held during Advent and Epiphany were advertised in the local press, with the footnote, 'These Mission Services are in no rivalry to others, which may be held by our Dissenting Friends. May a rich blessing rest on theirs and ours. W. Fox, Minister'.[75]

However, some of the curates-in-charge were not as tactful, and did much harm to the Church's position within the community. One such curate was the Reverend Charles Shaw, who stirred up the antipathy between Church and Chapel in Lanner once again, in 1891. The *Cornubian* of 9 January in that year reported that the Reverend C. Shaw had written to *The Church in the West* of 3 January, complaining that 'Dissenters' were being allowed to use the school in the parish while their chapels were under repair. The newspaper pointed out that the Church had freely used the schools in Cusgarne, St Day and Lanner, and that the Church was outnumbered in membership in Lanner by the 'dissenters' by something like 60-to-1. The newspaper said 'A fair exhibition of the Christian spirit of toleration might have good effect. Certainly the feeble piping of the Revd Gentleman in the *Church in the West* cannot possibly do him any good, but may do him a vast amount of harm. If the Dissenters at Lanner were to take revengeful measures, which it is to be hoped they will not, the church of Christ Church at Lanner would soon cease to exist'.

In spite of this, when Mr Shaw left Lanner, the *Cornubian* commented that he had been a distinct improvement on his predecessors, which made his indiscretion of 1891 such a shame, for the Revd C. Shaw had shown great philanthropy towards all the people of Lanner Parish. Still, his congregation had not multiplied, and the scant attendance of worshippers at the church had probably disheartened him. However, the pro-Methodist *Cornubian* could not resist a further dig at the vicar, remarking, 'the Reverend Shaw could never have been so profuse in his liberality towards the needy were he not possessed of private means'.[76]

It is interesting to speculate to just what extent the clergy were responsible for the poor attendance at Christ Church, its low standing in the community and its impoverished position. The Reverend Bayley Wallace certainly did not set an example of Christian living to his parishioners with his public divorce case in 1882 on the grounds of cruelty to his wife Mary Jane (née Bray), formerly his housemaid, whom he had married in 1880. She claimed he had been an absolute 'brute' to her, and alleged he had a violent temper, was abusive in the extreme, and as well as calling her by offensive names, had punched her, pulled her by her hair and spat in her face.[77] Many parishioners thought Wallace to have been worse than Hopgood, his predecessor, and attendance figures at his services were said to have been the worst in Cornwall. There was also a hint of scandal against Revd Charles Henry Shaw, who was accused of assaulting a woman from Breage, but had the case against him dropped due to inconclusive evidence. Indeed, an illuminating newspaper article seems to suggest that as far as the people were concerned, the clergy were to blame. In 1896 it was reported that there had been a successful bazaar at the church in Lanner, attended by 300 people, at which £36.18s.6d was taken. Lawyer Bray addressing those present commented:

> *... A cloud that has long hung over Lanner is beginning to lift... If the clergy treated the people of Lanner properly, they would get almost any help they wanted in return... Messrs. Eddy and Rendle had stuck manfully to the church when all others had left it in disgust... If it rose again on its foundations, a great part of the credit must be given to them for having in bad times kept the church from being obliterated.*[78]

However, in 1897 Lawyer Bray went much further and made his opinion on the clergy of Lanner Church perfectly clear. The Reverend Francis Thomas, Curate-in-Charge, was leaving for Werrington after four years at Lanner, which was a cause for universal regret. During his ministry, the congregation, which before his arrival had consisted of about four men and two children, had again assumed respectable proportions, the Sunday-School had risen from 7 to over 60 children and the Church building and the churchyard walls had been repaired and cleaned, and the debt paid off. In Hopgood's time the church door was reported to have been falling off:

> *To make a presentation to a clergyman in Lanner was as unusual as a record reign there', Lawyer Bray began, continuing, 'Unusual, not because of any fault or shortcoming of the people, but during the last 20 years the persons who had been in spiritual charge at Lanner (he spoke mildly because of the presence of ladies, but much stronger words would have better fitted his meaning), were either mentally weak or morally worthless men, whose mind no sane man would trust; men with whom no respectable person could or would associate; and with the assistance of a few outsiders as ignorant as they were officious, the Church and the Church people had been made a byeword for all that was filthy and neglected'.*

The Reverend F. Thomas was presented with a marble clock, an oak study chair, a pair of brass candlesticks, and an illuminated address signed by members of all the societies in the village. Mr Barrett of Lanner Band presented him with a Teacher's Bible, as he had been so instrumental in the formation of the village brass band, which then played 'God Save the Queen'.[79] With a succession of poor Curates-in-Charge after Hopgood's debacle, it is not difficult to see how this helped to contribute to Methodism's complete domination of the religious scene in Lanner by the end of the nineteenth century.

The Catholic Revival at Lanner Christ Church

We have detected evidence in Lanner, particularly during the Reverend J. Hopgood's ministry, of the continual strains in the Church of England caused by the diversity of religious practices ranging from 'High' or Ritualistic, to 'Low' Church.

In his scathing speech of 1897, George 'Lawyer' Bray had warned neighbouring 'High Church "jinks" not to interfere at Lanner Church, and promised trouble if they did. This Ritualistic sentiment reached its pinnacle during the early twentieth century with the 'Catholic Revival', a further reaction to the industrial revolution which had produced the Pre-Raphaelites and a Gothic style of architecture harking back to the period before industrialisation.[80] The rise of Anglo-Catholicism was another strand in the complex Cornish Revival of the early twentieth century. Instead of addressing the issues arising from de-industrialisation which severely affected Cornwall after the First World War, they chose to look back to the perceived glory of Cornwall's Celtic past. Cornish societies were formed which renewed links with other Celtic nations – Ireland, Brittany, The Isle of Man, Wales and Scotland. In the Church, there was a belief among some of the clergy that Cornwall should seek to rediscover its native culture, lost during the Reformation of the sixteenth century (see Chapter 1); this native culture was viewed by them to have been intricately bound up with Catholicism, the true religion of the Cornish people, usurped by Methodism, the church of industrialisation. However, as Garry Tregidga has pointed out, the Revivalists made a serious mistake in linking their movement to Anglo-Catholicism, 'for by looking back to a pre-industrial and Catholic past, they were distancing themselves from the Liberal Nonconformists: the only group which could possibly lead Cornwall into a Celtic future'.[81] Sadly, the Anglo-Catholic Movement only succeeded in causing more bitter denominational infighting and congregational schisms, as can be seen from Lanner's experience in the early 1920s.

In 1923, a spate of letters were published in the local press concerning the dispute raging at Christ Church. Frank Trethowan, the leader of the 'No-Popery Movement', the respected 'book man' at Tresavean Mine, and a member of the congregation, wrote to the *Royal Cornwall Gazette* stating that 'the Revd E. W. Stuart must modify his method of service in conformity with the expressed desires of the majority of the worshippers at the church.'[82] The great debate over the future form of service at the church found its way into *The English Churchman and St James Chronicle*, under the heading, 'The Cry From the Villages'. People took exception to some of the practices of 'Anglo-Romanism' which had been present during recent services there, which included 'the re-establishment of priestcraft, auricular confession with women like serfs and slaves kneeling at the feet of a clergyman, as seen a few weeks ago'.[83]

A Lanner person, presumably a church member and vociferous defender of the Catholic form, writing under the pseudonym 'Rough Street' was vehemently attacked in the local press by supporters of the 'No-Popery Movement', one of whom wrote that the Bishop of Truro was not at all in favour of Catholic practices, claiming he had written the following: 'I regret very much the alteration in the character of the services at Lanner. I do not agree with some of his (the vicar's) methods, nor do I hold that what is done in Lanner is the one and only legitimate thing in the Church of England.'[84]

Protest meetings were held in Lanner Square during the same year. The Rural Dean attended a Parochial Church Council Meeting to state that accusations of disloyalty to the Prayer Book and to the Church of England could not be sustained. The Revd E.W. Stuart's position became increasingly untenable at Lanner and he decided to move on, but even this did not run smoothly. At a Parochial Church Council meeting on 30 October 1923, the Council sent a resolution to the Bishop, that 'having heard that the care of the souls of the parishioners has recently been advertised for sale in the Press, desires to record its abhorrence of such a proceeding, which has long been regarded as a cause for scandal in the Church of England'. This referred to a notice in *The Times* of 'Advowson for Sale'.

There had been rumblings of disapproval in 1884 concerning the appointment of a new vicar, the churchwardens aggrieved that they seemed to have no say in the matter of church affairs, 'things being settled by strangers.'[85] By the early 1920s, the parishioners wanted to elect a Low Churchman, and the more palatable Revd F.E. Bury was appointed in 1924. He became known as the 'Evangelical Vicar of Lanner' and was greatly liked by the Methodists, who addressed him at their Centenary Service in 1928, as 'A good Protestant and a guardian of the Evangelical Faith'.[86]

At Christ Church, the pro 'Low Church' Martyrs' Memorial Trust Fund became patrons of the living, and this organisation saw to it that Low Churchmen were given precedence over Romish candidates. This won the unanimous approval of the Parochial Church Council, who in 1941 for example, sent the Trust a subscription of half a guinea to appreciate the interest shown by them in recently appointing the Vicar (Mr W.H. Greening).

At a Parish Meeting held on 5 November 1924 , there was evidence of a move away from 'High Church' practices. The meeting of parishioners fully endorsed the new Vicar's action in veiling the images and candles (including the Cross) until a faculty could be obtained for their removal. There was also unanimous 'hearty' approval of the church services as conducted by the Reverend F.E. Bury, who had made a real effort since his arrival to foster good relations with the village Methodist ministers. On 11 December 1925, a Faculty was granted by the Bishop of Truro for the removal from Lanner Church of a side altar, of the image of the Virgin and Child, altar covers, altar cross, candlesticks and other vestments and furniture. (The carved statue of the Virgin Mary was taken to St. Andrew's, Redruth.). This seems to have passed peacefully, in contrast to events at Cury and St Hilary; at the latter church in August 1932, a coach load of hired iconoclasts descended on the church and despoiled the interior.[87]

At the Annual Lanner Parish Meeting of 16 January 1930, a resolution was passed, 'regretting and condemning the action of the majority of the Bishops in authorising the use of the Revised Prayer Book in the face of its twice-rejection by Parliament, such action by the Bishops being both lawless and dishonest'.[88] In 1934, a parishioner offered to buy a brass cross for the altar at Lanner, but the schism which had divided the congregation during the Revd E.W. Stuart's ministry was still too fresh in the memory of some, so it was decided that it would not be advisable to have one 'at the present'. By 1945, 'there was a feeling in the Parish that the Cross should be restored to the altar', and one was finally made by Alf Bray in 1977–78 at South Crofty Mine, and he gave it to the church with the iron candelabrum which he had made.

Alterations in more recent years reflect a swing back towards a more 'High Church' approach; a new altar was installed in the church in 1992, and several choir and front pews were removed. The altar was brought forward, and the sanctuary area was re-carpeted. Interestingly, the services of 1998 again have a Catholic flavour, due in part to Lanner's incorporation into the Redruth Circuit, which is led by St Andrews which is quite 'High Church'. Perhaps this also emphasises the aims of the Western Church towards eventual reunification. However, it is interesting to note the comment of one of the ministers in 1997 'This area is most definitely a 'Nonconformist' one, and even the majority of the congregation at Christ Church could be said to have 'Nonconformist' hearts'.

A Renaissance of the Faithful

After the move away from High Church practices, the Church enjoyed growing membership. In 1924, the cleaner's salary was £11 a year, the organist was paid £10, the organ blower £2 and the churchyard work (not including grave digging) £4, and all salaries were supported within the Parish. Clearly the support for the Church was stronger and better organised than in the days of Reverend Hopgood. In 1924, there were two sextons, as there had been a demarcation dispute between the work of the grave digger (paid from the funeral charges) and the churchyard maintenance man. This problem was solved in 1926, when one of them died. The wages of the church cleaner (Mrs Vinson) were raised to 6s 6d per week in 1948. In 1951, the fee for digging graves by the sexton was fixed at £2 for a single grave, £2.15s. if bricked. The Reverend Oliver Roland Walkey replaced the Reverend F.E. Bury who left to take the appointment of the rectorship of Burton Joyce in Nottinghamshire in 1929.

The Reverend O.R. Walkey had done much missionary work in Tasmania, Brazil, Nyasaland and Portuguese East Africa, and was a keen supporter of the Lanner Auxiliary of the British and Foreign Bible Society. In the 1930s, church activity improved, but the parish was still impoverished, concern for this poverty being expressed at the annual Parish Meeting of 1930. In 1934, it was decided not to introduce new schemes of raising money, such as 'free will offerings', because of the level of unemployment throughout the Parish. In 1935, the *West Briton* reported that in 1934 there were 53 scholars and 6 Sunday School teachers at Christ Church, and in 1939, the Electoral Roll of the Church contained 109 names. There had only been 73 in 1934, but by 1944, the number was 111.[89]

The Second World War made things difficult for the normal continuance of church life; in 1940 the Young Men's Bible Class was forced to close, probably because many of its members were conscripted, but the work of the Sunday School went on steadily. Its numbers, and those of the Young People's Fellowship, showed large increases in participants. Midweek Lenten services were discontinued in 1942 due to the blackout and even after the war, hymn books on order in 1949 were held up for over twelve months, owing to the shortage of paper. During the war there were collections for the Bombed Church Fund. The year 1945 saw the Centenary of the Consecration of Christ Church and the establishment of a separate parish; the Centenary services were well-attended despite the war.

When the war ended, there was a big effort to improve the physical state of the church, including a redecorating scheme. It was also proposed that the British Legion be allowed to place a granite War Memorial on the western wall of the lych gate, to commemorate the men of the village who had lost their lives in the Second World War. This would join the War Memorial erected in 1920 for those who had perished in the 1914–18 war. A procession of the Men's and Women's British Legion members from Lanner, Perranwell and Redruth, headed by the Carharrack and St Day Band, marched from Trevarth Corner for the dedication service taken by Dr J. Holden.

The lych gate had been erected by John Tiddy, a local builder, at a cost of £75.10s., with £60.18s.19d raised through canvassing the villagers door to door for subscriptions.

In 1947, a new charismatic vicar, the Revd Colin Craven-Sands, came to Christ Church. He had been the vicar of Port Kembia, New South Wales, Australia, before coming to Lanner. In his report to the Annual Meeting on 12 January 1948, he stated that the Sunday School was the worst that he had ever seen. More teachers and helpers were required. When he arrived in Lanner a few months before, he did not like the place at first, but he and his wife were 'very happy now', and he hoped that there would be an increase in church congregations. However, there were a Girls' Club, a Girls' League, a choir, a Boys' Club (they were 'young and wild as young boys will be'), a bright hour following every service on Sunday nights, a Women's Fellowship, a new organ on the way, and there was a parish room at the vicarage, used two nights a week. Revd Craven-Sands quickly outlined plans to increase the activities of the church, and it was decided to publish a monthly Parish Paper and Newsletter for circulation in the Parish, and a Men's Enquiry Circle was formed which met at the Vicarage fortnightly to deal with current religious problems and questions about Christianity. During his ministry, the Lanner St John Ambulance Cadet Division led by W.N. Dunstan and H.E. Grigg was founded (in 1948), and a 'Busy Bees' group was formed to clean the churchyard, and were also put to work on the provision of a tennis court at the Vicarage for the use of the parishioners.

The Revd Colin Craven-Sands became very popular in the parish, and is still remembered with affection. The period from the late 1940s to the mid 1950s was probably one of the best eras for the church, as the Treasurer's report which appeared in the *West Briton* of 26 January 1950 confirms. There was a balance of £1263, which was almost twice as much as that of 1948, and six times greater than 1947. One hundred members of the congregation were using the weekly free will offerings. The congregation had increased in number, (but the vicar still considered that they were not as large and regular as they might be) and was composed mainly of people from working backgrounds, as opposed to the Chapel goers (the majority of whom were members of the former Wesleyan congregation), who were seen as more 'well to do' both by themselves but also the wider community. Many of them were local shopkeepers and businessmen – the middle class of the village. The old 'Bryanite' or United Methodist Chapel had closed, and many former members of its congregation found Christ Church more to their liking than Lanner Methodist Chapel, which perhaps proved the success of moving away from Romish practices. Many Lanner people appeared to view the Church as another type of chapel.

Sylvia Kessell, who attended the church with her parents, Harry and Ida Polkinghorne of Carn Marth, at this time, remembers the church being packed, and anyone arriving late for the evening service would sometimes find it difficult to find a place to sit down. Craven-Sands clearly enjoyed the company of his parishioners, occasionally playing cards, monopoly and dominoes with them, but strongly disapproved of dog racing, and vowed at the Parochial Council Meeting of 2 September 1948 to 'end the new menace to the district.' He set about forming a committee to raise money to prevent the proposed dog racing track planned for nearby Pool. He was also most vociferous in his opposition to fox hunting which did not win him any friends among the hunting fraternity, and he initiated a court case against leaders of a hunt which had crossed the Vicarage grounds, which he subsequently lost. This made his position at Lanner uncomfortable, and he did not remain in the parish for as long as his parishioners would have liked, returning to Australia in 1951. A new vicar (Reverend J. Vernon Shaw) was appointed in 1951, and F.G. Parr was made Secretary of the Parochial Church Council, as well as being Organist and Choirmaster. Freddie Parr became a major figure in the life of the village. A Parish Magazine was started, being sold for 2d per copy, and summer fetes became popular, raising much needed money through the sale of teas at 2d per cup and cakes at 3d each. There were annual Sunday School outings to Carbis Bay in August, harvest suppers and Christmas parties. By 1962, Sunday School numbers had increased to 29, from 15 the previous year, and the outing was to St Ives.

Years of Decline and the Creation of a Circuit Ministry

But the late 1960s were years of decline for the church. The Reverend J. Vernon Shaw died suddenly, placing Lanner in a very precarious position when a new vicar had to be appointed. The Parochial Church Council (PCC), writing to the patrons of the living, stated that 'the parish is traditionally Evangelical... it is not an easy parish to administer, and the PCC feels its needs would be best met by the appointment of a family man of energetic and resolute character who would be prepared to stay with the parish for a reasonable number of years'.[90] After four clergymen had turned the living down, the Bishop considered that Lanner should be united with, or held in plurality with, an adjoining benefice. While this was considered, the Vicar of Gwennap, the Reverend W.H. Greening, agreed to act as Priest-in-Charge.

The Parochial Church Council and the parishioners did not find the proposal to unite with another parish acceptable, and the Bishop therefore proposed that presentation to the benefice should be suspended for a period of five years, a suspension which could be terminated at any time. The Parochial Church Council had agreed to this proposal, but hoped that before too long a time had passed, there could be an appointment of a vicar to the parish. The lack of a resident vicar meant that there had to be an inevitable cut back in the amount of services, as in addition to Lanner, the Reverend Greening had to single-handedly run the two neighbouring parishes of Gwennap and Carharrack. Later in 1962, the Vicar of Gwennap, the Revd Greening, Priest-in-Charge at Lanner, left the area and the Bishop agreed to the Parochial Church Council's request that he review the five-year suspension. As a result a resident Priest-in-Charge, the Revd J.W. Fitkin, was appointed.

By 1964, the Women's Fellowship continued to have about 20 members, under the guidance of Mrs L. Lapham. But attendance at the church services had fallen off, to the concern of the Revd J.W. Fitkin, and he himself had been ill. The churchwardens felt that this was an important factor, and they asked him to retire, or at least take a period of complete rest. In 1965, the Revd W.H. Greening was again appointed Priest-in-Charge. The Bishop extended the suspension of presentation to the benefice for a further five years in 1967, in spite of the fact that the Martyrs' Memorial and Church of England Trust had asked him to consider whether the size of Lanner's population (approaching 2000) did not warrant a renewal of the appointment of a vicar.

The Parochial Church Council proposed in 1967 to the Diocesan Authority that the Church Green be handed over to the Camborne-Redruth Urban District Council, as the cost of upkeep had fallen heavily on the church, but no deeds were held by the Diocesan Board. In 1970, it was found that the trustees of the Green were the Patrons (the Church of England Martyrs' and Memorial Trust), who did not object to registration as Common Land. This was done, with the Parochial Church Council as trustees. 'The Green was now for the common use of the parish for recreation etc.'[91] About twenty years later, responsibility for maintaining the Church Green in Rough Street was taken over by the Lanner Parish Council, who fenced it off to stop cars being parked on it.

The Reverend D.C. Knight had taken over from the Reverend W.H. Greening as Priest-in-Charge in 1969, and remained in office until 1975. The idea of reorganising the parishes in the Camborne–Redruth area in order to save money had been mooted since the 1960s. A combined parish population of 42 000 was covered by 12 vicars and 3 curates, and it was increasingly felt that livings in small parishes such as Lanner could only continue if they were viable. The ultimate aim seemed to be that if any living became vacant it would be swallowed up by the nearest main church. In Lanner's case, it appeared that this was likely to have been Redruth. Indeed this is what happened in the early 1980s. Lanner is now included in a team ministry which includes St Stephens Treleigh, St Euny, Redruth, St Andrews, Redruth and Pencoys Four Lanes. Four team vicars share the responsibilities for ministrations at the Church – Father Roger Bush, Father Dennis Nichols and Father Colin Thurston. At the time of writing, Father Robert Sellars, the incumbent of Pencoys, had just left to take up the living at Devoran.

The congregation in the early 1990s was very small, scarcely exceeding an average of 15 communicants. The choir had been disbanded, Evensong was no more and there was no Sunday School. There were two services each week, on Sunday and Wednesday mornings. However, a team of dedicated, enthusiastic young ministers has been rewarded of late with increased membership, to add to the long-term workers, such as Mrs Gertie Crutchfield, who have helped to keep the Church going over the years. In 1995, the congregation celebrated the 150th anniversary of the Consecration of Christ Church with a number of special events, and the following year a new Sunday School commenced under the leadership of Mrs Penny Butt, which continues to grow. Evensong was restarted in April 1998.

An award of £5000 from the National Lottery Fund was announced in the autumn of 1997, to help towards the refurbishment of the kitchen and toilet facilities at the Parish Hall. Members of the congregation repainted the interior of the church during the summer of 1997 and the bell, which had been broken, was repaired. There is however, still a threat of an uncertain future hanging over Christ Church, and the congregation will have to work hard to raise the necessary finance to keep the church going in the Parish and thus ensure that the Church of England will enjoy a continued presence in Lanner in the twenty-first century.

Conclusion

Without a doubt, religion played a vital role in the development of Lanner, a Cornish mining parish. Methodism arrived in the village because of the geographical isolation of Gwennap Parish Church and acquired a stronghold which it has never relinquished. The Anglican Church has never made an enormous impact in the parish, the clergy of the nineteenth century in particular being partially to blame for this state of affairs. Lanner Christ Church has enjoyed periods of strength when it has had a 'Low Church' minister. The times in which it has been at its lowest ebb have been when it has had a Romish incumbent which created an automatic antipathy between the Church and the Methodist community. The Church of England has, nevertheless, held its own in the Lanner area and in 1998 has a decent sized congregation and growing Sunday School, but is nowhere near as high profile as the Church of England in other rural parts of Cornwall.

During the nineteenth century the Methodist Chapels in particular gave the growing middle class of the developing mining village a focus for their energies and enthusiasm for improvement, in both personal and social spheres. We see this manifested in the wide variety of chapel related organisations which flourished in Lanner, ranging from Mutual Improvement Classes, and Bands of Hope to Chapel Choirs and Burial Clubs. But in turn, such Chapel activities also helped working class families to provide the resources necessary to prepare strategies to cope with the pressures of a rapidly industrialising society, and so created the social solvent which bonded people together and helped to prevent growing class divisions. Methodist emphasis on thrift and hard work went some way towards allowing customary lifestyles (in Lanner's case, a traditional mining mentality of independence) to be maintained in the face of rapid economic change. Methodism can be viewed as a bridge from the traditional to the modern world, promoting liberal, individualist ideas, along with a maintenance of recognised structures of continuity and tradition. The Methodist Church therefore provided the third great pillar supporting life for its people – the others being the home and the workplace (for Lanner, this was the mine).

Church or Chapel was the channel for the Lanner people's love of music, and provided the main means of leisure and entertainment in the days before radio and television, as we shall see in Chapter 12. Places of worship played very important roles as regards education in the period before the opening of Lanner Board School in 1878, as we will discuss in the next chapter. The Church was also often seen as a source of employment, especially in the mid nineteenth century, when most of the chapel notables were connected with the local mines in one way or another. If your face was seen in chapel on Sundays, there might be a job for you at the mine.

The church was the great social institution which bound the community together, and fulfilled the spiritual, social and employment needs of many Lanner parishioners. During the twentieth century, interest in the churches has waned, especially since the 1939–45 War. Today the parish has but three places of worship; Lanner Christ Church, Lanner Methodist Chapel and the Kingdom Hall of Jehovah's Witnesses. The reasons for this are beyond the scope of this book, but it would be true to say that of all the religious places of worship remaining in the parish, Lanner Methodist Church has retained a strength of participation which, despite a recent decline in membership, is higher than the norm in Cornwall, never mind more generally in England.

REFERENCES

1 James, C. C., *History of Gwennap,* Privately Published, Penzance, Undated, p. 46.
2 Ibid.
3 Religious Census of Cornwall, AD 1676, Ref. No. C.274.23707, CSL, Redruth.
4 Rule, John, 'Popular Beliefs and Village Culture, 1800-1850', in Robert Storchy (ed.), *Popular Culture and Custom in nineteenth century England*, London, 1982, p.61.
5 Luker, David, 'Revivalism and Popular Belief, c. 1780-1870, D. Phil., Oxford, 1987, p. 396.
6 Munson, James, *The Nonconformists. In Search of a Lost Culture.* S.P.C.K., London, 1991, pp. 19-26.
7 Probert, John C.C., Redruth Methodist Businessmen: An Assessment, C.M.H.M., 1989, 11-17.
8 Pearce, J, 'The Wesleys in Cornwall', Bradford Barton, Truro, 1964, pp. 24-25.
9 Symons, R. 'Wesley's Ministerial Itineraries in Cornwall', 1879.
10 *Bible Christian Magazine*, January 1843, p. 232.
11 Ibid. 1867, p.88-89.
12 Ibid. 1891, p.180-1.
13 *Cornish Post and Mining News*, 30/6/1904.
14 MR/R/1463, CRO, Truro.
15 DD/PD/58, John Ryland's Library, Manchester.
16 *Cornish Post and Mining News*, 19/2/1903.
17 *Cornubian*, 31/7/1903.
18 Courtesy Michael Tangye.
19 *Cornubian*, 7/5/1903.
20 *Cornubian*, 21/11/1903.
21 *Cornubian*, 2/1/1903.
22 *Wesleyan Methodist Association Magazine*, 1837, p. 279; 1850, p. 100, RIC, Truro.
23 Probert, J.C.C., *Primitive Methodism in Cornwall*, Redruth, 1966, p.30.
24 Ibid, p. 31.
25 *Cornubian*, 18/9/1903.
26 *Redruth Independent*, 2/12/1887.
27 *Cornubian*, 25/11/1887.
28 *Cornubian*, 9/12/1887.
29 *Cornubian*, 16/7/1886.
30 *Cornubian*, 6/12/1902.
31 MR/R/1464, CRO, Truro.

32 MR/R/324, CRO, Truro.
33 MR/R/1467, CRO, Truro.
34 Probert, p.19.
35 MR/R/395, CRO, Truro.
36 *Cornubian*, 24/5/1889; 23/8/1889.
37 *Cornubian*, 16/11/1883.
38 Mitchell, J, 'A Cornishman Remembers' Campaign Literature, Saltcoats, Ayrshire, 1991.
39 *Cornubian*, 11/5/1888
40 *Cornish Post and Mining News*, 18/6/1903.
41 *Wesleyan Methodist Association Magazine*, 1849, p.558, RIC, Truro.
42 *Cornubian*, 26/5/1882.
43 Courtesy of Michael Tangye.
44 *Cornubian*, 29/4/1896.
45 *Cornubian*, 9/5/1902.
46 Courtesy of Michael Tangye.
47 Ibid.
48 *Cornubian*, 31/7/1891.
49 Courtesy of Michael Tangye.
50 Courtesy of Geoffrey Olds.
51 *Cornubian*, 24/1/1890.
52 Methodist Circuit Papers, held by CSL, Redruth, Courtesy of J.C.C. Probert.
53 Best G., *Mid Victorian Britain, 1851-70*, Wiedenfeld and Nicholson, London, 1971, p. 209.
54 P 79/81/1, 20/10/1840, CRO, Truro; *The Local Historian, Vol 27, No.2*, May 1997, p. 93.
55 Unidentified Newspaper Cutting.
56 Pearson, A., Old Cornwall, Volume IX, Autumn, 1982, p.338: 1983, Volume IX, Spring, p. 402.
57 James, C.C., p. 52.
58 Best, G. p. 211.
59 *Cornubian*, 29/6/1883.
60 *Cornubian*, 14/9/1883.
61 James, C.C., p.52.
62 Polsue, J., *A Parochial History of Cornwall, Vol II*, William Lake, Truro, 1868, p. 141.
63 James, C.C., p.52.
64 *West Briton*, 23/2/1847.
65 Francis, William, *Gwennap A Descriptive Poem*, J. May, Redruth, 1845, p. 136 & 137.
66 1851 Religious Census, CSL, Redruth.
67 Francis, William, p.140.
68 Probert, John C.C., *1851 Census, West Cornwall and the Isles of Scilly*. Privately Published, 1998.
69 *Cornubian*, 28/11/1888.
70 *Royal Cornwall Gazette*, 20/2/1875.
71 *Cornubian*, 26/6/1874.
72 *Cornubian*, 24/4/1875.
73 *Cornubian*, 3/5/1878.
74 *Cornubian*, 1/7/1887.
75 *Cornubian*, 9/9/1887.
76 *Cornubian*, 8/4/1892.
77 *Cornubian*, 10/11/1882.
78 *West Briton*, 9/1/1896.
79 *Royal Cornwall Gazette*, 1/7/1897.
80 Probert, Johhn C.C., *1851 Census, West Cornwall and the Isles of Scilly*. Privately Published, 1998.
81 Tregidga, Garry, 'Politics of the Celto-Cornish Revival 1886-1939', *Cornish Studies 5*, University of Exeter Press, 1997, p.137.
82 *Royal Cornwall Gazette*, 24/10/1923.
83 *Royal Cornwall Gazettee*, 26/12/1923.
84 *Royal Cornwall Gazette*, 24/10/1923.
85 *Cornubian*, 11/1/1884.
86 *West Briton*, 12/7/1928.

87 Walke, Bernard, *Twenty Years at St. Hilary*, Methuen Books, 1935, pp. 292-300.
88 P 112/7/2, CRO, Truro.
89 *West Briton*, 25/1/1935.
90 P.C.C. Minutes, 13/2/1961, held in the Church safe.
91 Minutes of the Annual Church Meeting, 24/2/1970.

Note: From 1923 to 1928, the minutes of Parochial Church Council meetings in Lanner are available as P112/7/1 in the Cornwall County Records Office, Truro. The Minute Book of the Parochial Church Council Meetings and the Annual Church Meetings from 1929 to 1951 are referenced P112/7/2, but from 1951 to 1972, the Minutes of the Lanner Parish Church Annual Meetings and Vestry Meetings are available as P112/7/3. Subsequent minutes of the Parochial Church Council and Annual Church Meeting are kept in the Church safe. Much of the information in the sections headed 'The Dissenters' was extracted from papers held in the Shaw Collection in the Courtney Library of the Royal Institution of Cornwall, Truro, and from information prepared for the '100 Years of Lanner' Exhibition, 1994, by members of the Lanner Methodist Church.

Fig.10.1. *Engraving of the Trevarth Grammar School, dating from the 1860s. Note the theodolite on the far right, indicating the mine surveying content of the curriculum. The building is Trevarth House, former home of John Paul, Esq., surgeon.* (© Royal Institution of Cornwall, Truro)

Chapter 10
Education

In the early nineteenth century there was a mixed quality of provision for schooling in England, which in effect mirrored the image of the class system which had grown out of the Industrial Revolution. Education became, in the Victorian period, a trump card in the great class competition. In the simplest terms, for the upper classes, the landed and wealthy, there were the famous public schools, Harrow, Rugby and Eton, providing a classical gentleman's education, and many new schools which sought to imitate these great and ancient institutions of Englishness. Lanner Parish could boast of none of these schools. For the middle classes, there were private 'grammar' schools, some of which were endowed, many more to which pupils were admitted on payment of fees. The state seldom interfered in the running of such schools, which often provided an education as good as, and in some cases, far better than the public schools. The working classes were educated in a bewildering assortment of private schools, attended by children who could afford to pay a few pence per week, These were often known as 'Dame Schools', being run by some 'good lady' or gentleman in the community. In addition, there were also small charity schools, endowed by local landowners, to which children were admitted free, or on payment of a few pence per week, or in kind. Sunday schools began in the eighteenth century, and even if the children worked during the week, they could be taught reading and spelling as an aid to reading the Bible. This was an important source of education in Cornwall, both for church-goers and dissenters, by the early nineteenth century.

The big issue of those times was that of bringing an adequate system of education to the masses. Where the provision of elementary education was concerned, Britain lagged far behind many of its industrialised European competitors, and by the 1860s, this state of affairs was thought to have been detrimental to the nation's future development. Very few working class children attended school regularly, and even fewer stayed at school beyond the age of nine or ten, as they were sent to work in mines and factories to help increase family earnings because of the rising cost of living, and were therefore deprived a solid basic education.

We have already noted, in Chapter 4, that children worked at the local mines. The area that was to become Lanner Parish had not developed into a sizeable community before 1800, so educational developments in our area were entirely based in the nineteenth century, and largely followed national lines, according to Parliamentary legislation.

John Hawken's Trevarth Grammar School

One of the first schools within the present Lanner Parish boundary was a private one, set up at Trevarth by subscription of mine agents and the emerging middle class of industrialists, self employed tradesmen and merchants who had made their money through the local mines. These men knew exactly what their young sons required by way of an education to succeed in the newly emerging world of industry and commerce. They wanted to have a 'respectable' school near their own homes, in which their children could obtain 'the rudiments of such scientific knowledge as bore particularly on mining operations, and at the same time to receive somewhat more general instruction than could be obtained from ordinary day schools'.[1] The exact year in which the school began is not known for sure, but there is convincing evidence that it was 1824 (see below), possibly making this the first mining school in Cornwall. In addition to the common elementary books, Chambers' Sciences and Nesbit's Mensuration were used, dialling, mapping, linear and perspective drawing were practised, and French and Latin were taught.

The setting up of this school clearly shows how the local mining industry had developed; the miner would need to know more than that which could have been learnt the traditional way by simply working alongside older men; better educated men were now required as agents, engineers and surveyors who were able to understand the rudiments of geology, engineering and metallurgy, and who were also competent in practical but complicated tasks such as dialling and surveying, both above and below ground. Such an education would have been difficult to achieve in an old fashioned Latin-oriented grammar school, so Trevarth School was breaking new grounds in terms of the quality and type of education on offer.

In 1840–41, the number of pupils on the books was 58, and 'the school appeared to be carefully conducted'.[2] An advertisement appeared in the *West Briton* of 6 March 1829, for 'Trevarth School, Gwennap', in which headmaster, John Hawken, 'begged leave to announce to his friends that his school would reopen after the vacation, on Monday 13 July'. John Hawken, a merchant's son born in Truro in 1794, had made arrangements to receive four pupils as boarders, who would be instructed in the general principles of school education, at twenty guineas per year. He was aided by a staff of assistant teachers; Richard Bennett, aged 20, is shown on the 1841 Census as resident with the Hawken household. Scholars generally attended Trevarth School from age seven or eight until the age of 16 and over, so the establishment was combining elementary instruction with the requirements of a secondary education.

The school was in a building enclosed by a courtyard, set back in a field, on the left immediately past the crossroads on the road from Trevarth to Carharrack. It appears that the school was abandoned by John Hawken sometime after the move to Trevarth House (see below) as the 1880 OS map shows two houses occupying the site. Today a bungalow also stands in the former grounds of the school, next to the two late Victorian houses.

Advertisements for Hawken's premier establishment appeared regularly in local and county newspapers from 1830 to 1838, but on 4 January 1839, the school was advertised with a new name, 'Trevarth Boarding and Day School'. Hawken begged to return his grateful acknowledgement to his kind friends, for the very liberal support which he continued to receive. He most respectfully informed them that his duties at this establishment would be resumed on Monday, 14 January. There was a vacancy for two boarders, and three months' notice was required prior to the removal of a pupil.

The annual prizegivings were always reported by the press. One such example appeared in the *West Briton* on 26 June 26 1840; the prizes on this occasion presented by the Revd T. Phillpotts, assisted by Capt. Arthur, RN. The First Silver Medal for Recitation was awarded to John Tregonning, of Trefula; Richard Mitchell, of St Day, won the First Prize for Maps; William Gill, of St Erme, had the Best Specimen Writing; John Mitchell, of Wheal Rose, was awarded the First prize for Cyphering, and William Whitford, of St Erme, showed 'greatest improvement'. In the *West Briton* report, 'an address composed for the occasion by H.J. Daniel was delivered by one of the pupils, aged 8, with considerable effect'.

On 1 July 1842, the Annual Meeting of the 'Trevarth Academy' took place, with the school 'appropriately decorated for the occasion'. A large number of recitations in every variety of style was given by the boys. An inspection of penmanship and mapping took place, cyphering books were displayed 'all of a very high standard'. Three silver medals were awarded, together with six books from Mr Hawken himself. 'Mr Tregellas told the boys that next year he would award a prize for the best drawing of Gwennap Church and adjoining scenery'. John Hawken, after consulting the boys, awarded a silver pencil case to Henry Paul, for general good conduct. This prize had been given anonymously for this purpose.

A mark of Hawken's success with his school was his announcement of 1842 'to inform Parents and Guardians of his having removed his Establishment to the extensive House and Grounds of the late John Paul Esq. surgeon, at Trevarth House, where he will be enabled to afford accommodations to an increased number of Pupils. The House is beautifully situated on a Play-ground Lawn of Six Acres, and possesses every comfort and advantage that can be desired for a Boarding School Establishment'. Hawken expressed thanks for the liberal manner in which his school had been supported for the last eighteen years, at Trevarth, which strengthens the argument for supposing the foundation to have been at least as early as 1824. The advertisement went on to say 'The course of instruction includes every item constituting a useful and solid English Education, which includes Land and Mine Surveying, Linear and Perspective Drawing, to which may be added French and Latin. Parents may rely on every attention being paid to the health, comfort, and morals of the Youths placed under Mr Hawken's care'. The Terms offered were: Annual Boarders 20 guineas per annum; Weekly Boarders 14 guineas; Day Scholars 4 guineas; Geography and Use of the Globe, 1 guinea per annum. A year's washing cost two guineas extra.[3] It should be remembered that at this time, the average miner's wages were two to three pounds a month, so that it would have been difficult for them to send their sons to Trevarth School (Fig.10.1).

The 1851 Census gives details of those living at Trevarth House. John Hawken, aged 57, was a widower, his wife Amelia having died in 1846, aged 40 years. His sons Charles (aged 9) and George (7) were scholars, along with eleven boarders, aged from 9 to 16, from St Agnes, Perranzabuloe, Falmouth, Truro, Mabe, Illogan and Gwennap. The boarders did not come from far away, but daily travel for most of them was probably out of the question at that time. This was certainly true of a twelfth boarder called Oslen, a 21-year-old from Norway. Ellen Coombe, 57 (a widowed housekeeper, the daughter of William Edgcombe, architect, who later became Hawken's wife), three house servants and a washerwoman were also living in. (Hawken's other sons John (20), Bryant (18) and William (15) had left home, John and William working for their grandfather, a grocer, in Truro).

The half-yearly examination results of 1856 provide a further insight as to what was taught at the school, with subjects ranging from arithmetic, English grammar and composition, as well as geography, English history and sacred history. An address to the boys at the conclusion of the prizegiving reminded all present that 'the prize boys at school generally proved the prize men of the world'.[4] The school rapidly acquired a good reputation within the county, and was widely seen as an establishment to which aspiring middle class gentlemen who wished to make a statement about their having 'arrived in society', sent their young sons. Indeed, over the following decades, its scholars successfully passed the Senior and Junior Oxford Local Civil Service, Preliminary Law and Pharmaceutical Examinations, and the local Oxford and Cambridge examinations. A certificate for a pass in any one of these examinations was considered a passport in society.[5] Hawken's son, Charles, won prizes for his studies in dentistry at Westminster Hospital.[6]

At the end of 1865 John Hawken decided to retire as the principal of Trevarth School. J. Tippett, the senior pupil, presented Hawken with a handsome and valuable silver inkstand as a parting gift from his scholars. The *Cornubian* reported on the sumptuous dinner, held in March 1866 at Tabb's Hotel, Redruth, at which 30 gentlemen, his former pupils, attended to present a testimonial to John Hawken. The Chairman, Philip Blamey, remarked in his speech that Trevarth Grammar School was regarded as one of the best educational establishments in the county, and M.R. Mitchell, a Redruth draper, noted that Trevarth School's reputation was admired worldwide, many of Mr Hawken's old pupils now being resident in every part of the globe.

An emotional John Hawken was presented with a heavy and richly ornamented silver tea and coffee service, upon which was engraved, on a shield, 'Presented to Mr John Hawken of Trevarth School, by his old pupils as a token of respect, and in recognition of the services he has rendered during a period of 40 years – Christmas 1865'.[7] Hawken died on 17 March 1867, aged 67.

'Daddy' Green

In 1866 Hawken instructed a sale by auction of the effects of Trevarth House, which was taken over by Richard Green from Bromley, Kent, and affectionately known as 'Daddy Green' by his pupils. Green, a talented man, was elected a Fellow of the Society of Arts on 13 April 1878.[8] The fine reputation the school enjoyed was continued by Green and was reflected in the numbers of pupils who were sent by their parents from places worldwide to receive a sound and comprehensive education. In 1871, a pupil was listed as being born of Cornish parentage in Chile, and in 1888, pupils from London, South Africa, Dublin and Brazil are noted on the school roll. Five languages were taught at the school, Latin, Greek, French, Spanish and German, emphasising its cosmopolitan connections, and providing a far broader range of instruction than the Latin-oriented grammar schools.

Trevarth Grammar School saw that its pupils were especially prepared for public examinations, and were offered both a sound classical and commercial education, the latter of especial importance to a rising middle class of industrialists, merchants, tradesmen and shopkeepers.

Sport was not neglected; Trevarth House Cricket Team was victorious over the Redruth Juniors in 1876 and the earliest rugby played in Lanner was that which took place on the lawns of Trevarth House Grammar School.[9] (Fig. 10.2.).

The school continued to operate after the 1870 Education Act and the building of Lanner Board School, an advertisement appearing in the *West Briton* in 1893 noting that young and delicate boys were given special attention. The school was listed for the last time in *Kelly's Directory* of 1897, and had perhaps suffered from the competition of the Commercial School, operated by William Carah Edwards at nearby Carharrack. This school offered a more modern

Education.

TREVARTH HOUSE GRAMMAR SCHOOL,
GWENNAP, REDRUTH.

ESTABLISHED more than fifty years. Situated in one of the most healthy parts of Cornwall. A lawn of nine acres. Affords a sound classical and commercial education. A public half-yearly examination. Prizes awarded to the most successful in each subject. Pupils prepared for public examinations. Moderate terms. For prospectus apply to R. GREEN, Principal. 63

Fig.10.2. *Advertisement from the* West Briton *of 2 December 1880. Pupils of Cornish Parentage from many parts of the world were sent to Trevarth School as boarders.*

curriculum than Trevarth, as lessons in music, chemistry and other scientific classes were available. One former pupil, James Hicks, architect, chose to send his stepson, Thomas Henry Jory, to the school at Carharrack rather than his old school at Trevarth.[10]

The *Cornubian* of 12 December 1902 referred to the widespread and deep regret at the departure of Richard Green from Trevarth House to live with his daughter in Liverpool:

> *He has been for 37 years a familiar figure in this parish and was held in very high esteem. He was a zealous worker in church matters and belonged to the Low Church Party. He read the lessons in Gwennap Church for upwards of a quarter of a century... Mr Green, it will be remembered, kept the well known Trevarth House Grammar School, and the greatest tribute that could be paid to his merit as a teacher and educationalist is to be found in the fact that his scholars – and they are legion – still keep up a correspondence... not a Christmas passes without his receiving souvenirs from them.*

The date of closure of the school is not known, but there is a record of a sale including school furniture about 1912, a decade after Green left, and after the house was no longer in use as a school. Baynard Evans recollected in 1966, that Trevarth House then became a home for inebriates.[11] It is now a private house.

Trevarth 'Old Boys'

The measure of the success of Trevarth Grammar School lies in the number of former pupils of Hawken and Green, who succeeded in high-profile careers, both locally and farther afield. And many of them were well-known figures, whose influence permeated through local society – a modernising bourgeoisie. John Simmons Tregoning, born in 1814, was a member of a middle class family of newly rich industrialists, and was a partner in the Firm of Clint, Tregoning & Co. of Liverpool, Metal and Ship Brokers, established in 1844, and later of the Llanelly Tinplate Works. His parents were among those who helped to set up Trevarth School in the early 1820s. John's brother, William Henry Tregoning, was also educated at Trevarth School, and was a partner in the small but successful Bissoe Tin Smelting Works. John Tregoning the Second, John's son, was also educated by John Hawken, and established the company of J.S. Tregoning in London in 1869. He was the High Sherrif of Cornwall in 1904–5.[12] Richard Manuel Blamey, the son of Philip Blamey, attended the school in the 1830s, and became an extra licentiate of the Royal College of Physicians, London, and held positions in Heidelburg, in 1842, and in Australia in 1844–48.[13]

James Hicks, who attended the school in the 1850s, rose to great prominence as an architect and surveyor (see Chapter 5, above), agent for the Treruffe and Trefusis Estates, businessman and entrepreneur, President of the Redruth Residents' Association and member of the new Redruth Urban District Council in 1895. Examples of his work were exhibited at the Royal Academy of Art, London.[14] John Waters attended Trevarth between 1844–1851. Born at Scorrier in 1835, Waters was the son of South American mine proprietor, Sampson Waters, and held various appointments in Chile, as well as becoming a successful poet, his major work being *The Refugee and Other Poems*, published by Longman of London in 1862.[15] Sir Arthur Carkeek, director of a major constructional company, one of Redruth's leading citizens and Chairman of Cornwall County Council, attended Trevarth in the 1870s.[16]

The Reverend William James was for a time educated at Trevarth, and after becoming a Bible Christian Minister, undertook seven years of missionary work in Cardiff.[17] William Wilton of St Day was noted as being the recipient of the a prize for penmanship in 1849; he later established a well known mathematical instrument business at St Day. Wilton's theodolites were sought after worldwide, and his son, William Henry Wilton, eventually declined business in Cornwall in favour of Valparíso, Chile.

Stephen Mitchell, of St Day, was the joint author of prize essays with Letcher Bros. on Mining Machinery and Tools and Cornish Mine Drainage. Former pupil John Teague, born in 1833, migrated to Grass Valley in 1856 where he set up a quartz mill and also became a gold broker. He later migrated to Victoria, British Columbia and joined the Gold Rush to the goldfields of Fraser Valley. He became a very important architect in Victoria, and many public buildings of note bear testimony to his great ability.[18]

One of Richard Green's former pupils was General Manning, Commander of military operations in Somaliland in the late nineteenth century, and another was Captain Egbert Barry Cornwall Hambley, born in Hayle in 1862. After leaving Trevarth, Hambley went to study at the Royal School of Mines at Kensington and, at 26, he was one of the youngest ever to be elected a life member of the Geological Society of London. He worked in London for Cornish mining entrepreneur J.J. Truran, who was an executive officer to many mining companies doing business abroad. In 1881 Hambley was sent as assistant manager to the Gold Hill Mines in North Carolina, and after three years attracted the attention of Messrs John Taylor & Sons who sent him to India as a engineer to the Indian Gold Mining Company of Glasgow. In 1887 he migrated to North Carolina, where he was at one time manager and consultant to eight different English mining companies doing business there. Hambley was also connected with various other enterprises in North Carolina – cotton mills, electricity companies, railroads, granite quarries, water power stations, farms, and banks.[19] His education, training and studies had prepared him well to be a civil and mining engineer, and in this, the instruction he received at Trevarth played no small part. For Trevarth Grammar School helped to mould and prepare the young men who were to play such an important role in industry, politics and public life, both in Cornwall and farther afield.

Early Education facilities in Gwennap Parish

A report in 1818, concerning the various schools in the Cornish parishes, noted Gwennap as having a parish school where 62 children were taught, the master being paid annually £25.4s. out of the parish rates.[20] A new Church School was built at Gwennap Churchtown in about 1826, under the auspices of the Reverend Martin. The school building was 60 feet long, 20 feet wide and 13 feet high, built of stone and covered with slate.[21] A Girls' School, for 60 scholars, was also in existence, operating along the lines of Mr Bell's plan (in which schools adopted a cheap and specific method of teaching with the aid of monitors), and was maintained by subscription. A new Girl's School was built in 1838 in the vicinity of the Vicarage grounds. (This school was demolished in 1890.).

In addition there were two further schools, at Gwennap and St Day, containing together 70 children. But these schools were over a mile-and-a-half in distance from the rapidly developing village of Lanner.

The 1818 report also mentions the existence of 6 schools in which 166 'free' children were instructed, and 11 schools kept by women (often widows), known as 'Dame Schools', comprising 169 children. Schools of this type were probably more widely used by Lanner's working-class children than the parochial schools at Gwennap Churchtown, because they were nearer to their homes. William Francis mentions the existence of one such Dame School at Trevarth in his poem of 1845:

Here memory recalls from the earliest day
The scenes of tuition, of pleasure and play;
Here the dame instructed her juvenile charge,
Severe in her school, she sought to enlarge
The infantile mind, and oft did she succeed,
Pupils reach'd her climax – the Bible could read.[22]

A Dame School at best taught the child to read and write in the most basic manner; at worst they were merely child-minding facilities, but were often the only provision for education open to the working classes, who paid one or two pence a week, or in kind. Such schools often operated in domestic surroundings, as the following example from the

Lizard area illustrates: 'Old Mrs Polkinghorne kept a good specimen of an old Dame's school. We sat in her small kitchen while she taught us and did her ordinary work at the same time. We read our lessons by her side while she washed her clothes'.[23] Later references to other Dame Schools in the area include a school at Trevarth, operated by Ann Trewartha, listed on the 1851 Census as a 44-year-old widow. Another school of this type appears to have existed at Pennance, operated by spinster Ann Treweek, aged 50, described on the 1851 Census as a tutoress.

It is not difficult to see why the standard of the provision for education of the poor was low and largely ineffectual within Gwennap in the early nineteenth century. Consider the comments of the Curate of Gwennap Church, the Revd J.J. Keigwin, to the 1818 report of the Select Committee, appointed to enquire into the Education of the Poor. This 'enlightened' gentleman stated that he conceived that the poorer classes: 'have quite sufficient means of educating their children and that they are satisfied with them'. The Minister also thought it 'more for the happiness of the poorer classes, that they should find their own education, than to have it found for them' and, incredibly, he believed that they might have been too well educated.[24]

Lanner Church School and Village Sunday Schools

The lack of education facilities for the poor in the late eighteenth century, and the largely ineffectual standard of teaching open to the poor in existing schools, prompted the churches to step in with provision for elementary education, for which pupils paid a few pence a week. In 1810, members of the Non Conformist Churches founded what eventually became known as the British and Foreign School. The following year, the Anglicans fought back with the establishment of their National Society for Promoting the Education of the Poor in the Principles of the Established Church.

As we have established in the previous chapter, Gwennap Churchtown, with its parochial schools, was geographically isolated from the rapidly growing village of Lanner, and there was therefore a need for a National School to serve the requirements of a population almost solely of mining families. A Church school in Lanner is mentioned in a letter from Gwennap Vicarage on 25 October 1838, addressed to the National Society which channelled Government funds for Church schools. The letter was in connection with proposals to build an Episcopal Chapel in Lanner. 'A very eligible piece of ground has already been granted by the Revd Canon Rogers; on part of this a National School-room has been erected, which, though originally designed for only 80 scholars and only opened within two years, already numbers nearly 200'.[25] In 1836 this school was granted a £5 annual allowance from the Gwennap Vestry. But the reasons for opening the schoolroom in Lanner were not necessarily purely philanthropic; for by providing a school the Church hoped to recover some of the ground which it had seemingly lost to Methodism.

Kelly's Directory of 1873 notes that there was a 'schoolroom attached to the church, with residence for a mistress' – Miss Grace Bray. The schoolroom was almost certainly the one now attached to the church in Lanner, currently functioning as the Parish Hall, and the mistress's 'residence', which contained a fireplace, is the two-windowed 'lean to' which now contains the kitchen and toilets. How 80 children, let alone 200, were supposed to get into that space is a matter for some speculation.

The National School at Lanner was not included in the Government survey of 1850, so it is not known what standard of education was achieved there. The Mistress would undoubtedly have been helped in her endeavours by a couple of monitors, and learning would have been mainly by rote. The parochial schools were largely concerned with religious knowledge based on the Bible, Prayer Book and Church Catechism, and the standards achieved were not always very high as evidenced by the following example quoted by Blewett, of a child's attempt to write from memory 'My Duty Towards God':

> *My duty towards God is to bleed in him, to fering and to loaf withold your arts, withold mine, withold my sold, and with my sernth, to wirchp and give thanks, to put my old trash in Him.*[26]

Nevertheless, parents were glad of the opportunity to send their children to the church schools, and the 1841 Children's Employment Commission noted several children employed at Trethellan and Tresavean Mines as having formerly attended the school at Lanner. Samuel Tippett, a 10-year-old in 1841, learnt to read and spell there, and Grace Bawden also attended school at Lanner New Church, and at 17 years old was found to read very well.[27]

In the previous chapter we have already noted the role the Sunday Schools had in providing education within Lanner and district. The importance attached to Chapel education can be seen when, in 1833, a Government enquiry noted that in Gwennap there were six Sunday Schools in which 540 males and 456 females received 'gratuitous instruction'.[28]

The first such school in Lanner was probably that of the Wesleyan Chapel, which commenced sometime in or soon after 1828. At Carn Marth, a Sunday School connected to the Church at St Day, and patronised by Miss Ann Williams of Scorrier House, was located in a cottage just below Sea View Farm, close to the lane which leads into Harvey's Quarry. The school, which operated under the National System, was reported to have had 85 pupils in 1833, and lay just inside the Lanner Parish boundary.[29]

The Primitive Methodists of Lanner Moor began a Sunday School in about 1858, in Tresavean Terrace, and included an alphabet class, which was in no way religious, but aimed at teaching the pupils to read. In the morning the scholars attended the Trevarth Wesleyan School. We have noted that a lease was granted in 1862 by Lord Clinton in connection with the opening of a Wesleyan Chapel. This was on the site of a school room, recently erected.

Levels of illiteracy were quite high in the early nineteenth century. This we can in great part attribute to the quickening pace of the Industrial Revolution which dictated that children, on the whole, went to work earlier, and had less free time at their disposal for learning. In 1846 there were 2000 children between the ages of 4–5 years and 14 years in Gwennap Parish, but William Francis, the headmaster at Gwennap Churchtown School estimated that only about 800 of them were attending school. He sympathised with the children, commenting in his 1845 poem that a figure of 800 was really too many:

and too much to expect where children must try
To get what they can as soon as they're able
To help their poor parents to furnish the table.[30]

The Factory Acts of 1802 were introduced to secure a minimum of instruction for children, but they were more often defied than obeyed. The problem of poor educational facilities in the nineteenth century lay not so much with the teachers as with the parents and the economy. Poor parents might have been able to afford the school pence for some of the time, but could rarely resist the temptation to put a child to work when it became old enough to earn a wage, particularly if a number of younger children were also at school, for whom 2d to 3d each per week needed to be paid in school fees. As we have seen in Chapter 4, the majority of juveniles employed at Tresavean and Trethellan mines were forced by necessity to commence work at the age of 9–10 years old. Many were found to have attended day school from between two to five years until they began work, and most relied on Sunday Schools to increase their learning thereafter.

A large percentage of the children, when asked by the Commissioner if they could read, answered that they could read the Testament or Bible tolerably well. This emphasises the influence of religious institutions in the provision of basic education in Lanner and District in the early nineteenth century. Those children who had not attended day school before commencing work, and who were reliant on only the Sunday School for their education, were less likely to be able to read. James Tresidder, aged 18, working at Tresavean in 1841, informed the Commissioner that he attended Sunday School but could not read. James Stevens, a Tresavean miner, was 15 years old, but could read very little, and only went to Sunday School occasionally.[31]

Nevertheless, we can see from Fig.10.3 that overall there were more children who could read to some degree (75 per cent) than who were illiterate (25 per cent), providing evidence that the early schools, such as the new Church School and the various Sunday Schools, had done some good in the community. (We see further evidence of this in Fig.10.4 which depicts adult signatories to the Lanner Marriage Register.).

There were also evening schools operating in the district, such as the one at Stithians Church Town in 1841, for which pupils paid 3d per week. One child, 12-year-old Mary Ann

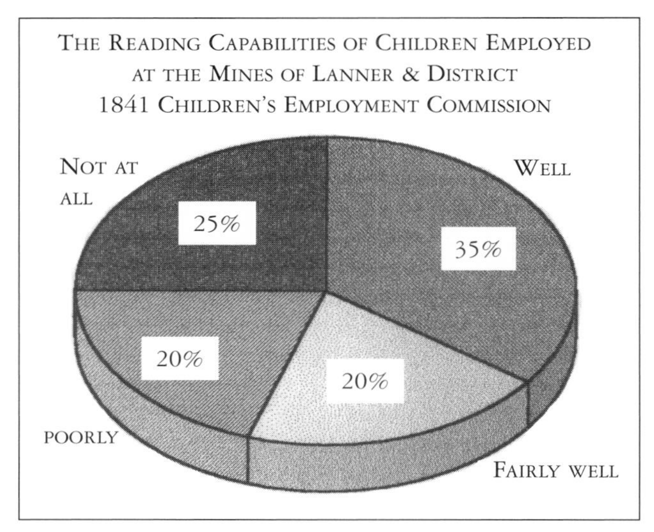

Fig.10.3. *Reading capabilities of children at Lanner's mines, 1841 (from the 1841 Children's Employment Commission, British Parliamentary Papers).*

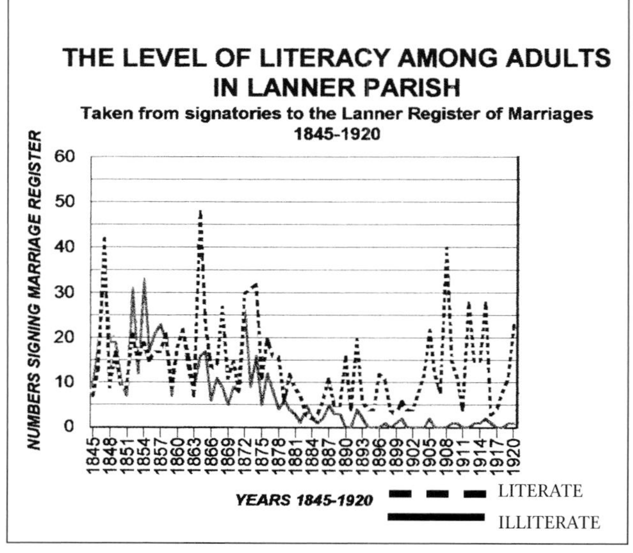

Fig.10.4. *Literacy levels in Lanner Parish, 1845-1920 (from signatories to Lanner Register of Marriages, Cornwall Records Office, Truro).*

Rescorle, replied to the Commissioner in 1841 that she had learnt to read in the Workhouse. All children who were admitted to the poor house were taught to read, one of the more positive and successful elements of policy in those harsh institutions. In 1807 it was estimated that more than 200 000 paupers were in English workhouses, taught by teachers who were themselves inmates of the workhouse. Gwennap's old workhouse was at Burnwithian, near St Day, and had such a pauper-teacher. The Lanner Church School probably ceased to function after 1878, when the Board School was built in the village in accordance with the terms of the 1870 Education Act. An advertisement in the *Cornubian* newspaper of 1888 notes a mission service as taking place at the 'Lannarth Old School'.

The 1870 Education Act and the Creation of Lanner Board School

The Forster Education Act of 1870 marked a notable advance which made its impact in Lanner, as elsewhere. For the first time, every child was to have a school within its reach, which it must attend. To achieve this aim, the Act required School Boards to be set up by parishes, or groups of parishes, with wide powers. Voluntary bodies were given six months to make up the deficiencies in a district, then the gaps were to be filled by School Boards, elected by town councils, and in rural areas, by vestries (in Lanner this was the Gwennap Vestry). The School Board could levy a local rate to build a school, and could accept the transfer of any voluntary school which wanted it.

Boards were free to decide whether religious instruction should be given in schools, and there was a conscience clause for children to avoid it. Gwennap decided to instruct its teachers that the Bible be taught and read daily. School fees within the Gwennap area were set at 1d per week for children under six, 2d for children aged six to nine and 3d for those over nine. Only parents who legitimately could not afford the fees were excused.[32] Education could be made compulsory in an area, and Boards appointed attendance officers – the 'School Board Man'. The attendance Officer for Lanner was W.D. Holman. The Act aimed to provide a basic minimum of education, and by 1892, education was both compulsory and free.

A suitable site upon which to build the new Board School for Lanner was sought. The preferred location for this was the Old Stamps Plot at Pennance, close to the main road, below Woodlands Terrace. But permission to build here was denied by Lord Clinton in 1874. An alternative area of waste ground, belonging to J.J. Rogers Esq., to the east of the road leading to Tresavean Mine, was also considered before the eventual site was chosen. The Lanner Board School was constructed in Little Garden Meadow, on the site of the present Henscol Estate, the entrance of which is almost opposite the present Village Hall. The leasehold for the land was purchased for the sum of £42 from farmer, Philip Bray. The architect was Silvanus Trevail, of Carne, Luxulyan, a prolific builder of schools, responsible for approaching 60 school buildings during the 1870s. Indeed, so many of his buildings were erected that they became known as 'Trevail's Landmarks'.

The builders of Lanner Board School were Messrs William Broad and William Guard of Helston, and the building was in granite, typical of many Cornish schools of that period, and surrounded by a yard with high, partly tarred, granite walls. The cost of the site was £130, and that of the building, £1500. The total cost, inclusive of the architect's commission and sundry expenses was £1900. The school bell was cast by N. Williams & Son, of Helston. The school furniture was purchased for £45, and books, stationary and apparatus were bought at a cost of £47.16.6d.[33]

The new school became yet another of Trevail's visible landmarks, dominating the skyline with its distinctive tower (Fig.10.5). But the interior was very stark in comparison to today's schools, for in the Victorian period, education was a

Fig.10.5. *Lanner, with Pennance Mine, top centre, on the slopes of Carn Marth, showing the old school site in the centre, c.1920.* (© Lanner Historical Society)

privilege to be taken seriously, and children were taught to be eternally grateful for being given the opportunity to learn. These schools were fortresses in the battle against illiteracy, and the pupils sat facing the teacher in a uniform manner on wooden benches. The emphasis was not on developing the skills or talents of the individual, but on collective development, so learning was mainly by rote which, if sufficiently drilled into a class, augured well for the teacher and the school during regular checks by an HMI (Her Majesty's Inspector), and payment was by results!

No colourful pictures adorned the walls of Lanner School in the Victorian period and there was little space allowed for free movement. The windows were designed to be high enough to avoid the distractions of the outside world, so the ceilings were lofty and the floors were of wooden tiles, or stone. Classrooms were therefore difficult to keep warm, the heat being provided by a small, open coal fire situated in the centre of the building. The rooms were lit by paraffin lamps, cleaned daily by the school caretaker. A teacher who stayed on after school had to work by candlelight.

The children's wooden benches had a drawer under them for storage of books, and the wooden desks had a groove along the top for a pencil or chalk to rest on. In the early days, much writing was done on slates. At play times, the boys used the top playground, and the girls and infants the lower one. Children were called in from the playground by the teacher striking a triangle. The school uniform for the girls was black boots and stockings and a white pinafore, and the boys wore black boots and a hat or cap.

A night of entertainment was held in the new school the evening before the opening, the proceeds of which went towards the fund for the proposed setting up of a Literary Institute for the village. The local press carried reports of the official opening on Monday, 15 July 1878, by the Chairman, Mr Trythall of Cusgarne. Also present were J. Rooke of St Day, J. Bawden of Scorrier, members of the Board, the clerk J.G. Edwards, several ladies and gentlemen, and about 80 scholars. 'The Chairman commenced proceedings with some very appropriate remarks to the master, mistress, teachers and children, and expressed a hope that the School they were about to open would prove a blessing to each one of them, and to the neighbourhood at large'. He was followed by J. Bawden, who pointed out to the children the advantages of education, and of the opportunities offered to children of the present day compared with those of their parents. He mentioned several instances that had come under his own notice, both at home and abroad, wherein persons with education had raised themselves from penury to positions of wealth and influence. After a few suitable remarks from the master, J. Richards, the Chairman, declared the School formally opened. 'The premises consist of boys', girls' and infant schools; they are spacious and well arranged, and are calculated to provide accommodation for 300 children'[34]

Despite the considerable improvement in basic education provided in the area by the Church and Chapels, in the mid nineteenth century there was still a degree of illiteracy, which made the need for Lanner Board School the more apparent. At this time a significant percentage of signatories to the Lanner Marriage Register could not write their name and merely made a mark. The Factory Act of 1844 stated that between the ages of 8 and 13, children were obliged to spend three days, or six half days, in school, but this legislation was widely ignored or flouted. Levels of illiteracy were already beginning to decrease, even before the opening of the Lanner Board School in 1879 as can be seen from Fig. 10.4, but after the provision of better quality basic education within Lanner there is a further improvement in the level of literacy.

School attendance figures gradually rose in the later decades of the nineteenth century, in part due to the presence of the 'attendance officer' and the reduction in school fees, but also due to the diminishing opportunities for children in the local economy, as the copper mines in particular shed large numbers of surface workers, while rising real wages helped families to survive without infant earnings.

Moreover, employers known to have been employing children of school age were prosecuted – Mr Goldsworthy of the Miners' Arms Public House was summonsed in 1902 for employing a boy named Pascoe, and in cases where the age of a child was difficult to ascertain, attendance officers were empowered to procure the child's birth certificate as proof of age and thus prevent truancy. Thereafter, the numbers of those unable to sign the marriage register decreased rapidly, resulting in very low levels of illiteracy by the early twentieth century.

The 1870 Education Act established an initial framework upon which free, compulsory elementary education for all was built, but it must be stressed that secondary education was still the prerogative of the better-off for over half a century. The 1902 Education Act abolished the School Boards, and responsibility for all elementary education (including the Church Schools) then passed to the County Councils which began to encourage the setting up of Secondary Schools. These schools, which became the Grammar Schools, were not free, but scholarships were awarded to the most gifted pupils. In our area, the boys attended the single-sex Redruth Grammar School, and the girls went to the Camborne Grammar School for Girls. Secondary modern schools, offering free places, gradually appeared after the 1944 Butler Education Act.

The Fisher Education Act of 1918 had fixed the school-leaving age at 14, with Local Education Authorities empowered to raise it to 15, though few did. No child below the age of 12 could be employed, and the Half-time System was abolished in 1922.

Masters, Mistresses and Monitors

The head teacher's pay in the Board Schools was linked to a Government grant, which was itself dependant on the numbers appearing on the school rolls. The first Government grants for education were introduced in 1834. In 1839, a

Committee of the Privy Council for Education was established, to distribute the grant. At Lanner Board School, Kate Gray was paid six shillings in 1884, for teaching in the afternoons for six weeks. In 1892, the annual salaries of pupil-teachers, who obtained their teaching qualifications by working at the school, rather than going to college (an idea rediscovered a hundred years later by a Government education minister), were between £7 and £13, depending on the years in teaching. Teacher Training Colleges were recognised by the Education Department in 1890.

In 1899, the Gwennap Board passed a resolution that Head Teachers would be paid by individual arrangement, and that Female Assistant Teachers who had passed the Queen's Scholarship examination, would receive £35 per annum, rising by £2.10s. annually to a maximum of £40. Ex-pupil-teachers who had not passed the Queen's Scholarship would be paid by individual arrangement, and pupil-teachers were paid the same as in 1892. Although their duties were basically the same, male pupil-teachers started at one pound a year more than females.[35] Monitors, older children, were essential, and helped the teacher where there were large classes of 30–40 pupils. In the 1890s, they were paid about 13 shillings a quarter out of School fees. Many well known public figures in the community were once monitors, including George Skewes, 'Lawyer' Bray of Lanner House, who became a solicitor. In 1893 Lanner School had 16 members of staff, including three department heads, aided by pupil teachers and monitors (Fig.10.6).

Fig.10.7. *The Girls' Class at Lanner School, 1890. Front row l-r: Clara Holman, Mabel Pryor and Janey Holman (aged 6, and later, Mrs T.C.Knuckey). The photographer came all the way from Yorkshire!* (© Mr and Mrs C. Williams, Lanner)

Teachers often complained of low pay, and as their wages were found out of the local rates, the board was keen to keep wages down so as not to increase the rate burden. In 1901, Miss Hilda Inch, of Lanner Infant's School, who had begun her working life in the Infant's Department as a monitoress in 1892, complained to the Gwennap Board that her salary as a fully qualified teacher was not on the same level as those of the others. Her petition for a wage increase was successful, despite one member of the Board, Mr Rooke, who considered that there were enough teachers there without Miss Inch. She was awarded an increase of £4 per annum.[36]

In 1893 the new head of the Girls School was appointed with a wage of £72 per year and the Infant Mistress was appointed the following year with a salary of £60 per annum. Yet the headmaster, doing a similar job to his female counterparts, was on a wage of about £100 each year. The assistant master received £36 a year in 1891. In 1908, Miss F.C. Phillips began her duties as an ex-pupil-teacher at an annual salary of £14.

But with low pay and more than one adult in the classroom, relations between the teachers and their assistants were sometimes strained; in 1901 Miss Noy complained of differences between herself and her new assistant, Miss Richards. The Board merely recommended that the women 'be urged to their utmost to work amicably in future'. The teachers in Lanner school were more often than not local, and those who were appointed from outside the area were almost exclusively Cornish.

Fig.10.6. *Staff at Lanner School, c.1902.* Back row, third from left, *Miss Trewren.* Next to back row, third from left, *Mr R T Richards (Head of Boys).* Seated on chairs, third from left, *Miss E B Polkinghorne (Head of Infants)*; far right, *Janey Holman (pupil teacher).* (© Mr and Mrs C. Williams, Lanner)

HEAD TEACHERS OF LANNER SCHOOL

Infants
1878-1887 E. Richards
1887-1894 E. Downing
1894-1928 E.B. Polkinghorne
1928-1952 L.J.P. Hensley
1952-1953 L.G. Opie
Girls
1878-1889 E.Hocking
1889-1893 J.Jenkin
1893-1894 D.B. Thomas
1894-1896 E.G. Whetter
1896-1905 Miss Noy
1905-1906 D. Simmon
1907-1909 Miss Williams
1909-1914 J. Hellings
1914-1930 J. Vague
1930-1935 J. W. Jose
1935-1966 G. Nicholls
Boys
1878-1889 J. Richards
1889-1924 R.T. Richards
1924-1927 H.E. Treneer
1927-1934 J.F. Richards
1934-1938 C. Andrew
1938-1959 A.G.S. Blatchford
1959-1986 T.P. Morgan
1986-present P.E. Lloyd

An Inspector Calls

Lanner School was subject to visits by School Inspectors, and the progress of the school was closely followed by the Gwennap Board. The School Log Book records such visits by the much feared School Inspectors, and they appear to have been vividly remembered by the pupils, as their accounts and reminiscences below clearly demonstrate. The HMI Report of May 1889 was quoted in the Log Book:

The proficiency of the children in the elements of Reading, Writing and Number and their manual dexterity alike deserve high commendation. A little more drill and more lessons on common objects given in a simple way would be useful. These children should be catechised not lectured, and even in young children the habit of answering rationally can be cultivated. Drill and some of the many exercises suggested in good manuals of infant instruction will be found most useful in maintaining order without repressing the desire for physical activity which in such a young child is only natural'.[37] (Fig. 10.7.).

Inspectors possessed almost the power of life and death over teaching staff, and these comments were obviously taken to heart by the Mistress (E. Downing), who reported in January 1890 that she had given an Object Lesson on the 'Hen' and the 'Duck'. In 1896, object lessons were given on 'Chalk', 'Horse', 'Tea' and 'Cat'. Another example of the power wielded by inspectors was in 1909, when a Mr R.J. Daniell visited the school at 3.45pm, 20 minutes after the time of closing. He found that the children had been so interested in the games they had in the last lesson that they had stayed on. Although they were just being dismissed, Mr Daniell had them all brought back and tested the registers. He found fault because one child had gone. The Board cautioned Mr Richards in 1890 after an adverse HMI inspection, warning him to do better and make improvements at Lanner Boys' School or his suitability would be questioned. In 1903, the HMI's report stated that the schools were in a 'serious state of inefficiency'.[38] The headmaster was advised that 'The abolition of square and slate work is strongly recommended. The acquirement of the power to observe accurately and to draw common things correctly should receive special attention.' Richards obviously made 'improvements' because by 1905, the HMI Report noted that 'This is a fairly good school'. However, the following recommendations were made: 'More scientific methods should be used in the teaching of number, and reading should in many cases be more natural in style, and better phrased. The speech of children also should be carefully trained. In hemming larger stitches should be employed.'

The Battle Against Truancy

To stamp out truancy and encourage regular attendance, in 1890 Gwennap School Board passed a resolution that prizes would be given as follows:

1). For every child who passes in three standards having attended 450 times in the year - or if living more than one mile from School 440 times.
2). For every child passing as above and attending 420 times or if living more than one mile 410 times.
3). For every child passing as above, attending 400 times, or living more than one mile 390 times.
4). Also for the child in each class who has in the current year made the greatest advance in attendance - the child's name having been on the books throughout both years - provided the child passes in three subjects.

The School Board further added, 'Prizes as above will in no case be given unless the School pence have been regularly paid or the child is duly excused and provided that the conduct of the child has been such as to meet the approval of the Board.'[39] In 1900 the Board introduced medals to reward those with exemplary attendance records. Clearly attendance, good behaviour and (before 1892) payment of fees were held in high esteem. In 1882, the average attendance figures for Lanner Boys was 81-9 out of a total of 116; 70-2

Fig.10.8. Lanner Boys School, c.1905. Jack Polkinghorne of Carn Marth, is fifth from left, second row. (© The Paddy Bradley Collection)

from a total of 120 in the Girls' Department, and 51-6 from a figure of 90 for the Infants' Department.

If a child was absent for more than three days, on the fourth day the 'Whipper-in' was called and sent to the child's home to give the parents a warning. Should the child not turn up at school the next day, the parents were sent to Court at Penryn, where they were fined ten shillings. Parents whose children had not attended regularly, or who had neglected to pay their school fees, were periodically called before the Board to explain why. A variety of excuses and pleas for clemency were entered in the Board Minutes, and some shed light on the sociological problems faced by many poor families at the time. In 1886, Catherine Jane Kemp, a widow with a large family, whose husband had died in November 1884 when her youngest child was but 6 weeks old, was struggling to keep the Carn Marth smallholding on which she lived. She pleaded with the board to allow her older sons to go to work, but the Board responded that it could not interfere in the matter (Fig.10.8).

In 1894 Edith Orme and Mary Ann Harvey had recently been kept at home 'for want of shoes' and Emily Wills' children, Minnie and Thomas, had no proper clothes to go in. Kate Blewett had not attended since the day of examinations 'for fear of being beaten by Mary Nicholls', and Laura Welch had been frequently 'stoned by Williams of Tretharrup' and was too terrorised to attend school thereafter. Many others attended infrequently because they were classed as 'delicate' or an 'invalid' whilst others such as Lucy Barnett, were absent because they were required to work locally or at home, or like Lena Rapson, needed at home to attend to a sick family member. Excuses devised by the parents more often than not fell on deaf ears, and only truly worthy cases were excused from paying the school fees. Legal proceedings were threatened on those parents who neglected to send their children to school regularly.

In order to stimulate the attendance figures and help to lessen non attendance, in 1896 a half holiday was granted on the first Friday afternoon in each month provided that the average attendance in the previous month was 90 per cent or more. In former days, there were no half term or Bank holidays, but the village children were allowed a free day occasionally for special events. In addition to the usual holidays of Easter, Christmas, Whitsun, Harvest Holiday and Midsummer, days off for Chapel tea treats and other important religious events were granted, and there were numerous other holidays noted in the school Log Book. Some examples include a day off for the opening of Truro Cathedral in November 1887, the 1895 visit of Mr J. Passmore Edwards (a well-known Cornish born philanthropist, who was responsible for financing many public buildings in Cornwall, and elsewhere) who came to open the 'Free Library' at Redruth, a free day because of the Local Board Elections in 1898, and a day off for the St Day Flower Show in 1901. On 6 September 1912, the school reopened after the Summer break, and the teacher commented, 'The children are so very backward after being away so long, that it is almost necessary to begin at the commencement of the year's work'. Some things appear to have changed very little!

Strict Disciplinarians

Teachers in the Victorian period were often strict disciplinarians and children caught misbehaving were swiftly punished. A group of boys who were caught climbing up to the school windows were lucky to have got away with a caution on 24 September 1878. After 1888, all children caught climbing on the school walls were punished. At times, punishments appeared to be arbitrary. James Harvey, of Rockfield, Carn Marth, who attended Lanner School in the early 1880s, once received a severe beating from John Richards, the headmaster, after his brother Thomas had played a prank on their school teacher. He had frightened her so severely that it caused her to faint. In order to revive her, the panicking prankster had plucked some 'guckoos' (bluebells) from a vase and given her the bitter water to drink! When she recovered, she thought that it was James who had played the joke, as the two brothers looked so alike, and swiftly reported his misbehaviour to the headmaster. Despite James's protestations of his innocence, he was caned by Richards. But he carried the memory of this injustice into adulthood. Years later, by a twist of fate, he ended up in the same mining town as Richards in South Africa, and could not resist the opportunity of giving his one time teacher 'a good pasting back'![40]

But some parents took exception to what they perceived to be the arbitrary and unjust punishment meted out to their children and the Log Book notes on 18 January 1879 that a woman had complained of her son being 'kept in'. In 1881, Susan Nicholls was sufficiently incensed to bring a complaint in person before the Gwennap Board Meeting, to voice her disapproval at the beating her child had received at the hands of Monitoress Mary Born. Assistant Mistress, Kate Martin, was also mentioned in connection with harsh punishment at Lanner School. The clerk was instructed to inform the Head Teachers that 'they are not to allow any pupil teacher or monitor under any circumstances to strike any child and that any breach of this rule be reported immediately by the Head Teacher to the Board'.

Mrs Job brought another complaint before the Gwennap Board Meeting of 7 December 1886, against the Assistant Master at Lanner Boys School, for inflicting severe punishment on her son. She demanded an enquiry, but nothing further seems to have been done. In 1886 E. Hosking, a monitor at Lanner Boys School, was reported to the Board to have inflicted corporal punishment on a scholar named Jorey. Hosking and his Head Teacher, John Richards, were ordered to attend the next meeting, but the monitor was not dismissed and Richards was merely urged to be more careful.

A case brought to the attention of the Board in 1899 by Philip Bray concerning the 'improper treatment of his son at school' was considered by the Board to have been 'comparatively trifling'. However it comes as no surprise to discover that some parents of this predominantly working class mining village took matters into their own hands and marched into the school to settle things themselves.

It is interesting to discover that in all instances recorded within the Board minutes, the parent was a mother, evidence of the tough, matriarchal character of nineteenth century Lanner. Indeed, in 1899 the clerk was ordered to warn Mrs Uren of Lanner not to enter the school premises during the hours of instruction, and in 1897 a case was brought against Mrs Curtis on behalf of Miss Noy, a teacher who claimed to have been assaulted by her.

Pupils who had misbehaved however, were not let off quite as leniently. In 1892 four boys, John Curnow, Edward Lawry, T. J. Daniell and Richard Vincent, were ordered by the Board to appear at school on Monday afternoon 12 September, to apologise for breaking and entering the school premises. This punishment was made all the more humiliating, as it took place in front of their peers. Moreover, failure to make this public apology would have resulted in legal proceedings.

Teaching Conditions

Examination of the Head teacher's Log Books reveal how difficult it sometimes was to continue the normal school routine, in the face of problems such as an insufficient budget, cramped classrooms, bad weather and inadequate heating. On 19 June 1896 it was reported that 'only half the children were present on Wednesday as it was heavy rain in the morning'. The entry for 21 October 1898 read, 'Capt. Bray (of Seleggan Tin Smelting Works) came to the School on Thursday afternoon to see about the stove and also about three new forms, as at present the children are much too crowded.' On 3 February 1902, a copy of the resolution which had been passed by the Board was noted: 'The Clerk was instructed to write to the teachers at the Lanner School and point out that the Board are of the opinion that the consumption of coal is much greater than is necessary – and this opinion is strengthened and confirmed by the comparison of the consumption of coal at the other schools'. However, the HMI report in May 1905 noted that the heating arrangements were insufficient for cold weather (so presumably the Board felt guilty). The entry for 16 June 1905 reports inclement weather: 'On Tuesday the weather was very wet. Less than 20 per cent were present in the morning and about 40 per cent in the afternoon, so no registers were marked.'

Bad weather commonly disrupted the normal school routine, as the following reports portray: 3 November 1905. 'No registers marked as weather exceedingly wet. Very few children came and the majority of those who did come had to have their things dried before they could do anything'. On 3 March 1909: 'Weather bad, three present in the morning, none in the afternoon, no registers marked'. 16 March 1909: 'Snow on the ground. Thirty two present, 3 had wet feet and could not remain in their classes. Thirty eight came in the afternoon, 16 had very wet feet, half were sent home, the other half dried themselves by the fire. No registers were marked'. 19 March 1916: 'No registers have been marked today as only 19 were present in the morning and out of 36 in the afternoon 4 were sent home as being too wet to stay, and 8 were forced to sit by the fire while their boots and socks were being dried'. 7 January 1929: 'Owing to deep snow and no running of buses, only 32 children were present today. Several of these cried with the cold and had to sit around the fire until warm. No registers were marked'. There was more snow in February, and attendance dropped to 42 (46.1 per cent of the School). The next day, the roads were in a bad state and the cold intense. On 31 January 1930: 'Very heavy rain this morning caused the river that flows under the playground to break through a hole recently made. The coal house was swamped and passage by way of the back door rendered impassable at midday'. Many families in Lanner were desperately poor, and inadequate clothing and footwear probably only added to the problems caused in bad weather (Fig. 10.9.).

Former pupils remember the old 'tortoise' stove with pipes going up to the roof for the smoke to go out. These burnt big buckets of coke, and sometimes the stove's top got red hot. And it was probably an open fire or dangerous old stove which was responsible for the entry in the teacher's Log Book of 28 January 1879: 'A child got sadly burnt this

Fig.10.9. *Lanner School Teachers, c.1920. Miss J Vague, Miss Gribble, Miss Trewren, Miss Lee, Miss Edwards, Miss Polkinghorne, Miss James, Mr R T Richards, Mr H E Treneer, Mr Blatchford.* (© Mrs A. Martin, Mawnan Smith).

Fig.10.10. *Lanner School Minstrel Troupe, 1933.* Back Row l-r: *1. 'Tiger' Riches; 2. W.J.Eddy; 3. ?; 4. Pat Craze; 5. Courtney Magor; 6. Des Bone; 7. ?; 8. ? McKenny; 9. Jack Richards (Headmaster).* Middle row l-r: *1. George Williams; 2. ?; 3. Jack Menadue; 4. Bert Bowles; 5. J.Cox; 6. Len Orme; 7. M.Matthews; 8. H.Adams.* Front row l-r: *1.Ken Minson; 2. H.Parminter; 3. R. Burgoyne; 4. S.Bear; 5. D. Bear; 6. R. Exelby; 7. D. Hocking; 8. E.Williams.* (© The Paddy Bradley Collection).

morning in the Infant Department.' The above details help to portray what an uncomfortable learning environment the children were expected to study in, a problem addressed in February 1956. In order to improve the heating in the schoolrooms, an 'Alicon' stove was installed, and a 'Courtier' stove was installed in the small infant room to replace the open fire.

But improvements to the school and the purchase of equipment had to be carefully balanced against requirements, as the money usually had to be found out of the rates. In order to address the problem of overcrowded classrooms, a partition was set up in 1879 to divide the classes, and in 1896 a new girls' classroom and a new boys' room were reopened by members of the Board. Mr Richard George engaged in prayer, followed by Mr Trythall and Rooke who addressed the children, who afterwards sang 'Trelawney'. In 1900 Lanner School ordered three harmoniums in oak cases by Hellier from Mr Kistler at a cost of £5.15s each.

By 1931, a report on the primary schools stressed maxims which few today would care to dispute: 'The curriculum is to be thought of in terms of activity and experience rather than of knowledge to be acquired and facts to be stored...the schools whose first intention was to teach children how to read have thus been compelled to broaden their aims until it might now be said that they have to teach the children how to live'.[41] (Fig. 10.10.). The result was to be that primary schools became far brighter and happier places than their nineteenth century predecessors, but Lanner School still had problems with overcrowded classrooms, inadequate heating, to say nothing of its Victorian cloakrooms and lavatories. In 1934, a 'new milk scheme' came into force, helping to ensure that children received the recommended daily amount of calcium, particularly important during the depression years of the 1930s. Former pupils remember their teachers placing the milk on top of the tortoise stoves to warm up.

Lanner New County Primary School

In 1944, the Butler Education Act established the Ministry of Education, and Primary, Secondary and Further Education were identified. The Local Education Authority were made responsible for securing that efficient education was available, and Primary and Secondary Education were gradually established in separate schools. As a result, the 5–15 year old range of ages in schools like Lanner's ceased, and when the Secondary Modern Schools became available it became a Primary School, taking pupils up to the age of eleven. On 10 September 1953, the Girls Department and Infants Department amalgamated, with a Head Teacher and three assistant teachers. A screen was erected to divide the main room into two separate classrooms.

On 16 April 1959, the School was renamed the 'Lanner County Primary Junior Mixed School' (reorganised from all-age to mixed Infants and Juniors), with 320 pupils. For the first time in its history, the school had a part-time clerical helper, Mrs M. Watters, from Redruth. She retired in 1994. Grants for sports were received from County Hall (£6.14s. in

1952). On 3 November 1953, the School was provided with a wireless and loudspeaker, and electric lights were switched on that same day. The new canteen (kitchen and servery) was opened in March 1957. A School crossing patrol officer was appointed in 1971, and strip-lighting was installed in every room, replacing the single 100 watt bulbs. A television set was delivered on 26 February 1974.

Yet for many years it was apparent that the school had become inadequate, being not large enough to accommodate its pupils, and in a poor state of repair. In January 1943, Mr Crispin, the County Building Inspector, and Mr Peters, the Chairman of the Managers, were called to inspect dry rot in one of the walls. Mr Peters and Mr Williams, a carpenter, came again in October 1948, to inspect the dry rot. The corner floor boards were removed and new ones fixed. In January 1950, it was reported that 'the baby room gallery was removed and the blocked floor replaced by cement, which is now drying and waiting to be tiled. As this room cannot be used, the whole school is working in the main room. This, with the extra children and furniture, is now overcrowded and the work of the school is disorganised'. It was not until September 1975 that the toilets were connected to the mains drainage. And in January 1978, the canteen roof was found to be unsafe, the latest in a long line of structural problems, and had to be supported by steel girders and scaffolding. On 20 June 1978 Mr Morgan, the Headmaster, was elated to report 'Have just heard new school to be built!'. There was cause for celebration in the School's Centenary Year.[42]

The new School was built on the site of a former farmhouse and its grounds between Bell Lane and the Lanmoor Estate at a total cost of £342 453. The old garden walls can still be seen (Fig.10.11). The architect for the 'state of the art school' was Mike Way of the county architect's staff, and the builders were K.H.J. Trethewey and Sons of St Erme.[43] Gone was the idea that a classroom was a square, and the rooms were deliberately designed with irregularly shaped walls, topped by a wedge-shaped sloping ceiling punctuated with a flood of natural light. A big area of glass in each room was designed to allow the children to see the outside world. 'The fine, airy building, with its modern facilities is meant to encourage learning in the nicest possible way', reported the *West Briton*. A far cry from the typical learning environment of the old Victorian village school. The new school premises was opened to 230 pupils on 8 September 1980, and a purpose built nursery unit was opened the following January. Attempts were made in the village to buy the old school from the County Council, for use as a Youth Club and Community Centre. Yet these attempts failed as there was insufficient support within the village, and the old school buildings were demolished. The site was subsequently sold for the building of the Henscol Estate.

In the eight years to 1994, the school numbers had grown from 179 to 204 (Infants and Juniors), and the new Nursery Class had risen from 36 to 50. The School maintains a very close relationship with the Lanner Pre-school Playgroup.

Fig. 10.11. *Lanner's new County Primary School, surrounded by the Lanmoor Estate, c.1980.* (© Lanner County Primary School).

The present Headmaster, P.E. Lloyd, has seen a significant change in management procedures at the School, following the Education Reform Act. Under the Local Management System, the school controls its own finances, and the budget administered by the Governors and Staff has risen from £10 000 to £250 000 per annum (1994). Sporting activities, formerly football and netball, now also include indoor bowls and chess. In 1994, the rugby team had only been defeated twice in eight years, and the cricket team were the South West Champions. The guitar, recorders, and the choir are important musical activities, and during their time at Lanner School, pupils have the opportunity to participate in an annual camp. The Friends of Lanner School give very valuable support to the work of the School, which continues to play a vital part in the life of the village, being its biggest employer, with a staff of about 30 people. The school still undergoes inspections, and in 1995, successfully passed the new-style OFSTED inspection introduced by the Government. In 1998, Lanner was placed 20th of 200 schools in the County League Table, a fine achievement.

Reminiscences of Lanner School Pupils.

In 1978, a number of Lanner people gave their reminiscences of their time as pupils of the School. These were published in the School's Centenary Document and provide often vivid and enlightening insights into the school life of yesteryear. The indignities suffered, the punishments meted out by the teachers, harrowing details of the first day at school, the daunting visits by the dreaded inspectors, as well as the type of activities and facilities the school possessed, are intensely illuminating and complement the School Log Books and the Gwennap Board Minutes, as they provide much missing information - how it felt to be a pupil at the Lanner Board School.

Thomas C. Knuckey was aged 96 years at the time of the Centenary, the oldest former pupil living in the village, and who lived on to celebrate his own centenary. A retired coal

Fig.10.12. *Thomas Knuckey, who was the oldest living pupil of Lanner School in 1978, cuts the Centenary Cake with Jonathan Rule, the youngest member of the school.* (© Lanner County Primary School)

merchant, Mr Knuckey started at Lanner School in 1885 when he was four years old. He remembered his teachers in the infants' department, Miss Downing and Miss Hocking, with affection, for they were, he said, gentle and kind. Each pupil paid one penny a week which was used to offset the expenses of the School Board. All books and writing materials were provided free, but these were often in very short supply and much of the written work was done on slates. The headmaster of the boys' school at this time was Mr Richards who shortly afterwards left teaching to enter mine management in South Africa where he provided jobs for several Lanner boys who had failed to find work at home. As Thomas Knuckey progressed through the school he remembered some of the teachers as 'tartars' but said that well-behaved children had little to fear. His favourite teacher was a Mr Philips who was firm but kind and who afterwards entered the Methodist ministry, first in Marazion and later in the Redruth circuit. The cane in Lanner School, said Mr Knuckey, was used more as a threat than a punishment. But one of Thomas' clearest memories was of an incident when the cane certainly was in vigorous operation, and that was when a boy gave the Headmaster, Mr Richards, a hefty kick on the leg (Fig. 10.12).

Thomas recalled that there were two important occasions in each year – the visits of the school inspectors, who would travel from Devoran on the Redruth & Chasewater Mineral Railway and arrive unheralded. Each child would be required to read and answer some general knowledge and mental arithmetic questions. He did not attend school very often after the age of ten because his widowed mother used to hire out a pony and phaeton and he was needed to look after the horse. The School had no piped water supply, no gas or electric lighting and times were hard but Thomas Knuckey had pleasant memories of his schooldays at Lanner.

Mrs Bishop and Mrs Mary Job (née Bray), aged 89 in 1978, were both well known village residents with clear memories of their formative years at Lanner School. They started school together in 1893. (Mary Job became the village's oldest resident, dying at the advanced age of 107, and always maintained a close link with her old school, addressing a large crowd assembled there on the occasion of her 100th birthday in 1989). In 1978, they remembered beginning as new infants in a tiny classroom. Their teacher was Miss Lily James, a much-loved character. The children's activities included chanting the alphabet, singing nursery rhymes and teasing threads of hessian cloth which were then used for stuffing cushions. Both boys and girls were taught sewing in the infants' department.

One of Mary Job's clearest memories of her first years in Lanner School was of the great day when members of the School Board arrived for an inspection. The children were in their Sunday best and each had been drilled in the party pieces with which they were to entertain the visitors, who included the vicar and his lady, and other local worthies. Mary remembered having learned a little poem and when her turn came she stood up to recite, only to find her mind a blank. But being a resourceful child, she recited the names of the Books of the Old Testament from 'Genesis' to 'Malachi' instead. What the distinguished visitors thought of this feat of memory we do not know, but the headmistress was unimpressed and Mary had no playtime for a week (Fig.10.13).

The two girls progressed through the school in the same class until they reached the age of fourteen. Then, having been told by the headmistress 'You'll never make a dressmaker, my dear', Mary Job left school determined to do precisely that and enjoyed proving her teacher wrong in the process! At fourteen, Mrs Bishop's life took a different turn for she was successful in a preliminary teaching examination and she returned to the infants' department as a pupil-teacher. In addition to assisting the class teacher, the pupil-teachers would have lessons set by the headmistress. Mrs

Fig.10.13. *Mrs Mary 'Minnie' Job, with her family on her 100th birthday in May, 1989. Lanner's oldest resident lived to the age of 107. She was educated at Lanner School, and spent some years in South Africa with her husband, before they returned to live in the village.* Back row l-r: *Michael Job, Gwen Kent (née Job), Rose Mitchell (née Job), William Kent, Patricia Job, Ivan Richards, Charles Job, Philip Job, Peter Job.* Front row l-r: *Joan Job (née Menadue), Millicent Doble (née Job), Mary Ann 'Minnie' Job (née Bray), Mavis Richards (née Job), Joan Job (née Kessell), Mary Job (née Bray).* (© Michael Job, Lanner)

Bishop remembered coming to school each morning at eight o'clock, when the headmistress would correct her work before the day's teaching began. After a probationary period Mrs Bishop attended for two days a week at a teacher's training college run in the schoolroom of Redruth Wesley Chapel. Following her training, Mrs Bishop spent some years teaching at Lanner School. She said that one of the chief innovations in education at this time was the replacement of slate pencils by chalk, and thus children did not need to spit quite so vigorously on their slates before wiping them. This was a very characteristic sound at a time when classrooms were very silent places.

Mrs Lillie J. Williams, of 4, Prisk's Terrace, Lanner was aged 79 in 1978, and recalled the following: 'I went to Lanner School at the age of five years, in 1904, and remained there until I was about seven (when my parents moved to Truro) but returned to Lanner again at the age of nine or ten. I well remember the old school bell would ring and we wouldn't be late, as we would get a black mark on the register. If on time we would get a red mark. On entering School we sang a hymn and said our usual prayer. We sat on a long seat with a desk, for about six or seven children. We were not allowed to talk in School, if we did we would have to stand outside facing the wall with our hands on our head for a time. If we ate sweets, and the teacher saw us, we would have to give them up to her to keep until we were going home, or else put them in the fire. You could almost hear a pin drop, everyone was so quiet.

The late Miss Janie Hellings was the head teacher for Standard 5, 6 and 7 and taught every subject. Geography, History, Arithmetic, Reading, Spelling, Scripture and Writing.

The afternoons were chiefly sewing, knitting, learning to darn and to do buttonholes, and occasionally we made garments. Sometimes we were told an inspector was coming and immediately he entered we would all stand and say 'Good afternoon, Sir' or 'Good morning, Sir'. We wouldn't dare to copy when doing sums or a composition; if so we would be put in another class who were doing a different subject. I used to feel sorry for our Miss Hellings who walked to and from Stithians every day in all winds and weather, brought her own packed lunch, and often arrived home in the dark. There were no school meals or free milk in those days. (Many children took pasties, which were heated up by the people who lived opposite the school). We had a month's holiday in Summer, a few days at Christmas and a few at Easter. No half term holidays then'.

Mrs Grigg (née Knuckey) who attended the school from 1912–18, remembered being sent home one day because her look at the teacher had been 'insolent' – she was not in any way rude, apparently. Later on during the day a girl was sent to bring her back to the school because the Inspector had arrived and Mrs Grigg was about the only one in the class who answered questions put by the Inspector.

Evelyn Abraham (née Rogers) – a scholar between 1914–1920, recounted how her brother, Jack, died at the age of seven years in 1913, in a diphtheria epidemic. On Empire Day, all children picked daisies and made chains for their necks and hair, and used to do country dancing in the yard.

Mavis Dorothy Bennetts (née Lawn) of 1 Hazel Terrace, Lanner, vividly recalled her first day at school:

I well remember the day I started to go to school, it was on 30 March 1919, I was then five years old. My mother took me at 9am and I didn't want to stay, so I just howled, but seeing I was five, I had to go. The teacher in the infants in the First Class was Miss Edwards, she was a very gentle soul, and took me and calmed me down, put me to sit in the front seat and gave me a rag doll (very crude) and a few doll's clothes, so that I could dress and undress the doll. Also a sand tray to draw something in. A sand tray was just like a baking tray, with some sand in it where we used to draw houses etc., with our fingers. We also had red clay to make models with and a drop of water to wet our hands to soften the clay, also slates and slate pencils to write with. I hated school from that day and hated it up to the day I was sixteen when I finished. I had to settle down and accept it, each year I moved to another class.

When I was in Standard 1-2, Miss Trewern was my teacher. She used to sit on my dress to keep me near her if she came to show me how to do something, because I was always restless and didn't pay attention to what she had to say. If we were naughty and deserved to be punished, she would either stand us in a corner facing the wall, or in a corner with our hands on our head, or give us a crack somewhere with a ruler. Some of the girls in the 5th, 6th and 7th Standards were very badly behaved and Miss Vague used to stand in fear of them, they were also very rude and cheeky to her. I have also seen them throw ink wells et cetera at her; she was an excellent teacher I believe, although I never reached her class. At twelve years of age I left Lanner School to go to the Camborne County School so was only in Standard 4 when I left. Our main lessons consisted of Reading, Writing, Arithmetic, Drill, and Games, Knitting and Sewing. We learned to knit on steel stocking needles, and with hard thick cotton, and when our hands got hot and we did it too tightly, it was a job to move the hard cotton over the needles. Our sewing consisted of darning wool stockings, doing buttonholes and patches, round and square. In the playground we used to play hop-scotch, rounders and do folk dancing. The school yard was very rough, not tarmac as it is now, and if we fell we had badly cut knees. The toilets were very bad, too, and I remember there were little ones with a step to get up to them for the infants and the wash basins were very dark brown earthenware, with cold water only and 'Lifebuoy' soap, which used to smell horrible. On wet days the children who lived a long way off and had to walk to school used to arrive with soaking wet feet and coats, and they had to sit in front of the open fire to get dry. I always wished I was one of them, but as I only lived a few yards away I never was. I remember there was one open fire and one slow but sure stove, which had a tortoise on the cover and a pipe which went out through the wall for the smoke to escape'.

Mrs Niddes (née Goodliffe) a scholar at Lanner from 1920–25, remembered a girl throwing an inkwell at the teacher, and it went all over her blouse. The girl came back two years later to apologise for her behaviour.

Mrs D. Uren (née Bear) went to Lanner School in the years 1924–1930. Because Mrs Uren was inclined not to listen, and to wander around the room, the teacher took her belt and tied her to the leg of the table. Mrs Uren's mother told her this was her own fault for not behaving herself, but her aunt was most annoyed about it and told the teacher in no uncertain terms. She also remembers rolling silver paper balls to make a necklace by stringing through cotton. She was not content with this so she decided to make earrings by pushing a ball of paper in each ear. She also put one up her nose. The story ended with the District Nurse having to come to the school to extract the balls from ear and nose.

Mrs Myrtle Grigg (née Martin) who attended the school from 1924-1930, recalled how on her way to school one morning, she took some apples from an orchard and hid them 'in her knickers' until she reached school. She then decided to give them to her friends, saving one for herself. When Miss Trewern began to take the first lesson, Myrtle decided to eat her apple, with the result that her apple and those distributed to her friends were confiscated and put on the open fire to burn.

Percy Smitheram recalled being unable to read a particular word in his reading book when he was in one of the higher classes. He was embarrassed by having to go to the baby class to ask them the word. He also remembered being sent, on his own, to the home of another child in the school, to find out why he was away.[44] In many ways, nothing changes, but it is worth noting how long indignities suffered at school are remembered.

The Rise of Technical Education

While the early elementary and Board Schools provided basic levels of literacy and numeracy, the more foresighted of Lanner's leaders realised the need for scientific and technological training and their opportunity came when the British Government, alarmed that foreign rivals were forging ahead in technical matters, gave money to the County Councils for scientific training. Cornwall, once at the leading edge of industrial technology, was lagging behind.

The members of the modernising bourgeoisie on the Council proposed a centre of excellence, employing first-rate staff of the highest calibre, who would tour the region to impart the latest scientific knowledge. But this chance to prepare Cornwall for the technology of the twentieth century was thrown away, Ronald Perry has argued, by internal rivalries. The 'city-state' mentality meant that Cornwall's towns could not agree on a site for the centre of excellence, and rival backwoodsmen, in a majority on the Council, wanted to spread the money thinly around Cornwall parishes, with the village schoolmaster imparting the rudimentary training required. An underlying attitude was that too much education might give labourers ideas above their station.[45]

Nonetheless, some of these trends trickled down to Lanner and helped to finance local evening classes. In the 1890s adult lessons organised by the Gwennap Technical Instruction Classes were held in the evenings at Lanner School and were strongly encouraged and supported by 'Lawyer' Bray and Mr Trythall of the Gwennap School Board. Classes included lessons in the principles of mining, vanning, mineralogy, machine construction, chemistry, geometry, human physiology, drawing, freehand writing, Pitman's Shorthand (elementary and advanced), mathematics

Fig.10.14. *Working on the Lanner School allotment behind Lanner Green, c1930.* Left to right: *Norman Pryor, Arthur Langford, Kenneth Angove, Eddie Dunstan, Jack Evans, Ernie ('Pete') Wales, John Bray, Bryant Opie, Bob Jago, Jack Williams, Charlie Job, Willy Pryor, Harry Vinnicombe, Leonard Tregonning, Jim Jago, Leonard Orme.* (© Jack Evans, Camborne)

and mensuration.[46] The money for prizes was subscribed locally, and not from the County Council grant. Lanner was noted as having had a 76 per cent attendance rate in 1896, and prizes were awarded for successful passes in the examinations which concluded the course.

Adult Education in Lanner

Adult, or continuing education, can be classed as those activities which are undertaken to improve knowledge, acquire skills and add to the education which has been given in adolescent years. Under the umbrella of adult education in Lanner appear obvious activities aimed at further education, such as the technical classes held at Lanner School in the late nineteenth century, and the shorthand typing school run in the 1930s. However, less obvious forms of education also existed, including the following of some cultural interest more associated with leisure and personal inclination. Therefore Bible classes, discussion groups, group meetings for 'mutual improvement', formal lectures and reading rooms may also be considered under the broader mantle of adult education. Continuing education was not new in the nineteenth century, but it was increased and developed on an entirely different scale.

A Miners' and Mechanics' Society began in nearby Carharrack in the 1830s, followed by reading rooms in Lanner, penny readings in the 1850s and 60s held in the Schoolroom at Rough Street and Bible classes attached to the various chapels. And Lanner Wesleyan Chapel had a thriving 'Mutual Improvement Society' in the nineteenth century (see Chapter 12), which organised evening lectures on a wide variety of subjects, with an emphasis on the further education of its members. The other chapels had similar societies. Organisations such as the above were created which mirrored the institutions of the nearby towns, particularly Redruth, and to a lesser extent, St Day.

There were few of the learned professional men from the upper stratum of society in Lanner in the mid nineteenth century, but these organisations were run by a new class of skilled workers which grew as mining itself grew increasingly technical. These men would be decidedly more educated in some 'secondary' way than the average miner, if only in technical skills and scientific knowledge related to their occupations. They included mine agents and captains, engineers, assayers, and men of the traditional trades, many of whom had acquired special skills adapted to mining, such as mine carpenters, blacksmiths, masons and so on. They were forming a class which could be recognised not only by their occupational skills but by their part in local affairs in parish and church, or more particularly, chapel. In many instances they might have been given more schooling in childhood, but many won their education by their own efforts after starting work.

Captain John Evans of Lambriggan House, Lanner, typifies this. He was for 40–50 years an agent to the copper company, Nevill Bruce & Co. of Llanelly, and was largely self-taught, acquiring the reputation of being a fine mathematician. In his zeal to master algebra, he at one time judged it necessary to rise at five in the morning in order to study.[47]

In the 1930s, a shorthand typing school was run from a premises in Lanner Square by Miss Philp. Miss Hazel Polkinghorne, of Carn Marth, trained as a typist there and secured a job as a personal secretary at Holmans, the Camborne engineering works. However, since the Second World War, the provisions for local adult education have diminished in Lanner, and are nowhere near as high profile as they used to be. With increased personal mobility, students went to evening classes in commerce, building, engineering and catering at Pool, where Cornwall College developed into one of the largest further education institutions in Britain, or to the smaller college at Falmouth. These colleges also offered wider horizons to Lanner youth. From the passing of the 1902 Education Act, which created the County Secondary Schools, a small minority of Lanner children, who passed the 11+ examination, went to the Grammar Schools for boys and girls at Redruth and Camborne. But from the 1950s an increasing proportion joined a widening range of full-time technical, commercial and general education classes at the Further Education College.[48] The parochial boundaries of educational life in Lanner have been dismantled during this century.

Nevertheless, there are still several groups in Lanner which endeavour to provide an opportunity of further education for their members, albeit in a leisurely manner. The village Historical Society holds monthly lectures aimed at furthering the knowledge of both local and county history and the WI monthly meetings have an educational element. The Writer's Group provides a useful forum for group discussion and activities for like-minded people interested in literature and journalistic endeavours.

Conclusion

The educational history of Lanner illustrates the fundamental differences in upbringing and learning that arose from the circumstances of the social classes and their relations to one another. The landed class, traditionally perceived as the governing elite, was the only class which was relatively well educated from childhood, and this was just for males; young ladies were merely 'educated' in the social graces and the kind of skills which would have enhanced their marriage prospects and made them suitable wives to their successful husbands. Therefore it was solely the male gentry who were at liberty to pursue leisure activities, with some educational element in their adulthood, before the nineteenth century. At first literary and philosophical, this later extended to natural philosophy, the sciences and particularly those subjects of relevance to an understanding of the local mining industry.

At the opposite end of the spectrum were the working classes, whose vocation to labour faithfully in their station was widely accepted before the nineteenth century. This attitude, which was bad enough for boys, was worse for girls, who were more likely to be kept at home to help out with domestic chores, or to nurse an elderly or sick relative, than a brother. In pre-industrial Lanner, and more so after the advent of industrialisation, women's labour was characterised as being unskilled, low status and low waged. And even for middle class females, education was often difficult to obtain. Therefore education for young girls was never more needed. The Church and Chapels led the way, providing the rudiments of an education to both sexes before Parliamentary legislation resulted in the building of Lanner's Board School and culminating in free and compulsory education for all by the mid twentieth century.

But the fundamental developments in education in the nineteenth century tended to rise from the energy and wisdom of the burgeoning middle classes. With their enterprise, zeal for independence, acquired expertise and working philosophy, the middle classes made a valuable contribution to local education. They required schools which were designed to suit their needs, leading to the foundation of learning establishments such as the Trevarth Grammar School, with its more 'modern' curriculum. And as members of the various Nonconformist chapels, they helped to set up schools for the working classes. For it was middle class concern over education which helped to bring the need for free and universal education very much into the political arena. Moreover, the setting up of reading rooms with their library facilities, evening technical classes and mutual improvement classes, were mainly organised by people from the ranks of the rising middle class but were intended to benefit those from all walks of life. In Lanner these enterprising people were, in many instances, self-made men who had made their money through and because of the local mining industry and who demanded improvements in education for their children, and also those of the working man, who were growing up in a world increasingly dominated by commerce and industry.

REFERENCES

1 Minutes of the Committee on Education, 1840-41, p. 195.
2 Tremenheere, Seymour, Report on the State of Education in the Mining Districts of Cornwall, London, BBP, 1840.
3 *West Briton*, 30/12/1842.
4 *West Briton*, 29/12/1856.
5 *Cornubian*, 8/1/1886.
6 *West Briton*, 17/4/1863.
7 *Cornubian*, 30/3/1886.
8 *Doidge's Almanack*, 1878.
9 *Cornubian*, 10/9/1876.
10 *Cornubian*, 3/8/1894.
11 F.L. Harris Archive.
12 Tregoning, E.A., *Two Centuries of a Cornish Family.* Edgar Backus, Leicester, 1950, pp. 5-6.
13 James C.C., James, C.C., *History of Gwennap*, Privately Published, 1944, p.74.
14 Schwartz, S.P. and Perry R., 'James Hicks, Model Victorian Architect and Entrepreneur'. To be published.
15 Boase, G. Clement, *Bibliotheca Cornubiensis.* Longmans, Green, Reader & Dyer, London, 1878, p. 854.
16 Gaskell, Ernest, *Leaders of Cornwall, Social and Political*, London, not dated, pp. 81-83.
17 Boase, G. Clement, *Collectanea Cornubiensia*, Netherton and Worth, Truro, 1890, col. 420.
18 Information courtesy of Dorothy Mindenhall, British Colombia, Canada.
19 *Salisbury Weekly Post*, North Carolina, 15/8/1906.
20 F.L. Harris Archive.
21 Ibid.
22 Francis, William, *Gwennap, A Descriptive Poem in Seven Cantos*, J. May, Redruth, 1845, p. 85.
23 Rowe, J., *Changing Times and Fortunes*, Cornish Hillside Publications, St. Austell, 1996, p. 47.
24 F.L. Harris Archive.
25 F.L. Harris Archive, National Society Files.
26 F.L. Harris Archive, quoting Blewett, *These Things Have Been*, 1968.
27 Children's Employment Commission, Report by Charles Barham, Esq., M.D., BPP, 1841, pp. 822-823.
28 F.L. Harris Archive.
29 Ibid.
30 Francis, William, *Gwennap, A Descriptive Poem in Seven Cantos*, J. May, Redruth, 1845, p. 130.
31 Children's Employment Commission, Report by Charles Barham, Esq., M.D., BPP, 1841, p. 825.
32 SRB/GWE/1, CRO, Truro.
33 Ibid.
34 *Royal Cornwall Gazette*, 26/7/1878.
35 SRB/GWE/2, CRO, Truro.

36 SR/GWE/2, CRO, Truro.
37 SR/GWE/4/1, CRO, Truro.
38 SR/GWE/4/2, CRO, Truro.
39 SRB/GWE/1, CRO, Truro.
40 Private communication with the late Mrs Minnie Haughton, interviewed when 80 in 1995.
41 Curtis S.J., and Boultwood, M.E.A., *An Introductory History of English Education Since 1800*, University Tutorial Press, London, 1964, p. 188.
42 'Lanner School Centenary 1878-1978', used here with kind permission by P.E. Lloyd, Headmaster.
43 *West Briton*, 18/9/1980.
44 'Lanner School Centenary 1878-1978' , used here with kind permission by P.E. Lloyd, Headmaster.
45 Perry Ronald, 'Regenerating Cornwall' in *Cornwall Focus*, Plymouth University, 1998.
46 *Cornubian*, 7/10/1897.
47 *Cornubian*, 9/11/1894.
48 L.P.S. Piper, *Cornwall College, A Short History*, Redruth, 1993.

Fig.11.1. *Lanner, looking northwards. Woodlands Terrace, with Oak Villa on the right. Early twentieth century.* (© Lanner Historical Society).

Chapter 11
The Development of the Community in the Twentieth Century

The first four decades of the twentieth century were characterised by war and economic depression. The Boer War (1899–1902), followed by World War One (1914–18), the Great Depression of the inter-war years and World War Two (1939–45) had long term detrimental effects on Lanner. The tendency to equate poverty, hardship and suffering with just the nineteenth century is an erroneous one. Those living in Lanner and mining villages like it in the early twentieth century faced problems and predicaments every bit as difficult and challenging as those faced by the parish's nineteenth century residents. These problems were partly caused by the wars, but the underlying common denominator was the unstoppable process of de-industrialisation, as the area's mining industry sank into a terminal decline. Lanner's premier mine, Tresavean, closed in 1928, and the closure of most of the mines in the wider Camborne–Redruth area led to mass unemployment, along with the demise of auxiliary industries situated inside Lanner Parish, such as the brick making industry at Pennance, but also those industries found outside the parish at which many Lanner people worked. These included the Seleggan Tin Smelting works, the Redruth Tin Smelting Works and the Perran Foundry. From a total population of 2710 in 1856, overseas migration and out migration from Lanner to other areas of Cornwall and Britain had caused a marked demographic decline; in 1881 Lanner's population figure stood at 1813, in 1931 at 1649, and by 1961 had sunk to 1589 (Fig.11.2).

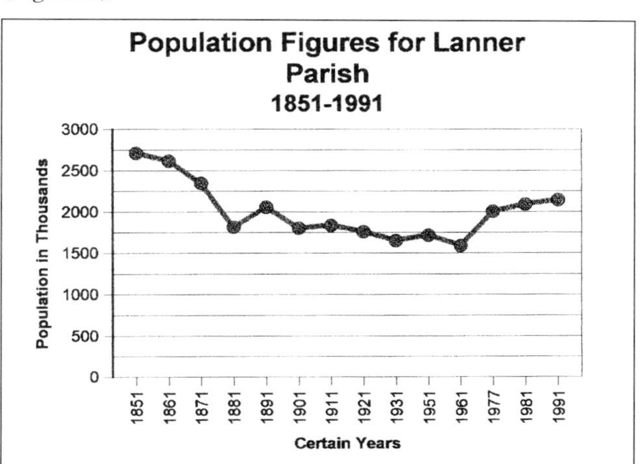

Fig.11.2. Population figures for Lanner, 1851–1991.

The inter-war years in Lanner were characterised by a fatalistic acceptance of this de-industrialisation, accompanied by economic stagnation due to the lack of a diversified economic base and a robust consumer market, caused by the aftermath of the calamitous crash of the over-specialised local copper mining industry. Beyond migration, nineteenth century Lanner had little answer to the crushing forces of de-industrialisation.

As a former mining district, still bearing the scars of extractive industries, Lanner was not likely to be an attractive prospect for the growth in tertiary industry, such as tourism, which was largely confined to the coastal regions. The quarry industry did creak on in our parish until the 1960s, and saw a very brief revival in the 1970s, but was not a large employer, being too distant from a major port, making the costs of transportation prohibitive.

The economic depression and gloom affected the village culturally; numerous clubs and societies ceased to function in the climate of economic uncertainty and poverty, and the lack of people able to form committees or to be active participants in such societies led to those which required considerable finance, in particular, not reappearing until the 1960s. It was during this time that the parish was woken from its slumber by an ambitious building programme, beginning in the late 1950s and continuing unabated throughout the 1960s. The population figures rose steadily thereafter, in 1977 reaching 2005, and by 1984, 2230, almost a return to the level recorded in its mining heyday.

Lanner's central position within the county, being less than 20 minutes away from Falmouth and Truro, and much less to Redruth, increased its attractiveness to people who could commute to work by car or bus. Lanner gradually changed from a community largely dependent on work within its boundaries in the nineteenth century, to a commuter-based economy. The increase in the parish population, as well as the proportion of its land taken up by housing, was the result of people wanting to live in larger properties (and in smaller numbers per house) than was possible in the more crowded areas of towns like Redruth.

One of the most positive things to come out of this expansion of the community was a distinct improvement in the village's municipal services. Over the ensuing years, post-industrial Lanner came to be increasingly viewed as a haven of rural peace and tranquillity, a perfect place in which to raise a family or retire, an ideal which was as far removed as possible from the parish's nineteenth century industrial condition, providing evidence that in people's hearts and minds, the process of de-industrialisation was complete. And this predominant perception of Lanner as a totally non industrial, rural location was highlighted when the proposed commencement of operations in one of the Carn Marth quarries in the mid 1980s came up against a barrage of opposition from many village residents, who had by now come to view Lanner purely as a residential community which would be marred by the presence of heavy industry, posing a dilemma which has its counterpart in many other Cornish villages.

Fig.11.3. *Mr Folley, the village postman, on his last round, 16 May 1912. The boy is Eddie Rogers. The photograph was taken at Southgate Street, Redruth.* (© Royal Institution of Cornwall).

Economic Depression and Cultural Deprivation

Although by the early twentieth century Lanner had an active and affluent middle class, it was small in comparison to the majority of the residents of the parish who were families from a mining background; the area thus retained a strong working class character and signs of poverty were still very apparent. Earlier this century, services at the Methodist Chapel often had to be stopped because of the noise and screaming coming from Church Row, where in one of the cottages a man regularly beat up his wife. In 1903, an alleged case of child neglect led to the premises of a local couple being searched by two policemen. Inside the badly cramped cottage were six children aged from 16 months to 11 years, all extremely dirty, and most half naked, with yellow, vermin-bitten skin. A baby in a perambulator had been almost suffocated by several cats, which when driven off, soon came back. The child was very thin; its face was caked with filth, and it appeared ill. On going into the bedroom, the policemen reported finding enough filth to fill a wheelbarrow. The children were removed to Redruth Workhouse where they could be better cared for.[1]

Again in 1915, a local woman with a family of seven children, of whom four had died, saw her filthy children clad in rags, and 'grafted with dirt', removed to the workhouse. Concern for the youngest, a mere baby, was expressed upon its being medically examined, and it was not expected to survive long. The baby had never received any milk, but was instead fed upon 'baked flour, a food commonly given to babies of poor families in Gwennap'.[2]

When the miners' dry at Tresavean burnt down in 1914, more concern was occasioned as to the loss of the clothing of about 40 miners, than the building itself, which was insured. And even in the 1930s and 40s, people did not always have an abundance of clothes. It has been brought to the attention of the authors that a poor lady in the village had but one cardigan to wear, and had to wait for a dry day in order to wash it. This particular lady was once invited to a relation's wedding, but felt she would have to decline, as she did not have anything suitable to wear. A kindly neighbour came to the rescue, and hunted out an old hat, frock and handbag for her so she could attend the special day.

Yet people who lived in Lanner during the hard economic times of the inter-war period would have liked to consider themselves respectable and well to do, and for many, a veneer of respectability had to be maintained at all costs. One resident remembers that many working people, when answering their doors, would go to great lengths not to allow the visitor so much as a glance down the hallway, in case the ragged rugs and carpets would be seen. Conversations took place on the doorstep (Fig.11.3).

Moreover, there were numerous people who did not have the money to buy elaborate hats and outfits for the more important social events which occurred in the village, but nevertheless devised ways to attend and still look elegant. One lady from the village who purchased a coat at West End, Redruth, on a Friday afternoon earlier this century, came back on the following Monday with the item saying that she was dreadfully sorry, but upon trying it on at home it was not quite as she had expected. She received her money back, but when the shop attendant looked in the pocket of the coat, therein was a folded programme bearing the details of The Lanner Sunday School Anniversary![3] Likewise, at a Primitive Methodist event, a lady thought she was being very discreet in slyly dropping a few cakes and buns into her partly folded umbrella, no doubt intended to supplement her meagre table at home. However, upon leaving the chapel it started to rain very heavily, and momentarily forgetting what was concealed in her umbrella, she hurriedly put it up, and to the amazement of several onlookers, a shower of cakes and buns joined the downpour![4]

There was a time, just after the Second World War, when it was impossible to leave anything outside the cottages of certain rows in the village, even items of limited value, as things simply went missing; scrubbing brushes, cloths and brooms would quickly vanish as people stole what they could not always afford. In one row a resident once spied the flowers from her garden, which had mysteriously disappeared, gracing the window of a neighbour's house a few doors away![5]

Even after the total cessation of mining, this one time mining community retained some of its former customs; in the 1950s and 60s, it was not uncommon to see bantam chickens, a sow and other livestock in the open gardens which lay at the back of the terraced cottages in the village, as people tried to collect eggs or rear a litter of pigs, as well as cultivate a few vegetables, especially potatoes, to supplement the table.

The poverty which persisted in the village until the 1960s was perhaps reflected in the lack of village organisations such as football, cricket and rugby teams, the Scouting movement and a brass band, all of which declined in popularity and had eventually disbanded by the post war period of the late 40s to late 50s, as we shall discuss in the following chapter. Such organisations required considerable financial outlay for uniforms and equipment, which proved too costly for an area hard hit by continuing economic depression and uncertainty. Below we will analyse some of the factors which created the continuing poverty outlined above.

World War One

After the uncertainty which had prevailed at the turn of the century caused by the Boer War, and the clear warning signals of the dangers posed to a culture overwhelmingly one of dependency, the reopening of Tresavean Mine in 1907 was cause for celebration in the area, as this was viewed as a return to prosperity for Lanner. After the mine was dewatered, development began, resulting in tin sales by 1914. Many Lanner men found jobs there.

Sadly, this progress at Tresavean Mine was to be frustrated by the First World War, and a number of Lanner men enlisted or were conscripted. A parish breakdown of the Mining Division in 1915 showed that Lanner had 55 men serving, or 7.88 per cent of its adult male population. Eighty-six eligibles remained.[6] This figure rose as many men who were working in American mines returned home to the village, as under the terms of the Anglo-American Draft Treaty, they had to serve either under the Stars and Stripes, or the Union Jack. Carn Marth man Wilfred Bray was one such

Fig.11.4. *The Bicycle Corps, Norfolk, after 1915.* Back row, 4th from left: *Lanner policeman, P.C.Kitt.* Front row, 3rd from left: *Wilfred ('Fred') Bray of Carn Marth.* (© Sylvia Kessell, Redruth).

expatriate who decided to come back to Cornwall from McGill, Nevada, and enlisted in the Bicycle Corps, serving as a dispatch rider. He was joined in his regiment by village constable P.C. Kitt, who became a military policeman.[7] The conscription of men led to labour shortages, resulting in the almost entire cessation of development at Tresavean Mine (see Chapter 3). (Fig.11.4.).

A Lanner War Committee was quickly formed with 'Lawyer' Bray as chairman. Held in the Wesleyan Schoolroom, the February meeting was informed that 142 garments had been knitted the previous month and 142 pipes had been collected to be sent to home defence forces at Old Sudbury, with a package of linen, three boxes of cigarettes and note paper and envelopes.[8] Regular concerts in the Wesleyan Schoolroom were held in aid of the Soldiers' and Sailors' Tobacco Fund. Recruiting evenings were held there also, one such evening seeing the visit of Lieutenant West and his Band of Pipers.[9] A children's concert in May 1916 was held in aid of the Belgian People many of whom had

Fig.11.5. *Schoolchildren helped to raise the morale of our soldiers, fighting in the First World War.* (© Mr and Mrs J. Craze, Redruth).

Fig.11.6. *Ex-Servicemen at Lanner Peace Celebrations in 1919, taken in the grounds of Melrose House.* Back row l-r: *Thomas Toy; seventh from left, John Whitford; eighth, Fred Dunstan.* Middle row, *left: Sidney Bone; second from left, Harold Langford; fourth, Mr Mugford; fifth, Joe Whitford.* Front row: *left, Mr Rogers; fourth from left, Bert Magor; sixth, Willie Treloar; seventh, Mr Blewett.* (© Arthur Langford, Redruth).

sought refuge in the West Country. A Lanner Ladies' Working Party was launched to provide knitted garments to the men at the front. By January 1915, over 500 garments had been made and dispatched to soldiers in India and sailors in the North Sea. Special parcels containing a few garments were made for Lanner men on active service.[10] (Fig.11.5.).

Certain commodities were rationed, whilst prices for many things soared, making maximum price fixing a necessity. In 1918, Mrs Margaret Jane, a grocer from Lanner Moor, was summonsed for selling bread at a price beyond the maximum. Upon being fined £10, she stood up in the courtroom and announced, 'I can't pay et. I'm not goin' rob my cheldrun.' 'Then you must go to prison for 14 days' replied the Judge. 'Then I will go' she said bitterly. 'You've 'ad my cheldrun who 'av fought and died, now you can 'av me!'[11] The cost to Lanner in human terms was high. Many men of the village lost their lives in the Great War: William H. Blight; Cecil H. Carbis; Pte James Collins, 10th DCLI 27/7/1916; Sapper William Geach, RE 31/1/1916; Lewis Gilbert, RNVR, 27/11/1916; Sapper John Thomas Glasson, RE, 10/12/1915; Pte John Morley Goldsworthy, 8th DCLI 10/5/1917; Pte Paul Morley Goldsworthy, 8th DCLI, 10/5/1917; Pte Osborne Greenslade, Machine Gun Corps 2/7/1916; Pte James Harris, 1st. DCLI 8/5/1917; William J. Herring; Lawrence Lampshire, ASC Transport 5/3/1918; 2nd-Lt Michael Innes Malton, DCLI 2/9/1918; Pte P.L. Malton; Pte James Martin, 1st DCLI 14/4/1917; Gunner Sydney Mitchell, RGA 26/4/1918; Sapper Stanley Peters, RE 30/4/1918; William Henry Tucker, Stoker, RNR, killed on board HMS *Goliath* 13/5/1915; Arthur Webster, Australian Force 12/10/1917.

The end of the War was warmly welcomed. Scholars at Lanner School were given a whole day for 'War Savings' on 31 October, and on 11 November, a whole day to celebrate the cessation of hostilities. On Armistice Day, the children were instructed as to the importance of peace to the nation and to solemnly remember those from the village and beyond who had given their lives to achieve it. Each year thereafter, the pupils kept two minutes' 'perfect silence' at 11am, as recorded in the log book in 1923 (Fig.11.6).

The Collapse of Mining

The end of the First World War might have brought peace to the nation, but the high price of basic commodities and low wages began to cause discontent among the mining population, even though the price of tin was to reach an all time high in February of 1920. This month witnessed scenes reminiscent of olden times, as Redruth Market erupted into violence. The protest was not spontaneous, but was organised by the Workers' Union, saw the participation of over a thousand people of the mining class, and arose over the price of butter and other commodities, sold at various prices in the weeks before the protest. The crowd demanded butter be sold at 2s.6d instead of 3s.3d per pound, at which it was retailing on the day. Butter dealers were attacked, and boxes were distributed in an ad hoc fashion by the crowd. After the event, the streets were described as 'strewn with butter and broken eggs trampled underfoot'.[12]

A delegation from the Workers' Union met local farmers to agree a fair price for butter in order to avoid a repetition of disorder. Many miners were described as earning about £2 per week, on which to maintain large families, and were

Fig.11.7. *Lanner Square, early twentieth century. Note the public drinking fountain. The tower of the school can be seen beyond the roofs of the buildings in the left background, and Phillips' Terrace had not yet been built.* (© Lanner Historical Society)

described as 'underfed, famished and pinched'. The demise of mining in Cornwall and the impoverishment of the mining workforce were the inevitable consequences of mining expansion elsewhere, particularly the exploitation of easily accessible alluvial sources of tin and open-cast copper mines. Therefore the outbreaks of protest, noted above, were the expression of the cumulative frustrations of years during which the labouring miner in Cornwall bore the consequences of the slow and painful de-industrialisation.

Worse was to come for mining areas such as Lanner which had enjoyed several years of high tin prices. The collapse in the price of tin on the world market sent the local economy into a downward spiral, resulting in numerous mine closures. In February 1921 came the news everyone dreaded – Tresavean gave notice to its 340 men and only planned to keep on a skeleton staff to keep the mine ticking over in the hope of weathering the economic storm (see Chapter 3). In addition to the closure of local mines, Holman's Number 3 works and the Seleggan Smelting Company's employees were forced to go on half time. These businesses employed Lanner men. The coal miners' strike in Wales further deepened the crisis at home as men who were working in Wales returned to the village with no job and no money, only to find that they were not eligible to receive the dole.[13] Those on the dole received 15 shillings a week and it was estimated that as many as 99 per cent of those unemployed in Gwennap were forced to draw on benefits of some kind. People found that they could not pay their rates, which were 6s.6d, but expected to rise by 8d. This added to the predicament faced by the local authorities who wished to employ those out of work within the parish on schemes such as road building, croft reclamation schemes and new water supplies.

Fig.11.8. *The Revd Butters and his wife in their motor car, the first to be seen in Lanner. Early twentieth century.* (©Royal Institution of Cornwall, Truro)

Mr Bree had this to say at a meeting in Gwennap in March: 'We are in a grave position caused by the cessation of operations at Tresavean and Poldice. Unless a permanent industry is established, I do not know what will happen'.[14] A deputation of four unemployed miners on behalf of Gwennap, which had been severely criticised by Redruth Parish for not doing enough in relief of its distressed, addressed the Redruth Rural Council to state that, unless relief was supplied in a few weeks, they would be forced to apply to the Board of Guardians for help. Two hundred children from Gwennap were being fed by Redruth, but Gwennap's contribution to the Redruth Rural District was less than £10. Gwennap Parish, of which Lanner was still considered a part, was described as a scene of desolation and dreariness in May 1921, 'the mines are of great depth and have been worked for ages, but they are all now stopped'.[15]

The effects of the depressions of the 1840s, 60s and 70s had been lessened somewhat by the emigration to foreign mining fields of hundreds of local miners and their families. But this time it was different. The 1914–18 War had severely disrupted migratory patterns, and the foreign mines, which had formerly employed many miners and engineers from Cornwall, were themselves the victims of low metal prices, and so were subject to the same economic factors as their Cornish counterparts. Therefore, for the over-specialised local miner, there was no longer the same level of opportunity of resorting to the age old remedy of migration to other mining fields. The Lord Lieutenant, J.C. Williams, aptly summed up the area's predicament in May 1921 in a letter to the Prince of Wales: 'their work [the miners] is of a highly specialised kind and it is not easy for them to take up other lines of industry... the men are out of employment through no fault of their own.'[16]

In the Mining Division in February 1921, it was reported that 4389 people were out of work, and in the Redruth District, of which Lanner was a part, 1307 men were unemployed, 83 women, 87 boys and 25 girls.[17] By June it was reported that 400 men were unemployed in Gwennap Parish alone. Very soon the poverty in the Mining Division began to tell. In March of 1921, a case came before the Redruth Guardians of a local schoolboy who had to wear a pair of boots, with practically no soles, to school in bitterly cold and wet weather. The school master, on discovering this fact, was reduced to tears and fitted the boy with a pair of boots.[18]

In Lanner, the bakery business of Charles K. Blewett went bankrupt, the Lanner Lamp Committee was reported to be in debt for the first time ever, and a man, who was aged just 20, was so depressed because he was unemployed, that he committed suicide in Martin's Quarry by throwing himself 30 feet on to the rocks. Farmers found life extremely hard, particularly those who had to send their fresh flowers, fruit and vegetables by rail to markets, such as Covent Garden, due to the coal strike reducing train services.[19]

A. K. Knuckey was having coal stolen piecemeal from his depot at the top of Lanner Hill. Two people from Wheal Buller were caught by Knuckey, who estimated they had stolen 70lbs of coal worth £2s.6d. They were later apprehended but had the case against them dismissed due to lack of evidence. The magistrate obviously viewed the case leniently due to the severe hardship prevailing in the area.[20]

Coal was rationed to 56lbs (half a hundredweight) per person per week, and people were to be seen cutting wood from the hedgerows or furze from the crofts instead, whilst many more combed the areas around the mines searching for 'cherks' – pieces of partly burnt coal.

Children living on Carn Marth were sent out to search for 'glows' (dried cow pats), a valuable fuel, and this practice persisted until the 1940s. Stories of hardship and deprivation filled the local papers. A local man who had been fortunate to obtain employment at Copper Hill Mine was found to have collapsed against a hedge en route to the mine, from exhaustion due to a poor diet. Another man who walked to Falmouth in the hope of getting a job, only to be turned away having to walk the eight miles back to Lanner, was so exhausted upon arriving home that he collapsed in a chair and began to haemorrhage.[21]

The economic crisis was alleviated somewhat through an appeal by the Camborne, Redruth and District Relief Fund to raise money for the unemployed miners. Joseph Cock, the Chairman of the Central Relief Committee, made a pathetic and impassioned plea to the Cornish worldwide, graphically describing the poverty which prevailed in the area: 'Until the price of tin is higher, and the prices of working material lower, there can be no revival of prosperity', he stated in June 1921, continuing:

> *'the closing of these industries means the extinction of a community. If you could imagine yourselves in the old towns of Camborne and Redruth and look to the North or South, the arrested toll would both pain and surprise you. Only here and there an engine works, and that only to keep the mine from flooding. No work means no money, and no money means the wolf at the door. Everywhere there is "a shortness of things..." the folk who nursed you in the Old Country are becoming too destitute for words'.* Ending the letter with the following passionate statement: *'The new economic conditions have hit us hard. The silence that is around us is like the silence which precedes the Last Watch. We are passing each other in silence - we dare not say how we are, or how our little ones fare'.*[22]

A Miners' Relief Fund was set up to provide assistance to those who were the most needy. Companies, individuals and organisations were lobbied to provide money for the fund. Lanner Wesley Chapel rose to the call, contributing £1.17s.9d, further boosted by the Prince of Wales who gave £300, and visited the depressed areas in the county in May 1921. But all around the district, in every town and village, reported the *Cornubian*, stood groups of men 'their faces pinched, drawn and haggard, staring with despairing eyes on the busy pavements of life in which they have no part, and with an outlook wholly hopeless'.[23]

A miners' choir was set up which toured the county and further afield, raising money for the unemployed and their families at concerts. John Trevena was one miner from the village who joined the choir. He had returned from South Africa and after a spell in the lead mines of Derbyshire, had secured a job at Tresavean only to find himself laid off shortly afterwards with no job to go to. Cornish organisations world wide, from Michigan and South Africa, to the gold fields of Kolar, India, helped their struggling kinsmen financially, and those overseas sent what little they could to family and friends in Lanner. A central food depot was established in May 1921, and by June had distributed 1000 parcels, each valued at 5 shillings, to needy families in our district.[24]

Some unemployed Lanner men counted themselves fortunate to be included on several schemes set up to alleviate unemployment in Gwennap. A road building project was implemented at Penstruthal, employing 11 men at £2 each per week. A scheme to reclaim croft at Clijah employed 50 more local men, and a similar project was launched at Carn Marth. A drainage scheme for Lanner was, however, considered too costly to the rates and was subsequently abandoned.[25]

The Government did eventually help Tresavean financially (see Chapter 3), but even with its reopening in 1922, the writing was on the wall. After well over a century of activity, Tresavean closed for good in 1928, throwing numerous Lanner men out of work.

The Great Depression

In the great global depression of the 20s and 30s, Cornwall was one of the worst-hit regions of Britain. Mines shut down, the loss of the American market crippled the china clay industry, the collapse of world trade decimated shipbuilding, and farming and fishing were in the doldrums. Lanner had its share of these problems. Much hardship prevailed, and a soup kitchen was opened in the village at the former Miners' Arms Public House. Women in the village volunteered to prepare and distribute the watery soup and a piece of bread to children on their way to school. Marion Blight was one such helper. A small orphanage for boys was run in 'Oak Villa' for a time in the 1920s.

During the 1930s, several of the local shopkeepers found that items put 'on the slate' remained unpaid for. It was said a great many people deliberately shopped at Mrs Tregoning's grocery shop because, being tender hearted, she seldom called in the debts and fed half the village in those hard times.[26] Mr Webster, the cobbler who had a shop in the Square, had a notice pinned on his wall which amusingly deterred requests for credit:

A man lives here who don't refuse
To mend our boots like wise old shoes.
The leather is good, my price is just,
But times are bad and I cannot trust.[27]

An elderly woman in Grays Terrace remembers seeing groups of unemployed men walking up Lanner Hill together on their way into Redruth to 'sign on' at the Labour Exchange. Lanner men, who walked to Falmouth seeking work at the Docks each day, would put boot polish on their ankles to cover any holes which might appear in their repeatedly darned socks. And hard times sometimes called for extreme measures. In the depression years of the 1930s, one woman in the village, whose absent husband was working overseas but sending irregular remittances, was so poor that she was forced by sheer necessity to entertain gentlemen. After such visits, her boys would be seen with a new pair of shoes, or a new jacket, or cap.... . There are stories from those hard times, still half-whispered even in the village today, of known cases of infanticide and burials of babies in the back hedges of cottage gardens.[28]

Many men and women from Lanner during this period would have found an empathy with the words of Blewett, quoting a resident from nearby St Day:

I am the son of a Cornish miner. I come from a long line of Cornish miners. I was born in a mining village in a two-roomed house. The month before I was born my father brought home 3/6 – a month's pay as a tributer. In our modern times we call such things the romance of history. We in St Day have a great store of them. But there are no vitamins in romance, and no proteins in history. The shock of that 3/6 must have passed into my blood. Now and again it has exerted itself in an indignation at the unnatural inequalities of life.[29]

Village Businesses

A person walking down through Lanner from Redruth in the mid 1930s would have seen a linear village, surrounded by fields, with footpaths joining the houses and roads, presenting a pleasant rural aspect. Prominent on the skyline would have been the school with its granite bell-tower, the Bryanite Chapel and the Wesleyan Chapel. Lanner Christ Church lay partially hidden by trees at the top of Church Row.

However, the 'stent' or debris thrown up in heaps by the mines on the broad hillsides on either side of the valley were still very apparent, as were a few of the engine houses which belied their location, providing a very visible reminder of the reason for Lanner's existence. Irene Williams has some vivid memories and recollections of what the village was like in the 1930s. From her description, we obtain a view of an essentially self-contained community, where most of the things needed for normal day to day living could have been easily purchased. But as with the nineteenth century, it was not possible to buy luxury items; these would have been bought at nearby Redruth.

Irene remembers that at the top of Lanner Hill behind the present Scout headquarters were two coal yards, those of Tom Knuckey who resided at Melrose House by the Wesleyan Chapel and Jim Rowe who lived at Stithians. Behind Rowe's coal yard was the yard of stonemason, Harry Blight, who polished granite for headstones (Fig.11.9). At Lanner Green was a family named Langford. This family were constructional engineers, specialising in the erection of mining and quarrying plant, the firm Langford & Sons, Mining Engineers, Builders, Carpenters and Undertakers, being

Fig.11.9. *John Tresidder (1888–1980), on the left, in his blacksmith's shop at the top of Lanner Hill. The calendar on the wall is dated December 1927. Tresidder emigrated to Seattle (USA) in the 1930s.* (© Royal Institution of Cornwall).

started in 1923. Walter Langford, a mine captain, had installed parts of the mill at Tresavean, and also did a lot of shaft-capping in the area. Walter celebrated his 80th birthday on his last job – building James Willoughby's fruit shop in the Square in 1950. Irene remembers going to Langford's workshops at Lanner Green to buy a bucket of lime to limewash the outside toilet. (The premises were later used by Goodyear Pumps, Westcountry engineers, headed by J.W. Goodyear who invented the Goodyear Pump, manufactured by Holman Brothers at Camborne, which was used for chemicals and 'difficult fluids').

Upon walking down into the village from Redruth, you could not have missed John James Willoughby's general store, and might have paused momentarily to gaze in admiration at the neat piles of sweets shaped into pyramids around the counter. Situated right below the schoolyard gates, Willoughby's was a very convenient place for the children to spend their pennies! Everyone in Lanner knew Willoughby, who used to go round the village with a large basket full of samples, enticing customers to place their orders. These he then delivered with his maroon Morgan van loaded to capacity, whilst his sister, Miss May Willoughby, ran the shop. His business was later relocated to his father's old blacksmith's shop, just down from the present Lanner Londis Shop.

Just past Willoughby's shop was the general stores run by Mr and Mrs Mitchell where Irene's mother used to buy their groceries. Irene was allowed tuppence worth of sweets when her mother settled the weekly bill. As a little girl, she remembers cutting the sweets in half to make them look more! On the opposite side of the road, was yet another general store, with the name of Kinsman over the door, and beyond this, the Bryanite's Chapel.

At the bottom of Lanner Hill a pedestrian would have passed the post office, newsagent and general store (now the Londis Shop) run by the Penna family (Figs. 11.10-11). A number of large barrels formerly stood outside this establishment, containing all manner of things. This was the base for the three village postmen, Mr Magor, Dick Reed and Mr Mounce, and one postmistress, Miss Emily Rowe. Behind the old Post Office and next to the Marigold Garages was the village blacksmith's shop of Jack Rogers. Just below the post office was a tiny butcher's shop owned by Braddon of St Day. And below Mitchell's stores, one would have happened upon a small shop owned by Mr and Mrs Dunstan, where Irene's family bought their shoes, especially new sandals for Whitsuntide to go to the fair at Redruth.

Next to what is now the Methodist Manse was the village bakery owned by the Grigg family 'who used to bake the best pasties and saffron cake for miles around' recalled Irene. A saffron cake would have cost four old pence. 'The Grigg sons would be all dressed up in white, with big high hats all floppy out on one side, but immaculately clean'. There had been a bakery at this shop for quite some time. Bill Harnden worked there in the early twentieth century as a skilled cake decorator. Edwin Harris ran the shop from 1902–1910, followed by Harry Veall until 1923 and between 1923 and 1935 by Joseph Williams, before the Griggs took over. Isaac Griggs' son, Julian, remembered working at the bakery as a young man. His day began at 4.00am, when he got the fires in the large ovens going and then made the pasties, yeast and saffron cakes, bread and other items. Summer was the

Fig.11.10. *Lanner Post Office on left, Willoughby's blacksmith's shop is the small white-fronted one-storey building between the rows of cottages on the left. Early twentieth century.* (© Lanner Historical Society) (Inset) Fig.11.11. *Lanner Post Mark – a rubber hand stamp, 'Lanner, Redruth, p.m., 9 May 1919'.* (from a postcard in the Derek Reynolds Collection)

Fig.11.12. *The Commercial Inn, Lanner Square (landlord, Henry Jenkyn), c.1910. Redruth Brewery Co delivering beers, wines and spirits.* (© Cornwall Studies Library, Redruth)

busiest time, with Chapels placing large orders for tea treat buns.[30] In 1939 the bakery closed because rationing limited the ingredients, a week's supply being limited to the amount used in a single day. After this, groceries and then wool, was sold from the premises by Mrs C. Snipp, then Beryl Thomas, until it was turned into a residence by T. Wearne.

In the Square was the Lanner Inn, run by the Bennett family at this time. The small shop attached to 'Malvern' was at this time a typewriting school run by Miss Philp, where many Lanner ladies learnt shorthand typing. Adjoining the school lived Mr and Mrs Pryor. Pryor was extremely skilled in mending clocks. In 1914 he had performed the extraordinary feat of dissecting and putting together a grandfather clock whilst blindfolded, in 80 minutes. He also made a model of the endless pulley block, a dual-winding engine dial, and model of a Cornish pumping engine. Sadly he did not have the necessary capital to patent his idea for the endless pulley block.[31]

On the end of the next cottage was a small shop which sold wool, run by Mrs Lapham, where Irene remembers buying wool for sixpence an ounce and a jumper pattern for tuppence. As many village ladies were not well off, Mrs Lapham would put back wool until they could afford to buy it. The shop in the corner of the Square was owned by the Jenkin family, and when Miss Jenkin became Mrs Veall, it operated as a general store. Around the back of this shop lived Mr Webster, who repaired boots and shoes.

On the opposite side of the road at the end of Grays Terrace was the wooden hut which was the Men's Institute. Irene's mother, Mrs Wilkins, was paid five shillings a week to clean the premises. Where the village Post Office is presently located was Tregoning's, a corn merchants' and general store. Irene remembers the huge double doors which opened inwards and a big crock coming down and hauling up goods and animal feedstuff to the store up over. It was possible to purchase paraffin and methylated spirits here too. Across the road in Woodlands Terrace was Ewart Opie and his egg collecting business. Ewart's brown van was a common sight in the village as he went around collecting eggs from all the farms and smallholdings. For a time in the early twentieth century, the small building attached to Mrs Opie's present house functioned as a social club.

The village fish and chip shop was in the same place as it is at present, with first the Minsons, then the Morrish's as owners. This premises had begun life as a hairdressers in 1926, run by Edwin Tucker, and it then became a shop selling woollen items and sweets. The Minsons installed a coal-fired range in the front section and the tiny area at the back was used as a restaurant, with wooden tables and benches – no refinements, just salt and pepper and a fork to eat your meal! The potatoes were peeled by a hand-operated peeler in the back yard of No. 6 Woodlands Terrace. Irene remembers it was possible to buy fish for four pence, chips for tuppence and a bottle of pop for a penny to take away. If eaten in the restaurant, the price of each was a penny dearer. Stewart Morrish built the present shop with an upstairs restaurant, since closed. Children who brought newspapers for wrapping the meals in to the Morrish's would be given a bag of chips by way of thanks. The Fish and Chip shop is presently run by Sylvia Clapp, daughter of Stewart Morrish.

At the entrance to Pennance Lane, Irene remembers Billy Williams' carpenter's and undertaker's shop (Fig.11.13). The figure of Billy Williams was indelibly etched in the

Fig.11.13. *Shop of W. Williams, wheelwrights, carpenters and undertakers. Lanner, early twentieth century.* (© Jack Evans, Camborne)

Fig.11.14. *Willie Eastman in front of his general store at Lanner Moor, 1934.* (© Mr J.J.D.Eastman, Redruth)

mind of young Irene – 'a very serious person, all in black with a high silk hat for funerals'. Next door was another general store operated by Mr and Mrs Willie Eastman. (Fig. 11.14) Occupying a strategic position at the corner of the playing field was a little ice cream shop owned by Willie Russell, who used to sell his ices in the village from a two-wheeled cart pulled by a pony.

At Lanner Moor was Owen Penglase's garage, and below that, the general store owned by his brother Sam Penglase (Fig.11.15). At the corner of the road up Tresavean Hill was the shop owned by the Daveys. The old Rogers' Arms Pub was at this time a dwelling, but the Luggs ran a taxi business from their home there. The Tiddy family once had a builder's yard opposite the present Lanner Moor Garage.

Beside the new garages around the back of the former mini market was Mugford's yard. Mugford was a fish hawker and used to sell fish which had come up from Newlyn. The sight of him coming up through the village with his pony and trap has long remained in Irene's memory, as has his familiar call: 'Pilchards a ha'penny each, all fresh for saltin' down in your bussa!'. He would nearly always give the small fish to the children. On travelling down through Lanner Moor, a pedestrian would have passed Lanner House (now the Coppice), the residence of Lawyer Bray, and a little further on at Treviskey, the tin streams with their water-wheels and red water, a reminder that this area was formerly dominated by mining. The Mounces lived beside the streams which were formerly where the Camper Van Centre is now situated, and had a small shop in a room in their house.[32]

Lanner before the Second World War was remembered as being a pleasant, close knit, cohesive community, a place in which everybody knew everybody else, people were more often that not related, and those with peculiarities of physical appearances, habits, speech, trade or occupation were given nicknames, as was common in all Cornish towns and villages. We have already mentioned 'Lawyer Bray', but there were many others: 'Shavins' the village carpenter, 'Jimmy I Knaw', 'Shaake Eye', 'Lord Eggshells' the village egg merchant, 'Jimmy Wireless' (the village electrician, sometimes called 'Jimmy Ten Percent'), 'The Western Morning News' (the village gossip), 'Lizzie Tray Cloth', 'Sick 'en Moyle' (who attempted to sell on weak and sickly hens), 'Ponto', 'Shiner' (who loved the women), 'Missus Limpet' (who presumably sold 'trigg' or shellfish), 'Henry Ditch', 'Bone Woman' and 'Snorter' (Willie Bray, the Organ Blower at Lanner Wesley).

'The Reverend Jewel' was a real character who lived in the old Pennance Mine Count House on Carn Marth and was famous for his monologues and skits, as well as for his home made metal 'contraptions', one of which happened to be a church, complete with mechanical weather vane, hence the name Reverend. There was also 'High Back Oliver' (who

Fig.11.15. *View looking towards the south of the village at Lanner Moor, 1930s. The garage was owned by Mr Owen Penglase.* (© Lanner Historical Society)

Fig.11.16. *Harry Polkinghorne, of Carn Marth, served as a special policeman in the Second World War. His job was to patrol the Carn to ensure that blackout was strictly observed.* (© Sylvia Kessell, Redruth).

'was rounded up like a chay wheel'), 'Miss "March" Bailey' (who always walked everywhere at top speed) and 'Willie Broth', who could not stick to the diet prescribed by his doctor, and was said to have proclaimed, 'wus thirteen lil baasins of broth you?' when questioned by his frustrated GP!.[33]

The Second World War

With memories of the First World War still fresh in the minds of many, the news of the outbreak of the Second World War must have caused dismay, but was accepted by the people of Lanner with a stoicism borne of hardship. Joan Martin of Bell Veor remembers people trying to continue their life as usual, but Jack Evans, who was a farmer, remembered the war changing everything. 'There was suddenly work for everyone. If you weren't conscripted to fight the Germans, then you were working at Falmouth Docks, Holmans, or Bickford Smiths, making the machinery and shells to blow them up'. The effects of this war were to ultimately change the village forever. Early on in the war, all railings and iron gates were removed from the Wesleyan Chapel to be used for scrap metal in Beaverbrook's hasty campaign to obtain iron for armaments. The railings around the gardens of some houses also disappeared, such an example being those of 'Calumet Villa' at Lanner Moor, and many more at South Downs.

Many essential items such as food (with the exception of bread, which remained cheap), fuel (petrol and coal) and clothing were rationed. Petrol was rationed according to car engine size. In 1940, the allowance was between 2 and 4 gallons per month. The same rations were allocated to everyone, with the exception of children, who were entitled to extra foods considered essential for growth, and expectant mothers, for whom special allowances were made. Children were issued with concentrated fruit juice, to provide them with adequate Vitamin C, which was distributed in Lanner by the newly formed WI. Each family registered their ration books with their own grocer and butcher, and could then get their supplies from them. Ration books contained pages and pages of coupons, printed with the date of the week in which they were to be used. Quantities were unspecified, as these were decided on by the shopkeeper and depended on what he could get. Shopkeepers clipped off coupons against whatever they supplied and inspectors checked that traders' coupons tallied with the supplies of food allocated. From time to time the Ministry of Food would announce how much a food coupon was worth.

As different types of meat were of a different quality, coupons were based on monetary value rather than weight, so that the amount of meat a housewife received depended on the price per pound. Inevitably, you could get more of the coarse cuts than of prime steak. A typical weekly ration of food per person: Meat 1lb; bacon or ham 4ozs; cheese, 3 ozs; eggs 1; cooking fat 2 ozs; butter 2ozs; sugar 8 ozs; tea 2 ozs.

Some of the older village residents remember clubbing together on rations in order to make Christmas and birthday cakes. Furthermore, rationing did not disappear immediately after the war; for example, sweet rationing remained in force until about 1953.

The Auxiliary Fire Service (AFS) was formed to assist the full-time Fire Service in tackling fires, etc., which might be caused by enemy action. The Lanner AFS assembled outside the present Post Office, using the telephone kiosk to receive instructions and pass messages. In Whitsun, 1944, they were called upon to assist in the massive blaze which occurred at Swanpool, Falmouth, when a fuel depot exploded following a hit by a German bomber. Mrs Sylvia Kessell (née Polkinghorne) can remember, as a small child, sheltering under the large wooden table at her Aunt Edie Polkinghorne's house next door. On hearing the air raid siren, her mother and her two sisters would run, in pitch darkness, down the narrow lane to their aunt's, because her mother felt less afraid in the company of her sister-in-law and her family, whilst her absent husband patrolled the carn in his capacity as a Special Policeman (Fig.11.16).

On one occasion, her father made the family shelter in a tunnel leading into Pennance Mine, where they were joined by some other neighbours, who also used it as a bomb shelter. The Polkinghorne's actually began to dig out a large pit for use as an air raid shelter, but it was never used. Sylvia remembers seeing the eerie glow of fires lighting the night sky over Falmouth from her home on Carn Marth.[34]

An elderly resident of the village recalled a parachute coming down behind Lanner Hill Garage. People rushed to the scene to grab pieces of the white silk of the chute which was made into all manner of garments. Shrapnel and the tail fin from an incendiary bomb were recovered from land adjoining Penhalurick Farm, farmed by Ronald Stephens.

Fig.11.17. *Lanner Civil Defence Corps, 1939–45. Taken at Melrose House. Back row l-r: W.J.Phillips, W.J.Pryor, Rev. G.Parrinder, L.J.Williams, R.Edwards. Middle row: W.Dunstan, W.B.Bennetts, C.W.Langford, S.Martin, W.Veall, P.Eddy, W.D.Penglase, W.J.Treloar, W.E.Bear. Seated: J.E.P.Dunn, W.H.Langford, J.F.Banfield, D.A.Phillips, T.E.Opie, Miss R. Lidgey, E.Dawe.* (© Arthur Langford, Redruth).

German Prisoners of War at Launceston.

The routine of life for many Lanner families was disrupted when they took in evacuees from the large cities, and the Lanner School Log Book contains numerous references to children who were evacuated:

September 4, 1939. Owing to the war, the schools in the Reception Areas are closed for another week, but the teachers are at their schools as usual, so that they can assist in the reception of evacuees. September 18, 1939. Owing to the Baby Room having been given up to the Roman Catholic evacuees, the babies now share the Main Room with Class 1 and miss the advantages of a separate room. June 13, 1940. Tomorrow one hundred and twenty or more evacuees are arriving in Lanner and the school, which is being used as a reception centre, is closed for the day. 24 June 1940. In order to accommodate the evacuee infants – the Roseberry Party 81, (a particular group of evacuees), we are working a double shift. School commences at 9am and finishes at 12.30pm. In the afternoon we have Physical Study and organised games, stories and poetry. March 3, 1941. Homer Row Roman Catholic School merged with IV/81 Roseberry Avenue party today and eight infants came into this school. May 21, 1942. Mr Hayman called this afternoon to say that in view of the demand of the Board of Education for the immediate return of 100 evacuated teachers from Cornwall, the girls of the L.C.C. unit at the Lanner Hill schoolroom will be merging with ours next week. July 11, 1944. Owing to the arrival today of 600 evacuees from Kent, the school closed at mid-day.[35]

The Lanner Civil Defence Corps (1940–45) met for instructions in their duties and in order to be kept up to date about Air Raid precautions at what is now the electrical shop, next to the Londis Shop, at the bottom of Lanner Hill. As part of the blackout precautions, motorists were required to fit masking covers to car headlamps (Fig.11.17).

Special Policeman, Harry Polkinghorne, was responsible for ensuring the blackout was enforced at Carn Marth. The old concrete Home Guard Hut is still visible on the slope behind Winn's Terrace on the Carn. The Lanner School Log Book has an entry for 13 November 1939 concerning the blackout: 'Today the afternoon session begins at 1.10pm and school will be dismissed at 3.35pm to enable children to get home before dark and to enable the Caretaker to sweep and clean premises without the aid of artificial light. This variation in time will continue for this term and until further notice'.

Owen Penglase's garage at Lanner Moor became a store for customers' cars, which had to be immobilised in case of an invasion. Tom Knuckey, the coal merchant, reverted to using a horse and cart to deliver his customers' orders to save on fuel. The Bryanite Chapel, then no longer in use as a place of worship, was used during the war by the Ministry of Food as a store for empty egg boxes, where local egg producers went to collect their boxes, in order that a record of the number of eggs being sold could be kept. The schoolroom adjoining the chapel was used by the local Home Guard, and became known as 'the Drill Hall'.

Recruits in the Women's Land Army worked the land in place of male farm workers who had been 'called up'. Irene Williams (née Wilkins) was the only member of the Land Army from Lanner, and worked on farms throughout Cornwall during the period 1943–45, working with thirty

Sheila Mooney, (née Dundon), was evacuated by train from Paddington, London, to Camborne with her sister the day before the war started. She remembers the traumatic selection process as the worse part, when the children were billeted out to various families.

Being in Lanner was like being in a different world' she recalled. *'We were placed with the Moyles who kept Bell Farm. Everything was quiet, green and tranquil compared to London. We fitted in as best we could, but my sister was only six and I was just eleven, and we were terribly unhappy at times. There were lots of other evacuees in the village which made being away from home more tolerable because we could at least play with our school friends. We attended Lanner school with the other children from the village, but travelled by*

Marigold bus to the Roman Catholic Church at West End. Our teachers, the nuns from the Holy Rosary School, were accommodated in a little cottage behind the Moyles' farm.[36]

This movement of population was to have lasting effects, as it brought the town and countryside closer together than ever before, and was the forerunner of subsequent population movements which ultimately altered the demographic balance and composition of Cornwall.

But it was not just people from up the country who lived for a time in Lanner. American soldiers were temporarily billeted at Tresavean and at Carn Marth, in the run up to D-Day. A more permanent base had been established at United Downs earlier in the war. They joined in with village life as well as they could, occasionally giving concerts in the Wesleyan Schoolroom. A percentage of the servicemen were black Americans. One such concert, at which the black GI's sang Spirituals, was at the Primitive Methodist Chapel at Lanner Moor in 1944, under the musical directorship of Sergeant Faust. A collection for the Moor choir fund realised £3.10s.[37]

To people in the village who had not ventured overseas, the presence of black GI's caused quite a sensation. Ida May Polkinghorne was quite surprised to meet one at the entrance to Carn Marth Lane. He proceeded to walk up the lane with her to the American Camp which had just been set up on the carn, on the croftland down behind Winn's Terrace. She remembered his courteous behaviour and his kind offer to carry the infant she was trying to manage as well as all her shopping, but was relieved when she reached her garden gate, as she was worried that someone would see her 'fraternising' with a black man.

Several Lanner women became pregnant out of wedlock after affairs with the servicemen, a few of whom had been black, and this had not met with the approval of some villagers, who, like many British people, considered the Americans to have been 'over-paid, over-sexed and over here!. Sadly some of those women who courted US soldiers found themselves deserted by their American boyfriends after the war. Likewise, an elderly village resident remembers the shock of finding herself in the company of numerous black Americans when the lights went on at the end of a concert at the Regal Cinema at Redruth.

Most people have pleasant memories of the GI's, especially those who as children were given candy and gum by the Americans, and some troops occasionally sold American preserves, tinned goods, packets of cigarettes, coffee and other items cheaply to residents on the Black Market, unspeakable luxuries for a population which had become used to getting by and making do for so long.

After the awful suffering witnessed in the First World War from poison gas, the fear of gas attacks by the Germans on the civilian population prompted the British Government to issue gas masks nationwide, and every Lanner resident received one. Sylvia Kessell can still remember the smell of her rubber mask in its cardboard box, and being loathe to give it up at the end of the war. Lance Bray remembers his 'Mickey Mouse' mask was red in colour, and the adults had black rubber ones. The School Log Book records that the children's gas masks were examined by an ARP Warden on 6 November 1941. Fortunately the masks never had to be used for their intended purpose.

Many men from the village served in the Second World War, and some lost their lives in defence of their country – Richard Curnow, Leonard A. Dunstan, George Mason and Edward D. Payne. Two Lanner men counted themselves fortunate to have returned home after the war. Charlie Job joined the RAF, seeing active service in the Far East. He was reported missing, and thought to have been taken prisoner of war by the Japanese. His mother Mary Job recalled vividly being told of her son's fate, and three long years of worry followed, when she did not know whether he was alive or dead. Mary remembered the Vicar of Lanner, the Reverend Greening, doing his best to console her, and they regularly prayed together for Charlie's safe return. After the war had ended, Mary received word that two prisoners of war would be returning to the village, and one of them would be Charlie. The other man was Charlie Andrews, who was taken POW by the Germans.

The village collected a large sum of money for the two men and planned a warm welcome home ceremony held at the Bryanite Chapel to celebrate their safe return. As a mark of his gratitude, Charlie Job decorated the interior of the old chapel some years later, after it had become the Village Hall.[38]

During the war years, the routine of village life was continued much as usual, with concerts to raise money which also provided a welcome distraction from the worries of war. The Teacher's Log Book for Lanner School records on 6 November 1941: 'This afternoon the children marched to the Wesleyan schoolroom for a concert, given by the RAF Band in aid of Wings for Victory week'. To boost village morale, there were three concert parties in the Lanner area during the war – the 'Victory' and 'Snowball' troupes as well as the Home Guard Choir. The Log Book for the village school provides evidence of the way in which the War disrupted and changed the routine of village life:

August 12, 1940. School opened today until 2nd September. During these three weeks scholars may make voluntary attendance, but teachers must be in attendance. No registration for these weeks. March 5, 1941. This afternoon all scholars with staff are visiting the Wesley Schoolroom in Lanner to see some films in conjunction with War Weapons Week. March 9, 1944. Owing to sickness in the house, and her husband's departure to join his squadron, Mrs Thomas did not arrive until 10.55 am. April 3, 1944. Mrs Thomas is absent from duty, owing to the reported loss of her husband in a raid over Germany. April 17, 1944. School Canteen open today in Lanner Boys' School for use of the three departments. Dinners are being sent in containers from Dolcoath Cooking Depot.[39]

During the War, a new radio station was built on the high ground above Lanner's valley, which had two 10 kW transmitters from which the BBC transmitted programmes for the Home Services and the Forces Network. The BBC planned to announce the news of D-Day as the troops were landing on the beaches of Normandy. Mary Baker and Phyllis Harding were on duty for four nights at the Lanner Transmitter in early June, 1944. They knew something was afoot, but were not sure what, as they had been instructed not to fall asleep on any account, but to listen to the music programme from Plymouth, and if a particular code was broadcast they would have to instantly power the Home Service Transmitter to radiate vitally important news. The women were sworn to absolute secrecy, but during their shifts nothing occurred. When the day shift arrived on day four, 6 June, the women remember chatting with their colleagues as the transmitter was powered, when they heard the message 'this is London' which heralded the news of the successful launch of D-Day. 'We were all dumb struck and shivering as we shook each other's hands,' recollected one of the women.[40]

When peace came to the nation in 1945, every town and village across the nation celebrated an end to war. On 8 and 9 May Lanner School was closed for the VE holiday and in the streets of nearby Redruth, people remember thousands joyfully dancing and singing to proclaim the end of hostilities. On 21 June 1945 a Garden Fete was held in Lanner in aid of the 'Home-coming Fund'.

Fig.11.18. *V.E.Day 50th Anniversary Celebrations, 1995. Former Japanese P.O.W., Charlie Job, on the left, in the procession leaving Lanner Square.* (photo. R.H.Parker)

Electricity and Gas

Electricity was one of the first modern services to benefit Lanner. Prior to this, parishioners had relied on candles or oil lamps (which ran on paraffin) to light their homes. The village adopted public lighting in 1894, by subscription, and the Lanner Lamp Committee were responsible for ensuring that sufficient money was raised to provide the oil for the lamps. By 1895, there were 14 lamps. Tom Osborne is remembered as the village lamp lighter, providing illumination at 6pm each evening in the winter months. The lamps were cleaned during the moonlit week each month, and the paraffin to light them was procured at 8d per gallon.[41] Old people in the village remember sitting together in the square for a chat under 'the Lanner Moon', the public lamp which was situated on top of the drinking fountain.[42] (There are plans afoot to restore the public fountain and to place a replica of the old 'Lanner Moon' in its former position.).

In about 1900 the Phosus Acetylene Lamp Co. was granted permission by the Lanner Lamp Committee to try one or two of their lamps by way of experiment, but the committee decided against changing from their oil lamps.

Around 1904 The Urban Electric Supply Co. attempted to interest the Lanner Lamp Committee with proposals to provide electric light, but the cost of £50 per annum, as against around £26 per annum for oil, was considered prohibitive. The cost of maintenance of the oil lamps in 1906 was 3d per lamp per night. The Imperial Light Co. also requested permission to try their burners which would have reduced the maintenance cost by 1d. Electric lighting only replaced the old oil lamps in the 1930s in the main streets of the village, but the long walk to and from Redruth via South Downs at night, without any light, is still remembered. 'It was good to see the houses lit up all along Clinton Road, which was modern compared with the villages'. In 1935, it was reported that another street lamp had been erected opposite the entrance to Bell Lane.[43] 'The road through the village is now well lit, but Rough Street and other roads away from the main road are still in darkness'. At the time of writing, they still are.

In 1903, Camborne and Redruth received mains electricity, but it was not until 1929 that domestic users in Lanner enjoyed electric lighting. The first use of electricity in Lanner Parish was industrial, at Tresavean Mine. Wayleave agreements made between various landowners and the Cornwall Electric Power Company, dated between 1912 and 1914, emphasise the importance the mining industry still had in the parish in the early twentieth century. Electricity was the preferred motive power for pumping and winding at Tresavean Mine during the last working, and was at first effected using an electrical power generating plant driven by three high-pressure Lancashire boilers. But the company later took their supply direct from the mains.

The first residences in the village to be lit by electric light were Melrose House and Leona Villa in 1929. Most homes still relied on candles and lamps at this time. Leona Villa had electric light in two rooms only, as two 'free' lights were allowed with the basic charge. The charges for electricity in 1936 by the Cornwall Electric Power Company (which had absorbed the West Cornwall Electricity Supply Company Ltd.) were 8d a unit flat rate for lighting, and 12d a unit for heating and cooking.

There was a distinction between 'power' and 'lighting' circuits and meters. The heating and cooking meter was supplied free, but the lighting meter had a rental of

2 shillings a quarter. As an alternative, a 'service charge' plus a one penny per unit charge could be paid. The service charge depended on the floor area of the house, starting at 40 shillings a year. Additionally, there was a cheaper unit charge for electricity used 'by approved thermostatically controlled heating apparatuses'. The minimum annual payment was £1.13s.4d. The first quarterly bill at No. 1 Glen View, Lanner, amounted to 17 shillings, for 23 units at the 8d flat rate.[44] Lanner Hill residents received electricity in 1936, Trevarth in 1939, but Carn Marth residents waited until 1976 for mains electricity, when once again, industry made this possible. The quarry facing Pennance reopened and electricity was required for the machinery. Residents had formerly depended on oil-fuelled generators for their electricity supply.

In 1911, the need of a telephone in Lanner was made obvious, when a young man was seriously injured at Tresavean Mine. Help had to be sent for at Redruth, resulting in a long delay in the giving of treatment. In 1929, plans were made for a public call box to be installed in Lanner at the earliest possible date.[45]

Although the first use of gas for domestic lighting in the world occurred nearby in Redruth, at the Cross Street home of engineer and inventor William Murdoch in 1792, this benefit has never reached Lanner. And the likelihood that a mains gas line will be brought down into the village by British Gas in the twenty-first century, at the present time of writing, seems remote. A feasibility study has concluded that the cost to homeowners of connection to the mains gas supply was too great, and not enough people had opted to do so, making the plan uneconomical to the company. But it might also underlie the fact Lanner has significant numbers of unemployed, poorer pensioners or families living on low income. Indeed, a report on Lanner County Primary School in the late 1980s commented that Lanner was a very large village, and that the community was a mixed one socially. 'Many parents commute to Falmouth, Truro and Redruth, but it is understood that the area is considerably affected by unemployment. Thirty-one of the 80 or so children who had school dinners received them free'.[46]

Water

In the mid twentieth century, as far as the provision of fresh water and the disposal of sewage was concerned, the residents of Lanner and district found that they lived in conditions remarkably similar to their nineteenth century forbears. Water was obtained from wells, chutes and standpipes, and Lanner had never had a proper sewerage system. Great strides forward were made during the late Victorian era as regards public health, and in the 1880s and 90s, nearby Redruth had benefited enormously from improved municipal services. Lanner and other neighbouring towns and villages were not as fortunate, and it is a damning indictment on the lethargy of the local councils that Lanner had to wait until the next century for improvements in the provision of basic sanitation.

The whole question of providing an adequate water supply for Redruth and district was a most contentious one, with local councillors and residents at each other's throats over the best plan and the cost of implementing it. Council meetings became a forum for bitter rivalries. Redruth received its water from four primary sources in the nineteenth century: Penstruthal, Gordon, Drump and Sandy Lane Adits. The latter location was of great importance to the town as demands for water rose with Redruth's late Victorian expansion centred on Clinton Road.

In 1887, it was reported that the Redruth Local Board had installed a 10-ton horsepower horizontal engine with a 10-inch cylinder, at Sandy Lane, powerful enough to work a 40 fathom lift. Eighty gallons of water a minute were estimated to have been drawn by this engine, and the water was reported to have been of good quality, although it contained minute traces of copper. Prior to this, Redruth had relied heavily on water drawn from Mount Carbis Mine in kibbles, which was then passed through an improvised filter of iron filings, coke and pieces of granite.[47] It was not long before Lanner was pulled into Redruth's battles over the water supply. In 1894, Lanner residents complained to architect James Hicks, the Chairman of the Redruth Ratepayers' Association, a constant thorn in the side of the Redruth Town Council, about the proposed plans to take water from the Penstruthal Adit which it was intended to divert to a large new reservoir in Sandy Lane.

James Hicks was a vociferous opponent of the new reservoir plan, brainchild of his arch rival, Arthur Carkeek, and gladly took Lanner's side in the battle, by arguing that it was unlikely there would be a surplus from a 4-inch wooden launder at Penstruthal, and drew the Redruth Board's attention to the fact that Lanner was also a crowded area which needed water.[48] But the new reservoir went ahead as planned, and Redruth residents benefited greatly from water which came from Lanner Parish, but ironically, Lanner people did not, and the water supply in the village continued to be most unsatisfactory.

Water was obtained from a variety of sources, many of which were not always close to home, and collecting it was a major inconvenience, especially for elderly people. Sylvia Kessell (née Polkinghorne), can remember feeling acutely sorry for her aunt, Lily Bray, who lived at Winn's Terrace, Carn Marth, and who had a family of nine children to care for. She spent many hours of each day trudging to and from Figgy Dowdy's Well with buckets of water. Women on Monday washdays would make numerous journeys to and from the nearest water source with pails in order to fill the 'copper' in the back wash house, in which the water was boiled to wash the clothes.

Water was therefore viewed as a commodity not to be wasted. Many people rigged up water butts outside their cottages in order to collect rainwater for washing vegetables, and for the weekly laundry. Few houses could boast a water cistern, exceptions being Lanner House, with a large tank, and West Trevarth Farm, which had an underground cistern.

Fig.11.19. *Lanner Village Square, c.1904. Note 'Maud's Water' (the water tap) on the right, the Commercial Inn, far left, and Lanner Wesley Sunday School, then only recently built, centre. The girl drawing water at the fountain is Florence Hodge.* (© The Paddy Bradley Collection)

One of the primary water sources in Lanner was the granite public fountain erected in the Village Square in 1901 by Miss Pascoe of Penstruthal in memory of her deceased sister Maud (Fig. 11.19). This became known as 'Maud's Water'. Nineteenth century Lanner had always suffered from a limited supply of water, and through the provision of a fountain in the square and a further two standpipes at Bell Lane and Pennance Lane, it was hoped to remedy the situation.[49] The public tap in the Square was used by people who did not have taps indoors. Lottie Benbow, of 2 Grays Terrace, often collected water from there for her elderly neighbours, 'a penny a turn'.[50] Some women used to gather there on Saturday in order to have water ready for the weekend and Monday's washing, as it was deemed unacceptable to queue there in public on a Sunday.

Other taps were situated on the corner of the road leading into Lannarth Glas, and can still be seen in the hedge going up Lanner Hill on the left; another already mentioned was sited at the bottom of Bell Lane where the bus shelter is presently sited, and a further tap was placed in Church Road. Water carriers came around the village selling water at the price of 1d a pail or pitcher, which had been collected from various chutes in and around the village. One such chute was situated at the entrance to the lane opposite the playing field, another at the bottom of Tresavean Hill and at Ivyhouse, Penstruthal. At the top of Pennance Lane was the Carn Marth Chute, and Thomas Henry Tresidder used to go there once a week with his cart containing a huge water barrel which he filled with enough drinking water for a week.[51] (Fig. 11.20.). The Blamey's of West Trevarth Farm also made the same weekly journey to this chute for their drinking water. The barrel stood outside their back door.[52]

Fig.11.20. *Thomas Henry Tresidder (1851–1916), water carrier and coal merchant, on his way to Carn Marth chute, where he collected drinking water every week.* (© Royal Institution of Cornwall)

Some parishioners were fortunate to have a well in their garden, and a public pump was situated at Lanner Moor close to the chapel. Trevarth was formerly poorly provided with water, and in 1892, it was noted in the *Cornubian* that the Redruth Rural Sanitary Authority considered it 'desirable that Trevarth residents should have a water supply without fetching it from a long distance'.[53]

The Trevarth chute was situated just below Gribble's Farm, on the opposite side of the road. Ethel Langford (née Evans) used the chute to make butter when she lived at Treviskey earlier this century. A well was situated at West Trevarth Farm which was used for irrigation purposes in the fields. On Carn Marth, Figgy Dowdy's Well was the principal water source for residents, but other wells existed, one in the garden of a cottage, now demolished, which formerly stood behind the dwelling, Carn Wartha, another on the Croftland close to Sea View Farm, and a further two at Dower's farm and at Gordon.

During hot summers the wells often ran dry causing considerable inconvenience to residents, who then had to travel longer distances to fetch water. In the summer of 1921, a severe drought caused the celebrated waters of Figgy Dowdy's Well to run dry. Someone had placed a notice on the ancient structure forbidding the drawing of anymore water 'hear' which caused considerable consternation amongst the carn's residents. Sammy Dower's Well further down the hill was also very low, and the residents of the carn then had the long walk down to Gordon's Well which was below the water table and therefore more reliable.[54] A public pump was later installed at Figgy Dowdy's Well.

In 1948, it was reported that the Carn Marth pump was in a bad condition and a notice was issued not to use it. In the mid 1950s, attempts were made by the tenants of Rockfield, on whose ground the well lay, to chain up the pump and thus prevent anyone from drawing water. This led to some spirited scenes of resistance, made all the more interesting since the tenants of Rockfield and their neighbours were mostly all related!

One can imagine that quarrels and rows frequently broke out amongst parishioners over the drawing of water from wells, particularly in times of drought. In 1892 a 17 year old named Harold Harvey had an altercation with the son of 'Muggy' Mugford of Carn Marth, over whose turn it was to draw water at Gordon's Well. This resulted in Harvey giving the boy 'a clip around the ear' for throwing a stone at him. The next day the boy's father 'Muggy' attacked Harvey with a shovel handle placing the youth's life in danger. Upon being charged for attempted murder and a warrant being issued against him, 'Muggy' absconded![55]

The quality of water from all these sources was often suspect, and sometimes the local authority placed an order forbidding people to draw from them. Water sources were graded in order of cleanliness, from 'excellent', to 'good', 'fair', 'suspect' and 'unsatisfactory'. Notices advising people to boil the water from the various taps, chutes and wells in the parish were frequent.

In 1947, some of Lanner's houses were connected to a mains water supply. In 1948, Melrose House, residence of coal merchant T.C. Knuckey, was the first in Lanner to have a bathroom with mains running water installed. In 1965, fresh water came from the shaft of old South Wheal Frances Mine, and was chlorinated at source. A 10-inch main came through Carnkie and down Buller Hill. At Sandy Lane it split, then came down Lanner Hill as far as Job's Buildings, while the other spur went around via Mount Ambrose, St Day, Carharrack, Trevarth, Lanner Moor and back to Job's Buildings. It was heavily used, and on Mondays, washing day, supply in some places 'dwindled to a drip'.[56]

In 1957, the Local Council received letters from W. Rule (Windy Ridge, Lanner Hill), E. Ralph (Gordon, Carn Marth) and W.J. Phillips (Endsleigh, Lanner Hill), together with a petition signed by a number of people residing in the Pennance area, asking for a piped water supply in their areas. The poor water facilities for an area which was earmarked for considerable development were obviously unacceptable, so to remedy the situation, a large water tank capable of storing two million gallons was built in the summer of 1965 at the top of Lanner Hill, and a small tank at Carn Marth. One thousand and fifty lineal yards of 8-inch diameter pumping main were installed between Lanner Hill reservoir and the Carn Marth reservoir, in conjunction with the Stithians reservoir impounding scheme. In 1966, a pumping station was built at Lanner Hill reservoir and the following year, the Annual Report of the Public Health Department of the Camborne–Redruth Urban District Council (CRUDC) stated that 40 yards of 3-inch PVC main had been installed at Lanmoor Estate, a new mains providing supplies of water to one of the village's largest housing developments.[57]

But it was not until 1976 that all Carn Marth residents received mains water. Figgy Dowdy's Well was closed by order of the local water board, who declared its water unfit for human consumption. This was only in part true. The well had become somewhat unreliable since operations in the quarry, opposite, had disturbed fissures feeding the natural spring, and at times the water was slightly muddy. Harry Polkinghorne of 'Hillside', defiantly continued to draw water from the well claiming that it 'was a good deal better than the tap water', which he considered reminiscent of bleach. Finally, the pump was partly dismantled, the granite front was mutilated and concrete slabs were placed over the entrance to the well to make access more difficult.[58] Harry Polkinghorne and his neighbours had to get used to chlorinated water, and the water bill.

Today's water supply is distributed from the covered tank at the top of Lanner Hill, into which treated water is pumped by night from the Stithians treatment works. The pipes are laid along the old Tresavean Tram track. In its turn, the reservoir at Stithians is topped up by water pumped across the county from the Colliford Reservoir in East Cornwall.

Sewerage

For the disposal of sewage, houses in Lanner had depended from time immemorial on earth and chemical closets tucked away in the corner of the garden, often close to a fragrant lilac tree and various species of scented flowers which helped to mask the ubiquitous smell emanating from the interior of even the cleanest and best kept 'thunder-box' during spells of hot weather. Many of these old privies can still be seen in Lanner's back gardens, now converted into sheds. The vast majority of Lanner's residents did not have indoor toilets or bathrooms earlier this century; an old tin bath hung from a nail in the wash house was a common sight in the village, well into the 1960s. One very 'grand' elderly lady who lived in the village some 30 years ago, was known to have made a daily trip into Redruth, ostensibly to go to Bartles' butcher's shop for 2ozs of ham, but her main intention was to use the public conveniences at Fish Cross. Villagers knew this, and

Fig.11.21. *Bear's Terrace, with Pennance terrace in the background. Note the old leat, with bridges to reach the houses. Early twentieth century.* (© The Paddy Bradley Collection)

often joked 'its a good thing she's regular!'[59] Many dwellings relied on cess pits and septic tanks, including the School, the two Methodist Chapels and the Village Hall. In 1965, it was reported that in Lanner it had become compulsory for new houses to have a tank, emptied free if only once a year – £1 per visit if more often.

However, some residents were not very careful when it came to disposing of their waste. The contents of a privy bucket were usually buried in the garden, a practice which was fairly safe if the excrement was buried deep enough. Problems arose when people emptied their slops 'up the bank' with no attempt at careful disposal, but the biggest hazard to public health was posed by those who discreetly made use of the 'leat', often during the night, which in effect became an open sewer. In 1957 the Gwennap Parish Council was forced to write to the Public Health Committee of the CRUDC to complain about the sewage nuisance from the leat running through Lanner. In 1965 it was stated that 'it needs little imagination to realise how this flow of easily accessible running water was abused. All types of people did so and are doing so in one way or another'.[60] (Fig. 11.21.).

This filthy channel was the abode of rats and other vermin and therefore posed grave danger to health, since it flowed in such close proximity to people's homes. We have noted the frequency of disease in the nineteenth century which arose mainly due to poor or inadequate sanitary provisions. The occurrence of infectious diseases was by no means purely a nineteenth century phenomenon.

The Lanner School Log Book provides ample evidence of the frequency of disease in the district. In 1904 diphtheria cases were reported in the village, with one fatality. People became nervous and so kept their children way from school, which was subsequently disinfected. In October 1914, the school closed for a month on the orders of the local Medical Officers of Health because of the reappearance of diphtheria in the District. In February 1915, the Infant Department was closed due to the prevalence of whooping cough, in October there were about 20 absent through scarlatina and a measles epidemic swept the village in 1918, causing the deaths of three children. Polio broke out in Lanner in 1948, and Ann, the daughter of the Revd C. Craven-Sands, was taken seriously ill in this outbreak of 'infantile paralysis'.

Since the middle of the nineteenth century, it had been patently obvious that Lanner needed a proper drainage system. However, little was done towards creating a sewerage disposal system, the reasons preventing this attributable to various factors primarily brought about by the collapse of the mining industry which left a trail of de-industrialisation in its wake. This in turn led to lack of finance, council inertia and a catalogue of false starts and promises, exemplified by an article in the *West Briton* in 1966, referring to a statement made in 1911 by Dr Arthur Permewan, the Medical Officer of Health for the District of Redruth. He had remarked that the drainage at Lanner was 'simply scandalous' with the existing system found to be totally inadequate and requiring regular attention, making a sewerage scheme a matter of great urgency. In response, the Rural Council visited Lanner some months later to view the situation and to devise a scheme for a safe and effective waste disposal scheme.

In May 1912, the *Cornubian* reported that the proposed scheme would have cost £2800, and the engineer H. Worth, had drawn up plans to provide an irrigation scheme at Little Trevince which would have taken sewage from Lanner to Gwennap and on to 8–10 acres of waste ground, with the effluent discharging into a stream.[61] However, nothing was done, chiefly through financial considerations.

It was again discussed in 1921, but dropped because considered to be too costly due to the prevailing woeful economic climate. The following decade, Dr C. Rivers, Medical Officer of Health for the newly-formed CRUDC, blamed the fall in the world prices of copper during the second half of the nineteenth century for the failure to provide adequate provision for the disposal of sewerage in the district. The new council called upon its engineer to prepare a feasibility plan for a new sewerage system, but in 1937, the scheme was again shelved due to insufficient funds. The Second World War delayed matters further, and after the war, the CRUDC had more urgent problems to contend with, foremost of these being the provision of more housing.

In the latter part of 1947, a sewerage disposal plant was constructed at Lanner to deal with waste from the local council's new units at Tresavean Estate. The plant was passed over to the Public Health Department in 1948, and comprised a septic tank, filter bed and humus tank. The effluent discharged into the nearby stream. In the late 1950s, N. Barret, Surveyor, submitted a new scheme, but without effect.

It was only in 1964, that the sewerage scheme received top priority. This was because Lanner was earmarked for considerable building development, which would not have been approved unless adequate provision was made to radically improve municipal services in the village and district. Mr Jeffrey, Chairman of the Housing Committee, pointed out to those present at the laying of the foundation stone of the new sewerage works near Gwennap in June 1966 that, 'the area might find itself, like Illogan, developing out of all recognition within a few years.' His words were indeed prophetic.

Finally, on 20 May 1965, the long-awaited drainage scheme for Lanner and St Day was inaugurated, and at the end of that year pipe-laying had reached as far as Comford, and the construction of the disposal works at Gwennap had commenced, constructed on ground belonging to Truro Rural Council. The sewerage scheme was expected to cost £350 000 of which 5 per cent was to be paid by St Day and Lanner people. Mr Jeffrey reminded those present at the stone laying ceremony, that the scheme was a continuance of a century of public health measures which had abolished the threat of cholera and reduced other major epidemic diseases to an occasional threat. 'Where health is concerned, money does not matter', he stated, continuing, 'there is a communal grave in Redruth, occupied by the victims of a cholera epidemic in the town'.[62]

At the time of Mr Jeffrey's stirring speech, it was over 120 years since those cholera victims had died in the great 1849 epidemic. It is hardly a commendable thing, that in an age in which man had split the atom and travelled into space, that people in our area were still emptying buckets of waste in their own back gardens. Lanner had had to wait 136 years for such a vital municipal service.

Inhabitants were urged to connect their properties to the new sewer as it was being laid. Many engineering difficulties were encountered, including problems with solid rock, mine shafts, culverts and flooding, but in 1966, five miles of pipe had been laid, and the scheme, involving a total of almost 12 miles of pipe, was to be completed by the end of 1967, serving 1400 houses and a population of 5000. One major branch of the main sewers was laid through Lanner, and the other from St Day and Carharrack through Sparry Bottom where they joined to run on to the sewerage works, built on mine wasteland between Gwennap Churchtown and United Downs. It was expected that at least two-thirds of the houses would be connected to a main sewer, the expense of constructing it being the Council's responsibility. Householders who wished to be connected to the main sewer had to meet the cost themselves.

The problems posed by the notorious 'leat' which conducted water from Penstruthal and Bell Vean Mines through the village and on to the sea at Devoran were finally tackled. The Bell Vean and Penstruthal adits flowed past the church green and joined part of the Wheal Beauchamp adit beneath the square. The Wheal Beauchamp adit flowed from the top of Lanner Hill, under the old school yard, underneath the Village Square, past the present Post Office and ran open to the entrance to Bell Lane where it crossed beneath the road at the end of Grays Terrace. It then passed under Woodlands Terrace to Pennance Lane and from then on ran open from the present Garden centre through Lanner Moor to Comford.

Residents very soon felt the benefits of the scheme to clean up the noisome leat and the banishment of the rodents inhabiting it banks. When the leat was being enclosed, rats swarmed through the village and one resident got a particularly nasty shock one evening whilst visiting his outside privy; he was bitten by a rat which had found its way into the bucket beneath. In 1960, the road at the upper end of the village was widened to allow the construction of pavements, and concrete pipes were installed to deal with the adit water. 'Here the leat is just a bad memory, and the only reminder one gets nowadays is the sight and sound of rushing water at the semi-closed places at each end of Prisk's Terrace, but the occasional rat may still be seen darting in or out'.[63]

However, it appears that the money allocated by the County Council for the scheme to pipe the leat ran out before the whole length was covered, and for the next five years, at the lower end at Lanner Moor, contaminated waters continued to run alongside garden gates bridged by granite slabs, highly dangerous especially for children or people venturing out at night.

Several older residents of the village can remember falling into the leat. In 1965, it was covered along most of its length, going under the road at Bray's Terrace and then under front gardens in some places, but further problems were encountered at Lanner Moor when work resumed from Trevarth Corner; a resident refused permission for a garden entrance to be broken to make way for the pipe, and work ceased. By February 1966, work had still not resumed, and the leat was therefore not fully enclosed until the late 1960s.

On the Buses

The development and improvement of the local roads resulted in great changes in employment patterns, as people from the village were able to travel longer distances to work in the new coaches which plied the improved routes. A group of old friends were sitting in the Square under the Lanner Moon earlier this century when one of the 'new' buses came up through the village, gears clashing, backfiring and emitting copious amounts of black exhaust fumes. 'I've seen 'em come and I shall see 'em go', commented one of the old timers as he watched the bus disappear out of sight.[64] Of course he did not, and in no time the buses became as much a part of life as the horse and cart had been. Moreover, much was done to accommodate such new vehicles which altered the narrow lanes and changed the look of the countryside forever. In 1934 a cottage at the corner of Lanner Moor opposite the Coppice was demolished by the County Council to facilitate the clear passage of the large buses en route to Carharrack, and in 1959 the main Falmouth to Redruth Road (A393) was widened and pavements laid down by order of the Local Government Act of 1933. Mrs M. E. Blight of Lambriggan House lost 30 square yards of her front garden in this road widening scheme, receiving compensation of one shilling, although the Council had to rebuild the boundary walls in their new position.[65] Just what a drastic change this was to the local roads can be seen by looking at Fig. 11.22 of South Downs, which was changed beyond recognition.

Howard Manley operated the Lannarth Bus Company, or 'Lannarth Tours', after he had left the firm run by Newton Trewern during the 1930s. His buses were painted a chocolate brown colour. But Newton Trewern's Marigold Buses will long be remembered by people in the Redruth area, owned and operated firstly by Newton and then the Stephens family of 'Rose Cottage', Lanner Green. Newton Trewern had been employed as a carpenter at Falmouth Docks, and travelled there daily with many other village men. At first

Fig.11.22. *South Downs, showing the old turnpike road, now the busy A393. Note the Wesleyan Chapel on the right, now the Kingdom Hall of the Jehovah's Witnesses. The row of cottages on the left was pulled down in 1984. The two girls on the road are Miss Lilian Vincent (left) and Miss Lilian Trudgeon.* (© The Paddy Bradley Collection)

Fig.11.23. *Marigold buses in Lanner Square. Llewellyn Tamblyn in doorway; Harold Stevens, far left; Jimmy Stevens, David Polkinghorne; last man, unknown.* (© The Paddy Bradley Collection).

he gave lifts to his colleagues on motorbike and sidecar. Seeing that this was a potential source of money, he bought a Model 'T' Ford before the Second World War, and built a special covering for it. Newton guaranteed people from Lanner a free ride to Falmouth Docks to seek work, with the understanding that if they were employed, they would agree to travel with him afterwards for a moderate return fare. After some time, he judged the concern was lucrative enough to allow him to give up his full time job at the Docks and the Marigold Bus Company was born.[66] Business expanded and these buses took many village men to work each day, not just at the Docks, but other places of work such as Bickford Smiths, and Holmans, before the war, continuing a trend towards a commuter-based economy for Lanner's residents.

In 1959 Harold Stephens bought the Marigold Coach business from Newton Trewern who was retiring. Harold Stephens acquired a total of eight coaches, seven Bedfords and one Commer, plus the garage in Ankervis Lane which is now used by Keith Abrahams, coal merchant. The eight bright-orange coaches, picked out in black, were a familiar sight in the district. Drivers on these buses over the years included Harold and his brother Jimmy Stephens, brothers Willie, Dick and John Bray, Mr Hooper, Charlie Barnes, Glen Thomas, L. Tamblyn, Bill Bullock, David Polkinghorne and Steve Daly. Other staff included Jo Craze, as a mechanic, and Irene and Mary Williams, as conductors.[67] (Fig.11.23.).

Harold Stephens had regular contracts with Falmouth Docks, the Rank Factory at Pool, local nursery gardens and schools. And in addition to these, he also ran services to Truro, Falmouth, Camborne and Redruth. Lanner to Redruth was a service run every half an hour on Fridays, 9.00am–9.00pm. and Saturdays 1.30pm–10.30pm. The coaches were occasionally booked by local groups, and in the summer, he operated services to Porthtowan and Portreath for the locals. There are many amusing stories about what happened on the routes plied by these buses, but the following was particularly well known. Late one night, a bus driven by Jimmy Stephens was on one of the routes which ran to Devoran. A female passenger kept repeatedly reminding him not to miss her stop. 'Es Missus, all right, I shan't miss 'un' he replied in his familiar reedy voice. But for some inexplicable reason, Jimmy drove right past the bus stop in the pitch darkness, stopping somewhere else. The door opened and thinking she was at her stop, the woman stepped off and fell straight into a river up to her waist. 'What 'ee doin down theer Missus?' was all the surprised bus driver could say![68]

Each morning the coaches were filled with diesel from the garage in Ankervis Lane and driven to the Square, and lined up. The drivers were then given their instructions for the day prior to their departure.

At 60, Harold Stephens decided to retire and sold the coach business to Mr and Mrs Hartland who had recently come to Cornwall from London. But the cuts at Falmouth Dockyards and the Rank Factory at Pool meant that the Marigold Company could not continue to run these routes profitably. In about 1980 the concern was bought out by a much bigger concern, Grenville Motors of Camborne, ending one of the businesses which had put Lanner on the map.

Many more of the services which gave Lanner a unique identity and independence from nearby Redruth have also vanished. We now no longer have a resident policeman, who once lived at Phillips Terrace, and The Lanner Hospital Committee, formed in 1943, was disbanded in 1948 because of the commencement of the National Health Act. The Lanner and Gwennap Nursing Association which had begun in the early twentieth century was also disbanded 1948 when the National Health Act created a central body, dispensing with the need of rural services such as that at Lanner, increasing reliance on Redruth or Camborne for many of its services.

The Exploding Village

By the end of the nineteenth century, Lanner contained a variety of housing, from the detached and humble smallholder's cottage, in varying degrees of dilapidation, terraced cottages more substantially built, and smart houses and villas which were the abodes of the new middle class. At this time Lanner's housing developments could still be divided into distinct areas. There was a concentration of buildings focused on the Square, at Pennance and Lanner Moor, and fanning out between these areas were terraced cottages and solitary houses, found along the main roads connecting them. Rough Street, the area around the Turnpike Road (now the A393) from Lanner Moor to South Downs, and along Pennance Road had witnessed ribbon development, but Pennance Lane had very few houses along its route. Bell Lane and Bell Veor were largely undeveloped and the area between the A393 and Pennance Road was mainly open fields. Trevarth remained a separate hamlet with signs of terraced development along the road leading from Trevarth Village to Carharrack. Carvannel, Brewer, Penstruthal and Carn Marth had remained largely undeveloped, with a few scattered farms and homesteads.

The story from then on has been the gradual in-filling of the open areas, a process which still continues today. As had happened in the village during the nineteenth century, new phases of building and development occurred when Tresavean Mine was in production. Several new rows of housing were constructed during the final phase of Tresavean's working (1907–1928), including Phillips Terrace, built in 1912, Hazel Terrace and the two houses on the left side of the road, opposite the Londis Shop, built in 1914. The *Royal Cornwall Gazette* reported in 1915 that 'A few villa residences have been erected (in 1914), which certainly add to the significance of the village, but the all important factor – workmen's dwellings – is still a matter of theory'.[69] Later that year, the freehold of some 30 cottages at Lanner Moor was sold, the same newspaper commenting, 'scarcely any of these is modern'.[70] After the closure of Tresavean Mine in 1928, the process of de-industrialisation resulted in a declining population and very little building development was to occur until after the Second World War.

As noted above, many people in Lanner lived in overcrowded cottages with extremely basic facilities. Very few had indoor bathrooms or toilets, or even an indoor water supply. This was common throughout Cornwall, the 1951 Census revealing that 55 per cent of the population had no access to a bath and a staggering 33 per cent of households lacked exclusive use of a sink (this compared to 13 per cent in England and Wales), whilst 34 per cent lacked piped water (17 per cent England and Wales).[71]

After the war, the Council was forced to address the issue of those local families living in poor or substandard accommodation, and it became top priority to re-house them. In 1950, the Vicar of Lanner, the Reverend Colin Craven-Sands, was Chairman of the District Council's Reconstruction Committee, so Lanner's needs must have been heard in the corridors of power. Winn's Terrace, formerly Pilcher's Row on Carn Marth, was declared unfit for habitation in the late 1950s and condemned by the council. People continued to live there until the early 1960s and were eventually rehoused on newly built council estates circling Camborne and Redruth. Derelict cottages, such as the couple in the terrace opposite the square, and the Miners' Arms and McKenny's below the post office (named after the family which last lived there), were demolished. Newton Trewren built 'Huish' (now the Methodist Manse) on the former site and H. Shipp built 'Timbertops' in 1965 on the latter.

But the first building project of any magnitude which occurred independently of mining operations in Lanner, was that of the council housing estate, built in 1947–48 on mine waste land at Tresavean, and aptly called the Tresavean Estate. Fourteen 'traditional' homes and eight bungalows, all complete with the modern conveniences of indoor bathrooms and running water, were erected by the CRUDC under a scheme prepared and carried out by Major R.C.H. Greet, the Chief Surveyor.[72] Many local families were rehoused there, along with people from neighbouring areas.

Cornwall in the mid-twentieth century was enjoying a rare taste of prosperity. Mining was making a recovery, china clay production was expanding, farming was benefiting from Government subsidies, shipbuilding and repairing were doing well and hard rock engineering was supplying world markets.[73] Jobs were plentiful and the great drive to improve the housing stock continued, to clear slum housing, make good war damage (of which there was not a lot in Cornwall) and to increase family housing due to the post war 'baby boom'. The Government attempted to attract investment in the Cornish economy by encouraging branch factories (such as the Rank factory at Pool), and indirectly through strategies of population-led growth. The philosophy of new jobs to attract workers from outside Cornwall, economists believed, would create a knock-on effect of generating increased demand for goods and services, resulting in a more buoyant Cornish economy. Within a ten mile radius, Lanner people could commute to big firms. In Camborne, Holman Bros. employed up to 3000 workers (mainly men) and the television component factory at Pool, then well over 1000 workers (mainly women). Falmouth shipyards had nearly as many workers as Holmans, again mainly men, and a number of smaller firms offered hundreds more jobs.

By the mid sixties, Cornwall County Council began to promote voluntary settlement into Cornwall, which was marketed as an attractive place in which to set up a business and to settle down. The policy of prior allocation of land for house building which accompanied this strategy was the main reason for the huge building developments in Lanner in the 1960s.

'Foreigners' from 'up the country' were attracted to Cornwall in their thousands and many saw Lanner as an ideal place in which to live. People were buying their own cars, reflected in the number of planning applications for domestic garages, so it was easier for them to commute, to work outside the parish. Some found jobs to come to, some came expecting to find jobs (they were often disappointed), whilst others came here to retire to their 'bungalow in the sun'.

It wasn't by the sea, but property was relatively cheap in Lanner. The price of a new bungalow on the Valley View Estate in the mid 60s was £3750, and two-bedroom bungalows built in Bell Lane were £2900.[74] And it wasn't far to either the north or south coast. Lanner enjoyed a central position in the district and lay on the main bus routes into numerous other local towns and villages. As early as 1894 this fact was pushed to effect house sales in Lanner, which was advertised as being 'situated where omnibuses pass daily'.

People's expectations of their standard of living had improved since the war, and they wanted to live in larger dwellings, and in fewer numbers per dwelling, prompting Harold Macmillan, in an address the nation, to inform the people that they had 'never had it so good'. Plastered and painted bungalows, rather than houses, very different from the old miners' cottages of granite and killas, were fashionable, and not just for older people who could not climb stairs. As a result of these trends, the number of people living on a square foot of land had dropped, so that today, Lanner, which contains twice as many dwellings as it did 50 years ago, has about the same number of inhabitants as it did in the mid nineteenth century.

Population Turnaround

We saw earlier in this chapter that the population of Lanner had been 2710 in 1856, had dropped rapidly thereafter but had almost returned to the levels of the mid nineteenth century by 1977, reaching 2005. The 1960s saw a dramatic reversal in Cornwall's demographic path. After a century of decline or stagnation, the population increased by over 40 per cent in the next three decades. The increase entirely resulted from in-migration for, left to itself, the ageing population would have fallen. Over 70 per cent of the incomers were aged 55 or under.

In the 1960s, there was a significant increase in the number of planning applications for domestic building in the parish. The names of the developers included Messrs Opie and Abrahams, R & T Jacob, Bell and Pascoe, and W. F. Wright. In 1961, Freddie Johns was building four bungalows at Tresavean and during 1962, 1963, and 1964, building at Bell Lane and Pennance continued unabated, whilst the development of Bell Veor continued for several years. Almost all units were bungalows, the term 'chalet' bungalows appearing for the first time at Pennance at this time. In 1964 a spate of planning applications appeared and Lanner followed this trend, with Freddie Johns obtaining permission to build the first half dozen houses and bungalows in the Lanmoor Estate, built on former farm land. This became Lanner's biggest housing development, and the building continued throughout the remainder of the 1960s.

At the same time, the Valley View Estate, also once farming land, was being built by P. Quick, who had his plans to develop this estate into a self-contained area with four lock-up shops quashed by the Council. In 1966 he was granted permission for just one lock-up there. Penmayne Parc, off Pennance Lane, was completed by the late 1960s.[75]

Yet the old terraced miners' cottages did not diminish in popularity, and were being gradually 'done up' during this time. Doors and window frames were being 'modernised', and electric doorbells were replacing knockers. Brightly coloured paintwork was then very *en vogue*, and thus Gray's Terrace was nicknamed 'Rainbow Row'. Floors were lowered to increase the height of rooms and front passages with a stairway to the upper floor, replaced stairs leading up from the back room. The old open fireplace and hearth was filled in and plastered over and replaced by a smaller grate of brick or tiles, and Cornish ranges were ripped out to be replaced by modern and cleaner gas or electric ovens.[76]

With the arrival of a piped water supply and sewerage system, people began to install bathrooms and lavatories.

Kitchenettes were built on and the era of 'do it yourself' was ushered in. The records of the Planning Committee contain numerous references for permission given in 1966 and 1967 for the installation of bathrooms and kitchens in cottages in Hazel Terrace, Brays Terrace, Murtons Terrace, Pentreath Terrace, Pennance Terrace and at Lanner Moor.[77] Once done up, such cottages 'fetched a good price'.

This was the era of mass tourism to Cornwall. The annual total of visitors grew 1 million in the 1950s to nearly 3.5 million by the late 1970s. The CRUDC confidently welcomed motorists with the road-sign 'Welcome to Camborne–Redruth: Centre for Industry and Tourism'. Yet Lanner, with its inland location, situated on the outskirts of the old industrial conurbation of Camborne and Redruth, was perhaps not best placed to cash in on the tourist boom. The holidaymakers who came to Cornwall, the 'bucket and spade brigade' as some called them, were looking for a specific type of holiday – sun, sea and sand, not industrial archaeology. However, Lanner families hoped to attract tourists to generate income to replace the loss of village businesses and other jobs, such as the decline of employment opportunities at Falmouth Docks. Bed and Breakfast signs were appearing in the village throughout the late 60s.[78]

The old residence of 'Lawyer' Bray, Lanner House, became the Lanner House Hotel. This hotel, with its 130 year old rhododendron – the largest in the county, is now known as the Coppice. Outline permission for a residential licensed hotel below the Lanmoor Estate, was granted to Freddie Johns in 1968, but the building did not go ahead as it became obvious that Lanner was not going to attract great numbers of tourists, who preferred to be nearer to the beaches.[79] The Bed and Breakfast signs also disappeared and the new village school was built on the site of Freddie Johns' proposed hotel in 1980.

A Dormitory of Redruth?

After steady demographic growth from the 1960s, Lanner's population stood at 2230 by 1984. On the one hand, this increase of people breathed new life into the community and gave an impetus village organisations, and some new businesses were created, such as the garden centre, opened by the Price Family from the South East of England, and the Lanner Moor Garage, owned by the Stacey Family from Wales. 'Critical mass' had again been reached. This was the beneficial side of the building development. On the other hand, many people in the village were concerned by the issues which accompanied the development.

Under the title 'The Exploding Village', in 1974, the Lanner Village Association voiced its concern in a village newsletter about some of the negative factors seen to be affecting the community. 'What do you do when you see a quiet Cornish village changing before your very eyes? What do you do when you see it erupting almost overnight into a suburb? When the Cornish hedges and greensplatts turn into fences and asphalt plateaus with concrete kerbstones? When the little school, so beloved by previous generations, becomes totally inadequate for the swarms of new life bursting out of the bungalows and cramming into classrooms likely to split at the seams? What do you do when a close rural community, accustomed to mining and farming, gets plastered over with 'foreigners' from faraway places like Folkestone – or Falmouth?'[80]

Furthermore, there was little employment in the village; if anything, the number of shops was decreasing at this time. In 1968 permission was given to Mr and Mrs Dibble to change the use of a shop at 1, Phillips Terrace, to living accommodation and this trend has continued. What future did Lanner have with its businesses closing, its main street a racecourse for an ever increasing volume of traffic and the housing developments creeping up over the valley sides, swallowing up the green fields and crofts?

After a temporary lull in building developments in the 1970s, the development continued. May Gardens was completed in the 1980s, and the Henscol Estate was constructed on the site of the old village school in the late 1980s, on the way up Lanner Hill. The 1990s have witnessed yet more development, with the arrival of the new estate of houses built by a housing association at Strawberry Fields between Penmayne Parc and Valley View, in three stages of development, with phase two completed in 1997, in spite of the objections raised to the District Council about the lack of adequate services and road access. Another huge bungalow estate at South Downs near Sandy Lane, The Paddock, is still being built in 1998, plus several new houses on the junction with Sandy Lane, named Beauchamp's Meadow. Although Lanner is already one of Cornwall's largest villages, several new sites for possible future development are designated on a draft structure plan, which threatens to further undermine the rural character of Lanner.

Although Lanner has witnessed such rapid growth, the decrease in village businesses became more acute in the 1980s and 90s, with the loss of the butcher's shop, once owned by Foster Hooper, and latterly by Ralph Gilbert, and the village hairdressers' shop in the square; the latest casualties are the Lanner Moor Mini Market and the garden centre.

Competition from out of town shopping posed by the new industrial parks such as those at Pool, have really hurt Lanner businesses, which cannot compete with the lower prices of larger stores, and this has been a contributory factor in the diminishing focus of Lanner as a separate village community. Reaching out of town supermarkets is no inconvenience for those with a car, but what about those without a vehicle who have to rely on buses, which are expensive? Many people fear Lanner will go the same way as Illogan Highway, and will become but a dormitory of Redruth.

And the changes continue apace. The square, an open space in the heart of the village, was considered by some residents to be a danger because of haphazard parking and cars driving through it. With Council approval, a new layout with raised pavements of pink paving bricks set in a herringbone pattern, pink-blossomed hawthorns, and new seating, bordering painted and tarmaced parking bays, went ahead. Although people agreed the square posed a danger to motorists and pedestrians, not everyone was in favour of this modification. Some people felt that the unique Cornish village atmosphere generated by the old square was lost with this development, similar to the kind which can be seen anywhere in urban England, leaving the square little more than a car park. Others argued that the atmosphere of the old village square had been lost long before, as vehicles, especially large lorries, regularly used it as a car park. They argue that the square is now much safer. But recently, Probus village residents voted not to make alterations to their square in order to retain Probus' unique Cornish village character.

The Revival of Industry, Sub-urbanisation and the Green Card

Many people have bought property in Lanner because they relish the rural aspect of this one time mining parish, but on the whole, they have no desire to see a return to extractive industries. Such an attitude brought a dilemma common to many parts of Cornwall and rural Britain. Having escaped to a rural environment, many new arrivals in Lanner wished to keep it that way. But local people, used to exploiting their own land to make a living, as miners, clay-workers, farmers and fishers, valued employment higher than environment. 'You can't eat scenery', summed up their position. That the area was once a heavily industrialised one, indeed one of a constellation of villages surrounding the industrial towns of Camborne and Redruth, might be of interest historically to some people, but few nurture any desire to encourage industrial pursuits which would disrupt or shatter their pleasant rural life.

This sentiment was clearly evidenced when local residents discovered that there were plans to purchase and reopen the Pennance Quarry at Carn Marth which had last operated in 1976 (see Chapter 5). Coming at the same time as fears about the insidious onslaught of sub-urbanisation, a remarkable coalition of village residents, and people from the wider neighbourhood, voiced a number of concerns posed by many projects to create or reopen industrial sites in rural Cornwall.

As the campaign to stop the quarry gathered pace, environmentalists expressed concern for the carn's wildlife, arguing that the 'despoliation of a popular and well-used area of natural beauty' would have resulted if the quarry worked again.[81] Many people began to view Carn Marth in a different light. A Carrick and Kerrier Newsletter which contained a 'potted history' of Carn Marth, attempted to justify the anti-industrial position by endowing the place with an aura of timelessness, of ancient peoples and Celtic mystery. It hinted at the remote possibility that the carn might have been the burial place of the Celtic King Mark and was definitely a beacon used for the Celtic Midsummer festival, as well as making numerous references to relics of prehistory; the ancient Figgy Dowdy's Well and the three tumuli which were once located near the summit, thought to have been the burial places of ancient Bronze Age chieftains. Nothing was mentioned about the more visible 'relics' of our modern industrial heritage; Pennance Consols engine house, which is the most visible building on Carn Marth did not feature in the article.[82]

This view of the carn as a wild and rugged outpost steeped in prehistory, coupled with the 'green card' of the environmental lobby, made for an impressive alliance and certainly grabbed people's imagination, as it seemed to epitomise the threat people felt from out-of-control development and the danger posed to the countryside. Carn Marth was thus transformed from a hill covered with the scars of nineteenth century industry, to an area of outstanding natural beauty, further enhanced by the strong links with the culture and heritage of Celtic Cornwall which must be preserved at all costs as 'a lung for Lanner'.

Yet to some people the creation of the Carn Marth Protection Group, which successfully secured several thousands of pounds from councils both locally and further afield to prevent quarrying operations on the Carn 'for ever', was a most worrying precedent. Cornwall County Council's unprecedented grant of £10 000 to the group was considered to be the continuance of a trend which was insidiously 'sanitising' Cornwall of all signs of industry, as industry was at variance with the rural theme park of peace and tranquillity, of ancient stones and mystic places, wild and rugged unspoilt countryside and picturesque villages, which had been vigorously promoted by local and regional councils and the Cornwall Tourist Board since the Second World War. As early as the 1960s, Cornwall County Council were warning off the clay industry from further development because it would jeopardise the tourist trade, now recognised as Cornwall's primary industry.[83]

'Not only does it seem that preservationists these days oppose virtually all development that offers the chance of jobs for the Cornish people outside of a theme park or hotel, but they now demand and get ratepayers' money to help them create their rural paradise of "peace and quiet", read a letter in the *West Briton*, commenting on the Pennance Quarry development, and continued, 'The logical end of this is a gentrified, sanitised museum – devoid of living communities. Is that really the Cornwall we want to see in the future?'[84]

But the fact that quarries are not like factories, capable of being moved to any location, seemed to have been lost in all the hue and cry made by those who did not oppose quarrying as an industry, nor jobs for local people, but simply wanted it to be sited somewhere else, and 'Not In My Back Yard'.

This issue split the community, for although everyone wanted the best for Lanner and its residents, people could not agree on what the best thing was. Nevertheless, quarrying has ceased and the Carn Marth Protection Group now owns much of the area near the summit, and oversees Harvey's and Martin's Quarries and the surrounding areas. Due to the efforts of the Carn Marth Protection Group, Carn Marth is now included in the County Council's draft structure plan as an area of outstanding natural beauty and plans to clean up and restore Figgy Dowdy's Well are currently on the table.

There seems little likelihood of mass building developments or a return to extractive industry on Carn Marth, but just what the future holds for other areas of the parish is uncertain.

REFERENCES

1 *Cornish Post and Mining News*, 19/2/1903.
2 *Cornubian*, 4/2/1915.
3 Private Communication with Mr J.C.C. Probert.
4 Ibid.
5 Private Communication with Mr G. Olds.
6 *Cornubian*, 10/6/1915.
7 Research on the Bray Family, by S.P. Schwartz.
8 *Cornubian*, 11/2/1915.
9 *Cornubian*, 15/4/1915.
10 *Cornubian*, 7/1/1915.
11 *Cornubian*, 4/4/1918.
12 *Cornish Post and Mining News*, 28/2/1920.
13 *Cornubian*, 28/4/1921.
14 *Cornubian*, 3/3/1921.
15 *Cornubian*, 19/5/1921.
16 Ibid.
17 *Cornubian*, 24/2/1921.
18 *Cornubian*, 24/3/1921.
19 *Cornubian*, 10/2/1921; 24/3/1921; 26/5/1921; 30/6/1921.
20 *Cornubian*, 2/6/1921.
21 *Cornubian*, 15/9/1921.
22 *Cornubian*, 16/6/1921.
23 *Cornubian*, 3/12/1921.
24 *Cornubian*, 30/6/1921.
25 *Cornubian*, 3/3/1921; 10/3/1921; 7/4/1921.
26 Private Communication with Mrs Rhona Blatchford, 1998.
27 Information collected at the '100 Years of Lanner Exhibition', May 1994.
28 Private Communication with Mrs Rhona Blatchford and Mr G. Olds, 1998.
29 *West Briton*, 28/7/1938.
30 *West Briton*, 1/2/1996.
31 *Cornubian*, 5/2/1914.
32 Private Communication with Mrs Irene Williams.
33 Courtesy Mr Michael Tangye and Mrs Sylvia Kessell.
34 Private Communication with Mrs Sylvia Kessell.
35 'Lanner School Centenary 1878–1978', used here with kind permission of Mr P.E. Lloyd, Headmaster.
36 Private Communication with Mrs Sheila Mooney, 1998.
37 'Lanner School Centenary 1878–1978', used here with kind permission of Mr P.E. Lloyd, Headmaster.
38 Private Communication with the late Mrs Mary Job, interviewed when 101.
39 Information collected at the '100 Years of Lanner Exhibition', May 1994.
40 D. Carter, V. Acton, *Operation Cornwall*, Landfall Publications, 1994, pp. 145–6.
41 *Cornubian*, 16/2/1894.
42 Courtesy Mr Michael Tangye.
43 *West Briton*, 31/1/1935.
44 Information courtesy of Mr Paul Langford.
45 *Cornish Post and Mining News*, 11/5/1929.
46 Department of Education and Science, Report by HM Inspectors, S908/2209/02, 1986, C.S.L., Redruth.
47 *Cornubian*, 15/7/1887.
48 *Cornubian*, 21/9/1894.
49 *Cornubian*, 27/7/1900.

50 Private Communication with Mr G. Olds.
51 Courtesy RIC Photograph Archive, Truro.
52 Private Communication with Mrs Prudence Danby.
53 *Cornubian*, 10/6/1892.
54 *Cornubian*, 21/7/1921.
55 *Cornubian*, 12/8/1892.
56 Lanner Women's Institute Document, 1965, courtesy of Mrs A.M. Opie.
57 District Council Minutes, C.S.L., Redruth.
58 Courtesy Mrs Sylvia Kessell.
59 Private Communication with Mr G. Olds.
60 Lanner Women's Institute Document, 1965, courtesy of Mrs A.M. Opie.
61 *Cornubian*, 30/5/1912.
62 Information courtesy of Mr Paul Langford.
63 Lanner Women's Institute Document, 1965, courtesy of Mrs A.M. Opie.
64 Information courtesy of Mr Michael Tangye.
65 Courtesy Mrs Rhona Blatchford, daughter of Marion Blight.
66 Private Communication with Mr Lance Bray, 1998.
67 Information courtesy of C. Stephens.
68 Information courtesy of Mrs Sylvia Kessell.
69 *Royal Cornwall Gazette*, 7/1/1915.
70 *Royal Cornwall Gazette*, 4/2/1915.
71 William, M, Housing the Cornish in, *Cornwall Since the War*, Philip Payton (ed), Dyllansow Truran, Redruth, 1993, p.157.
72 *Cornubian*, 29/1/1948.
73 Perry, Ronald, 'Cornwall Circa 1950', in *Cornwall Since the War*, Philip Payton (ed), Dyllansow Truran, Redruth, 1993, chapter 2.
74 Lanner Women's Institute Document, 1965, courtesy of Mrs A.M. Opie.
75 District Council Minutes, C.S.L., Redruth.
76 Lanner Women's Institute Document, 1965, courtesy of Mrs A.M. Opie.
77 District Council Minutes, C.S.L., Redruth.
78 Lanner Women's Institute Document, 1965, courtesy of Mrs A.M. Opie.
79 District Council Minutes, C.S.L., Redruth.
80 Lanner Village Association Newsletter, 1974, C.S.L., Redruth.
81 *West Briton*, 13/5/1986.
82 Carrick and Kerrier Newsletter, No. 3, March 1989.
83 Perry, Ronald, in Garry Tregidga (ed), *The View From Hensbarrow*, to be published.
84 *West Briton*, 5/2/1987.

Chapter 12
Leisure and Entertainment

In recent years much has been written about culture and the construction of place.[1] As Deacon has pointed out, place is a powerful source of identity, giving rise to local, regional and national identities.[2] This chapter will attempt to provide the reader with an insight into the kind of place Lanner has been over the past 150 years by exploring some of its leisure pursuits. We will also explore the cultural effects of the mining collapse and economic stagnation which followed in its wake, and what effect this had on Lanner's village identity.

For our nineteenth century forbears, there was a wide array of leisure activities available. These ranged from the traditional rural pursuits of antiquity, which, during the nineteenth century were challenged by new forms of 'respectable' leisure growing both directly and indirectly out of Methodism, which had a big impact on Lanner. But towards the end of the century, new 'secular' pastimes emerged to challenge both traditional and respectable spare time activities, and which were to become very popular and important leisure pursuits in the twentieth century, many recognisable to the reader of today. These have helped to give Lanner its distinct village identity.

Hunting and 'Tide-times'

Prior to the industrialisation of Gwennap, the area was predominantly rural, as were the pastimes. Hurling with men of the neighbouring parish of Stithians was reputed to have occurred from early times at Trebowland Round, and bell ringing and bowling were also popular. Bell ringing at Gwennap Churchtown, according to William Francis, was the chief amusement of the inebriated, thoughtless and dissipated. William Francis mentions the St Day Fight as being an echo of former times which were far more bloodthirsty and boisterous. The fight was a custom which lasted in the Gwennap area until the late eighteenth century, the antagonists being men of neighbouring parishes such as Redruth, and casualties were not unheard of.[3] It is of interest that the folklore of events such as the inter-village fights persists, and even effects the perception of 'the sort of people' who live in villages like Lanner.

Cruel sports such as cock fighting, badger baiting and dog baiting were dying out in the area during the last century, but the third of these, described as 'a particularly disgusting spectacle,' was witnessed at Redruth Whitsun Fair as late as 1877.[4] Hunting, however, was enjoyed by all classes, from the local squire down to the farm labourer or tinner with his shotgun who indulged in rabbit shooting, and maybe the occasional spot of poaching, which although illicit, was a necessity when there was a surplus of labour and wages were low; shooting or trapping often meant the difference between rabbit pie and no meat at all. Francis, in his 1845 poem, mentions that hunting regularly occurred at Pengreep, home to one of the Williams family:

> *then the whooping of huntsmen in shrill sportive sounds,*
> *The trampling of horses, and baying of hounds,*
> *In the chase full eager were heard in the grounds.*[5]

William Williams of Scorrier House, leader of the Four Burrow Hunt in the late nineteenth century, would not allow any fox seen on Carn Marth to be shot, even if it had attacked and killed poultry. He would in such cases award a sum of money to the smallholders who had suffered any loss, upon seeing the head, wings and legs of a dead fowl.[6] Fox hunting was still a common sight in the village in the mid twentieth century. In 1929, the Four Burrows Hunt met in Lanner Square for the first time in the history of the pack, where a large crowd had gathered to witness the occasion. The Master, Mr G. Percival Williams, led the hunt in a gruelling chase, in which the unfortunate creature was finally bowled over in Lanner, after evading the hounds for two hours

But this ancient rural leisure pursuit did not meet with the approval of everyone. Fox hunting was a sight which was so abhorrent to Lanner's Revd Craven-Sands, that he felt compelled to speak out against its cruelty, alongside that of dog racing, in the 1950s. In Lanner, where hunting was so popular, most cottages contained a gun and accidental shootings were common. In 1862 the death of an 18 year old, James Nicholls, accidentally shot by his best friend upon leaving his house to go out shooting, led to the foreman of the inquest, the village vicar Revd J. Tucker, to comment upon the wisdom of keeping a loaded gun in the house and going about the neighbourhood carrying one.[7]

Other popular activities included rabbit coursing, at which a pack of hounds would chase a rabbit or hare, and bets were usually placed. The Gwennap Rabbit Coursing Society's annual meeting held at Comford was always well followed in the area; an advertisement in the *Royal Cornwall*

Gazette for 1896 noted that entries had to be registered with J. H. Odgers of Rough Street, Lanner, and James Hicks, architect, was noted as the President in 1894. This event probably gave the local pub at Comford its former name of The Hare and Hound.

As a rural or semi-rural dweller, the miner and his family participated in the activities, events and festivities that marked the country year. From some of these, such as the harvest home, they gained important additions to their diet in the form of rabbits, trapped in the small area of crop left standing at the end of the harvest, and by participation in the substantial repast laid on by the farmer's wife. From others, such as market and feast days, they gained the reciprocal benefits of social interaction.[8]

Miners were able to participate quite fully in the rural life of Gwennap, due to the degree of independence they were able to exercise over the regulation of their working time as 'self-employed' tributers in the mines. Local people looked forward to the traditional and highly popular annual Tide-times with great anticipation. Gwennap's feast day was on Whit-Sunday which was later changed to Whit-Monday. At such Tide-times a variety of sports were held, including boxing, Cornish wrestling, cudgel playing, donkey races and pole climbing, usually accompanied by excessive drinking.

The Midsummer celebration, an ancient custom which involved the lighting of a large bonfire, along with furze bushes and numerous tar barrels, became the miners' unofficial holiday and usually took place at Carn Marth. Fireworks and dynamite were let off liberally, and accidents involving the latter were not uncommon. The midsummer bonfire custom was dying out by the mid Victorian period, probably due to the changing nature of employment in the mines, with working time being increasingly regulated by the mine management. But bonfires were still lit to herald important news, such as the occasion of the marriage of His Royal Highness, Albert Edward, Prince of Wales in 1863, and a monster bonfire was also lit to commemorate Queen Victoria's Jubilee in 1887, chiefly through the exertions of Captain John Richards of Trefulla.

But Midsummer was not the only rural event to suffer at the hand of the changing nature of mine working hours. Other casualties were the ancient feasts and fairs at nearby Redruth, patronised by Lanner's working class; the Goose Fair and the Mazzard Fair, which were noted in 1893 as being scantily attended. By 1919 Union officials were endeavouring to make the national holidays of Whitsun and August Bank Holiday days off with pay for the miners, thus undermining and diminishing the opportunities for participation in such traditional, pre-industrial celebrations. However in 1929 the Midsummer bonfire ritual at Carn Marth was revived by the Redruth Old Cornwall Society, on this occasion being lit by Sir Arthur Carkeek at 10.00pm.[9]

This organisation, which grew out of a milieu of Cornish and Pan-Celtic Revivalism, conducted the ancient ceremony in the Cornish language, but surprisingly the venue for future Midsummer events was changed to Carn Brea, even though fires ignited on the summit of Carn Marth can be seen from far greater distances.

'Winks' and the Mock Mayor Ceremony

Rural life traditionally revolved around the village inn and its proprietor. Numerous beer shops, or 'kiddleywinks,' which were important centres for games and sports, were common throughout the mining districts. Tributers often divided the earnings of their 'pare' in local pubs and 'winks' which encouraged heavy drinking, wages being spent on beer and gin. Skittles, dominoes and card games were widely played in the public house by miners in their out of core time, but their wives often sought their company and entertainment there too, a visitor to the Gwennap mining area commenting on the habit in the mid nineteenth century: 'Their wives are dressed out in tawdry silks and flank away in the alehouses, between rows of obedient fiddlers'.[10]

Innkeepers were likely to arrange Cornish wrestling matches, card games and other events, which often involved gambling. The Gwennap Parish Vestry Book of the early 1830s contains numerous entries pertaining to disorderly doings at the winks and pubs of Lanner. 'Joseph Morcom, Constable, is requested to call John Beer, William Bray and William Gray, Beer Sellers, before the Magistrates for disorderly conduct and drawing beer during Divine Service on Sunday 27 August, 1836', reads a typical entry.[11]

Lanner had several public houses in the nineteenth century, among them the Commercial Inn (now the Lanner Inn), and the Miners' Arms, which faced each other across the square (Fig.12.1). The latter, which stood on the site of the present Methodist Manse, had a skittle alley, and the former also had a skittle alley, in a building at the back of the premises (Fig.8.8), together with the first radio in the neighbourhood around which local people gathered in the early decades of the twentieth century to hear the latest news.

At Lanner Moor on the corner of Tresavean Terrace and Tresavean Hill, was a public house named the Prisks' Hotel, later the Rogers' Arms. It was known locally as 'Uncle Joe's,' (after one of the landlords, Joseph Prisk), and because it was

Fig.12.1. *Lanner Wesleyan Methodist Band of Hope. The Miner's Arms public house is the building behind the banner on the left. Early twentieth century.* (© Paul Annear, Probus).

popular as a drinking establishment for Tresavean miners in the last century, their wives and mothers used to gather outside in the courtyard on 'setting day' to take their earnings before they were spent on beer. Today it is a dwelling.

The Hare and Hound, now the Fox and Hounds, at Comford, and the Six Bells Inn at Gwennap Church Town, the latter since closed, were other favourite drinking places nearby. And in addition, there were also numerous 'kiddleywinks' (beer houses) operating out of peoples' homes. Half way up Lanner Hill, on the right, is a building which was once the rowdy 'wink' of William Bray mentioned above, and is now a dwelling named 'Treruffe'. William Winn of Pennance, who ran a kiddleywink in his house, was called before the Magistrate in 1837 'for pulling beer at an inappropriate hour'. The habit of heavy drinking once prevalent in the Lanner area was one which greatly concerned the Methodists, as we shall see below.

A more recent vestige of a former rural custom centred on a village beer house, and an occasion which afforded considerable entertainment, was the 'Mock Mayor Ceremony'. This annual village event took place at the Miners' Arms, and was maintained until the close of the nineteenth century, usually occurring on Boxing Day. The custom was reputed to have been started by one of the Edwards family in the dim mists of time, the mayoral chain of office having been presented to the 'Corporation of Lanner' by him. Every year since then, it was reported that the chain of office had been 'handed down with the greatest regularity'. The Mayor was 'elected' by a crowd of villagers assembled at the pub, who then customarily blackened his face and placed a large white collar and a cow's chain with a tin pendant around his neck. He was then ready to make his 'parade' through the village.

Often such parades were heralded by a man who rang a bell. He led the participants, many dressed as black slaves, who would be called upon to make the proclamation 'in ancient form', of His Worship's style and rights. The mayor was followed by a motley procession of carts and wagons to the tunes from the local fife and drum band, creating much noise and revelry, as he ceremonially performed the customary tour of his 'boundaries'.

The following proceedings were reported in 1888, the start made about eleven o'clock from the Miners' Arms Inn. On this occasion, the Mayor was Mr Richard Lean, whose attire was said to have been magnificent. 'Amongst his decorations were five medals... the "Mayor" occupied an easy chair which was fixed in a vehicle drawn by three horses and a donkey.' The party proceeded to Mr Taylor's Hotel (The Rogers' Arms), stopping for refreshment which was generously provided by the proprietor, after which the procession headed back to the Miners' Arms to partake of a "banquet" for all, given by the Lord Mayor at the expense of the community, for

While he feasted with the great
He ne'er forgot the small.

'After dinner, persons presuming to enter the presence of the Lord Mayor without an invitation, were compelled to provide a gallon of beer each for the benefit of the company, the Lord Mayor and his friends, for the nonce, condescending to drink it, in order to make the punishment of the intruders more severe.'

On occasions, passers by would be arrested and brought before the Mayor's Court, or as it was known, the 'Cuckle's Court,' which passed a sentence. This often resulted in the 'offender' having his face blackened and being locked in the spence (a small cupboard under the stairs)! Strangers had their money confiscated for attempting to pass counterfeit coins, and this went into a kitty to pay for the drink which was to come. All drinks ordered found their way into a huge 'cuckle's cup', made by a local potter, from which all drank after the Mayor had made his speech, usually containing ludicrous suggestions, and toasted the health of those present.

The 1888 report relates that after the banquet was completed, the revellers, most of whom were very drunk, adjourned to a field adjoining the banquet room 'to witness the civic sports for which prizes were awarded. These included pigeon shooting, greasy pole climbing, Cornish wrestling, donkey races etc.'[12] This strange custom, once common throughout many of the towns and villages in the county, but now moribund, probably had its roots in antiquity, its meaning most likely already lost to our Victorian forbears. In Lanner the Mock Mayor Ceremony, centred on the Miners' Arms, only died out with the closure of this drinking establishment in the early twentieth century.

Royal Events and 'Show-time'

The more generalised seasonal activities such as Midsummer, being so rurally based, could not survive the industrial transformation of the mining industry, but the love of festivity and parades was not vanquished, but rather channelled into a type of popular culture which was far less wild than the old rural pursuits. In the late Victorian and Edwardian periods these found expression in elaborate events which were assiduously planned by committees got up months in advance to organise celebrations to commemorate Coronations, Royal Marriages, Jubilees, etc. In August 1902, it was reported that Lanner was once again *en fête*, for the third time since June, for the occasion of the Coronation of Edward VII. The fronts of most of the cottages were decorated and flags were hung in almost every garden. A parade around the village, headed by the Lanner Brass Band, and the Lanner Lodge of Odd Fellows in full regalia, was joined by some 750 children and adults; 483 children received coronation medals. On return to the field from which the start had been made, the children were given a bountiful tea.

The adults' tea, for about 350, followed, held in the open in a field in front of the Wesleyan Chapel, to which all the old people from the village had been invited. The Chairman of the committee, G. S. 'Lawyer' Bray addressed the large gathering and 'God Save the King' was sung. In the evening, the children indulged in games to their hearts' content, and at 9.20pm, a beautiful display of fireworks took place at Comford Burrow. 'For nearly an hour and a half, rocket coloured fire and set pieces illuminated the neighbourhood, and a correspondent says it was one of the best displays seen west of Plymouth' reported the *Cornubian*. From about 10pm until midnight, the majority of villagers illuminated the fronts of their houses, making a beautiful effect.[13] In such reports, one can perceive a sense of civic pride, with Lanner vying to outdo neighbouring villages in terms of excellence.

In 1897 the school was closed for The Queen's Jubilee, and pupils enjoyed a week off for Edward VII's Coronation. The Lanner School Log Book provides further evidence of the popularity of royal events in the life of the village. In July 1903, the visit of the Prince and Princess of Wales to Cornwall produced a day off. In 1911 a week's holiday for the Coronation of George V was granted at the request of the King, and in 1923, Lanner School was closed for the marriage of the Duke of York. The Royal Family continued to provide the excuse for holidays and ceremonies: the wedding of HRH the Duke of Kent (1934), the Jubilee of George V (1935), the wedding of HRH the Duke of Gloucester and Lady Alice Scott (1935), the funeral of King George V (1936), the Coronation of King George VI (1937), the funeral of King George VI (1952), Queen Elizabeth II's Coronation (1953), and a visit of the Queen and Prince Philip to Truro (1956).

Royalty of a different kind made occasional visits to the village. Travelling entertainers often had equipment, which was at the cutting edge of Victorian and Edwardian science and technology, bringing the world of the town into the heart of the countryside. This included steam-driven rides, ornately decorated fairground organs, magnificently illuminated at night, and colourful and exotic side shows. The Whitsun Fair at Redruth was always keenly awaited. Village proceedings were further enlivened by the visits of travelling showmen, the Hancocks, Birchalls and Brewers, who pulled into the square or playing field with their highly popular steam-driven dobbies and beautiful organs. Sometimes they were invited to 'open' village tea treats (Fig. 12.2).

Fig.12.2. *Steam driven roundabout, complete with gondolas, in Lanner Square, c.1905.* (© The Paddy Bradley Collection)

Fig.12.3. *Lanner Carnival Queen float, post-Second World War. Violet Bray on far right.* (© Royal Institution of Cornwall)

On one occasion, Joseph Brewer, on his way to Falmouth, spied Birchall in Lanner Square doing brisk business with his ride. Worried that he might miss the opportunity of making money, he pulled into the present day playing field at Lanner Moor, and opened his roundabout in direct opposition! His remarkable 'three abreast' had a number of centaurs fixed to the outside row after the Boer War, sporting the heads of generals in a patriotic flavour.[14]

The Lanner Carnival, organised by Lanner and District Silver Band, is a similar modern popular village entertainment, in which most organisations, including the Chapel and school, participate (Fig.12.3).

Respectable Leisure – 'Self-improvement' for a Penny

By the 1830s a new leisure culture was emerging, centred on the Methodist Chapels, the Church of England and various philanthropic societies, and was organised by people from the emerging middle class who adhered to a philosophy of 'self-help and improvement', not just for themselves, but for the working man too. 'Rational Recreation' became their favourite phrase for spending 'out of core time', time which could be profitably spent in catching up on lost schooling, technical improvement and self-improvement in secular as well as religious respects. Many of the traditional forms of leisure were abhorrent to such people, who disliked their boisterous and violent nature, particularly those involving heavy drinking. Methodism in particular made an important impact in the Gwennap area, and a variety of societies and events were organised with self-improvement and social philanthropy in mind. These set out to challenge the older forms of leisure, and to provide new and challenging spare time activities. For much of the nineteenth century these two spheres of leisure were forced into an uneasy coexistence.

In 1839, a Miners' and Mechanics' Society was set up at Carharrack, the first of its kind in the Gwennap area. This was probably inspired by the success of similar societies that were spreading through the industrial towns of the North of England, aimed at attracting the artisan sector of the working class and self-employed tradesmen. Mining in particular was becoming increasingly sophisticated, and it was felt that an organisation devoted to a greater understanding of mining technology would be of benefit to miners who wished to rise through the ranks from tributer to captain. For subscribers to the society, a wide range of books were available, including works on the arts and sciences, natural and experimental philosophy, metallurgy, astronomy, geography and architecture.[15]

Penny readings were given in the schoolroom at Rough Street (now the Church of England Parish Hall), *Doidge's Directory* of 1866 noting that they took place on alternate Tuesdays. However, a visitor to one such reading was shocked by the behaviour of many people at a talk given by James Johns of Redruth, which prompted a letter to the *Cornubian*. 'We thought we had found our way into a room frequented by a lot of roughs for betting purposes and gambling', commented the visitor, who described the antics of an audience of singing, dancing, whistling and hooting young men as disgraceful, whilst the activity of one, who was beating a nearby desk with a piece of evergreen, resulted in the speaker having to stop several times to regain order![16]

Perhaps this provides evidence of Lanner's rough working class character. Yet the *Cornubian* of 19 December 1875, contained a retort to an earlier letter accusing the youth of Lanner as being content to 'lounge about the highways'. 'Where can we go to spend an hour with our associates but to the pubic house?' asked the writer of the letter, entitled 'Lanner Loungers', going on to say:

> *There is no Institution in the neighbourhood of Lanner with a population of more than two thousand people, nor even a circulating library, although there was one some years since which was soon stopped, its only support being a contribution of I think, two pence per month, by from twelve to fifteen members. About five years since there was a step made towards establishing an Institution by holding special services, &c., the proceeds of which was something better than £20; but because a few narrow-minded men could not get it conducted under the chapel trust, the scheme was abandoned, and a portion of the proceeds applied to the use of the Wesleyan Chapel.*

The writer of the letter concluded with the comment 'How many labouring men are there in Lanner who have the means of purchasing books to study without depriving themselves or their families of many real necessaries of life?' So in response to this sentiment, in 1883, Lanner parishioners voted unanimously to set up a public reading room for the use of the inhabitants, and it was decided to open the schoolroom at Rough Street for the purpose.[17]

Libraries were becoming more common throughout the nineteenth century, and were used by increasing numbers of people as standards of literacy improved. In addition to books, such reading rooms also held pamphlets and newspapers. One copy of a newspaper might have been read by numerous people, for in the mid nineteenth century they were subject to tax, and therefore expensive. In 1838 a Redruth newspaper, the *Cornubian*, cost 4½ pence, a price well beyond the means of most of the literate working class. It was only after 1855 that the newspaper tax was abolished and newspapers such as the *Cornubian*, more affordable at its new price of 1d, saw an increase in readership, in 1870 enjoying a weekly circulation of about 12 000 copies.

Many of the Methodist Chapels had comprehensive libraries; that of the United Methodist Free Church at Redruth had seven shelves of books, with over 450 volumes on a variety of subjects for those who subscribed as members. As well as the obvious works aimed at respectability – titles such as *Self Improvement* and *Lectures on Intemperance and Teetotalism*, there were a wide variety of religious works, commenting on the Christian, Judaic and Islamic worlds, numerous Biblical commentaries, as well as a wide range of non religious books. We can speculate that the reading room at Lanner would have held a library of similar content, opening, to those who could read, a rich world of learning.[18]

Methodism, Mutual Improvement and Teetotalism

There had been few leisure activities arranged by the Methodist Churches in the first 100 years, but all that changed as Methodism acquired a 'social' element, chiefly through its exertions to raise money. Prayer meetings and Love Feasts gave way to tea treats, anniversaries, Band of Hope parades, and concerts. Later came bazaars and garden fetes, which as well as being increasingly important and lucrative social events, still retained a religious element. Prayers were often said, for example, at the opening and closing of bazaars and fetes. Many of these events, the Wesleyan Sunday School Anniversary in May for example, became almost legendary in the district and helped to create Lanner's unique village identity.

In 1886, a Mutual Improvement Class under the auspices of the Wesleyan Chapel was inaugurated, with its President the Reverend T. Clarke, Vice-President, Captain W. Edwards, Treasurer W. Vivian and Secretary J.H. Tregonning. The founder members were mainly drawn from the literate middle class, and indeed, the society was intended to attract those who were concerned with upward social mobility.

The idea to inaugurate such a society at Lanner was probably inspired by the success of similar societies in nearby towns such as Redruth. Lectures were given on a variety of topics including decorum, the importance of education, social advancement and respectability, as well as a broad ranging itinerary intended to increase members' knowledge in diverse subjects. One such lecture was entitled, 'Mental and Moral Culture', and another, given by C.C. James of Comford in 1890, was entitled 'Cornish Legends, Charms and Superstitions'.[19]

For many Methodists, the biggest bar to self-improvement was alcohol abuse, and concern over the evils of drink was of paramount importance. William Francis in his poem of 1845 is strongly critical on the subject of alcohol, articulating the feelings of many of his concerned contemporaries:

Oh, ye! who support a system so fraught
With woes and with crime, I entreat your calm thought:
Is it not wiser to remove the chief cause
Of crimes, than to punish transgressors of laws
Excited by drinking, and drunkards' applause?...
...These liquors are hurtful, not useful for food;
Without them do millions health's vigour enjoy,
And with them do myriad's health's vigour destroy: [20]

As early as 1839, the Gwennap and Redruth Teetotal Society met at Carharrack Chapel yard and formed a procession to Gwennap Pit, where a public meeting was held and the company addressed in furtherance of the principles of total abstinence from intoxicating liquors.[21] Such support for temperance continued throughout the nineteenth century. The British Women's Temperance Association made a visit to Lanner in 1888, and in front of a packed meeting 13 signatures to the pledge were taken.[22] References to Temperance Sunday were still common in the minutes and newspaper reports of the Lanner Chapels in the early twentieth century. The Mock Mayor Ceremony was looked upon with total disdain by teetotal villagers, and in 1888 female relatives of the man who was chosen to have the 'gown and chain', B. Bird, prevented him from making a fool of himself by locking up his clothes![23]

It appears that Lanner Wesley had a Band of Hope in 1868, when they held a meeting in Frogpool Chapel and in 1869, membership stood at 60. But this organisation seems to have petered out, because in 1893 there was a discussion in the village concerning the setting up a Wesleyan Band of Hope, which was formed in March of that year. (The Lanner Bryanites and the South Downs Wesleyans already had such an organisation.). The President was Captain Edwards, Vice President, C. Dunstan, Treasurer, W.D. Holman (the Board School Attendance Officer) and the Secretaries, W. Puckey and S. Opie. By June, the society had over 70 members, and the following month it was reported that membership numbered 120.[24] (Fig.12.4).

Through membership of this society, it was hoped to save young people from sinking into the puerile pastimes of the local beer-shop or alehouse: 'improvident habits thus easily gain, a sway o'er the mind, which long they retain.'[25] Members took a pledge never to partake of alcohol, and it was customary to sing hymns from Temperance hymn books; in 1894 for example, a recitation was given by two little girls entitled 'No More Wine'. The concerts given by the Wesleyan Band of Hope held at Lanner School were always well attended in the village, being great musical occasions. The late Tommy Martin, who took part in the concerts in the 1920s, admitted in 1995 that he greatly enjoyed himself there. Joan Martin remembers that the highlight of the calendar were the Good Friday concerts, one in the afternoon for the youth and one in the evening for the adults. A faith tea always followed.

The YMCA and Village Philanthropic Societies

The growth of Lanner from a rural backwater to a village of considerable importance, which could boast of a community brimming with talented, able and tireless workers from many societies was evident by 1892. The YMCA had decided to set up two experimental village branches, one in Devon and one in Cornwall. Underhays near Totnes was chosen for the Devon branch, and Lanner was picked to be the Cornish location. For as a place, Lanner was marked for its strong migratory tendencies. 'The advantages open to members who leave their homes and go away ought alone, in a village like Lanner where so many young men leave their homes, to be a sufficient inducement to join.'[26]

A public meeting was held at Lanner Wesley Chapel for the purpose of inaugurating the Lanner association. The Chairman was John Williams and the Secretary, W. H. Roberts. The Temperance Committee generously proffered the use of their room, situated in the heart of the village, to the YMCA as a reading room and classroom, if they agreed to share the rent. It is likely that this reading room was connected to either the Bryanite or Wesleyan Chapels. Conversational Bible Classes were held every Tuesday. It is not known how long the YMCA continued at Lanner, no further mention being made to it in the press.

Societies aimed at social philanthropy were once quite common in the area, and were formed as a result of the poverty once so prevalent in the mining districts, to help to ease pressure on families and individuals who feared admission to the Union House, or loathed the sour

Fig.12.4. *Lanner Wesley Band of Hope, before 1907.* (© Royal Institution of Cornwall).

bread of charity. They were mainly middle class led and played an important part in the focus of Lanner as a self-supporting mining village. In 1885, it was reported that the Wesleyan Dorcas Society (which made and distributed clothing, linen etc., to poor and needy families) had distributed upwards of 130 garments among the poor of the district.[27] The Lanner Odd Fellows, Lodge number 5295, Truro District, was formed mainly by mine agents, shopkeepers, businessmen, and self-employed tradesmen who had made their money through the local mining industry and were desirous of channelling their new found confidence towards helping the working man and his family.

Described as a lodge in a very prosperous state in 1889, the organisation was 'open to elect miners as well as tradesman as members, if approved of'.[28] Lodge members were nominated to serve as sick officers to aid those members and their families who were in some way incapacitated. In 1897 membership numbered 150 and there was £1200 in the Sick and Funeral Fund. The *Cornubian* of 19 February 1903 reporting on the statement of the Loyal Lannarth Lodge of Odd Fellows for 1902, mentioned that the sick pay to the members had been extraordinarily heavy, with £153.5s. being paid in sickness benefits. There had been six deaths – five men and one woman. Total membership was 195. Money was paid to the widows of members who had died.

It was customary for members of the Loyal Lannarth Lodge of Odd Fellows to make an annual parade headed by a local brass band. A collection was always made en route by the ladies of the community on behalf of the Miner's Hospital at Redruth. However in 1950, the decision was taken to amalgamate with the larger Cornubian Lodge at Redruth, due to the paucity of members. Although possessing a small membership, Lannarth Lodge of Odd Fellows was reported to have had substantial financial resources. The society had played an important role in village affairs for over 70 years; Fred Pryor who had been a member since 1905, had served as sick officer for 38 years. Doubtless the unstoppable process of de-industrialisation and subsequent emigration had been the main contributory factor in declining membership.

Lanner Philanthropic Society's 'Valley of Hope Lodge, number 34' was noted as having a membership of 67 in 1876 not long after their formation, following the collapse of the copper mines in the 1860s and the decline of the remaining tin mining industry from the mid 1870s. Formed mainly by miners, the express aim of the society in 'assisting each other in sickness and distress, and thus obviate the need of seeking parochial relief,' led the members to feel that their society should be patronised by the well-to-do, by paying into the funds of the society as honorary members.[29] The society had disappeared by the early twentieth century.

In July 1924, the Royal Antediluvian Order of Buffaloes (RAOB) Bell Lodge 5278, was begun at Lanner Inn by 12 miners from Tresavean Mine, probably in response to the dire economic situation which had prevailed throughout the Mining Division in the early 1920s. They took their name 'Bell' from the name of the lane in the village, and have continued to meet in the same room over the pub ever since. Many local charities have benefited from their successful fund raising activities. It is the only philanthropic society to survive in the village.

Horticultural Societies

Gwennap, as a rural industrial area, had several garden and horticultural societies, started in the mid Victorian period by self-improving cottagers and smallholders. These were encouraged by landlords who benfited from the increase in well cultivated land. Prizes were usually awarded to men who had brought large areas of poor or fallow ground into a state of fertility. Gwennap had a Cottage Garden, Horticultural and Poultry Society which ran an annual competition, at which entries for vegetables, flowers, fruit, poultry, and the best kept garden and allotment, were awarded and the organisation continued to remain popular well into the twentieth century. In 1917, The Gwennap Flower, Vegetable and Fruit Show was inaugurated, with two classes – one for 'cottagers', the entries of none other than working men, and the second, open to all comers. The 1921 event was opened by Major J.A. Ford, and was followed by a tea and sports. The participants were treated to music by the Illogan Military Band.[30] Lanner had a Gardeners' and Allotment Holders' Association in the early twentieth century, which in 1921 enjoyed a membership of 30. The President was George 'Lawyer' Bray, and the Chairman, A. Hooper.[31] In 1958, the Lanner Horticultural Show was established as a annual event, taking place at the Village Hall, and continuing to be held each year until 1980.

The Primrose League

The year 1887 saw the inauguration of the Carn Marth Habitation of the Primrose League (a Conservative political organisation) for the Redruth District, under the auspices of Lady Beauchamp.[32] This organisation never established itself strongly in the area and did not really have a strength in Cornwall beyond Bodmin, Truro and Penryn. The rise of the Primrose Leagues coincided with the onset of the Catholic Revival in the Anglican Church, which harked back to the glory of Cornwall's Catholic or 'Celtic' past, and was mainly patronised by the landed classes (of which there were comparatively few in our area). The Primrose League could never have hoped to gain a popularity in an area so staunchly Methodist and overwhelmingly Liberal in its politics. In 1914, Lanner was reported to have been one of the brightest spots of Liberalism in the division.

Primrose League Meetings often took place in the grounds of Trevince House, home of the Beauchamp Family, and were grand occasions attended by the cream of local society. The 1890 meeting was attended by Mrs Basset of Tehidy, accompanied by Miss Somerset, the Revd Canon Rogers and Mrs Rogers of Gwennap, and the Revd and Mrs Shaw of Lannarth, local clergy, and Mr and Mrs Ford of Pengreep. A very plentiful and substantial repast was provided in the dining room and adjoining apartments, and afterwards games and amusements were arranged, with dancing on the tennis courts. The Ponsanooth Brass Band attended the occasion, ending a most pleasant evening by playing the National Anthem as twilight fell.[33]

The Challenge of Mere Entertainment

The setting up of reading-rooms, Mechanics' Institutes, gardeners' and allotment societies, Bands of Hope, and the giving of public lectures at Mutual Improvement classes testified to the strength of the idea that leisure should be devoted to self-improvement, not self-indulgence. However, by the latter decades of the nineteenth century in Lanner, this form of leisure was losing out to mere entertainment as it had done in the big towns and cities across Britain from the mid century. For example, by the twentieth century the tee-total element of the Lanner Wesley Band of Hope had diminished somewhat. Joan Martin of Bell Veor, a member of the organisation in the early decades of the twentieth century, did not remember such an emphasis on teetotalism. She recollects the annual parade in which the children marched around the village to the music provided by a brass band. At the end of the parade, a tea would be laid on and games organised for the children, which Joan remembers as being virtually identical to those of the annual Chapel tea treat.

After a hard day at the mine, people did not relish the idea of quitting their fireplace for a lecture, or to frequent the reading room to tax their weary minds further. What they wanted from their leisure time was entertainment, enabling them to relax and enjoy themselves. The Church and the Chapels in particular, had to move with the times, and, as a result, from the late nineteenth century, we see music, dance, plays, fetes, and trips away from the village, beginning to achieve a more prominent role. Lanner School Teacher's Log Book noted that the various tea treats and other church events occasioned scant attendance at the school if a day off was not given (Fig. 12.5).

Fig.12.5. *Lanner Carnival group outside the Commercial Arms, Lanner Square, 1930. 'Lanner Boys' Army', with wooden guns made by Mr Reg Minson: Back row, on right, Mr Levy. Middle row l-r: Ken Minson, Jack Menadue, Michael Job, Ronnie Goodland, Bertie Bowles. Front row l-r: Don Bear, Stanley Bear, Joe Eastman, Eddie Williams, 'Jock' McKenny , unknown, and ? Bray.* (© Mr J.J.D.Eastman, Redruth)

We have already noted the success and appeal of the yearly Church and Chapel tea treats, as well as the Sunday School anniversaries, all great events in the annual calendar which were highly popular forms of entertainment. By the twentieth century, tea treats had developed into a whole-day event, and with the creation of better roads and the advent of the motor vehicle, Chapel and Church members were able to travel considerable distances. The seaside proved to be a popular destination, but the community atmosphere and cultural reciprocity had been eroded by taking the venue out of the village (see Chapter 9). Annual trips for chapel choirs were similar. The choir and friends of Lanner Bible Christian Chapel, numbering about 30, were reported to have left Lanner Square at 6.30am for a day out at Porthscatho in 1901. Mr Hugo, the proprietor of Tabb's Hotel, Redruth supplied the Jersey car. Lunch was taken at Kea, and a day on the beach was followed by dinner at the Peter's Hotel.[34]

By the early twentieth century the Wesleyan Guilds for adults and youth were highly popular in the village and had developed out of the Mutual Improvement classes of the nineteenth century, providing lectures and 'socials' much looked forward to (Fig. 12.6). The organisation still retained an educational element, as can be seen from typical lectures of the 1920s, which included 'The New Testament Apocrypha' by C.J. Davey, 'Gray's Works', a paper by J.F. Richards, headmaster of Lanner School, Shakespeare's *The Tempest* by H.H. Chappel; Miss K. Wickett presented a paper on *Paradise Lost*, and J.C. Phillips talked about Thomas Hardy. 'The League of Nations' formed the subject matter of another lecture, and Mr Williams talked about 'Some Naval Occasions'. Yet new and exciting forms of entertainment in the form of magic lantern shows, gramophones and films were also enjoyed by guild members, and the organisation prided itself on being very avant-garde in bringing to the village the newest inventions in the world of entertainment. The Wesleyan Guild disbanded during the Second World War, but re-formed again shortly afterwards.

Annual concerts and plays were great crowd pullers, and afforded considerable excitement in the village, as did the annual 'Pageant', an event which is still popular in the village today. These long plays were almost a return to the old Cornish miracle plays and were often held over two or three days. In 1908, the subject was the Life of King Constantine, performed in the grounds of Melrose House. (Fig. 12.7) The tradition is continued to the present day with that of 1997 entitled 'David and His Greater Son', held over two evenings. Concerts in which the Guild members dressed up in costume were highly popular events which drew large crowds who loved to peep at the elaborate clothes donned by the chapel actors. In 1928 'The Lord Mayor's Banquet' was performed to a packed audience, and the Guild also entertained the community with the film 'The Guv'nor', staring George Arliss. The late Ewart Opie will long be remembered for his part in making the Guild one of the village's most successful social organisations in the early twentieth century. The Primitive Chapel at Lanner Moor had a

Fig.12.6. *Lanner Wesley Guild 1925–26.* Back row l-r: *Edmund J. Harvey, Lilian Curnow, Enid Knuckey, Ena Curnow, Cyril Davey, Enid Spargo, Percy Rogers, Hazel Curnow, Dorothy Angove, Willie Knuckey, Joan Tiddy, Janey Manhire, Willie Angove, Lily Jenkin, unknown.* Row 2. *John Vivian, Edna Andrew, Audrey Lawn, Willie Whitford, Flo Rogers, Stanley Whitford, Lily Chapple, Hubert Chapple, Alice Tamblyn (Tredeague), Wm. John Chapple, Wm. John Andrew, Mossy Tiddy, Bob Tresidder.* Row 3. *Mr Eastman, unknown, Sylvia Penrose, Doris Trethowan, Sylvester Martin, Ruth Langford, May Willoughby, Ewart Opie, Annie Dower, Julia Lawn, unknown, Gwen Webster, T.C.Knuckey, Olga Curnow, unknown, William Ripper, Mrs Tiddy.* Row 4: *Mary Andrew, Beatrice Opie, Joan Langford, Hannah Peters, Bessie Collins, Helen Buzza, Nicholas Buzza, Josiah Bawden, Susan Jane Dunstan, Bessie Clark, Minnie Edwards, Margaret Annie Vivian, Annie Towan Chapple, Nellie Gribble, Katie Trewren, ? Harvey, Willie Gay.* Row 5: *Amelia Kelly, Jane Curnow, Morcom Richards, Amelia Andrew, Miss Axford, Miss Muggeridge, Ernest Williams, Lily Jane Collins, Edward Charles Williams, Wm. Harold Curnow, Wm. Harold Andrew, James Gribble, Miss Pryor, Rufina Martin, Emma Jane Andrew, Mrs Angove, ? Harvey.* Row 6: *Miss Hitchens, Jane Collins, Joe Dunstan, Millie Bear, Mr Dunstan, Miss Halse (or Halls), Winnie Gribble, Percy Collins, Rev. J. Coombes, Mrs J. Coombes, Sarah Ann James, Catherine Barrett, Mary Ann Dower, Bessie Philips, Mrs Andrew, Johnny Andrew.* Front row: *Emily Jane Martin, Kitty Tiddy, Teddy Blenes, Tommy Martin, Evelyn Lawn, Bob Blight, Jimmy Philips.* (© Mr and Mrs Michael Veall, Gwennap).

Fig.12.7. *'The Conversion of King Constantine', the Pageant of 1908, at Melrose House.* (© Lanner Historical Society)

Fig.12.8. *Lanner pageant in the grounds of Melrose House, early 20th century.* (© The Paddy Bradley Collection).

Fig.12.9. *Miss Rigby's Music Class. Miss Rigby is on the far right, c.1935.* (© The Paddy Bradley Collection)

Christian Endeavour Society, and the United Methodists had their Young People's League, which presented an itinerary of events similar in content to that of the Wesleyan Guild.

In the 1930s Miss Amy Ribgy arranged shows for charity at the Wesleyan Schoolroom and the Bryanite Chapel (Fig. 12.9). Older villagers remember attending her plays and concerts which included 'Jack and the Beanstalk', 'Aladdin', 'Princess Ju Ju' and a 'Black and White Minstrel' show. Baby shows helped to raise money for the churches, such as one held in 1916, resulting in a half-day holiday for the pupils of Lanner School, and a garden fete held at the Vicarage in 1950 raised £50 for Church funds. The Church also arranged whist drives to raise money in the 1950s, possibly not viewed favourably by some of the more austere chapel-goers, who might have perceived a degree of decadence in the playing of cards, even if for a good cause.

Music for the Masses

Evenings of song and music in which a programme of various items were performed by choirs, or villagers playing cornets, pianoforte and violins, and singing solos and duets, formed the regular entertainment slot in the days before television or radio, and introduced classical music to a broad cross section of the parish for the first time.

The annual meeting of Lanner Auxiliary of the British and Foreign Bible Society saw the presence of the combined

Fig.12.10. *Lannarth Male Quartette, c.1950. Left to right: A. Bray, A.Knuckey, D.Martin, T. Grigg. Winners, Cornwall County Championship, 1950; Camborne Wesley Eisteddfod, 1949.* (© Lance Bray, Lanner)

Anglican, Primitive, United Methodist and Wesleyan Choirs in 1928, described as a stunning spectacle, under the conductorship of J. Ivan Gill, the Organist of Lanner Wesley.[35]

Several glee groups and quartets, choirs and a crop of outstanding musicians have grown out of such a milieu of Church and Chapel music. The Lannarth Quartet of Alf Bray, A. Knuckey, D. Martin and T. Grigg, won the Camborne Wesley Eisteddfod in 1949, and the Cornwall County Championships in 1950 and were the only local quartet ever with a score of 88. They regularly provided evenings of entertainment on behalf of funds for Lanner Church (Fig. 12.10).

In the mid 1950's, skiffle groups were all the rage, and Lanner's first was formed in 1956. Known as 'The Vikings', featuring Reggie Barrett as lead vocal, John Beckingsale, guitar/vocal, Peter Benbow, guitar, Norman Graham, washboard and Vic Graham on the tea chest bass, their first concert in the Village Hall was a huge success. Encore after encore was requested for yet another chance to hear Reggie singing 'Butter Fingers' (Fig. 12.11).

Fig.12.11. *'The Vikings' skiffle group concert at the Village Hall. Left to right: Peter Benbow, Vic Graham, Reggie Barrett, Norman Graham and John Beckingsale, c.1956.* (© Peter Benbow)

About 1958 Peter Benbow started another skiffle group with colleagues Peter Grenfill on bass, Tony Grenfill on drums, Brenda Polkinghorn, guitar/vocals, Bunny Thomas, vocals, and Tinky Thomas on guitar. This band was known as 'The Live Jives'. More recently, the New Life Group of young musicians who had been converted in 1986 at a 'Saltmine' concert at Redruth Cinema, continue a great musical tradition in the village. This successful youth group which was connected with Lanner Methodist Chapel, released a cassette of contemporary Christian Songs in 1988, entitled 'More Love. More Power', songs from which were regularly aired on Radio Cornwall.

Music has always been a most important part of the life of Lanner people, and many very talented musicians who began their musical lives entertaining the village residents at traditional 'socials' have distinguished themselves both within Cornwall and beyond. Lanner could also count itself thankful for the talented teachers of music who have helped to develop the skills of many young villagers. Miss Amy Rigby taught piano, banjo or violin to her pupils, and Miss Alice Ripper, later Pappin, was a piano teacher. E.J. Williams formed and conducted the Lanner Home Guard Choir which performed in the area during the Second World War, and also composed their signature hymn tune 'Lanner'. He taught pianoforte and brass instruments, and tutored his son Eddie to such a high degree that he eventually went on to play with the famous Black Dyke Mills Band, the Fairey Works Band, and the All Star Brass Band under the baton of Harry Mortimer. Eddie's mother, Martha May Williams, was also an accomplished musician, having been a member of the Bible Christian Chapel Choir, her beautiful contralto voice winning her many trophies. Eddie regularly played 'The Spinning Wheel', a solo for tenor horn composed by his father, and eventually became the Musical Director of a successful Cornish Brass Band, St Dennis.

Alan Opie began his career in music as a young boy in the South Downs Wesleyan Choir. By the age of 16, he had won his first major festival for singing at Cornwall Music Festival at Penzance in 1961. He gained a scholarship at Cambridge, and then at the Guildhall School of Music, London, where he trained for three years. In 1969, his fine baritone voice won him the Cinzano Scholarship to the London Opera Centre. He appears regularly with the English National Opera, after making his professional debut as Papageno in 'The Magic Flute' with the Saddler's Wells Opera.

Donald Bennetts, organist and choirmaster at Lanner Methodist Chapel, has been there in this capacity since 1947. As well as being a talented organist, he has also composed several hymn tunes, among them, 'Cynthia', a tribute to Cynthia Maddern, born in the village in 1952, who attended the Royal College of Music, London. He has enjoyed his time with the Methodist Chapel, and the people with whom he has worked over the years. 'What wonderful people from whose presence I did not wish to be parted,' he wrote in 1995, reminiscing over his career. 'A large and efficient Cornish Choir who tackled, with honours, all I asked of them. It is not possible to forget such a disciplined and devoted group of first class singers – good comrades. We presented numerous sacred concerts and cantatas at Lanner and at other places. Practising for perfection was indeed hard work – but it was always executed gracefully and dutifully. The writer was never let down.'[36] A fitting tribute to Lanner's musical residents.

In the days before Government and Council grants, the task of raising money for necessary local projects fell to the community, and concerts were seen as a useful way to raise money not just for Church and Chapel concerns, but for much needed local schemes, such as those performed on behalf of the Lanner Lamp Committee. Joan Martin, of Bell, can remember such evenings of entertainment in Lanner School earlier this century, held to raise money for the oil to light the street lamps in the era before electricity. And it was customary for this organisation to hold an annual dinner, which by all accounts was a grand occasion, as the following sardonic report suggests: 'It is whispered that our "Let there be (lamp) light" people will hold their annual feast on the first Saturday in the New Year, and that after that date, they will not fear starvation for another 12 months'.[37] In 1928 a minstrel troupe from Falmouth, numbering about 30, gave a concert at the Lanner Boys School to raise money for the provision of a new playing field at Lanner Moor.[38]

Lanner Village Hall, a Venue for 'One and All'

One of the most positive moves to provide a centre for a varied range of leisure pursuits within the village was the acquisition of the old Bryanite Chapel in 1945 by a group of villagers, headed by T.C. Knuckey and Frank Trethowan. These gentlemen could see the potential of this building as a multi-purpose village hall. Thirty residents agreed to share payment of the £300 asked by the vendors, the Redruth Methodist Connexion, by giving £10 each as a tax free loan, and work began straight away to create the new hall.

An inaugural dance and social evening took place after the alterations were completed, launching the new village leisure facility, which has remained a popular venue. One of the first groups to use the hall was the newly formed Lanner Amateur Dramatic Society. Various villagers worked very hard to maintain the success of the hall, including T.C. Knuckey, the first Chairman of the Trustees, Messrs F.C. Parr and F.L. Smitheram, and Mrs A.G. Bear, office holders. From 1964 Alice M. Opie has acted as general secretary, and holds the record as the longest serving member of the Trustees and the Management Committee, and secretary of both.

Lanner Church held dances in the Village Hall in the early 1950s, at which J. Treloar's Band from South Downs was regularly invited to perform old time and modern dance music. The cost of admission was in the region of 2 shillings, not including refreshments, and usually lasted from 7.30pm to midnight. People would come from far and wide, and they were ideal occasions at which to meet a prospective partner. The Lanner Men's and Women's British Legion also used the Village Hall to hold dances and socials after the Second World War, and one such social held there, in April 1950, raised £12.4s.2d, much fun being afforded by the judging by F.C. Parr and Mrs Dore of an 'ankle competition'.

The Village Hall was the setting for a social and dance set up by Mrs W. J. Thomas in 1950 to raise money for the Cornwall Cripples' Fund and the British Sailors' Society. Stalls. Humorous songs and sketches saw the largest amount ever raised in the Village Hall to that date, the sum of £62, which was split evenly between the two organisations.

The rise of 'secular' leisure

As we have seen, since the 1870s the almost austere, or 'improving leisure', of the mid Victorians, and the disapproval of the gambling and drinking culture of the village pub, was challenged by a population who wanted, in the main, light entertainment, enabling them to unwind and relax. By the close of the nineteenth century, people were able to chose, not just between entertainment provided by the chapel and lecture room, or the older and less respectable public house and fair, but were able to consider new options. Some of these blended 'respectable' and new secular forms of leisure pursuits, finding expression through organisations such as the Men's and Women's Institutes and the Scouting Movement. Many however, had crossed the Tamar from the industrial North of England and Wales, and found a ready home in the mining centres of Cornwall. Brass bands, male voice choirs, and spectator sports such as football and rugby merged with the older Methodist-mining culture to produce some of the leisure activities with which we are familiar today, and which have played a very important part in Lanner's village identity. The rise and popularity of such activities are also indicative of the fact that there was more money around in late nineteenth century Lanner, much of it remitted from South Africa, and it is no surprise that their decline, in the first quarter of the twentieth century, coincided with de-industrialisation, migration and poverty, resulting from the demise of the local mining industry.

The Village Brass Band

Brass Bands were great institutions in industrialised working class areas, particularly in the colliery towns and villages 'up country'. Brass Bands brought classical music to the working masses, and proved to be a similar attraction in the mining areas of the music-loving Cornish. Lanner had both a brass band and a fife and drum band in the nineteenth century. In 1965, two former members who had played cornets in the latter were still alive; Thomas Knuckey of Melrose, and his brother who had emigrated to Australia.

The first Lanner Brass Band had been set up in the mid 1890s by William Barnett, his father and brother Anthony (who left the band in 1898 to travel to South Africa), with much encouragement from the Reverend Francis Thomas of Lanner Christ Church. From his youth, William, who became a miner at the Basset Mines, maintained an interest in the band, becoming its bandmaster. The band performed at Band of Hope parades, Lanner Church events, Sunday School anniversaries and village tea treats, such as that of Lanner Wesley in 1901. They also paraded the streets of the village in 1901, playing the Dead March in 'Saul' on the occasion of Queen Victoria's death, and celebrated the Coronation of Edward VII.[39] In 1902, Barnett retired, and the band broke up but quickly reformed under the conductorship of Mr Bray of Sunny Corner, but disbanded again shortly after.[40]

The de-industrialisation and the decline in the level of remittances coming from places abroad, such as South Africa, which characterised the area in the following decades, probably prevented the reformation of Lanner Brass Band. As well as requiring players, the village brass band would have needed a number of people capable of forming a committee, plus significant financial resources to provide instruments and uniforms for the players. But emigration had seriously depleted the number of would-be musicians and committee members. Early twentieth century Lanner was a dependency culture, an impoverished area, incapable of financing a village brass band until the economic upswing of the 1960s saw a rise in the general standard of living, in part due to the building programme, providing local employment and turning the demographic balance in favour of cultural revival. There followed the reappearance of several village activities, beside the brass band, including the cricket club, a football club, the scouting movement and the rugby club.

So it was not until 1965 that another brass band was formed under the able conductorship of Tommy Martin, a former bandmaster of Carharrack and St Day Silver Band, and an extremely skilled cornet player. A lifelong interest and passion for brass bands had begun when he was just a schoolboy, and he brought his first cornet from John Jennings for 17s.6d. He took lessons with Clifton Allen and soon joined the Carharrack Temperance Band.

Nominated by Lanner Village to be Conductor and Instructor, he chose the title, 'Lanner and District Silver Band' for the new band, inspired by the heading 'Lanner and District' which appeared weekly in the *West Briton*. L. Williams was appointed Secretary; T. Paull and R. Williams were the Treasurers. The first practices, comprising about 12 players, were held in his front room at Bell Veor, while individual lessons were given to improve the overall standard. Twelve instruments were purchased from St Just Old Town Band at a cost of £100, together with a few extra instruments donated by village residents. The first Gala Day held in the Village Hall was followed by an evening concert at which enough money was made to clear the debt for the instruments.

Tommy Martin's front room proving to be too small to accommodate increasing numbers of musicians, the venue for practices was switched to Daisy Moyle's concrete chicken shed at the bottom of her garden in Ankervis Lane. The building was 12 foot by 15 foot, but once cleaned, chairs provided, and batteries found by Mr Penglase to supply electricity, practices continued! Later in 1965, a large Nissen Hut was offered to the band for use as their headquarters. It was brought from Falmouth, and eventually erected on a piece of land at the top of Lanner Hill, the freehold of which was obtained from H.L.D. Beauchamp of Trevince, the band's President. In 1984, the band acquired the old Primitive Methodist Chapel at Lanner Moor as their HQ, purchased from the Methodist Circuit for £13 500. After improvements and repairs bringing the total cost to £16 000, the new premises were opened on 5 May.[41]

Dedication and hard work over the years have built Lanner and District Silver Band into one of the county's better bands. Dick Hancock has been a major figure in the organisation of the band for many years, in addition to his work for the parish as Chairman of the Lanner Village Association, and more lately, of the Parish Council. Numerous musical directors followed Tommy Martin, including A. Bedding, R. Perry, T. Rule and Joe Anderson, who was formerly a euphonium player with the famous Cresswell Colliery Band. Sadly, he did not live long enough to see his band achieve the greatest achievement of his musical directorship, playing at the National Finals at Pontins. Derek Greenwood stepped in to conduct the players so they could still compete.

Musical Directors Messrs K. Hamlod, Faro, R. Trelease and Richards continued to maintain the band's good reputation. In 1995, the musical director was C. Harris, the band competing in the first section of the National Finals in London for the first time. A flourishing youth band gives the young of the village a wonderful opportunity to learn to play an instrument, as well as an educational hobby with a good social life (Fig. 12.12).

The band, from its humble nineteenth century origins, revived as a village institution, adds colour to the life of Lanner, organising the annual carnival as a part of their band week activities. It also provides the poignant reminder of our fallen heroes on Armistice Day by marching through the village to the tune of a stirring march, and contributes to the Christmas season by playing carols around the village. Tommy Martin was responsible for a crop of talented young players who have succeeded in the musical world, among them Alan Pope, a military bandsman, Roy Williams who became the Musical Director of the Gweek Silver Band, and Philip Penglase and David Tonkin who both now play in orchestras.

Rugby

Organised sport grew out of a need to tone down the boisterous nature of many pre-industrial games. Controlled sports with rules still provided great excitement and added a little zest and thrill to a way of life increasingly dominated by the workplace clock. In the context of regional or local identity, sports, it has been argued, perhaps better than any other single activity, reflected the reality of community life.[42] These spectator sports remained within the parameters of respectability because they appeased the innate craving to vent one's energy, but in a controlled and constructive way, which was very necessary for an industrial society which needed to occasionally 'let off steam'. Spectator sports were to become very popular nationwide in the twentieth century. Seward notes that sport contributed to an enhancement of an individual's sense of identity with, or belonging to (either within a group or collectively), a district, village or town, class, colour or country.[43]

Fig.12.12. *Lanner & District Silver Band's finest hour. Taking part in the Finals of the National Brass Band Championship of Great Britain, at the Wembley Conference Centre, London, 22 October 1995. The test piece was 'Plantagenets'. Musical Director: Chris Harris; soprano cornet, Leslie Kneebone; principal cornet, Ian Hooper; solo cornet, Lee Rouse, Simon Hampton, Ellen Bray; repiano cornet, Sharon Hooper; flugel horn, Roland Woods; second cornet, Mark Solway, Rachel Hills; third cornet, Shane Wills, Angela Kneebone, Gemma Bosworth; solo horn, Alison Richards; first horn, Simon Osborne; second horn, Sharon Gilbert; solo euphonium, Graham Allen; euphonium, Andrew Staples; first baritone, Jeremy Gilbert; second baritone, Matthew Ager; solo trombone, Leon Youlton; second trombone, Nicholas Solway; bass trombone, Mark Osborne; Eb Bass, Victor Ellis, Francis McWilliams; BBb Bass, Shaun Jenkin, Arthur Osborne; drums, Wayne Morris; percussion, Julie Ellis.* (© R. J. Hancock, Lanner)

Fig.12.13. *Lanner Rugby Football Club, 1925–26.* Back row, l-r: *W.I. Whitburn (Chairman), F. Pryor, W. Downing, F.M. Trethowan (Hon. Sec.), W .Hitchens, W.G. Ingram.* Middle row: *G.W. Blatchford, T.J. Tregoning, E. Lampshire, C.G. Lampshire, F. Dunstan, P. Prophet, R. Perry, P. Rogers.* Front row: *W.S. Rogers, J.C. Hocking, L.M. Curnow (Captain), The Revd F.E. Bury (President), A.Moyle, D.Downing.* On ground: *A. Harris, F. Ellis, H.B. Moyle (Vice-Captain), W. Downing jr.* (photo Opie Ltd, Redruth. © Mrs R. Blatchford, Lanner)

Lanner has had a long tradition of sporting activities, particularly in rugby. This sport was introduced into West Cornwall from 'up the country' in the early 1870s by returning public schoolboys and professional men. In 1875, Old Cliftonian Henry Grylls and W.H. Willimott formed the Redruth Rugby Football Club, successfully obtaining a ground from the Redruth Brewery Company. Over the succeeding years, the town became the home of Cornish rugby, and although it owed its existence to the initiative of Redruth's modernising bourgeoisie, it was readily adopted by the working class as their sport. Culturally, rugby has provided the vehicle for expressing a powerful sense of place and identity, the best example being the passionate support for the Cornish rugby team at the County Championship Finals at Twickenham in 1991, 1992 and 1998.[44]

The enthusiasm for rugby in Redruth spilled over into the surrounding villages, and one of the earliest mentions of rugby in Lanner is the report of a match played between the students of Trevarth House Grammar School and the Redruth Junior team in 1877, played in the grounds of Trevarth House. On this occasion the home team were defeated by three goals and five tries to nil.[45] A rugby club was formed in Lanner soon after and made great progress. During the 1894–95 season, a report in a February edition of the *West Briton,* halfway through that season, remarked that Lanner had played nine matches, won six and drawn three, a good record.[46]

Matches between Lanner and neighbouring St Day were guaranteed to draw a good crowd to enjoy the atmosphere of friendly rivalry for sporting supremacy and pride manifested by the players and supporters of the two mining villages.

By the turn of the twentieth century, the Lanner team continued to function in spite of losing numerous key players through emigration. Many of these former players, including Thomas Curnow and Sam Job, continued to play rugby for teams formed in the mining towns of the Rand, South Africa. William Wallace Curnow who migrated to South Africa, was reported to have been one of the first men to play rugby for Lanner,[47] and William Blatchford, a player and a former Tresavean engineer, migrated to Malaysia following Tresavean's closure in 1928.

After the Second World War, the popularity of the game in the village seemed to wane, and the club faded away in the mid 1950s. This demise of the village rugby club was subject, like the brass band, to the effects of industrial collapse, migration and economic paralysis. The focus of Lanner as a village had diminished, hundreds of its sons and daughters deserting the village for distant shores, and although there a few talented individuals remained in the village, there were not enough key players, or dedicated and capable individuals to form a committee, necessary to ensure the club's rebirth. This is a completely different picture from the confident, vibrant village community, brimming with talented and enthusiastic workers of the previous century, and provides further evidence of the way in which the process of de-industrialisation had effected the village culturally.

However, Lanner Rugby Club was revived in 1967 by Johnny Quintrell of 'Buena Vista', Lanner Moor, a great figure in the history of sport in the village. He was the inspiration and driving force behind rugby in Lanner for the next twelve years, and when he eventually resigned, the club ceased to function. The Rugby Club were originally based at Mewton's Farm, Tresavean, but moved in 1970 to Ting Tang, at the top of the Trevince Estate. In 1972, the club moved again to a field opposite the Fox and Hounds Pub at Comford, before crossing the road to use the area alongside the pub, until the the club ceased. However, many Lanner men have achieved rugby fame outside the village, at local, county and national level.

Douglas Martin won an Under 15 International cap for England Schools in 1929–30, and later became one of Lanner Rugby Club's most dedicated officials.
Harold Curnow and Percy Rogers are well known names to those familiar with Cornish rugby. Both played for Redruth and Cornwall in the 1920s and 30s, Harold awarded 23 County Caps, and Percy 14. Howard had the honour of captaining Cornwall and was also picked as an England reserve. A wonderful all-round sportsman, he was noted for his skill in Cornish wrestling, and continued to referee rugby

matches for several seasons after his retirement as a player. Calvin Martin, a pupil at Redruth School, played in both the Under 15 and Under 18 Schools' County sides. He played for Redruth as a hooker before leaving the county, in 1965 being selected for the England squad.

Lanner lad Adrian Curtis played all his 'club' career with Redruth, and as a versatile flanker played for county 16 and 18 Schools' groups and the County Colts. Between 1983 and 1988, he played no less than 29 times for the full Cornwall County team. Alan Buzza is the latest in a line of villagers to distinguish himself on the rugby pitch, playing for the England Schools Under 18 group in 1984, and 19 times for Cornwall between 1984 and 1988. He had the honour of captaining Cambridge University against Oxford, and has been a member of England's national squad twice.

The loss of the village rugby club means that prospective players are now forced to look to Redruth for inclusion in the town squad, yet another example of Lanner's dependency on Redruth.

Soccer and Cricket

The earliest evidence of organised soccer in the village is part of a programme bearing details of a Lanner XI. The game was played during the Second World War on the Recreation Ground at Redruth. Frank Bowden, Michael Veall, Johnny Quintrell, Dougie Smale, Archie Oats, Jimmy Pascoe (Captain), Cap'n Oates, and Aubrey Williams have been identified as being team members. The adult game seemed, in common with rugby, to have diminished in importance from the early 50s onwards until it was revived in Lanner in 1980. Messrs Broomhead and Darlington played an important part in this, and the team joined the local Mining League, with one team in each of the two divisions. In 1986–87, Lanner won the Division 1 title. The club then decided to leave the Mining League, and instead play in the Helston/Falmouth League. A new football pitch was secured by Lanner Parish Council on the site of the former dressing floors of Tresavean Mine, which was 'landscaped' in 1991. Football was also played by the boys of Lanner School. Since 1974, the boys of the village have been fortunate enough to have organised football. Hugh Mabely and Johnny Dodds formed a team, and the boys play competitively throughout the county.

A cricket club was formed during the mid 1920s in connection with Lanner Christ Church, the Revd F. E. Bury being its President and a playing member. The club petered out before his departure in 1928, probably due to the loss of key players through emigration, and another club was not formed until after the Second World War, in 1948. Lanner Cricket Club enjoyed a successful season in 1959, narrowly losing to Longdowns in the final of the Andrew Cup. In 1961 and 1964 the club won the Falmouth and District League. F. C. Parr who was the club President and Johnny Quintrell, the Secretary, played an important part in the running of the club in its successful years (Fig.2.15). In recent years its fortunes have waned, and in September 1998, after several years of falling further down the league table, the club was disbanded.

Various grounds have been used as a cricket pitch. The top half of a field belonging to Kitto's Farm was first used, before activities were centred on a field at Trevarth, where the brick works once were. Some time after this, the venue for games was switched to a field behind Lanner Hill Garage, and then to one behind Tresavean Estate. From here, the club moved back to Kitto's, and finally to Clijah Croft, where they were based for about 20 years.

Alternative Sports

Lanner had a lawn tennis club in 1907, and grass courts at the Vicarage were used for the purpose. There were also tennis courts at Trevince. Croquet was played by many of the more well-to-do residents, and was participated in by schoolgirls, a croquet iron being found by Susan Gribble on her Trevarth farm, thought to have come from a school which might formerly have existed there. Croquet lawns were likely to have been found in the grounds of houses such as Trevince and Trevarth.

Numerous more modern sports have become fashionable over recent years, among these Judo, gymnastics, netball and badminton. The Parish Hall was a venue for the Lanner Ladies Netball Club, and a table tennis club for a time in the 1950s, and the Village Hall has provided the forum for indoor sports such as judo, gymnastics and badminton. Andrew Dodds, who played at Lanner, became one of the best young badminton players in Cornwall, being included in the County First Team.

A more recent addition to Lanner's sporting repertoire has been the introduction of Carpet Bowls, which was augmented in 1988 at the Village Hall, and became a regular Tuesday night slot. Membership is limited to 36, owing to the small size of the hall, and competition and friendly matches are held, resulting in the club competing in the Premier Division of the Camborne–Redruth League. Lanner has four teams spread over three divisions of the league.

Cross country running and athletics have become popular leisure time activities for village residents over the past two decades, the terrain around Lanner being ideally suited for training. Several talented runners have achieved great success, but because there is no club in the village, athletes have had to represent Redruth School and local athletic clubs, and have progressed to eventually distinguish themselves at club, county, national or international level. Among those to do so are Kevin Heather, who was the South of England Champion in the 1500 metres Steeplechase at Crystal Palace in 1977. David Buzza became the British Universities' 1500 metre champion in 1985, and has since represented Britain in the World Cross-country Championships in New Zealand, finishing 34th. In 1991, he ran for the United Kingdom in the World Cup Marathon, finishing 16th in a time of 2hr.12min.37sec. In the same year, he came 20th in the World Marathon Championships in Tokyo. In 1993, he came 6th in the London Marathon, and followed this by coming in 10th in the World Marathon Cup with his best time of 2hr.11min.6 sec. In 1994 he was selected to represent England in the Commonwealth Games in Vancouver and in 1998 in the European Championships Marathon in Budapest.

Kerry Marshall has won both the Cornwall Schools' and the Cornwall AAA's 1500 metre races, and in 1993, she represented the county in the South West Region Championships, finishing 11th. In 1993–94, Kerry won the Cornwall Schools' Cross Country Championships.

Lanner Men's Institute

In 1906, Lanner Men's Institute was founded in a wooden building which formerly stood on the site of the dwelling 'Bellair', at the Southern end of Grays Terrace, and was opened in January of that year by Miss Bray, who was presented by Mr Hooper with a silver key with which to unlock the building.[48] In 1915, the total membership was 65, and the Treasurer, Mr E. Job, presented the financial statement which showed a balance in hand of £8.14s.4d. The President was R. Opie, and the Secretary, James Lawn.[49] Money was raised by the Men's Institute for charitable causes, and in 1915, the Cornwall County Patriotic Fund received the sum of £5 from the Institute, the Belgian Relief Fund £1.14s.6d, and the *Weekly Dispatch* Tobacco Fund, £11s.6d. (Fig. 12.14.).

The Institute provided a much needed place of retreat and camaraderie for the village men, particularly during the troubled inter-war period, when increasing numbers of young men faced unemployment as the mining industry sank into a terminal decline. A reading room was provided for the men, and the 1915 accounts show that the sum of £2.15.6d had been spent on the provision of newspapers. In 1921, it was decided to erect a proper reading room for the members, measuring 12 ft by 12 ft, at an estimated cost of £50. This proposition came during very hard times in the village and, in order to raise the necessary capital, a grant was applied for, and subsequently the sum of £42.15s. was awarded from the United Services Fund for the project, leaving a small balance which had already been raised. Mrs Malton, the Vicar's wife, was asked to open the reading room on 27 December 1921. 'We have already erected a memorial to the dead,' stated former-Lieutenant Toy, 'this will serve as a memorial to the living'. The membership numbered about 80 at this time. In 1907, the men obtained a snooker table, and the sport, a new form of leisure activity, has had a good following in the village ever since. In the early years, the members played in the Gwennap and District Billiard League, and in 1915, it was reported that Lanner was the top of the league.

Probably the best snooker player to emerge in Cornwall was Barry Scarlett of Bell Lane. By the late 1970s, he was a member of a successful County Youth team, and in 1982, competed for the Senior County team which defeated Hampshire. In 1984, he won the Senior and Youth County Individual Championships, and was forced to move to London in order to maintain a competitive edge, by playing with better quality opposition. The Lanner men now play in the Truro and District Snooker League.

In addition, the institute provides a chance to play darts, dominoes, draughts and card games, which were once played widely in pubs. In 1922, Lanner Men's Institute draughts' team was comprehensively beaten by 20 games to 4 by the Redruth British Legion's team.[50]

In 1962, the old wooden building which had been the Institute for over 50 years had become very dilapidated, and concern was mounting among members for the safety of the snooker table. Councillor William Hart, a trustee of the Village Hall, received general support for his proposal to accommodate the Men's Institute in the Village Hall, by constructing a room in the disused gallery of the old United Methodist 'Bryanite' Chapel, from which the Village Hall had developed.

The members of the Institute were to benefit greatly through the generosity of a local builder, who donated the proceeds of the sale of the site of the original wooden building, which was channelled into funds to renovate their new premises. The Institute pays an agreed annual rental with the Village Hall, and are by the constitution forbidden to sell or consume alcohol on the premises. In 1966, separate doors were built into the old main doorway of the chapel. The Lanner' Men's Institute continues to remain a main cultural focus for numerous village men.

Fig.12.14. *Lanner Men's Institute, possibly in the 1920's. This was the Institute's original building. Back row 4th from left: John Henry Whitford. Front row 4th from left, Stanley Whitford; 5th, Bennett Moyle; 9th, George Goodland.* (© Lanner Historical Society)

Lanner Women's Institute

At the end of the Second World War, many women in the village thought that the ladies needed a social organisation of their own as the men had their Institute. As village life was felt to be quite dull, the Women's Institute's object was to brighten it. The organisation of Women's Institutes had earlier set out to be more than just another regular lecture spot, and did not plan 'to play gramophone music to a lot of middle aged women'; the Cornish Women's Institute meeting of 1921 agreed to pay the entertainment tax, and so enable the Institute to lay on a full, varied and interesting itinerary of events. 'Without paying the entertainment tax, we cannot foster or continue the social side and neglect to do this will kill the movement'.[51] The movement grew from strength to strength, and on the evening of 23 November 1945, a group of village women met in the Lanner Wesley Schoolroom to discuss the idea of starting a Women's Institute (WI) in Lanner, following its popularity in other rural and semi-rural areas of Britain. A fortnight later, the Lanner Women's Institute was born, with Mrs E.M. Barbary elected as its first President, and with a committee of nine.

By the end of 1946, membership stood at 42, and the new organisation soon entered the mainstream of village life, being called upon to help distribute free orange juice on behalf of the local Food Office. A rota of seven volunteers continued to help with the scheme until 1947. The WI prided itself on providing a broad range of leisure activities, which in the 1950s, included concerts containing monologues, skits, sketches, music and dance, which were well patronised by local residents. The Lanner WI was successful, because it provided entertainment at affordable prices, and any money raised at the events helped to finance the Village Hall, the WI meeting place, which was then a relatively new village amenity. Annual summer parties and New Year Parties were included in the programme between 1947–1965, and outings were taken by Marigold bus to various places in the South West. Today, annual parties are held at hotels, rather than the former venue of the Village Hall.

Fund raising activities of the WI at Lanner have helped many local worthy causes, among those to benefit being The Green, at Redruth, and St Julia's Hospice, residential homes for the elderly; Cornwall Air Ambulance; NSPCC and Autistic Children; The Devon and Cornwall Caviton Appeal, and the Diabetic Appeal at Treliske Hospital, Truro. Most recent in a long line of fund raising activities was the organisation of a collection point for items to be sent to the former Yugoslavia, to help the women and children of Bosnia. The WI at Lanner has participated in various county wide events, and have achieved several commendable results.

In 1955, Lanner came fifth in the Baker Cup with a Dutch evening, which saw the members dressed in Dutch national costume. Food, music, crafts and stories continued the Dutch theme. In 1965, Lanner again entered the Baker Cup, with a historical project entitled, 'A Scrapbook About Your Village', edited by Alice Opie. This provides much useful information concerning the village during a period of great change (see Chapter 11). The year 1991 saw all the WI's in Cornwall being asked to participate in a project called *The Cornish Village Book*. Jeannie Hopkins, using material collected by Sheila Barnard, agreed to write a brief history of Lanner, which was included in the book.

Lanner WI's banner, made in 1965 at a cost of £2.65 in time for the Golden Jubilee organised by the County WI, reflects Lanner's history, and was the collective work of eight members. It is an affirmation of Lanner's rich mining heritage, and the members' cultural construction of Lanner's place in Cornwall. The banner is proudly displayed at all important events and functions.

The aim of the WI movement is to give members nation wide, a venue for entertainment and an opportunity for personal achievement and adult education, as well as providing rural communities with a social framework just for women. Several Lanner ladies have taken the opportunity over the years of attending the WI's own residential college in Oxfordshire, where they have participated in a wide variety of courses, including music, science, marketing, the Treasures of Britain and china restoration.

Monthly social evenings at which a speaker is invited to present a slide show, display or lecture, are given at the Village Hall on a diverse range of subjects. Many Lanner ladies have helped to make the WI in the village a success, and none so more than Alice M. Opie, who was President from 1954–1965. She was afforded the honour of representing Lanner WI at the Royal Garden Party at Buckingham Palace on 31 May 1965. Mrs P. Rogers' contribution to the organisation was acknowledged by a lasting tribute to her in the form of a clock for the Village Hall, and a chain of office, purchased in 1990, following her death. Like the Men's Institute, the WI performs a very important role in keeping Lanner's village identity alive.

Darby and Joan

In 1954, a meeting was called in the back room of the Village Hall to consider the formation of a Darby and Joan Club, aimed at providing a social forum for the senior members of the village. Mrs Shaw, the Vicar's wife, became the leader of the new club, and fortnightly meetings continued to be held in the same room. At the early meetings, games such as bingo and beetle drives were held, played on tables donated by the Redruth WVS. Quizzes were also organised, and the atmosphere was a convivial one, which led to an increase in membership and a change of venue to the main Village Hall. Leaders of the Club included Mrs E. Lapham of Lanner Square and Mrs L. Phillips of Bell Lane, before Mrs J. Shaw, a Methodist minister's wife, took over the leadership. Mrs Shaw had been very involved with Age Concern committees, and she completely changed the complexion of the club. The name was changed to 'Lanner Good Companions', and the itinerary was expanded to include entertainment, speakers and some help and education for its members concerning the many state and other benefits available to them. Membership was open to all those over 50.

A determined effort has been made in the village to make this one of the most successful institutions which is able to meet the leisure needs of a growing elderly population in Lanner, as well as providing a framework of philanthropy for the aged, reflecting the popularity of the village as a retirement location. The strength of this organisation also underlines the changing patterns of the village's demography, from a relatively youthful community in the nineteenth century, to one which is presently very much older.

In 1989, the Council of Community Services Minibus was introduced to provide transport for members to and from meetings, and also a shopping trip on alternate weeks, and organised coach trips are also popular events. Members have contributed to a local charity by knitting toys for Save the Children, and many hours go into preparations for their stall at the Community Fayre. Mrs Shaw decided to retire and her position was taken by Mrs E. Gilbert. This organisation enjoys one of the best followings in the village today, and its membership numbered over 85 in 1994.

Leisure for children

For Victorian children, there was little organised entertainment outside of the chapel. Games, which probably had their roots in antiquity, were played in the street, including leap frog, marbles, hop scotch, Lily Mount (a game resembling rounders), quoits (played with steel rings about 8 inches in diameter, which had to be thrown on to a small stick set at a required distance), and Duck Stones, which involved knocking a stone from a prominent position with another.

Leisure events for children have developed enormously in the village during the twentieth century, as it became apparent that they needed a form of entertainment to keep them out of trouble. Children in the present century have far more leisure time than that enjoyed by their Victorian predecessors, who as we have seen, worked long hours.

We have already noted the large groups of young men who hung around in the village square around the turn of the century making a nuisance of themselves. One of the first attempts to address the problem of youth facilities in Lanner was the provision of a playing field at Lanner Moor in 1928. In the 1920s, Frank Trethowan, who worked in the office of Tresavean Mine and was a leading light in Lanner Church, campaigned vociferously for a playing field for Lanner after seeing the success of that of neighbouring St Day. An area was purchased at Lanner Moor as a playing field soon after, and his efforts were further rewarded in 1935, when a grant for £180 was given to Lanner for the purchase and erection of playing field equipment from the National Council and Social Service, providing a much needed amenity for the village youth.[52] The children of Lanner School were given a half day off to attend the opening ceremony.

Scouts, Cubs, Rainbows and Drama

In 1924, Reggie Bury, the son of the Vicar, introduced the Scouts to Lanner. The Troop consisted of 12–15 boys, who all wore the traditional scout uniform of the day. Meetings took place in the Parish Church Hall once a week, and Mr Gordon Opie, a member of the Troop from 1924–1928, remembers regular church parades, games of tennis on the Vicarage tennis courts, tracking on Tresavean, and camps at Carvannel and Maenporth. He especially enjoyed the camps, particularly cooking over an open camp fire, and the tracking exercises. The special hike from Maenporth to Falmouth provided the boys with the chance to earn their hiker's badge. Sadly, when the Bury Family moved from the village in 1928, scouting ended too. The fact that scouting was not continued in the village is probably indicative of the depressed times in the village, with Tresavean Mine closing the same year, to be followed by the depression of the 1930s. In common with the fate of the sports teams above, scouting was not revived until the rejuvenation of the village following the building programmes of the 1960s.

In 1972, the organisation was restarted under the auspices of Michael Richards, who had a young son and felt that there was a need of a scouting movement in such a large village. He asked the leaders of Lanner Methodist Chapel to sponsor his idea of forming the first cub pack in the village. A public meeting was called, to which Chapel leaders, District scouters and interested parents were invited, and in due course, the 1st Lanner Wesley Cub Pack was formed. Weekly meetings were held at Lanner Methodist schoolroom. From this new beginning, a scout group was revived once more, but independent of the Chapel. It raised its own money through scout fetes and other events, and enjoyed district camps at Tehidy Woods and Carwinnon. However, interest in the Cubs began to wane around the late 70s, numbers dropped and the pack closed.

The Scout group continued under the leadership of two local lads, Simon Moss and Brian Rogers, who were both well respected Venture Scouts in the area, yet despite their energy and the events organised by them which included camps, interest was increasingly difficult to maintain, and membership numbers declined. Had not Tony Martin decided to inaugurate the cub pack once again in 1980, it is doubtful whether the Scout pack would have survived. With many of the older boys moving on from the Cubs to become Scouts, more help was required with the latter group. Ian Walsh agreed to run the Scouts with Tony Martin following the death of 'Skip' Wilson, a much respected senior scouter, who had contributed greatly to the movement in the District. Sheila Barnard took over as leader of the Cubs with assistance from Susan Rule and Roger Barnard, a senior patrol leader within the Scouts. The organisation proved so popular that Lanner was one of the first villages in the District to start a Beaver Colony for boys of pre-Cub age, under the auspices of the late Angela Williams.

With such a rapidly expanding organisation, it was felt that the group needed its own premises. The old band room at the top of Lanner Hill was vacated by the Lanner Silver Band in 1987, and in the following year, planning permission was granted for a change of use, and the 1st Lanner Wesley Scout Group moved from the Wesley Schoolroom to their new base. At this time the organisation's name was changed to that of 1st Lanner Hill Scout Group. In 1988, Phil Mitchell assumed leadership of the Scouts, and excelled at organising a number of exciting activities aimed at capturing the imagination of the village boys. Camps, hikes, canoeing courses, swimming galas, participation in gang shows and community service projects, as well as weekly scout training and Church parades, gave the village youngsters a chance to obtain personal achievements, which have resulted in 11 Scouts earning their Chief Scout awards.

In 1995, the Cub pack was run by Linda James, and the Beavers by Julie Mugford. Phil Mitchell runs the Scouts, and also the group as Group Scout leader. A total of 70 boys of all ages are involved. In 1997, a Rainbow Guide group for girls aged five to seven was set up. The leader is Penny Butt and weekly meetings are held in the Parish Hall.

A children's theatre workshop was begun in 1989 by Doreen Fiol, with sessions which include mime, improvisation, drama games, script work, group and solo work. There is a strong emphasis on confidence-building, social communication, reliability and fun. Plays are conducted in local halls and at the Carn Marth Quarry Theatre, and the scripts and most of the music and lyrics are written by Doreen.

The problems of providing entertainment facilities in Lanner today, especially for its teenage population, are most pressing. The Village Hall as a venue has proved so popular that it is at times impossible to book the hall for an evening. The Methodist Chapel has recently started a youth club in the Methodist Schoolroom, in response to the wishes of many of the parents of the new Strawberry Fields Estate. But Lanner Parish Council are considering the problem, and are initiating plans for Lanner, one of Cornwall's fastest growing villages, to have a purpose-built youth centre.

The ever-changing nature of Lanner's Leisure: a summary

The nineteenth century was one of great change, particularly in the mining industry which was gradually transformed from the 1840s onwards. The restructuring of this industry, with less tribute and more contract work, was reflected in the way in which people chose to spend their leisure time with the result that many of the traditional forms of leisure which were carried on in time honoured fashion, such as the Midsummer celebrations, disappeared. But this disappearance did not occur at once; many ancient rural activities coexisted with newer forms of leisure for many years. It is only relatively recently that events focused upon the pubs have been confined to the pages of history – the Mock Mayor Ceremony and Cornish wrestling matches.

The number of public houses in the area has declined; Lanner now has but two drinking establishments, the Lanner Inn, and the Coppice, the latter having also a restaurant with a venue room, and was once the home of Lawyer Bray. The Fox and Hounds pub at Comford falls outside the parish boundary.

Even hunting, the countryside's great leisure pursuit, is coming under fire from animal rights' groups, and at the time of writing, there is great debate over the right of urban Britain to attempt to inflict change on traditional rural communities, whose time honoured way of life is seen to be under threat. We hear no more of badger-baiting, rabbit shooting and coursing or dog baiting, although it must be noted that many of the old rural activities did however maintain a high profile right throughout the nineteenth century, despite the criticism levelled by self-improving campaigners connected to the Church and Chapels.

Gone too are the Mechanics' Institutes and reading rooms, as mass education has dispensed with the need for such village facilities for self-improvement. Educational evening classes, no longer offered in Lanner, are centralised at places such as Cornwall College at Pool. 'Respectable' leisure still makes up a part of village life, albeit in many cases merged with more modern and secularising influences, although it must be noted that the activities centred on the chapel are by no means as high profile as they used to be. This is common throughout the country, as twentieth century society has become far more secular in its outlook. Bands of Hope, Mutual Improvement Classes, tea treats and the annual Sunday School Anniversaries have vanished, but the Lanner Methodist Church still endeavours to play an important part in community life. However, some of the leisure events which would have been immediately recognisable to our Victorian forbears remain today, including the annual pageant, bazaars and evenings of song and entertainment.

It is interesting to note that the gradual decline of certain leisure activities in the early to mid twentieth century were those which required significant capital, either collectively or individually. The village brass band would have needed a considerable amount of finance to purchase instruments and uniforms, as would the rugby and football clubs, for strips and boots, and the cricket club, for expensive equipment, plus the rental of premises for meetings. Even belonging to the village Scouts would have required members to have a uniform and necktie, an unwanted expense for working class parents.

In this atmosphere of economic gloom and resignation, people had adopted and championed a philosophy of 'getting by and making do', which had important sociological implications.[53] By the twentieth century, Payton notes that instead of being 'vigorous icons of an assertive identity', elements of popular culture had become increasingly private affairs, in many cases mere shadows of their former splendour, as Cornish society turned in on itself. Brass bands, rugby football clubs, and even Methodist events (such as Lanner Show Fair), became introverted expressions of a fossilising way of life, as communities like Lanner sought to come to terms with their economic plight in the face of continuing de-industrialisation.[54]

It is significant that such activities did not reappear in Lanner until the period of revival in the village following the building developments of the 1960s which led to a much needed demographic increase. This generated a better standard of living through improved housing and employment opportunities, which in turn led to an increased affluence, confidence and a cultural revival for the parish. This development saved Lanner, which was fast becoming a fossilised community, paralysed by the effects of de-industrialisation resulting from the collapse of the area's mining industry.

Yet paradoxically it is this very expansion which has led to fears about the 'exploding village' which could fall victim to the forces of sub-urbanisation, and become just another dormitory of Redruth with no real life of its own. This anxiety looms large in the minds of many, who are aware that this fate has already befallen many villages on the outskirts of large towns 'up the country'. The car has liberated many peoples' lives, and given twentieth century citizens the opportunity of choosing the venue for their entertainment, and it does not necessary follow that this should automatically be in one's home village.

In order to maintain and strengthen its village identity, it is vital that Lanner should retain a variety of leisure activities to ensure that the village does not culturally become but 'a suburb of Redruth'. Through activities such as the brass band, Women's and Men's Institutes, Good Companions, football club and Scout Movement, Lanner's unique village identity can be maintained. This will help to avoid total dependence on nearby Redruth. Hopefully a little of the community atmosphere which had been on the wane since the troubled times earlier this century has been regained.

Moreover, a new leisure pursuit has developed in the late twentieth century which is challenging all of the above forms of spare time activities – that of home entertainment. Television, satellite dishes, video recorders, hi-fi systems and home computers increasingly mean that people do not need to leave their home in order to be entertained. This, probably more than anything else, has done much to harm the attendance numbers at village organisations, particularly those which occur in the evenings. Numbers of people leaving their home on a night which has cup football or a film or drama premiere showing on television, are likely to be few. Local shops stock videos for home viewing, and an increasing number of homes in the village sport a satellite dish. Where formerly Lanner residents looked to the community and to their friends and neighbours for the provision of leisure and entertainment, the trend now is far more insular and solitary, to the detriment of many village organisations. This arguably poses more of a danger than sub-urbanisation to the various organisations and societies which today endeavour to maintain Lanner's village identity and community spirit.

Fig. 2.15. Mr Johnny Quintrell with the garden seat presented to him by Lanner Cricket Club to mark his retirement after 42 years as Secretary, 20 April 1991. (© Mr Malcolm Quintrell, Lanner)

REFERENCES

1 Westland, Ella, (ed..,), *The Cultural Construction of Place*, Patten Press, 1997.
2 Deacon, Bernard, And Shall Trelawney Die? The Cornish Identity, *Cornwall Since the War*, Payton (ed.,), University of Exeter Press, p. 201.
3 James, C.C., *History of Gwennap*, privately published, undated, p. 123.
4 *West Briton*, 24/5/1877.
5 James, C.C., *History of Gwennap*, privately published, undated, p. 92.
6 *Royal Cornwall Gazette*, 19/8/1897.
7 *West Briton*, 10/10/1862.
8 Burke, G., The Cornish Miner and Cornish Mining Industry 1870-1921. PhD Thesis, London University, 1981, p. 282.
9 Jenkin, Hamilton A.K., *Cornwall and Its People*, David & Charles, Newton Abbot, 1970, pp. 439-440.
10 *Mining Journal*, 22/2/1840.
11 P 79/81/1, CRO, Truro.
12 *Cornubian*, 28/12/1888; James, C.C., 'History of Gwennap', p.141.
13 *Cornubian*, 15/8/1902.
14 Olds, G., Fair Play is Good Play! *Echoes of the Past, 3*, 1997.

15 *West Briton*, 22/2/1839.
16 *Cornubian*, 10/1/1868.
17 *Cornubian*, 23/2/1883.
18 Methodist Circuit Papers held at CSL, Redruth, Courtesy of Mr J.C.C. Probert.
19 *Cornish Post & Mining News*, 17/1/1890.
20 Francis, William, *Gwennap, A Poem in Seven Cantos*, p. 104.
21 *West Briton*, 2/6/1839.
22 *Cornubian*, 23/3/1888.
23 *Cornubian*, 28/12/1888.
24 C.M.R.C., July 1893, Shaw Collection, RIC, Truro.
25 Francis, William, p. 132.
26 *Cornish Post & Mining News*, 1/10/1892.
27 *Cornubian*, 20/2/1888.
28 *Cornubian*, 1/1/1890.
29 *Cornubian*, 30/6/1876; 27/7/1883.
30 *Cornubian*, 28/7/1921.
31 *Cornubian*, 21/7/1921.
32 *Cornubian*, 17/2/1888.
33 *Cornish post & Mining News*, 26/9/1890.
34 *Cornubian*, 30/8/1901.
35 *Cornubian*, 6/12/1928.
36 Information from an interview with Mr Bennetts in 1995.
37 *Cornubian*, 19/12/1903.
38 *Cornubian*, 13/12/1928.
39 *Cornubian*, 8/2/1901.
40 *Cornubian*, 21/2/1902; 15/5/1903.
41 Taken from interviews with Mr T. Martin in 1995.
42 Metcalfe, *Sport and Community: A Case Study of the Mining Villages of Northumberland, 1800-1914*, Williams and Hill, (ed..), 1996, p.175.
43 Seward, Andy, Cornish Rugby and Cultural Identity: A Socio-Historical Perspective, quoting T. Mason, (ed..,) Sport in Britain, Cambridge, 1988, p. 118, *Cornish Studies 5*, Philip Payton (ed..), University of Exeter Press, 1997.
44 Deacon, Bernard, And Shall Trelawney Die? The Cornish Identity, *Cornwall Since the War*, Philip Payton (ed..), p. 201.
45 *Cornubian*, 23/2/1877.
46 *West Briton*, 14/2/1895.
47 *Cornubian*, 29/4/1915.
48 *Cornubian*, 11/1/1906.
49 *Cornubian*, 4/2/1915.
50 *Cornubian*, 23/3/1922.
51 *Cornubian*, 15/9/1921.
52 *West Briton*, 28/2/1935.
53 Bernard Deacon, 'And Shall Trelawney Die?', in Philip Payton (ed.) *Cornwall Since the War*, Redruth, 1993, pp. 200-223.
54 Payton, Philip, Paralysis and Revival: the Reconstruction of Celtic-Catholic Cornwall 1890-1945, in Ella Wesland (ed..), *The Cultural Construction of Place*, Patten Press, 1997, p. 26.

Much of the material contained within the above chapter was taken from the '100 Years of Lanner Exhibition', held in 1995. The following people contributed information concerning many aspects of leisure activities, clubs etc. in Lanner: The Lanner Writer's Group, Mrs J. Hopkins; Lanner and District Silver Band, Mr L. Rouse; Lanner Good Companions, Mrs E. Gilbert and Mrs O. Burrell; Lanner WI, Mrs S. Barnard and Mrs J. Russell; Sport, Messrs M. Buzza and M. Quintrell; Choirs and Music, Mr and Mrs K. Minson; The Children's Theatre Workshop, Mrs Doreen Fiol; Lanner Brownies, Scouts, Cubs and Beavers, Mrs Hill and Mr P. Mitchell and the RAOB Lodge, Mr D. Menhenott.

Epilogue

This book has sought to trace the development of Lanner over some two centuries, by examining the effects of rapid industrialisation on Cornwall, but an industrialisation which, as Philip Payton has argued, was imperfect, incomplete and over-specialised, leading to a slow and painful process of de-industrialisation from the last quarter of the nineteenth century. The post industrial period witnessed an economic and social paralysis, which posed, and continues to pose, myriad problems for the old mining areas.

Lanner changed rapidly from being a small and insignificant rural community of farmers and tinners, to a dynamic, virtually self-contained mining parish, albeit one with many of the problems endemic to Victorian Britain, but one largely dependent on an export commodity – copper – for its economic well-being. The gradual cessation of mining and all heavy industry created long-term employment problems for Lanner and communities like it throughout the old Central Mining District. Even as this book is being written, we are informed that Cornwall's last tin mine, South Crofty, near Camborne, has closed with the loss of over 300 jobs, bringing almost 2000 years of tin mining to an end in Cornwall.

As we approach the new millennium we might pause to ask ourselves, 'where now Lanner?' The question of local needs and viable alternatives to traditional forms of employment, plus housing for a population which still continues to grow, is one which has yet to be properly answered. There seems little possibility of extractive industries returning to Lanner, with parts of the parish – Carn Marth for example, now considered an area of outstanding natural beauty. But to date, Lanner has not received the spin-offs from the fastest growing industry in Cornwall – tourism. Yet in recent years, two of the old mineral tramways which traverse the parish, have been included in the Mineral Tramways Project, a programme which aims to upgrade and rehabilitate about 37 miles (60 kilometres) of trails for recreational walking, cycling, horse riding and educational uses, as well as sites of industrial-archaeological interest which lie on these routes. Pennance Consols engine house is one example of an industrial landmark earmarked for restoration.

In addition, the Tin Mining Country Tourism Association, established in 1997, aims to promote and protect the heritage of the area spanning Camborne, Redruth and the north coast at Portreath. In partnership with Mineral Tramways, it envisages meeting the needs of the local community as well as providing an invaluable tourism asset in which local businesses will directly benefit. 'Coast, countryside and a rich industrial legacy combine here to make Tin Mining Country a unique holiday or day trip destination', reads their colourful brochure. This marks a clear departure from the Cornish Riviera approach of the past, with its emphasis on golden sandy beaches fringed with palm trees, and draws attention to the unique character of the hinterland of Cornwall. And the £1.1 million Mining Villages Regeneration Scheme plans to restore confidence and pride in villages like Lanner, by renovating sites of historic interest and improving village facilities, such as the renovation of the Lanner Band Room and the provision of new bus shelters. This, it is hoped, will have a knock-on effect of engendering a more positive attitude amongst local communities which have suffered economically since the collapse of the mining industry. And the message that the old mining areas have much to offer prospective tourists means that places such as Lanner might well benefit from the environmental/industrial tourists of the new millennium.

Lanner now has its own democratically elected Parish Council as a forum for ideas to be developed by its inhabitants, unlike former times, when the only political forum was the Camborne Redruth Urban District Council. There is widespread scepticism about the use of Parish Councils, but they are there to influence the organisations who take decisions which affect the community.

The aim in writing this book is to remember the main reason for Lanner's existence – its roots as a Cornish Mining Parish, a community firmly established in its land and its traditions, which must not be submerged or annihilated in the drive towards yet more development in the twenty-first century. Only careful land-use planning, and suitable economic policies will address the unique needs of rural communities such as Lanner.

Index

Subscribers

Glynn And Paulette Abrahams, Lanner
Viv And Bob Acton Penpol, Devoran
Sandra K. Albrant, Michigan, U.S.A.
Patrick Allen, Lanner
J. Andrew, West Trevarth, Lanner
J.R. Anson, Lanner
Ray Atkins, Lanner
Vernon Baldry, Padstow
Mrs Pat Banks, Perth, Western Australia
Kevin Barnard, Seaford, East Sussex
Roger Barnard, Battersea, London SW8
Mrs Sheila M. Barnard, Lanner
David Barrett, Mullion, Helston
A. Jean Barrett, Falmouth
William Peter Benbow, Redruth
Frank and June Bentley, ex Lanner
Billingham Family, Lanner
Stuart Bishop, Lanner
Elizabeth and David Blake, Redruth
Mrs Rhona Blatchford, Lanner
Mr K.J. Bosher, Lanner
Chris and Helen Bosworth, Lanner
Ivor Bowditch, Tregony, Truro
Mr and Mrs L. (Jim and Betty) Bowles, Carnon Downs
John Bray, Redruth
Lancelot H. Bray, Lanner
Mrs L. Bray, Helston
Michael Bray, Redruth
Wilfred Bray, Wales
Patricia A. Bridger, Redruth
Mr And Mrs N. J. Brokenshire, Lanner
Stephen J. Brooking, Lanner
Mr L.E. Broomhead, Lanner
Mr S.D. Broomhead, Lanner
W A Telfer Brunton, Idless, Truro
Ivor Bryant, Redruth
Jane Buchanan, Penzance
William R. Bullock, Lanner
Shaun and Wendy Burgess, Lanner
Mr and Mrs P. Burrows, Lanner
Mrs Joan Butt
Margaret C. Buzza, Lanner
Jack Buzza (Family History Researcher), Truro
Mr J.V. Calvert, Asst. CSO Technical, Kerrier District Council
Mr J.C. Carbis, Chelsea, London
Mr K.N. Carlyon, Lanner
Andrea Chamberlain, Sutton, Surrey
Alison J. Chapman, Victoria, Australia
Ken Clark, Higher Pennance, Lanner
Dorothy M.H. Clemence, Four Lanes, Redruth
Paul Cockerham, Penryn
Patricia Coleman, Lanner
Mr Peter Collins, Redruth
Brian and Janet Coombes, Bodmin
Paul Raglan, Cornwall Mining Services
Carole E. Cowan, New Zealand
Lisa Cowling, Cairns, Queensland, Australia
Mrs Christine Cowls, Camborne
Catherine Cox, Bristol
Mrs J. Crowder, Lanner
Mr Monty Curtis, Lanner
Dorothy Curtis, Redruth
DuncanCurtis-Richards, Lanner
Mary G. Dale, Lanner
Prudence Danby, Trevarth, Redruth
David I. Darlington, Four Lanes, Redruth
Richard D. Dawe
Johnathan and Paul Dengate, Lanner
Nina And Ian Dibble, Lanner
C.D. Downing, Falmouth
Denis Dunstan, Lanner
David K. Dunstan, Lanner
J.J. Dower Eastman, Redruth
Sue Edelman, Lanner
David and Brenda Edwards, Lanner
Patience Ellis (née Martin), Cambridge
Michael J. Evans, Camborne
J.L. and D.B. Fiol, Trevarth, Lanner
Jay Foote, Lanner
Mrs C. Gajardo, Carnon Downs, Truro
M. Gale, Essex
Richard and Lesley Gardner, Lanner
Mr and Dr C. Glasson, Dulwich, London
Ronnie and Dorothy Goodland, Redruth
Marjorie Goss (née Goldsworthy), Lanner
Albert Graham, Lanner
Joyce A. Green, Stithians, Truro
Mr and Mrs M.E. Greenhalgh, Carn Marth, Redruth
Violet Greenwood, Lanner
Gribbles of Trevarth, Redruth
Rodney M. Grigg, Redruth
Mr Anthony Grigg, Yorkshire
Sandra Anne Grigg, Lanner
John M. Grigg, Portishead, Bristol
Mildren J. Grigg, Redruth
Mr and Mrs William Grout, Ontario, Canada
Mr T.H. Hart MBE, Lanner
David Harvey, Exeter
Mr H.E. Harvey, Paignton, Devon
Mr and Mrs T. A. Harvey, Sevenoaks, Kent
Desmond Hawken, Carshalton, Surrey

Glyn R. Hayes, Lanner
Mr and Mrs C. Heather, Surrey
Mrs Glynis Hendrickson, Ballarat, Australia
Mr and Mrs E.D. Hill, Redruth
Mary Hodgson, West Trethellan, Lanner
Dr Hugh Hollingsworth, Redruth
Anita T. Hooper, Lanner
Arthur R. Inch, Haywards Heath, Sussex
Institute of Cornish Studies, Truro
Louise Ireson, Lanner
J. Ireson, Lanner
Mr and Mrs J.C. Ivey, Truro
Pamela James (née Martin), Moose Jaw, Canada
Mr R.D. and Mrs J.M. Jenkin, Redruth
Ann Trevenen Jenkin, Hayle
Mr M.L. Jervis, Lanner
Mr and Mrs R.H. Jewell, Lanner
Mr C. Jewell and Ms D.W.Frutschi-Barlow, Lanner
Mr W.M. Job, Lanner
Francis Peter Job, Lanner
Pat Job, Lanner (now Australia)
Stephen A. Johns, Lanner
Barbara J. Johns, Lanner
Vyvyan C. Jones, Swansea, Wales
Mrs A. Jones, Camborne
Eirian A. Jones, Lanner
John Juggins, Lanner
John Julian, Illogan
Mrs B. M. Juzefatous, Camborne
Joyce Kellow, Lanner
Barrie T. and Sylvia Kessell, Redruth
Petula K. Kessell, Redruth
D. And S. King, Lanner
Robert Knight, Trevarth, Lanner
Roger Lacy, Newquay
Diana M. Laity, Gwennap
Wendy and Jon Langford
Arthur Langford, Redruth
Gillian and Paul Langford, Lanner
Lanner C.P. School, Lanner
Ross and Helen Lawn, Christchurch, New Zealand
Liz Lawson, Lanner Moor
Shaun C.W. Lean, Lanner
David Lean, Redruth
Miss D. Lenderyou, Camborne
Philip E. Lloyd, Frogpool
Catherine Lorigan, Delabole
David C.E. Lugg, Lanner
Deborah Macdonald, Eire
Alan Manaton, Pennance
Sylvia Mann (née Martin), Swanley, Kent
Dennis Martin, St Day
Mrs Joan Martin
David and Anne Martin, Mawnan Smith, Falmouth
A.D. Martin, Truro
Revd Jim Martin, Cockermouth
Janice Martin-Essoui, Swindon, Wilts.
Geoff and Steph Mason, Trevethan, Redruth
David Matthews, Totnes, Devon
Mrs P.E. Maynard, Redruth
Damian J. Mccurdy, Golborne, Warrington
Gage Mckinney, California, U.S.A.
Sheila and Ivor Merrin
Eleanor J. Mill, Lanner
Dorothy Mindenhall, Victoria, BC, Canada
Ken and Barbara Minson, Lanner
Peter and Joan Mitchell, Chacewater, Truro
Rosemond E. Mitchell, ex Lanner
Geoffrey F. Mitchell, Lanner
Mr and Mrs S.J. Mitchell, Redruth
Mr and Mrs Malcolm G. Moorehouse, Trethellan
Dorothy and Garfield Moyle, Lanner
Mr and Mrs I.R. Moyle, Menerdue
Morley Mugford, Murtons Terrace, Lanner
Desmond H. Nancholas, Redruth
David J. Nunn, Mabe
Graham and Angie O'Callaghan, Crosshaven, Lanner
W.G. Olds and N.F. Pender, Lanner
Mary Oliver, Truro
Mrs A.M. Opie, Lanner
Albert H. and Phyllis G. Osborne, Lanner
Mr Murray L. Owen, St Austell
Christopher Parker, Bristol
Michael Parker, Cardiff, Wales
Mike and Pat Pascoe, Lanner
Peter Pascoe, Chequers, Camborne
Mrs V. Patterson, Wyke Regis, Dorset
Philip Payton, Illogan Highway
Mrs B. Pearce, Falmouth
Joan and Gerald Pearce, Lanner (1959-1988)
W. Joan Pellow (née Langford), Redruth
Mrs M. Alison Penaluna (née Corey), Exeter, Devon
N.F. Pender, Redruth
Joe Pengelly, Plymouth, Devon
John Penglase, St Day, Redruth
Ron Penglase, Redruth
Philip Penglase, Hinckley, Leicestershire
Percival Penpraze, Lanner
R.H. Penpraze, Lanner
A. T. and J.F.F. Percy, Bellvean, Lanner
Mr Ivan D. Perry, Helston (formerly of Stithians)
Dr Ronald Perry, Truro
Peter, Stella and Mark, Lanner
G. Stanley Peters, Lanner
Mrs D. Pope, Guisborough, N. Yorkshire
Hal and Diane Popna (née Polkinhorn), West Chester, USA
Sylvia Pover (née Webber), Portreath
Frank and Susan Prisk, Four Lanes, Redruth
John C.C. Probert, Redruth
Malcolm Quintrell, Lanner
Eric Rabjohns, Carharrack
Mrs Yvonne Rafferty, Lanner

David R. Raven, Lanner
F.R. Rayner, Perranwell, Truro
Brian Reed, Town Farm, Redruth
Y.V. Reynolds, Lanner
Ernie and Kathleen Richards, Bell Lane, Lanner
Elida Robinson, Lanner
Marcus D. Rogers, Redruth
Lee Blatchford Rouse, Lanner
George W. Rowe, Mousehole
Steven J. Rule, Lanner
Russell Family, Lanner
Richard J. Sandow, Trevarth, Lanner
Richard Saunders, Lanner
Emma Saunders, Lanner
John and Pat Saunders, Lanner
Ruth Sawley Kadina, South Australia
Fr Robert Sellers, Christchurch, Lanner
Rev and Mrs T. Shaw, Perranporth
William P. Shield, Lanner
Mrs S. M. Simmons, Falmouth
Mr Calvin Stephens, Falmouth
David R. Strout, Lanner
Kevin R. Swain, Lanner
Derrick A. Swan, Tresavean Farm, Lanner
Mrs Melanie Sweet Carharrack
Henry Ottley Tallett, Lanner
Moira Tangye, Newquay
Mrs Pauline Taylor, Illogan, Redruth
Joe Thomas, Illogan
June E. Thomas, Bodmin
Charles Thomas, Truro
Brian Thomas, Illogan, Redruth
John and Janice Thomas, Lanner
Mr C.M. Thomas, Lanner
Graham Thorne, Maldon, Essex
W John Tonkin, St Austell
John Travis, Lanner
Dr Garry Tregidga, Institute Of Cornish Studies, Truro,
Linda M. Trelease, St Day, Redruth
Miss S. Treweek, Sutton, Surrey
David H. Uren, Maghull, Merseyside
John H. Veall, Redruth
Mr and Mrs M. E. Veall, Gwennap, Redruth
Mr C.J. and Dr Veall
Mr Frederick C. Walker, Trevarth
I. Walsh, Lanner
Mac Waters, Foxhole
Janeen Watkins, Utah, USA
Michael O. Webber, Lanner
Jennifer Whitelegg, Knockholt, Kent
Nigel and Julie Whittaker, Lanner
Sandy Whyte, Ponsanooth, Truro
Mrs E.J. Williams, Lanner
Patricia and George Williams, Lanner
Irene Williams, Lanner
Jeremy Williams, Redruth
Dr Lynn Willies, Matlock, Derbyshire
Shaun Wills, Barnstaple, Devon
Michelle Wills, Lanner
GloriaWills, St Erth, Hayle
Mrs C. Worden, Redruth
Elizabeth Worth, Torrington, North Devon
Mr Graham Young, North Country, Redruth